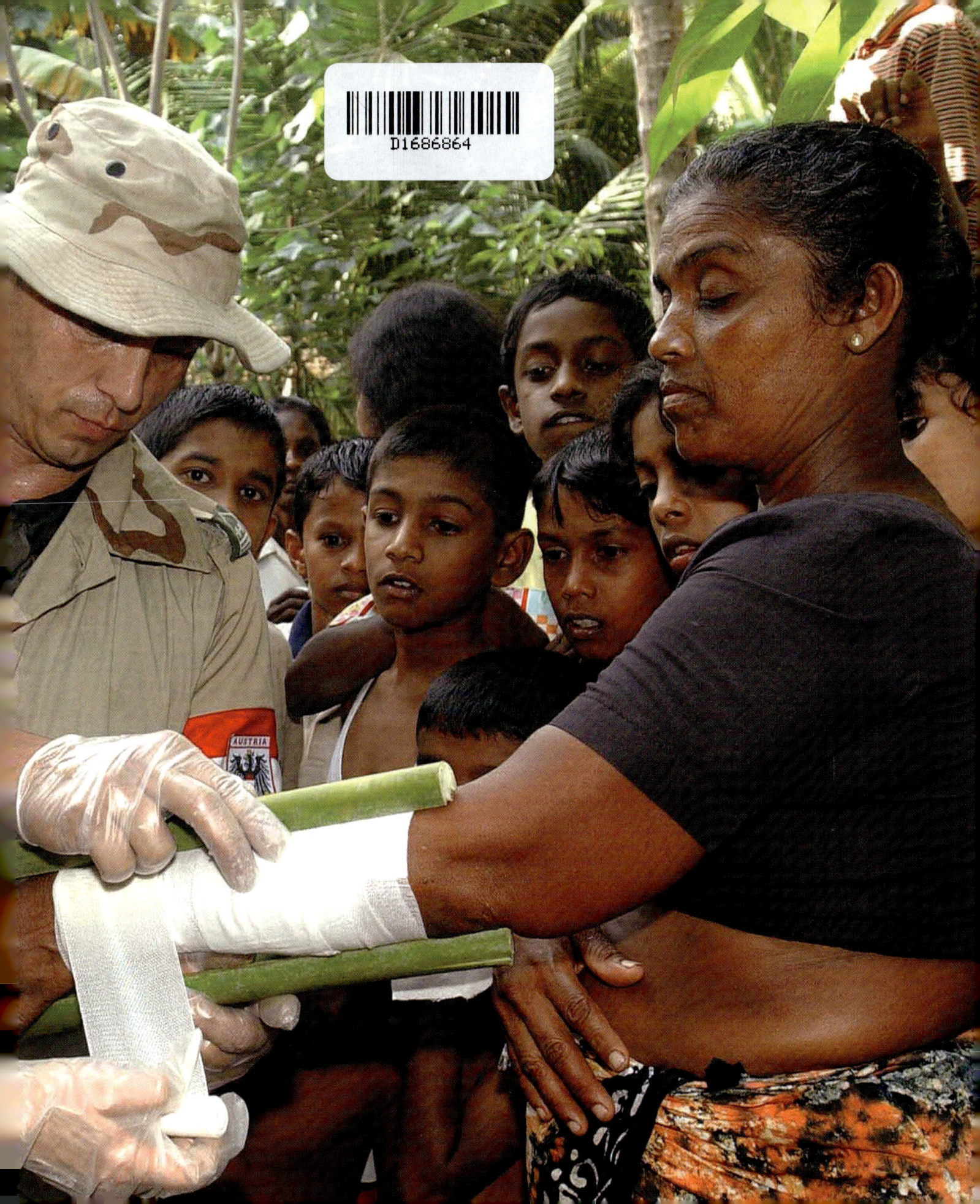

Rolf M. Urrisk-Obertyński

EVER READY!

The Austrian Armed Forces at Home and Abroad

Operational 24 / 7

Weishaupt Publishing

Exclusive edition
commissioned by the
Federal Ministry of Defence and Sports

Title picture: Austrian Patrol in Kosovo (picture: Thomas Rakowitz).
Front leaf: A military doctor and a medical noncommissioned officer care for a women who broke her arm during the tsunami disaster in Sri Lanka in January 2005.
End leaf: Engineers push a bridge piece after a flood disaster.
Back of dust jacket: Because the dam broken after a flood disaster in March 2006 near Dürnkrut is no longer reachable by land, "Black Hawk" helicopters reinforce the 80 m long site of the break with anti-tank tetrahedrons.

Dust jacket design: Dipl.-Graph. Prof. Franz Stierschneider.
Translation: Jessica Hedrick.
For assistance with military terminology, we thank Mag. Gernot Fridum,
National Defence Academy, Language Institute.

ISBN 978-3-7059-0337-1
English edition of the 3rd expanded German edition © Copyright 2011
Production: Weishaupt Publishing, A-8342 Gnas,
Tel.: 03151-8487, Fax: 03151-84874.
e-mail: verlag@weishaupt.at
e-bookshop: www.weishaupt.at
Printing and binding: Theiss Printing Press GmbH, A-9431 St. Stefan.
Printed in Austria.

Contents

Greeting of the Federal President and Commander-in-Chief of the Austrian Armed Forces 7
Foreword of the Federal Minister of Defence and Sports 8
Foreword of the Chief of the General Staff 9
Foreword of the Director General Operations 10

Domestic Deployments 11
    Revolt in Hungary, 1956 13
    Flooding in Carinthia and East Tyrol, 1965 23
    Attacks in South Tyrol, 1967 24
    "Prague Spring", 1968 29
    Congestion on the "Guest Worker Route", 1969 36
    Collapse of the Viennese Reichsbrücke, 1976 37
    Foot-and-mouth Disease, 1981 39
    Nuclear Power Plant Accident at Chernobyl, 1986 40
    Catastrophic Thunderstorms, 1989 42
    Catastrophic Storm, 1990 43
    Border Area Surveillance, 1990 – 2007 44
    War in Yugoslavia, 1991 56
    Railroad Accident, 1993 64
    Deployment to Ensure the Transit of IFOR and SFOR Troops, 1995 – 2007 66
    Catastrophic Flood, 1997 70
    Visit of Pope John Paul II, 1998 71
    Mine Accident in Lassing, 1998 72
    EU Presidency, 1998 74
    Catastrophic Avalanche in Galtür, 1999 75
    Y2K Precautions, 1999/2000 80
    Austrian OSCE Chairmanship, 2000 82
    Funicular Disaster on Kitzsteinhorn, 2000 83
    Anthrax Alert, 2001 – 2009 85
    Serious Forest Fires, 2002 87
    "Hundred Year Flood", 2002 88
    European Economic Forum, 2002 90
    Interception Deployment, 2004 91
    Heavy Snowfall, 2005 92
    Austrian EU Presidency, 2006 93
    World Economic Forum in Davos, 2006 94
    Flood in Lower Austria, 2006 95
    Forest Fires, 2006 98
    Storm "Kyrill", 2007 99
    Visit of Pope Benedict XVI, 2007 100
    Schengen Expansion, 2007 – to date 101
    European Football Championship "EURO 2008", 2008 102
    Heavy Storms, 2009 105
    Research Project, 2009 107
    Longest Bailey Temporary Bridge, 2009 108

Deployments Abroad 109
    ONUC (Opérations des Nations Unies au Congo; United Nations Operation in the Congo), 1960 – 1963 110
    Earthquake Deployment in Skopje, 1963 118
    UNYOM (United Nations Yemen Observation Mission), 1963 119
    UNFICYP (United Nations Force in Cyprus), 1964 – to date 120

UNTSO (United Nations Truce Supervision Organization), 1967 – to date	132
Medical Deployment in Biafra, 1968 – 1970	135
UNEF II (United Nations Emergency Force II), 1973 – 1974	136
UNDOF (United Nations Disengagement Observer Force), 1974 – to date	138
Earthquake Deployment in Friuli, 1976	152
Earthquake Deployment in Titograd, 1978	153
Earthquake Deployment in Calabritto, 1980	153
UNIT (United Nations Inspection Team in Iran and Iraq), 1984 – 1988	155
UNIIMOG (United Nations Iran Iraq Military Observer Group), 1988 – 1991	155
UNGOMAP (United Nations Good Offices Mission in Afghanistan and Pakistan), 1988 – 1990	159
OSGAP (Office of the Secretary General in Afghanistan and Pakistan), 1990 – 1993	159
Earthquake Deployment in Armenia, 1988	162
UNIKOM (United Nations Iraq – Kuwait Observation Mission), 1991 – to date	167
UNAFHIR (United Nations Austrian Field Hospital in Iran), 1991	175
UNSCOM (United Nations Special Commission), 1991 – 2000	180
UNMOVIC (United Nations Monitoring, Verification and Inspection Commission), 2000 – to date	180
UNGCI (United Nations Guards Contingent in Iraq), 1991 – 1992	184
MINURSO (Misión de las Naciones Unidas para el Referéndum del Sáhara Occidental; United Nations Mission for the Referendum in Western Sahara), 1991 – to date	185
UNAMIC (United Nations Advance Mission in Cambodia), 1991 – 1992	190
UNTAC (United Nations Transitional Authority in Cambodia), 1991 – 1993	190
UNMLT (United Nations Military Liaison Team in Cambodia), 1993 – 1994	190
UNOSOM I (United Nations Operation in Somalia I), 1992 – 1993	198
CSCE/OSCE Skopje (CSCE/OSCE Spillover Mission to Skopje), 1991 – 1995	203
UNOT (United Nations Office in Tajikistan), 1993 – 1994	204
UNMOT (United Nations Mission of Observers in Tajikistan), 1994 – 2000	204
UNOMIL (United Nations Observer Mission in Liberia), 1993 – 1994	207
UNAMIR (United Nations Assistance Mission in Rwanda), 1993 – 1996	208
CSCE/OSCE Mission to Nagorno-Karabakh, 1994 – 1996, 2000	213
CSCE/OSCE Mission to Georgia, 1994 – 2001, 2008 – 2009	218
UNOMIG (United Nations Observer Mission in Georgia), 1994 – to date	220
UNOMSA (United Nations Observer Mission in South Africa), 1994	222
UNMIH (United Nations Mission in Haiti), 1994 – 1995	223
ECMM (European Community Monitoring Mission in former Yugoslavia), 1995 – 2000	225
EUMM (European Union Monitoring Mission in former Yugoslavia), 2000 – to date	225
UNDAC/Laos (United Nations Disaster Assessment and Coordination Mission in Laos), 1995	229
IFOR (Peace Implementation Force), 1996 – 1997	230
SFOR (Peace Stabilization Force), 1997 – 2001	230
UNDAC/Africa (United Nations Disaster Assessment and Coordination Mission in Africa), 1996 – 1997	242
MINUGUA (Misión de Verificacion de las Naciones Unidas en Guatemala), 1997	243
UNDAC/Malawi (United Nations Disaster Assessment and Coordination Mission in Malawi), 1997	244
UNMAC/BiH (United Nations Mine Action Center in Bosnia and Herzegovina), 1997	245
MPF (Multinational Protection Force in Albania), 1997	246
ATHUM/PL (Austrian Humanitarian Contingent/Poland), 1997	249
OSCE/BiH (OSCE Mission to Bosnia and Herzegovina), 1998 – to date	251
UNDAC/Afghanistan (United Nations Disaster Assessment and Coordination Mission in Afghanistan), 1998	253
ATHUM/CRO (Austrian Humanitarian Contingent/Croatia), 1998	254
KVM (OSCE Kosovo Verification Mission), TFK (OSCE Task Force for Kosovo), 1998 – 1999	255
AFOR (Albanian Force), 1999	256
WEUDAM (Western European Union Demining Assistance Mission in Croatia), 1999 – 2000	263
UNAMET (United Nations Assistance Mission in East Timor), 1999	264
OMIK (OSCE Mission to Kosovo), 1999	266
KFOR (Kosovo International Security Force), 1999 – to date	267
UNMIK (United Nations Interim Administration Mission in Kosovo), 1999 – 2002	291
AFDRU/TU 1 (Austrian Forces Disaster Relief Unit/Turkey 1), 1999	293

Mission	Page
ATHUM/TU (Austrian Humanitarian Contingent/Turkey), 1999	296
S+R/TW (Multinational Search and Rescue Unit/Taiwan), 1999	297
AFDRU/TU2 (Austrian Forces Disaster Relief Unit/Turkey 2), 1999	298
UNDAC/MZB I/II (United Nations Disaster Assessment and Coordination Mission in Mozambique I/II), 2000	300
ATHUM/MOC (Austrian Humanitarian Contingent for Mozambique), 2000	301
OHR/BiH (Office of the High Representative for Bosnia and Herzegovina), 2000 – 2002	305
UNMEE (United Nations Mission in Ethiopia and Eritrea), 2000 – to date	306
RACVIAC (South-East European Regional Arms Control Verification and Implementation Assistance Center), 2000 – to date	310
UNMOGIP (United Nations Military Observer Group in India and Pakistan), 2001 – 2002	311
ISAF (International Security Assistance Force), 2002 – to date	313
ISAF II (International Security Assistance Force), 2005	320
EUFOR "Concordia" (European Union Mission in FYROM "Concordia"), 2003	322
MINUCI (United Nations Mission in Côte d'Ivoire), 2003 – 2004	324
UNDAC/Algeria (United Nations Disaster Assessment and Coordination Mission in Algeria), 2003	325
AFDRU/AG (Austrian Forces Disaster Relief Unit Algeria), 2003	326
EU-Operation "Artemis" (European Union Military Operation in the Democratic Republic of the Congo "Artemis"), 2003	327
UNDAC/Iran (United Nations Disaster Assessment and Coordination Mission in Iran), 2003 – 2004	328
AFDRU/Iran (Austrian Forces Disaster Relief Unit Iran), 2003 – 2004	329
UNAMA (United Nations Assistance Mission in Afghanistan), 2004 – 2006	330
UNDAC/Bangladesh (United Nations Disaster Assessment and Coordination Mission in Bangladesh), 2004	331
Hum/Beslan (International Humanitarian and Disaster Relief for Beslan/Ossetia), 2004	332
EUFOR "ALTHEA" (European Union Force Operation "ALTHEA" in Bosnia and Herzegovina), 2004 – to date	333
ART (Austrian Rescue Team/Thailand – Administrative Assistance Team), 2004 – 2005	340
UNDAC/Thailand (United Nations Disaster Assessment and Coordination Mission in Thailand), 2005	341
AFDRU/Sri Lanka (Austrian Forces Disaster Relief Unit in Sri Lanka), 2005	342
HUM/ALB (Humanitarian Aid Contribution in Albania), 2005	343
AMIS II (African Union Mission in Sudan), 2005 – 2007	344
UNMIS (United Nations Mission in Sudan), 2005 – 2006	345
EU-AMM (European Union Monitoring Mission in Aceh), 2005 – 2006	346
AFDRU/PAK (Austrian Forces Disaster Relief Unit in Pakistan), 2005	347
EU-BAM Rafah (European Border Assistance Mission for the Rafah Crossing Point), 2005 – 2006	350
EUDAC/Indonesia (European Union Disaster Assessment and Coordination Team in Indonesia), 2006	351
ATHUM Cyprus (Austrian Humanitarian Mission Cyprus), 2006	352
EUFOR RD Congo (European Union Forces in the Democratic Republic of the Congo), 2006	353
UNOWA (United Nations Office for West Africa), 2006 – 2009	354
UNMIN (United Nations Political Mission in Nepal), 2007 – 2008, 2009 – to date	355
KST (Crisis Support Team)	356
EUSEC RD Congo (European Union Security Sector Reform Mission in the Democratic Republic of the Congo), 2007 – to date	357
EUDAC/Peru (European Union Disaster Assistance and Coordination in Peru), 2007	358
ATHUM/GR (Austrian Humanitarian Contingent in Greece), 2007	359
EUFOR/TCHAD/RCA (European Union Force "Tchad/Republique Centralafricaine"), 2008 – 2009	361
UNDAC/Albania (United Nations Disaster Assessment and Coordination Mission in Albania), 2008	369
OSCE/GEO (OSCE Mission to Georgia), 2008 – 2009	370
MINURCAT II (United Nations Mission in the Central African Republic and Chad II), 2009	371
UNDAC/Namibia (United Nations Disaster Assessment and Coordination Mission in Namibia), 2009	373
EUMM/GEO (European Union Monitoring Mission in Georgia), 2008 – to date	374
UNDAC/Pakistan (United Nations Disaster Assessment and Coordination in Pakistan), 2010	374
ATHUM/HU (Austrian Humanitarian Mission Hungary), 2010	375
ATHUM/ALB (Austrian Humanitarian Mission Albania), 2010	375
KST/EGY (Crisis Support Team/Egypt), 2011	375
KST/LBY (Crisis Support Team Libya), 2011	375
ATHUM/JPN (Austrian Humanitarian Mission Japan), 2011 – to date	376
EU IT OHQ (European Union Italian Operational Headquarters), 2011 – to date	376
UNOWA (United Nations Office for West Africa), 2011 – to date	376
EUCPM/CYP (European Civil Protection Mission Cyprus), 2011 – to date	376

*Dedicated to my comrades,
who always have and always will give a good account
of themselves, even in the most impossible situations,
often with inadequate resources,
but always with idealism and improvisational talent.*

*True to the once sworn oath
"Loyal to the death!"*

Rolf M. Urrisk-Obertyński

Greeting of the Federal President and Commander-in-Chief of the Austrian Armed Forces

Whenever I am on state visits in countries with which the Austrian armed forces have close contact, I am assured in numerous encounters and conversations of the great appreciation for the competence and ability of our armed forces in foreign deployments.

This international recognition is undoubtedly very pleasant. For 50 years now Austrian male soldiers – and in recent times increasingly more female soldiers – participate in humanitarian aid deployments and peacekeeping missions of the United Nations, and through this support the efforts of the international community to enforce and ensure stability and human rights even in far distant crisis regions. Conflicts are to be stabilized and the effects of violent hostilities on the civilian population held in check.

In these years the Austrian armed forces has worked with competence and endurance in the spirit of the mission mandate "in the service of peace". In 1988 the valuable engagement of the United Nations peacekeeping troops was also suitably recognized and honored with the award of the Nobel Peace Prize.

It is not last this helpful work which has contributed in the last years and decades to fixing a positive image of the Austrian armed forces in the population at home as well. This connection is expressed particularly clearly at public events such as the yearly exhibition on the national holiday at the Vienna Heldenplatz.

How much the armed forces are valued and respected is particularly shown during the mastery of challenging domestic deployments. Again and again in the past we have had to experience crisis situations such as precarious snow or flooding situations. And again and again the armed forces have moved out with soldiers, in order to helpfully support the population often around the clock.

I am therefore pleased with the interesting documentation at hand. It is simultaneously a reference work and a performance record and strikingly shows where and how Austrian soldiers are deployed in their domestic and foreign missions or contribute technical-humanitarian aid in crisis situations.

All this demands the highest degree of commitment and professionalism, and I would like to use this publication as an opportunity to express my thanks and my recognition to all soldiers.

My thanks also apply to the author, Brigadier General ret. Prof. Mag. Rolf M. Urrisk-Obertyński for the valuable and interesting documentation.

I very heartily congratulate and combine this with my best greetings to the readers!

Dr. Heinz Fischer
Federal President of the Republic of Austria

Foreword of the Federal Minister of Defence and Sports

"The Austrian Armed Forces – A Success Story"

The history of the Austrian armed forces' deployments at home and abroad strikingly demonstrates what great feats the soldiers have accomplished in the last 55 years. It is a balance which is more than presentable and from which it is clearly visible that the Austrian armed forces need not shy away from comparison with other armies. In the 120 foreign deployments which have been completed since 1955, many officers and noncommissioned officers were able to avoid an international intensification of a conflict situation through thoughtful action. On the contrary, they were able to work towards conciliation. Very important during this was also the good cooperation and the functioning crisis management that the Defence Ministry has operated with the Foreign Ministry and the Ministry for the Interior during deployments.

Something for which many armies across the world envy us is the integration of the armed forces into the population. The mixture of soldiers who belong to the Austrian armed forces professionally and those who, after their use, return to their civilian professions, contributes to the anchoring of the armed forces in the population and enables the armed forces to access varied civilian skills, knowledge and experiences. This is of especially great importance during deployments, domestically and abroad.

I would like to very heartily thank Brigadier General ret. Prof. Mag. Rolf M. Urrisk-Obertyński for the production of this book and also pay him my great respects. This is a comprehensive documentation which shows the many-sidedness of the domestic and foreign deployments according to their type, duration and intensity – and above all makes one thing clear: The Austrian armed forces of the Second Republic are a success story!

Vienna, in September 2011

Mag. Norbert Darabos
Federal Minister of Defence and Sports

Foreword of the Chief of the General Staff

As Chief of the General Staff my supervisory responsibility leads me to our contingents abroad with a certain regularity. One is almost tempted to brush this off as the simple routine of military business, but far from it: Again and again I discovered new facets of our troop's deployments. It is of course true that much occurs, and must occur, in a daily routine. Nevertheless commanders and troops must constantly prove themselves anew in the most varied situations and exhibit a high amount of flexibility. And once again I recognize the unique professionalism and high motivation that has always distinguished Austrian soldiers when they approach the accomplishment of their assigned duties. Just recently this was confirmed to me once again by the Filipino Force Commander as well as the Syrian Chief of the General Staff on the occasion of my troop visit to the Golan Heights. The reputation of these soldiers is also what makes Austria in demand worldwide as a troop contributor, albeit not all of the requests submitted to us can be fulfilled, since a small country like Austria simply does not have unlimited resources.

The foundation for this outstanding reputation is laid by the troop divisions, the academies and the schools of the armed forces, who compensate for often small resources with personal initiative and improvisational talent as a requirement for the successful fulfillment of a mission at home or abroad. In addition to this is the intensive mutual exchange of experience with foreign armies, international organizations, domestic and foreign civilian educational institutions.

The Austrian soldier is meantime used to working in a multinational environment. Partial units and whole divisions are regularly tested internationally within the framework of deployment preparations or deployments, and so prove their interoperability. The term "interoperability" has meanwhile become a key term when the topic is the personnel and material direction of modern armed forces for the future – and among these I justifiably count the Austrian armed forces.

Although foreign service is given a stronger focus, recently there has been the notable phenomenon of the growth of the domestic deployments, above all within the framework of disaster relief. We must acknowledge this fact and make the appropriate deductions.

The keyword domestic deployments leads me to the "Blue Light Organizations", with which the Austrian armed forces cooperates in an outstandingly concerted way during deployments as well as during exercises. I may therefore use the publication at hand to express my thanks for this profitable cooperation for the benefit of our population. By the same token I thank the civilian partners of our divisions for their support, above all during the fulfillment of domestic duties.

Mag. Edmund Entacher
General

Brigadier General Prof. Mag. Rolf M. Urrisk-Obertyński paints a comprehensive series of pictures of the many-sided deployments of the Austrian armed forces, which lets us look on them with pride. At the same time this is a comprehensive documentation of the ability of our soldiers, which is to be preserved in the present and future.

Foreword of the Director General Operations

Years ago when Brigadier General Rolf M. Urrisk produced the 1st edition of his work "The Deployments of the Austrian Armed Forces at Home and Abroad", the author of these lines found himself in the interesting situation of seeing his own work area represented in a broad way, often illuminated in detail, and rounded off by numerous photos as well as maps.

Now a 3rd, expanded addition is appearing, which is even more detailed than before and represents the years up to 2010, drawing on a row of new documents and other writings. Especially the legal backgrounds are given great attention, with good reason.

With no small pleasure I am also able to feel that this book from Rolf M. Urrisk is an essential part of my life story, since I have now been engaged with the preparation, planning and leadership of deployments at home and abroad for around 28 years as an officer of the armed forces, since February 1st, 2008 in the position of the director of the Deployment Section.

If the political foundations have also shifted in a way that seemed hardly possible, even downright unrealistic in the eighties of the 20th century, so nevertheless despite all changes one thing has remained unbroken: The good spirit of our armed forces, which often displayed a notable posture of perseverance in duty even under difficult conditions and in a situation of radical change, and which constantly fulfilled the difficult jobs assigned in an exemplary manner, from which a pleasing continuity developed, as one could hardly have wished to be better.

Thanks and recognition to our comrade Brigadier General ret. Rolf M. Urrisk-Obertyński!

Mag. Christian Ségur-Cabanac, LTG

Domestic Deployments

AUSTRIAN ARMED FORCES IN THE WEB

www.bundesheer.at

- News
- Missions
- Photos & Videos

If you want to be up to date about the Austrian Armed Forces you should refer to the following web address: www.bundesheer.at. The website doesn't just offer information about the challenges, missions and armed forces' structures. You can also find information about the Minister of Defence, the Austrian Security Policy and the career opportunities in the Austrian Armed Forces - just one click away!

Revolt in Hungary

Preliminary Events

At the end of World War 2, Hungary remains occupied by the Soviet army. In the summer of 1948, all democratic parties are dissolved. On the 12th of June, 1948, the Social Democrats and Communists are unified as the "**Hungarian Working People's Party**"; on August 18th, 1948, Hungary becomes a People's Republic. A preliminary phase of "democratization" ends with the political participation of the Communists, and leads to a Stalinist dictatorship under Matyas Rakosi. Centralization and nationalization further lead to economic decline. These developments go hand in hand with political oppression and purges within the party and the army. Among others, 10 generals and 19 other high-ranking officers are executed. 16,000 soldiers are imprisoned for "political offenses" between 1951 and 1955 alone. At the same time, a rebuilding of the army is carried out, so that it finally reaches a strength of 210,000 men. Not until Stalin's death does hope for a better future begin to take root in the population. Imre Nagy, the Communist reformer, takes Stalinist Rakosi's place in mid-1953. Nagy promises economic and political reforms to benefit the population.

On the 14th of May, 1955, one day before the signing of the Austrian State Treaty, the **Warsaw Pact** (WaPa) is chartered. The troops previously stationed in Austria shift to Hungary. As a result, the reins are tightened within the Warsaw Pact. On May 18th, 1955, Imre Nagy resigns and is expelled from the party as a "dissenter". Rakosi takes power again and continues on his old course.

At the 20th convention of the Communist Party of the Soviet Union (CPSU) in February 1956, First Secretary of the Party Nikita S. Khrushchev breaks with Stalinism, waking new hope for change. In Hungary, communist youth organizations, in particular the so-called **"Petöfi Circle"** (named after the most famous Hungarian revolutionary poet of the 1848/49 Revolution), organize public debates on the independent course to be pursued. Yugoslavia's successful emphasis on its own path, the Soviet withdrawal from Austria and the declaration of Austrian neutrality, the 1953 uprising in the German Democratic Republic, and the events in Poland (heavy unrest among workers in Posen on June 28th and 29th, 1956) all serve as models. Above all, Austria's neutrality seems to be a promising course. After all, the Soviet Union suggested just last year that Turkey, Iran and Iraq also transition to policies of neutrality. Domestic tensions lead to a crisis of the Stalinist regime under Rakosi, so Moscow sends Anastas Mikoyan to Budapest in July to assist with the "reestablishment of stable conditions". Rakosi resigns as First Secretary of the Party in July 1956 "because of health concerns", but his successor, Ernö Gerö, pursues the same course and delays the previously conceded reforms.

The call for a fundamentally different Communist party policy, including acknowledgment of its unique national identity, grows in strength within the Hungarian army, supported by political officers' schools and the General Staff college. In contrast, the **border guards** and the **secret police** (AVH) remain firmly in the hands of officers who hold fast to the stiff Communist party line, so that not only the differences, but also the tensions and mutual distrust between them grow.

On the afternoon of October 23rd, 1956, a student demonstration takes place in Budapest, which, despite prohibition, begins at the memorial to General Bem (leader of the Hungarian army in the revolution of 1848/49). Around 100,000 people gather in the square. The student union, having already resigned from the Communist youth organization, distributes pamphlets with a **14-point program** (that ties in with the 14 Points of American President Wilson). Among other things, the immediate removal of Soviet troops (legally, the Soviet Union should have withdrawn their troops from Hungary within 90 days of their removal from Austria, since the reason for their presence according to the Treaty of Paris – see next paragraph – had fallen away), new elections, a reordering of international relationships and the economic system, freedom of opinion, and the removal of the Stalin Monument in Budapest. When this leads to the destruction of this monument (incidentally, the material for the monument was obtained by melting down statues of Emperor Charles VI, Maria Theresa, Emperor Francis Joseph, and Empress Elisabeth), troops from the AVH open fire on the demonstrators; several hundred people are killed. Another group lays siege to the radio station and demands the announcement of the program. The bloody skirmishes finally lead to a national uprising. On the morning of October 24th, Imre Nagy takes over the office of prime minister. The jails are opened; the most prominent prisoner, Cardinal Mindszenty, the Primate of Hungary, is led to his official residence by an exultant crowd. Troops from the Honved, the regular national army, refuse to advance on the revolutionaries, army warehouses are opened, the revolutionary masses arm themselves. The battle for freedom begins.

The Soviet occupation troops are stationed in garrisons around Lake Balaton, primarily the **"Special Army Corps"** (Osobyj Korpus) with 1 armored division (92nd) and 2 motorized infantry divisions (2nd and 17th) with approximately 50,000 men under the common of General Pyotr Lashchenko (who had already moved his headquarters here from Baden near Vienna in September 1955). The command is in Stuhlweißenburg (Hungarian Székesfehérvár). No Soviet garrisons stand in Budapest itself. The "Special Army Corps" is under the direct control of the Soviet Army General Staff in Moscow. The deployment goes back to the Hungarian Peace Treaty, concluded between the victorious powers in Paris in 1947. This treaty regulates, among other things, the rights of the Soviet Union – including just this deployment of troops on Hungarian territory – who have the task of militarily securing supply lines with the Red Army in Austria's eastern occupation zone. More recent sources show that plans of attack existed in case of a Hungarian uprising. The outbreak of unrest, therefore, does not surprise the Soviets. Parts of the Red Army stationed in Czechoslo-

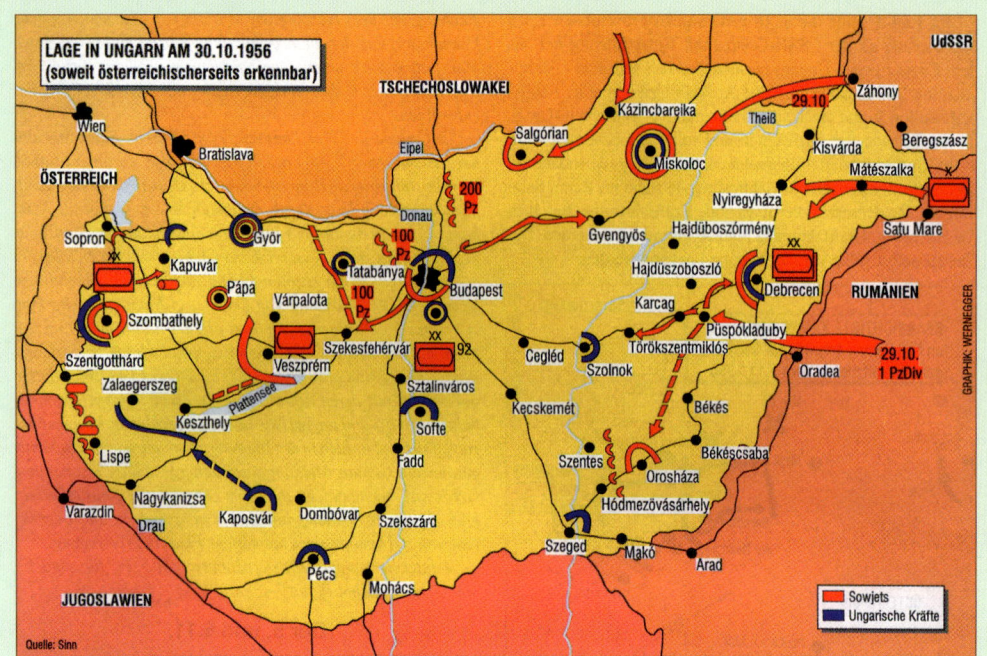

Liebe Österreicher!

Ihr waret die Ersten, die sich von der ersten Minute unseres Freiheitskampfes auf unsere Seite gestellt und aus aller Kraft geholfen haben. Für Eure aus Herzenstiefe kommende, opferwillige Hilfsbereitschaft und für Euer Mitgefühl bedanken wir uns mit aller Wärme unserer Seele und unseres Herzens. Eure Hilfe tut sehr viel in unserem Kampf und lindert unsere Not.

Im Namen des geprüften ungarischen Volkes die Jugend der Universität von Sopron.

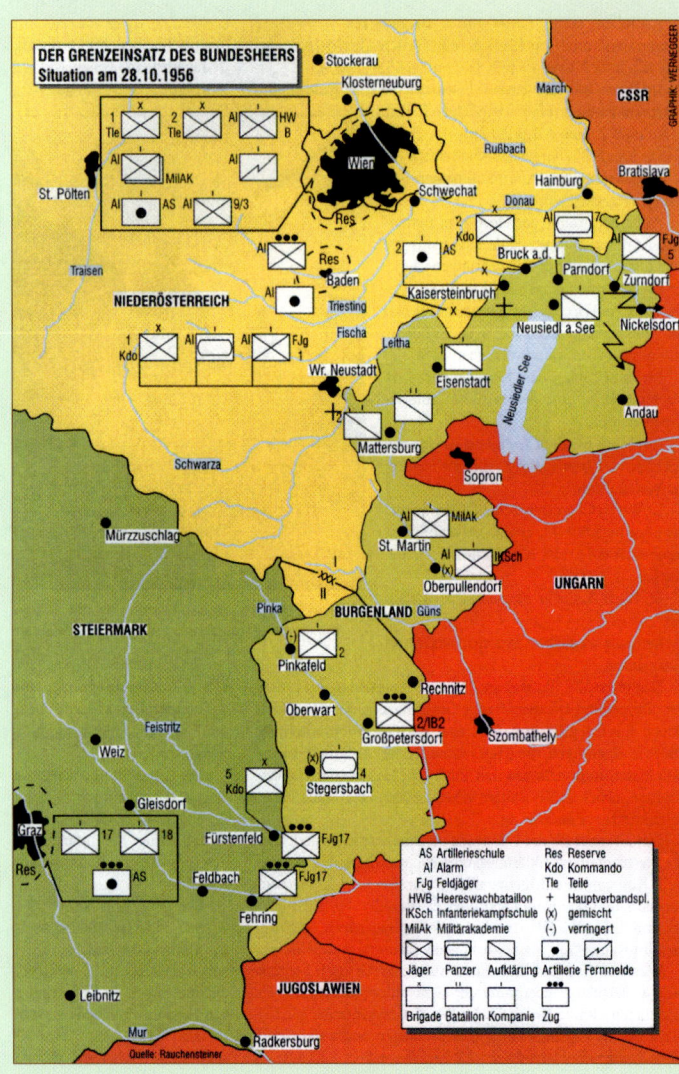

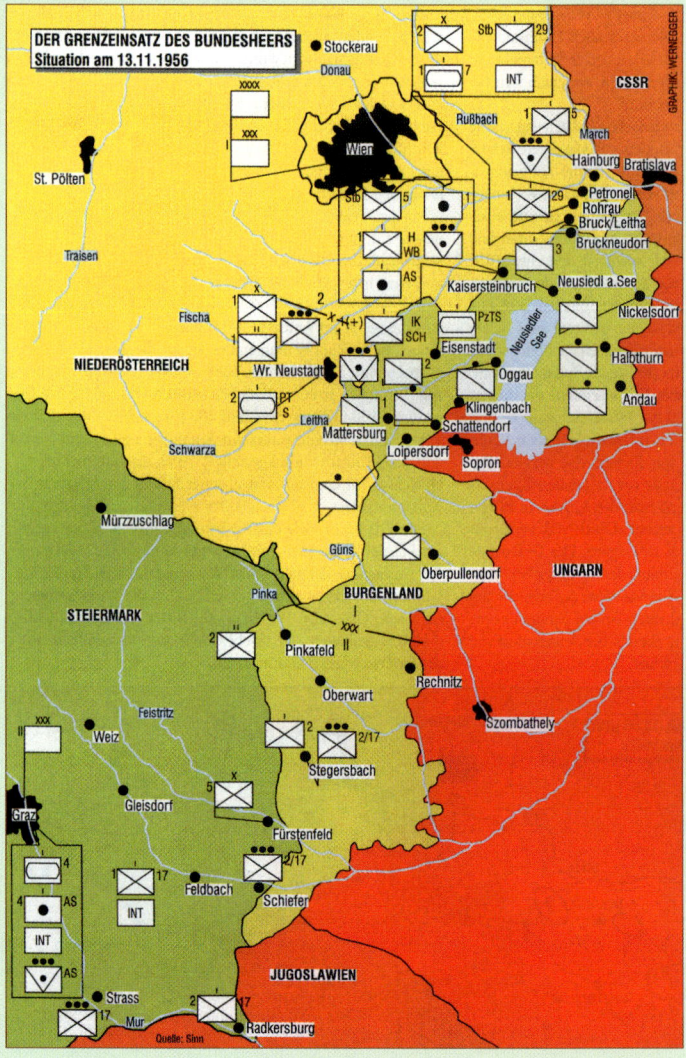

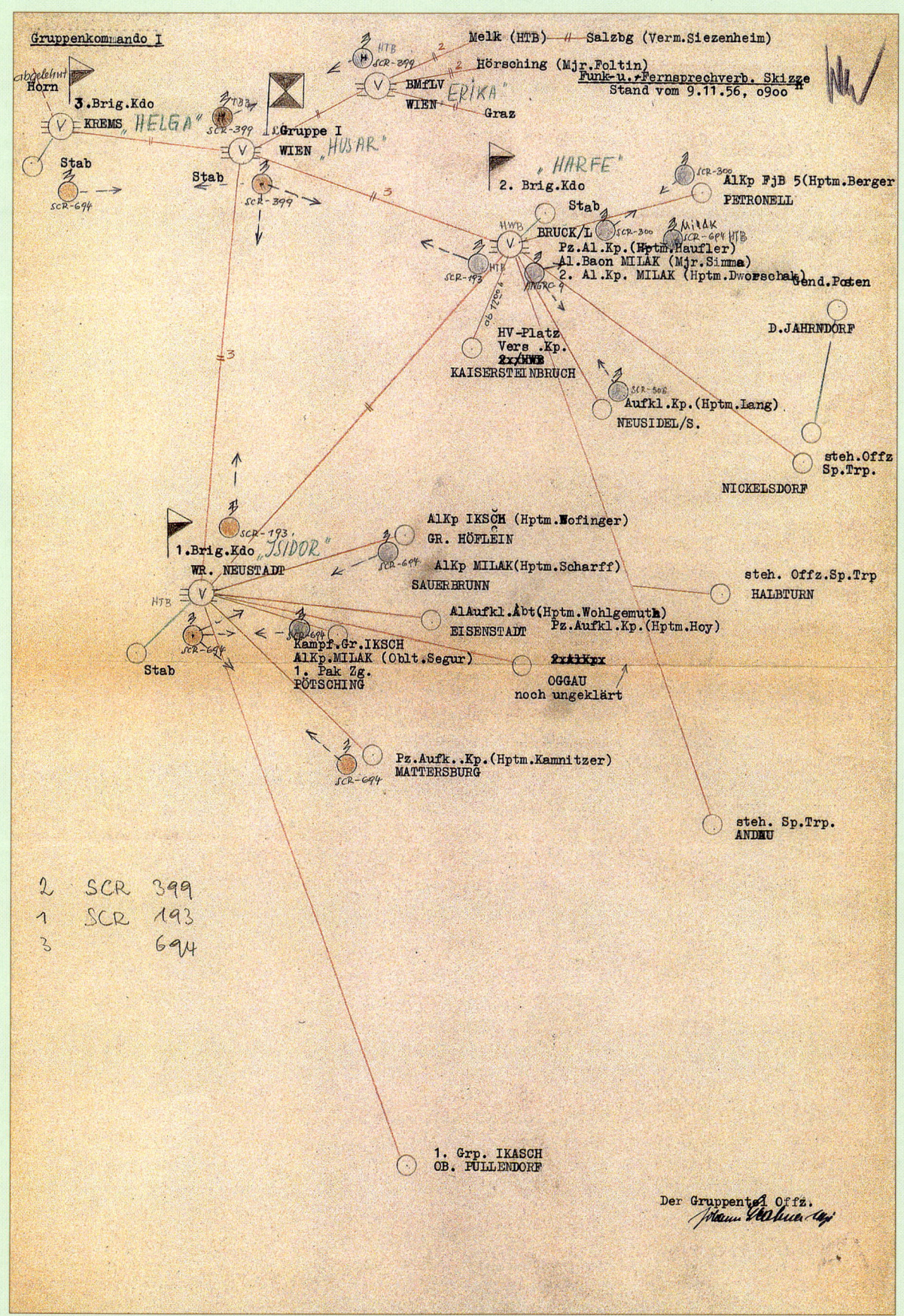

vakia, in Carpatho-Ukraine, and in Romania were already placed on alert the day before. Already, the night before October 24th, the First Secretary of the Hungarian Communist Party appealed to the Soviet military attaché to deploy the Soviet Army to reestablish order. By the wee hours of October 24th, Soviet divisions arrive in Budapest and occupy all the nerve centers of the city. At the same time, Anastas Mikoyan, the Soviet-deputized prime minister, Suslov, the chief ideologue of the Communist Party of the Soviet Union, and General Serov arrive in Budapest to sound out the situation and lead political talks for consolidation. The **"written request for assistance"** required by Khrushchev is signed by prime minister Hegedüs, in the meantime already deposed, on October 26th and backdated to October 24th. General Lashchenko orders six motorized infantry regiments to Budapest and also moves his headquarters to the capital. For the time being, the Soviet troops are unable to end the revolt. The revolutionaries provide them with fierce resistance and drive them back again and again. The Russian soldiers have no training in urban warfare, possess only outdated street maps, are inadequately supplied, and are indoctrinated and confused by the Russian-speaking Hungarian students. Troop morale sinks to almost nothing. The **"Compass"** plan of operation becomes a disaster. The uprising spreads through the entire country. On October 27th, Austrian customs officers in Klingenbach are able to watch as Hungarian border guards ceremonially raise the Hungarian flag and tear the Soviet star from their caps. And on October 29th Nagy, with the backing of the Soviets, attempts to unify rebels of all camps, in order for them to make Hungary a free, neutral, but socialist country.

As a result of their heavy losses, the Soviet leadership decides on October 30th to withdraw their troops from Budapest for the time being. After a two-day marathon conference, the Moscow Central Committee decides on the 31st of October to end the Hungarian revolution by violent means. While the Soviet Union outwardly consents to the withdrawal of their armed forces, new divisions (initially the 128th and 138th motorized infantry divisions from the military district of the Carpathians) are simultaneously sent to Hungary. However, their deployment is delayed, since the insurgents often destroy railway lines. On November 1st, in an act of desperation, Prime Minister Nagy declares Hungary's withdrawal from WaPa and the neutrality of his country after the Austrian model.

On November 2nd, the Russians slowly, and for the Hungarian population hardly noticeably, begin their intervention. Soviet tanks first close the road from Nickelsdorf to Budapest, and then seal off the border with Austria. By the evening of November 3rd, a Hungarian negotiating delegation, which includes the newly appointed defence minister General Pal Maleter, the chief of the General Staff, and other high-ranking officers, resorts to the Soviet headquarters in Tököl, having been invited by the Soviets (!) to negotiate the final withdrawal of the Soviet armed forces. Despite their protected parliamentary status, KGB General Serov has them arrested immediately after their arrival. Imre Nagy flees to the Yugoslavian embassy (from today's perspective, he was probably lured there under false pretenses after a Yugoslavian-Soviet arrangement). Cardinal Mindszenty seeks protection in the American embassy.

Then, during the night of the 3rd into the 4th of November, a large-scale advance of Soviet troops ("Operation Heavy Gale"), who had previously been strengthened to over 200,000 men (2 armies and 1 Army Corps with 17 divisions and approximately 2,000 tanks, as well as 1 air army), is successful under General Lelyushenko. The battles in Budapest last until November 11th, when the revolution is finally suppressed. Whole districts of the city are reduced to rubble in the process. The battle continues on in the provinces until November 15th. Scores of rebels continue to fight a guerilla war against the occupying forces for some time. The Soviet losses are unexpectedly high: 720 soldiers killed in action, 1,540 wounded. Roughly 50 Red Army soldiers flee with Hungarian help to Austria, from whence they are brought to safety in the USA.

After the end of the battles, Janos Kadar returns to Budapest, where he is named prime minister. On November 23rd, Nagy and his coworkers, seemingly under false hopes or promises, willingly leave the Yugoslavian embassy and are immediately arrested, carried off, and on June 16th, 1958, hanged in Budapest, along with 29 officers and soldiers (including General Maleta). Imre Nagy and his companions are later fully rehabilitated by the Communist government of Hungary.

International Reaction

At this point in time, however, the world is looking at the crisis in the Middle East: on October 28th the Suez Crisis begins, on October 29th Israeli troops advance on Egyptian territory towards the Suez Canal. At this time, Egypt is allied with Russia. On October 31st, after Egypt does not accept their ultimatum, French and British troops also attack Egypt at Israel's side. Cairo, Alexandria, Port Said, Ismailia and Suez are bombed in air strikes. On November 5th, French and English paratroopers parachute over the Suez Canal. The Soviet Union threatens the use of intercontinental rockets. The military entanglement of England and France in the Middle East thus makes any decisive campaign in Europe impossible. In the USA presidential elections are imminent on November 6th. Therefore America has only a limited ability to act, however it realizes that the possibility of a direct confrontation with the Red Army exists. There are several plans about how the Hungarians could be helped, among others with an airlift. However, since it must be considered that this would only be possible through Austria, which has unmistakably declared its intention to prevent all intrusion into its territory, this suggestion also remains on the drawing board. The Hungarians come to the bitter realization that they cannot count on any outside help.

Therefore only two countries react immediately: Yugoslavia and Austria. Yugoslavia has already broken with Moscow and struck out on an independent Communist course. It now hopes that Poland and Hungary will go down a similar path, following its example. With this, Yugoslavia would no longer be the only dissident and could even imagine itself as the center of a belt of nations. On the other hand, in case of a massive attack of the Red Army on Hungary, a threat to Yugoslavia's own independence could also occur.

Austrian Reaction

Political Measures

Relations between Hungary and Austria already begin to worsen in the early 1950s as a result of the constant border incidents, often set off by the mine belt directed against Austria (especially during floods, mines were often swept into Austrian territory). Relations improve in the summer of 1956, as, among other things, the mine belt along the "Iron Curtain" (a term that incidentally goes back to Goebbels) is cleared and replaced with a "less dangerous" signal system in the interior of the country.

After the signing of the Austrian State Treaty, the National Council enacts the Defence Act on September 7th, 1955. According to this, the Minister of Defence is assigned the power of disposition over the national armed forces, within the authority accorded to the national government, while the Federal President is the commander-in-chief (to whom the conscription of all those eligible into extraordinary military service for the purposes of Sec. 2 of the Defence Act falls). A corresponding authorization is first chartered in 1959. A **National Defence Council** is established in the Office of the Federal Chancellor. It should devise suggestions for action in military affairs. On September 22nd, the federal law on the formation of the **National Defence Agency** is agreed upon as Section VI of the Federal Chancellor's Office. The future General of the Artillery, Privy Councilor Dr. Emil Libitzky, is commissioned as its director. At the same time, the renaming of the Gendarmery schools as provisional army reserve divisions takes place on May 27th, 1955, from which the national armed forces' body of troops consequently arises. Finally, the organization of the national armed forces is established by a ruling of the Council of Ministers on January 11th, 1956. However, guidelines for the acceptance of applicants in the national army were not laid out until June 2nd, 1956. Members of the 1st national army were given preferential consideration in the process. On the other hand, the "Colonel Rule" applied to former members of the German army (accordingly, officers with a rank of Colonel or higher were not allowed to be taken over into the national army), as well as an inspection of possible close ties to the National Socialist German Worker's Party (NSDAP). Therefore only younger and "unencumbered" former German army officers are taken over. On July 15th, 1956, the National Defence Agency is transformed into a distinct **Federal Ministry for National Defence** (BMfLV), at the head of which stands Dr. Ferdinand Graf, a politician, as first Minister.

At first, like all other governments as well, the Austrian federal government is surprised by the events in Hungary. In addition, as a result of the interruption of all diplomatic ties between Hungary and Austria, only sporadic and conflicting pieces of information arrive. Federal Chancellor Raab is on a state visit to Germany, Foreign Minister Leopold Figl at the Council of Europe in Strasbourg. The fact that Vice-chancellor Dr. Adolf Schärf still sets off on a trip to East Asia on October 28th shows that the political situation is still judged as "not too serious". Nevertheless, on October 24th, Minister for the Interior Oskar Helmer and Defence Minister Dr. Graf meet with Vice-chancellor Dr. Schärf in order to discuss the situation. To keep border trespasses under control, a strengthening of the Gendarmery forces in Burgenland and a "preventative" alert of military forces is decided upon. It is initially assumed to be a **supportive deployment of federal armed forces** according to Sec. 2 para. 1 sub-para. b of the Defence Act for support of the Executive. While the Minister for the Interior possesses the authority to deploy and shift his forces, the Defence Minister must first gather the agreement of all his present fellow ministers by telephone.

On October 27th, the first border crossings in larger numbers begin. 600 – 800 Hungarians, including soldiers, customs officials and security forces, cross the border at St. Gotthard, in order to organize a "demonstration of friendship" with Austria. Around 3,000 Hungarians appear two days later in Rattersdorf, in order to celebrate a "friendship festival" with the citizens living there. In Lutzmannsburg, 200 Hungarians want to take part in religious services. In all of these cases, the Executive is able to bring the Hungarians to return to their native country without threats or the use of violence. Only a few are awarded political asylum. To prevent further "incidents" in the future and to avoid any appearance of contributing to an open border, the federal government orders the creation of a "prohibited area" along the border, which is eventually spread across large portions of Burgenland, and which one is only allowed to enter with a special pass. The intention is 1. to hold off the curious, 2. to secure the unimpeded deployment of the armed forces and the Executive, 3. to document the fulfillment of their duties as a neutral entity in any case, and finally 4. to create conditions for the most orderly acceptance of refugees possible. At the same time, the national borders are marked with red-white-red flags. On the same day, the federal government convenes for a special session, where they release, among other things, an appeal from the federal government, which is promptly handed over to the new Soviet ambassador, Sergej J. Lapin, as he presents his credentials. In it, the federal government demands the "normalization of conditions in Hungary and the reestablishment of freedom in line with human rights". On October 30th, the foreign military attachés accredited in Austria are invited to visit the prohibited zone for a briefing in the planned deployment of the armed forces to prevent border trespasses and to control the flow of refugees. On November 1st those in authority in Austria are still of the opinion that conditions in Hungary will stabilize, even though the Ministry of Defence has already been informed about Soviet troop movements since October 29th. This changes, as on the same day the Soviet Union, on the basis of an issue of the "Volksstimme", the newspaper of the Communist Party of Austria, levels heavy charges against Austria for acting non-neutrally (incidentally, the issue of the "Volksstimme" in question is confiscated, and the responsible editor is charged with treason and sedition and sentenced to 14 days imprisonment without parole). The Austrian ambassador in Moscow is subsequently directed to file a most strident protest in Moscow against this libel. Nevertheless, propaganda against NATO (also in connection with the Suez Crisis) and Austria increases. This, together with observed mobilization measures in the Czechoslovakian army, makes an escalation of the situation and an attack against Austria seem possible from a military point of view. The population reacts with panic; the stores are very quickly sold out.

Simultaneously, roughly 180,000 Hungarians flee to Austria in the time between the beginning of the Soviet attack and the suppression of the revolt, and are accommodated here, housed in refugee camps, and provided with supplies, often at the cost of private, personal sacrifices. The fact that Honved soldiers are also among the refugees forces the federal government to construct internment camps, according to the Hague Convention of 1907.

Military Measures

Until the middle of 1956, the **military organization** can be considered as a whole. After taking effect on August 1st, the federal armed forces organize themselves in three group commands, eight brigade commands, supply troops, academies and schools as well as support forces. The Ministry itself must serve a double function as an administrative agency and as a military command agency. The military command leadership of the federal armed forces is assigned to the **General Troop Inspector** according to the assignment of duties. The first holder of this function is the colonel of the higher military service (as the General Staff service is first shamefacedly described), Erwin Fussenegger, on July 21st, 1956. The Border Patrol and Organization departments are combined into a **"Command Department"**, the leader of the Operations department takes over the role of a **"Chief of Staff"**. The available number of officers allows only minimally occupied continuous service. Some of the officers must even provide their services in civilian clothes, since they do not possess uniforms yet. They first receive pistols after two weeks. The larger problem, however, is with the "support personnel", which consists almost entirely of civilians, who hold themselves to office hours. Because of the lack of communication facilities, connections to command posts are created over the public networks, thanks to exemplary work with postal service stations. In the radio sector, the connection takes place over the stationary **"Homeland Radio Network"**. The federal Gendarmery network is available for teletype messages within a limited area. As a first step, the newly created GTI enacts the **"General Directive"** for warfare in case of an attack from the area of Czechoslovakia and/or Hungary. Despite initially very limited prospects, the Armed Forces **Intelligence Group** is able to make timely descriptions of the intentions and movements of the Soviet reinforcements. This directive provides for the deployment of Group I (based in Vienna) south of Vienna, with the mission to lead a campaign of delay to the east and then a stalling campaign to the west of Vienna. If under enemy attack, the bridges on the Danube should be destroyed. Group II (Graz) should fall back while resisting to the area of Graz – Klagenfurt – Villach; Group III (Salzburg) should be deployed in the area of Linz – Enns – Steyr. In reality, the brigades and troop groups are only made up of commands and a few portions of cadres at this time (the first men eligible for military service are not drafted until October 15th, 1956). Air forces in the true sense do not exist. The military possesses only a few Russian Yakovlev Yak-11s and British and American helicopters that were left behind by the occupation troops.

On October 24th, during a meeting between the Minister for the Interior and the Defence Minister concerning the situation in Hungary, a **strengthening of the security measures** in Burgenland is decided upon. After consulting with his fellow ministers by telephone, the Defence Minister issues the following directive at 3:00 PM:

- preparations for the formation of alert units (1 company per battalion);
- deployment of an infantry platoon in Fürstenfeld to strengthen the Border Gendarmery;
- provision of one (!) Yak-11 airplane for training and strafing missions and one helicopter for reconnaissance and investigation purposes.

Concrete arrangements are:

- the 1st, 2nd, 5th, and 7th Brigades form alert units with a strength of one company per battalion;
- the Army Engineer Battalion (AEngBn) provides a company of engineers, and the Infantry Battle School provides a mixed company;
- the 5th Infantry Brigade sends an infantry platoon to Fürstenfeld;
- the Military Academy of Enns forms (fully motorized) alert companies out of the 1st and 2nd enrollment classes and holds them in readiness;
- the Tank Troop School of Hörsching provides a reconnaissance company;
- the Artillery School forms an (alert) battery;
- the Air Force holds a helicopter and a fixed-wing aircraft (Yak-11) ready for reconnaissance and investigation purposes;
- all commands remain occupied until further notice.

The alert companies are composed of roughly 100 cadre soldiers. The General Troop Inspector issues the first assignments. Since the Minister's directive, which comes in at 5:00 PM, conflicts with the GTI's assignments, he orders at 5:45 PM the provision of a half-hour readiness to move out for the Guards Battalion, the Infantry Battle School, the 1st Light Infantry Battalion and 2nd Infantry Battalion, the Artillery Troop School, and the Army Telegraph Battalion. The alert readiness for the 5th Light Infantry Battalion and the 1st Engineer Battalion is rescinded.[1] However, since the events in Hungary seem not to rush[2] any further forward, the readiness of the alerted units is rescinded again on the following day. By the same token, the Homeland Radio Network is turned off, the Intelligence Group stops the monitoring service.

Not until the next day (it is the 26th of October, the "Day of the Flag") does the military leadership realize that the situation is developing to the contrary. Because of the recent worsening of the internal Hungarian conflicts and the threatening Soviet troop

---

1 See: War Log, October 24th, 1956.
2 By the morning of October 25th, Hungarian radio is already reporting the suppression of the revolt and the end of the fighting.

movements, a new **Alert for Federal Military Units** (including an "Alert Academic Company" from the Military Academy in Enns[3], as well as an "Alert Tank Company" from the Tank Troop School in Hörsching) and their relocation to the Austria-Hungary border is ordered. The alerted troops' advance is improvised. Due to a lack of military drivers, the owners of civil drivers' licenses without driving experience must steer the American vehicles. Despite extremely difficult weather conditions, the deployment takes place without traffic accidents. The units are assigned to support the public security institutions in the prohibited zone in the transfer of a large stream of refugees into Austria, and to prevent the sudden development of hostilities in Austrian territory. Independent of these tasks, the actual deployment of the armed forces in the sense of Sec. 2 Defence Act (DA) begins now as well. The formations also receive a directive for **use of deadly force** in this situation: *"Use of deadly force is only to occur when armed individuals or formations cross the border and do not obey orders to retreat across the border or lay down their weapons, or immediately after intruders open fire against anyone in Austrian territory."* This order is clarified two days later: *"Deadly force is also to be used against Soviet units..., if they do not withdraw and continue to fight. The intruders are to be repelled and disarmed as necessary."*

In the meantime, further alert units are placed in half-hour readiness to move out, or employed for border patrol as necessary. On October 27th, the 1st Infantry Brigade is directed to send three Officer Scout Troop units to patrol the border area between Pinkafeld – Oberpullendorf – Neusiedl/See. The mass of the deployed troops had reached their duty positions on the evening of October 27th. Over the course of the day, roughly 1,000 Hungarians cross the border at Mogersdorf to celebrate their supposed freedom. A military police company is set on the march to make the Hungarians leave the territory of the state. The night of October 28th, the military academy receives the order to create two further alert companies out of the executive enrollment class and to establish their one-hour readiness to march.

As hostilities break out in Hungary, the strictest self-control is imposed on the Austrian soldiers. Apart from motorized patrols and specific posts, the units are not allowed to go closer than 500 meters to the border, so as not to unintentionally become involved in gunfights. The units continue scouting activities and training in the following days. The disarmament and internment of combatants plays a special role. Following the federal government's directive, the military constructs specific **internment camps** for escaped members of the Honved and border security troops at the military training ground at Bruck/Leitha, in the barracks at Feldbach and Oberwart, and in the engineer troop school in Klosterneuburg.

On November 5th, the situation comes to a head. Worrying news arrives at the Defence Ministry, which does not eliminate the possibility of a Soviet attack against Austria. The US military attaché speaks before the ministry and warns of a possible escalation in Europe in connection with the events at the Suez Canal. Mobilization measures in Czechoslovakia strengthen the threatening situation. In the Defence Ministry, two possible deployment variations for **the defence of the border against Czechoslovakia** were devised. A **command staff** was established in the ministry, which was to fulfill the duties of an army command. The GTI (a Colonel) had already called for this on November 3rd, but it was prevented by the director of Section I (a General!). Such animosities also seem to be traditional.

Since the Parliament had given no authorization for deployment the day before, Defence Minister Dr. Graf acts independently and signs the **deployment order for the federal armed forces** in the late afternoon of November 5th. Accordingly, the following is scheduled for November 6th:

- Withdrawal of deployed forces to the general line of Sauerbrunn-Großhöfein, Bruck/Leitha-Petronell;
- Relocation of Group II troops to a stance protective of Graz;
- Leadership of the forces in the area of Linz – Enns – Steyr by Group III;
- Preparation for destruction of the bridges on the Danube outside Vienna;
- Transfer of operative leadership to Group III in the case of obstruction of the command staff in the Defence Ministry;
- Evacuation of the barracks and movement into encampments close to garrisons, so as not to become targets for air attacks;
- Continued occupation of the immediate border area only for tank reconnaissance companies and motorized scout troops already deployed;
- Provision of an echelon of military drivers in case of a possible relocation of the command staff.

At 6:45 AM on November 6th, the formation of Groups I and II report their defence readiness. However, the night remains quiet, except for a few smaller shootings, so that by day the defence preparations, disguised as **"night march practice"** can already be ended again. The units remain in their new duty positions, however. The reconnaissance companies take over surveillance on the national border. Officer scout troops are advanced from the assembly areas back to the border.

The "withdrawal of deployed forces" is a result of the dilemma caused by an imprecise definition of duties in the Defence Act. According to the Defence Act, the primary purpose of the armed forces is the "protection of the borders of the republic" instead of for instance the "perpetuation of sovereignty". So at first, formations were placed on the border to take up their task there. However, when the crossover of hostilities into Austrian territory is feared, this "border defence" is given up as not practically viable. A measure that is incomprehensible for the affected (and endangered) population in the border area. However, political mistakes are imputed to the military.

---

[3] The removal of the emergency military academy company is contrary not only to economy of force, it leads – according to their debriefing – to problems with the neutrality policy. The appearance of this then most powerful formation in an area thoroughly unsuitable for defence is seen by the neighbors as a sign of a coming Austrian offensive advance to cut off the Ödenburger Gates (see Anton Leeb: "Ten Years Ago – Deployment on the Hungarian Border", Truppendienst 6/1966).

As a result of the further relaxation of tensions, the alert companies of the Military Academy of Enns can be released to continue their officer training on November 12th. At the same time, the alert companies are reorganized into companies according to the organizational plan, in that they are filled with young men who until then were intensively trained in their home garrisons.

On November 13th, therefore, 2,740 soldiers are deployed. Readiness measures are slowly reduced. The defence preparations are nevertheless continued, and the engineer inspector receives the order to devise a **blockage plan "East"**, assuming a massive enemy attack from the east. Its survey takes place in civilian clothing to keep from agitating the population.

Besides the military measures, the military also supports **humanitarian facilities**, so loading teams are placed at the Schwechat airport in order to transfer relief supplies from around the world from airplanes into trucks; on November 22nd the refugee camp Kleßheim in Salzburg is opened and on November 26th the Stiftskaserne in Vienna is evacuated for the admittance of refugees.

On November 23rd, a further **reduction of units** is ordered, the command of the 1st Infantry Brigade is removed from Wiener Neustadt to Eisenstadt, that of the 2nd Infantry Brigade from Bruck/Leitha to Vienna and that of the 5th Infantry Brigade from Fürstenfeld to Graz. On the same day a serious border incident happens in Rechnitz: Three Soviet soldiers pursue Hungarian fugitives into Austrian territory and attempt to rob and rape a young girl. They are confronted by a Gendarmery patrol. One soldier can be captured and disarmed, two attempt to flee, despite "calls to stop" and shots fired. One of the soldiers is hit and dies in transit to the hospital, the other escapes. Shortly thereafter the security directorate alerts the armed forces. The 2nd Infantry Battalion receives the order to shift a platoon to Rechnitz to calm the distressed inhabitants and protect against possible further encroachments. On November 24th, a further reduction takes place. The standing scouting troops are withdrawn from the border towns, readiness reduced and forces removed to their home garrisons. Only motorized scouting troops continue to patrol the border, where the drives simultaneously serve as training for the drivers. The Defence Ministry officially declares in the "Wiener Zeitung" that the Hungarian embassy in Vienna has informed them of the official end of hostilities in Hungary. Therefore, on December 7th, 12:00 AM, all internment camps are disbanded in accordance with human rights regulations. All the interned are questioned in the presence of representatives of the International Committee of the Red Cross (ICRC) about whether they want to return to their native country.

Only 103 out of around 1,200 people decide to return. They are immediately sent through Nickelsdorf back to Hungary. On December 10th the Defence Ministry orders the cessation of the remaining patrol activities, to take effect on December 15th, 5:00 PM, and the deregulation of the tactical interception border on December 22nd, 12:00 AM. The 13th Light Infantry Battalion is the last formation to shift to its home garrison, on December 24th. In total 70% of the cadre personnel are deployed at the height of the crisis, while the remaining 30% carried out the training of the first young men.

By the beginning of 1957, the political relationship between Hungary and Austria had already worsened again. The border is less porous as a result of the "Iron Curtain", but also more dangerous. The Hungarian border authorities make more use of their firearms to hinder escape attempts. As the result of a decision made by the Council of Ministers on January 15th, 1957, a prohibited zone is again established along the shared border to prevent illegal border crossings and suppress the smuggling of people and goods as well as the illegal foreign exchange trade. The security directorates of the Gendarmery forces assist in the affected sectors. The armed forces establish renewed signal heads in Deutschkreutz, Eisenstadt and Andau.

From February 14th there then followed a **supportive deployment** to assist the customs officers, in which Group Commands I and II supplied personnel in 14-day shifts. The assignment is to support the customs officials in the carrying out of customs duties, particularly with patrol duty for border observations and surveillance. In addition, precaution is taken that during border incidents a swift gathering of military forces, as a reserve of intervention under military command, is possible as support for the Executive. The end of the supportive deployment of the armed forces, and thereby the end of the military deployment as a result of the events in Hungary in October 1956, does not end until April 23rd, 1957 at 12:00 PM.

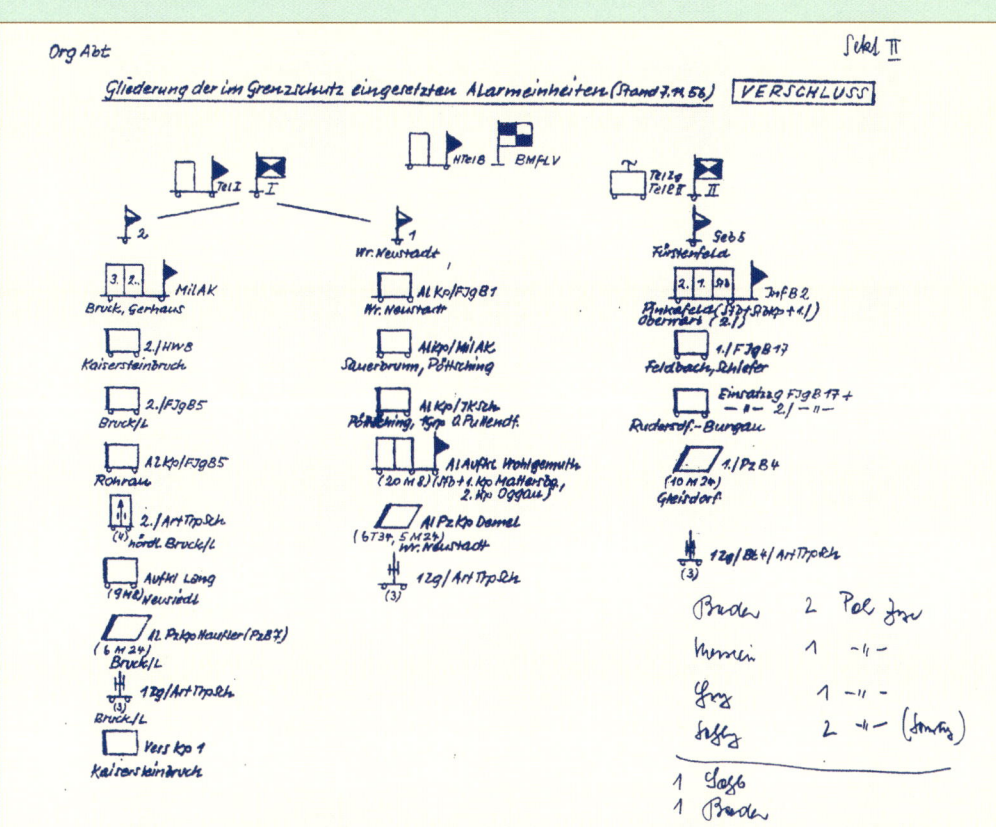

The armed forces are, with a few exceptions, equipped with American light and armored vehicles. Light vehicles from Jeep, Dodge and GMC are deployed on the Hungarian border.

The armored vehicles consist of 29 M8 armored reconnaissance vehicles (m.l.) as well as 21 M24 reconnaissance tanks from America and 27 T34 battle tanks (m.r.) from the Soviet Union. Patrol on the national border, marked with a red-white-red flag (b.l.).
The mistake: American uniforms and American equipment – those must be American soldiers (b.r.).

Basis for deployment:	Discussion between Minister for the Interior and Defence Minister on October 24th, 1956; retroactive approval by the Council of Ministers (CM) on October 28th, 1956 of all measures taken by the Defence Minister.
Type of deployment:	Supportive deployment according to Sec. 2 para. 1 sub-para. b DA, from October 26th, 1956, also security deployment according to Sec. 2 para. 1 sub-para. a DA.
Mission:	Defence of the Austrian Republic's borders.
Duration of deployment:	October 24th, 1956 – December 24th, 1956 and February 14th – April 23rd, 1957.
Contingent strength:	2,740 (as of November 13th, 1956).

Equipment and Armament

The still young military is almost exclusively equipped with weapons left behind by American occupation troops. The tank soldiers also wear American uniforms at the outset. A red-white-red cockade is only fixed[4] to the head coverings. Being mistaken for regular American troops is therefore preprogrammed. Not only by Hungarian refugees, but in some areas also Austrians fall victim to these mistakes. While Hungarian soldiers often specifically demand to be handed over to the American troops in Austria, the Austrians are happy to learn that the soldiers in American uniforms are their own. The "Volksstimme" even uses this situation to spread the allegation that American troops are already in Austria throughout the world. This is gratefully taken up by the Soviets and used against Austria.

Scouts in a 1/4t all-terrain truck (Jeep), armed with a 7.62 mm MG M1919A4.

---

4 See: Rolf M. Urrisk: "The Uniforms of the Austrian Armed Forces from 1952 – 1995", Weishaupt Publishing, Graz 1995.

Flooding in Carinthia and East Tyrol

Preliminary Events

At the beginning of September 1965, catastrophic storms break over Carinthia and East Styria. An intense, continuous rain, reaching up to altitudes of 3,500 meters, drops 400,000 cubic meters of rainwater in the 24 hours between September 2nd and 3rd in the district of Lienz alone.

10,000 cubic meters of rock mass are swept away with the first flood wave. National and regional roads in the district of Lienz are broken in 131 places along a distance of 20 km, in Upper Carinthia 14 crossings over the Drava are destroyed.

Political Measures

Immediately after the start of the catastrophe, a supportive deployment of units of the federal armed forces is requested by regional and district authorities.

Military Measures

Due to appropriate civil and military emergency plans, the armed forces are deployed without delay.

Basis for deployment:	Request of the affected provincial governments and district administrations.
Type of deployment:	Supportive deployment according to Sec. 2 para. 1 sub-para. c DA.
Mission:	Construction of temporary bridges; transportation of people and goods of all types; installation of telephone cables; repair of roads and ways.
Duration of deployment:	September 2nd, 1965 – September 28th, 1965.
Contingent strength:	2,500.
Contribution:	The soldiers contribute a total of 900,000 work hours, while the deployed vehicles cover 500,000 km. 3,288 people and 171 tons of goods are transported with helicopters. 5,000 people are transported with ferries, 129 bridges and 55 km of roads are repaired by the engineers. The telecommunication forces install 180 km of telephone wire. Through the assistance of the soldiers, the effects of the damage are limited and the normal course of public life can be restored in the shortest possible amount of time.

Attacks in South Tyrol

Preliminary Events

After the 1st World War, the territory of the former Austro-Hungarian monarchy is assigned to the newly formed states in the **"Parisian Suburb Treaties"**. In doing so, it is assumed that that only "nationally pure" regions should form states, and that the people's right of self-determination has the highest priority. These principles, however, have no effect on the case of South Tyrol. South Tyrol, despite its very large German-speaking segment of the population, and against the wishes of those affected, is left to Italy, more or less as a "reward" for entering the war. Austria must renounce integration with South Tyrol in the **"Treaty of Saint-Germain-en-Laye"**. Italy subsequently carries out a massive "Italianization" in the interwar period. Italians are settled in South Tyrol, to change the proportion of the nationalities to Italy's advantage. World War 2 does not change the situation either. Austria's hopes for a reintegration of South Tyrol after the end of the war are not fulfilled. The intentions of the western powers are clearly against it. So Austrian foreign minister Dr. Karl Gruber settles the accord on South Tyrol with his Italian counterpart, Alcide de Gasperi, on September 5th, 1946.

This **"Gruber-De Gasperi Agreement"** arranges for equality between German-speaking South Tyroleans and Italians that should be expressed in the equal position of the German language in the bureaucracy and education and an economic boost to the region from Rome. The agreement is accepted by the Conference of Foreign Ministers in Paris on September 13th, 1956, and is added as an appendix to the peace treaty with Italy on February 10th, 1957. The Italian implementation of South Tyrol's autonomy takes place only very slowly. After a declaration from the Austrian Foreign Minister, Dr. Lujo Toncic, before the General Assembly of the United Nations, the negotiations between Austria and Italy show a certain amount of progress. Nevertheless, groups form in South Tyrol for whom the process is too slow, and who also do not shrink away from violence. South Tyroleans, but also North Tyroleans, belong to the **"Committee for the Liberation of South Tyrol (BAS)"**. The BAS begins to organize bomb attacks. An intensive cross-border "cooperation" and brisk smuggling activity develop. Over the years the explosions, known colloquially as "banger activity", shift from electrical pylons and statues to assassinations of Italian politicians or other public figures who either openly or supposedly oppose South Tyroleans' right to autonomy. This leads to a renewed escalation of the tense relationships. The negotiations are not in fact broken off, but Italy begins to put Austria under political pressure to take measures against the terrorists' illegal border crossings. The attacks reach a sad culmination with the bloody assassination attempt at the Porzerscharte, in which, on the night of June 25th into the 26th, 1967, four Italian soldiers lose their lives.

This assassination triggers clear outrage in the South Tyrolean regional parliament as well as in Rome. At the same time, Austria seeks a treaty of association with EEC. Italy takes this as an occasion for Foreign Minister Fanfani to announce on June 28th that Italy will boycott the current association negotiations with Austria at the EEC Foreign Ministers' Conference on June 28th. This tandem measure is subsequently introduced at the conference of the European Coal and Steel Community and the committee meeting in Brussels. On July 8th the Italian ambassador in Vienna delivers an official **note of protest,** in which above all Austria's inactivity in the fight against terrorism is criticized.[5] The note is rejected by Austria. In a new note of protest on July 18th, Austria is even accused of allowing terrorist outposts in Austria. A further escalation occurs when Italy cancels their participation at the Viennese trade show (astoundingly, however, takes part in the opening of the trade show in Klagenfurt, which takes place on the same day). Not until Austria's announcement that it will put Italy's veto on the agenda in the Council of Europe does Rome take a more conciliatory posture. In December 1967, Italy resumes the expert-level bilateral negotiations.

Austrian Reaction

Political Measures

On July 4th, 1967, the federal government decides on the placement of a Gendarmery Special Unit and deliberates on a possibly deployment of the armed forces beginning on July 5th, 1967. A corresponding request is already being posed in some newspapers, most of all in the "Presse" and the "Tiroler Tageszeitung". Federal Chancellor Dr. Josef Klaus and Austrian People's Party Secretary-General Dr. Hermann Widhalm confirm the government's plans. Through these measures, Austria's efforts for a peaceful solution to the South Tyrol Problem should be demonstrated to the world at large. Naturally, the Italian tandem measure in the EEC plays a substantial role in this. The actual decision is made in the Council of Ministers on July 11th, under the chairmanship of Vice-Chancellor Dr. Fritz Bock after an application from Minister for the Interior Franz Hetzenauer. In doing so, they call upon Article 79 of the Federal Constitution Law (FCL) 1920, in the 1929 edition, in which a **supportive deployment** is allowed for when the civil powers can no longer fulfill their duties with their own forces. The deployment of more than 100 men requires a formal decision of the Council of Ministers, which is given with the passing of the resolution on July 11th. The necessary briefing of the Federal President according to the FCL takes place immediately following the meeting of the

---

5 "Italian Memorandum Delivered in Vienna", in: Tiroler Tageszeitung, July 10th, 1967.

Council of Ministers, first personally through the Vice-Chancellor and shortly thereafter in written form (with a designation of the deployed formations) through the Defence Minister.

In this deployment, the domestic political situation also plays a large role. For the first time, the Austrian People's Party rules as the sole party in power. The Socialist Party of Austria is in the opposition. It also sees not the conclusion of the decision for a supportive deployment, but rather the goal of the deployment as conflicting with the constitution. According to the opposition, guarding the border from illegal border crossings is not the duty of the national armed forces. The fact that *"soldiers could detain and search civilians is unthinkable in normal times in a democracy."*[6] Dr. Kreisky expresses the worries of the Socialist Party of Austria in this way: *"We want to prevent the federal armed forces from being used for political, in this case international political considerations of gain. Many of us have experienced what it means for a constitution to be trifled with."*[7] This reason is certainly grounded in the trauma of 1934, when soldiers of the federal armed forces had to advance on the workers' party. A further point of criticism from the SPÖ's viewpoint is the inappropriateness of the deployment. The SPÖ argues that the terrorists know the terrain like the backs of their hands, while the soldiers on the other hand possess little knowledge of the terrain. The true reason for the criticism, however, presumably lies in the the fact that the SPÖ was not included in the decision process. At any rate, no criticisms are put forward at the sitting of the international political committee. On the contrary, in the same sitting the SPÖ votes for the purchase of interceptor planes of the "Draken" type (the armed forces actually first receive these planes 20 years later – over heavy protests from the SPÖ). As Foreign Minister, Dr. Kreisky instigates the deployment of the military to the Congo, in order to gather international rear cover for his South Tyrolean policies before the General Assembly of the United Nations (see the ONUC deployment of the Austrian armed forces).

The deployment has a positive psychological effect, however at first the various legal opinions reach no consensus about protection of the measures promised by the Italian side in the South Tyrol question. Not until 1969 does it come to the conclusion of the "South Tyrol Package".

Military Measures

Immediately after the sitting of the Council of Ministers on June 11th, a meeting takes place in the Defence Ministry, in which the command structure and the mission order are established. The 6th Infantry Brigade for North Tyrol and the 7th Infantry Brigade for East Tyrol are specified as the leading commands. Group Command III leads a platoon to the border of Salzburg with Italy (the reason this takes place is no longer comprehensible today). This platoon is shortly thereafter subordinated to the 4th Infantry Battalion. The length of the supportive deployment is set at six weeks for every battalion. This is to be seen as a compromise. A shorter duration would have affected more divisions and hardly allowed time for the overlap necessary for orientation in the area of operations. Although less divisions would have been affected through a longer deployment, the deployment training would have suffered in indefensible ways. Therefore, three cycles are initially specified:

- July 11th – August 24th: 4th, 23rd and 24th Infantry Battalions;
- August 21st – October 5th: 13th Mechanized Infantry Battalion; 2nd and 19th Infantry Battalions;
- October 2nd – November 15th: 17th, 21st and 26th Infantry Battalions.

The deployment of the (Viennese) 4th Infantry Battalion, for whom personnel with alpine qualifications had to be introduced, is surprising. The reason must have been that at first they consciously wanted to make no use of Tyrolean divisions.

From the beginning it is clearly expressed that the brigades receive their **orders from the security directorate of the Tyrol or the district administration of Lienz**. Therefore the soldiers are only "indirectly" subordinate to the civil entities. The "General Service Regulation (ADV)" continues to apply. As a regulation of the federal government, the ADV binds the other ministries as well. As a result of this comprehensive application, it is not necessary to enact specific regulations, for instance for the use of weapons. The rights and responsibilities of the soldiers in the area of operations conform to those of the military guards. Every soldier receives an **information sheet**, where these rights and responsibilities are summarized. Initially, the patrols always begin with officials of the Gendarmery, until all soldiers are familiarized with the border routine. Later Gendarmery officials are only assigned in delicate situations.

The mission order follows the alert of the divisions. The 4th Infantry Battalion is moved by train, the other two infantry battalions march through the streets to the area of operations. Because of the unusual character of the deployment, no heavy weapons are taken along. Deployment readiness is provided until July 13th, on July 14th the supportive deployment begins. The 6th Infantry Brigade relies on the cooperation of a helicopter squadron, the 7th Infantry Brigade on two helicopters. The border is divided into engagement bands, staging posts are established at the most important border crossings, and the territory in between is monitored with patrols. As a result of the offset in depths, the surveillance system proves to be very efficient, changes in circumstances can be quickly and effectively responded to. The bands and patrols, carried out at irregular times, take place during all weather conditions and at every time of day.

The soldiers' accommodations are provided in mass quarters. Where infrastructure issues or the tourist industry make these impossible, the accommodations are in tent camps in group tents. These are heated with tent stoves, the middle post of the tents

---

[6] Paul Blau, Editor-in-Chief of the "Arbeiterzeitung", on July 15th, 1967.
[7] Bruno Kreisky's answer to Dr. Klaus' comments, "Arbeiterzeitung", July 18th, 1967.

Right: Since the deployment is carried out according to instructions from the Federal Ministry for the Interior, all assigned soldiers wear white armbands with the official seal of the Security Directorate of the Province of Tyrol, in order to make this subordination to the civil authorities outwardly visible as well.
Below: Overview sketch of the area of operations on July 15th, 1967 (Sketch: Wolfgang Zecha in "Truppendienst" 2/1997).

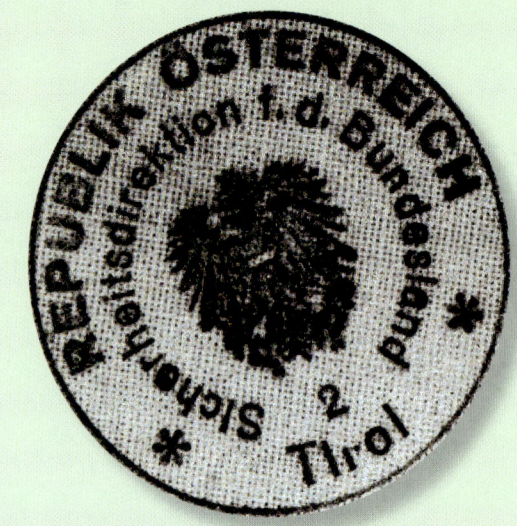

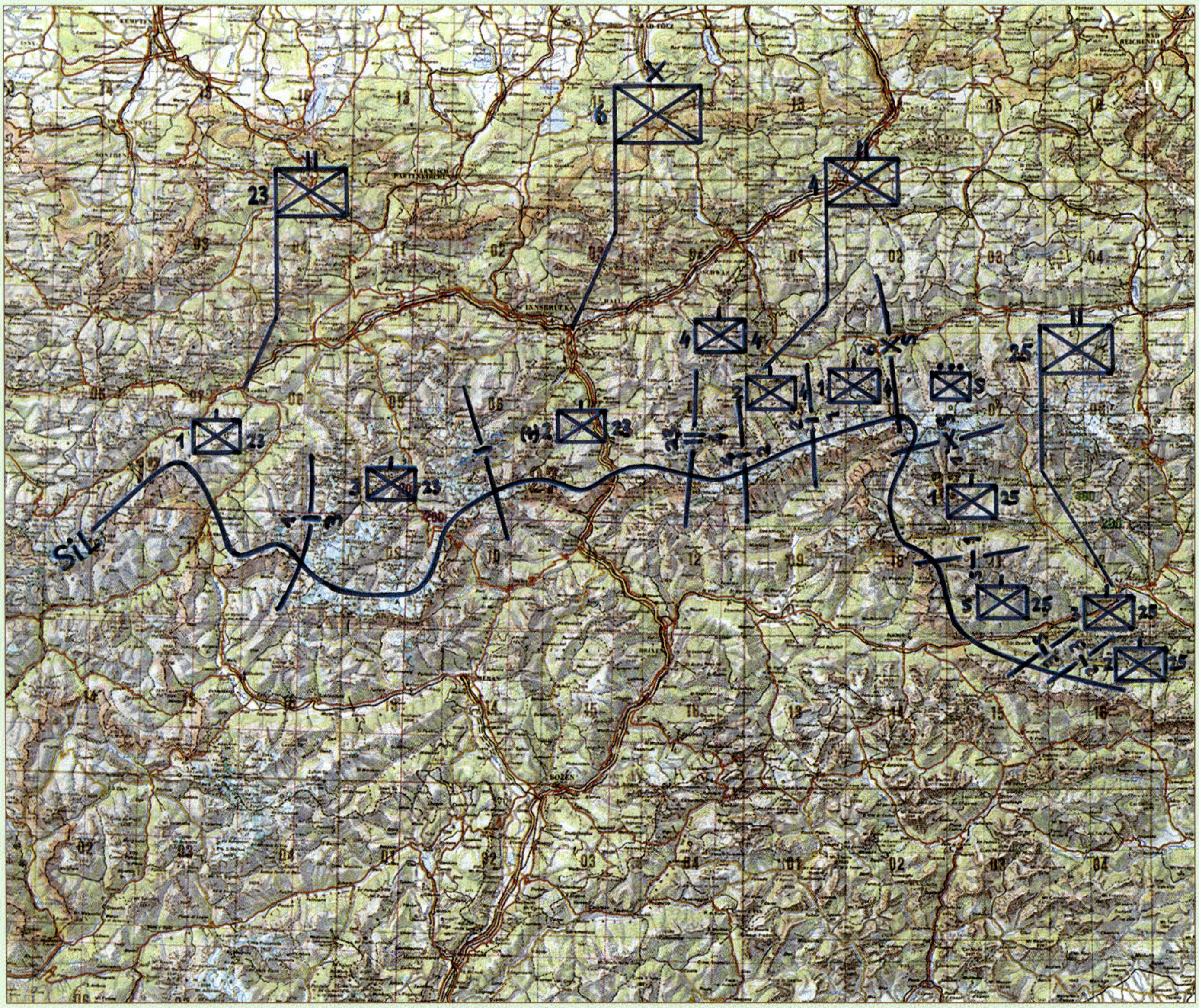

The "Haflinger", whether on four wheels or four legs, is an indispensable form of transport in the mountains (l.t.). Consultation between Gendarmery, Border Patrol and Armed Forces (l.b.).

A patrol goes off duty according to protocol. Discipline even high in the mountains (r.t.).
Surveillance also takes place from the air. SE-3130 Alouette II helicopter with crew (r.m.).
Rolls of barbed wire are laid extensively as barriers (r.b.).

are also designed as chimney pipes. As it becomes clear that the deployment will stretch into the bad season, bivouac huts ("bivouac boxes") are constructed in the tent camps for protection against the weather conditions. 20 of these pre-made huts, as well as a few of the smallest quarters, are provided for the scouts. Since reserve tents were also brought, dry, shower, and provision tents can also be set up. For the detainees, transfer points are established.

As well as patrol activities and the preservation of camp order, the time is also used for ongoing training at the staging posts (alpine troop training, exercise duty, orientation in the terrain, ADV, homeland and citizen studies, weapons drill, security and observation duty as well as self- and comrade-assistance) and at the military training ground in Lizum (shooting and battle duty up to group parameters). The soldiers are equipped with the normal man's gear. Because of the weather conditions the battalions take a large supply of changes of clothing with them. To secure the sanitation provisions, the companies are assigned practical doctors and dentists by location. Furthermore, there are constant inspections from military doctors from the military command. The veterinary care of the pack animals is carried out by the Pack Animal Company of the 6th Headquarters Battalion. Meals are prepared in the central cook sites of the battalions and picked up from there by the divisions. The platoons' staging posts and the standing scouting troops in the high alpine regions are brought their meals with the 0.5t all-terrain vehicle of the Puch "Haflinger" type or by pack animals of the same name. Due to great distance, Staging Post A/1 (Krimmler Tauernhaus) and the standing scouting troop B/2 (Dristelbachalm) are reliant on commercial meals. Besides this, every staging post is equipped with a "package of provisions for independent cooking" free for the taking, consisting of bacon, raw eggs, onions, potatoes, flour and lard.

On August 24th, a **change of leadership structure** takes place. The responsibility for leadership is transferred from the infantry battalions to the military commands of the Tyrol and Carinthia, so as not to endanger the division training of the brigades. Since the military command of the Tyrol has two battalions to lead, a regimental command "South" is formed.

The camps and staging posts are already checked for avalanche safety in September. During this it comes out that only ten are safe against avalanches. Some, however, are very threatened by avalanches, since they were established in summer according to their usefulness for the supportive deployment. In these cases a shift to a safer area takes place. Since ever more border soldiers are being withdrawn from the Italian side as a result of the worsening weather, a reduction of the Austrian forces also takes place. Only individual companies remain, who are directly led by the military commands. The military leadership reduces the forces to seven staging posts in North and three in East Tyrol on November 14th. In total, 180 men remain in North Tyrol, 90 in East Tyrol. These are subsequently further reduced. At Christmas the official end of the supportive deployment is ordered and announced for December 31st, 1967.

The success of the deployment is difficult to quantify. Doubts are naturally cast by the socialist media "Arbeiterzeitung" and "Express." The daily reports offer a better picture. According to them, searches happen practically every day between July 14th and the end of August, twelve arrests are verifiable. The official "Wiener Zeitung" writes of six arrests and 594 luggage searches, as well as several discovered weapons caches. It is hardly possible to determine to what extent a preventative effect was produced, but at any rate illegal border crossings were made more difficult. After camouflage as "tourists" falls away in the middle of September, it is not possible even for natives to cross the border without regulation. The political effect of the deployment is substantial. The Italians' willingness to negotiate as of September is to be attributed in large part to the signal sent by the supportive deployment.

Basis for deployment:	Council of Ministers on July 11th, 1967.
Type for deployment:	Supportive deployment according Sec. 2 para. 1 sub-para. b DA.
Mission:	Suppression of the illegal movements of people and goods from Austria to Italy and back, especially to prevent or discover terrorist attacks.[8]
Duration of deployment:	July 12th, 1967 – November 15th, 1967.
Contingent strength:	Around 1,400.

---

8   See Information Sheet for the Supportive Contribution of the Armed Forces to the Monitoring of the Austrian-Italian Border.

"Prague Spring"

Preliminary Events

Since 1948, the year the Communists took power, an intellectual resistance has been developing in the Czechoslovak Socialist Republic (ČSSR). In addition, tensions between the Czechs and the Slovaks are growing within the Communist Party of Czechoslovakia (KPČ) under president and party chief Novotny. The Union of Czechoslovak Writers proclaims their demand for the introduction of a "democratic Communism" for the first time in June 1967. After Novotny is removed, Alexander Dubcek is elected the new First Secretary of the KPČ on January 5th, 1968. This begins a meaningful break in the KPČ's domestic political situation, which results in many measures, such as the abolishment of censorship on March 1st, or important personnel replacements (in this way, economist Oldrich Cernik becomes prime minister of a newly-formed cabinet). In public, a discussion begins about a possible future neutrality of the nation. Within the army the hardliners lose ground after Major General Sejna's escape to the west in February and Colonel General Janko's suicide in March 1968.

In 1968, the Czechoslovakian leadership under Alexander Dubcek attempts to create a "socialism with a human face" in the so-called **"Prague Spring"** (this name comes from an annual music festival that takes place between May 12th and June 3rd since 1946). This leads to "concern" from the leadership in Moscow under the direction of Leonid Brezhnev, who fear a weakening of the Warsaw Pact (WP).

Serious threats against the government of the ČSSR are already taking place – although still cryptic – at the conference of state and party leaders in Dresden on March 23rd, 1968. The first preparations for a military deployment already begin in the Soviet Union on March 20th, 1968, through the general staff of the Soviet army under the leadership of Defence Minister Marshal Grechko, as a result of a directive from the Politburo of the Central Committee of the Communist Party of the Soviet Union. The work takes place without the involvement of the high command of WP, because the Soviet leadership eliminates the participation of Romania from the beginning. Therefore, no document mentions the "Warsaw Pact", only "allied troops". On May 7th, General Yepishev, Chief of the Main Political Directorate of the Soviet Army and Navy, speaks of possible "assistance" for loyal Communists in the ČSSR. Marshal Grechko's supposed probes between May 17th and 25th can be seen (from today's perspective) as possible preparatory steps towards intervention. On June 20th, 1968, the mass **staff maneuvers "Sumava"** (Bohemian Forest) begin. Around 16,000 Soviet soldiers with 70 tanks and 4,500 vehicles enter the nation as a result. The withdrawal of the divisions is "delayed". Despite consultations between the leadership of the ČSSR and the other members of the WP at the Conference of Čierna nad Tisou (Schwarzau an der Theiß) and Bratislava (Pressburg) in summer 1968, which proceed in a "relaxed atmosphere" and should deceive the whole world about the tense situation, the preparations for a possible military intervention in the ČSSR are continued. Operational plans exist by the middle of May, the actual preparations begin in the middle of July. The governments of Bulgaria, the German Democratic Republic, Poland, and Hungary are "asked to participate in the exercise".[9] **Propaganda measures** which are meant to simulate an impending intervention of NATO troops in Bohemia start at the beginning of July. Extensive **Soviet provisioning maneuvers in West Ukraine** are to disguise the deployment of the Soviet divisions. On July 27th, the Soviet general staff orders the provision of raised deployment readiness, and the implementation of a concealed mobilization for its partner countries. On August 18th, the deliberations of the party leaders and government heads of the five participating nations abruptly end in the decision for armed occupation of the ČSSR. Only the Hungarian head of state, Janos Kadar, at first speaks out against intervention, presumably remembering the events of fall 1956.

In the night before August 21st, 1968, the troops of the Warsaw Pact begin the occupation of the ČSSR. This is carried out largely without a struggle, although not without problems.[10] The military intervention begins on August 20th, 1968, 1 hour before midnight, with border crossings at 18 points under the leadership of the commander-in-chief of the Warsaw Pact troops, Marshal Yakubovsky. At least 14 Soviet divisions are involved (8 of the "Group of Soviet Troops in Germany (GSTG)", 5 divisions from the military district (MD) of Carpathia, an air assault division from the military district of Leningrad, and parts of four divisions of the "Southern Group of Troops (SGT)", four Polish, two Hungarian and parts of a Bulgarian division). Within 48 hours the troops reach their ordered areas and stop 10 km from the respective national borders of neighboring countries. The provided 7th Tank Division and 11th Motorized Infantry Division of the German Democratic Republic's (GDR) National People's Army (NVA), contrary to previous plans, are not deployed in the territory of the ČSSR; to them falls the "sealing of the border area". An advance command of the Soviet air assault division occupies the Prague airport with a surprise attack at 9:30 PM. An Antonov-24 from Aeroflot lands unannounced and without permission to land. Its crew brings the airport under

---

9 Since the WP is a pure "defence alliance", the charter does not provide for an intervention in the internal affairs of a member nation. Therefore the term "exercise" must be chosen, since it is the only legal title under which movements of WP troops into the territory of a member state without their consent can take place.

10 As a result of faulty coordination, in some places it comes to an exchange of fire between troops of the occupation army (see: Pachmann Ludek: "What Really Happened in Prague: Illusions and Facts from the Dubcek Era", Freiburg im Breisgau 1978).

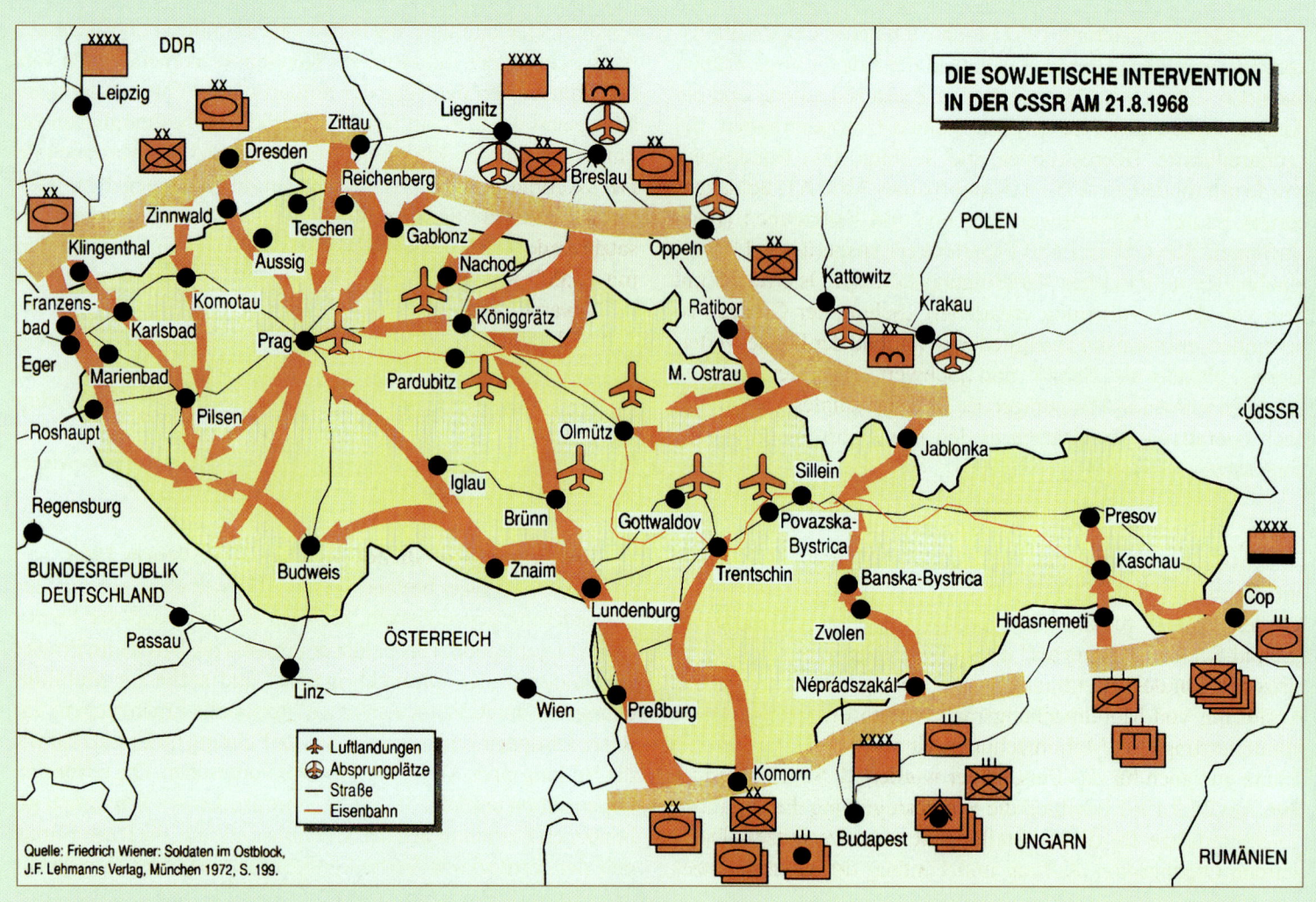

DIE SOWJETISCHE INTERVENTION IN DER CSSR AM 21.8.1968

Quelle: Friedrich Wiener: Soldaten im Ostblock, J.F. Lehmanns Verlag, München 1972, S. 199.

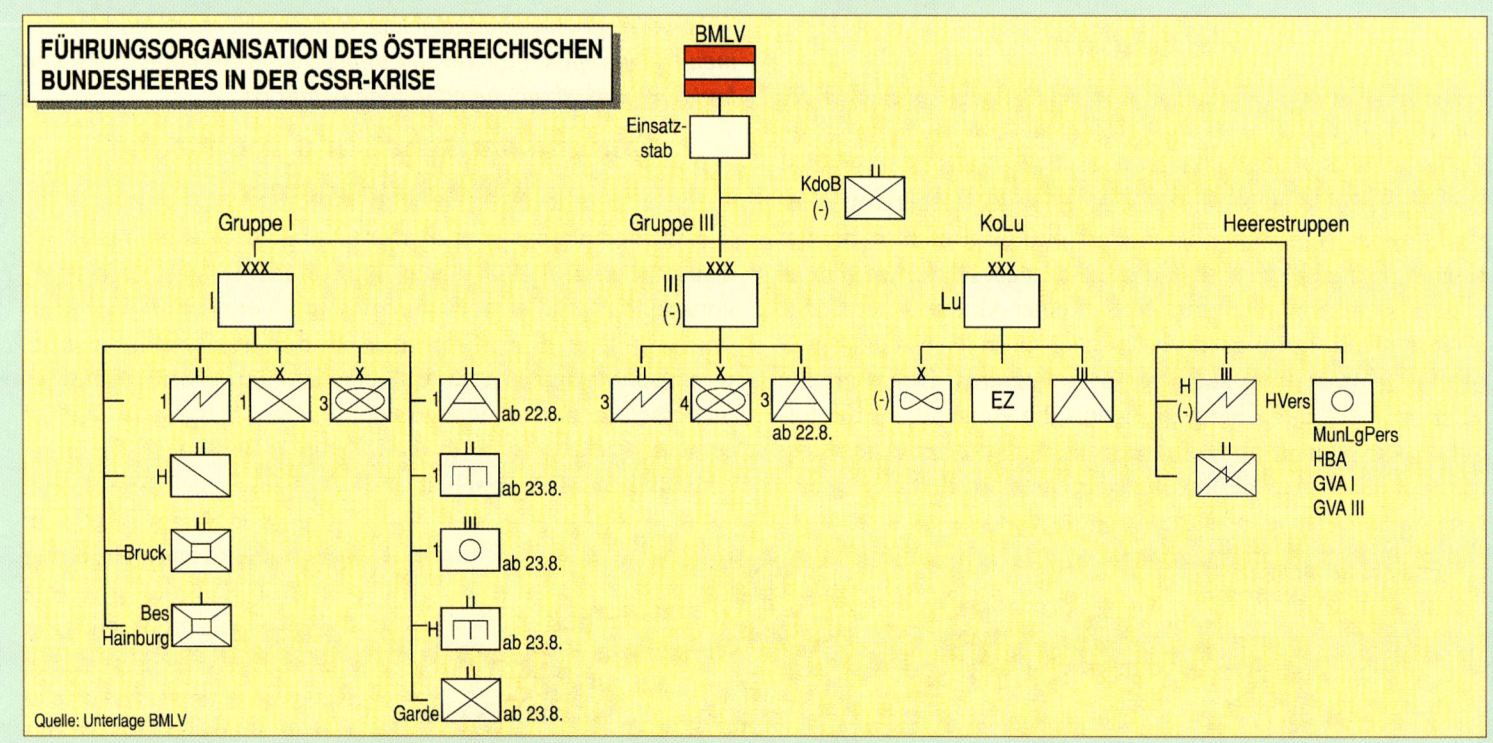

Legende:
- Luftlandungen
- Absprungplätze
- Straße
- Eisenbahn

FÜHRUNGSORGANISATION DES ÖSTERREICHISCHEN BUNDESHEERES IN DER CSSR-KRISE

Quelle: Unterlage BMLV

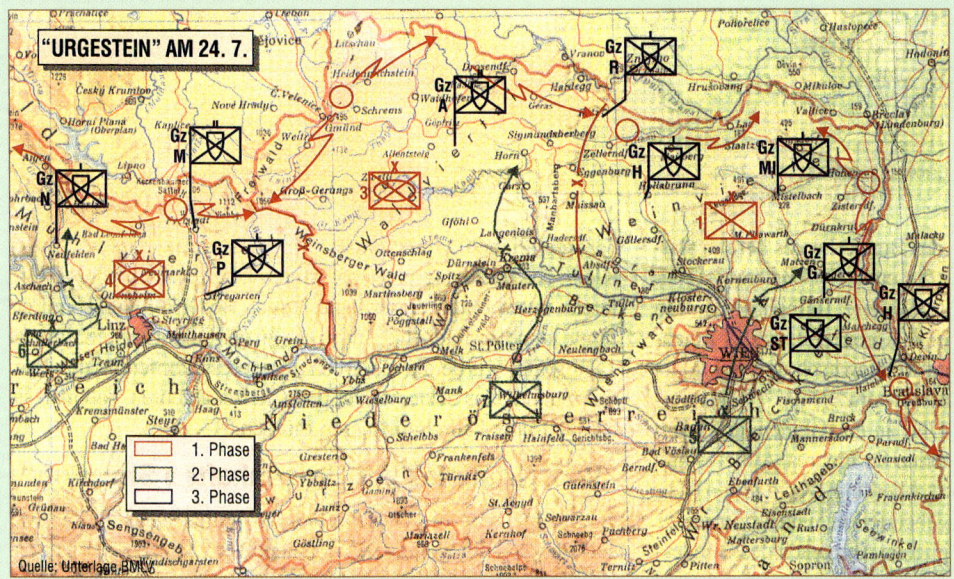

Since it is apparent that the scope for preparations is limited by political considerations, the Defence Minister issues instructions that for the next two months troop formations appropriate to Saturdays, Sundays or holidays are to be held ready to march at the military training grounds in Bruck/Leitha and Allentsteig respectively (officially for exercises). In the directive of July 24th, 1968, which circulates under the code words "Prehistoric Rock", all preparatory measures for deployment of the armed forces to secure the border with Czechoslovakia are taken.

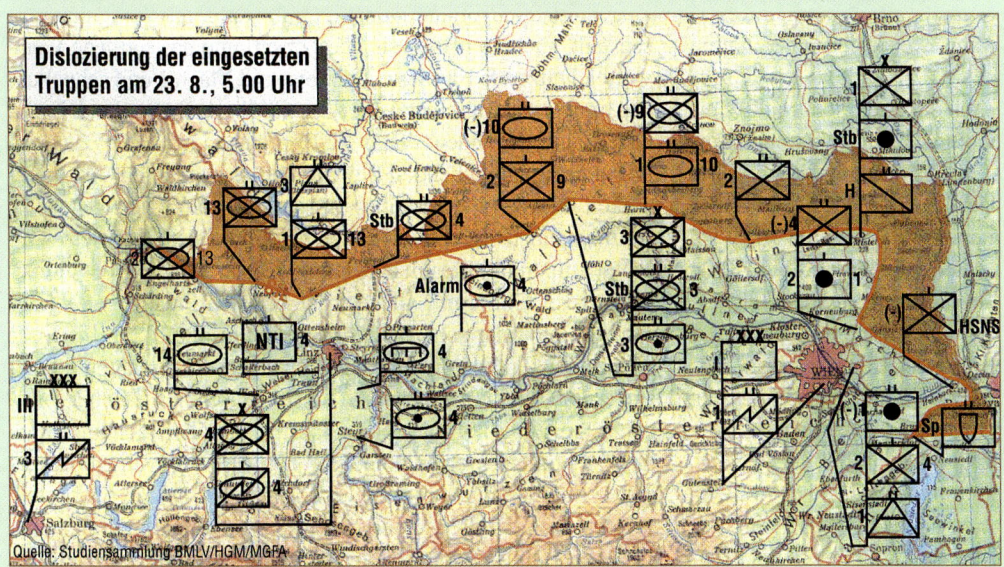

The military forces are already prepared for deployment after 1 1/2 days. For fully incomprehensible reasons, the federal government establishes a 30 km zone along the border, which their own soldiers are not allowed to enter (orange area).

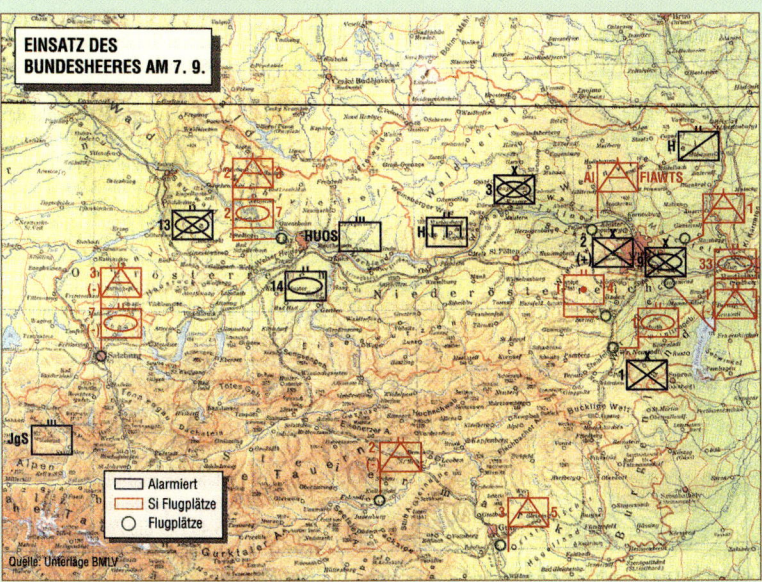

On September 7th, the situation is aggravated after a report from the Bavarian border police that an army of Soviet tanks have begun to march in the direction of Germany. Redeployments in the ČSSR and the GDR offer an unclear picture. Since air attacks cannot be ruled out, divisions of the armed forces take up position around the airports of Schwechat, Wiener Neustadt, Vöslau, Aspern, Deutsch Wagram, Graz-Thalerhof, Zeltweg, Hörsching and Salzburg.

their control. Only an hour later 250 transport planes begin landing minutes apart. A complete air assault division is landed in this manner. Their open rejection by the population leads to strong frustrations among the soldiers of the occupation army. Finally, however, the impressive civilian resistance is broken with the use of massive military force. While there are no exact calculations of the Czechoslovakian population's losses, the Soviet troop losses through "hostile civilian action" are given as eleven dead and 87 wounded.[11]

As a result of the invasion, there are considerable refugee movements. 162,000 Czechoslovakians flee to Austria alone. Within the Czechoslovakian People's Army (CPA) there are considerable "purges", in which 11,000 officers and 30,000 noncommissioned officers are discharged.

By the end of 1969, the "normalization" is completed. For the next 20 years the ČSSR is again a full-fledged and "secure" member of WaPa and COMECON.

International Reaction

Once again, the West is taken completely by surprise. American troops have been deployed in Vietnam since the beginning of the '60's. The "Tet Offensive", begun on January 30th, 1968 by Viet Cong and North Vietnamese divisions, is brought to a standstill by American and South Vietnamese troops, the Communist troops are crushed. Nevertheless, there is growing resistance from ever more powerful population groups in the USA to the military engagement in Southeastern Asia. The murder of Martin Luther King in March 1968 and of Senator Robert Kennedy in June 1968 causes serious shock in the nation. The situation in the Middle East does not quiet despite Israel's clear-cut victory in the "Six Day War". On March 12th, 1968, the heaviest fighting yet takes place between Israeli and Jordanian or Palestinian troops in Al-Karameh (northeast of Jericho).

In Europe, the rebellious stance of the younger generation increases. In Germany an assassination attempt on student leader Rudi Dutschke leads to the formation of left-leaning terrorist groups. France sinks in chaos in May 1968, as student demonstrations in Paris set off a general strike across broad sections of the country.

A unified campaign against the intervention in the ČSSR is therefore unthinkable. In addition, in the eyes of the "West" as well as those of the "East", the matter is a purely "internal" affair within the Soviet Union's "sphere of control".

Austrian Reaction
Political Measures

At the instigation of Minister for the Interior Franz Soronics and Defence Minister Dr. Georg Prader, a meeting takes place between representatives of the two ministries on July 23rd, 1968, in order to discuss and coordinate preventative measures for the maintenance of Austria's security in the case of an armed conflict. In the process it becomes clear, as already during the Hungarian crisis, that the Defence Act, which orients itself largely on the laws of the 1st Republic, and which says among other things that: *"The purpose of the armed forces is to protect the borders,..."*, serves neither military developments since the Second World War nor the political demands of neutrality. This mission is impossible to fulfill. For this reason, already in the Hungarian crisis the larger part of the troops had to be withdrawn to "easily blocked" terrain in the night before November 6th, 1956, since the "defence of the borders" was practically impossible to carry out. However, after the end of the Hungarian crisis, the opportunity to amend the purpose of the armed forces to, for instance, "maintenance of sovereignty" is neglected. During the meeting on July 23rd, which takes place under the chairmanship of the General Director for Public Security, Dr. Kurt Seidler, and in the presence of General Anton Leeb, the following details are determined:

- Strengthening of the Executive in the area of the Austrian-Czechoslovakian border in the shortest amount of time;
- Preparation of 10,000 red-white-red flags for clear designation of the border line;
- Transfer of military units to the designated security zone north of the Danube;
- Shared patrol activities with Gendarmery and Border Patrol;
- Motorization and equipage of the designated standbys of the Executive with radio equipment;
- Alert of the district governmental authorities;
- Immediate activation of an administrative staff in the control room of the Ministry for the Interior.

The invasion of Warsaw Pact troops is correctly perceived by the Ministry for the Interior as well as the Defence Ministry (in contrast to NATO). While the military preparations take place as planned, serious mishaps take place on the political level. It is holiday time and *"the military intervention of the Soviet government in Czechoslovakia is – just as for the rest of the world – a surprise for us."*[12] Federal Chancellor Dr. Josef Klaus and the Defence Minister are to be found at their weekend houses – both without telephones. Federal President Franz Jonas and Vice-Chancellor Dr. Hermann Widhalm are on holiday. So the decision about a deployment of the military is delayed. In contrast, the measures planned for the protection of the border by the Ministry of the Interior are carried out with a hitch. The first emergency meeting cannot begin until 5:45 AM, under the chairmanship of the

---

11 See: Pauer, Jan: "The Invasion of the Warsaw Pact: Background – Planning – Implementation", Bremen 1995.
12 Foreign minister Dr. Kurt Waldheim in a speech before the Council of Ministers on September 10th.

Federal Chancellor (in addition, he must, like other members as well, first be flown in by military helicopter). A further meeting begins at 8:00 AM. Differences of opinion in judging the situation and conflicts of responsibility delay the planned and possible 8:00 AM decampment of the military by eight (!) hours (during this time the soldiers sit in their vehicles). The government reaches no unanimous decisions on whether to mobilize the border protection divisions and debates on whether the Defence Minister, the federal government, or the Federal President should give the order to march. The question is a politically explosive one, since an SPÖ Federal President stands opposite an ÖVP one-party government. Not until an irregular Council of Ministers, which gathers at 1:30 PM, is it finally agreed that the issuance of the order to march falls in the Defence Minister's sphere of authority. There are also problems with the prescribed terminology. Finally it is spoken of only as a *"critical situation"*, differing from the concept of a broad national defence, which distinguishes between crisis, neutrality, and defence cases.

In the same way, information is kept from the population, which promotes the uncertainty of the border population. Despite appropriate advice, the Federal Chancellor only resolves on a press conference 14 days later, in which he must finally admit to this mistake.[13]

Therefore, while the population longs for the deployment of the armed forces on the border, the military leadership urges it and the military is ready to decamp, the political leadership delays. With the knowledge (or the hope?) that the WP's attack on the ČSSR will be limited, they want to avoid a possible escalation through incidents on the border. In a meeting of the National Defence Council on February 25th, 1958, Minister for the Interior Oskar Helmer already emphasizes *"the necessity of giving the population living near the border a feeling of security"* in the process, in light of the experiences of the Hungarian crisis. On the other hand, no one wants to provoke the Soviet Union, or, as the former Federal Chancellor Julius Raab once expressed it: *"One shouldn't step on the bear's tail."*

In retrospect, the judgment proves to be correct; the course of action however is to be classified as risky. Had the executive committee of the PKC's call to submit to the invading troops not been ignored, or had groups of ČSSR troops attempted to take evasive action into Austria, this over-carefulness could have had (life-) threatening consequences. The threat is not just limited to the land, however. Foreign Minister Waldheim must already protest against the numerous **violations of air space** on August 21st. If the first flyovers could be imputed to disorientation, it becomes clear in the following days that TU-16 reconnaissance flights are taking place against military facilities in the area of Linz, Steyr, Waidhofen/Ybbs, St. Pölten, and Vienna.

For the first time, **"psychological warfare"** is used against Austria as well. The Soviet literary magazine "Literaturnaja Gazeta" claims in an article on August 28th, 1968, that American special forces are being trained by American and German officers in the Schwarzenberg barracks in Salzburg, disguised as tourists, armed, and smuggled into the ČSSR to support the "reactionary forces". In addition, the Soviet party newspaper "Pravda" writes that 22 mobile transmitters were brought into the ČSSR through Austria. Both accusations are completely baseless and are decidedly repudiated by the Austrian federal government.

Military Measures

In light of the political developments in Czechoslovakia and supported by the ongoing assessment of the situation by the communications group, the military leadership introduces appropriate measures prematurely. Already on May 13th, 1968, the Defence Minister discusses the situation with the General Troop Inspector, General Erwin Fussenegger, and the commander of Group I, General Leo Waldmüller. Since it is apparent that the scope for preparations is limited by political considerations, the Defence Minister issues instructions that for the next two months troop formations appropriate to Saturdays, Sundays or holidays are to be held ready to march at the military training grounds in Bruck/Leitha and Allentsteig respectively (officially for exercises).[14]

In the directive of July 24th, 1968, which circulates under the code words "Prehistoric Rock", all preparatory measures for deployment of the armed forces to secure the border with Czechoslovakia are taken. Within, Point 3b reads: *Mission: "Safeguarding the northern border, with emphasis on crossing areas and surveillance of the territory in between... The deployed forces are to disarm crossing armed divisions as well as military individuals on entering sovereign Austrian territory and to accommodate them in collection camps..."*

The first report from the Communications Group (the officer on duty that night is the father of the author) takes place on August 21st, 1968 at 1:50 AM. At 3:00 AM the staffs and commands are forewarned, at 3:40 AM the alert is carried out by Brigadier General Johann Freihsler, the leader of the Operations Group, who, as chief of the deployment staff, from this point on leads the **"ad hoc army command"** which is to be formed in case of deployment.

In an alteration to the "Prehistoric Rock" instructions, by political request, the **"order to reinforce the garrison areas north of the Danube"** is issued on the afternoon of August 21st. Consequently only the garrisons north of the Danube are "reinforced" in the 1st phase of the "critical situation" (August 21st – September 2nd). Since the order to march is not issued until 4:00 PM to troops ready to march out since 8:30 AM, these troops cannot occupy their security positions in the area of Freistadt, Weitra, Allentsteig, Horn and Mistelbach in full measure until that night, while Soviet troops already reach the Austrian border across from Lower Austria that morning, and in the area of Upper Austria by early evening.

---

13   Undersecretary ret. Johann Ellinger, personal recollections, Reichenau on February 10th, 1998, quoted by Andreas Steiger: "From Border Protection to Area Defence", Dissertation, Vienna 2001.
14   File note from COL GS Maerker on May 14th, 1968/Secret. Document from the military history research division through the study collection of 1968.

The military divisions receive the (political) instruction to go no closer than 30 km to the border (only survey troops and signal corps are at the border – although in civilian clothing). An instruction that the population, most of all, cannot understand. An officer of the border patrol expresses their feelings as: *"There may be many reasons to keep the army away from the border. But none of them change the fact that we are left here alone."* In contrast to the Hungarian deployment, the government gives no instructions for an "order to fire". The use of weapons is simply directed in the sense of Sec. 30 of the General Duty Regulations (GDR) as allowed for self-defence during unambiguous attack or at the order of the unit commander on the appearance of battalion-strength foreign land or air armed forces. While the divisions conduct themselves according to their mission, the border defence develops a striking momentum: the reservists are conscientiously prepared for possible threatening cases, including a threat from the ČSSR. In the Mühlviertel, the oldest border defence battalion stands as a "demonstration model". Plots of land and buildings in the gathering areas are rented in anticipation. The reservists have their uniforms and equipment at home.[15] The first reservists therefore immediately betake themselves to their area of operations and begin preparations for deployment without a particular order, but just as they have learned and often practiced. They even bring their own provisions, in order to be self-sufficient until the expected follow-up supplies. However, they do not meet their (active) commanders and comrades, since these are forbidden to enter the 30 km zone. As they find out from the political authorities about the new situation and the alterations to the "Prehistoric Rock" orders, the reservists come to an existential crisis. The question arises why they took everything upon themselves, sacrificed some holidays and invested so much free time in the business. But unfortunately here, to tell the truth, it must be observed that the military, in the person of Brigadier General Freihsler, is the one who answers Federal Chancellor Klaus' question of whether the activation of the Border Defence is necessary in the negative.[16] Not until afterward does Klaus decide against their mobilization. A reason for this decision also lays in the declaration of the Soviet ambassador in Vienna, Boris Fyodorov Podzerob, on August 21st at 12:30 PM, in which he officially apprises the federal government that the WP troops will not invade Austria.

The Austrian Air Forces endeavor to supervise a preassigned restricted flight area north of the Danube from August 23rd to September 3rd, with the available Saab J29F "flying barrel". During this time they succeed in keeping 18 airplanes ready for deployment daily, in view of the total number of 21 airplanes an outstanding accomplishment for the technicians. The airplanes cannot in fact be deployed against intrusions, due to their low speed, inadequate armament and the lack of an onboard radar, but thanks to their cameras it is at least possible to document the airspace infringements. With these politicians can deliver the records and proof they need for protests against the Soviets. The presentation of the photos in the Kremlin also leads to a discontinuation of these sovereignty infringements in the air, initially described as "technical errors". In addition to the deployment of the "fighter-bombers", the three stationary radar stations in the Stift Barracks, near Hellmonsödt and on Kolomannsberg, together with two mobile directional radar devices are put into use. In the time between August 24th and September 29th, 7,965 non-identifiable headings are identified at least. There are many radar disruptions against it; obviously the WP is experimenting with how it can "make the Kolomannsberg blind". For the time period between September 7th, 12:00 PM, and September 9th, 8:00 AM, strict readiness is ordered as a result of special information from the Ministry of the Interior.[17] This is based on the testimony of the former leader of the Department of Disinformation of the CPA, Major Ladislav Bitman, who previously defected. According to his information, the Soviet Union intends to hermetically seal the borders of the ČSSR, disarm the border troops, and drive them back onto Austrian territory, where it could come to armed hostilities with the Austrian military. This in turn would be a pretext for an occupation of eastern Austria. At the same time amplified immigration, despite all hindrances, is observed. On September 7th, the situation is aggravated after a report from the Bavarian border police that an army of Soviet tanks have begun to march in the direction of Germany. Redeployments in the ČSSR and the GDR offer an unclear picture. Security measures of all kinds are taken, with the most attention given to the airports, since measures similar to those taken in Prague on August 21st are feared. Divisions of the armed forces take up position around the airports of Schwechat, Wiener Neustadt, Vöslau, Aspern, Deutsch Wagram, Graz-Thalerhof, Zeltweg, Hörsching and Salzburg. A tank company and an armored infantry platoon of the 9th Mechanized Infantry Brigade (in total 17 armored vehicles), who are stationed at Schwechat Airport, receive the concrete mission to "destroy" landing military aircraft.

In the process two dangerous incidents occur: in the night from the 7th to the 8th of September, an "Aeroflot" airplane prepares to land unannounced. Not until the last minutes does the pilot realizes his "error", he actually wanted to land in Pressburg. To what extent this was only an excuse and the attempted landing a test, can no longer be determined. More explosive still is the unannounced landing of an American airplane. Because of the order to identify himself or be fired upon, the pilot feared that Schwechat was already occupied by Soviets. Here as well a catastrophe is successfully avoided (the M60-tanks already have orders to fire on the airplane). There are "only" American journalists on board the plane.

How unsatisfactory the legal situation is can also be seen in another occurrence, which takes place in the area of Vöslau: There

---

15 With a ruling of November 21st, 1961, the Council of Ministers agrees to the transfer of equipment and apparel, not however weapons, to the personal custody of those liable to military service in the reserves.

16 "It is perhaps interesting that the same man who carried the main responsibility for the military measures on August 21st and the days afterward, and who was ideologically close to opposition leader Kreisky, was then made Defence Minister by him", Manfried Rauchensteiner: "Shield without Sword", Styria Publishing, Graz 1991.

17 Report of the Defence Minister before the National Defence Council on September 13th, 1968.

While some soldiers of the 4th Infantry Battalion in Maria-Theresa Barracks in Vienna follow the news reports after preparing to decamp (t.l.), the connection to other divisions is already being established through radio-teletype MFF-1 (t.r.). Meanwhile, in the 33rd Tank Battalion in Zwölfaxing preparations are being made to decamp (m.l.). The time until decampment is used for quick field training with the new conscripts (m.r.).
The first divisions of the 9th Mechanized Infantry Brigade leave their garrison (b.r.: Armored Air Defence Gun Battery of the 9th Tank Artillery Battalion in Baden) and move into their area of operations (b.l.).

a battery of the 9th Tank Artillery Battalion is in position. Several times it must be determined that the security connections for fire control are broken. Patrols observe that field wire has been cut out of the connections by the meter. After the Gendarmery get hold of the culprits, they cannot be charged with sabotage, although from the viewpoint of the soldiers it was a life-threatening, even state-endangering action, but only with "malicious destruction of property". While for the soldiers a deployment is in force, the population is at peace. An intolerable situation, which it turns out is not remedied through the decades.

Although the acute danger seems at an end in September, the available conscripts are kept in the troops past their demobilization date. At the suggestion of the federal government, Federal President Jonas orders the following on September 10th, 1968: *"According to Sec. 23 para. 2 DA... I temporarily postpone the return to the reserves for all those liable to military service who would have been returned to the reserves between September 26th and 30th, 1968 after the orderly completion of their military service, until October 28th, 1968."*[18] However, this measure was annulled again on October 21st.

As would later become clear, concrete preparations for an intervention in Austria existed, but these had no connection to the previously described redeployments. The fact is that a "supply infiltration" was among the preparations: numerous Soviet towboats with weapons, munition, and tank replacement parts lie along the Donau and anchored in the ports of Vienna and Linz. More than 1,000 t of raw meat are stored in cold storage in Salzburg, Linz and Vienna for provisioning the Red Army. However, these measures must be qualified by the consideration of a possible deliberate "disinformation" campaign.[19]

Even though the soldiers of the federal armed forces again contribute all that is humanly possible, the method and manner in which this deployment took place led to a large loss of trust from politicians, the population, and the reservists. The consequence is the initiation of a referendum on the abolishment of the armed forces, on the creation of an committee to reform the armed forces, and on the shortening of mandatory military service from nine to six months (plus 60 days of weapons training) as a consequence of the parliamentary elections of 1970, in which the SPÖ, with Dr. Kreisky's motto "6 months are enough!", comes out as the clear victor.

Basis for deployment:	Council of Ministers on September 10th, 1968.
Type of deployment:	Protective deployment according to Sec. 2 para. 1 sub-para. a DA.
Mission:	Defence of the Austrian Republic's borders.
Duration of deployment:	August 21st, 1968 – October 21st, 1968.

Congestion on the "Guest Worker Route"

Preliminary Events

Shortly before Christmas there is an above-average amount of snowfall in Styria. This coincides with the journey home for foreign workers who work in Germany and want to spent the Christmas holidays with their families. The heavy snowfall and the large number of vehicles, which mostly do not possess the appropriate winter equipment (many vehicles are furnished with summer tires), leads to chaos, above all on the infamous "guest worker route" between Spielfeld and Leibnitz.

Political Measures

The district administration petitions the armed forces for assistance. This deployment is notable not because of the cause, but rather because of another peculiarity: the Defence Act envisions a supportive deployment of not more than 100 men as the result of a petition from the district administration. In this case, however (by mistake) more soldiers are deployed. Accordingly, this deployment would have to have been approved by the federal government. Strictly speaking, this deployment is the **first and as of yet only extralegal deployment of the armed forces or a part thereof.** The success and the purpose "sanctify" the means, however.

Military Measures

The Styrian military command immediately alerts the standby units always in readiness in the 17th Infantry Battalion and the 2nd Artillery Regiment. Over 100 men from the 17th Infantry Battalion and two mechanized infantry combat vehicles from the 1st Rocket Launcher Battery are deployed.

---

18 FLG No. 342/1968.
19 Andreas Steiger: "...Chosen for the Defence of the Borders?", ÖMZ, Issue 5/1998, Vienna 1998.

Basis for deployment:	Petition of the district administration.
Type of deployment:	Supportive deployment according to Sec. 2 para. 1 sub-para. c DA.
Mission:	Street clearance and recovery of jammed vehicles; care of the affected vehicle occupants.
Duration of deployment:	December 21st, 1969.
Contingent strength:	108.

Collapse of the Viennese Reichsbrücke

Preliminary Events

Most Austrians believe it to be a late April Fool's joke, as the morning news of Sunday, August 1st, 1976, broadcasts news of the collapse of the Viennese Reichsbrücke. This very bridge belongs, like St. Stephen's Cathedral or the Riesenrad, to the seemingly everlasting emblems of Vienna, which survived even World War 2.

Political Measures

At 8:00 AM a crisis staff under the chairmanship of the Viennese mayor meets at city hall. The armed forces are requisitioned for supportive activities. The clearing of a shipping channel through the detonation of bridge fragments is requested for the navy, in order to help with the construction of a temporary bridge with D-bridge equipment for the streetcars, and in order to support the civil bridge specialists in the search for the causes of the collapse.

Military Measures

At 6:30 AM the military command is alerted in anticipation. Engineer units from all across Austria are transferred to Vienna for the deployment and, together with the Engineer School, placed under the Military Command of Vienna for the duration of the deployment. The collapse of a bridge of this size presents the soldiers with previously unknown technical problems and demands their highest expertise and precision. The engineers succeed, with support from civil firms, in securing the alternative transport system over the Danube within four months. The temporary bridge provides its service for five years. It is dismantled again in June 1982 by soldiers of the 2nd and 3rd companies of the Army Engineer Battalion in Melk.

Basis for deployment:	Petition of the Viennese provincial government.
Type of deployment:	Supportive deployment according to Sec. 2 para. 1 sub-para. c DA.
Mission:	Clearance of a shipping channel for ships through the detonation of bridge fragments; construction of a temporary bridge with D-bridge equipment for the streetcars; support of the civil bridge specialist in the search for the causes of the collapse.
Duration of deployment:	August 1st – September 20th, 1976 (deployment after the collapse); November 17th – December 10th, 1976 (construction of the street replacement bridge); June 1st – June 9th, 1982 (dismantlement of the street replacement bridge).
Commander:	Major General Karl Schrems, military commander of Vienna.
Contribution:	In 130,312 man hours, 10,830 transfers between the two banks of the Danube are carried out, among other things. A two-lane street bridge with a total length of 372 meters was constructed over the Danube. On the right bank of the Danube, a street bridge with a length of 120 meters and a width of 7 meters was built. In the process, 39 panels of D-bridge come into use.

Here the Reichsbrücke once stood, one of the emblems of Vienna (t.l.).
The picture on the top right shows the temporary bridge constructed by the engineers out of D-bridge pieces.
Even the M88 Recovery Tank has no chance against this type of destruction. Only necessary safety rope work takes place with it (m.l. and m.r.). Through the engineers, a ferry service to the midstream investigation sites is ensured (b.r.).

Foot-and-mouth Disease

Preliminary Events

At the beginning of March, 1981, thousands of farmers and agriculturists are horrified by the evil tidings that foot-and-mouth disease has broken out in Lower Austria. The small towns of Thalheim, Ziegelhausen, and Untermiesting are especially affected.

Political Measures

The mayors of the affected communities are apprised of the catastrophe by the responsible member of the provincial government and the regional governor on the evening of March 2nd, 1981. Shortly thereafter the mayors alert the volunteer fire departments and the Gendarmery of the region. All town access roads, freight lanes, and paths to the farms are immediately closed off. Sawdust is collected from a nearby sawmill by the fire departments, a troop procures the sodium hydrate necessary for the application of the disinfection carpet from all the pharmacies in the area. The disinfection carpet is already applied that night. The Gendarmery supervises the blockade measures. Finally the provisions for the enclosed population are secured. Animal cadaver utilization vehicles transport the infected animals (the affected include 451 swine, 165 cattle, and 15 sheep) to be destroyed. The disinfection carpet must be renewed every four hours, since it is seriously battered by the animal cadaver utilization vehicles. At a situational briefing, some of the firemen express their fear that they could contract the disease during blockade duty and introduce it in their own agricultural businesses (2/3 of all deployed firemen are agriculturalists). The mayors are therefore requested to petition the armed forces for support, which then occurs. On March 16th, the disinfection mat and the blockade are removed by order of the head of the district. At 5:30 PM the infected area can be deregulated again.

Military Measures

At the petition of the mayor, soldiers are placed to supervise the disinfection mat.

Basis for deployment:	Petition of the mayors of the communities affected by the disease.
Type of deployment:	Supportive deployment according to Sec. 2 para. 1 sub-para. c DA.
Mission:	Supervision of the street blockades and disinfection mat; support of the volunteer fire department during the renewal of the disinfection mat; provisioning of the population.
Duration of deployment:	March 6th, 1981 – March 17th, 1981.
Contingent strength:	Unknown.

Disinfection Mat

A so-called "disinfection mat" is laid at all the approaches to the foot-and-mouth disease infected areas. All pedestrians and vehicles that want to leave this area must past through this mat. In this way, the spread of the disease should be prevented. For this purpose, at every approach 6/8 stacks are anchored parallel to the street at a distance of 8 m. In between, wood shavings are poured ca. 10 cm high. 1,000 l of water is then sprayed with fire engines. Afterwards, chalk is scattered on the wood shavings, and finally a solution of water and sodium hydrate in a proportion of 1:50 is poured on top with a watering can.

The problem of foot-and-mouth disease is unfortunately topical again today, and keeps Europe breathless.

Nuclear Power Plant Accident at Chernobyl

Preliminary Events

On April 25th, 1986, at 11:10 PM, an experiment is run in Block 4 of the nuclear power plant at Chernobyl: it is tested how far the kinetic energy of a running reactor turbine can be used to ensure an emergency power supply for the reactor. No one is informed of this attempt other than those involved. On April 26th, at 1:23 AM, a catastrophe occurs as a result of a row of faulty reactions from the reactor personnel in Block 4. The reactor, having become critical, runs away, the first fires arise in the reactor hall. As hydrogen gas is released, an electrolytic gas explosion occurs that destroys the reactor's casing. Through the burning of the moderator graphite block a fire develops that releases radioactive byproducts.

These byproducts are pushed to a height of up to 1 kilometer in the atmosphere through a "stack effect", and from there carried by the wind over thousands of kilometers. Many of the nuclear power plant's employees lose their lives in the accident. Europe first becomes aware of the elevated radioactivity through routine readings taken in a Swedish nuclear power plan on April 28th, 1986. Detailed information on the cause is not available at first. Not until midnight does the Soviet news agency TASS publish a first communique, which speaks of a "loss" in the nuclear power plant in Chernobyl. Not until much later does information about the momentous catastrophe in the USSR come to light.

Political Measures

On April 29th, the Austrian radiation early warning system shows rising levels, that reach their high point on April 20th with level values of 2 – 3 and finally sink again. The Federal Ministry for Health and Environmental Protection (MHEP) activates the radiation alert plan and verbally petitions the Defence Ministry for support on May 1st, in writing on May 5th.

Military Measures

The radiation alert for the armed forces is triggered as a result of an instruction from the Commander-in-Chief of the Army in the evening hours of April 30th. The deployment readiness of the nuclear, biological and chemical (NBC) weapons defence troops is immediately prepared, instructions for the limiting of training in the open country and special hygiene measures are distributed and regular measurements of the radiation levels in the area of military buildings are ordered.

MHEP's request for support on May 1st can therefore be immediately complied with. After the alert of the NBC defence troops, eight decontamination and 23 detection troops come into use in the provinces of Lower Austria, Upper Austria and Burgenland on May 2nd (three decontamination and ten detection troops are held in reserve in the other provinces), in order to, together with the Border Patrol, Gendarmery and Fire Department, inspect vehicles, freight, but also people at the borders to the ČSSR and Hungary for radioactive contamination and, when necessary, to decontaminate them as well. Furthermore, a "foodstuff testing relay" is established. For this purpose, two fixed-wing aircraft of the type PC-6 "Pilatus Porter" and two helicopters are deployed, which transport the samples from Vorarlberg and Lienz through the provincial capitals of Innsbruck, Salzburg and Graz to the Seibersdorf Research Center.

Further, two Saab 105OE jet planes with radioactivity sensors mounted outside stand at the ready, in order to be able to take air samples from great heights at any time. In Vienna, specialists from the NBC defence troops are placed at the Federal Office for Environmental Protection, the City Information Office, the Atomic Institute and the Bacterial-serological Research Institute. A decontamination area is established in Eisenstadt, a detection unit is deployed at the Berg/Hainburg border crossing.

Basis for deployment:	Petition of the Federal Minister for Health and Environmental Protection.
Type of deployment:	Supportive deployment according to Sec. 2 para. 1 sub-para. c DA.
Mission:	Transport of foodstuff samples in the area of the provinces as well as from the provinces to the central foodstuff inspection areas; NBC detection deployment and decontamination of vehicles (and when necessary people) on the border-crossing points and supply of experts for the investigation of possible contaminated samples.
Duration of deployment:	April 30th – May 23rd, 1986.
Contingent strength:	500.
Commanders:	Lieutenant Colonel Norbert Fürstenhofer, commander of the NBC Defence School.
Contribution:	The soldiers contribute 84,340 man hours. During this time, 842 land, 134 water, and 121 air measurements are carried out, 17,010 vehicles, 15,670 railway carriages and 153 people are inspected. 157 decontamination deployments take place. From the military air force, 8.4 t of foodstuff tests are transported in 308 flight hours and 54 flight hours are used for detection deployments.

```
ARMEEKOMMANDO
     G-Luft
     AK/GL
RINDERHOFER, Obstlt
```

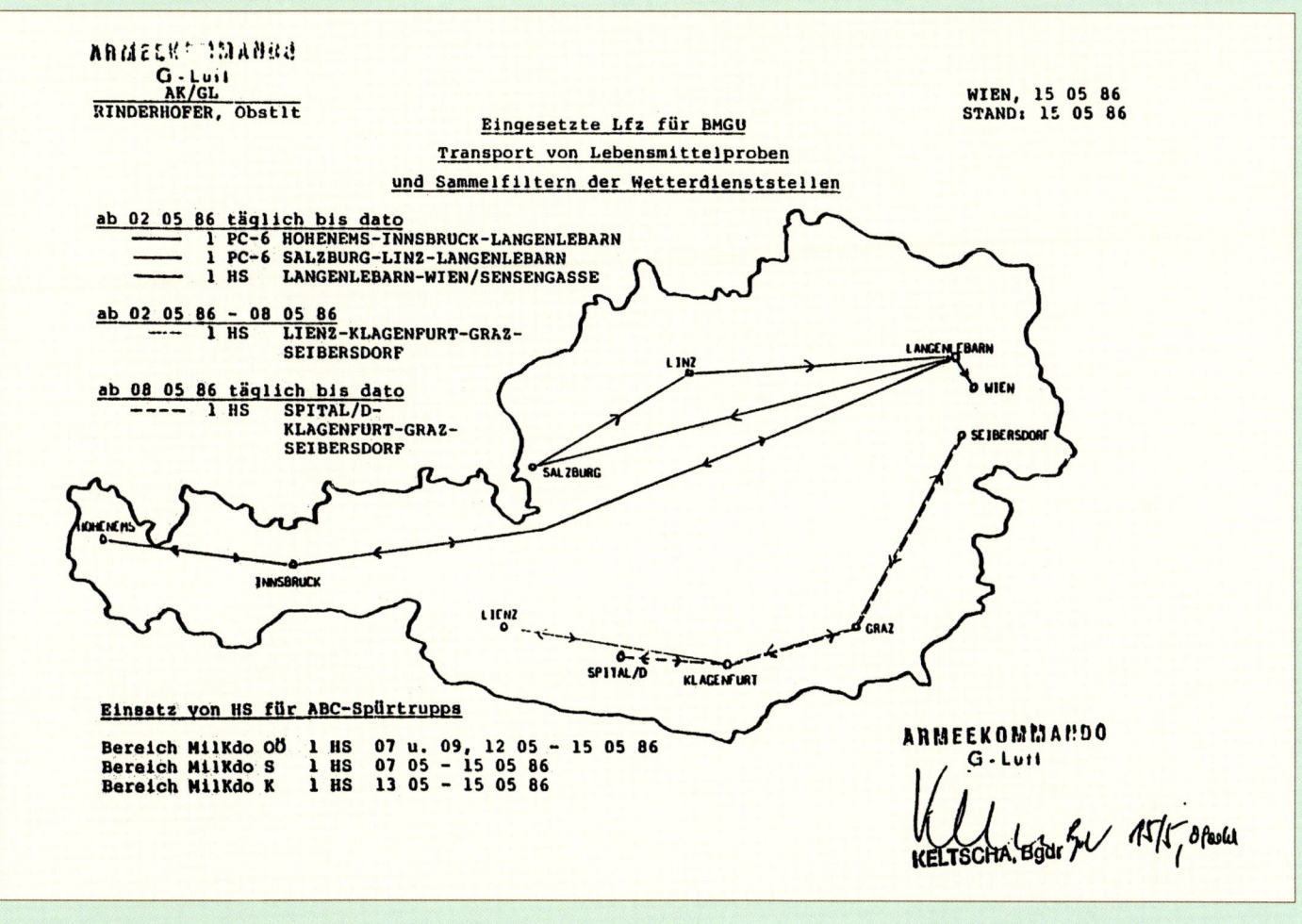

                                Eingesetzte Lfz für BMGU   WIEN, 15 05 86
                              Transport von Lebensmittelproben   STAND: 15 05 86
                             und Sammelfiltern der Wetterdienststellen

ab 02 05 86 täglich bis dato
 ———   1 PC-6   HOHENEMS-INNSBRUCK-LANGENLEBARN
 ———   1 PC-6   SALZBURG-LINZ-LANGENLEBARN
 ———   1 HS   LANGENLEBARN-WIEN/SENSENGASSE

ab 02 05 86 - 08 05 86
 ----   1 HS   LIENZ-KLAGENFURT-GRAZ-
                 SEIBERSDORF

ab 08 05 86 täglich bis dato
 ----   1 HS   SPITAL/D-
                 KLAGENFURT-GRAZ-
                 SEIBERSDORF

Einsatz von HS für ABC-Spürtrupps

Bereich MilKdo OÖ   1 HS   07 u. 09, 12 05 - 15 05 86
Bereich MilKdo S   1 HS   07 05 - 15 05 86
Bereich MilKdo K   1 HS   13 05 - 15 05 86

```
ARMEEKOMMANDO
    G-Luft
```
KELTSCHA, Bgdr

A soldier during the radiation measurement of a truck (l.b.) and in heavy protective gear during decontamination (r.b.). In the meantime valuable insights can be won: so it is determined that higher values appear in cars in the areas of the radiator, wheelhouses, and air filter.

Catastrophic Thunderstorms

Preliminary Events

Catastrophic thunderstorms devastate whole swathes of land in Salzburg. In the night before July 14th, 1989, deluges of rain wreak damages worth millions around the Attersee in Upper Austria and in the Lower Austrian District of Scheibbs. Within a short time such gigantic masses of water fall that numerous streams overflow their banks, bridges are washed away, farm buildings closed off from their surroundings by mudslides.

Political Measures

The catastrophe alert is immediately given by the affected district administrations. The deployment coordinations goes into action in the various catastrophe districts. The responsible military commands are petitioned for support.

> **Basis for deployment:** Demand for support from the affected district leadership.
> **Type of deployment:** Supportive deployment according to Sec. 2 para. 1 sub-para. c DA.
> **Mission:** Construction of temporary bridges; securing of weir systems and bank slopes; cleanup and clearing work.
> **Duration of deployment:** July 13th – 21st, 1989.
> **Contingent strength:** 173.
> **Commander:** First Lieutenant Reinhard Pfanzagel.

Donation Collection

In this deployment soldiers not only help through their personal service around the clock. The large number of onlookers, who specifically travel into the disaster zone in order to watch the engineers at their dangerous work, and in so doing also not insignificantly obstruct them (at times the valley in the area of Kirchberg/Wechsel must even be blockaded in order to be able to work without danger) are quickly "asked to pay up". The soldiers spontaneously organize a charity drive among the "audience". Within two hours 7,600 schillings come together in this way, which are handed over from the soldiers to the mayor of Kirchberg for the needy victims of the catastrophe. In this way it is once again shown that soldiers are not only at work with their knowledge and skills, but also with their hearts, when it comes to helping where others no longer can.

Military Measures

The alert of the military forces takes place through the MoD. Among others, the Army Engineer Battalion (AEngBn) in Melk is assigned to provide support in the District of Scheibbs.

The soldiers of the AEngBn construct nine temporary bridges and carry out bank securing measures, access roads to arms must be excavated and log jams eliminated. 4,500 cubic meters of rubble are removed in total. In Molzbach a complete weir field is constructed. Since the thunderstorms occur in the middle of the holiday and therefore travel season, it also comes to problems for some tourist groups. In Randegg, for instance, a tourist group is surprised by a mudflow. The flood made a bridge in front of the tour bus unpassable. The way behind the bus is also no longer drivable due to the rainfall. The approach must first be made passable again by forces of the AEngBn. After the rescue of the tour bus the bridge is temporarily repaired again.

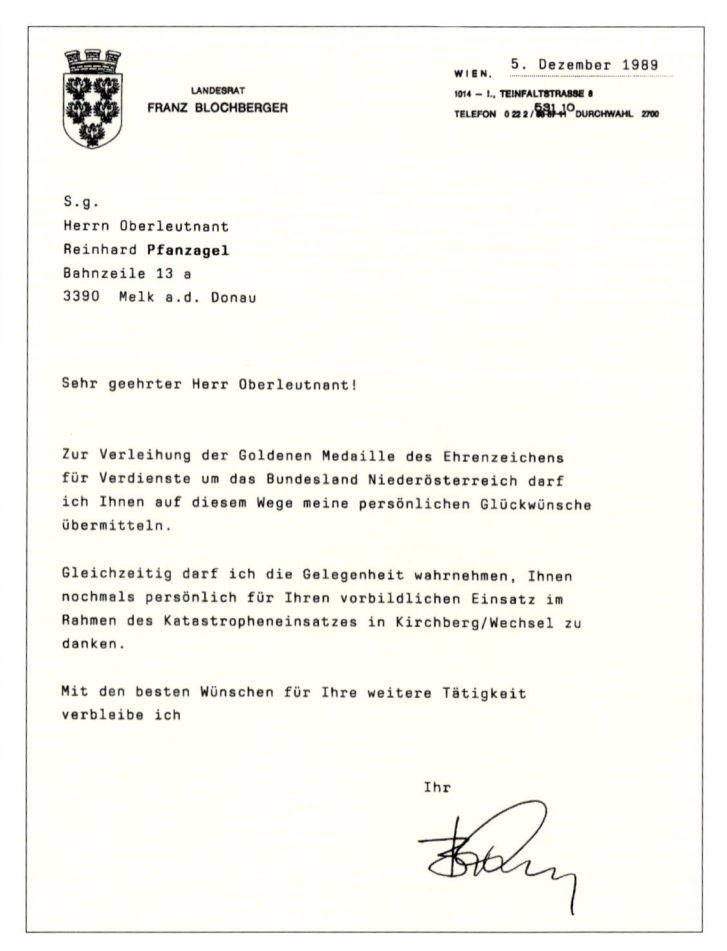

```
                                              WIEN,   5. Dezember 1989
        LANDESRAT                    1014 - I., TEINFALTSTRASSE 8
     FRANZ BLOCHBERGER               TELEFON 0 22 2/ 631 10 DURCHWAHL 2700

S.g.
Herrn Oberleutnant
Reinhard Pfanzagel
Bahnzeile 13 a
3390 Melk a.d. Donau


Sehr geehrter Herr Oberleutnant!

Zur Verleihung der Goldenen Medaille des Ehrenzeichens
für Verdienste um das Bundesland Niederösterreich darf
ich Ihnen auf diesem Wege meine persönlichen Glückwünsche
übermitteln.

Gleichzeitig darf ich die Gelegenheit wahrnehmen, Ihnen
nochmals persönlich für Ihren vorbildlichen Einsatz im
Rahmen des Katastropheneinsatzes in Kirchberg/Wechsel zu
danken.

Mit den besten Wünschen für Ihre weitere Tätigkeit
verbleibe ich

                                                       Ihr
```

The outstanding work contributed by the soldiers after catastrophes of all types finds due recognition always and everywhere: farmers invite soldiers over as thanks, from this some friendships develop. Letters of thanks arrive from public authorities, clubs and the like and remind of each personal contribution. Exceptional contributions are commemorated in the award of medals. Many soldiers receive honor or service awards from the respective provincial governments, the provincial fire department union, or the Red Cross after such a deployment (see also Volume 8, "The Cultivation of the Traditions of the Austrian Armed Forces from 1918 – 1998").

Catastrophic Storm

Preliminary Events

On March 1st, 1990, a hurricane also blusters over Upper Austria, devastating the work of generations and wreaking damage worth millions. The forest, the emergency reserve for many farmers, is nothing more than a tangle of uprooted stumps and shredded trunks. The amount of damaged wood caused by the hurricane is estimated at around 2 million solid cubic meters. Over 100 communities are directly affected by the damages.

Political Measures

The provincial governor of Upper Austria petitions the military command of UA for support. The support applications of the affected communities goes to the Provincial Forestry Authority, which, after evaluation of the respective damages, arranges the applications and deployments directly with the Contribution Staff. As a result of the constant increase of support applications the military commands of Carinthia, Salzburg, and the Tyrol are also petitioned for help. Since the support troops possess no special equipment, the Upper Austrian provincial government quickly helps out and procures 150 protective suits from the resources of the catastrophe fund, which are placed at the disposal of the soldiers for the duration of the deployment.

Military Measures

Immediately after the catastrophe became known, the military commander of Upper Austria orders that training be ceased and readiness to decamp be prepared in the Upper Austrian garrisons. Around 1,100 men in four engineer and 27 support platoons are affected by this. In the chancellery of the chief of staff a deployment center is established, which stands in constant contact with the provincial government and the Provincial Forestry Authority. Since after a short time all available soldiers in Upper Austria are already deployed, further forces are added on March 7th. The engineer platoon (EP) of the 2nd Engineer Battalion out of Villach assists in Gilgenberg am Weilhart, a engineer platoon (EP) from the military command of the Tyrol assists in Altheim with specialized tools, and an EP from the 3rd Engineer Battalion out of Salzburg assists the farmers in Neukirchen an der Enknach and Uttendorf. Furthermore, from March 13th, soldiers from the 26th Infantry Battalion and 71st Militia Training Regiment (MTR) from Carinthia, 3rd Supply Regiment and three recovery troops from the 7th Light Tank Battalion from Salzburg, and two platoons of the 62nd MTR from the Tyrol help the farmers of Traunviertel and Innviertel go to work. The soldiers make superhuman contributions. They are constantly deployed for ten hours a day, sometimes in life-threatening situations. The work is also – willingly – continued over the weekends. How dangerous the work in the storm-damaged forests is, is illustrated by the injuries that numerous soldiers suffer: there are cuts from power saws, bruises, pulled muscles and the like. The problem lies in the fact that though the engineer platoons indeed possess the appropriate protective gear for work with power saws (head, hand and leg protection), the support platoons do not. A swiftly accomplished procurement from the provincial government brings help.

> **Basis for deployment:** Petition of the provincial governor of Upper Austria.
> **Type of deployment:** Supportive deployment according to Sec. 2 para. 1 sub-para. c DA.
> **Mission:** Clearance work after a catastrophic storm.
> **Duration of deployment:** March 1st, 1990 – March 23rd, 1990.
> **Contingent strength:** 1,660.
> **Organization:** 7 engineer platoons, 36 support platoons, 5 "Greif" recovery tanks and 1 M 88 recovery tank, 3 engineer tanks, 300 wheeled vehicles.
> **Deployment leader:** Major General Dr. Karl Schoeller, military commander of Upper Austria.
> **Contribution:** 200,000 man hours.

Unusual Episode

40 Tyrolean soldiers experienced an "unusual type" of disappointment as they were quartered in the Steyr barracks during their deployment from March 13th – 18th: as they wanted to go out on their free evening, a club owner refused them entrance in uniform. The deployment leadership discloses this incident in the media. They report on the incomprehensible lapse, for which the (not only immediately affected) population can find no understanding.

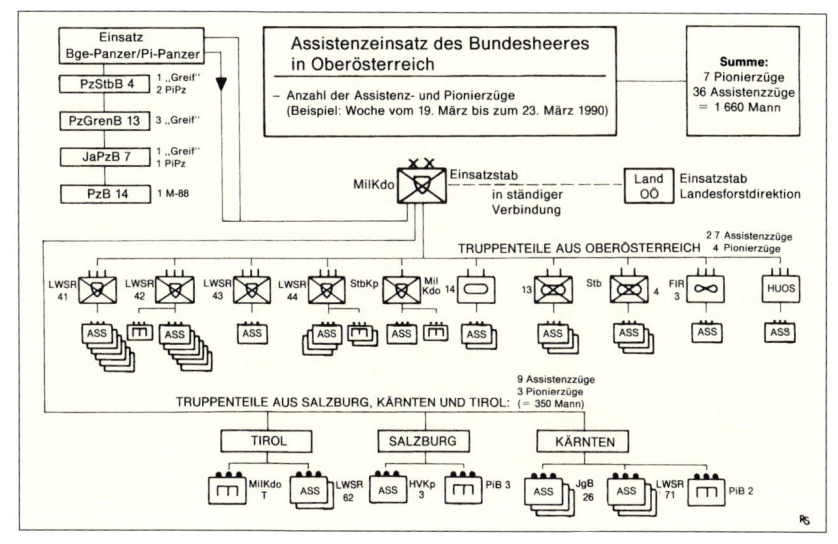

Border Area Surveillance

Preliminary Events

With the collapse of the Communist economic and political system in East Europe and the breakup of the Soviet Union the postwar order in Europe, frozen since the Yalta and Postdam Conferences draws to a close at the end of the 1980's. The fall of the Iron Curtain triggers jubilation, the freedom of travel and movement connected with it is initially only tentatively claimed. For the first time, major traffic routes lead through the up to now "dead" borders. Alongside the aspects to be embraced, however, come a row of problems. The opening of the border leads to illegal migration of people who seek a better future, but also to transnational crime (from narcotics smuggling to organized auto theft and burglary in the border areas to organized people smuggling). Through this a massive uncertainty develops in the affected border population. In June 1990 alone 1500 illegal border crossers (IBC) are picked up. At the end of August it is assumed that 50,000 foreigners are already illegally staying in Vienna. The mass of the IBC are set out by smuggling organizations near legal border crossings, then cross the border mostly in darkness in the area of the crossing, in order to finally be picked back up by the smugglers in Austrian territory and brought into the interior of the country.

International Reaction

On June 14th, 1985, as a result of a German and French initiative, the **"Schengen Agreement"** is signed in Schengen in Luxembourg. Together with Belgium, Luxembourg and the Netherlands, the abolition of border controls in internal traffic is agreed upon for January 1st, 1990. The agreement is subsequently designated as "Schengen I". As a result of the perceived security deficiency in the implementation, the "Schengen Implementation Agreement" – "Schengen II" is agreed upon on June 19th, 1990. This comes into effect on March 23rd, 1995, and regulated the complete phase-out of the monitoring of persons on the mutual internal borders and the reduction of monitoring in the traffic of goods.

These monitors are, however, transferred to the external borders of the EU at the same time. In this way, the responsibility for security within the EU is transferred to countries with external EU borders. On the borders a "dragnet" that encompasses the border territory is established. For better use of data a central computer ("Schengen Information System – SIS") is established in Strasbourg. The European Union attempts to master the ever growing illegal immigration and organized crime with these measures.

When the **"Amsterdam Treaty"** comes into effect on May 1st, 1999, the Schengen Agreements I and II are expanded to the limits of the EU.

Austrian Reaction
Political Measures

The ever more critical situation on the border leads the responsible Federal Minister of the Interior, Dr. Franz Löschnak, to take up the question in August in discussions on the highest official level of whether the armed forces would be prepared to respond to a possible call for support. The deployment should orient itself in the process by the summer 1967 supportive deployment. Since there is already a legal opinion from this time that such a deployment of the military would be seen as appropriate to the prevailing laws, the Minister of the Interior introduces the appropriate request for a supportive contribution of the armed forces on September 4th, 1990. The Council of Ministers, in its 158th session, registers the oral report of the Minister of the Interior on the order for the participation of the soldiers of the armed forces in the monitoring of the national border between Deutsch Jahndorf and Lockenhaus according to Sec. 2 para. 1 sub-para. b Defence Act 1990, FLG No. 150, as amended, for a duration of maximum (!) ten weeks.

For the coordination of the entire deployment (Gendarmery, Border Patrol, Armed Forces) a "deployment control room" is established by the Federal Ministry of the Interior (FMI) in the provincial Gendarmery command for Burgenland in Eisenstadt.

Already three weeks later, on September 25th, the security area must be widened to the Danube. The federal government decides on November 13th for a (1st) extension of 26 weeks. The border area in southern Burgenland can still be monitored with the forces of the Executive.

As a result of the growing concentration of illegal border crossings at the less monitored border sections in the south, it is necessary to expand the supportive deployment to the districts of Oberwart, Güssing and Jennersdorf in November 1991 (the supportive deployment is extended by the federal government to the length of one year with minor content specifications in the meantime). Therefore, with the exception of the 4 kilometer long section of the border directly before the Slovenian border, the entire national border with Hungary, with a length of 346 km is increasingly monitored by 2,000 men.

Although the foundation of a separate border Gendarmery occurs in 1997, this does not lead to any personnel relief for the supportive deployment. It only leads to a new separation of the assignments between the executive monitoring bodies. From the perspective of time it also seems more reasonable, should it come to a displacement of the "Schengen border" to the east with a possible acceptance of Hungary into the EU. If one placed executive officials at the border instead of soldiers, around 2,000 posts and workplaces would have to be created, which after the acceptance of Hungary would no longer be needed. The financial burden on the armed forces is worsened by the resolution of the Council of Ministers on November 12th, 1996, wherein it is determined that the supportive deployment will continue with "strengthened deployment of forces" (at first until December 31st, 1997). A further burden develops out of the petition from the Federal Minister of the Interior in the summer of 1997 for the *"participation of the armed forces in the strengthened monitoring of the 'green' border from the air through helicopters"*. This call for support is justified by the obligation to effective safeguarding of the external EU border resulting from the Schengen Agreement. The helicopters are needed not only for surveillance, but also for the swift movement of deployed forces. This supportive deployment is formally resolved upon, together with a new extension of the existing deployment, on November 18th, 1997 by the Council of Ministers, and in consideration of their similar goals, both supportive deployments are connected under the generic term **"measures for the heightened monitoring of the eastern EU border"** as a unified military contribution of help. The envisioned end of this supportive deployment is given as the "removal of the need to secure the outer borders to the Czech Republic, Slovakia, Hungary and Slovenia according to the provisions of the Schengen Implementation Agreement". In this way, a supportive deployment initially planned for only ten months becomes a "long-term temporary solution". On September 24th, 1999, the supportive deployment is once again expanded, this time to the north, where from that time on, 74 km in Lower Austria, from the confluence of the Morava with the Danube until just beyond the three-nation convergence of Austria, Slovakia and the Czech Republic, are monitored with an additional 170 men. This produces a total length of some 480 kilometers.

The smuggling organizations possess state-of-the-art electronics to scout out the locations of the soldiers. The military, in contrast to the Border Gendarmery, can do little to counter them. In December 2000, Defence Minister Herbert Scheibner therefore repeatedly demands the same equipment that the Border Gendarmery has. Likewise, the Minister once more points out that the border service is not the job of the military. The deployment serves only to bridge the gap that is necessary for the full development of the Border Gendarmery. On December 19th, 2000, the Council of Ministers therefore decides on only a three-month extension for the time being (normally the supportive deployment of the armed forces is extended by the Council of Ministers by a year at a time). A policy decision on the continuation of the border deployment should take place by March 2001. However, in the Council of Ministers on March 27th again only an "interim solution" occurs: the supportive deployment is initially extended until December 31st, 2001. A task force is supposed to reach an agreement on further organization by the end of June 2001. By January 2002 the armed forces should be withdrawn "step by step". For this purpose, 100 million schillings are allocated for the procurement of night vision and heat sensing equipment for the military.

Military Measures

As a result of the previous meetings between the Federal Ministers for the Interior, Finance, and Defence, the **"Army Order No. 1 for the Supportive Deployment of Military Forces for Securing the Borders According to Sec. 2 para. 1 sub-para. b DA 1990"** is signed immediately after the Council of Ministers on September 4th, 1990, at 2:25 PM, by Commander-in-Chief of the Army Gen-

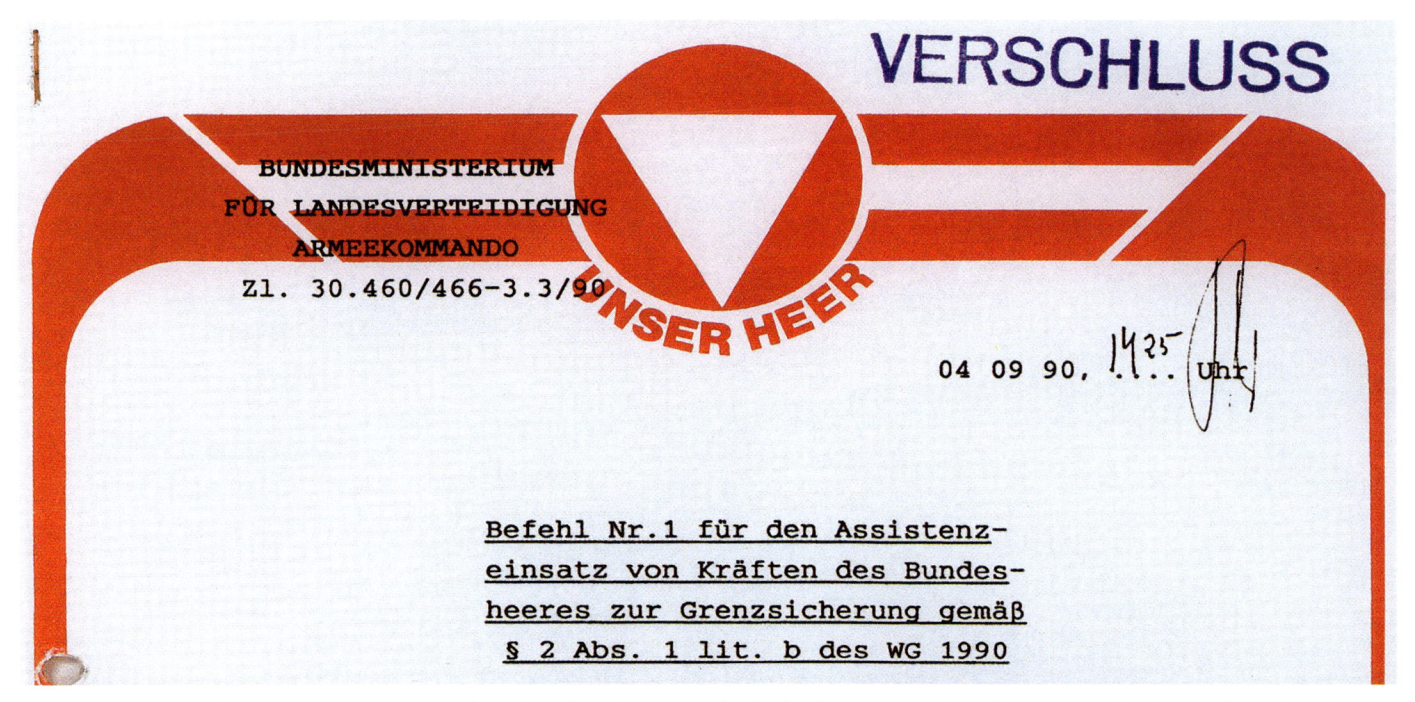

The following copy of the heading of this order shows how fast the army order had to be sent out. The order was mistakenly copied on a letterhead of the Public Works Division (AK/G5), that by chance remained in the paper tray of the copier from an earlier copy job. The personal entry of the time of dispatch by General Philipp is noteworthy.

eral Hannes Philipp. Among other things, this says that: *"The army command prepares to lead a supportive deployment of several weeks in cooperation with the Ministry of the Interior, in the form of border supervision with an initial emphasis between Deutsch Jahrndorf and Lockenhaus, under the formation of a territorial deployment staff with 2 support battalions on a line of security and a battalion-strength reserve held in readiness in the southern section, in order to create the conditions for the prevention of illegal border crossing in the aforementioned area."* In order to be historically accurate, it must be mentioned that this order goes out to the troops before appropriate basic instructions for the GTI (administered in the interim through Lieutenant General Siegbert Kreuter) are ruled on through Federal Minister Dr. Robert Lichal, and that this order has essentially preserved its validity to this day. From this viewpoint the replacement of General Philipp and the dissolution of the army command in June 1991 seems still less understandable.

The support troops are subordinated to the responsible security authorities (district administrations). This accounts, irrespective of the military hierarchy, for a certain authority of the security authorities over the soldiers in security police matters. The authority consists above all of concrete regulations adapted to the respective situations with specific regard to the **Security Police Capacities**, certain methods of behavior as well as the use of weapons. In addition to this an information sheet based on the regulations from the year 1967 is handed out through the FMI. The soldiers deployed to monitor the borders enter the legal status of "institutions of the public safety"; they therefore enjoy the same rights that are accorded to the security institutions (higher legal protection, executive capacities). The soldiers nevertheless carry out no monitoring activities directly at the border monitoring posts. This falls to the institutions of the Ministry of the Interior. With respect to the **use of weapons** the specifications of the General Duty Regulations apply. The specifications with regard to independent military action according to Sec. 2 para. 4 of the Defence Act as well as Sec. 3 Criminal Code (self-defence) remain untouched by this regulation.

The military leadership structure is adapted to that of the civilians. This means that the Burgenland Military Command (BMilComm), as the command leading the deployment, is led directly through the **Army Command**. As a result of the dissolution of the Army Command, the BMilComm is subordinated to the **Operations Division in the Federal Defence Ministry**. To secure uninterrupted leadership ability for all domestic and international deployments, a **"Operational Center (Land)"** is established in General Körner's command building. Within the BMilComm, a **"deployment staff"** is installed to support the commandant in the fulfillment of his leadership duties.

At the beginning of the deployment, 3 support commands ("North", "Central", "South"), each with a support battalion, are formed. Each support battalion (SuppBn) consists of a battalion command, reduced headquarters company with liaison officers for the executive authorities and the 1st – 3rd support companies (SuppCoy). The SuppCoys consist of a company command, supply groups and the I – IV support platoons, each with 4 support groups. Both SuppBns "North" and "Central" each possess a communicative helicopter and a medical helicopter. Furthermore, 4 transport helicopters and a light fixed-wing aircraft are ready for aerial photography in Langenlebarn. The SuppBn "South" is in an assembly area, is held in readiness as a reserve for the time being and is only deployed on the border as occasion warrants. On September 11th, 1990, the SuppBn "South" is dissolved. Both remaining support commands now possess 4 SuppCoys each.

The situation on the national border with Hungary makes an extension of the military border area surveillance (BAS) necessary in October 1991. Therefore, the forces are redeployed under the formation of a third SuppCd. With a decree from November 7th, 1991, 13th MTR is commissioned with the formation of SuppCd South and HQCoy. By the beginning of 1992 the supportive deployment is led with 3 SuppCds (each 1 SuppBn with 3 SuppCoys each).

On the basis of the appropriate guidelines of the security authorities, the number of soldiers supportively deployed can be initially reduced to 1,500 in fall 1993. For this reason, the number of the SuppCoys is decreased from 9 to 6 (2 SuppCoys per SuppBn), with the retention of the three support commands. In spring 1994 the "Central" SuppCd is dissolved, the two companies are divided between the two remaining commands.

After the situation demands the increase of the number of support companies to 8 in November 1996 (with a total of 35 SuppPls), and that of the deployed soldiers to 2000 in March 1997, the organizational structure can be described as follows: The SuppCd "North" is assigned the area from the Danube to the Herrentisch (east of Sieggraben) as its security area. For this is has access to 4 SuppCoys. The security area of SuppCd "South" reaches from the Herrentisch to Raabtal. This SuppCd also has 4 subordinate SuppCoys. In addition, a reconnaissance platoon "ELO" is subordinated to the BMilComm. This platoon supports the BAS in particularly sensitive areas through the use of heat imaging and radar technology.

On October 1st, 1997, the **"helicopter border deployment"** initially begins independently and later, as a result of the ruling of the Council of Ministers on November 18th, as a part of the already occurring supportive deployment. On December 1st, 1997, the full operation is taken up with night-flight capable helicopters adapted especially for the border deployment, from two staging areas in the Waldviertel and in southern Burgenland.

The further expansion of the border area to be monitored into parts of Lower Austria across from Slovakia leads to the establishment of a separate SuppCoy, which is initially subordinated to SuppCd N as the **5th SuppCoy**, and which takes up its duties on September 23rd. Since this makes SuppCdN's responsibilities too great, the border between the two SuppCds is shifted to the north. Consequently the SuppCdN leads 4 SuppCoys and SuppCdS 5 SuppCoys. The SuppCoy has a strength of 200 soldiers, 170 of whom perform duties directly on the border.

The length of a deployment cycle is initially established as four weeks at the beginning of the deployment, to which another approximately two weeks for preparation and debriefing are added. As a result of the experiences had, the **cycle length** is lengthened to six weeks in June 1999.

The **tactical approach** of the BAS must continually be adapted. At the beginning of the deployment the presence of the soldiers alone has a strong deterrent effect externally and a calming effect internally. The soldiers are commanded to confront the IBC humanely, even in a friendly manner. This initially leads to IBC coming openly to the soldiers, in order to be taken up and, as they believe, rescued. This quickly changes as professional bands of smugglers carefully study the behavior of the soldiers and subsequently use the situation to systematically introduce citizens of the Third World. Smuggling has in the mean time become the largest line of business for organized crime (OC). The approach of the smugglers, as well as the illegal border crossers, changes drastically through the years. Exclusively organized smugglers attempt to smuggle illegals over the border today. There are many levels to be seen in the process: The "leadership level", which transports the IBC from their homelands to the vicinity of the "West" with the help of ultra-modern communications technology and optimally equipped counterfeiting workshops; the "distribution centers", which exist in the border regions and observe the military and spot their tactics with their own reconnaissance organization, and the "border smugglers", who are at the other end of the hierarchy and carry out the "onsite work".

In order to constantly adapt to these changes, the military must continually react flexibly and professionally. Instead of the former "open" demeanor, it now depends on the correct tactical behavior of each individual soldier. The deployment therefore increasingly needs the best infantry-trained, physically capable, resilient and motivated soldiers. Commanders at all levels must constantly judge the situation anew and lead their soldiers quickly and with initiative as the situation develops. The deployment leadership of a SuppPt receives great importance. In the place of the posts and patrols, a system of powers on the border in switch lines in the depths, with quickly accessible reserves, comes into place. Constant planning for combing through the terrain as well as for unnoticeable shift changes is necessary. Flexible leadership makes the reconnaissance activities of the smuggling organizations and prevents illegal border crossings or makes the arrest of these criminals possible.

The **circumstances of the deployment** are difficult and demanding. The deployment takes place at the time with around 80 double patrols during the day, 160 double patrols at night. Alongside the deployment on foot, motorized patrols or bike patrols are carried out. At time mounted patrols on Haflingers from the Pack Animal Echelon of the 24th Infantry Battalion out of Lienz are also deployed. The soldiers perform their duties around the clock and in all weather. The most intense service takes place at night, since the mass of the IBC naturally use the cover of darkness. The supportive deployment offers an excellent opportunity to test and improve the leadership ability of the cadre personnel under even extreme circumstances. The lower-level commanders are especially constantly under pressure, since they are after all for 4 to 6 weeks the (often only) contact person and role model for the recruits entrusted to them. Since the confrontation with poverty and misery or the separation from home can sometimes be great, military chaplains and psychologists are available around the clock over their own **"Help Line Service"**.

On the other hand the loss of training time of up to two months should not be underestimated. This time is missed above all with the training of specialists. The premature wear of materials in deployed equipment muss also be included in calculations. Below the line, however, the deployment conforms to the expectations of the population, namely, to be there for their "protection and help".

For the duration of the deployment, the professional soldier is initially due a **deployment fee**, graduated according to family status. All other rights to extra fees remain intact. This means, however, that the extra fees, such as overtime compensation, reach an indefensible magnitude, while professional soldiers with a right to a usage bonus (such as the battalion commanders) receive no financial compensation for the often serious overburdening of their time and responsibility. For the soldiers who are used in the supportive deployment during their mandatory military service, generally only a uniform higher deployment pay is provided.

As a first legal salary improvement, a deployment compensation is introduced for contract soldiers in fall 1990. Subsequently, it is attempted to do justice to the overburdening and moments of danger with a qualified higher salary. As a result of experience to date in supportive deployment and security deployment in 1991, a new salary regulation comes into force on July 1st, 1992, in the form of a **deployment fringe benefit law**. Afterwards uniform deployment fringe benefits are introduced, which take the place of most of the extra fees. The deployment fringe benefits also appertain to the time spent directly preparing for deployment. For soldiers contributing their mandatory military service, a deployment monthly allowance is planned, the deployment compensation introduced in 1990 for contract soldiers is raised to the amount of the deployment fringe benefits for the professional soldiers. In this way, a practically oriented deployment compensation can largely be realized. An amendment allows the inclusion of militia soldiers in the course of voluntary weapons drills in supportive deployment since March 2001. This allows for deployment experience for the militia and to a noticeable relief of the active cadre.

In the course of the public services law amendment of 2000, a demand of many years' standing from the Public Service Union also comes to account: the **security services assistance law** is expanded, so that as of September 1st, 2000, henceforth *"soldiers, who are deployed in a supportive deployment according to Sec. 2 para. 1 sub-para. b of the Defence Act of 1990, FLG No. 305, for the maintenance of public order and safety"* are also included in the provisions regulations of the aforementioned law. This amendment ensures that soldiers who suffer an accident in the exercise of these security police measures during border duty, in case of an incurred injury and damaged health (or alternatively in case of death, the bereaved) are equated with the security service workers in view of their outstanding assistance. In individual cases the one-time federal payment can reach up to 1.5 million schillings.

The unusual character of the deployment (above all the ban on leaving the area of operations) also demands special considerations with respect to **troop entertainment**. So each SuppCd possesses its own budget contingent for cultural and athletic entertainment. Television sets and video recorders are available beginning at the platoon level. The military print shop produces its own field postcards. The post office delivers letters and cards that carry the

All soldiers that are in the SuppD wear a red-white-red armband on their left bicep. The vehicles are identified through red-white-red flags that are fitted in front of or above the engine hood. The patrols occur on foot, with vehicles, bicycles, and sometimes on horseback. The expansion of the monitoring zone makes observation by water necessary as well (b.l.). Especially noteworthy is the outstanding cooperation with the Executive (b.r.).

stamp **"Army Post"** and that are mailed from established "Army Post Offices" for free. For the connection to home a prepaid telephone card is made available to every recruit.

Since this SuppD deals with a current deployment, the current detailed organization, exact equipage, and deployment procedures cannot be enlarged upon.

Basis for deployment:	CM of September 4th, 1990.
Type of deployment:	Supportive deployment according to Sec. 2 para. 1 sub-para. b DA.
Mission:	Preventative deterrence of illegal border crossers, cessation of illegal border crossings.
Duration of deployment:	September 4th, 1990 (full operation since December 1st, 1990) until December 21st, 2007.
Contingent strength:	Between 1,200 (end of 1995) and 2,200 (1999 – 2002).
Total strength:	334,903.
Organization:	Burgenland deployment staff, reconnaissance platoon, Support Command "North" with 4 SuppCoys, Support Command "South" with 5 SuppCoys, Lower Austrian support company.
Commander:	September 4th, 1990 – February 28th, 2003: Major General Friedrich Dialer, military commander of Burgenland. March 1st, 2003 – December 21st, 2007: Brigadier General Mag. Johann Luif, military commander of Burgenland.
Contribution:	90,648 illegal border crossers (IBC) from at least 11 countries.
Cost:	661.4 million Euros. Too little is said about this in public: The **financial costs** of the supportive deployment which is carried out by the armed forces for the Ministry of the Interior, must be drawn from the (smallest in Europe) defence budget. Money that the armed forces lacks for the most urgently necessary investments (keywords: helicopter, armored personnel carrier, radio equipment, interceptor plane…).

The deployment occurs at the **cost of training**, however. After all, up to seven weeks are lost in basic military service (with two-time deployment up to eleven weeks). Time that can never be recovered and the loss of which will have an effect on the deployment readiness in line with a mobilization. At the same time the counterargument for deployment experience under "extreme" conditions (physical and psychological "pressure") can only be given limited acknowledgement. Obviously this cannot be denied. Constant duty under often the worst weather conditions, cohabitation over a longer period of time in the smallest amount of space, confrontation with human suffering, these are all factors that play a role. The label "under the most extreme conditions" alone shows that this peacetime (!) burden often goes past the limits of these young people. On the other hand, this deployment often occurs at the expense of the fundamental training for a "real" deployment. It is to be hoped that this deficiency never shows itself to be life-threatening.

The Military Command of Burgenland, as the command leading the deployment, is initially led directly by Army Command. With its dissolution in 1991 the Operations division in the Federal Ministry of Defence takes over this agenda until the creation of the Land Forces Command in the year 2002. Since 2005 the Military Command is subordinate to the newly created Land Forces Command.

Electronic Surveillance

Since December 1st, 1997, the full operation of the "Schengen-compliant" border zone monitoring also takes place from the air. The helicopter deployment is carried out above all at night along the 1,257 km long EU external border with the Czech Republic, Slovakia, Hungary and Slovenia. This is a part of the supportive deployment. The **BAS from the air** takes place from the staging points in the Waldviertel and Punitz in southern Burgenland. A helicopter each from the northern and southern sections is deployed at night. For tactical reasons, and in order to keep the noise pollution to at ground level as low as possible, they fly around 300 m above the ground. During each flight a member of the Gendarmery is on board as the operator, who sends his observation results directly to the deployed forces on the ground.

The helicopters deployed in BAS, of the types SA.316B "Alouette III" and OH-58B, are especially adapted for this deployment. They possess a quick-hitch for the swift mounting of a part of the so-called "Schengen equipment". This consists of the following components:

- Heat imaging equipment and daylight TV camera (AN/AAQ-22);
- Video recorder for recording and analysis;
- "Nightsun" Searchlight with infrared filter;
- "Airscout" Global Positioning System (GPS) with "Moving Map" map reading equipment;
- Radar height gauge;
- Additional radio equipment for the connection to the Executive;
- "Goggles" Night vision goggles for pilots (currently being procured).

The AN/AAQ-22, video recorder and searchlight are not permanently mounted, but are mounted for the respective deployment on the helicopter's quick-hitch. The deployment of these helicopters shows a highly deterrent effect, and the deployment forces on the ground can be led with meter-by-meter accuracy to the IBCs detected from the air.

In Wiener Neustadt an AB.212 is also available, with which forces of the Gendarmery Deployment Command (GDC) can be flown into the border area as needed.

"Schengen border surveillance outpost" with heat imaging camera (t.) and analysis area (r.).

Makeshift observation at night with the driver's periscope (night vision equipment) of a MBT M60A3Ö (b.l.).

Battlefield radar tool Thorn MSTAR (m.).

Heat imaging tool / large, consisting of a TV camera, heat imaging tool and laser distance gauge (b.r.).

50

Helicopters of the types SA.316B "Alouette III" (t.) and Bell OH-58B (b.l.) with "Schengen Equipage". In the pictures (t.r.) the spotlight and (r.) the observation stand in an "Alouette III" are visible. In order to be able to mount the heat imaging tool AN/AAQ-22 (b.r.) below the OH-58B, the skid landing gear must be raised (b.l.).

Battlefield Reconnaissance System (BRS)

The lack of appropriate electronic surveillance devices severely impairs deployment at night or in bad weather. So initially one must improvise (once again): Some support forces help themselves with makeshift night vision equipment by using tank periscopes on tripods. Subsequently divisions that are equipped with PAL "Bill" or FAL "Mistral" are allowed to use these heat imaging systems for Border Area Surveillance (BAS) for the intensification of the electronic surveillance. Not until 1997 is the Battlefield Reconnaissance System introduced for BAS on the ground. The goal of the BRS is the detection of illegal border crossers at night as well as the personnel-sparing surveillance of open and wide-ranging areas of terrain, in order to free up forces for use in more personnel-intensive deployments, for instance in the forest. The BRS consists of three components:

- Battlefield radar (BR);
- Heat imaging tool/large (HIT/large);
- Heat imaging tool/small (HIT/small).

With the **battlefield radar tool (Thorn MSTAR)** people can be spotted from a distance of up to 10 km and vehicles from up to 20 km. As long as the "targets" are in movement, an exact calculation of their direction of movement, distance and the respective current whereabouts is possible. The BRT is especially superior to a HIT at discovering targets in bad weather.

The **heat imaging tool/large (RTV-445 LORIS)** is a combination of TV equipment, a heat imaging tool and a laser distance gauge, that is mounted on a remote-controlled vertical and horizontal directional system. The HIT/large is suitable as a passive sensor, supported by the ground or a vehicle, for reconnaissance missions of up to 6 km. Its especial strength lays in its high detection and identification abilities in darkness. The exact identification of the targets can take place by description, number, type and activity.

The **heat imaging tool/small (MILCAM HHTI)** is, like the HITs of the PAL "Bill" and FAL "Mistral" as well, above all for the surveillance of no-visibility areas, but can also be used for infantry deployments (for instance by scouts). These machines have a range of 1,500 – 2,500 m. Experience during border duty has shown that the connection of an external monitor considerably improves the efficiency of observation (during a daily use of 10 – 15 hours!)

In addition the forces that are directly deployed to pick up the IBCs are above all equipped with night vision binoculars or night vision goggles respectively. The night vision binoculars (NVB 87) are optical precision instruments with 2.4-time magnification. The "LUCIE" night vision goggles function on the principle of residual light amplification. With the help of a headset LUCIE can be worn handsfree and so allows for use during all kinds of work as well as the steering and driving of vehicles at night.

902 Weeks and a Day[20]

On December 22nd, 2007, an expansion of the Schengen Area occurs. The neighboring countries of the Czech Republic, Slovakia, Hungary and Slovenia enter the Schengen treaty as well. In this way, the Schengen outer border shifts from the eastern border of Austria further to the east. With this, the intensified border surveillance is no longer necessary. The supportive deployment/border area surveillance is therefore concluded and transferred to the **Supportive Deployment after the Schengen Expansion (SuppD/SchE)** (see page 101 ff).

After 6,315 days and the presentation of all data it is therefore time to sum up.

Personnel

In total 334,903 soldiers from all of Austria were supportively deployed for border area surveillance. Including their family members and friends, the "supportive deployment initiates" must be the fourth largest group of people in the alpine republic, after football, ski and political experts. The number of deployed soldiers per cycle varied between ca. 1,200 (end of 1995) and at times more than 2,200 (1999 until 2002) soldiers. At least as late as the reduction of the required military service from eight to six months in January 2006, the military would have been unable to accomplish the supportive deployment in the required numbers without militia soldiers! On average the militia participation lay around six percent. Until 1995 still laying around one percent, the participation of militia soldiers in the supportive deployment climbed to 15 percent in the year 2007. 387 times, bodies of troops from all of Austria formed a support command.

The supportive deployment yielded much: joy and tears, successful experiences and frustration, worry and boredom, conflict and forgiveness. Sweat and blood were shed, friendships sealed and marriages split up. Father and son stood in uniform on the eastern border, at times also father and daughter. The supportive deployment was also advertisement, advertisement for the Austrian military, Burgenland, and the Weinviertel. Over 300,000 soldiers got to know the east of Austria. Some hated it, but many became fond of it and returned. The came to show their parents, girlfriends, children or grandchildren where they "froze their asses off" or where they bravely "took up" a group of illegal border crossers.

Most tragically, 49 soldiers died during supportive deployment. 15 of them lost their lives outside of their service demands, 13 alone in traffic accidents, 22 soldiers committed suicide. They should all be remembered at this point (author's comment).

The deployed soldiers were also specially identified, namely with armbands. According to tactics, either with a red-white-red one, in order to be recognized as border area surveillance soldiers, or with an olive green one, in order to operate secretively and whenever possible not to be recognized. (In this, however, the appropriate combat behavior of the soldiers was more important than the color of the armband.)

---

20 Manfred Roth: "902 Weeks and a Day" (in extracts).

Area of Operations

The area of operations stretched first from Geschriebenstein (884 m, highest point in Burgenland) to the three-nation convergence of Hungary – (then still) Czechoslovakia – Austria in Deutsch Jahrndorf. Three weeks later it was expanded northwards to the Danube and on October 25th, 1991 into the district of Jennersdorf until the three-nation convergence of Hungary – Slovenia – Austria. With the last expansion on September 21st, 1999 to the north along the Morava until Hohenau, it reached its final length with ca. 470 border kilometers.

Result

By all means necessary, it was attempted to make the border area as impassable as possible for illegal border crossers. The soldiers made rounds on foot, they patrolled on horseback, with bicycles and with engineer boats. Pack animal echelons and infantry command forces were deployed, and from September 1997, regular observation flights with helicopters, equipped with Forward Looking Infrared (FLIR) took place. In some cases ground sensors and drones were also tested.

Through these measures 90,648 illegal border crossers (IBCs) from at least 111 countries of the world were taken up by soldiers while or after crossing the border. Nearly 75,000 of them came merely a handful of countries: the mass of them from Romania, the successor nations of the former Soviet Union, from Afghanistan and the ex-Yugoslavian nations. For almost 3,000 illegal border crossers their identities were either not determinable or verifiable by the Austrian authorities. Sometimes it also happened that illegal border crossers were taken up more than once. The estimated number of unknown cases of illegal entry, unrecognized by soldiers and the Executive, can only be speculated over with a border length of over 470 km and a maximum occupation at night of 312 troops – statistically therefore only two soldiers on every 1.5 km.

Cooperation with Foreign Border Patrols

In December 2001 the security authorities issues the order, when possible to hinder illegal border crossers while they are still crossing the border. As a result of this mission, beginning in the year 2002, the attempt is undertaken to detect illegal border crossers in a timely manner while still on the other side of the border, in order to fulfill the requirements for a seizure of the illegal border crossers while still on their national territory by the respective foreign border patrol. From the year 2002, at least a fifth of the illegal border crossers were prevented from entering Austrian national territory with this method of "rejection". The foundation for this was, among other things, the security partnership between Austria, Hungary and Slovakia as well as the resulting close cooperation of the domestic and foreign security authorities and Burgenland Military Command. That it was not always so is shown by the fact that on Christmas Eve 1990, after an intervention of the representative commander of the Hungarian Border Patrol in the Security Directorate of Burgenland, the then-commander of the "Central" support command had to take back the sweets handed out from Austrian to Hungarian soldiers on the day before.

Military Driver Service
In order for the soldiers to carry out their duties at observation posts or on foot patrols in the border area, they generally had to be brought to their deployment location with vehicles and be picked up again there after the end of their duty shift. Breakfast and dinner were also picked up from faraway cooking sites and brought to the soldiers. The mail and every replacement part was transported, the commanders were driven to meetings or briefings and the soldiers to amusement facilities in the time without planned service demands. Despite appropriate consolidation of trips, a total of 133,000,000 kilometers were covered. The equator was therefore purely statistically circled ca. 3,324 times. In the process, 371 accidents occurred, unfortunately also those with injuries and deaths, from which 62 were to be attributed to third party fault. The record with respect to accident-free driving was established by the 13th Militia Training Regiment and 19th Infantry Battalion, with 1,105,972 km!

Medical Service
During the supportive deployment, cooking was done in the field and the provisions delivered in hay boxes. During this time there were only two salmonella epidemics and two cases of salmonella whose causes could not be determined. In total it came to loss of 446 work days as a result of illness. From a total of about 12,000,000 work days a negligible number, which stands as proof of the quality of the general hygiene, the professional provisions preparation and delivery as well as the constant supervision in this delicate area.

A comparison of the "doctor's visitors" or the sick certificates in the barracks with those in supportive deployment shows a further, highly interesting aspect: The soldiers in supportive deployment had a three-day duty rhythm with twice twelve hours and twice six hours of duty (36 hours) as well as 36 hours of readiness. The readiness time was primarily thought of as rest time. Practically, the soldiers had to prepare themselves for duty in this time (briefings, inspection of tools, weapons, munitions, etc.), be brought to the border and picked up from the border again (including an up to 15 km march) and follow up on their duty (ensuring the safety of weapons, cleaning and surrender of weapons and munitions, cleaning of equipment and clothing, etc.). This reduced the actual rest time considerably. The soldiers also had serious difficulty finding a sleep rhythm as a result of the constantly changing rest times, which sometimes led to sleep disorders. In addition the soldiers were exposed to all weather and environmental conditions: heat and mosquitoes in summer, snowstorms and biting cold in winter, as well as the, for many soldiers unaccustomed, almost constant wind all year. Nevertheless the soldiers in the supportive deployment visited the troop doctor noticeably less than those soldiers who performed their service in barracks.

Public Interest
Far more than 800 delegations with almost 11,000 people received orientation in the specifics of the supportive deployment. The interest of the media was no less. The "Ganze Woche", and the "Rennbahnexpress", the "Los Angeles Post", "Le Figaro", "Krone" and "Kurier" – to name only a few – sent journalists. Half the world could hear and see articles on the supportive deployment of the armed forces through radio and television. It speaks for itself that these reported not only on the specifics of the deployment, but also on incidents such as saved lives and contributions of help from soldiers, brawls, the burning of toll huts or observation stands, accidents with trucks and weapons, or the discovery of war relics.

Infrastructure and Accommodation
The tactical demands made a central, and at the same time near to the border, location of the platoon, company, and supportive commands, as well as the provision facilities, necessary. The military therefore had to fall back on the civil infrastructure, although the civilian accommodations often not even approached the requirements and – limited by the short terms of the contracts – the rental costs were at first immensely high (cadre soldiers were quartered in the guest rooms of inns and bed and breakfasts, recruits in rented mass quarters). The closed lodging of the platoons on one property was only successful in a few cases. In many places adequate sanitary facilities were lacking, sometimes no warm water was available for personal hygiene. Many accommodations were also not adequately heated. The repair of vehicles and the operation of the field kitchens often took place under shed roofs in the open air. Construction, fire safety and other security regulations were hardly or not at all followable. As a result of these unreasonable conditions for the soldiers and with the apparent longer duration of the deployment, Burgenland Military Command (BMilComm) began to better the infrastructure and administer it centrally.

The necessary adaptations were carried out by engineers. For the new construction of properties or the required adjustments yearly sums between 100,000 and a million Euros were spent.

Furthermore, the maintenance of the infrastructure demanded roughly 100,000 Euros per year, while the costs of the upkeep of the rented properties were partially to be shouldered by the landlords. The yearly total outlay for rents and operating expenses was ca. 2.4 million Euros. This sum, which seems huge at first sight, corresponds to about (a cheap) 3.50 Euros per soldier and day.

The first trailer camps for the accommodation of deployed soldiers in Deutsch Jahrndorf and Rattersdorf came into being in 1994 through close cooperation between Burgenland Military Command and the Military Construction and Measurement Agency. The container camp in Punitz for helicopter crews followed in 1997, and in the year 2001 camps for the support platoons in Baumgarten and Schandorf.

Through the years the soldiers, command posts, horses, storage, and helicopters were housed in over 120 (overwhelmingly civilian) properties in 75 towns in the area of operations. Through the constant improvement of the infrastructure of the command posts and accommodations a standard was soon reached that was at least equal with or in some areas even exceeded that of the barracks.

Dugouts and Raised Stands
By their service directly on the national border and away from any infrastructure, the soldiers were exposed to every kind of weather. In order to protect themselves from wind, rain, snow and icy cold to some extent, they constructed temporary tents. Group tents were likewise set up, and small huts (the so-called high felt huts) – with a floor space of hardly a square meter – also served a the first suitable weather protection. Border Patrol huts had floor space of four square meters and were heated with wood ovens, which the soldiers were allowed to use just weeks after the beginning of the deployment. So that the soldiers, above all on the plains of the Weinviertel or in Burgenland, could observe as far as possible across the terrain, they first made use of higher civilian observation points (such as grain silos). These were nevertheless subsequently forbidden, not lastly for reasons of security. The observation thus took place only with the raised stands constructed by the Austrian military. For the construction and positioning of a raised stand of wood an engineer group needed around one and a half weeks. The material costs for these were ca. 3,500 Euros. At the end of the deployment in December 2007, 204 dugouts and raised stands were in the inventory of the Austrian military: three observation containers, 146 Border Patrol huts, two raised stands of metal and 54 raised stands of wood.

Foodstuffs
For breakfast the soldiers were delivered fresh bread and drinks. The border guards received a warm meal (of more than one course), prepared in the troop kitchen, for dinner. They had to prepare all other meals themselves. In exchange, every platoon commander could daily order foodstuffs from a list (incidentally in a variety that was hardly to be found in a private household). In total the soldiers consumed over 55,000 tons of foodstuffs of all kinds, including 24,480,000 rolls and happily also 5,875,200 kg of fruit. 2,464 coffee machines provided for the duty readiness of the soldiers, who filled them with 856,800 kg of coffee. 1,121,280 rolls of toilet paper were consumed. 8,480 brooms cleaned a total of 120 occupied properties in 75 different towns. Since the mass of the foodstuffs and commodities were drawn from the area of operations, a considerable economic factor for the region can be spoken of. True to the old farmers' rule: *"Better a good maneuver than a bad harvest."* (Author's note)

Army Post
Army post offices were established for the handling of private mail for the soldiers, which were also used for official mail. Through them, around 600,000 letters and 5,800 packets were dispatched.

Thanks!
In conclusion, all the many people who selflessly and unbureaucratically supported the soldiers in their work and eased their stay away from home for over 17 years must be thanked! *"All Burgenlanders bake for the military"* and *"Border guards with family connections"* wrote Peter Zehrer in the daily newspaper "Die Presse" on December 23rd, 1990.

That this "adoption" of the soldiers did not end over the years is also to the credit of those women – from the soldiers lovingly named the "little basket women" –, who supplied the "defenders of the nation" with many additional regional goodies over the years. A thank you for all those natives who remain publicly unknown and who simply once invited the soldiers to lunch or coffee and cake, and who were patient listeners and replacement parents for many a soldiers with the problems of late puberty.

The "little basket woman".

Representative of all the helpers and supporters of the soldiers is a special thank you directed at Brigadier General ret. Otto Herzog and his family, who showed especial proof of openheartedness and hospitality. In the times of the SuppD/BAS, far over 1,000 (!) soldiers of all ranks, functions and from all Austrian provinces – as it stands, after all, x amount of times in their chronicle? – *"were heartily taken up, abundantly feasted and lovingly cooked for by the women of the house"* at the "Herzogs"! Over 1,000 soldiers, who in thousands and thousands of hours joked, laughed, sang, eat and drank with the "Herzogs." And over 1,000 soldiers for whom the "Herzogs" were an endearing relief from the dull everyday soldiery far from their homelands. This is documented in three fat ring binders and a folder full of thankful and commemorative certificates, designed with much love and creativity. After a resolution of the provincial government of Burgenland, the medal of the province of Burgenland was conferred on Brigadier General Herzog by provincial governor Niessl for his dedication to the support troops.

This thanks also applies to the mayors and "customs workers", the fire department commanders and gendarmes, hunters and landowners as well as all the others who realized and aligned their behavior to the fact that the soldiers did not stand on the border for personal reasons, but had a mission to fulfill: A mission not least for the well-being of the population.

War in Yugoslavia

Preliminary Events

Yugoslavia is created after the collapse of the Central Powers in November 1918, by incorporation of parts of the former Austrian monarchy and the entire former kingdom of Montenegro into the kingdom of Serbia.[21] The borders are fixed in 1919 through the Treaties of St. Germain en Laye (against Austria and Italy), Trianon (against Hungary) and Neuilly (against Bulgaria). They are definitive after the Carinthian Plebiscite, the Rapallo Treaty (1920) and the Treaty of Italy (1921). With the words, *"The long-desired liberation and consolidation in a unified nation state has been fulfilled,"* the Serbian Prince Regent Alexander Karađorđević proclaims the newly created "Kingdom of the Serbs, Croats and Slovenes (SKS)"[22] on January 6th, 1919. However, shortly afterwards the new creation resembles a powder keg. The strong position of the Serbs runs into resistance from the non-Serbian ethnic groups. In the Second World War the differences, previously only suppressed with effort, deepen. While Croatia becomes an "independent", Serbian-antagonistic nation by the grace of Hitler under the Fascist Ante Pavelic, the Communist partisans under Josip Broz "Tito" resist the German invasion in 1941.[23] In 1945, Tito declares a "Democratic Federal Yugoslavia". Until his death, he succeeds in holding his "commonwealth", which consists of six republics, five nationalities, four languages, three religions, two alphabets and one party, together.

After the death of Prime Minister Marshal Tito, the peoples of Yugoslavia drift apart. The ethnic instabilities lead to dangerous situations. The Yugoslav People's Army (YPA), as a result of the ethnic mixture of its soldiers, despite Serbian dominance in the leadership cadres, can also only conditionally discharge its role as the "clamp of the nation". The YPA prepares itself for war. So behind the scenes a staff drill under the codename **"Bedem 91"** (Firewall 91) was run. The plan, characterized as "secret and extremely confidential" is also sent to the troops. In it, the soldiers are informed that Slovenia and Croatia, after a declaration of independence, will invite the neighboring countries and NATO to intervene militarily. Austria will annul its treaty and join NATO.

The proceeding democratization of individual constituent republics goes hand in hand with the independence efforts, which lead to ceremonial declarations of independence on June 25th, 1991, in Slovenia and Croatia. In the night from the 26th to the 27th of June, parts of the YPA stationed in Slovenia use this as an occasion to attempt to occupy or take into their own hands the capital, Ljubljana, the airport and the border crossings to Austria and Italy. A first report of large troop movements and tank deployments comes from former member of parliament Karel Smolle, who is in a hotel in Ljubljana at the time.[24]

This report, which goes to the Foreign Office as well as to the on-duty officer in the Defence Ministry, is confirmed by Slovenian politicians shortly thereafter. Further reports speak of tank columns, which move from Croatia in the direction of Slovenia, particularly Ljubljana, and the borders to Austria and Italy. During the course of June 27th the situation escalates, it comes to the first combative actions between members of the Slovenian Territory Defence and Troops of the YPA, also in close proximity to the Austrian and Italy border crossings. The anxiety of the population in the area of the border of Yugoslavia climbs considerably. Furthermore, in the evening hours the first airspace violations through YPA helicopters take place, who are documented during **radar plotting**.[25] At midday a further, this time much more serious airspace violation occurs: A Yugoslavian fighter jet invades Austrian airspace as far as Graz. At the same time, heavy battles occur directly on the border.

Despite the failure to accomplish the goals of the YPA, the noticeable provisioning shortages, and the sinking will to fight of the soldiers ("battle against our own people"), a further escalation cannot be ruled out. Yugoslavia begins an CSCE suit because of Austria's supposed provocations and interference in Yugoslavian domestic matters. On June 29th, the Austrian ambassador in Yugoslavia is cited in the Foreign Office in Belgrade, where he must accept the protest of the Yugoslavian government against the "troop concentrations" on the Austrian border.

On July 2nd, the verbal attacks against Austria are continued. For instance, the representative commander of the 5th Army Division, Lieutenant General Andrija Raseta, claims in a special broadcast on Yugoslavian television that the Austrian armed forces are supporting the Slovenian Territorial Army. At the same time, the YPA divisions reluctantly withdraw to their barracks. Some surrender to the Slovenian troops. On the other hand, in Bosnia, Herzegovina and Serbia, a mobilization of the so-called "dependable troops" occurs, in an initial amount of 200,000 men; the YPA forces in Slovenia are commanded to persevere. On July 3rd, after the elimination of the politically legitimate authorities, leadership is taken over by the army in some cases. "Since the early morning hours, division-size powers from the area of Belgrade have been shifted towards Slovenia, with sections towards Vojvodina. The

---

21 See "South Slavia (Yugoslavia)" in Concise Political Dictionary, Vol. 2, Leipzig 1923.
22 Stefan Sauer: "Powder Keg from the Beginning: Too Many People for Just One State", Kölner Anzeiger of March 27/28 1999.
23 Heinz Brill: "The Balkan Conflict and the Interests of the Powers", ÖMZ 5/2000, Vienna 2000.
24 See Christian Ségur-Cabanac: "Military Security Deployment 1991", Truppendienst 2/1992.
25 Graphical representation of air activity.

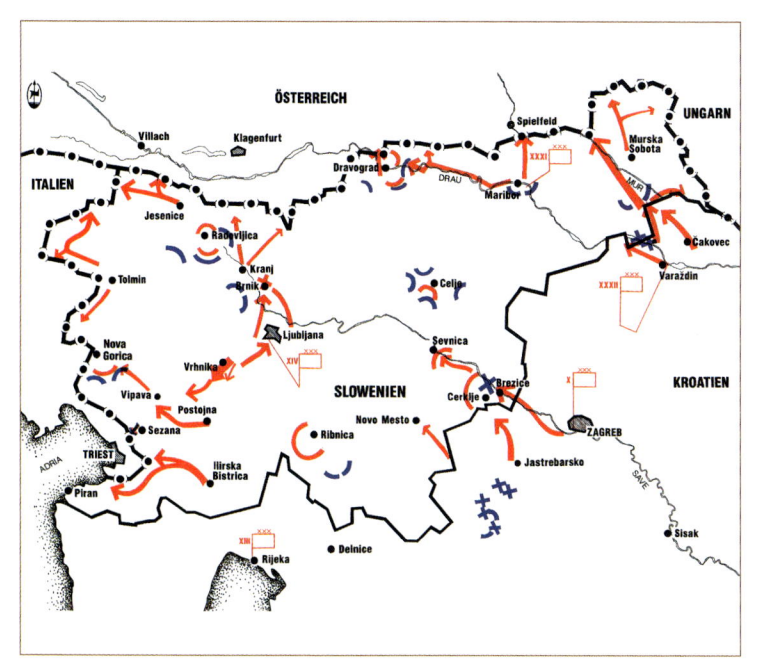

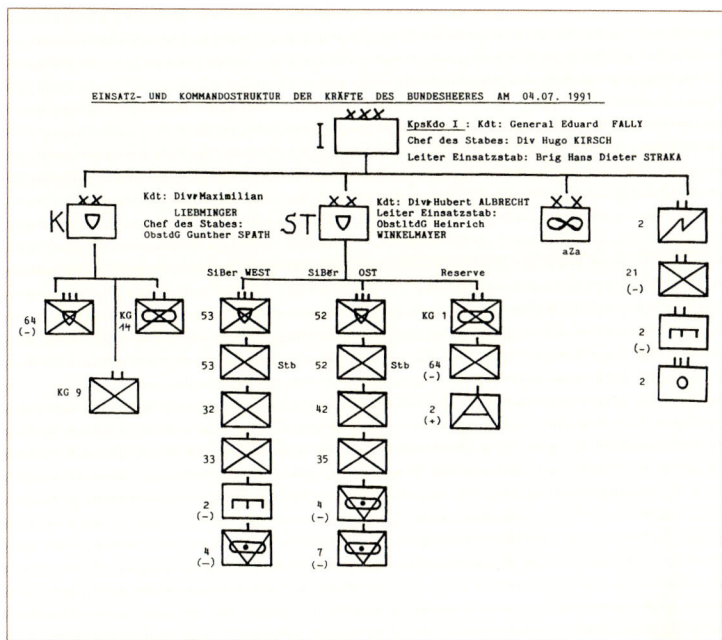

The main lines of attack of the YPA during the battles in Slovenia from June 26th – July 3rd, 1991 (left graphic).

troop movements make attempts at decisive battles on July 4th at least seem possible."[26]

By July 6th, the altercations shift from the military into the political arena. The Yugoslavian army almost completely withdraws into its barracks. Slovenia does not accept an ultimatum from Belgrade, wherein the surveillance of the border crossings should have been handed over to the national army. In Croatia there are sporadic battles. On July 9th it comes to a noticeable relaxation of tensions.

International Reaction

In the nations of the European Union and the USA, the altercation is initially trivialized as a regional conflict without effects on the surrounding nations. However, the so-called "EU Troika", the foreign ministers of Luxembourg, the Netherlands, and Italy arrive in Belgrade the night before July 1st for a meeting with the Yugoslavian foreign minister Loncar. An CSCE ambassadors meeting is called for the same evening in the Viennese Hofburg. Out of consideration for the Hungarian minority in Yugoslavia, Hungary collects no troops on its borders; Italy alerts its troops on the borders and increases patrol activity.

Austrian Reaction
Political Measures

This development of the situation does not come as a surprise. For years the situation in Yugoslavia has been intensely observed and evaluated by both the Foreign Ministry as well as the Defence Ministry. On May 7th, Defence Minister Dr. Fasslabend declares after a meeting of the Council of Ministers that they are following the conflicts in Yugoslavia with concern, however no direct provocation for *"outwardly visible activities"* of the military exists. Moreover, the minister references the ruling of the federal government, which took place at the end of May, which plans for an increase of the support troops by up to 4,000 men. Appropriate preparations for a well-adapted, flexible reaction, however, are out of the question. The graduated scheme initially envisions a supportive deployment which could later cross over into a defensive deployment. On June 26th, 1991, the Defence Council registers the dissolution of the Army Command and the Command of the Mechanized Infantry Division during the simultaneous creation of a third Corps Command in Baden as a first step to a reorganization. On the edges of the meeting, the situation in Yugoslavia is also discussed.

The development of the situation on the night before June 28th causes the government to give up the restraint it had shown out of political caution in favor of the security needs of the affected border population.

---

26   Excerpt from the situation report for the junior commands of the Defence Ministry on July 3rd.

Bad Radkersberg (Gornja Radgona), Austrian and Yugoslavian/Slovenian, separated by the Drava, a peaceful border crossing, open for the population on both sides – suddenly the border between "war and peace".

In order to emphasize its own defensive intentions, foreign military attachés accredited in Austria are briefed on the defence precautions.

Unimaginable a short time ago: The tank blockades, memories of the concept of territorial defence, are activated, armored antitank vehicles of the army drive into position directly on the border and secure the blockades of the border crossings.

Furious callers threaten to arm themselves if the military is not finally deployed.[27] At the same time, an inquiry takes place by the Security Directorate into whether, during armed conflicts between the Territorial Defence and the YPA, the first opportunities for defection to Austria can be granted and if so, under which conditions. It can also be noted at this point that these scenarios were also played through beforehand.

The airspace violations and the battles in the direct area of the borders lead the federal government to enact guidelines for the basic **"Authorization of the Defence Minister for National Defence with respect to the Deployment of the Armed Forces"** according to Art. 79 para. 1 FCL for the protection of the Austrian-Yugoslavian border on June 28th. As a result of the subsequent deployment directive of the Defence Minister, appropriate measures are issued on June 30th through the responsible administrator for the affected district administrations; so entrance and residence bans are issued for the protection of the threatened physical safety of people and property as well as for the guarantee of military security.[28] With this, the long-standing legal uncertainty over the military authority while deployed is cleared away.

On the provocation of the airspace violations, the Defence Minister makes it clear that *"any further airspace violation will be prosecuted with all the methods at our disposal"*. The time may have come where *"restraint no longer seems at our disposal"*. The Yugoslavian ambassador is cited in the Foreign Office.

In a crisis meeting of the Council of Ministers on June 29th, the Defence Minister discloses that he *"sees no reason for the mobilization of more sections of the armed forces for the time being. A flexible reaction to developing changes is possible at any time with the currently available forces in the area of operations."*

The federal government, for its part, puts an CSCE suit for the containment of the conflict between nationalities into motion. Because of the Yugoslavian complaint against Austria in the CSCE, a detailed briefing of the military attaché corps accredited in Austria takes place directly on the national border on July 1st. Through this, the appropriateness of the military measures is to be demonstrated.[29]

In the meeting of the Council of Ministers on July 2nd, 1991, they decide to formally comply with the Defence Council's suggestion of June 26th: the Army Command and the Mechanized Infantry Division are dissolved and the III. Corps created.

Military Measures

In the Army Command (AC), the deployment staff is formed and preparations made for constant staff operation. Around mid-day on June 27th, the Defence Minister orders preparatory measures in the garrisons in the domain of the Military Commands of Styria and Carinthia: *"To secure possible infrastructure needs or territorial duties and for security forces, constant duty readiness in the border garrisons of Command Areas 5 and 7 is necessary and to be secured by the barracks commands until further instruction. This especially affects the garrisons of Villach and Klagenfurt (...) as well as Bleiburg, Wolfsberg, Strass, Radkersburg, Leibnitz, Fehring and Feldbach."* With this, deployment readiness is to be secured around the clock during the next week. At the same time the junior commands issue the order to raise deployment readiness from parts of the military to preparation for deployment according to Sec. 2 para. 1 sub-para. a and b DA. This order leaves the possibility of a military deployment (sub-para. a) as well as that of a supportive deployment on the example of Burgenland (sub-para. b) open. In all considerations it must also be criticized that on June 28th the soldiers from the January 1991 draft are to be released and the draft of a thousand soldiers is to be prepared for July 1st.

The formation of strengthened forces in the amount of two support battalions with a short march readiness follows. A SuppBn of the CoyCd I with 800 men is formed and held in readiness in southern Styrian garrisons. A SuppBn, also in a strength of around 800 men, is formed from soldiers of the 3rd MechInfBrig. A mixed battalion-strength battle group is formed from the exercise sections of the troops in the area of Carinthia from June 17th – 28th for the yearly graduation exercise of the Theresian Military Academy, and held ready north of Klagenfurt in an assembly area. Parts of the Academic Battalion are formed to an infantry engagement force. Intensive radio surveillance and airspace observation create the conditions for a constantly up-to-date picture of the situation. Supplying running counter to all routines and the smooth operation of all leadership connections is noteworthy.

In the night before June 28th, railroad transport space is secured as a precaution for one of the two defence battalions in northern Lower Austria and the loading of the vehicles ordered by June 28th, 9:00 AM.

As a result of the authorization of the federal government, the Defence Minister issues a deployment directive on June 28th, 1991, which is then converted to a **deployment order**. For the first time in the history of the armed forces a deployment order is issued on the basis of a **"directive of the Defence Minister for a deployment of the armed forces for military national defence"** and an appropriate **"regulation with regard to the tolerance and use laws and encroachment on the rights of third parties"** is made. Under this title, Zeltweg Airfield's runway is also lengthened after lengthy delays, and a platform, including access road, is constructed for a mobile radar station.

---

27   See Military Defence Deployment 1991.
28   According to Art. II Sec. 4 para. 2 VÜG of December 7th, 1929, FLG No. 393/1929, in connection with Sec. 15 of the Authority Transition Act, FLG No. 94/1945.
29   At this time just under 6,500 men are in the defence deployment.

> "According to Art. 80 para. 2 FCL the Defence Minister is authorized, in view of the critical situation in the Socialist Federal Republic of Yugoslavia, to take immediate measures for a military deployment according to Art. 79 para. 1 FCL. The area of operations comprises the area of every district administration which shares a part of the Austrian-Yugoslavian national border...
> The goal of this deployment is to secure the Austrian-Yugoslavian national border and to prevent the crossing of troops or parts of troops into Austrian national territory, as well as to strengthen the feeling of security of the population in the affected area. For this purpose, available deployment-ready forces are to be shifted to the area of operations in necessary numbers, whose main focus is to secure the border crossings as well as to conduct reconnaissance in the areas between these border crossings. Moreover, the necessary measures for increased airspace surveillance as well as the prevention of airspace violations are to be taken.
> The deployed troops are authorized to take measures militarily necessary for the deployment in the area of operations; these measures are to take place under the highest possible preservation of the rights and defence-worthy interests of the general public and the individual. In case of a fundamental alteration of the situation, the federal government is to be involved once again."

Authorization of the Defence Minister by the federal government.

As a reaction to the increasing airspace violations, antiaircraft defence forces are alerted on June 28th, formed into battle groups, and set on the march for the protection of the deployment airfields in Graz, Klagenfurt and Zeltweg. The border surveillance with helicopters and fixed-wing aircraft, among them Saab 35OE "Drakens" and Saab 105OEs, is intensified. Further, forces are sent to the national border. For psychological reasons, demonstration rounds are carried out with tanks as well. On the evening of the 28th around 3,500 soldiers are in the area of operations. In addition to the already named forces, there are also part of the 21st InfBn (Kufstein and St. Johann), as well as part of the 4th Mechanized Infantry Brigade and the 4th Light Tank Battalion (LTkBn) from Graz.

In the night before June 29th, all border crossings are secure and intensive battle reconnaissance carried out. As a reaction to the increasing escalation a strengthened mechanized battle group is formed in Upper Austria and sent to Klagenfurt by rail. The strength of the forces now already amounts to almost 5,000 soldiers. In the area of the province of Carinthia, in addition to the resident forces, there are two battle groups from parts of the 3rd and 4th MechInfBrig as well as parts of the 7th LTkBn. They move into a security line along the border at Wurzenpass, Rosenbach, Loiblpass, Seebergsattel, Bleiburg, Lavamünd, with emphasis on the border crossings with surveillance of the territory in between. The MilComC has access to further forces, formed from members of the TherMilAc, as engagement troops and a battery of the 1st Antiaircraft Battalion. In the area of MilComSt, in addition to the resident forces, there is a battle group from parts of the 4th LTkBn, the 2nd Engineer Battalion, and two companies from LA. These are complemented by forces from the 2nd AArtBn. The security line in this area reaches from Soboth, Radlpass, Langegg, Spielfeld, Mureck, Radkersberg, Sicheldorf, Goritz, St. Anna until Bonisdorf (Burgenland). In addition the I. Corps organizes a battle group, consisting of parts of the 21st Infantry Battalion, two further companies from the Tyrol and Upper Austria, parts of the 2nd AArtBn and 2nd SignBn. Further, the Corps has access to an AA battle group in Zeltweg. In the night before the 30th, three foreign military persons are taken up by Austrian soldiers and interned. On June 30th a freeze on holidays is ordered for all members of the military. In response to a petition from the I. Corps, the divisions of the peace organization (essentially the 5th and 7th Infantry Brigades) responsible for mobilization of the deployment organization are preemptively alerted. At the same time the formation of a further mechanized battle group is ordered. The intensified airspace surveillance leads to a sudden reduction in airspace violations.

The ruling of the Council of Ministers with reference to the dissolution of the Army Command and the Command of the MechInfDiv is in this situation – almost the high point of the Yugoslavian crisis – somewhat surprising and must, since it is given a deadline of 12:00 AM, be converted in the shortest possible amount of time, in order to allow no moment of weakness in the leadership to appear. During this, the leadership of "Security Deployment South" and "Border Area Surveillance East", is handed over to the deployment staff as a part of the highest leadership in the Defence Ministry, with the maintenance of their personnel assignments. Only the Army Commander, Chief of Staff and the Head of the Operational Directorate are relieved of their previous responsibilities.

On July 3rd, 12:00 AM, leadership through the Defence Minister with the support of the Administration/Deployment Staff with direct access to the troops takes effect. As a result of the unclear situation the Defence Minister causes the movement of the already alerted mechanized battle group of the 9th MechInfBrig (with battle tanks, armored antitank vehicles, and armored howitzers) into the area of operations. In this way, the total strength is raised to around 6,000 men.

With regard to the battle-worthiness of the deployed forces, despite the disproportionately high cadre participation, the fact must still be considered that those serving their mandatory military service were only in their fourth month of training. A growing psychological pressure is detected in these soldiers, of course active battles must still be counted upon at this time. However, as before there is no willingness from the political side to prepare divisions for mobilization, since heavy consequences for the affected regional economy are calculated.

As a result of the relaxation of tensions, the withdrawal of forces begins on July 9th. The mechanized sections of the 9th MechInfBrig make the start, when they are shipped into the metropolitan area of Graz that afternoon. The reduction is continued until July 10th, the

While tanks go into position on all border crossings and provide fire protection, positions are quickly enlarged by the infantry and tank blockades constructed. Who would have thought after the collapse of WaPa that these could be deployed again?

At this time it is especially important to "fly the flag" (t.l., m.) as proof of the will to defence against a possible aggressor and to reassure the domestic population. Even if life in the towns close to the border seemingly goes on as normal (t.r.), for the soldiers it is an emergency.

Especial meaning is accorded the protection of sovereignty in the air with the BAS airplanes of the type Saab J35OE "Draken". Although the stationing of the "Draken" was initially resisted with all available methods, in the final analysis one is still glad to have them here in particular. That the provincial governor suddenly called for "his" Drakens in this situation is one of history's little jokes after the fact.

21st Infantry Battalion and parts of the AA defence of the airports are returned to the barracks. At the same time, however, the addition of forces in the case of an escalation is prepared.

The last phase of the deployment is characterized through the consolidation of the deployed forces, the heightening of training condition and with that deployment readiness. The holiday freeze is raised on July 10th. The members of the military academy assigned to commanding functions are broken up and return to the TherMilAc. On July 12th the mechanized and infantry forces held ready with short march readiness on the military level are released from deployment status and introduced into peacetime training. The last units are withdrawn step by step until July 31st.

Nevertheless, in order to be able to react at any time, a tank destroyer company for the area of Styria and an infantry company for Carinthia are held in readiness again from August 1st; the patrol activities on the border and in the air are continued. This deployment was also mastered with bravery under difficult conditions. Above all the military earns the full trust of the affected population. This even finds an echo in the foreign press.[30] In Austrian newspapers one finds headlines like "A Miracle Called the Armed Forces" (Hans Werner Scheidl in "Die Presse", July 3rd), "From Dearest Enemy to Good Friend" (Franz Ferdinand Wolf in "Kurier", July 6th) or "Necessary Army" (Humbert Fink in "Kronen Zeitung", July 2nd). Ernst Sittinger phrases it this way: *"The soldiers – a large part are inexperienced draftees from the April 1st draft date – are hit with a wave of unashamed sympathy from the population... As "Draken" interceptors fly over the main square, there is spontaneous applause."*[31] Provincial Governor Dr. Krainer's cry (one of the strongest opponents of the "Draken" procurement) after a MIG 21 is spotted over Graz: *"Where are my Drakens?"* is already legendary. Dr. Krainer has tears in his eyes as the "Drakens" finally circle Graz. A late sign of insight.

It must not be neglected to point out that this is not the only deployment at this time: Around 2,000 soldiers are in supportive deployment on the Hungarian border, some 1,000 men are performing duties within the framework of UNO, 200 members of the armed forces are in Iran and operate a field hospital there. In addition, there is a catastrophe deployment in Austria. All four deployment varieties take place at the same time and succeed without mobilization. The fact that, instead of the trained and deployment-ready militia, untrained draftees are deployed, is to be sharply criticized in hindsight.

Basis of deployment:	Authorization of the federal government on June 28th, 1991.
Type of deployment:	Security deployment according to Sec. 2 para. 1 sub-para. a DA.
Mission:	Protection of the borders of the Austrian Republic.
Duration of deployment:	June 28th, 1991 – July 31st, 1991.
Contingent strength:	Max. 7,700 with 1,400 wheeled vehicles, 150 track vehicles as well as 60 aircraft.
Commander:	General Eduard Fally, Commander of the I Corps.
Contributions:	Flight contribution: 150,000 km / 1,000 flight hours, up to 60 deployments / day. Rail transport: 41 special trains with 725 cars and 24,000 total tons transported. Munitions: 1,250 t. Resources: 2,700 cubic meters. Provisions: 700 t. Mail: 300 administrative circulars, 35,000 field postcards.

On June 29th, 2001, a ceremony takes place in Spielfeld on the occasion of the 10th anniversary. During the celebrations Federal Minister Herbert Scheibner awards the **deployment medal**, newly established with the decree of June 13th, 2001, to all soldiers who took part in the deployment at that time.

Award of the deployment medal by Federal Minister Herbert Scheibner.

---

30 "One looks with some pride on the otherwise so often criticized armed forces that protects the border with Slovenia. The presence of the army has a calming effect on the population, which is confronted with the conflict within visibility range", in: "Neue Zürcher Zeitung" of July 3rd, 1991.
31 "Der Standard", July 4th, 1991.

Railroad Accident

Preliminary Events

On February 13th, 1993, at 8:03 AM, 350 m west of the train station in Melk, a serious train accident takes place. As a result of the carelessness of the engine driver of a freight train, it collides at around 60 km/h with an express train coming from Pöchlarn traveling at 80 km/h. The accident causes three deaths (including that of the engine driver of the express train) and 21 injured, some very seriously. The two locomotives are wedged in each other, some cars stand on end or are crushed. Since the freight train was loaded with grain, flour and sugar, the accident site is shrouded in a thick cloud.

Political Measures

Already, 15 minutes after the accident, the district administrator of Melk, Privy Councilor Dr. Lechner takes over the deployment administration.

Military Measures

This deployment is an example of a classic independent intervention of military troops. 1/LT Teply and WO I Poscher are in the nearby engineer's barracks in Melk at the time of the accident, a Saturday. There they hear the sound of the crash, which initially seems like an explosion. Both go immediately to the accident site. At 8:10 AM, the available sections of the Army Engineer Battalion (AEngBn) in the barracks are alerted. By 8:25 AM an engineer platoon from the 1st AEngBn and the members of a course of instruction being carried out with the 3rd AEngBn arrive and immediately begin to support the civilian emergency teams. Captain Pfanzagel, who lives in the neighborhood of the train station, goes immediately to the accident site after the sounding of the sirens and takes command of the supportive deployment of the armed forces at 8:40 AM. The soldiers help with the rescue of the injured as well as with the collection of pieces of luggage. Since numerous onlookers impede the clearance work, or even attempt to steal things laying about, the Gendarmery is also supported with traffic regulation and sealing off the accident site.

At 8:50 AM the garrison officer at the Military Command is informed of the independent deployment. The official order does not come through until February 15th.

To support the rescue efforts of the Austrian Federal Railways, at the petition of the district administration of Melk, TkBn 10 in St. Pölten is also alerted. By 1:00 PM two M88 recovery tanks, which were brought from St. Pölten to Melk on flat-bed trucks, are ready at the accident site. However, they can first be used at 4:00 PM, after the release of the accident site by the criminal bureau.

At 1:10 PM, after disconnecting the power lines, the recovery of the dead begins. At 5:30 PM a wheel loader also arrives, which is in uninterrupted use from 2:45 AM the following day until the end of the support. In order to continue the rescue work during the night as well, lighting through an AEngBn power unit is installed by the soldiers. While the cadre is continuously deployed for sometimes up to 40 hours, duty shifts must be ordered for the recruits. The supportive deployment can finally be ended on February 15th at 12:30 AM, only the lighting is still maintained by four men until 8:30 AM.

Basis for deployment:	Independent intervention according to Sec. 2 para. 4 DA.
Type of deployment:	Supportive deployment according to Sec. 2 para. 1 sub-para. c.
Mission:	Support of the Red Cross and the fire department in the rescue of the injured; support of the Executive in traffic regulation and the sealing off of the accident site; support of the Austrian Federal Railways (ÖBB) in the recovery of the locomotives and cars.
Duration of deployment:	February 13th – 15th, 1993.
Contingent strength:	117.
Organization:	Parts of the Army Engineer Battalion, the 10th Tank Battalion and the 3rd Tank Headquarters Battalion.
Commanders:	Until 8:40 AM First Lieutenant Rupert Teply, afterwards Captain Reinhard Pfanzagel.
Contribution:	4,025 man hours.

The pictures suggest the extent of the horrible train catastrophe: a M88A1 recovery tank and a wheel loader are used. In the top right pictures the transport of the M88A1 recovery tank with a 55t heavy load transport system can be seen.

65

Deployment to Ensure the Transit of IFOR and SFOR Troops

Preliminary Events

Differences between the Yugoslavian central government and the constituent republics as well as between the individual constituent republics lead to the final collapse of the Yugoslavian government in 1991. Subsequently armed battles take place in Slovenia, Croatia, and Bosnia-Herzegovina, which are often accompanied with ethnically motivated violence.

International Reaction

On November 20th, 1995, the wartime enemies of the Bosnian War sign the "General Framework Agreement for Peace in Bosnia and Herzegovina" under the patronage of the USA in Dayton/Ohio. This forms the basis for the multinational peace-keeping deployment on the territory of the former Yugoslavia. On December 15th, one day after the ceremonial signing in Paris, the UN Security Council adopts Resolution 1031/1995, with which the deployment of international peace-keeping troops under Chapter VII of the Articles of the United Nations is decided upon.[32] NATO, in cooperation with other nations, is entrusted with the implementation. The resolution also includes a call on the nations in the regions to support the necessary transit for troop deployment.

The operation, running under the name **"Joint Endeavor"**, is initially comprised of about 60,000 soldiers, among them 20,000 Americans, 13,000 British and 10,000 French, who are largely already in the area of operations under the framework of UNPROFOR.[33] Germany dispatches 4,000 soldiers. The operation is implemented in five phases:

- Dispatch of advance commands,
- Transfer of the main contingents to Bosnia-Herzegovina,
- Separation of the parties in the conflict and establishment of a buffer zone between them,
- Surveillance of the territory that is vacated by the parties in the conflict,
- Surrender of responsibility to the civilian institutions and withdrawal.

Within the framework of the dispatch, started on December 4th, of the advance commands for the NATO peace-keeping troops of IFOR, 1,400 soldiers are initially shifted to Bosnia-Herzegovina and 1,200 to Croatia. They primarily have to secure logistical missions and the establishment of the headquarters. The stationing of the US ground troops turns out to be far more complex. In total, 32,000 US soldiers are dispatched to Bosnia-Herzegovina, Croatia and Hungary. In addition, there are 11,000 men from Marine aircraft squadrons who are already in the area, as well the crew of the US aircraft carrier "USS America" with its escort ships, which have been circling in the Adria since the 1st half of December. In Kaposvar in southern Hungary US soldiers, using the former air force staging post of the Warsaw Pact in Taszar, establish a logistical base for around 20,000 soldiers.[34]

In the international media, there is targeted disinformation to a previously unknown extent about the readiness of Austria to collaborate with the international community for the peace process in Yugoslavia out of solidarity. So Dan Rather – a star journalist for CBS – reports on December 8th during the main news hour that Austria is hindering troop transports through Austria, since there is not yet a resolution approved by the UNO.[35]

Austrian Reaction
Political Measures

Consultations already begin in November 1995 under the coordination of the Federal Chancellor's Office. During these it becomes apparent, among other things, that the existence of a UN Security Council resolution must be adopted as the prerequisite for the conclusion of an appropriate agreement with NATO. However, this can first be formally decided upon after the signing of the peace treaty. For all activities previous to December 15th, therefore, the mandate of the UN Security Council for UNPROFOR is drawn upon as the legal basis.

As a consequence of previous experience, the composition and adoption of a **"Status of Forces Agreement – SOFA"** and a federal constitutional law on "cooperation and solidarity in the dispatch

---

32 See also p. 230 ff.
33 See also p. 225.
34 Christian Ségur-Cabanac: "Operation Joint Endeavor" – The Organization of the Military Transports of Troops and Equipment for Deployment in Bosnia, speech manuscript, May 1996.
35 Ibid.

The IFOR/SFOR transports through Austria take place on the streets and the rails. On the highway the columns are piloted by the Gendarmery and military patrols (t.l.). In the top right picture a formation equipped with Bradley Fighting Vehicles loaded onto railway cars can be seen in front of the Church of St. Francis of Assisi in Mexikoplatz in Vienna.
On the march to Hungary the soldiers are provisioned by the armed forces and their vehicles are refueled as needed. Both pictures in the middle show the entry and refueling in Kaisersteinbruch. During this comdradely encounters between US soldiers and the members of the Austrian support troops also happen (b.l.).
But much is also happening in the air. A US military "Black Hawk" helicopter is refueled by an Austrian airfield tank troop in Langenlebarn (b.r.). The soldiers naturally do not pass up the opportunity to look at this type of helicopter, which the armed forces will soon be receiving.

of units internationally" (as a replacement for the federal constitutional law on "the dispatch of units of the armed forces for assistance internationally" from the year 1965). On December 12th, the Council of Ministers authorizes an agreement with NATO on the privileged and immune status of the units and persons traveling through Austria in the framework of the multinational peacekeeping mission (IFOR) in Bosnia. Further, the Council of Ministers authorizes in the same meeting a transportation agreement with NATO. In this, the legal requirements for unhindered travel of units and persons of IFOR through Austria within the framework of the existing Austrian legal situation is established. The agreement grants NATO unhindered travel by land, water and air for personnel, freight, equipment and replenishment of supplies. At the same time, all transports are exempted from certain requirements (for instance in the areas of trucking, traffic, toll, dues, customs, visas and residence). Permission to carry weapons is provided for in the agreement only within the limited constraints of the generally accepted rules of international law; weapons and munitions are to be stored separately in any case. The wearing of uniforms and the display of national emblems is also granted to NATO. The egregious allegations in the American media are immediately countered by the Federal Chancellor and the Foreign Minister. Federal Chancellor Dr. Franz Vranitzky explains verbatim in the "Mittagsjournal": *"When anyone claims that there are difficulties here, he is subject to a one hundred percent error. All the government agencies that have anything to do with the troop transports are working orderly together."* And Foreign Minister Dr. Schüssel indicates that there have been flyovers from NATO transports since December 4th, for which orderly clearances were obtained in Vienna. It is regrettable, but also characteristic, that the false reports cause agitation in the domestic media and among various opposition politicians. While the journalists from the "Kurier"[36] or the "Presse"[37] deal more with Austria's role as a "nervous recruit in questions of security politics", the exponents of the Communist Party of Austria[38] or the Green-Alternatives see this already as a "stealthy entry into NATO and betrayal of neutrality". No word about the solidarity otherwise so highly praised and constantly demanded from just this sector.

Military Measures

By the start of November, all the preparatory measures for **ensuring the transit of the IFOR troops** are already begun. In the Operational Center / Land a separate communications office is established, in which an American officer performs service. At the same time an Austrian communications officer each is assigned to the logistics command of the US military forces in Europe in Kaiserslautern, as well as to the Hungarian Honved in Budapest and to the US logistics base in Kaposvar. Between December 15th and 20th, 1995, therefore right at the beginning of the transit, delays in the area of the Hungarian-Croatian border lead to a backup of the railroad transport trains in Austrian territory. So up to six trains must be parked on military training areas in Bruck/Leitha, Langenlebarn, St. Pölten/Spratzern, Hörsching and Wels, and appropriate provisions made for the US soldiers. But traffic congestion also develops with the street transports. As a result of the extreme winter weather conditions there is comprehensive care of the soldiers affected here as well. The "media jangling" is deplored at the highest political and military levels and the outstanding work of the Austrian stations highlighted. The NATO Commander-in-Chief, General Joulwan, directs a personal letter to the GTI on January 1st, 1996. In it, the highest ranking American officer in Europe gives the Austrian armed forces his thanks and his acknowledgement for their support in connection with the IFOR deployment (this letter hangs framed as visible motivation for the on-duty officers in the situation room of the Operational Center / Land).[39]

Since December 11th, 1995, military transports pass almost daily on the streets and sometimes on the rails of Austria. They are not only connected to American soldiers, but also soldiers from Belgium, Denmark, Germany, Finland, Great Britain, the Netherlands and the Czech Republic. The military special trains, which are always accompanied by Austrian officers, operate on the Westbahn, the Tauernbahn, and over the Semmering. The street transports take place for the most part on the Westautobahn and are escorted by the Highway Gendarmery. The Benedek Barracks in Bruck/Neudorf and the Hessen Barracks in Wels are available for overnight stays, refueling and repairs.

Basis for deployment:	CM from December 15th, 1995, MC from December 15th, 1995.
Mission:	Securing of transit for IFOR/SFOR troops through Austria.
Duration of deployment:	December 11th, 1995 – December 1st, 2004[40].
Commander:	December 11th, 1995 – November 30th, 2002: Brigadier General Mag. Christian Ségur-Cabanac, December 1st, 2002 – November 1st, 2004:[41] Mr. Karl Michael Hruza.

---

36 Christoph Kotanko: "Why the Americans Don't Quite Trust Us."
37 "Nervous Recruit in the Way."
38 Walter Bayer: "With the NATO troops it is a question of... a cold annexation of Austria into NATO"; KPÖ press release of December 11th.
39 Christian Ségur-Cabanac: "Operation Joint Endeavor".
40 On December 2nd, 2004, the NATO-led SFOR will be replaced by the EU-led EUFOR Althea.
41 Subsequently the Host Nation Support (support for foreign troops who pass through Austria on the march to the actual area of operations, including accommodation, provisions, sanitation, etc.) will be put into place, so that no more stays by these troops occur.

BUNDESMINISTERIUM
für LANDESVERTEIDIGUNG
Operationsabteilung

WIEN, 15 01 01

IFOR/SFOR TRANSPORTE
Leistungen des ÖBH von 11 12 95 bis 31 12 00
in Zusammenarbeit mit den ÖBB und der Exekutive

1. BAHNTRANSPORTE:

Anzahl der Züge:	US	NL	GE	DK	B	NO	FIN	GB	SLO	CH	IT	S	A
1309	1309												
209		122	47	18	4	5	5	4	4	1	38	3	
7													20
1525													

VeO:	US	NL	GE	DK	B	NO	FIN	GB	SLO	CH	IT	S	A
684	580	50	24	17	3	2	4	2	2	0	1	0	0

2. STRASSENTRANSPORTE:

		US	BE	DK	GE	FI	UK	NL	NO	SW	AUSLO	CZ	CA
Anzahl der Transporte:	2735	2735											
	3144		770	152	91	17	11	1734	132	9	175	51	2
	5879												
Kfz:	14.632	14632											
	12.305		4129	332	217	51	154	4879	305	39	2109	84	6
	26.937												
Soldaten:	18.146	18146											
	21.823		8757	644	409	82	296	6230	336	64	4757	242	6
	39.969												

		US		DK				NL					
zusätzlich Zivilbusse:	5.880	5880											
	25			23					2				
	5.905												
Soldaten:	115.908	114.917		881					110				

3. BEGLEITUNGEN:

		US	BE	DK	GE	FI	UK	NL	NO	SW	AU	CZ	CA
Exekutive:	504	203	80	92	43	4	4	32	39	2		3	2
MilStrf:	24	10			2			4			8		
	528												

4. LUFTTRANSPORTE:

147.417	gemeldete Überflüge
52.903	tatsächliche Überflüge
1.661	Landungen

5. UNTERBRINGUNG von Soldaten in Kasernen:

		US					BELGIER		SCHWEDEN		FINNEN	
		BN/INN 1)	AM/GÜ 2	St PÖL	GRAZ	FIH	AM/BN 3	KIDF	KIDF	B N	STRASS	B N
	21.645	20.767	16	276	66	520						
	6.790						3042	5542	16	39	36	24
	28.435											

		BELUGA/HELBA							NIEDERLAENDER			GE
		BLU/HAL 4	KI/L 5)/W	GRAZ 6)	VIL/KL 7	KREMS	SZBG	WIEN 8)	SZBG	KI/VL 9)	B N	VL
	1.813	100	224	799	295	134	33	79	12	19	4	114
	1.813											

Gesamt:	30.248

6. VERPFLEGUNG:

		US					BELGIER		SCHWEDEN		FINNEN	
		BN/INN	AM/WE	St PÖL	GRAZ	FIH	AM/BN	KIDF	KIDF	B N	STRASS	B N
Frühstück:	37.903	27.960	16	276	43	758	2727	6008	16	39	36	24
Mittag:	7.552	5.061	236	343	30	1846	36					
Abend:	31.759	23.672	16	28	30	533	3030	4335	16	39	36	24

		BELUGA/HELBA							NIEDERLAENDER			GE	Gesamt:	
		BLU/HAL	KI/L/W	GRAZ	VIL/KLA	KREMS	SZBG	WIEN	SZBG	KI/VL	B N	VL		
Frühstück:	2.674	200	223	1221	588	149	33	76	12	23	8	141	Frühstück:	40.577
Mittag:	2.563	192	169	1261	602	149	33	76	6			75	Mittag:	10.115
Abend:	2.806	135	250	1337	634	149	33	76	6	19	2	165	Abend:	34.565

7. SANVERSORGUNG:

26	25 US-Soldaten, 4 Soldaten ambulant
12	7 US-Soldaten stationär, davon 4 an zivile SanEinr weitergegeben
	1 dt Soldat 3 Tage stationär 1 gr Soldat 3 Tage stationär

8. BETANKUNG:

		US	BE	GE	UK	NL	SW		HELBA	
Kfz:	17.469	15.989	1428	52						BENZIN
	2.883.288	2797221	15816	3719	792	159			65.581	DIESEL
	4.443	4441		2						ÖL
	48	48								FROSTSCHUTZ

		US	BE	GE	NL					
LFzg:	1.379.055	1315825	4610	56840	1780					AVTUR
	2.380	2380								Turböol

Catastrophic Flood

Preliminary Events

At the beginning of July 1997 a "hundred year flood" devastates the districts of Lilienfeld, Mödling, St. Pölten, Amstetten and Baden in Lower Austria, but also broad areas of Styria, like the region of Mariazell, and Steyr in Upper Austria. Up to 263 liters of water per square meter fall from the sky. Through strong rainfall the Danube climbs to 2.5 m in a few hours. On July 6th the first streets are flooded up to 1 m high. At 5:30 PM the first federal roads must be closed, some rail lines must be shut down. On July 7th the flooding alert is given. The basic cause of the flood lies in log jams (shifting of the stream or river bed by floating refuse), which quickly lead to overflows, broken dams, scouring (undermining of banks) and bridge collapses. The log jams partially arise from deficient maintenance of the riverbanks, a too low flow-rate profile of the bridges as a result of rubble accumulation, or untimely use of the weir system. One reason for the great damage done to residential buildings is also the too heavy settlement of flood-threatened areas. Hydrologists speak of the kind of flood that occurs once only every 100 years.

Political Measures

Until July 8th the communities initially attempt to clean up the existing damages in their areas independently, with the help of the fire departments and volunteers. The continuing rainfall and the ever more numerous inundations finally cause the mayors to call for support from the armed forces. After the full extent of the damages is assessed, the district administrations take over the deployment administration. Here the damage reports are now collected, evaluated and the support measures coordinated. The provincial warning center supports the assessment of the situation, coordinates the deployments in case of damaged areas over more than one district, and continuously delivers flood information, such as water levels and prognoses on the foreseeable further development of the flood.

Military Measures

Immediately after the alert, communications officers are placed with the deployment staffs, first surveys of the area of operations are carried out, and their results are reported to the military deployment administration. Parts of the alerted troops relieve the fire departments, which has already been constantly deployed for more than 24 hours. 600 men of the 9th MechInfBrig and troops of the III. Coy, with recovery tanks and helicopters among other things, are deployed in the most heavily affected areas, Mödling and Baden, alone. A further 100 soldiers of the Flight Division contribute help in Langenlebarn and Judenau. The 3rd Artillery Regiment from Wiener Neustadt and the 3rd Logistics Regiment from Zwölfaxing are alerted as well. Engineers construct dams at the entrances to the Viennese Forest in the Piesting and Triesting valley, secure bridges, and reestablish vital connections. In some towns "Meals on Wheels" can only be secured through special vehicles from the armed forces. Through the Military Command of Upper Austria, around 170 recruits serving their mandatory military service are deployed, especially in the district of Ried/Innkreis, largely to support the district fire department in building dams and pumping out cellars. Sandbags are filled by the remaining troops in the barracks and loaded on trucks, so that they can be brought to the threatened areas in case of further rising of the flood. Further forces monitor the threatened levees. Liaison helicopters are deployed for surveys and to rescue trapped people.

On July 9th, a release of tension occurs. The military helicopters remain in continual deployment, among other things trapped people must be flown out. On July 12th, there is a renewed catastrophe alert. The situation is especially dramatic in Trofaiach in the district of Leoben and in Bruck/Leitha. In addition to providing assistance, soldiers must also stand guard in the devastated shopping center in Lilienfeld to hinder looting. Nevertheless, on the weekend the soldiers can be allowed a rest, after which the clearance work continues. On July 16th the levees on the Leitha break at multiple places between Deutsch-Brodersdorf and Wampersdorf. Firemen and soldiers are again constantly deployed to close the holes with sandbags. On July 22nd the soldiers march out once again: seepage water erodes the Sulzbach dam near Dürnkrut. 120 soldiers of the 3rd ReconBn come to help the firemen.

New flooding occurs on July 23rd as a result of the opening of full-to-bursting flood retention ponds in the Czech Republic and Slovakia. The Morava reaches a water level of 6.63 m. Now also soldiers are deployed around the clock to rescue what can be rescued; in this situation alone a further 4,000 sandbags are laid.

Basis for deployment:	Call for help from the communities.
Type of deployment:	Supportive deployment according to Sec. 2 para. 1 sub-para. c DA.
Mission:	Support of the civilian emergency, rescue, and clearance work; securing of dams; rescue of trapped persons; repair of roads, paths and bridges; illumination at night; decontamination.
Duration of deployment:	July 8th, 1997 – July 24th, 1997.
Contingent strength:	Max. 2,200 soldiers.

Visit of Pope John Paul II

Preliminary Events

Known internationally as the "speedy" Pope, John Paul II made it a goal from the beginning of his pontificate to visit as many dioceses around the world as possible, in order to personally carry the gospel to many Catholics. This pastoral visit is the third (after 1983 and 1988), that the Pope pays to Austria.

Political Measures

As the worldly head of the Vatican state, all the protocolary honors of a head of state are due to the Pope. In accordance with this, the Pope is welcomed not only by the Catholic Church of Austria, but also by the political leadership. For this reason, political as well as pastoral meetings are on the agenda.

Military Measures

Since this is a state visit, the armed forces support the organizer in implementation.

Basis for deployment:	CM ruling.
Type of deployment:	Assistance as a result of a petition from the "Task Force for the Papal Visit 1998".
Mission:	Protocolary duties (reception and farewell with military honors, battery salute, honor guards); construction of grandstands in Salzburg, St. Pölten and Vienna; transports of all kinds.
Duration of deployment:	June 15th, 1998 – June 23rd, 1998.
Contingent strength:	730.
Organization:	Honor Company of the Guards, engineer forces from the Engineer Troops School as well as the 1st and 2nd Engineer Battalions, working commands from MilCom of Vienna, the 2nd Logistics Regiment and the 3rd Headquarters Battalion, communications forces from the 2nd Signal Battalion, aircraft (2 AB-212, 1 PC-6).
Contribution:	6,235 work hours are contributed by the soldiers in 712 man/days, 5,000 km are covered with 70 vehicles. The aircraft provide 6 flight hours.

This deployment does not remain hidden from the Holy Father (himself the son of an Imperial noncommissioned officer), as proven by his farewell words to the Military Bishop before his return flight from Schwechat Airport:

"Mr. Military Bishop, I thank your stalwart soldiers."

"During the 1st pastoral visit on the occasion of the Austrian Catholic Convention in 1983, the entire air transport of the Pope also lies in the hands of the armed forces. For this 10 transport version AB-212s, 2 medical version AB-212s and 1 communications helicopter are deployed. The flying forces are supported with 3 flight management troops, 1 water pump and 2 firefighting vehicles and 4 medical trucks. Engineers construct, among other things, two 400 m long temporary station platforms and a pedestrian overpass for the visitors who come by train to the mass in the Donaupark." Within the framework of the Catholic Convention the armed forces introduce themselves to the broader public as a separate **"Military Diocese of Austria"**.

Reception of Pope John Paul II with all military honors.

Mine Accident in Lassing

Preliminary Events

On July 17th, 1998, the most serious mine accident ever occurs in Austria. In Lassing in Styria, the underground shaft system caves in. One comrade is buried. The mine accident even causes great dismay abroad and leads to international help. So assisting forces from the volunteer fire department of Berchtesgaden, the Federal Border Patrol, the Federal Police of Munich, and the Marina Military are deployed.

Political Measures

Initially, disagreements over authority between the civilian institutions in Lassing develop. As a result of a poor assessment of their own possibilities, the help of the armed forces is at first waived. The actual call finally takes place through the Regional Mines Authority of Leoben on July 20th, at 12:30 PM, far too late, as is publicly criticized. The immediate area of operations is declared a restricted area.

Military Measures

On Saturday, July 18th, at 7:00 AM, the engineer officer of Styrian Military Command is alerted from holiday and ordered to Lassing. At 3:00 PM he is relieved by the S3/NBCDefO/MilComm ST. Since during the survey no concrete manner of support by the armed forces can be envisioned, this is broken off at 10:00 PM. On July 20th, a petition of the deployment administration for the dispatch of a engineer platoon takes place. Since the 1st Engineer Battalion from Villach is on a division exercise, the 3rd EngBn in Melk is alerted. Contrary to the desire to first begin the deployment on July 21st, the engineers are already transferred to the area of operations on July 20th. With this, the entire night can be used for construction work. A 25-t ferry is established in the hole by the engineers as a floating platform for the fire department's suction pumps, and a lighting arrangement is constructed. In addition, there are a number of transport duties on land and in the air as well as the direction of the German military helicopters, which are transporting rescue equipment. More than once, the deployment must be temporarily broken off and the rescue teams evacuated because of the acute danger of landslides or as a result of the measured difference in the levels of the mountain and ground water.

On July 22nd, the necessary parts for the constructions of a central reporting state and a sound ranging troop are sent. On the same day, parts of the Special Operations Forces Training Center from Wiener Neustadt arrive at the accident site with the pressurized diving chamber.[42] At 2:00 AM the duties of the fire department are taken over, on July 23rd also the complete provisioning preparations for the assisting forces deployed in Lassing (up to 300 people). This offer of the military deployment administration is necessary so that the constant disbursement of additional provisions is maintained. On July 25th, in the course of the administrative assistance, the technical supplies of the RuBSD/EZ/B (alkali cartridges, explosion warning devices, and mine rescue radios) are delivered. On Sunday, July 26th, with the cooperation of the armed forces[43], the rescue of trapped comrade Georg Hainzl finally takes place. Despite repeated rescue attempts, help is unfortunately too late for the 10 miners who entered to free him.

> **Basis of deployment:** Call for support from the Mining Authority of Leoben.
> **Type of deployment:** Supportive deployment according to Sec. 2 para. 1 sub-para. c DA.
> **Mission:** Operation of a central reporting station; construction of a floating platform and hose bridges; deployment of emergency boats and supply of emergency equipment; assumption of transport duties and provisions preparations for all support forces.
> **Duration of deployment:** July 20th, 1998 – August 5th, 1998.
> **Contingent strength:** 30.
> **Organization:** Deployment administration, half-platoon of engineers with 4 half-pontoons and an aluminum tool from the 3rd EngBn, diving troop with pressurized diving chamber from the Special Operations Forces Training Center, sound ranging troop from NBCDefPl/MilComm ST.
> **Commander:** Captain Gaugl.
> **Contribution:** 440 man/days are contributed by the armed forces and 16,806 km driven during this time.

Consequences

The mine accident leads to an evaluation of the national crisis management (Crima) under the leadership of the Federal Chancellor's office. The emphasis during this is on the clear delegation of authority and the introduction of deployment staffs in the provincial and district catastrophe administrations. It is once more shown that no conclusions are drawn from the experiences of the troop experiment which took place in East Tyrol in 1977/78, which concerned itself with coordinated leadership on the district level.

---

42 This is added at the request of the Department of Hyperbaric Surgery at the Provincial Hospital of Graz. It cannot in fact be used, since it is currently undergoing modification work. However, experience can be added and meaningful new insights won for deployment.
43 For the rescue, additional alpine equipment must be brought and deployed.

On July 17th, 1998, the most serious mine accident ever in Austria happens in Lassing. A engineer platform for the fire department's suction pumps is constructed by army engineers under most difficult and dangerous conditions (t.). The German Armed Forces transport recovery equipment with a helicopter of the type CH-53 (m.).

Pressurized diving chamber from the Special Operations Forces Training Center (b.l.). An occasion to smile in this depressing situation is given by this little dog, for whom the safety of his master is obviously a concern (b.r.).

EU Presidency

Preliminary Events

Austria becomes a member of the European Union on January 1st, 1995. The assumption of the EU presidency for a half-year is included in this. This duty falls to Austria from July 1st to December 31st, 1998.

Political Measures

An array of meetings on the most varied levels is to be organized by the federal government. The high point of every presidency is the orderly convention of the Council of the European Union, in which the heads of state and government of the member nations take part. The date is planned for the 11th and 12th of December, the Austria Center Vienna ("UNO City") and the Wiener Hofburg are considered as the location. At the explicit wish of the majority of the member nations, the Hofburg is finally given precedence.

Military Measures

In the time between June 15th – 17th, 1997, a survey already takes place in Amsterdam, in order to study needs and experiences there. Subsequently various construction projects take place. Two trailer villages (with 120 and 160 trailers) are constructed in the Hofburg's library courtyard for the communications center; in the Summer Riding School a large tent (in cooperation with a Dutch firm) is raised. The catalog collection of the Austrian National Library (138 catalog cabinets) must be removed from storage. The vehicle fleet must be picked up from firms in Germany.

> **Basis for deployment:** Petition of the Federal Ministry for Foreign Affairs.
> **Type of deployment:** Administrative assistance.
> **Mission:** Assumption and operation of the vehicle fleet; construction and operation of the communications center in the Vienna Hofburg; construction of stands; transport and security duties.
> **Duration of deployment:** January 1998 – December 1998.
> **Contingent strength:** 150 noncommissioned officers as drivers.
> **Commander:** Brigadier General Mag. Christian Ségur-Cabanac, Head of the Operations Directorate in the MoD.
> **Contribution:** 7,871 work hours in 870 man/days.

In the Viennese Hofburg all the cables for the entire presidency are laid, 310 telephones, 30 fax machines, 33 PCs as well as 225 journalist workspaces are arranged. In the European Parliament itself there are 1,487 telephones, 161 fax machines, 1,050 journalist workspaces. During the rest of the meeting across Austria 2,083 telephones, 217 fax machines, 239 PCs and 1,332 journalist workspaces are installed. The drivers contribute 5,934 man/days and cover 600,000 km with 72 BMW limousines (16 armored) and 29 Chrysler minivans during this time. The signal corps contributes 81,602 work hours, the engineers 7,291. 219 people are transported with 18 helicopters and 1 PC 6 transport airplane in 85 flight hours.[44]

Danube Crossing

Within the framework of the EU presidency an informal meeting of the Council of Environmental Ministers takes place on July 19th, 1998. The transport of persons is accomplished through inflatable boats from the Donau-Auen GmbH, the naval security by the Naval Police. The engineers construct an "aluminum staircase" near Haslau a. d. Donau to board the inflatable boats, operate two engineer boats for accompanying journalists and distribute 100 life vests to delegation members.

Uniform

The desire for the noncommissioned officers assigned as drivers to appear in uniform does not conform to the wishes of the Federal Chancellor.[45] Therefore, the drivers are equipped with the formal dress that was introduced for competitive athletes (blue blazer, gray pants). The state coat of arms with the inscription "Armed Forces" is sewn on the breast pocket of the blazer. Moreover, the national emblem of the armed forces with the side wings is put on the right sleeve.

Logo

Since it is customary for each presidency to choose a logo for itself, after the appropriate announcement and selection, a concept is chosen. To publicly demonstrate the support of the armed forces, all military vehicles are equipped with a sticker that shows this logo and an additional inscription.

---

44 According to the final report of the Defence Ministry.
45 Although the wearing of the dress uniform was originally ordered, this must be changed at the "petition" of the Federal Chancellor, since he would like to avoid a too "military" appearance.

Catastrophic Avalanche in Galtür

Preliminary Events

After days of heavy snowfall and strong winds leading to snowdrifts, avalanche alert level 5, the highest alert level, is called for the provinces of Upper Austria, Salzburg, the Tyrol and Vorarlberg. As a result of street blockages connected with avalanche flows, many towns are no longer reachable by land. Among others, the access roads to Stanzertal from Pians, the Lech valley in the area of Warth, Lech and Zürs are interrupted on February 11th, and by February 12th the access road to Paznaun valley near Ischgl. By February 22nd the avalanche situation visibly escalates as a result of the increasing growth of new snow in West Tyrol and Vorarlberg.

On February 23rd and 24th, 1999, multiple massive avalanches flow in the Paznau Valley in the Tyrol within 24 hours. On February 23rd, around 4:00 PM, a powder avalanche around 800 m wide devastates large parts of the town of Galtür. During this, 31 people lose their lives. The immediately deployed rescue measures, however, can only be carried about by the locally available forces, since the disastrous weather situation makes flying in support forces impossible. Nevertheless it is possible to rescue 22 people in the first hours. In the afternoon hours of February 24th, a further avalanche flows in Valduz, a small hamlet between Ischgl and Galtür. It costs 7 people their lives.

Political Measures

The crisis staff meets in Landeck. As a result of the extensiveness of the catastrophe, the provincial governor directs a petition for supportive contributions on the Military Command of the Tyrol.

Military Measures

On February 12th the armed forces are deployed with up to twelve helicopters of the types Agusta Bell AB.212 and Aerospatiale SA.316 "Alouette III" to provision the trapped towns. About 700 people are flown out of the areas acutely threatened by avalanche and around 75 t of foodstuffs, medicines and other vital goods are transported into the isolated towns, until the cancellation of flights because of the extremely bad weather on March 23, at 3:30 PM. The avalanche deployment troop set on alert readiness in Landeck must wait at first. A helicopter that nevertheless attempts to start must turn back around. On the morning of the next day the snowfall abates far enough for satisfactory flight visibility conditions to be given. At 6:30 AM the first helicopters with assistance teams, as well as civilian helicopters, start out for Galtür. Through this 370 people (two military avalanche deployment platoons, Alpine Gendarmes, emergency doctors, mountain rescue, Red Cross volunteers and avalanche search dogs), technical equipment and medicines are brought into the catastrophe area. On each return, injured are simultaneously flown out. The minor wounded are transferred into emergency vehicles in the Landeck barracks, the seriously wounded are flown directly to the surrounding hospitals. In this way, 1,089 people are able to leave the threatened area in the first nine hours alone.

Survey flights show that the access road to Galtür is heavily buried, the introduction of support teams can therefore not be thought of. In view of the amount of the transport flights to be expected, it is proven once again that the transport space of the armed forces is much too small. The military helicopters also cannot transport the urgently needed heavy equipment, such as diggers or snowblowers. Therefore, in the night before February 24th, the leadership staff in the Defence Ministry decides to send a verbal note to Germany, France, Switzerland and the USA with a request for the dispatch of large transport helicopters. All of the contacted nations immediately declare their readiness to help. By the afternoon, a "Super Puma" from the Swiss Air Force arrives and immediately begins to fly out trapped persons in Vorarlberg. Somewhat later German and American military helicopters arrive from Germany. As a result of the coming darkness and the once again worsening weather conditions, they nevertheless cannot be deployed. On the morning of February 5th the weather conditions allow the resumption of the provisioning flights.

A deployment center is established in Pontlatz barracks in Landeck, staging posts in the Walgau barracks in Bludesch and in Imst. However, especial attention is paid to the airfield established on a part of the Inntal Highway (Call sign: "Highway Imst"). For this end this part of the highway is blocked off for traffic. In addition, sections of the guardrails and street signs must be removed and trees cropped. Since some of the foreign pilots possess only limited mountain flight experience, they are briefed by Austrian pilots. Finally, there are four avalanche deployment platoons and four platoon-strength support teams with 350 men in the Tyrol and seven avalanche deployment platoons and support teams with 350 men in Vorarlberg, in constant deployment. In addition, three avalanche deployment platoons as well as support forces in a strength of 420 men in the Tyrol and four avalanche deployment platoons or 24 support platoons (engineer, logistics, NBC, communications, and infantry forces) with a total of 700 men in Salzburg are readied for deployment.

In total, this deployment is the largest **airlift** ever to be carried out in Austria, with international participation under Austrian leadership into the bargain.

*The avalanches leave a trail of devastation (t.l. and t.r.). The access roads must be blocked off (m.l.).
Soldiers in the nearby garrisons are alerted in the night, as well as members of the infantry school in Saalfelden (m.r.).
Those buried are despairingly searched for with sensors (b.l.) and search dogs (b.r.).*

All available helicopters are deployed. They transport the emergency teams in the closed-off regions (t.l.) and fly out holiday-makers surprised by the catastrophe. While the rescued leave the aircraft, these are simultaneously loaded from the other side with foodstuffs for the trapped (t.r.). The helicopters fly with the maximum load of people and materials until late in the night (m.r.). To that end, the airfield is secured and illuminated by the fire department (m.l.). In the flight deployment center all flight movements are centrally directed and coordinated (below).

After its own helicopter capacities are found to be insufficient, Austria asks for international help. Germany, France, Switzerland and the USA send helicopters for support. On a part of the Inntal Highway an airfield (Call sign: "Highway Imst") is established, from which the foreign helicopters operate. From Germany, among others, come three CH-53s (above), from the US Army nine UH-60 "Black Hawks" (m.). Since some the foreign pilots possess little mountain flight experience, they are briefed or alternatively piloted by Austrian pilots (b.l.). After the end of the deployment a ceremonial tribute and farewell to the foreign occupants (b.r.) takes place.

Basis for deployment:	Petition from the provincial government of the Tyrol.
Type of deployment:	Supportive deployment according to Sec. 2 para. 1 sub-para. c DA.
Mission:	Flying in search and emergency teams; provisioning of the isolated towns and huts; flying out the casualties and holiday makers; rescue and emergency deployment.
Duration of deployment:	February 19th, 1999 – March 12th, 1999 (the preparations already begin in July 1996).
Contingent strength:	1,820.
Organization:	47 helicopters: twelve aircraft of the type AB.212, two AB.204Bs and six SA.316B "Alouette IIIs" from the Austrian armed forces; five aircraft of the type CH-53 and six UH-1Ds from the German armed forces as well as two AS.332 "Super Pumas" from the German Border Patrol, nine aircraft of the type UH-60 "Black Hawk" from the US Army, two aircraft of the type SA.330 "Puma" and three AS.532 "Cougars" from the French armed forces; an aircraft of the type AS.332 "Super Puma" from the Swiss Army, three avalanche deployment platoons.
Deployment director:	Major General Richard Neururer, military commander of the Tyrol.
Contribution (Galtür and Valzur):	18,132 people and 270 t of provisions (medicines, emergency materials and foodstuffs) are transported with 3,232 landings in 910 flight hours; 10,200 civilians are catered to and cared for; the deployment forces are dispensed 8,600 daily rations; the avalanche deployment platoons contribute ca. 45,000 man hours.[46]
Contributions (previously):	16 military helicopters transport 700 people and 75 t of freight.

Deployment Exercises

During this extensive deployment of international forces, the experiences gained in past years during the **NATO PfP exercises** "Cooperative Chance" and "Cooperative Key" could be applied to an emergency. Multinational cooperation during the planning and carrying out of operational and logistical procedures and the carrying out of support and provisioning activities, as well as emergency and rescue measures from the air could be practiced during these exercises.

Particularly notable is the outstanding **cooperation with the civilian deployment administration** (provincial governor, district administrator, emergency organizations). This is also the product of constant coordinated exercises with civilian and military deployment forces.

Experiences

As a result of the experiences that were had in the deployment in Galtür and Valzur, a **military catastrophe deployment center** is established one year after the accident in the Pontlatz barracks in Landeck. With this deployment center, the military possess an institution in which separate bunks and connections are present for all support forces and from which all systems can be coordinated and led. This leads to an intensive information exchange between decision makers and those carrying them out. Besides this command center, conference rooms and break rooms for free shifts are available. Separate from this is a press and information center. In addition to this, the Tyrolean provincial government is also working on a unified digital trunked system that should overlie the available wire-bound cables.

As a further consequence of the tragic events, the federal government manifests readiness to introduce the **acquisition of a newer, larger transport helicopter** for the armed forces. A specification sheet is produced and a public call for bids carried out. As a result of the evaluation process, the choice is finally reduced to two types: the American UH-60 "Black Hawk" and the French/German AS.332 "Super Puma". Both aircraft were deployed in Galtür. The decision finally falls on the "Black Hawk". With this, the (logical) military demand for a military multipurpose (battle and transport) helicopter asserts itself over the demand from "some" politicians for a purely "civilian" transport helicopter. The first aircraft will come in 2002.

---

46 Homepage of the Defence Ministry on March 12th, 1999.

Y2K Precautions

Preliminary Events

Worldwide, problems are feared in computer systems during the transition from December 31st, 1999 to January 1st, 2000.

International Reaction

Millions of US dollars are invested in the review of all systems that are equipped with the most diverse types of chips. Particular attention is paid to nuclear power plants and atomic weapons. Russia even invites US technicians, who are supposed to assist with the inspection and when necessary, the readjustment of their atomic weapons' guidance systems, to eliminate even the slightest chance of a faulty reaction. It can generally be determined that most of the primary security systems of the 430 nuclear power plants worldwide normally function independently of the date and are not usually controlled by computer. The old reactors of the Soviet design work with hard-wired systems. This is however not the case for all access or control systems. These must therefore be made "Y2K secure".

China takes a somewhat unusual path: It requires among others all managers of the national airline to celebrate the new year in one of their aircraft. In this way they hope to be sure that through their managers, all necessary checks are administered and the most security possible is guaranteed.

Austrian Reaction

Political Measures

In Austria as well, all necessary measures are taken. Furthermore, the situation is used to examine all alert plans and emergency measures. From the side of the responsible Federal Chancellor's office ("coordination of crisis precautions and national crisis management as well as political security foundations" group) it is determined that no additional security precautions are necessary or to be undertaken on the federal level for the 2000 year change, since events of an unusual magnitude (NPP disruptions, large chemical disasters, etc.) can be ruled out with "the closest probability bordering on certainty".

Military Measures

From the side of the Defence Ministry all alert plans also undergo inspection. Since the Federal Chancellor's office rules out unusual events, individual precautionary measures are neither possible nor reasonable. Therefore, only measures to assure the functioning of the on-duty system and in the operation of emergency power are taken. So all private branch exchange systems possess devices which ensure operation even after a long power outage. The addition of emergency power aggregates by the signal corps in the case of a longer outage is ordered, all duty instructions are appropriately amended. An additional (call) readiness for key and maintenance personnel is also available.

The actual internal military preparations begin even earlier. They concern

- the information technology (IT) system (host, server, PC) with the network components;
- the integrated radio infrastructure of the airspace surveillance system "Goldhaube";
- the "embedded system" (heating controls, entrance monitoring systems, etc.) and
- the "intelligent" measuring systems (computer-controlled sensors, automatic test systems, etc.).

The Y2K problem is used for a thorough renewal of the essential areas of the IT infrastructure. In addition, targeted measures for year 2000 capability have been taken in the department' data processing centers since 1996. In connection with this, projects worth ca. 230 ATS are conducted. The successful integration test takes place between September 24th and 26th, 1999. The test of the integrated radio infrastructure then succeeds between October 9th and 10th.

A complex problem is posed in securing the year 2000 capability of the airspace surveillance system "Goldhaube", together with Austrocontrol, the central institution for meteorology, Geodynamik, the data distribution system of the German weather service, and Austrocontrol/Technical University Graz for the lightning positioning system and the weather radar group. The appropriate tests run from November 15th to December 13th.[47]

In order to be armed against all cases, the **present organization** of the military on January 1st, 2000 and the alert-able **cadre intervention forces** for protection of members of the military on military property are specifically determined and publicly published. These forces encompass primarily the signal, engineer, and NBC defence troops.

---

47 Homepage of the Defence Ministry on December 16th, 1999.

Parts of the Radio Troop School (RTS) have a special deployment. The "radio crew" spends New Year's Eve with the partner company of the RTS, "Energy Supply Lower Austria (EVN)". In the course of "assistance within the framework of training", the EVN is supported in overcoming possible communications problems as a result of the year change. The soldiers of the RTS construct and operate three radio circuits (two shortwave and one VHF circuit). All equipment is remote-controlled. This means that the beaming parts (antennas and senders) are assembled before the facilities of the EVN, OMV and the associated companies. The public agencies, however, can communicate with each other from their respective workplaces. After an appropriate survey the preparations already begin on December 30th, 1999. On December 31st, at 1:30 PM, all connections are ready for operation. Finally, at 2:00 AM on January 1st, the "all-clear" can be given. The soldiers can celebrate the year change with the workers on duty in the partner company in peace. In the early morning hours the disassembly takes place, which is ended at 8:30 AM. This shows once again how seriously the armed forces and their allies took the Y2K problem. The radio troop is the only one in Austria capable of accomplishing such a deployment (operation of a closed telecommunication network over radio without fixed cable connections).

Basis for deployment:	Petition of the affected company.
Type of deployment:	Assistance within the framework of training.
Mission:	Securing of radio contact within the EVN, OMV and associated companies.
Duration of deployment:	December 30th, 1999 – January 1st, 2000.
Contingent strength:	28.
Organization:	10 MFF-1A-0, 1 KFF-19, 2 KFF-32.
Commander:	Major Christian Wally.

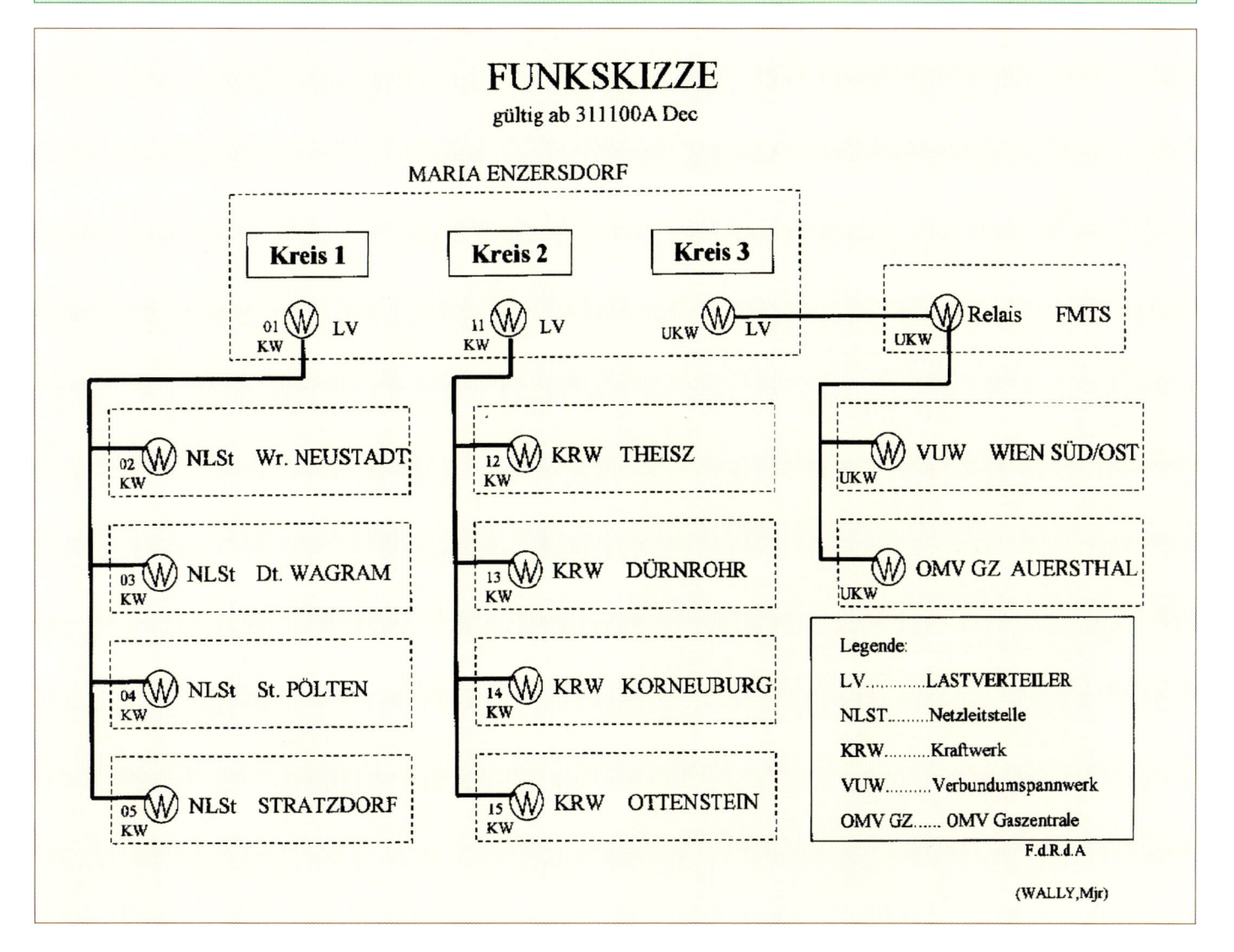

FUNKSKIZZE
gültig ab 311100A Dec

MARIA ENZERSDORF

Kreis 1 — 01 KW — LV
Kreis 2 — 11 KW — LV
Kreis 3 — UKW — LV — Relais UKW — FMTS

- 02 KW — NLSt Wr. NEUSTADT
- 03 KW — NLSt Dt. WAGRAM
- 04 KW — NLSt St. PÖLTEN
- 05 KW — NLSt STRATZDORF

- 12 KW — KRW THEISZ
- 13 KW — KRW DÜRNROHR
- 14 KW — KRW KORNEUBURG
- 15 KW — KRW OTTENSTEIN

- UKW — VUW WIEN SÜD/OST
- UKW — OMV GZ AUERSTHAL

Legende:
LV............LASTVERTEILER
NLST.........Netzleitstelle
KRW..........Kraftwerk
VUW..........Verbundumspannwerk
OMV GZ...... OMV Gaszentrale

F.d.R.d.A

(WALLY, Mjr)

Austrian OSCE Chairmanship

Preliminary Events

Every year another member of the OSCE has the chairmanship. The high point of every presidency is the OSCE Ministerial Council, which is carried out in the capital of the chairmanship nation. Ministers and diplomats from all 54 member nations and the nine cooperative nations take part in this conference.

Political Measures

In the year 2000 Austria receives the chairmanship of the Organization for Security and Cooperation in Europe (OSCE). Accordingly, numerous events take place in this year. One is the OSCE Ministerial Council on November 27th and 28th in the Viennese Hofburg. This event has broad public interest, not least through the worldwide intensive news coverage. Accordingly, everything possible is undertaken by the federal government to make this conference a success.

Military Measures

Such a major event is no longer doable in any country in the world today without the support of the army. Analogous to the support of the armed forces on the occasion of Austria's EU presidency, various supportive contributions are brought by the armed forces in connection with the OSCE chairmanship. The motor pool this time consists of 65 Audi A8 Quatro 4.2 long version limousines (some armored), 65 Audi T4 mini-vans as well as six to eight Audi A6 security trucks. The vehicles are accepted by their assigned drivers directly from the production company in Ingolstadt on November 22nd and transferred to Vienna. The withdrawal and return takes place on November 30th. The communications deployment already begins weeks before the conference. Soldiers of the staff communications leadership, supported by the Military Radio Regiment, provide all the telephone, ISDN, fax and internet connections needed by the conference participants and journalists from the Viennese Hofburg to the entire world.

Basis for deployment:	Petition of the Ministry for Foreign Affairs.
Type of deployment:	Administrative assistance.
Mission:	Operation of the "Audi fleet" (A6 and A8 limousines, minivans); signal corps appropriate development of the conference site and the press center in the Hofburg and the National Library in agreement with the Siemens company and Post/Telekom AG., transport and removal of conference equipment; deployment of 70 liaison officers to individual delegations; pilots, doormen, guards; air transport.
Duration of deployment:	November 17th – December 1st, 2000.
Contingent strength:	147 (drivers), 550 (signal corps), 250 (engineers), 48 (airmen).
Commander:	Brigadier General Mag. Christian Ségur-Cabanac, Head of the Operations Directorate in the MoD.
Contribution:	In 1,710 man days 14,199 work hours are contributed.

In contrast to the EU presidency, the assigned drivers wear the "dress uniform". All other assigned soldiers, on the other hand, wear "service uniform 75". As practiced before during the EU presidency, all military vehicles that are deployed for support are distinguished with appropriate stickers. In order bring home the deployment to a wide public, the vehicles are already supplied with the stickers during the military exhibition on October 26th.

Funicular Disaster on Kitzsteinhorn

Preliminary Events

An extensive "snowboard opening" is planned on Kitzsteinhorn for November 11th, 2000. More than 2,000 skiers and snowboarders are already on the glacier, as a tragedy occurs at 9:30 AM in the tunnel of the funicular railway: the funicular, which leads through a 3.2 km long tunnel 3,000 m above sea level to the glacier skiing region of Kitzsteinhorn, catches fire for unclear reasons, about 600 m past the entrance to the mountain. Only eight of the 163 passengers manage to rescue themselves and get out through the bottom of the tunnel. 155 passengers burn helplessly in the train or fleeing up the mountain. The entire train burns itself completely out, only the iron chassis is left over. The fire also paralyzes the electricity supply of the mountain station. There three further deaths through carbon monoxide inhalation are to be lamented, since the suction effect in the tunnel pushes the smoke up the mountain like a chimney.

Political Measures

The crisis staff of the Salzburg provincial government meets immediately. A massive deployment of help is released. 165 paramedics, 25 emergency doctors, 480 firemen, 110 gendarmes, 40 psychologists and 14 helicopters take part. Through the Federal Chancellor, in agreement with the Federal President, national mourning is declared.

Military Measures

After the alert through Salzburg Military Command, a team of specialists (air rescuers, alpinists, NBC defence soldiers – all with deployment experience) is put together. At first the identities of the dead are unknown. A DNA analysis, which is compared to samples of relatives, first brings clarity. In addition it is necessary to recover the earthly remains of the almost totally burned victims. This succeeds through recovery teams from the fire department, Gendarmery and armed forces, who must work around the clock under the heaviest psychological and physical burdens. The soldiers' mission is the laborious removal of the corpses from the tunnel as well as their transfer to the coroner. In addition they must first climb about 700 m on 2,000 steps. After their release by the criminalists, the corpses are packed in body bags by teams of two and carried up around 100 steps on a steep, only 60 cm wide, supply staircase in the tunnel. Finally the soldiers must build their own assistance elevator to overcome the next 500 vertical meters to the transverse tunnel. Breathing protection, darkness, the narrow tunnel and the confrontation with death pushes the soldiers to their psychological and physical limits for six days. Therefore, teams of psychologists and military chaplains stand ready for the recovery teams. From the mountain station, the dead are taken by helicopter to Salzburg to the coroner. The soldiers also lay communication and lighting conduits to the accident site, as well as secure the material transports. Finally the soldiers perform one final duty to the American comrades that are unfortunately also among the dead: The earthly remains are given a farewell with full military honors and surrendered to the US Army. The armed forces were assigned to this difficult deployment, because they can "sustain a breath longer", as the military commander of Salzburg, Major General Roland Ertl, expresses it in his final press conference.

Basis for deployment:	Petition of the Tyrolean provincial government.
Type of deployment:	Supportive deployment according to Sec. 2 para. 1 sub-para. c DA.
Mission:	Recovery and removal of corpses; transport of materials; registration of the returning athletes; provisioning of all helpers and journalists; construction and operation of communication and illumination conduits.
Duration of deployment:	November 11th, 2000 – November 17th, 2000.
Contingent strength:	146.
Organization:	Recovery teams (two shifts of four groups each with six to eight soldiers), paramedic troop, psychological support team (military chaplains and psychologists), logistics team and photography troop.
Deployment director:	Major General Roland Ertl, military commander of Salzburg.
Commander:	Colonel Friedrich Bieler.
Contribution:	The recovery and removal of all 155 victims succeeds without accident or injury. Through the six deployed helicopters 407 takeoffs and landings take pace in 81 flight hours under most extreme conditions (foehn storms with up to 140 km/h as well as a landing pad of only 5 x 5 m directly under the cables of a funicular at the middle station). During this, 19 t of load are carried. During the entire duration of the deployment, all helpers and around 500 media representatives are provisioned by the troop kitchen of the infantry school.

The helpers are flown to the accident site with military helicopters; the earthly remains of the victims are then brought to Salzburg. To reach the accident site, up to 2,000 steps must be overcome. Every catastrophe of this type, even more so when many foreigners are affected, draws reporters and camera teams – in this concrete case around 500 persons – from around the world. In order to curtail this disaster journalism, as was already successfully practiced in Galtür, the "military film and and photography station of the armed forces" is exclusively allowed access. Through this, a serious and respectful photojournalism can be ensured. The diverse attempts to obtain the most bloodthirsty pictures possible, through bribery or other unspeakable means, can also be curbed in this way. How disgusting and inhuman some of sensationalism hungry "journalists" approach this is shown through the following example: A photographer and a commander of the military contingent are each offered 4 million Schillings in cash to give photographers the opportunity to take photos in the tunnel. When both decline, their families are even put under pressure. Despite the offered sum no one agrees to this "proposal". The soldiers are committed only to their mission and their honor.

Anthrax Alert

Preliminary Events

In October 2001, shortly after the horrible terrorist attacks in New York and Washington, a new horror story speeds around the world: in the USA an American dies after contact with the biological weapon anthrax. Further cases of anthrax contamination are announced almost hourly. As it comes out in the investigations, pieces of mail were used as the bearers in all cases. So, pieces of mail are also issued this way to important American politicians. Consequently, still more people die. In the general hysteria after September 11th the suspicion is voiced that this is a further terrorist act against the USA. The FBI determines, however, that all the mail was sent from the USA, some of it before September 11th. In other countries as well, including Austria, there are subsequent anthrax alerts.

International Reaction

In all the countries in which anthrax alerts occur, these are naturally taken seriously from the political side, and they proceed accordingly. After the investigations that later occur, these actions luckily turn out to have been either completely false alarms or the actions of so-called copycats.

First the samples are collected (picture right), securely packaged, and sealed (picture b.l.). The further examination then takes place in the lab (picture b.r.), who – in only one case – adduce the evidence of anthrax spores.

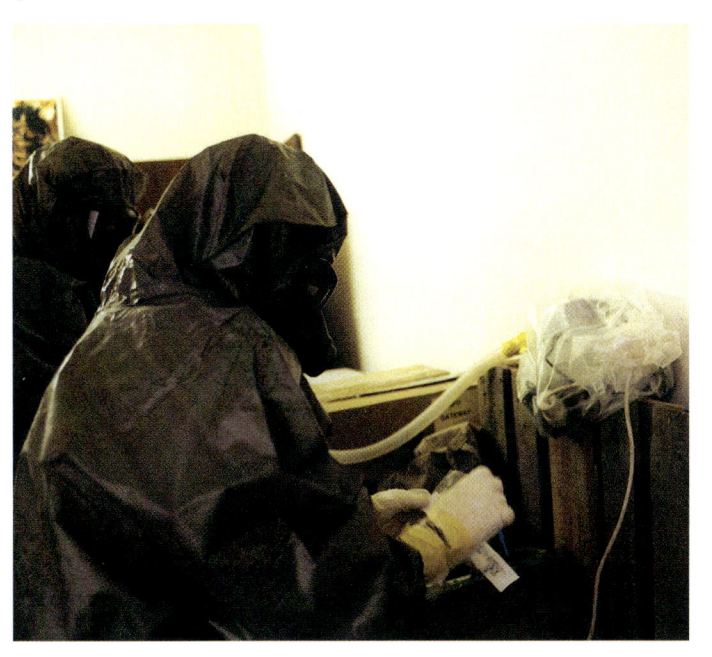

Austrian Reaction
Political Measures

As a result of the deadly cases and the general hysteria that runs rampant in the USA, concern also develops among the population in Austria. This leads to the fact that wherever anyone supposedly finds some strange powder on the ground, an alert is immediately sounded. Obviously no politician can be responsible for negating these. From the side of the federal government, therefore, all measures are taken to immediately secure and analyze samples and so to give the population the feeling of security. Although this is initially a purely national deployment, it takes on an international dimension when an anthrax alert is activated from the institutions of the American embassy in Vienna.

On October 13th, 2001, as the result of an agreement between the Ministry of the Interior and the Defence Ministry, a supportive deployment for all the NBC defence troops is ordered.

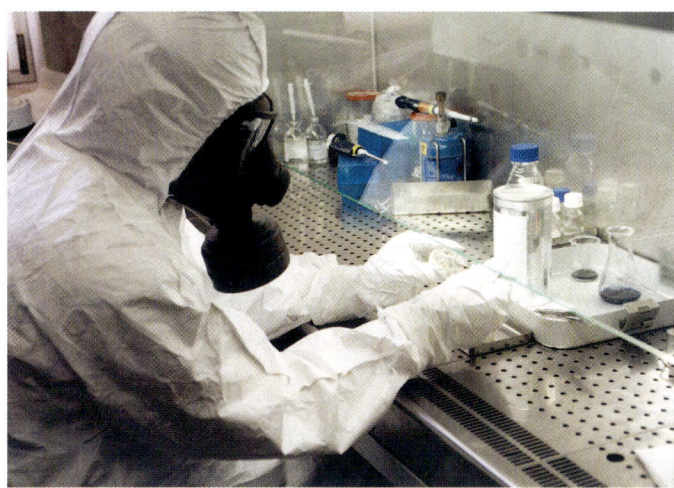

Defence Minister Herbert Scheibner takes the current anthrax case in the US embassy in Vienna as an occasion to press for the implementation of an already agreed-upon heightening of the capacities of the NBC Defence School.[48]

In the Health Ministry a separate "anthrax hotline" is established.

Military Measures[49]

As an answer to the scenario it is ordered from the side of the Defence Ministry to make all personnel and material alert preparations of the current NBC defence forces. In the same way, measures for parts of the infantry, special forces, flight and logistics troops are ordered. As a result of the accord with the Ministry for the Interior, the entire NBC defence troops of the Austrian armed forces are ordered to supportive deployment on October 13th, 2001. For the coordination of the deployments through the entire nation, a leadership element, and since the majority of those to be supported are in Vienna, a "quick intervention group" are formed at the NBC Defence School in Vienna. These forces are on duty around the clock. The NBC defence companies and NBC defence platoons, for their part, form mixed detection and decontamination elements, in order to be able to react swiftly to possible support needs.

The specialists of the NBC defence troops have the mission of carrying out a first evaluation of the situation and detection activities, taking samples, and taking decontamination measures. Subsequently, the substances suspected to be anthrax, or alternatively the pieces of mail, are analyzed by the military laboratories of the Office of Defence Technology (ODT) and the Federal Institute for Veterinary Examination in Mödling as well as the laboratories of the Universities of Graz and Innsbruck.

Anthrax in the American Embassy

After the terrorist attacks, first discussions between the Defence Ministry, or rather the NBC defence troops and the American embassy, already take place with respect to aligning the deployment procedures for possible attacks on American institutions. Since the diplomatic mail of the US embassy comes from the post office in Washington affected by the attacks and a contamination is therefore not to be ruled out, the mailroom of the embassy is sealed. Through representatives of the embassy, a petition for support is lodged with the Ministry of the Interior. The Defence Ministry is requested to take necessary decontamination measures in accordance with the previous agreement. With this, the "international" part of the anthrax deployment begins on November 8th. A first evaluation of the situation takes place through specialists of the NBC Defence School. On November 12th, work in the embassy is begun. During this various special problems must be solved, such as the decontamination of a pneumatic mail tube. Since the danger is given that pieces of mail were already sent on this way to various places in the embassy, the question quickly becomes how one can proceed here. The solution is found, in that a mail tube cartridge is covered with the appropriate decontamination agent and sent through the system. This may well have been the first usage of that method worldwide. In the course of further work air, material, and swipe samples are taken from the office, some 90 suspected mailbags secured, and finally analyzed. This work requires a few weeks. In one case (concretely, it is the 338th[50]) in the ODT, traces of anthrax are discovered. This is confirmed through a reference test in Mödling (among other things, a white mouse is infected, who within 24 hours shows a "specific bodily reaction"). All further examinations give negative results, no further germs or signs of the anthrax infection are identified.

Basis for deployment:	Call for support from the Ministry of the Interior and the US embassy in Vienna.
Mission:	Securing of the suspicious pieces of mail, detection activities, taking of samples, decontamination.
Area of operations:	Entire nation.
Duration of deployment:	October 13th, 2001 – 2009.
Contingent Strength:	Around 350.
Commander:	Colonel Norbert Fürstenhofer.
Contribution:	540 deployments (as of 2009).

---

48   APA release on December 14th, 2002.
49   Gerhard Ruhm: "Anthrax Alert in Austria – Supportive Deployment of the NBC Defence Troops"; in: The Soldier, the Independent Soldiers' Newspaper of Austria, No. 1, Vienna 2002.
50   Andrea Waldbrunner, Eva Linsinger: "Anthrax: Another 60 Mailbags Wait", in: Der Standard, edition of December 15th/16th, 2002.

Serious Forest Fires

Preliminary Events

Between February 2nd and 3rd, 2002, a forest fire breaks out on Stragor, a southern foothill of the Kreuzeck group in the Carinthian Drau Valley above the market town of Steinfeld (Spittal/Drau District). The fire may have been caused by sparks from the fireplace of a nearby mountain shelter. The partially inaccessible terrain and the weather conditions initially hinder swift combat of the fire. This is additionally fanned through the dryness and the constantly changing wind directions (after sunset the wind turns and blows downhill). In the course of the following days ca. 70 ha of spruce and larch forest are destroyed. The forestry service estimates the damages caused at around 500,000 €.

Political Measures

The fire department and the mountain emergency response service are alerted through the affected district administration (DA). After they cannot master the fire, the military command is petitioned for support. After it seems on February 8th that the fire can be extinguished, the "fire out" signal is initially given. Nevertheless, on February 9th hidden pockets of embers begin to burn anew, so that the extinguishing deployment must be ordered again. The area around the Weissensee is also blocked by the DA at times, so that military aircraft can collect water for the extinguishing deployment from a hole which was previously knocked in the ice sheet. Not until February 12th can "fire out" finally be given.

Military Measures

After the request for support is accepted, engineers from the 2nd Engineer Battalion from Villach and helicopters as well as light fixed-wing aircraft are deployed to fight the fire. After the rekindling of the fire a helicopter with a heat imaging device is also deployed to detect underground pockets of embers. In total this is the largest deployment of this type.

Basis for deployment: Petition of the district administration of Spittal/Drau.
Type of deployment: Supportive deployment according to Sec. 2 para. 1 sub-para. c DA.
Mission: Support of the local forces in firefighting.
Duration of deployment: February 8th, 2002 – February 12th, 2002.
Contingent strength: 42.
Organization: Engineer platoon, up to eight helicopters of the types Agusta Bell AB-212 and Alouette III with fire fighting water containers on outer load hooks as well as up to four light fixed-wing aircraft of the type Pilatus PC-6.
Deployment director: Colonel Josef Lindner.
Contribution: 5,000 work hours, 2.5 mill. liters of water are dumped from the helicopters and fixed-wing aircraft over the fire sources.

To fill the fire fighting water containers, a hole is knocked in the ice sheet over the Weissensee.

"Hundred Year Flood"

Preliminary Events

In March 2002, first flooding events occur in Upper and Lower Austria. Before the damages can be fully cleared away, heavy precipitation occurs in June in southern Lower Austria. In July heavy rainfall spreads across the entire nation. In Carinthia, the Tyrol, Salzburg, Upper and Lower Austria as well as Styria, serious mudslides and flooding occurs. By August 6th, the massive cumulative flow of water reaches a previously unimaginable magnitude. The Danube reaches the record mark of the flood of 1991 on August 13th at 12:00 PM. The hydrographic service determines that events of this kind are qualified by experts as happening only once every 500 to 1000 years. As a rule, however, protective measures for settled areas are only designed based on events happening once every 100 years. The flood waters become the most serious national catastrophe to devastate Austria since the Second World War. Over 10,000 houses are most seriously damaged, the infrastructure of entire regions are heavily battered. In the area of public rail traffic, over 80 km of the transport network are fully submerged. Massive hindrances occur on the highways and expressways. Through numerous bridge collapses, many towns are cut off from their surroundings. Valuable cultural assets cannot be brought to safety in time and are destroyed.

Political Measures

Immediately after the start of the heavy rainfall, the affected provincial warning centers (permanently occupied catastrophe protection facilities on the provincial level) under the leadership of the provincial governors begin warning and alerting the population as well as coordinating the deployment of assistance and emergency forces. The majority of the burden of these activities, however, lies with the communities. The constantly occupied federal warning center immediately takes over the coordination of all provincial facilities and acts as an information platform for all federal and provincial agencies and the deployed organizations. In the Federal Chancellor's Office an Austrian telephone line for information on the coordination of the assistance measures is established. Subsequently, the shipping on the entire Danube must be suspended by the Ministry for Transportation, Innovation and Technology (MTIT). From the side of the federal street maintenance the "large floodwater duty" is declared. All branch offices are occupied around the clock. All dams are constantly monitored. On August 8th, the first petition for support is lodged with the Defence Ministry.

On August 14th a special sitting of the Council of Ministers is called for in order to decide upon the necessary supportive measures for redressing damages and reconstruction. On August 19th, the coordination of all further measures takes place in a special sitting of the provincial governors' conference together with the members of the federal government and under consultation with the city and community union. Resources are drawn from the catastrophe fund. A bill for the passing of a floodwater compensation and reconstruction law is introduced by the federal government and then passed by Parliament. The Federal Ministry for Public Achievement and Sports grants all federal employees who voluntarily provide aid special leave. The Federal Ministry for the Interior (FMI) coordinates the deployment of the Executive, especially in the area of directing and securing traffic.

ORF calls for the as yet largest charity drive, which finally brings in over 60 mill. € for the victims of the floodwaters.

In total, around 140,000 deployed forces, including 2,700 members of the executive, 120,000 firemen and women, and 5,200 Red Cross workers battle the floodwaters. The total cost of the damages caused by the floodwaters is estimated at ca. 8 billion €.

Military Measures

Beginning on August 8th, the first calls for support from the provinces and communities arrive at the military commands. They are immediately answered. If only 300 soldiers are deployed at first, the number finally climbs to 12,000. With the stabilization of the weather conditions, the allocation of missions shifts from protection to help. If the main focus is initially on evacuation and shoring up dams and bridges, it subsequently becomes a question of provisioning the affected population, treating water, constructing bridges and taking up the clearance work. Alongside this, the armed forces provide unoccupied duty apartments and barracks accommodations for homeless families; 600 sleeping bags and 800 sweaters are donated to the Red Cross from military inventories. To support the aid contributions in Germany, 50,000 sandbags are filled by soldiers and loaded in airplanes in Schwechat on August 19th.

Since 1,500 wells are contaminated with fuel oil or chemical residues in Lower Austria alone, drinking water purification sites are operated by the NBC Defence School in Gmünd, in Spitz and Krumau, and in Upper Austria in Haid near Mauthausen. In Gmünd alone 80,000 liters of water per day are provided for the local hospital. In Krumau the destroyed water conduits are rebuilt. 250 cooks in 10 field kitchens provision rescuers and victims alike. Within the framework of a military "Meals on Wheels" program, 1,500 meals are cooked in the barracks of Allentsteig, Horn, Amstetten, Melk and St. Pölten and delivered by boat to the trapped victims of the floodwaters.

During the catastrophe deployment, the Engineer Bridge 2000, which was first delivered to the troops the year before, is deployed. A partnership that is one-of-a-kind in the military and in Europe, between MilCommLA and Raiffeisen Holding LA-Vienna, proves itself anew: Since the beginning of the flood, the construction holding Strabag, a daughter company of Raiffeisen (whose general director is also a militia officer) unbureaucratically provides the armed forces with a wide variety of equipment. This comprises heavy earth-moving equipment as well as mini-diggers or medical and accommodation trailers. The machines are controlled by Strabag employees and soldiers. The ORF charity drive is supported by 120 guard soldiers, who man the charity telephones between 8:00 AM and 11:00 PM in the ORF center.

For the care of the deployed soldiers, the constant availability of the military psychological service is assured. This deployment is the largest in the history of the military.

As thanks, 15,000 free tickets for a liner cruise on the Danube are presented to Brigadier General Ségur-Cabanac by the Austrian Transportation Office on October 7th.

Basis for deployment:	Petition of the provincial governments, district administrations and communities.
Type of deployment:	Supportive deployment according to Sec. 2 para. 1 sub-para. c DA.
Mission:	Support of the local forces.
Duration of deployment:	August 8th, 2002 – August 21st, 2002 (locally beyond that).
Contingent strength:	11,277.
Organization:	5 engineer tanks, 6 recovery tanks, 7 wheel loaders, 2 field generators, 2 heavy decontamination vehicles, 5 fire trucks, 26 low-loading systems, 8 dump trucks, 3 walking excavators, 35 heavy engineering machines, 814 trucks, 2 engineer bridge 2000s, 10 field kitchens and 4 water purification systems.
Deployment director:	Major General Hubertus Trauttenberg (commander of the II. Corps assigned to leadership).
Contribution:	81,000 man days. Evacuation of 13,000 people. 262 people in deadly peril are rescued from roofs and trees with cable winches on transport and liaison helicopters in 174 deployments in 350 contributed flight hours, 1,340 people are flown to safety and 5,535 freight transports are carried out. Around 125,000 food rations are produced and handed out. Furthermore, 30 bridges with a total length of 788 m are constructed and 195,000 sandbags laid.

The new Engineer Bridge 2000 is deployed for the first time. With this bridge system the armed forces have access to the most modern equipment, that in addition to war-related deployment can also be used in wide ranges of engineer technical assistance where quick reactions count. The engineer bridge wins approval with high mobility, short construction times, low personnel needs, high load bearing capacity with a low mass, high transportation capacity, a variable span adequate for most applications, closed lanes and low space requirements for construction (top picture). The major elements of the system are the bridge sections, the 6.9 m long inner section (middle piece) and the 6.7 m long ramp section (ramp piece). A bridge unit (bridge column) consists of a bridge-laying vehicle and four transport vehicles with two ramp pieces and four middle pieces (picture below).

European Economic Forum

Preliminary Events

From September 15th to 17th, 2002, the European Economic Forum 2002 takes place in the city of Salzburg.

Political Measures

Extensive security measures are arranged through the federal government and the Salzburg provincial government, in order to ensure the undisturbed activity of the convention. On the part of the MI, a petition for assistance and support during the implementation with aid contributions of help and/or supplies of military goods, is issued to the DM.

Military Measures

The DM immediately responds to the MI's petition. At the request of the organizer, extensive protective and supportive contributions are arranged through the DM. Besides the classic military security measures the armed forces provide accommodations for the 1,800 executive officials who are additionally gathered from the entire nation. Military kitchens provision around 2,800 policemen and gendarmes. The equipage of the executive is supplemented with mobile blockade materials (SB rollers, Spanish riders) and radio equipment. Numerous vehicles are placed aside for the transport of personnel and materials. Two helicopters of the type "Alouette III – Owl" with heat imaging cameras and six transport helicopters of the type AB-212 fulfill flight missions for the Ministry of the Interior.

Especially noteworthy, however, is the deployment of the Saab 105OE and Saab 35OE "Draken" armed fighter jets for the protection of Salzburg's airspace. In addition the military airspace surveillance system "Goldhaube" is also set at higher readiness from September 13th. The heightened airspace protection is a part of the security standard since the devastating terrorist attacks of September 11th, 2001. Without such measures no major international event will be awarded. This is registered by all politicians, who now sacrifice general populism for the badly necessary replenishment of interceptor planes. The political and economic consequences of the postponement are not foreseeable at this time.

The argument that Austria is only surrounded by friends is carried out ad absurdum through the following event: In the course of the preparations for the NATO summit in October 2002 in Prague, a petition is issued by the Czech government to NATO that they obtain from Austria permission for the Czech Air Force to operate in Austrian airspace as necessary during the summit, in order to intercept unidentified flying objects in a timely manner. This would one of the requirements for the summit to take place in safety. In a heated answering note from the director of the air division, Brigadier General Erich Wolf, it is made unmistakably clear from the Austrian side that Austria itself is in a position to provide for the security of its airspace. The example shows that the "friendly" neighbors do not share this opinion with us. Without its own fighter jets, there will therefore be no more major international events in Austria in future. The deployment of foreign airplanes in Austria is only to be expected when the affected country feels itself directly or indirectly threatened by Austria, surely not in the case of a threat to Austria.

For close to 18 years the Saab Draken 35OE flies in Austria without accidents. During this time, 250 alert takeoffs with "A" priority and 23,545 flight hours are completed by military pilots on the jet. At the end of 2005 the Delta wing goes into retirement. With it ends one of the most eventful chapters in the history of the military aviation of the armed forces.

Interception Deployment

Preliminary Events

In the course of the state visit of Israel's President Moshe Katzav an incident occurs on October 20th, 2004, on a helicopter flight to Mauthausen: During the landing of the assembly airspace surveillance suddenly reports an unknown flying object on a collision course. Since the airspace along the flight route is closed for civilian air traffic and the unknown pilot does not react to radio contact, an attack cannot be ruled out.

Military Measures

Airspace surveillance is the duty of the Austrian armed forces according to Sec. 26 Military Powers Act, it occurs around the clock. A heightened airspace surveillance and/or airspace security operation in connection with flight restrictions and no-fly zones is arranged by the MoD after coordination with the Ministry for the Interior (in this process senior to the Federal Office for Defence of the Constitution and Suppression of Terrorism) and the Ministry for Transport, Innovation and Technology. With reference to the incident mentioned above, a priority "alpha" flight (prio "A" flight) is ordered. This is the flight of military aircraft for direct fulfillment of military missions. Such deployments occur 40 – 80 times yearly on average. This includes deployments for identification as a result of a lack of radio contact for civilian flight security or escorts.

A squad of Saab 105OEs ready for deployment, cleared for takeoff on the ground and deployed in the air (Markus Zinner). The onboard guns in the containers under the wings are loaded with live ammunition. A frequency is painted on the containers, with which the pilot of the aircraft to be identified can initiate contact with the alert squad.

Basis for deployment:	Sec. 26 Military Powers Act.
Type of deployment:	Priority "Alpha" flight.
Mission:	Interception.
Duration of deployment:	October 20th, 2004.
Contingent strength:	2 Saab 105OEs.

Progression of deployment:

- 3:35 PM: Armed Saab 105 jets are in the established patrol area.
- 3:45 PM: Takeoff of the transport convoy in Vienna towards Mauthausen.
- 3:50 PM: An unknown aircraft flies northwesterly towards Vienna on the border of the closed airspace. It has contact with the civilian air traffic control and is informed of the existing restrictions.
- 4:02 PM: The unknown aircraft flies into the closed zone. Air Traffic Control Vienna wants to make the pilot aware of the situation, but no longer reaches him.
- 4:04 PM: The military control centers are informed. The airplane flies in the direction of the presidential assembly.
- 4:05 PM: The prepared Saab 105s are called for.
- 4:08 PM: The military jets reach the airplane and identify it. The plane does not comply with the first orders to change its course.
- 4:10 PM: After a further order the sport airplane can be pushed aside.
- 4:13 PM: The rerouted plane is released a safe distance from the transport convoy.

Heavy Snowfall

Preliminary Events

In the beginning of February 2005, heavy and long-lasting snowfall occurs throughout the country. The heavy snowfall leads to massive hindrances of the rail and street traffic throughout Austria. The deployment of technical clearing devices is pushed to its limits. Numerous communities are trapped by the masses of snow, many holiday makers are prevented from returning home.

Political Measures

Constant call for support come from the side of the offices of the affected provincial governments and district administrations.

Military Measures

At the beginning of the first snowfall, avalanche deployment platoons in numerous garrisons are already put on alert readiness. In Styria alone the authorities are able to fall back on 800 soldiers in case of emergency. In Upper Styria above all the paramedic Pinzgauer high mobility all-terrain vehicles are held ready for patient transport in support of the Red Cross in Liezen. From Vorarlberg to Ried im Innkreis members of the military shovel against nature. So the train stations of Saalfelden, Selzthal and Kitzbühel can be navigated again. As soon the weather situation improves, the air forces carry out survey and provisioning flights in the trapped settlements.

> **Basis for deployment:** Petition of the authorities.
> **Type of deployment:** Sec. 2 para. 1 sub-para. c DA.
> **Mission:** Freeing of the transportation connections, provisioning of trapped persons and surveys from the air, carrying out of evacuations.
> **Duration of deployment:** February 3rd, 2005 – February 9th, 2005.
> **Contribution:** Ten helicopters of the type Alouette III, six Agusta Bell AB-212 and four S-70 "Black Hawks" evacuate 887 people and transport ca. 20 tons of freight. In the more than 100 flight hours besides transport of persons and equipment, the avalanche situation is surveyed, avalanches disrupted, as well as foodstuffs and water transported.

Race with nature: The Austrian Federal Railways (ÖBB) petitions among other things for snow clearance at the Selzthal train station. Since the clearance of transportation routes has priority, this petition is answered. Soldiers clear paths, tracks and stations (Wolfgang Grebien). After the weather has improved somewhat, ski tourists trapped on the Upper Styrian Planneralm can be rescued on February 4th by military helicopters. Minute by minute eight AB-212 and "Black Hawk" aircraft bring around 280 people to Aigen safely. There the affected – among them 230 schoolchildren on a ski course – are provisioned by the Red Cross and can then begin the trip home safe and sound.

Austrian EU Presidency

Preliminary Events

For the second time since Austria's admission to the European Union on January 1st, 1995, Austria takes over the EU presidency for a half year on January 1st, 2006.

Political Measures

A range of meetings on the most various levels are to be organized through the federal government.

Military Measures

The focus of the Defence Ministry during this is the active continuance and further development of the European Security and Defence Policy (ESDP). The particular attention of the Austrian presidency lies on ESDP operations, civilian-military coordination and the development of military capacities. In his speech before the foreign defence attachés, Defence Minister Günther Platter explicates the "management of operations", the Balkan focus of the Austrian EU presidency, and explains that Austria will profit from the joint EU defence policy. "Inner security through outer security" is therefore the motto in the Defence Ministry.

In line with the Austrian EU presidency the defence ministers of the European Union meet on March 6th and 7th in Innsbruck. In the process, the following themes are dealt with: civilian-military coordination (catastrophe assistance and crisis management), EU operations in the west Balkans and Africa, military capabilities of the EU (Headline Goal 2010, Battle Groups). Furthermore, a meeting of the European Defence Agency is on the agenda in the Tyrol. The Austrian armed forces present themselves as a dependable partner for security and stability in Europe.

In connection with the defence ministers' meeting Platter meets his counterparts from Turkey, the former Yugoslavian republic of Macedonia, Croatia, Iceland and Norway, to inform them of the results of the talks. Javier Solana and Platter's successor as council chairman, Finland's defence minister Seppo Kääriäinen take part in this meeting. A meeting with the defence ministers of Albania, Serbia-Montenegro, and Bosnia-Herzegovina subsequently takes place at the end of March.

On June 28th, 2006 Defence Minister Günther Platter hands over the EU chairmanship to his Finnish counterpart. "The security and defence policy is an essential motor of European integration", Platter emphasizes during the handover. Both ministers discuss the central themes of the European defence policy during the two day visit. Among these is Civil-Military Co-operation (CIMIC). The collective initiative of the three successive chairmanship nations Great Britain, Austria, and Finland considerably improves the Union's crisis management. In particular during the reaction to natural catastrophes, the first hours are decisive. At the end of the meeting with the Finnish Prime Minister Matti Vanhannen, Platter symbolically hands a baton over to his counterpart Seppo Kääriäinen, on which the logos of the Austrian and Finnish EU presidencies as well as the EU flag are pictured.

Basis for deployment: Petition of the Ministry for Foreign Affairs.
Type of deployment: Administrative support.
Mission: Securing of airspace, protocolary duties, contributions of help of all kinds.
Duration of deployment: January 1st, 2006 – June 30th, 2006.
Deployment director: Major General Mag. Christian Ségur-Cabanac, Director of Joint Command and Control Staff.
Contribution: 118 flights in 156 flight hours. In the process, among other things, 99 passengers are flown to conferences.

During the chairmanship, the conference sites and accommodations of high-ranking guests are inspected for NBC agents by military specialists and the Ministry of the Interior before every conference. Depending on the assessed threat level at least one NBC detection troop or NBC defence platoon is held ready for a decontamination after a possible terrorist attack. The "EU-Latin America-Caribbean Summit" and the visit of the American president in line with the "EU-USA Summit Conference" are classified as especially threatened. As a result, nine helicopters for transport and evacuation purposes as well a paramedic and connection helicopters are also deployed by the armed forces.

Defence Ministers' Meeting

For the meeting of the defence ministers, soldiers of the armed forces lay around five kilometers of cable and establish computer and telephone networks. Furthermore they transport all the equipment that is necessary for events of that type. The panoply ranges from signage to background walls or placards. For representatives of the media, more than 70 online workspaces and personal advisors are readied. Besides Innsbruck, the military supports all other events during the Austrian presidency. Among other things employees of the armed forces take over all transports in the air and on the streets. The 260 deployed drivers are mostly noncommissioned officers with special training.

World Economic Forum in Davos

Preliminary Events

From January 25th – January 29th, 2006, the World Economic Forum (WEF) meets in Davos in Switzerland. The WEF is a private trust with a seat in Geneva. It has the status of a non-governmental organization (NGO), which among other things advises the United Nations Economic and Social Council. The forum's yearly conference is also a meeting for the economic, political and intellectual leadership of modern society. The Swiss Air Force carries out an airspace security operation to secure the airspace during this conference. Since Davos is only 15 kilometers away from Austria, the Austrian Air Force is asked for aid.

Military Measures

The armed forces therefore actively and passively support the Swiss airspace safeguarding during the conference. This support is routine since 2002. During active support, jet planes of the types F-5E "Tiger" and Saab 105OE, fixed-wing aircraft of the type PC-7, as well as S-70 "Black Hawk" and OH-58 "Kiowa" helicopters are deployed. The passive support encompasses stationary and mobile radar stations and camera systems. In addition, a mobile mean range radar station and a low-flying radar acquisition tool are shifted from Salzburg to Vorarlberg. All radar data converges over satellite connections to the deployment center "base area" in St. Johann im Pongau. There the information is processed, evaluated and sent to the leadership center. To raise efficiency, the current pictures of the air situation are exchanged with Switzerland over a specially created data connection. Furthermore, in line with the deployment, precautions are taken for various flight incidents, in which the provincial warning centers of the Tyrol and Vorarlberg are also included. The planned and prepared deployment of anti-aircraft forces is not activated as a result of the concrete evaluation of the situation. In line with the operation, an area of restricted airspace is established in a part of Vorarlberg. The leadership of the deployed forces takes places through the Air Force Command in Langenlebarn.

An S-70 "Black Hawk" in front of a mobile radar station (left). Coordination of active and passive airspace surveillance: Two F-5E "Tigers" pass the stationary radar station on Kolomansberg in the Salzkammergut (b.r.). After the retirement of the SAAB S35 "Drakens" it is necessary to find an interim solution to maintain the active component of the airspace surveillance. The airspace surveillance duty is carried out by 12 F-5E "Tigers", which are rented from the Swiss Air Force. The official presentation of the planes takes place on July 9th, 2004 at Nittner Air Base in Graz-Thalerhof. With a so-called "flyout", the official return of the "Tigers" to the Swiss Air Force takes place on June 30th, 2008 in Graz. In those four years, 4,983 of the agreed-upon 5,000 flight hours are accomplished with an average of 66% operability. Fire control radar of the "Skyguard" type provides for seamless surveillance (b.l.).

Flood in Lower Austria

Preliminary Events

At the end of March 2006, as a result of heavy rainfall, substantial floods occur in Lower Austria.

Political Measures

New calls for support are issued almost hourly from the offices of the Lower Austrian provincial government and the directly affected district administrations.

Military Measures

The Military Command of Lower Austria organizes the deployment staff and coordinates all assistance measures. Five S-70 "Black Hawks", two Agusta Bell AB-212s, two AB-206 "Jet Rangers" and one Alouette III are deployed by the Air Force. All the bodies of troops stationed in Lower Austria take part in the safeguarding and clearance work along the Thaya in the towns of Raabs, Waidhofen, Liebnitzmühle and Eibenstein, along the Kamp in the city of Zwettl and along the March in Stillfried, Grub, Drösing, Angern, Sierndorf, Zwerndorf, Dürnkrut, Mannersdorf and Jedenspeigen.

In Raabs and Waidhofen/Thaya soldiers construct sandbag barriers with the local deployment forces through the night, in order to intercept the masses of water. Such barriers are also positioned in Zwettl. The dams resist the streaming mass of water of the Kamp, but are battered by the current. In order for them to continue to hold, the sandbags displaced from their original positions by the force of the water must be brought back to their original positions and porous areas sealed up. In the towns of Liebnitzmühle, Eibenstein and Waidhofen/Thaya alone, the military helpers construct many hundreds of meters of walls. With the help of over 3,000 sandbags the flooding of entire urban districts can be largely prevented.

Because of the continuing flooding, a dam of the March breaks in the early morning of April 3rd, 2006 in Jedenspeigen in the district of Gänserndorf, which leads to flooding of the town of Dürnkrut. Soldiers support the local deployed forces since the morning hours. "Black Hawks" discharge around 400 anti-tank tetrahedrons and far over 3,500 Big Bags in the dam holes. Further soldiers are constantly brought into the catastrophe zone. In addition, recovery tanks are deployed. With their help, the already begun protective barrier around the town is finished as fast as possible. Furthermore, the soldiers provision the population and all deployment forces with foodstuffs and drinking water. More than 3,500 meals per day are prepared and distributed for the civilian population and other support forces.

Basis for deployment: Call for support through the office of the Lower Austrian provincial government.
Type of deployment: Sec. 2 para. 1 sub-para. c DA.
Mission: Safeguarding and clearance work.
Area of operations: Along the rivers Kamp, March and Thaya.
Duration of deployment: March 30th – March 31st, 2006, April 3rd – April 19th, 2006.
Contingent strength: On peak days 750 men.
Organization: NBCDefPl/MilComm LA, 10th TkBn, 9th MechInfBn, 1st ATkBn, 3rd and 9th TkArtBn, 12th InfBn, 3rd ReconBn, 3rd EngBn, Allentsteig military training area. 62 wheeled vehicles, three military recovery tanks, four diggers and two boats.
Deployment director: Major General Prof. Mag. Johann Culik, military commander of Lower Austria.
Contribution: In around 80,000 man hours, among other things, far over 600,000 sandbags are filled, built into protective walls or used to secure dams; the Air Force transports 1,108 people and 4,620 t. of total material (including 450 anti-tank tetrahedrons and 4,000 Big Bags).

"Land underwater" – Dürnkrut in April 2006. Soldiers and civilian deployed forces work together to finish the previously begun protective wall around the town of Dürnkrut.

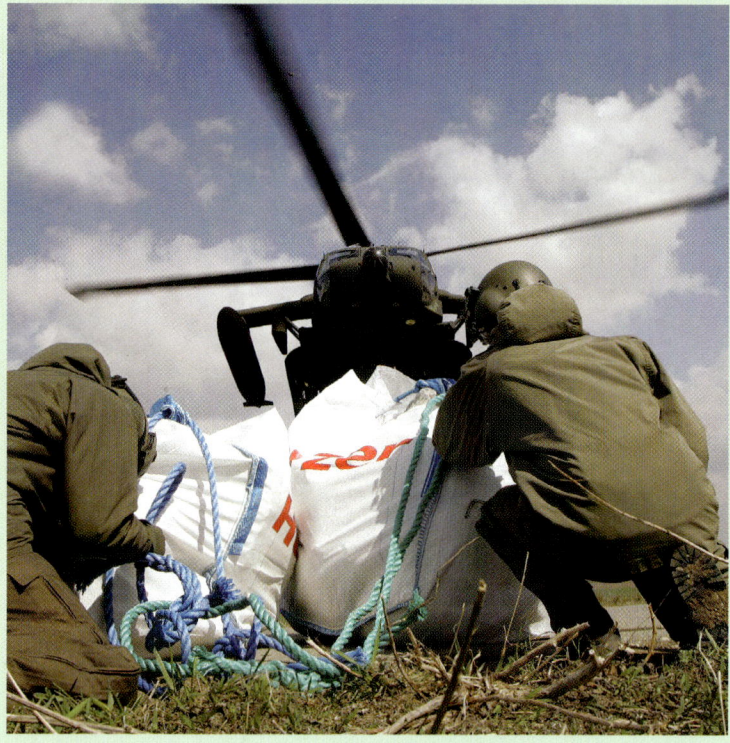

Between the anti-tank tetrahedrons "Big Bags" are then laid. These are large bags which are filled with sandbags and rocks (all pictures Dragan Tatic). The Big Bags are gathered by the "Black Hawks" and laid piece by piece in a row by the pilots. At the same time, engineer divers scan the old dams for crumbling places and reinforce weak areas with additional sandbags. Because the broken dam is no longer reachable by land, "Black Hawk" helicopters strengthen the 80 m long breach with armored blocks. In total, 2,000 tons of "Big Bags" and 300 anti-tank tetrahedrons are transported and laid at the breach near Dürnkrut (top right side).

After the "Black Hawk" helicopters have ended their flood deployment, the engineers attempt to close the broken dam near Mannersdorf from land. For this, a so-called "foldable street" is laid along the dam crest. On this artificial road the soldiers can advance with heavy transport vehicles up to around 80 meter broad breaches and close them. Before the foldable street can be laid, however, the crest of the soaked dam must be appropriately broadened through an embankment of crushed rocks. The street-laying system serves to assure the trafficability of soft, swampy, sandy or snow covered terrain. In this it is also perfectly suited for catastrophe deployments. In total, the engineers have eight folding street systems deployed. Each one possesses over 50 meters of road, which is immediately drivable after being laid. The engineers' night shifts paid off: The dam near Mannersdorf is closed. Thanks to the folding street the engineers can introduce around 1,300 cubic meters of fill material (which corresponds to some 90 truckloads) into the breach near Mannersdorf in one night.

Forest Fires

In July 2006, the lasting heat leads to forest fires in multiple provinces. The military air force support the deployed forces in multiple areas with helicopters and fixed-wing aircraft. The area around Ebensee in Upper Austria is affected by several fires at once. In the late afternoon of July 18th a forest fire ignites on Großsonnberg near Taxenbach, which quickly spreads. By the morning hours of the following day ca. 5 ha of forest are already in flames. 150 helpers, among them 43 soldiers of the Infantry School out of Saalfelden and four Alouette III helicopters out of Aigen im Ennstal, are in firefighting deployment. The mission of the mountain guides is to provide for the security of the firefighting forces in the difficult to reach, steep terrain at 1,700 m above sea level. After the deployment forces cannot bring the fire under control in the following night, additional soldiers are demanded the next day.

Because of the lasting heat and the lack of precipitation forest fires break out anew on July 26th, 2006. There is burning in Upper Austrian Ebensee again, this time between Offensee and Almsee. In Bleiberg and Imst two each of the Alouette IIIs, AB-212s and S-70 "Black Hawks" support local fire departments through firefighting missions from the air. In Imst an Alouette III from the staging post in Schwaz in the Tyrol is in constant deployment. After it also begins to burn in Brückl near Völkermarkt, additional fires break out on the weekend in Imst, Spittal/Drau, Arnoldstein, on Hochobir under the Eisenkappler Hütte and on Sattelnock in the Carinthian Gitsch Valley.

Many hundred thousands of liters of water are dropped over raging forest fires or smoldering pockets of embers by the pilots. In total the military craft are deployed at eight fire sites. It lasts more than a week in total until "fire out" can be given.

A "Black Hawk" collects water from the Offensee, in order to distribute it later over the source of the fire. The firefighting bucket contains 4,000 liters (top). An AB-212 transport helicopter also comes to help (b.l.). The "Alouette III" is especially suited for very precise deployments (b.r.).

Storm "Kyrill"

Preliminary Events

In the night before January 19th, 2007, hurricane "Kyrill", with gusts of up to 202 km/h, leaves a path of destruction through Europe and causes heavy damages in Austria as well.

Political Measures

Support from the military is petitioned on the part of the district administration authorities.

Military Measures

Especially in the provinces of Salzburg, Upper Austria, and the metropolitan area of Vienna, there are deployments of the armed forces.

Protection of the protected spring area of the Viennese Spring Water Administration: Through "Kyrill", a windfall amount of several tens of thousands of solid cubic meters of wood are destroyed in the protected spring forests of the city of Vienna under the purview of the Wildalpen Forestry Administration in Upper Styria. The situation in the area of Hirschboden is especially problematic. Here 8,800 solid cubic meters of wood is destroyed in an area of 20 hectares. According to an extensive geological and hydrological evaluation, since this area is extremely exposed, an environmentally sound removal of the unusable wood is urgently necessary to prevent an imminent massive proliferation of bark beetles. The responsible Municipal Bureau 49 – Forestry Office of the City of Vienna can remove a portion of the damage. However in situations without forestry roads, where as a result of the spring protection no roads are permitted to be constructed, the felled wood cannot be removed. However, to avoid a bark beetle proliferation – and subsequent damage to the healthy forest – these tree trunks must be stripped of bark. Because if the five millimeter long bark beetle should infest the healthy trees as well, landslides and ground erosion are to be feared. The ecosystem would no longer be in balance, the consequences in decades irreparable. If helped in a timely manner, the ecosystem can recover again.

> **Basis for deployment:** Call for support through the city of Vienna.
> **Type of deployment:** Supportive deployment according to Sec. 2 para. 1 sub-para. c DA.
> **Mission:** Stripping the trees of bark.
> **Duration of deployment:** May 14th, 2007 – July 13th, 2007.
> **Contingent strength:** 139.
> **Commander:** First Lieutenant Birgit Jedinger (2nd Engineer Battalion).
> **Contribution:** In 4,408 man days, 43,527 work hours are contributed.

The first challenge for the armed forces is the construction of a trailer village at 1,600 m above sea level. In total, 15 office, sleeping, and materials trailers are transported piece by piece to high clearings with a "Black Hawk" helicopter before the deployment forces can begin with the forest work. From the camp, the soldiers must cover 800 vertical meters daily to their workplace (above). Mayor Dr. Michael Häupl honors deserving soldiers for their great service to protect Viennese drinking water. In the picture below Warrant Officer I Ewald Himmelreich, commander of the Construction Engineers Platoon of Viennese Military Command, receives a commendation from the hands of the mayor.

Visit of Pope Benedict XVI

Preliminary Events

On the occasion of the 850th anniversary of the basilica of Mariazell, Pope Benedict XVI is invited by the federal government as well as from the Austrian bishop's conference.

Political Measures

As the worldly head of the Vatican State, the Pope is due a reception with all military honors.

Military Measures

For the armed forces two occurrences come together: the visit of a head of a state and a major event. The spectrum of duties to master is accordingly broad: They span from the Honor Guard Formation which advances to receive the Pope with all honors, to the interceptors and other planes that secure the airspace, to the paramedics and musicians. Furthermore, military emergency medical helicopters and NBC defence specialists are ready for emergencies. Further soldiers help with the construction of press centers and support the preparations in Vienna and Mariazell. Finally, the Musicians' Guard and their comrades from the military musicians of Carinthia and Lower Austria provide the correct tone.

Basis for deployment: CM resolution.
Type of deployment: Assistance as a result of the request of the organizing committee.
Mission: Fulfillment of all planned protocolary duties in line with a state visit, ensuring the protection of airspace and of aid contributions in emergencies, supportive contributions of all kinds.
Duration of deployment: September 7th, 2007 – September 9th, 2007.
Contingent strength: 1,350.
Deployment director: Major General Mag. Christian Ségur-Cabanac, Director of Joint Command and Control Staff.
Contribution: 15,860 man hours or alternatively 1,838 man days.

Schengen Expansion

Preliminary Events

On December 21st, 2007, the neighboring countries of Slovakia, Slovenia, Hungary and the Czech Republic, among others, join the Schengen Agreement. As a result of this, the EU outer borders are pushed away from Austria to the eastern borders of these countries. With this, Austria is no longer along the outer border of the EU.

Political Measures

In anticipation, the Council of Ministers already decides on all the measures connected to the Schengen expansion in November 2007. Included among these is a security police supportive deployment. This deployment follows seamlessly on the security police supportive deployment/border area surveillance (SuppD/BAS).[51] The purpose of the support is to support the security authorities in the prevention of illegal migration and the abatement of cross-border crimes. The concrete supportive missions for the troops are issued from the district administration authorities as security authorities.

Military Measures

The supportive deployment for border area surveillance operating up until now (see page 44 ff) is no longer necessary through the movement of the EU outer border, and is therefore ceased or rather leads into the supportive deployment after the Schengen expansion (SuppD/SchE). Only around 1,500 soldiers are still deployed by the armed forces. Around half of the soldiers are directly in the area of operations. The other half are held in readiness as reserves in their home garrisons. In order to strengthen the population's sense of security, show a presence in the area of operations and appropriately support the executive during hazard control, sensitive properties and areas are monitored with reconnaissance and patrols, abnormalities noted and reported directly by means of mobile telephone to the executive for intervention. Furthermore, suspicious preparations for committing property crimes are observed, and according to relevant criminal investigation requirements, reconnaissance is carried out. 156 troops of two men each are deployed daily for a duration of 12 hours. In addition, the surveillance of the "green border" as well as the deployment of specially equipped military helicopters is planned in case of a time and locality limited reestablishment of border controls according to Art. 23 of the Schengen Border Codex, such as the occasion of the European football championship 2008.

The soldiers – in contrast to the previous supportive deployment/border area surveillance – are entitled to no executive powers. The powers of military organs in line with military self-defence and its forced employment are nevertheless undisturbed.

> **Basis for deployment:** CM of November 7th, 2007.
> **Type of deployment:** Supportive deployment according to Sec. 2 para. 1 sub-para. b DA.
> **Mission:** Support of the security authorities; surveillance of the green border.
> **Appellation:** Supportive deployment after Schengen expansion (SuppD/SchE).
> **Area of operations:** The political districts of Gänserndorf and Bruck/Leitha, Neusiedl, Eisenstadt/Umgebung, Mattersburg, Oberpullendorf, Oberwart, Güssing, Jennersdorf and the cities of Eisenstadt and Rust.
> **Duration of deployment:** December 22nd, 2007 – to date.
> **Contingent strength:** Up to 1,500[52].
> **Total strength:** 10,106 (as of March 2010).
> **Organization:** Territorial headquarters company, 1st – 4th Infantry Companies.
> **Deployment director:** Brigadier General Mag. Johann Luif, military commander of Burgenland.
> **Contribution:** 2,400 security police activities, 1,800 alerts of the police, over 330 demands through the police, 63 life-saving measures, first aid at 47 accidents, 26 fire reports (as of May 2010).

Changing of the Guard in the Sky above Burgenland

During the border area surveillance, a multipurpose helicopter "Alouette III" from Aigen im Ennstal is deployed among others. The area of operations of the helicopter reaches from Hainburg in the north to Spielfeld in the south. Since February 25th, 1998 the new outpost for military helicopters is in Punitz in south Burgenland. The "Alouette III" is specially equipped for this deployment. It possesses a heat imaging camera and a searchlight – equipment, that also makes surveillance flights at night possible. After 18 years of border area surveillance the "Alouette" returns to its home staging post on September 5th, 2008. In total 15,000 flight hours on the border were flown with the helicopter, 4,454 of them at night. The "Alouette" is relieved by an OH-58 "Kiowa" out of Langenlebarn, which takes over the surveillance flights for safeguarding the border area until further notice.

---

51 See page 44 ff.
52 Around half of these are directly in the area of operations. The other half are held ready in their home garrisons and are first deployed at an escalation of the situation on the border.

European Football Championship "EURO 2008"

Preliminary Events

After an official bid, Austria is awarded the hosting of the European Football Championship 2008. This demands that the host nation is in the position to provide safety against attacks of all kinds on land, on water, or in the air.

The "EURO 2008" represents a major event in a class by itself. 51,000 people at the games in Ernst-Happel Stadium and thousands of visitors in the fan zone and the many "public viewing" squares represent a challenge for paramedics, police, the fire department, and all others involved. In order to be as prepared as possible, all organizations to be deployed begin thinking about possible scenarios many months before the event and work out the necessary deployment plans.

Political Measures

To secure the European championship, restricted airspace zones are decreed around the event locations.

Military Measures

The military prepares itself for all imaginable incidents that could not be mastered by any other organization. An administrative agreement is made with the Ministry for the Interior with regard to the use of the military infrastructure by the executive. The support of the provincial governments is secured through direct discussions with the respective military commands.

> **Type of deployment:** Assistance.
> **Mission:** Airspace surveillance, readiness of paramedical personnel and NBC defence specialists, supportive contributions for the executive, protocol duties.
> **Duration of deployment:** June 7th, 2008 – June 29th, 2008.
> **Contingent strength:** Up to 3,000 (per game day, variable by event location)
> **Composition:** Two NBC companies, patient decontamination element, anti-aircraft division, two stretcher carrier companies.
> **Deployment director:** Lieutenant General Mag. Christian Ségur-Cabanac, Director General Operations.
> **Commanders:** Military commanders of Carinthia, Styria, the Tyrol and Vienna.
> **Contribution:** 31,850 man days, 680 flight hours.

Safeguarding the Airspace

To secure the airspace over the stadiums and for transport duties a total of 40 helicopters and 25 fixed-wing aircraft are deployed, including Eurofighters for the first time. During this, the Air Force completes 680 flight hours. In total, eight violations of the restricted airspace zone are observed. The aircraft illegally flying in are identified and escorted out of restricted airspace. Furthermore, during the final game a hot air balloon is forced to land in the area of the Vienna Woods.

Paramedic Supply

In the provinces the military holds 200 stretcher carriers and in readiness according to game location and game day, as well as 400 stretcher carriers on game days and 100 stretcher carriers on non-game days in Vienna. In addition emergency medical vehicles, patient transport buses and helicopters are available. The military hospitals and emergency medical facilities are brought up to full admission capacity.

Measures of the NBC Troops

Their main duty is to be prepared for contact with nuclear, biological, or chemical weapons (NBC). The NBC defence company of the 4th Tank Headquarters Battalion is in the Maria Theresia Barracks, where it is always in a position to move out for decontamination with its special vehicles. Among them is the all-protected transport vehicle (APTV) "Dingo 2" with a new special equipage for such cases. This vehicle is a mobile laboratory, which can evaluate environmental poisons with an external sensor and at the same time offers four-member crew the highest level of safety. A further NBC defence company is in Baden near Vienna. In total, three decontamination units are prepared, which are in the position to detoxify 135 people per hour. Furthermore, ten detection troops are ready as the guards for purported decontamination. In the case of a deployment, these detection troops can ascertain that only decontaminated persons enter the hospitals and protect the patients there from carryover of the environmental toxins. These measures are coordinated with the city of Vienna and already trained in the general hospital before the EURO 2008.

At the petition of the Ministry of the Interior, a chemical laboratory for identification is held ready for deployment through the Office for Armament and Army Engineering.

An alerted wing of two intercepters „Eurofighter Typhoon" over the Viennese Hanappi Stadium (top). The Polish president Lech Kaczynski comes to the EC Poland – Austria game on June 12th, 2008. After a visit to Federal President Dr. Heinz Fischer the state guest is flown into the Prater stadium with an S-70 "Black Hawk" (right). An military emergency medical bus can transport up to 20 patients (b.l.). Paramedics escort the stretcher carriers to the military emergency medical helicopter. Everyone pitches in (b.r.).

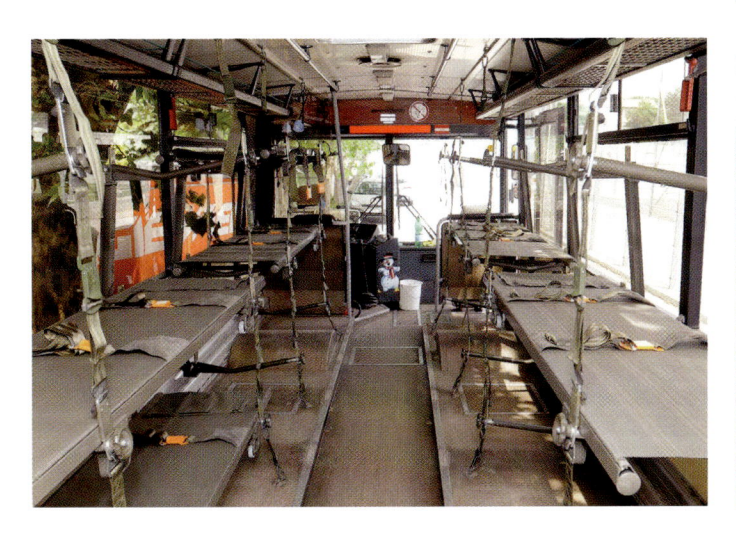

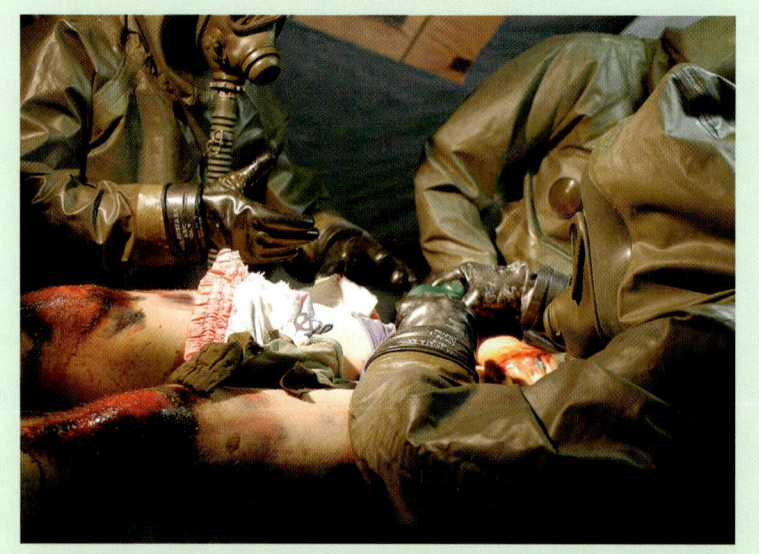

The AC Dingo – an all-terrain armored laboratory (t.l.). The decontamination platoon tests their equipments. In the picture is an NBC decontamination vehicle on the chassis of an all-terrain heavy truck from ÖAF (t.r.). Emergency medical decontamination has a special use: This process is employed by the Emergency Medical Institute of Salzburg to decontaminate injured persons. It was perfected by military employees over ten years of development and first deployed for the EURO 08. Armies all across Europe orient themselves according to this system. The protective suit makes everyday movements difficult. Nevertheless the optimal treatment and care of the patients can be ensured, since the equipment and medicines are adapted to these special conditions (m.l.). The armed forces also care for all deployed forces (b.l.). The deployed recruits can follow the games on a projector in their free time (b.r.).

Heavy Storms

Through the long-lasting rains beginning on June 23rd, 2009, the flood threat rises from hour to hour in broad sections of Lower Austria as well as southern Burgenland and southern Styria. The situation in the alpine foothills and Wachau is especially precarious.

The armed forces immediately prepare for a possible flood deployment. On June 24th a supportive platoon from the NBC Defence School out of Korneuburg is set on the march to Gresten (district of Scheibbs). The soldiers are equipped with special vehicles and support the locally deployed fire departments with pumping and safeguarding activities. Soldiers of the NBC defence company out of Mautern support the deployed civilian forces in Weißenkirchen (district of Krems). In the community of Zelking (district of Melk), engineers from Melk construct flood protection, and in St. Valentin (district of Amstetten) soldiers from the 12th Infantry Battalion out of Amstetten are busied with protection work in the area of the Danube. In addition, survey troops are on the move in the Wachau and the area of Ybbsitz (district of Scheibbs). In these areas helicopters out of Langenlebarn are also deployed for survey flights. They should provide the leadership staffs and deployment administrations with a current picture of the situation from the air. In Hafnerbach near St. Pölten a dam breaks. Sandbags are dumped from the air with "Black Hawk" helicopters to close the dam again.

As a result of the weather situation the Lower Austrian Military Command raises the number of available deployment forces to around 3,000 for coverage of further calls for support on the part of the authorities. In Upper Austria, three support companies of the 4th Mechanized Infantry Brigade as well as one support company each from Air Support Command and the Upper Austrian Military Command are held ready with six hour deployment readiness. In Salzburg soldiers out of Saalfelden, Tamsweg and St. Johann are gathered together. In Styria a support company of the 1st Logistics Regiment and a company consisting of forces from the 17th and 18th Infantry Battalions as well as the 7th Reconnaissance and Artillery Battalion prepare themselves.

A fixed-wing aircraft of the type PC-6 is sent from Zeltweg to carry out photographic documentation in the area of the Danube. Through this, the authorities should be given the basic information for further planning of the deployment forces. After the heavy storms, a dam breaks on July 4th in Mold (district Horn). An S-70 "Black Hawk" helicopter out of Langenlebarn flies "Big Bags" in, in order to close the breach and shore up the dam together with the deployed forces. In this way a dam near Hafnerbach is also shored up again.

Heavy rainfall leads to new flooding on July 6th, 2009 in the district of Krems. Near Weißenkirchen the B3 is blocked due to mudslides. Army engineers are occupied with clearing mud and rubble from the Danube shore road there. In Senftenberg NBC defence troops out of Mautern support the local fire departments with pumping work and remove prior log jams at bridges along the Krems valley. In the meantime the clearance work in Spitz and Mühldorf goes on unabated. The Lower Austrian Military Command additionally transports 20 dehumidifying devices from Raiffeisen-Holding NÖ-Wien into the community of Mühldorf, in order to distribute them to the most heavily affected households.

In Trandorf the masses of water batter a bridge such that it is no longer trafficable. An appropriate temporary bridge is constructed by engineer forces out of Melk in the direct vicinity of the damaged bridge. Up until July 9th, 137,000 work hours are contributed by the soldiers. Per day more than 700 soldiers on average help in the affected communities, at peak times even up to 1,200. They are supported in this by seven helicopters, who ferry more than 200 persons and transport 60 tons of freight in 120 flight hours. In the districts of Feldbach and Fürstenfeld soldiers, along with fire departments and other deployed organizations, stand in constant deployment. The devastating rainfall has made around 500 slopes begin to slide, flooded swathes of land and destroyed numerous traffic routes. On July 9th engineers construct a "Bailey" bridge over the Pickelbach in Studenzen on the Raab, since the original bridge was destroyed by floodwaters.

Because of the continuing storms, the support forces of the Austrian military extend their deployment into the middle of August. In the catastrophe zones of Styria almost 150 soldiers from divisions out of Carinthia and Styria are still helping the affected population. In the districts of Feldbach, Deutschlandsberg and Graz-Umgebung 85 damage areas are to be remedied. Sliding cliffs in Krennach (district of Feldbach), Greith and Tobisegg (district of Deutschlandsberg) are stabilized by soldiers with the help of various techniques. A destroyed bridge in Stiwoll (district of Graz-Umgebung) is newly constructed by the engineers. A further bridge in Graz-Andritz is also reconstructed. In Gröbming the experts of the Styrian Military Command judge the work conditions as especially difficult because of the terrain situation.

Deployment of the Military Geographic Entity

The experts of the Institute for Military Geography examine the reported damage areas and note their position with the help of GPS devices. Furthermore, they photograph the battered hillsides and document the gradient, exposure and other characteristics. In total the investigation troop evaluates 494 landslides. In the evenings in the control room the gathered geodata is evaluated and prepared in order to keep the current situation in the most up-to-date condition for the civilian deployment director, district administrator Dr. Plauder. Subsequently the data goes to the province of Styria for documentation in the landslide register there. With this, the military geo-experts contribute their part in line with the flood assistance and deliver important basic information for future area planning in landslide-prone zones with their quick documentation.

In Weissenkirchen soldiers pump out water (Andy Wenzel). Anti-tank tetrahedrons stop the slippage of slopes (Dragan Tatic).

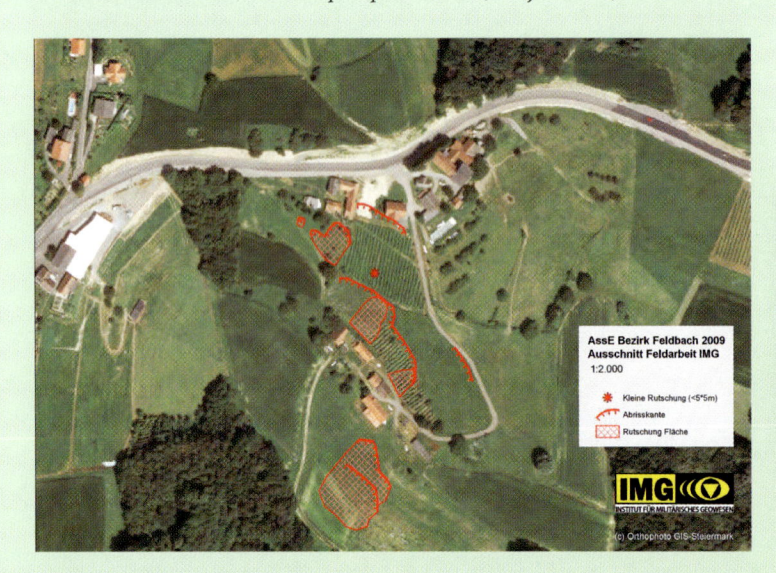

On this picture from the air (m.l.) discovered slope slippage is noted. In Graz-Andritz engineers construct an almost 28 meters long bridge (m.r.) (Gerald Ehling). A "Black Hawk" flies in so-called "Big Bags" to close a dam (b.l.). Heavy equipment – like this digger – is deployed to remove the damages (Mathias Kolle).

Research Project

The Styria research society Joanneum Research carries out an experiment to investigate the satellite reception quality in broadband signals, high frequencies, and mobile reception for the European Space Agency (ESA). In the center of the experiment is a C-130 "Hercules" transport place from the Austrian armed forces, which represents the satellite: On the underside of the "Hercules", a test transmitter is attached and the technical equipment for the experiment is in the loading area. The director of the experiment, Dr. Michael Schönhuber, decides on the military on the basis of their flight ability and good experiences with military pilots. In total six flights are available in July 2009 for the experiment.

The "Hercules" out of Hörsching is brought into the precisely calculated flightpath for the experiment, while a receiver on the ground measures the data. The beneficiaries of the experiment are internet and cellular network users who want to use mobile phones and laptops in the most remote areas of the world. From there in the future they will be provided with signals from space via satellite.

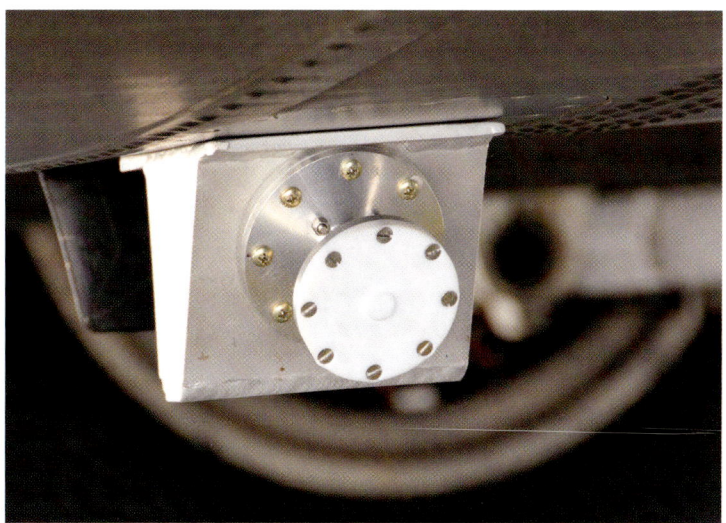

The equipment on board the aircraft (t.l.) and the transmitter on the underside of the "Hercules" (Gerhard Simader). The armed forces possess three transport airplanes of the type C-130 "Hercules". At a traveling speed of 540 km/h it has a range of around 3,000 km (ca. 18 t payload) and 6,000 km (ca. 10 t payload). The aircraft can transport 16,369 kg or 92 passengers or 64 parachute troopers or 74 stretchers with two paramedics. Measurements: length: 29.79 m, height: 11.66 m, wingspan: 40.41 m.

Longest Bailey Temporary Bridge

Preliminary Events

Over decades, increased numbers of Bailey and D bridge systems are bought through individual provincial governments and left to the military for training and deployment purposes. As a "trade-off", the engineers must build temporary replacement bridges for free during provincial bridge renovations. With this training goals can be reached under deployment requirements.

Political Measures

Through the office of the Styrian provincial government, the construction of a replacement bridge is ordered.

Military Measures

In Styrian Bruck an der Mur on November 23rd, 2009, army engineers build an over 80 meter long temporary bridge together with the bridge maintenance crew of the province of Styria. With this span, it becomes the longest Bailey bridge ever built in the Second Austrian Republic. After the planned three week construction time a temporary bridge with two walls and two levels on two bridge trusses with a roadway width of 3.8 meters and a maximum bearing load of 60 tons is completed. The structure serves for three years as a replacement for a blocked bridge which is generally renovated. The Bailey bridge, named after the British army employee Donald Coleman Bailey, is a transportable emergency or temporary bridge of preassembled lattice supports. The construction is consistent with a modular construction system, all individual components are connected with bolts.

Deployments Abroad

Opérations des Nations Unies au Congo (ONUC)

United Nations Operation in the Congo

Preliminary Events

In the 19th century the Belgian King Leopold II attempts to bring African countries, such as the Congo, under his control. Without having ever visited this country, which is 76 times larger than his own kingdom, he makes the "Free Congo State" into his private colony. In order to obtain ivory and wild rubber for the king in the expected amount, the Belgian colonial regime establishes a system of terror and forced labor. In 1908 the Congo reform movement succeeds in forcing King Leopold II to a formal renunciation of "his" colony, but the perfidious forced labor system continues as the Belgian state follows in the footsteps of the king. During Leopold's rule and in the time afterwards no less than 10 million people lose their lives, often in the most brutal ways. In this way, the Congo becomes one of the largest places of destruction in the modern era.

Not until February 21st, 1960, does the Belgian government in Brussels come to the decision to release the colony of the Belgian Congo into independence on June 30th, 1960. In May 1960 the first parliamentary elections take place in the Congo, Joseph Kasavubu is elected president. On June 29th, 1960, one day before independence, Belgium and the Congo sign a friendship treaty, which among other things allows Belgium to retain two military bases in Kamina and Kitona. But already on the day after independence heavy civil war-like unrest develops, which spreads quickly in view of the traditional differences between the peoples of the giant state. After a mutiny, black soldiers arrest their white officers, in order to protest against the discrimination against black soldiers in promotions. On July 6th Lumumba dismisses all white officers and noncommissioned officers, two days later all remaining members of the Congolese National Army (Armee Nationale Congolaise) are promoted a rank, subsequently low ranking and noncommissioned officers are called unprepared to high officer placements. Over night it devolves from one of the best trained armies to a disintegrating heap; with the army the state also falls. On July 10th, 1960 Belgian paratroopers occupy the most important airports. Further Belgian soldiers are flown in to protect the remaining Belgians in the Congo. On July 12th, as a result of the Belgian intervention, the Congolese government petitions UNO for military assistance against the outer threat to independence and the secession movements of individual provinces that have begun in the meantime; on July 14th the diplomatic ties to Belgium are broken. By the end of August the Belgian troops leave the country, since in the meantime further UN soldiers have arrived – the operation spreads ever further and even reaches a height of almost 20,000 men in the middle of 1961. At the end of September a further domestic political crisis occurs: President Kasavubu dismisses Prime Minister Lumumba. Lumumba's followers form a government in exile in the province Orientale in October 1960, which is promptly recognized by the Soviet Union and other "socialist nations". The Soviet Union offers Lumumba 29 Ilyushin Il-14 "Crate" transport planes, 100 heavy trucks and 200 technicians as support for the reconquest of the province of South Kasai. Lumumba is arrested on November 28th, 1960 and murdered on January 17th, 1961. Afterwards great unrest develops throughout the nation. The secession efforts of Katanga continue. The Katanga Gendarmery is led by white officers and is tightly organized. The advance of the Katangese can be stopped by UNO again and again. In October 1961 Congolese troops invade Katanga, but avoid a direct confrontation with the Katanga Gendarmery. Instead they carry out a massacre against the civilian population. On December 21st, 1961, the Katangese Premier Tschombé indeed recognizes the Congolese central government, but this brings no final solution, just as little as the plan for national reconciliation from the new UN Secretary General U Thant (his predecessor Dag Hammerskjöld lost his life in a plane crash in 1961 during his intervention efforts in the Congo). Not until the UN deployment can the conflict be ended.

In summary, it must be determined that the background for the domestic conflicts lies in the political and ethnic differences of the second largest state in Africa with its 14 million inhabitants, 70 ethnic groups, and 400 languages or dialects, and in the fact that the Congo is released unprepared into independence after 75 years of colonial rule.

International Reaction

On July 14th, 1960, the UN Security Council (SC) enacts Resolution 143 (1960). ONUC is set up and the withdrawal of Belgian troops is demanded. In mid-July the first blue helmets arrive. The mission at first is only to ensure the disengagement of Belgian troops and to support the Congolese government during the reestablishment and preservation of peace and order. Later the mission is expanded to include the maintenance of the Congo's territorial integrity and the prevention of a civil war. With this the mission goes far further than previous UN deployments. The Secretary General would like above all to use the UN measures to prevent the Congo from becoming a secondary theater of war for the "Cold War". Again and again the UNO troops succeed in temporarily providing peace and order. In order to prevent the secession attempts of the Katangese, however, fighter jets from Sweden, India and Ethiopia must also be deployed by UNO through the years after 1961. Not until

1963 is Katanga's secession ended; during the battles and conflicts 234 UNO soldiers lose their lives. The UNO operation is slowly reduced in 1963/64 and finally ends on June 30th, 1964, although the situation is the Congo is still far from peaceful.

Basis for deployment:	SC Resolution 143 (1960) of June 14th, 1060[53];
	SC Resolution 145 (1960) of July 22nd, 1960;
	SC Resolution 146 (1960) of August 9th, 1960;
	SC Resolution 161 (1961) of February 21st, 1961 and
	SC Resolution 169 (1961) of November 24th, 1961.
Mission:	Ensuring the withdrawal of Belgian troops; support of the government; protection of the integrity and political independence of the state; prevention of a civil war.
Duration of deployment:	July 14th, 1960 – June 30th, 1964.
Participating nations:	Argentina, Austria, Brazil, Burma (today Myanmar), Canada, Ceylon (today Sri Lanka), Congo-Leopoldville (a battalion of the Congolese National Army), Denmark, Ethiopia, Ghana, Guinea, India, Indonesia, Iran, Ireland, Italy, Liberia, Malaya (today Malaysia), Mali Federation (today Mali and Senegal), Morocco, the Netherlands, Nigeria, Norway, Pakistan, the Phillipines, Sweden, Sierra Leone, Sudan, Tunisia, United Arab Republic, Yugoslavia.
High point:	19,828 soldiers and 1,300 civilians (as of July 1961); finally 5,871 workers.
Headquarters:	Leopoldville (today Kinshasa).

Austrian Involvement

Political Measures[54]

On August 6th, 1960, the Secretary General of the United Nations petitions Austria to dispatch a veterinary team and a field post office. This request is nevertheless not acceded to, since month-long negotiations between the Foreign, Defence and Transportation Ministries lead to no conclusion. After a renewed request is placed shortly thereafter on August 26th, this time for the dispatch of a 400 bed field hospital, the Austrian federal government decides on September 20th to respond to this request. But here again it is debated too long, so that in the meantime an Indian and an Italian hospital are sent. UNO therefore reduces their request to 100 beds. On September 20th, 1960 the Council of Ministers orders the dispatch of a paramedic contingent.

The Austrian participation in the UN operation in the Congo goes back to an initiative of Foreign Minister Dr. Bruno Kreisky and is to be seen against the backdrop of the South Tyrolean question. Italy denies Austria any right to mix itself up in this "purely Italian issue". In fall 1960, therefore, Austria brings this problem before the UN General Assembly, in order to gather international backing for its South Tyrol policy (this, it should be mentioned at the start, is successful and is the starting point for the "South Tyrol Package", concluded in 1969). So participation in the UN operation, seen in this light, seems like a fitting method to encourage sympathy for Austria's position against Italy.

From October 12th to 22nd, a delegation of representatives of the Ministries of Foreign Affairs, Defence, and Social Administration stay in the Congo to survey the requirements for the deployment. On October 13th, 1960 the federal government releases a call for volunteers. On November 20th, 1960 the first foreign deployment of the Austrian armed forces begins.

As a result of the outstanding work of the Austrians, the Secretary General twice requests the extension of their posting. The federal government therefore decides on the continuation of the Congo deployment. A renewed petition from UNO on May 1st, 1962 is equally positively answered on May 15th. Only the request for the dispatch of 5 additional doctors cannot be complied with, since it has already been most difficult to summon up the necessary doctors for the 4th continent. The UNO request which arrives on January 8th, 1963 for a renewed extension of the deployment of the Austrian contingent is responded to on January 22nd. In April 1963 a further extension becomes apparent (6th contingent), but no longer carries any weight.

Military Measures

The first contingent is assembled under the title **"UN Medical Contingent of the Republic of Austria"**. The contingent, like all those after it, consists only of volunteers. Since the federal constitution does not allow for a deployment of the armed forces outside the borders of the republic, the military volunteers are placed on leave and subsequently reemployed under special contracts. Only some few doctors (among them experienced tropical specialists) and two medical technical assistants (at the same time this is the first deployment for women in a military division, in which these also have an officer's rank) do not belong to the military. The adjustment to both women brings problems. While a kind of uniform

---

53 Resolution of the United Nations Security Council, subsequently identified as SC resolution.
54 Erwin A. Schmidl: "Blue Helmets, Red Cross: The Austrian UN Paramedic Contingent in the Congo 1960 to 1963", Innsbruck Studies in Recent History, Volume 13, Österreichischer Studienverlag, Innsbruck 1995. This book is the most detailed single scholarly study to date on a deployment of the Austrian armed forces abroad.

is prepared for them out of the state resources, they each receive 1,300 öS in cash for the purchase of underwear (the submission of receipts is generously waived). Finally 124 volunteers are assigned. The planning envisions a two-part division of the contingent: 69 people for Stanleyville (today Kisangani) in the province of Orientale and 55 for Bukavu in the province of Kivu. At the beginning of December the "1st UN Medical Contingent of the Republic of Austria" is ready to move out.

On November 20th the advance command leaves. While the departure of the field hospital intended for Stanleyville is delayed again and again due to the unrest in the province of Orientale, the main contingent leaves Vienna-Schwechat on December 11th in five C-130 Hercules transport planes of the American Air Force. Despite a few small incidents (on one C-130 two engines fail, on another the stern ramp does not close, so that it is bitterly cold on board) the flight shapes up to be uncomfortable indeed, but still memorable. On the evening of the 14th and into the 15th of December, the **1st Contingent** arrives in **Bukavu**. As a result of the general hostility towards whites (earlier incidents already took place with Irish UNO soldiers) the arrival of the Austrians proceeds in a tense atmosphere. Shortly after arrival, while setting up in a bungalow compound, the first disagreements with local authorities already take place. These order the Austrians to immediately leave Bukavu again. Before new instructions arrive from UNO, the contingent is surrounded by the Congolese Gendarmery, who suspect the Austrians of being disguised Belgian paratroopers. The Austrians are in fact armed (everyone possesses a Walther PPK pistol on their person and a Thompson machine gun disassembled in their duffel bag), but quickly realize that any fired shot would cause a bloodbath. The contingent commander, Colonel Ferdinand Foltin of the General Staff, therefore orders them not to offer any resistance. Finally they are taken prisoner and transferred to the local jail (picture below left). Subsequently the commander of the Nigerian UNO Battalion (5th Battalion, Queen's Own Nigerian Regiment), Lieutenant Colonel J.T.U. Aguiyi-Ironsi, and the civilian UN chief, Robin T. Miller from New Zealand, negotiate with the Congolese. Although the provincial president, Jean Miruhu, intermittently promises the release of the Austrians, this is prevented by Congolese soldiers; finally the Austrian contingent is freed on December 16th by Nigerian troops after six hours of fighting. It must be added, however, that the Nigerian headquarters company consists almost only of "system upholders" (cooks, clerks, military musicians) and possesses only two Bren machine guns as armament. Therefore a further company from Goma is brought as reinforcement. The leadership of the operation is incumbent upon the acting battalion commander, the British Major Roderick Galloway. The Nigerian attack is faced with fierce resistance at first, which is why the operation does not quite go according to plan. Finally, thanks to a resolute leadership, the Nigerians carried the victory over the somewhat well-trained but badly led Congolese. The blue helmets suffer one death and three badly wounded; the losses of the Congolese add up to at least eleven dead and some fifty wounded. For this deployment, Lieutenant Colonel Ironsi and Major Galloway receive the Decoration of Merit in Silver of the Republic of Austria, the fallen Nigerian soldier Madugu Zonkwa posthumously receives the Silver Medal for Services to the Republic of Austria.

The contingent is then moved on December 17th through Burundi – Rwanda to Leopoldville, where they can recover from their exertions for the time being (after they are also still being shot at during the flight, one plane receives two hits.) Before, however, the entire equipage, including the private possessions of the soldiers, is confiscated by the Congolese. The Congolese take the water filtering equipment for a new type of cannon and sink it in Lake Kivu; pieces of underwear later surface in the native market, where one could have bought his socks and shirts back at high prices. Defence Minister Ferdinand Graf initially wants to call the UN

In this prison the Austrians are confined after their arrest as supposed Belgians (photo: Major [ret.] Geoffrey Norton). Happy faces after their release: Left "Lieutenant" Pieber (photo via Vukovits).

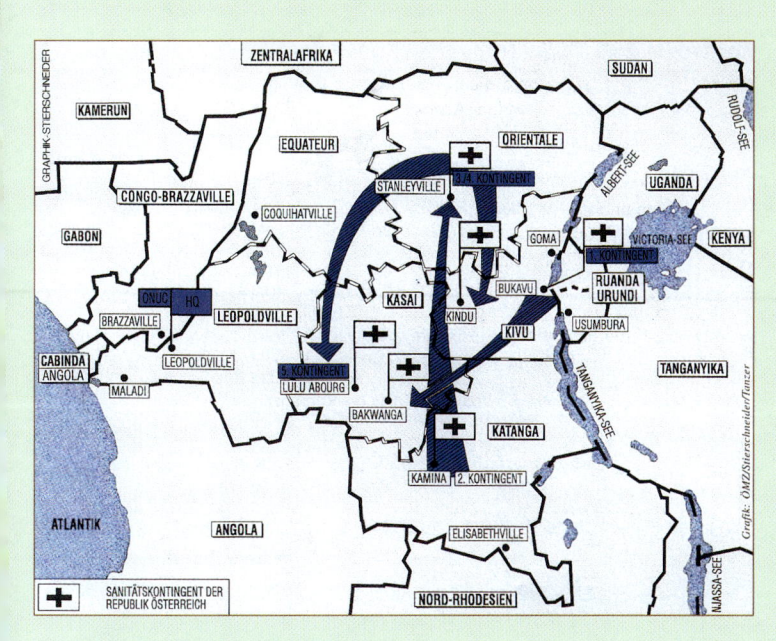

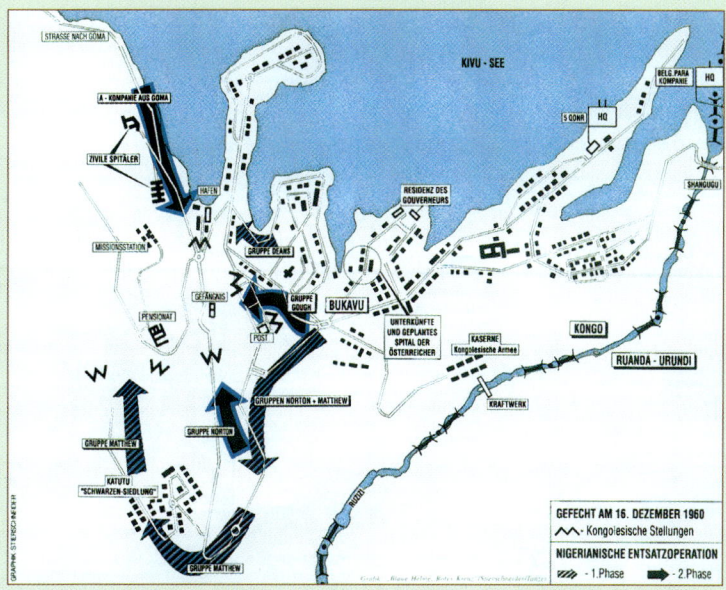

Outline map of the deployment of the Austrian medical contingent in the Congo 1960 to 1963 (t.l.). The battle at Bukavu on December 16th, 1960 (t.r.). Identification card for ONUC members (m.r.). Members of the Austrian UN contingent in the uniform specially created for the ONUC deployment (b.l.). Medicine dispersal from a medical noncommissioned officer (b.r.).

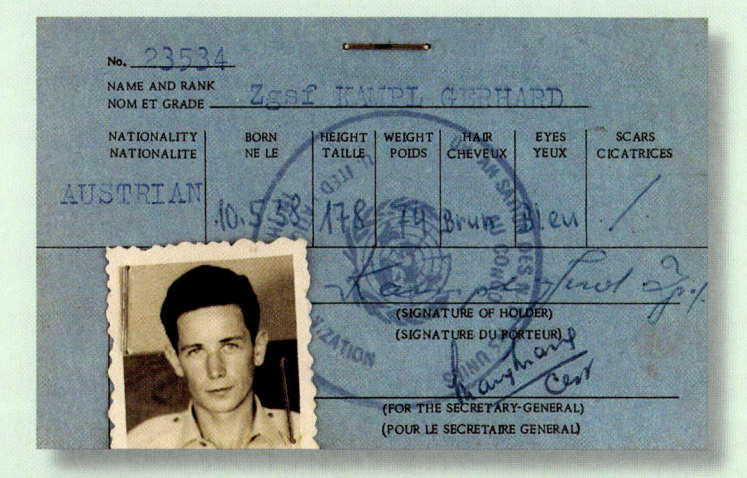

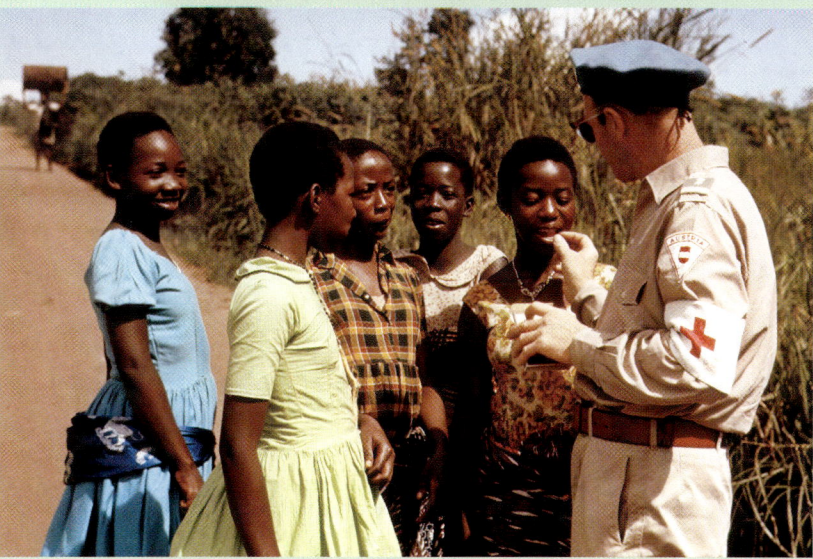

113

contingent back home, but Foreign Minister Bruno Kreisky manages to bring him around with the mention of the honor of the armed forces (!). So, with a rallying cry of *"Hold on, this is for South Tyrol"* from Vienna, the Austrians are sent on January 17th, 1961 into their new area of operations in Bakwanga, the capital of the diamond republic and residence of the "God King" Albert Kalonji, where they are deployed to care for refugees until May. Besides refugee care, a tent hospital in the area of the Disele hospital and a mobile Red Cross station are operated. A branch office develops in Miabi. Between 700 and 800 patients are cared for daily in all three establishments.

Since the situation continues to worsen (the Congolese show an ever greater dislike of the UNO) and since the extent of the cases of death and illness have significantly sunk thanks to the work of the medical contingent, UNO decides to remove the Austrian contingent together with the Ghanians and Pakistanis. After the transfer of the hospital to the local authorities, therefore, the Austrians prepare themselves for their evacuation. The removal is planned with two Douglas DC-4s. In the end the movement of the medical contingent takes place first with land march through Luluabourg into the Kasai region with a Pakistani transport column, from whence it continues to Leopoldville on May 15th with two UN planes. There the ceremonial award of the UN Service Medal "In the Service of Peace" on a striped Congo ribbon takes place (incidentally, 41.50 schillings' worth of revenue stamps must be paid for the personal right to bear it in Austria). Finally, after an ample recovery phase, the return trip to Austria can be entered upon on May 26th. How successfully the Austrian contingent worked can be inferred from the fact that the South Kasai government asked Austrian Colonel Dr. Pervolseko during the farewell to be sure to send the next contingent back to Bakwanga.

On July 14th, 1961, the **2nd contingent** is set on the march in the direction of the Congo and deployed in **Kamina** (Kaminaville), a large (previously Belgian) air force base, in a UN hospital together with doctors from Denmark and Sweden. After battles around Kamina, it is then finally possible in September 1961 to shift the contingent to **Stanleyville** (today Kisangani), where it takes up its work on October 1st. There the Austrians, besides assuming leadership of the field hospital, also assume parts of a civilian hospital transferred to them, the dispensary, and the hygiene department of the province of Orientale, as well as the medical care of the Ethiopian contingent. Around 500 patients are treated in the health care center monthly. Furthermore, around 200 captive Gizenga Gendarmes are treated, some of whom were faced with terrible mistreatment. From October 18th, 1961, a further branch office is staffed on the left bank of the Congo river, the "Rive Gauche". But already by December 16th, this work is forbidden by the Congolese authorities because of supposed "spy activities to benefit the West". At the same time Colonel med. Dr. Fill, the commander of the contingent, becomes the UN medical chief for the province of Orientale.

At the turn of the year, the next replacement takes place. This **3rd contingent**, besides the previously detailed duties, must also come to terms with enormous work during the serious flooding catastrophe of the Congo river. So the supplies of drinking water and electricity are also secured. From February 4th, 1962 a branch office in Kindu is also operated, in which the military medical treatment of the local UNO troops is carried out. The worst deployment also falls to them in this time: On February 23rd, 1962 the corpses of 13 Italian pilots, who were previously tortured in the most cruel manner by revolting Congolese of the 6th (Watsa) Battalion and afterward murdered, must be exhumed under the oversight of the Austrian military doctor. The contingent also takes over the intensive treatment of the whites who remain behind in the eastern province.

The **4th contingent** reports for duty on July 21st, 1962. On October 11th, 1962 the branch office in Kindu receives the status of a separate UN hospital; this is also to be attributed to the outstanding work of the Austrians. Besides the medical care all general medical duties of the health service are performed. These stretch from latrine construction to organization of garbage disposal, the set-up of the cold storage house to inspections of the bakeries and foodstuffs. But it is also imperative to instruct the patients and their family members in the most basic questions of hygiene: so it must be considered that no Congolese goes to the hospital alone. He brings his family with him, who spend the night under his bed, the meals are consumed together. In December 1962 the activities of the branch office in Kindu end, while the main hospital in Stanleyville remains until the beginning of 1963. Simultaneously with the transfer of the 4th to the 5th contingent, the Austrian area of operations is shifted anew, this time to **Luluaburg** in the province of Kasai. Here the Austrians are again entrusted with the leadership of the UN hospital and the treatment of the civilian population. In addition to this there is rat extermination, since the number of rats represents a serious problem.

During this, action must also be taken against the Africans, who trap the rats and sell them at the market as delicacies (from Major Karl Wimmer's report, who was responsible for the general health service). Because of the closing of the hospital in Kindu the status of 5th contingent is reduced to 29 men (in reality, their status fluctuates between 26 and 36). The inadequate accommodations, in which hygienic conditions are also disastrous, and the low contingent strength demand the Austrians' all. Since the UNO drastically reduces their troops in the Congo in summer 1963, the deployment of the Austrians also ends in September 1963.

During the reception in their homeland, Foreign Minister emphasizes that the deployment of the Austrian medics in the Congo *"brought great honor to the name of Austria and, which is much more important, helped tens of thousands of poor people plagued by terrible illnesses to stay alive at all."* Before Defence Minister Graf had already asserted that: *"It is impossible to make agreements on paper only, but be unwilling to fulfill these commitments as well. Such behavior would seriously endanger the laboriously won prestige of our Fatherland."*

Basis for deployment:	CM[55] of September 20th, 1960 (dispatch), CM of June 25th, 1963 (end of deployment).
Mission:	Construction and operation of field hospitals; ensuring the medical care of the UN armed forces, the population, and refugees.
Appellation:	**UN Medical Contingent of the Republic of Austria.**
Form of posting:	Special contract after leave placement.
Area of operations:	Bukavu, Kamina, Stanleyville, Kindu, Luluaberg.
Duration of deployment:	November 25th, 1960 – May 26th, 1961 and July 14th, 1961 – September 18th, 1963.
Contingent strength:	Up to 55, in addition up to 200 local assistants.
In total:	166 (of which 33 doctors and – in the 1st contingent – two technical medical assistants).
Composition:	Command, signal corps, administration group, vehicle and mechanic's group, laboratory and blood bank, dispensary, walk-in clinic, surgery group, X-ray group, dental station. Intermittently also a group for internal medicine, gynecology, and ear-nose-throat.
Commanders:	1st contingent: December 11th, 1960 – December 24th, 1960 Lieutenant Colonel GS Ferdinand Foltin
	December 25th, 1960 – May 26th, 1961 Colonel med. Dr. Werner Pervulesko
	2nd contingent: July 14th, 1961 – January 15th, 1962 Colonel med. Dr. Maximilian Fill
	3rd contingent: January 15th, 1962 – July 21st, 1962 Colonel med. Dr. Maximilian Fill
	4th contingent: July 21st, 1962 – February 21st, 1963 Lieutenant Colonel med. Dr. Josef Mayer
	5th contingent: February 21st, 1963 – September 18th, 1963 Lieutenant Colonel med. Dr. Robert Wech
Contribution:	Some 200 UN affiliates, but also up to 4,000 Congolese patients handled monthly.

Uniform

As previously mentioned, a new uniform is necessary for the Congo deployment. The khaki uniform introduced for this closely models the uniforms of the German Afrikakorps in the Second World War and is very similar to the Belgian. As symbol of nationality a rounded strip with a red border and "AUTRICHE" in red lettering is worn. This is also supposedly the reason for the imprisonment: the Austrians were taken for Belgians and (from the Congolese viewpoint) treated accordingly. Since the Austrian five-point rank insignia are not suitable (detachable tabs are first introduced in the armed forces in 1965), square ones are introduced on epaulets. These new rank insignias also have their good sides: One of the members of the then-current contingent, Gerhard Kampl (today First Warrant Officer) reports that as a platoon leader with his three stars he was taken for a captain while off-duty in Leopoldville and therefore received entry into one of the few hotels of the city. Supposedly this is the reason that new rank insignia on the shoulder of the left sleeve for noncommissioned officers are introduced in 1962. In view of the incidents in Bukavu minor changes of the uniforms also occur at the dispatch of the 2nd contingent. The streamer inscribed "AUTRICHE" on the left bicep is replaced with a white triangle with the inscription "AUSTRIA" and the red-white-red striped shield.

Farewell to the ONUC contingent from Defence Minister Dr. Prader at Schwechat airport. Note the new rank insignias on sleeves, introduced in 1962, and that some soldiers wear a red-white-red cockade on their berets instead of the UNO emblem.

---

55   CM=Council of Ministers.

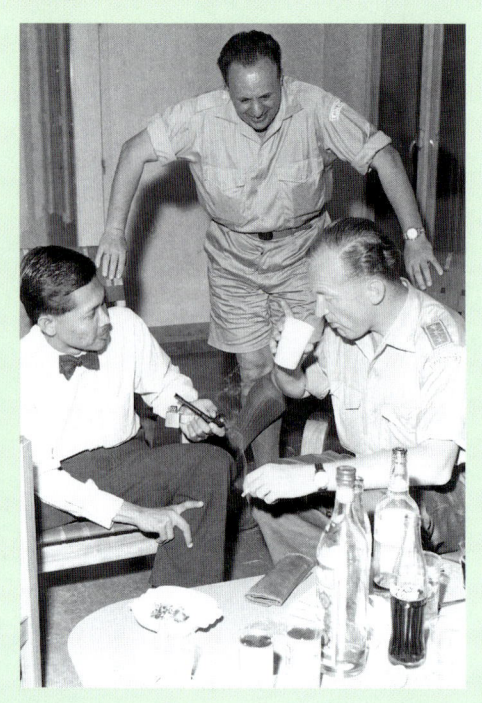

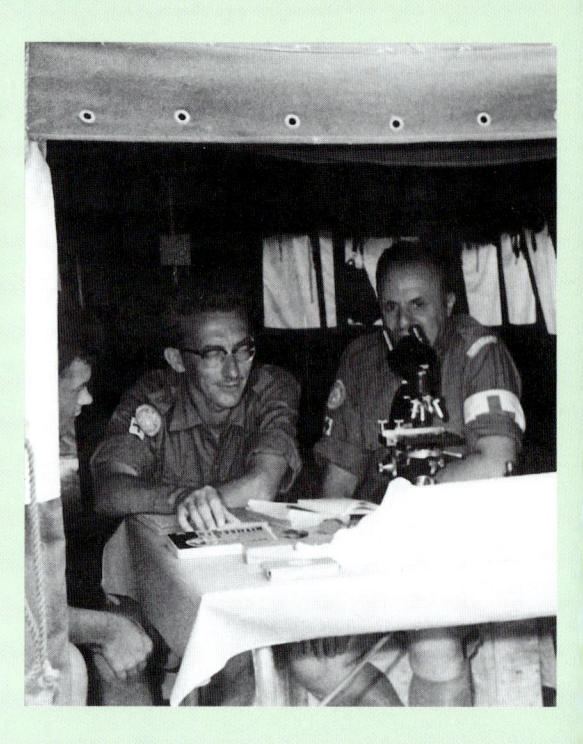

Two nurses also belong to the 1st contingent, who are given the rank of "Lieutenant" for the duration of the mission (t.l.). Officer representative with rank insignia on sleeves (b.r.) Captain with epaulet rank insignia and the nationality insignia "AUTRICHE" worn by the 1st contingent (t.m.). The tents of the Austrian field hospital (m.l. and t.r.).
Major med. doctor with the old nationality insignia "AUTRICHE" and Lieutenant with the new insignia "AUSTRIA" worn from the 2nd contingent on (b.l.).

The transport of equipment to the Congo takes place in US transport airplanes of the "Hercules" type (t.). The hospital facilities must also be unloaded (m.). Besides all-terrain trucks (Haflinger AP 700) and 3/4 t medical vehicles (VW 271), 1/4 t all-terrain trucks (Jeep) and 3/4 t all-terrain trucks (Dodge WC-51) are deployed in the Congo. Naturally the contingent must also depend upon itself for technical services (b.r.).

Earthquake Deployment in Skopje

Preliminary Events

On July 26th, 1963 at 5:17 AM a heavy earthquake jolts the capital of the Yugoslavian constituent republic of Macedonia, which is flattened. This is the third earthquake in the history of Skopje. The first was in the year 518, when Skopje was still named Skupi. The second took place in the year 1555. The third now costs more than 1,000 lives and makes 200,000 citizens homeless. All telephone, telegraph, and radio connections are interrupted. With the help of the army and the police 6,000 people can be rescued. On August 1st (the first day of the Austrian deployment), renewed, somewhat heavy earth tremors occur at 12:35 AM, which repeat themselves once more at 12:45 AM. During these, numerous houses in Skopje collapse, nevertheless no damage is done to people.

International Reaction

International relief organizations immediately start an extensive rescue campaign.

Austrian Participation

Political Measures

The Austrian Red Cross spontaneously decides on a relief operation and petitions the armed forces for support within the framework of the international aid campaign.

Military Measures

Through a telephonic petition of the Austrian Red Cross, the Defence Minister commissions the Air Defence Troop School (ADTS)[56] with the selection of a rescue and recovery group. The deployment group is put together as a result of voluntary enlistment (90% of the members of the ADTS immediately report for the deployment) and professional experience. The selected personnel then receive special leave and carry out the deployment under the auspices of the Red Cross.

The movement into the area of operations begins on the evening of July 29th, 1963 and takes place by train. As a result of the relatively late arrival in the area of operations the Austrians can only participate in the recovery of the dead, where they are above all assigned to the recovery of buried foreign holiday makers from the destroyed hotel "Macedonia". 2/3 of the four-story hotel have collapse, the stories lay in stacks of ca. 60 cm on top of each other. The deployment takes place together with Yugoslavian soldiers and recovery workers. Besides their own vehicles, five Caterpillars (among others D8), a driveable crane and a fire engine from the local fire department are available. Unfortunately, only two of the dead can be recovered on the 1st day of deployment. On the 2nd deployment day, Skopje is again shaken by a serious earth tremor at 12:35 AM, which is followed by another of the same strength at 12:45 AM. The main assignment of the Austrians is subsequently to break through cellar walls, in order to penetrate these rooms and search them for survivors. The Austrian team impresses with training and equipment suitable for the deployment. The experiences had are immediately incorporated into the further design of the rescue and recovery training at the ADTS.

Basis for deployment: Petition of the Austrian Red Cross.
Mission: Recovery of those buried.
Appellation: None.
Form of posting: Special leave.
Area of operations: Skopje.
Duration of deployment: July 29th, 1963 – August 5th, 1963.
Contingent strength: 9 (1 officer and 8 noncommissioned officers) as well as one civilian technician.
Total: 9.
Composition: 1 clearance and rescue group.
Commander: First Lieutenant of the Technical Service Wilhelm Jagisch.
Contribution: 4 recovered dead.

---

56 Predecessor of today's NBC Defence School.

United Nations Yemen Observation Mission (UNYOM)

Preliminary Events

After the death of the Imam on September 1962, the Republic of Yemen, supported by revolting army units, is declared in spring 1963. In the following civil war, the royalists are supported by Saudi Arabia and the republicans by the United Arab Republic of Egypt.

International Reaction

The UNO and USA accomplish a cease-fire and an agreement on a demilitarized zone along the Yemeni-Saudi Arabian border. The UN Security Council decides on June 11th with Resolution 179 (1963) to post an observer group, which must supervise the cease-fire, the disengagement agreement and the demilitarized zone.

Basis for the deployment:	SC Resolution 179 (1963) of June 11th, 1963.
Mission:	Surveillance of the troop disengagement agreement between Saudi Arabia and the United Arab Republic, the withdrawal of foreign troops and the demilitarized zone established on the border with Saudi Arabia.
Duration of deployment:	July 4th, 1963 – September 4th, 1964.
Participating Nations:	Australia, Austria, Canada, Denmark, Ghana, India, Italy, the Netherlands, Norway, Pakistan, Sweden, USA, Yugoslavia.
High point:	189 soldiers, including 25 military observers; lastly 75 workers.
Headquarters:	Sana'a.

Austrian Participation

Political Measures

On June 17th, 1963 the UN Secretary-General requests the dispatch of a doctor from the Austrian medical contingent in the Congo for a maximum of four months to UNYOM. Since this only means a temporary change of area of operations, no further political measures are necessary. The dispatch therefore takes place without involvement of the federal government.

Military Measures

The Defence Ministry orders the temporary duty assignment of one doctor from ONUC to UNYOM.

Basis for deployment:	Duty assignment.
Mission:	Medical treatment of mission affiliates.
Appellation:	None.
Form of dispatch:	Continuation of the dispatch to ONUC with special contract.
Area of operations:	Sana'a.
Duration of deployment:	July 30th, 1963 – November 7th, 1963.
Contingent strength:	1 doctor.
Total:	1.

United Nations Force in Cyprus (UNFICYP)

Preliminary Events

Cyprus, the beautiful **"Island of Aphrodite"**, is conquered by the Ottomans in 1571 and incorporated into the Ottoman Empire. The island is inhabited by Greeks and until the conquest was under Venetian influence. The thousands of Ottoman soldiers and officials who now come to the island become the germ cells of a Turkish minority. Cyprus acquires strategic meaning for Great Britain in 1869 with the opening of the Suez Canal. It is placed under British administration in 1878 by the Congress of Berlin, however remains under Ottoman sovereignty for the time being. As Turkey joins the First World War in 1914 on the side of the Central Powers, the island becomes a British colony, in 1925 it becomes a crown colony. In the year 1931, the Greek majority of the island first attempts to break free from England in the "October Revolution". The British government building is set on fire. The revolution fails. In 1950 Makarios II becomes Ethnarch (as the leader of the ethnic group he is the political as well as the spiritual head of all Greek Cypriots). In a poll organized by the church, 96% support the annexation of Cyprus by Greece ("Enosis"). In 1953 the **Greek-Cypriot underground movement "EOKA"** is grounded under General Grivas. In 1954 Greece brings the Cyprus problem before the UNO. This group, however, argues against a direct intervention and references the British responsibility. In 1955 Turkey demands the division ("Taksim") of Cyprus. In 1956 Makarios is exiled.

From 1955 – 1959 the EOKA leads a guerilla war with Greek support under Colonel Costas Grivas against the British administration and for **Enosis** (this conforms with the "Megali Idea", the "Big Idea" from the 19th century, to unify all Hellenes in one nation). Despite the Greek 80% majority of the population, Great Britain declines an annexation of the island to Greece, with a view to the Turkish minority and the role of Turkey as the most easterly NATO member.

In 1959 a compromise takes place between Greece, Turkey, and Great Britain as well as Cypriot Greeks and Cypriot Turks in the Zürich and London Agreement: Cyprus is released into independence on August 16th, 1960 as the "Independent Republic of Cyprus" within the framework of the British Commonwealth. The Turkish-Cypriot minority is protected through special constitutional clauses. Among other things it is established that the president must be a Greek (Makarios III) and the vice-president a Turk (Kücük). In the army and administration the offices are occupied on the basis of various formulas (such as a 70:30 clause for the political field or a 60:40 clause for public service). Enosis and Taksim are forbidden. The treaties signed on August 16th, 1960 award the three protective powers wide-ranging authority and responsibility: Great Britain leaves the island, however according to the treaty it retains two sovereign military bases in Dekhelia and Episkopi/Akrotiri. Greece and Turkey, in contrast, provide contingents for the armed forces on Cyprus.

Between 1960 and 1962 there is a relaxation of tensions between the ethnic groups. Makarios' foreign policy is "neutral", friendly to the USSR and Arabs and hostile to NATO.

When the Cypriot president, Archbishop Makarios III, wants to strengthen the Greek-Cypriot position through a change in the constitution at the end of December 1963, an outbreak of open hostilities between the two ethnic groups on Cyprus occurs, which increasingly reaches civil war proportions. Displacements, kidnappings and the creation of enclaves for Cypriot Turks take place. This leads to the posting of UNO troops in 1964. In 1964 Turkey plans an intervention, but gives it up as a result of international pressure. President Makarios calls on the British to intervene as a guarantor power. At first they do succeed in calming the two aggressors. In November 1967 a serious crisis again occurs, as units of the (Greek dominated) Cypriot National Guard and the Greek troops on Cyprus ("ELDYK") occupy Turkish settlements. Once more the situation is able to be settled. In 1972 EOKA-B is founded. Despite the presence of UN troops, the disputes increase from April 1974. General Costas Grivas escalates the terror of his EOKA-B, while the special forces of President Makarios appear ever more ruthless. The unrest finally leads to a putsch of the Greek National Guard from extremist right Cypriot Greeks on July 15th, 1974. President Makarios is deposed and flees to exile in England. Sampson becomes president. The goal of the putsch is the declaration of a Hellenistic Republic of Cyprus. Serious assaults and massacres of the Turkish population take place.

Since the British refuse to intervene, an **invasion of Turkish troops** takes place on July 20th, 1974. This begins on 5:45 AM with the bombardment of Nicosia and the dropping of paratroopers over the Nicosian airport, over Bogaz and Gönyeli. Parts of the Turkish navy land in Kyrenia. At the same time battles break out around the Turkish enclaves throughout Cyprus. On July 22nd at 4:00 PM a general cease-fire takes effect. The Turkish ethnic group surrenders after heavy losses, in Mari for instance not until repeated interventions of the infantry company stationed there under Captain Brell. On July 24th an Austrian observation troop is captured by Turks in Pergamos and held hostage, in order to force a constant UN presence there. The hostage situation is first ended through massive intervention. In July and August negotiations on a troop withdrawal and the establishment of a UN buffer zone take place in Cyprus and Geneva, which finally fail. The Turkish invasion troops use this time to increase the territory conquered before the cease-fire with the "Salami" tactic: they advance by 100 m per night, raise their flags and maintain that they were always there. On August 13th the invasion troops continue their attacks despite SC Resolutions 353 and 354. On August 16th at 6:00 PM a final cease-fire is concluded upon, however the battles continue sporadically. On August 26th the UN Secretary-General Dr. Waldheim himself arrives in Nicosia. By that point the Turks have conquered the entire northeast of the island (ca. 38% of the area) until the line of Lefka – Nicosia -Famagusta ("Attila Line"). In December 1974 Makarios III returns as president. In 1975 the "Turkish Federate State of Cyprus" is founded, Denktash becomes its "president". In 1977 Makarios III dies.

On November 15th, 1983, in the Turkish occupation zone the **"Turkish Republic of North Cyprus"**, only recognized by Turkey, is one-sidedly declared under "president" Rauf Denktash. In 1988 Vassiliou becomes president of Cyprus. He pursues a policy of detente. In 1990 Cyprus applies for membership in the EU. In 1993 Clerides becomes president of Cyprus.

In August 1996 numerous demonstrations of Greek Cypriots take place against the continuing occupation of North Cyprus by Turkey. In the course of two especially violent demonstrations in the area of Dherinia a Cypriot Greek is beaten to death and shortly thereafter another is shot while climbing a Turkish flagpole. At the end of 1996 Cyprus orders two Russian S-300 rockets, which are seen as a direct threat by Turkey as a result of their proximity. In January 1997, therefore, Turkish battleships circle before Famagusta, in the following year Turkish fighter jets constantly infringe upon Cypriot airspace. Finally Turkey threatens, in case of the installation, with air attacks on the rocket's positions. Nevertheless, with Russian help, the area of Paphos is developed for S-300 positions and the airport appropriately adapted. The Russians also survey places for Russian radar systems (it must be additionally noted that a British radar stands on Mount Olympus and American U2 and Black Hawks are stationed in Akrotiri). On December 28th, 1998 the Cypriot government, after massive international pressure (USA, NATO), decides to "temporarily" station the rockets on Crete.

When, in June 2000, the agreement of the Turks or alternatively the Turkish Cypriots is not sought for the extension of the UNFICYP mandate, the irritated Turkish Cypriot leader Rauf Denktash causes all zone crossings in (Austrian) Sector 4 to be blocked for UNO soldiers. The only crossing left for the Austrians is therefore the central corridor in Nicosia. This blockade has direct effects on the Austrian contingent: not only leisure time activities are heavily restricted by this, but the supply paths are noticeably lengthened and above all the leadership of the battalion seriously hampered.

International Reaction

Already in 1954 Greece brings the Cyprus question before the UNO. This group, however, argues against a direct intervention and references the British responsibility. After civil war-like conflicts a settlement takes place in 1959 between all conflict parties in the London Agreement. The unrest which jolts the island at the end of the year 1963 first represents the triggering moment for the posting of UNFICYP.[57] On December 29th, 1963 a neutral zone ("Green Line") is established. In January 1964 a peaceful solution is sought in a conference in London. An international peacekeeping troop is meant to be posted for stabilization. The first thought is of a deployment within the framework of NATO, which all three involved powers belong to, after all. Archbishop Makarios, however, decidedly rejects a NATO deployment and pushes through his wish for a UN troop. Finally, at the beginning of 1964 the UN Security Council concern themselves with the Cyprus problem and pass Resolution 186 for the posting of a peacekeeping troop unanimously on March 4th, 1964. A delegation is already sent to Cyprus in January, which has the mission of surveying the fundamentals of a stationing of UN forces. This mission is named **"United Nations Cyprus Observation Mission (UNCOM)"**. On March 27th, 1964 the deployment of UNFICYP begins. Since the bloodshed is reaching a high point, blue berets are simply put on the British troops on the island and they are declared to be the 1st UNO contingent. This naturally arouses a dislike of UNO among the Cypriots, which first dwindles when the first "real" UN soldiers from Denmark, Finland, Canada, Austria and Sweden land in Cyprus.

In 1967, under pressure from the USA, NATO, and the UNO, Greece orders General Grivas to withdraw his illegal troops from the enclave areas. In 1971 the "Lisbon Conference" takes place, during which Greece and Turkey, without the involvement of the two Cypriot parties, agree on a solution. The terrorism escalates, however. The escalation of the situation in April 1974 naturally has an effect on the UN soldiers stationed on Cyprus. The UN troops (Austria is already providing its 5th contingent – UNAB 5) are placed on raised alert readiness "Blue" on July 15th, on July 20th "Orange" is ordered. The UN troops are directly entangled in the battles. In connection with the de facto cease-fire of August 16th the so-called "Attila Line" is established as the cease-fire line. During the battles from August 14th – 16th around 180,000 Greek Cypriots flee from the Turkish army into the Cypriot government-controlled south of the island. Along the "Attila Line" a buffer zone exists between the Republic of Cyprus and the Turkish occupied area in the north. This buffer zone, in which the UNO troops are deployed, takes up about 3% of the island, including the most fruitful farmland. In 1975 in Vienna, numerous talks take place between the two ethnic groups, in which a population exchange in large style is agreed upon: all those Greek Cypriots who did not flee and still live in the north will move to the south, all Turkish Cypriots from the south to the north. Only around 20,000 Greek Cypriots remain in the north (predominantly in Karpas) and around 400 Turkish Cypriots in the south. The moral and material care of these two minorities is handed over to UNFICYP.

The UNFICYP's mission reads, in the interests of the maintenance of international freedom, to use all means necessary to prevent a flareup of the battles and, as far as is required, to contribute to the preservation and reestablishment of law and order as well as a return to normal conditions. The fulfillment of the mission is made considerably more difficult since no formal cease-fire agree-

---

[57] Alfred Plienegger: "UNFICYP 1981, the United Nations in Peacekeeping Deployment on Cyprus"; Österreichische Militärische Zeitung, Vol. 4/1982, Ueberreuter Verlag, Vienna 1982.

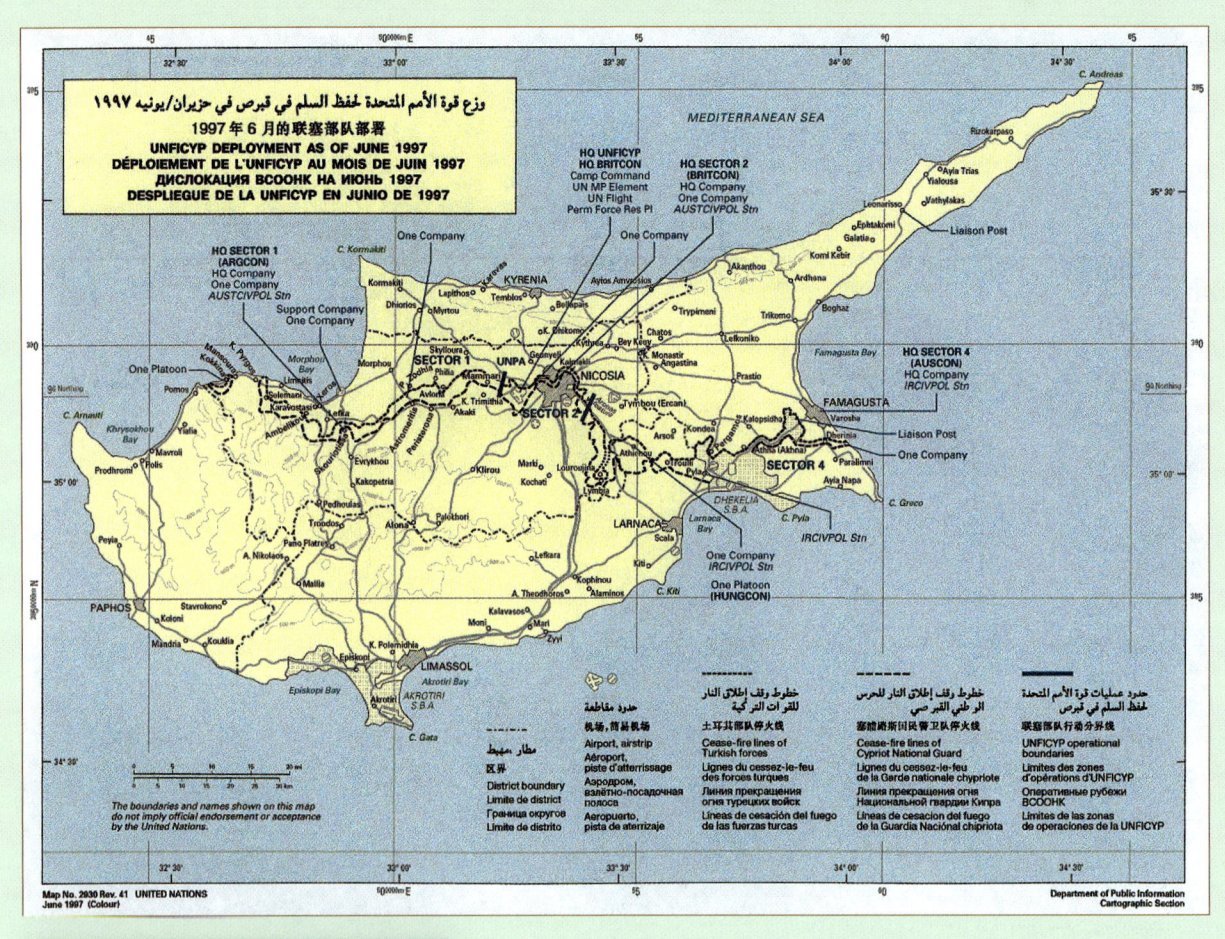

Official UN map of the deployment of UNFICYP in the year 1997 (top).
Trilingual sign (English, Greek, Turkish) at a UN checkpoint (m.).
The commander of the 2nd InfCoy/UNAB at the position map (b.l.).
The deployment of UNAHSB in Sector 4 (b.r.).

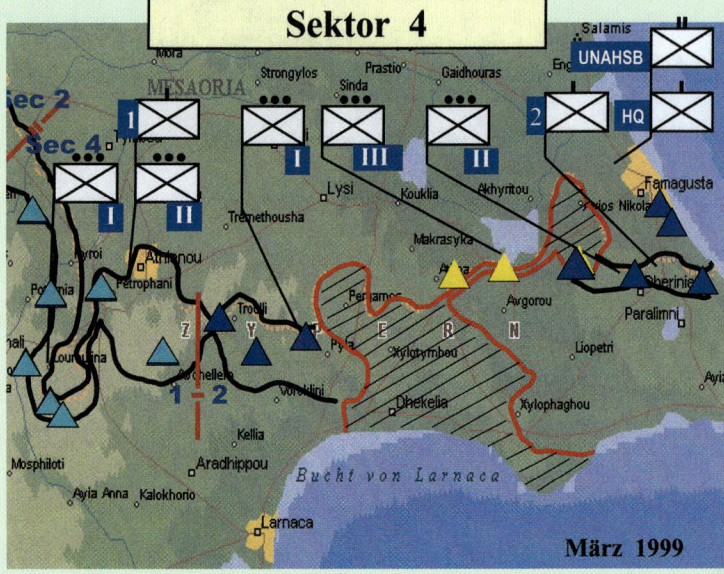

ment exists. A problem also develops for UNFICYP in the fact that the functioning of the water and electricity utility services, which are connected beyond the buffer zone, is to be ensured. Further, the UN troops are to participate in humanitarian aid programs in cooperation with the Office of the UN High Commissioner for Refugees (UNHCR) and the International Committee of the Red Cross (ICRC).

On April 22nd, 1981, the ethnic group talks are taken up again, on August 9th, 1980 an accord is reached on the establishment of a committee to investigate the fate of missing persons. This, like all further talks, remains unsuccessful to this day.

As a result of the declaration of the Republic of North Cyprus in 1983, the fronts harden anew. In May 1989 a UN deconfrontation program takes place, in the course of which a part of the – at points only a few meters broad – buffer zone inside the city of Nicosia is demilitarized and 24 OPs[58] are subsequently closed. In 1992 unified sovereignty and citizenship as well as the bicommunal and bizonal federation are regulated in SC Resolution 750.

In 1973 the Irish contingent is withdrawn, the Finns leave the island in 1977 and the Swedes in 1987. In 1992/93 the Danish and Canadian contingents are withdrawn. The Danes are relieved by Argentinians, the duties of the Canadians are transferred to the British and Austrians. Currently the "deployment" of UNFICYP looks as following: The Argentinian contingent is responsible for Sector 1 in the west of the buffer zone (until about 15 km west of Nicosia), the British (with a Dutch company since 1996) for Sector 2, the metropolitan area of Nicosia, and the Austrians for Sector 4 in the east of the buffer zone (until about 10 km east of Nicosia).

Numerous pushes for disarmament and the solution of the Cyprus question – for instance a UN proposal on trust-building measures in 1993 – remain without lasting success. In December 1998 a new aggravation of the crisis occurs because of the planned (and then not carried out after all) posting of Russian S-300 rockets in the South. The EU decides to accept Cyprus onto the list of membership candidates and begins negotiations in connection with this.

A special position is taken by the UN civilian police, who are deployed in UNFICYP for the first time as an independent component of the UN peacekeeping mission. In contrast to UN military police, who are only deployed for the maintenance of order and discipline inside of UNFICYP, the civilian police are concerned with the tracking of crimes committed between members of the two ethnic groups and fulfill police duties in the buffer zone since 1974. The Cyprus question is still a dangerous potential crisis in the eastern Mediterranean to this day.

Basis for deployment:	SC Resolution 186 (1964) of March 4th, 1964; Consensus of August 11th, 1964; SC Resolution 422 (1977) of December 15th, 1977; SC Resolution 750 (1992) (sovereignty); SC Resolution 831 (1993) of May 27th, 1993 (regulation of finances) and SC Resolution 1331 (2000) of December 13th, 2000 (extension until June 15th, 2001).
Mission:	Prevention of the renewal of hostilities; reestablishment and maintenance of law and order; protection of the security and the well-being of both ethnic groups; cooperation with the UNHCR and the ICRC during humanitarian aid programs.
Duration of deployment:	March 27th, 1964 to date.
Participating nations:	Argentina, Australia, Austria, Canada, Denmark, Finland, Great Britain, Hungary, Ireland, New Zealand, Slovenia, Sweden.
Contingent strength:	Max. 6,411 soldiers and civilian workers (status June 1964); 1,165 soldiers, 35 policemen and 341 civilian workers (status April 30th, 2001).
Headquarters:	Nicosia.
Force Commander:	March 1st, 1981 – April 11th, 1989: Major General DI Günther Greindl.

Austrian Participation

• Dispatch of a Field Surgical Hospital

Political Measures

On March 3rd, 1964 UN Secretary-General U Thant inquires in Austria if the federal government would be prepared to select a troop contingent of 700 – 800 men. Should this not be possible, the dispatch of a medical contingent is requested. Initially a decision is made on March 17th to dispatch a field surgical hospital.

In addition, in the time from April 14th, 1964 – July 27th, 1977 a total of 639 officers from the gendarmery and police are dispatched within the framework of AUSCIVPOL.

---

58 Observation Post.

Military Measures

The armed forces assembles a field surgical hospital with a strength of 54 men – initially still with special contracts as in the Congo. In March a survey command (Envoy Dr. Gudenus, LTC med. Dr. Wech and CPT Kloss) is dispatched to Cyprus. After a long search Dr. Wech finds a fitting place, a former stopover camp for EOKA fighters, which, if also with a great amount of work, can be made into a field hospital. Shortly thereafter the actual advance command is transferred, which immediately begins the construction work. And beginning on April 14th, the contingent follows them to Nicosia. The contingent consists partly of soldiers who could already gather experience in the Congo. So LTC med. Dr. Robert Wech is assigned as 1st commander. Dr. Wech was the last commander in the Congo. Congo "veterans" are also in other contingents. So it can come to pass that Austrian and Irish UN soldiers make themselves understood in Swahili. In summer 1964 the field hospital achieves the same configuration as before in the Congo. UNO delivers refrigerators, a large kitchen is constructed and a laundry organizaed. The good reputation of the AFH is confirmed by the visits of prominent patients: General Thimayya, commander-in-chief of the army, General Rikhie, military advisor of the UN Secretary-General U Thant, the Swedish envoy Bundy, members of the American and German embassies, and many others. The population is only treated in emergency cases, since the health system of both ethnic groups is well organized. At the direction of HQ during the battles in August 1964 wounded "Turkish fighters" are also operated on and then transferred to the Turkish hospital.

In this time a team with two ambulances is also placed in the battle zone with the Swedish battalion there, in order to carry out transports of the wounded and refugees. Medicines and foodstuffs are also affected by the economic blockade of the Turkish by the Greeks. So medicines from UNO and Austrian supplies are to be brought over the border zones, to prevent the outbreak of epidemics.

Basis for deployment:	CM of March 17th, 1964 (dispatch), CM of November 30th, 1965 (mission duration), CM of April 1976 (end).
Mission:	Securing the medical care of the mission.
Appellation:	**Austrian Field Hospital (AFH).**
Form of dispatch:	Special contracts as in ONUC, from 1965 according to Foreign Deployment FCL 1965.
Area of operations:	Kokkini Trimithia, about 15 km west of Nicosia.
Contingent strength:	55 (from June 26th, 1968 Austria also places staff personnel in the HQ/UNFICYP).
Total:	1,071.
Commanders:	May 16th, 1964 – November 17th, 1964 — Lieutenant Colonel med. Dr. Robert Wech
	November 18th, 1964 – April 2nd, 1965 — Lieutenant Colonel med. Dr. Benno Nußbaumer
	April 3rd, 1965 – July 9th, 1965 — Colonel med. Dr. Otto Renth
	July 10th, 1965 – September 19th, 1965 — Lieutenant Colonel med. Dr. Erich Narodoslawsky
	September 20th, 1965 – March 22nd, 1966 — Major med. Dr. Leo Effenberger
	March 23rd, 1966 – August 28th, 1966 — Colonel med. Dr. Robert Wech
	August 29th, 1966 – December 14th, 1966 — Colonel med. Dr. Otto Renth
	December 15th, 1966 – September 14th, 1967 — Colonel med. Dr. Benno Nußbaumer
	September 15th, 1967 – June 24th, 1968 — Colonel med. Dr. Robert Wech
	June 25th, 1968 – December 26th, 1968 — Lieutenant Colonel med. Dr. Leo Effenberger
	December 27th, 1968 – December 26th, 1969 — Colonel med. Dr. Benno Nußbaumer
	December 27th, 1969 – June 26th, 1970 — Colonel med. Dr. Robert Wech
	June 27th, 1970 – June 27th, 1971 — Lieutenant Colonel med. Dr. Leo Effenberger
	June 28th, 1971 – December 26th, 1971 — Colonel med. Dr. Robert Wech
	December 27th, 1971 – September 25th, 1972 — Colonel med. Dr. Benno Nußbaumer
	September 26th, 1971 – April 16th, 1973 — Colonel med. Dr. Hans Schallaböck
	April 17th, 1973 – October 18th, 1973 — Colonel med. Dr. Josef Mayer
Composition:	Surgery station, internal station, X-ray station, dental station, laboratory, dispensary.
Contribution:	Some 65,000 patients are treated in the duration of the deployment.

• Dispatch of a Field Medical Center

From October 19th, only a field medical center is operated in the UNFICYP headquarters anymore. At the request of Austria these activities are discontinued in April 1976 and transferred to the British and Canadian contingent.

Mission: Securing the medical treatment in UNHQ.
Appellation: UNFICYP Medical Center (UMC).
Form of dispatch: Foreign Deployment FCL 1965.
Area of operations: Nicosia.
Duration of deployment: October 19th, 1973 – April 10th, 1976.
Contingent strength: 14.
Total: In total 1,071 soldiers performed duty in the AFH and UMC.
Commander: Colonel med. Dr. Josef Mayer.
Contribution: During the length of the UMC deployment 14,200 patients are treated.

• Dispatch of an Infantry Battalion

Political Measures

After Ireland reduces its contingent from 400 to 100 men at the end of 1971, a new request on the part of UNO occurs on January 12th, 1972, if Austria would this time be prepared to send 300 – 400 men. On February 15th the UN Secretary-General, the Austrian Dr. Waldheim, again concretely requests the selection of a battalion in the strength of 270 men. The Defence Ministry initially makes its doubts known in view of the personnel situation. On the other hand it does not seem politically defensible for Austria to deny the request of the Austrian Secretary-General. It is also hardly thinkable for one to prepare an appropriate division for 6 years for a possible deployment, but then deny this when the opportunity finally arises. The Austrian federal government therefore agrees to the deployment with a ruling of February 29th, 1972. For financial reasons the federal government of 2000 decides to let the Austrian participation in the Cyprus deployment run out in 2001.

Military Measures

The armed forces have already previously formed a UN battalion, on the basis of the deployment law of 1965, which is to be available to the United Nations as a **"stand-by" troop** on the Scandinavian model. 2,000 volunteers report by March 1966. In the time from March 24th to 25th, the first weapons exercise ("Inspection and Instruction") takes place in Vienna. The battalion is to be ready for deployment within a month, with a strength of 623 men (31 of which are officers). In 1967 the time frame for deployment is shortened to 7 days. This unit subsequently practices regularly, but for lack of an appropriate UN operation, is not however deployed. On December 1st, 1966 the designated commander of UNAB, Major Hans Dreihann-Holenia reports to the Austrian UNO ambassador Dr. Waldheim in a letter: *"The battalion is ready for deployment, presents arms and waits for dismissal."*[59] As a result of the decision of the federal government to dispatch a UN contingent to Cyprus, the assembly staff is established on March 2nd, 1972 in Vienna at the 2nd Training Regiment. The possibility of recourse to the stand-by battalion considerably eases the preparations. So the forward command with a strength of 35 men can already be set on the march on March 24th. On April 25th the battalion is shipped from Rijeka (Fiume) to Limassol, the equipment arrives on April 29th in Famagusta. On May 3rd the Austrian take over the district of Paphos from the British.

Basis for deployment:	CM of February 29th, 1972, MC[60] of March 15th, 1972 (dispatch); CM of November 3rd, 1999, MC of November 18th, 1999 (extension); CM of December 5th, 2000, MC of December 15th, 2000 (end by December 2001, dispatch of staff members by December 31st, 2001).
Mission:	Surveillance of the border zone between the Turkish Cypriot and Greek Cypriot cease-fire line as well as Varosha, the former hotel quarter of Famagusta, which since August 1974 is occupied and closed off by Turkish armed forces and since then decays as a "ghost city in the forbidden zone".
Appellation:	**Austrian Contingent (AUSCON),** **United Nations Austrian Battalion (UNAB)** – Appellation of the battalion without the parts at HQ/UNFICYP until November 1995, **United Nations Austrian Hungarian Battalion (UNAHB)** – after the addition of a Hungarian contingent (HUNCON) on November 14th, 1995, **United Nations Austrian Hungarian Slovenian Battalion (UNAHSB)** – since the addition of a Slovenian contingent (SLOCON, since spring 1998 SICON) in September 1997.
Form of dispatch:	Until April 1997 according to Foreign Deployment FCL 1965, after April 1997 according to FCL-CSD 1997.
Area of operations:	District of Paphos (west part of the island).
Duration of deployment:	May 3rd, 1972 – December 2nd, 1973.
Contingent strength:	283.
Composition:	Battalion command, headquarters company, 1st Infantry Company in Camp Duke Leopold V., 2nd Infantry Company in Camp Alpenland in Polis.

The outbreak of the Yom Kippur War makes a swift transfer of soldiers to Egypt necessary in October 1973. Among those are also 205 volunteers from AUSCON, who subsequently are deployed in line with the (second) United Nations Emergency Force (UNEF II) and since 1974 as part of the United Nations Disengagement Observer Force (UNDOF) on the Golan Heights. This transfer makes a regrouping of UNFICYP necessary, which also affects the Austrians. The Austrian contingent is immediately brought to the status of 270 men through volunteers.

---

59 Erwin A. Schmidl: "Blue Helmets, Red Cross".
60 MC = Main Committee of the Parliament.

In Rijeka the contingent waits to be shipped out; custody is secured through Yugoslavian military police (t.l.).
The Steyr diesel trucks on the sea transport to Cyprus (t.r.).
The members of the AFH during the construction of the field hospital and during the first exercises (m.l. and r.). Much value is placed on hygiene in the deployment as well, even when it is not so simple (b.l.).
Parades on the occasion of the awarding of the UN medal ("medal parade"). The carrying of sabres must have been unheard-of in this area (b.r.).

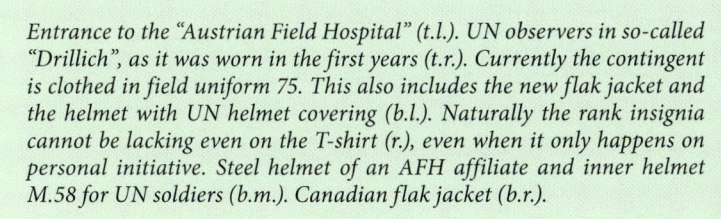

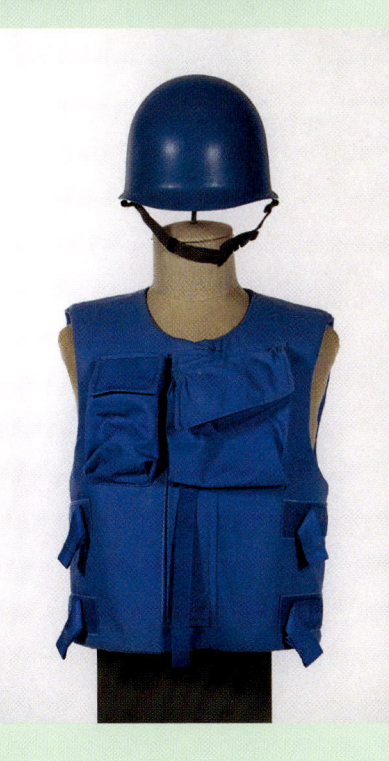

Entrance to the "Austrian Field Hospital" (t.l.). UN observers in so-called "Drillich", as it was worn in the first years (t.r.). Currently the contingent is clothed in field uniform 75. This also includes the new flak jacket and the helmet with UN helmet covering (b.l.). Naturally the rank insignia cannot be lacking even on the T-shirt (r.), even when it only happens on personal initiative. Steel helmet of an AFH affiliate and inner helmet M.58 for UN soldiers (b.m.). Canadian flak jacket (b.r.).

127

Area of operations:	District of Larnaca.
Duration of deployment:	December 3rd, 1973 – October 17th, 1977.
Contingent strength:	270.
Composition:	Battalion command, headquarters company, 1st and 2nd Infantry Companies on the border of the city of Larnaca. A part of the 2nd Coy moved into a camp in Zyyi by summer 1974. On December 29th, 1975 a small camp is constructed by the 1st Coy in Athienou.

In the course of the invasion in July 1974 the UNAB is directly involved in the hostilities. The firefights are carried out directly through the Austrian camp, because a Turkish bunker is directly next to it on one side and positions of the National Guard are on the other side. Within the UN camp vehicles and buildings are hit, the medical building alone is bored through by over 120 shots. In the course of July 21st a cease-fire occurs under the agreement that the "Turkish fighters" are disarmed by UNAB and placed under their protection. On July 22nd the general cease-fire takes effect. The disarmament and internment of the "Turkish fighters" (at least nearly 1,000 men), is, when improvised, continued. On July 24th an Austrian observer troop is captured by Turks in Pergamos and taken hostage. After massive interventions the soldiers are set free again. After a mediation attempt in Goshi an Austrian patrol is attacked by Turkish fighter bombers on August 14th, 1974. Three of the four occupation affiliates in the Land Rover, 1/LT Johann Izay, Master Sergeant Paul Decombe and CPL August Isak, are killed during this attack.

On October 1977 the Finns withdraw their Contingent. A regrouping leads the Austrians and Swedes to exchange sectors.

Area of operations:	District of Famagusta (Athna coast).
Duration of deployment:	October 18th, 1977 – June 18th, 2001.
Contingent strength:	241 (status as of February 1st, 2001).
Total strength:	15,245.
Composition:	Battalion command, headquarters company, 1st and 2nd infantry companies in Famagusta. This camp is also, like all previous camps in Cyprus, given the rich in tradition name of Duke Leopold V. The 1st company receives the Athna line, the 2nd company is assigned the Dherinia line to the sea.

In spring 1987 Sweden also withdraws its contingent. On October 8th, 1987 Austria takes over the eastern part of this sector as well. For this, AUSCON is supplemented by 100 men. The area of operations now stretches from Athienou until the coast south of Famagusta. The 1st Coy occupies the area from the Lacarna – Nicosia street until SBA Dekhelia and has a small camp in Athienou, which is called Camp Izay since spring 1989 (named after 1/LT Izay, who fell in the air attack on August 14th, 1974). A platoon (Pyla platoon) is deployed in Pyla and its surroundings. The 2nd Coy occupies the Athna line from Dherinia on and the Dherinia line until the sea.

In 1992 a reduction from 4 to 3 sectors (Canada, Great Britain, Austria) takes place in the course of the withdrawal of DANCON, in 1993 CANCON is withdrawn and replaced with an Argentinian contingent (ARGCON).

In the middle of 2000 the situation with UNAHSB can be described as follows: UNAHSB observes the buffer zone in **Sector 4** between the border to Sector 2 near the Almyros river and the coast as well as the areas of Athna, Strovilia, Varosha and Karpas in the Turkish controlled zone, and in the British sovereignty area the "Link Road" under the deployment of the 1st (HU) company in the area of the Almyros river – UN 91 – Louroujina Salient – Athienou – Karavous Pass (including UN-118), the 2nd (A/SI) company from Karavous Pass (excluding UN-118) – Troulli – Pyla until the SBA border of Dhekelia, along the Link Road from Akhna through UN 139 until the SBA border Ayios Nicolaios – UN 140 through UN 142 (Dherinia) until UN 146. Further: Operation of a liaison post in Strovilia (SI) and on Karpas (A), holding two attack platoons in readiness in order to prevent a flare-up of hostilities as well as changes in the status quo.

In June 2000 a new evaluation of the extent of the foreign deployments takes place as a result of the duties which result from international commitments and the budget resources which are available for them. Since the concept "New Beginning" now only plans for one unit for a classical peace-keeping deployment, the decision is made on June 5th to end UNFICYP by September 2001 at the latest. Hungary and Slovenia are asked if they will take over the Austrian participation, however they make it clear that in that case they will also end their participation. The UN Secretary-General is informed of these measures by the Minister for Foreign Affairs, Dr. Ferrero-Waldner. In his answering letter he expresses his understanding and at the same time his thanks for the lengthy support. On June 18th, 2001 the ceremonial act of ending the deployment and the transfer of the command to a Slovakian unit takes place in Cyprus. A final command remains until the end of July in the area of operations.

All-terrain 1 t truck (710 Pinzgauer) at the entrance to Camp Duke Leopold V. (t.l.). Patrol, consisting of a Ferret armored car and a radio vehicle (VW 231/235) (t.r.). UNAB possesses a wide variety of vehicle types: light military vehicles (VW181) and all-terrain trucks (PuchG/LP) (m.l. and r.). 1 1/2 t. all-terrain medical vehicles (712 Pinzgauer) (b.l.). In addition there are a number of civilian vehicles, among others some from Mitsubishi (staff vehicle b.r.) and Citroën.

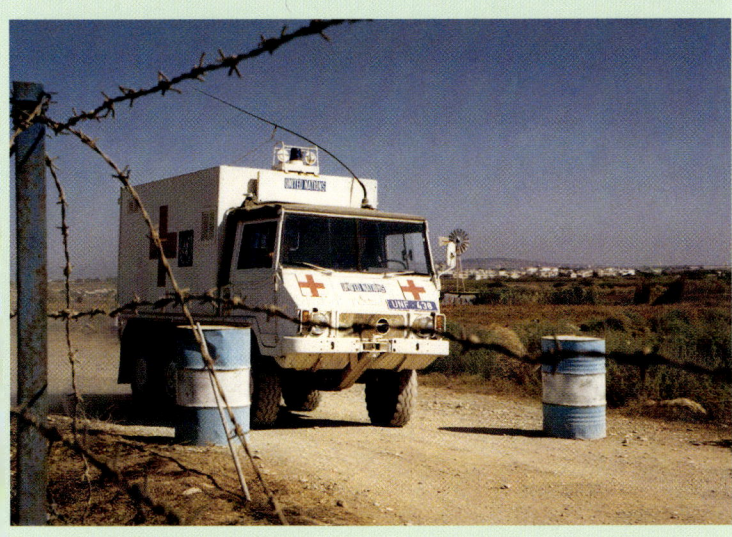

Hungarian Contingent (HUNCON)

Since November 14th, 1995 Hungarian soldiers are also integrated in the Austrian contingent. At first a Hungarian infantry platoon (34 soldiers) takes over the duties of I platoon of the 1st company (Louroujina/Camp Berger); four staff functions (depBCdr, depCoyCdr, doctor, logistics officer) are occupied by Hungarian officers. On September 30th, 1997 HUNCON is expanded to 107 people; the contingent takes over the duties of the 1st Coy, further staff functions in UNAHB and in HQ/UNFICYP. As of August 1st, 2000, 111 Hungarians are with UNAHSB.

Slovenian Contingent (SLOCON, as of spring 1998 SICON)

On September 30th, 1997 a Slovenian infantry group takes over the duties of 3rd Grp/IIPt/2nd Coy (Position 126/Camp Marie-Therese) and four staff functions (depCoyCdr, depPtCdr, duty officer, field equipment officer). On September 22nd, 1998 SICON is expanded to platoon strength (27 soldiers). SICON takes over the duties of the IIPt/2nd Coy and two staff functions in HQ (duty officer, UN/military police).

Commanders:		
	March 24th, 1971 – May 20th, 1972	Lieutenant Colonel Franz Burgstaller (advance command)
	May 21st, 1972 – April 26th, 1973	Lieutenant Colonel Alfons Kloss
	April 17th, 1973 – October 25th, 1973	Lieutenant Colonel Dr. Erich Weingerl
	October 26th, 1973 – January 14th, 1974	Lieutenant Colonel Walter Fritz
	January 15th, 1974 – January 17th, 1976	Lieutenant Colonel Franz Rieger
	January 18th, 1976 – May 7th, 1977	Lieutenant Colonel Walter Fritz
	May 8th, 1977 – July 25th, 1978	Lieutenant Colonel Heinz Oberwinkler
	July 26th, 1978 – April 24th, 1979	Lieutenant Colonel Walter Fritz
	April 25th, 1979 – July 27th, 1980	Lieutenant Colonel Helfried Satter
	July 28th, 1980 – July 31st, 1981	Lieutenant Colonel Karl Pokorny
	August 1st, 1981 – July 31st, 1982	Lieutenant Colonel Helmuth Weber
	August 1st, 1982 – October 31st, 1983	Lieutenant Colonel Ingo Buttinger
	November 1st, 1983 – November 2nd, 1984	Lieutenant Colonel Theodor Dorfmeister
	November 3rd, 1984 – November 2nd, 1985	Lieutenant Colonel Werner Brandner
	November 3rd, 1985 – November 1st, 1986	Lieutenant Colonel Werner Machly
	November 2nd, 1986 – November 1st, 1987	Lieutenant Colonel Alfred Gröbming
	November 2nd, 1987 – June 20th, 1988	Lieutenant Colonel Johann Schipper
	June 21st, 1988 – November 26th, 1989	Lieutenant Colonel Erich Dallinger
	November 27th, 1989 – December 6th, 1990	Lieutenant Colonel Maximilian Pacher-Theinburg
	December 7th, 1990 – August 12th, 1991	Lieutenant Colonel Klaus-Josef Holzer
	August 13th, 1991 – July 12th, 1992	Lieutenant Colonel Gerd Rieszland
	July 13th, 1992 – July 5th, 1993	Lieutenant Colonel Helmut Hossinger
	July 6th, 1993 – November 3rd, 1994	Lieutenant Colonel Andreas Kloss
	November 4th, 1994 – November 10th, 1995	Lieutenant Colonel Ernst Eder
	November 11th, 1995 – January 24th, 1997	Lieutenant Colonel Wolfgang Wildberger
	January 25th, 1997 – January 23rd, 1998	Lieutenant Colonel GS Robert Prader
	January 24th, 1998 – March 5th, 1999	Lieutenant Colonel Heinz Hufler
	March 6th, 1999 – March 2nd, 2000	Lieutenant Colonel Helmet Plieschnegger
	March 3rd, 2000 – June 18th, 2001	Lieutenant Colonel Josef Kienberger

Police Training

Major demonstrations, which result in numerous injured UN soldiers, demand consistent enhancement of training in the direction of demonstration control. For this, the elite troop of the Viennese Police, WEGA, confronts a training block in which the classical topic of "crowd control" is taught. The equipment of the men is also customized: helmets, shields, arm, leg, and groin protection has been available for UN soldiers for some time now.

Equipment

Besides their own vehicles, the Austrian UN contingent on Cyprus has access to a row of vehicles which do not count as the equipment of the armed forces. Among these are the Station Wagon Pajero 2800, Double Cabin Pick Up L 200, Lancer Saloon 1298, Minibus L300 and Van L300, all from Mitsubishi, and the Jumper 35LH25 from Citroën.

Professional Internship

In December 1999 six students of the Vocational School for Electrical Engineering on Mollardgasse in Vienna complete a special type of internship: Under the supervision and direction of two teachers they bring the electrical wiring of the camps in Famagusta and Pyla as well as two observation posts up to date. Among other things, sixty electrical outlets are provided, the existing wiring system reinforced and lighting strike protection installed. The materials are supplied by professional firms, the UNO absorbs the transport costs and provides accommodation and provisions. Besides advanced professional training, this "deployment abroad" offers the students the possibility to make contacts with the UNO troops.

Similar internships also exist in Golan. There not only the electrical wiring, but also the gas and water installations are renovated by a further professional school and with this, important work is contributed for our UNO soldiers on-site.

The Better Argument

Cyprus 1976. Among the duties of the A-01 platoon command post is to observe the water supply for around a dozen towns in the Turkish-occupied part of the island. The problem is that the pump stations necessary for this lie in the Greek part of the island. And it can very well occur that an ailment "suddenly" develops at the pump station or the fuel runs out. During such an examination the pump attendant is met in front of his hut, wringing his hands. "No petrol, no petrol," he whines. The examining noncommissioned officer then pretends to leave. Nevertheless, after a few meters of driving he stops, gets out, brings his weapon up to a firing position, and aims right at the supposedly empty fuel tank. The horrified tank attendant, who has watched him closely, runs towards him with raised arms and screams: "Petrol inside, petrol inside." The water supply is immediately resumed.[61]

• Dispatch of Staff Personnel

---
61 Otmar Ulrich: "The Better Argument", "Blue Helmet News", 3/2000.

Basis for deployment: CM of December 5th, 2000, MC of December 15th, 2000.
Mission: Staff activities in HQ/UNFICYP.
Form of dispatch: Foreign Deployment FCL 1965.
Duration of deployment: June 18th, 2001 – to date.
Contingent strength: Max. 4.
Total: 148 (including the staff personnel who have already been carrying out duties since 1972 within the framework of AUSCON).

• Dispatch of Military Observers

Basis for deployment: CM of November 30th, 1993, MC of December 1993 (dispatch); CM of November 15th, 1994, MC of November 18th, 1994 (end).
Mission: Support of the battalions in their zones, especially with respect to the contacts with the conflicting parties, formation of longer-term present element to improve the basis of experience.
Form of dispatch: Foreign Deployment FCL 1965.
Duration of dispatch: August 6th, 1993 – December 31st, 1994.
Contingent strength: Max. 4.
Total: 5.

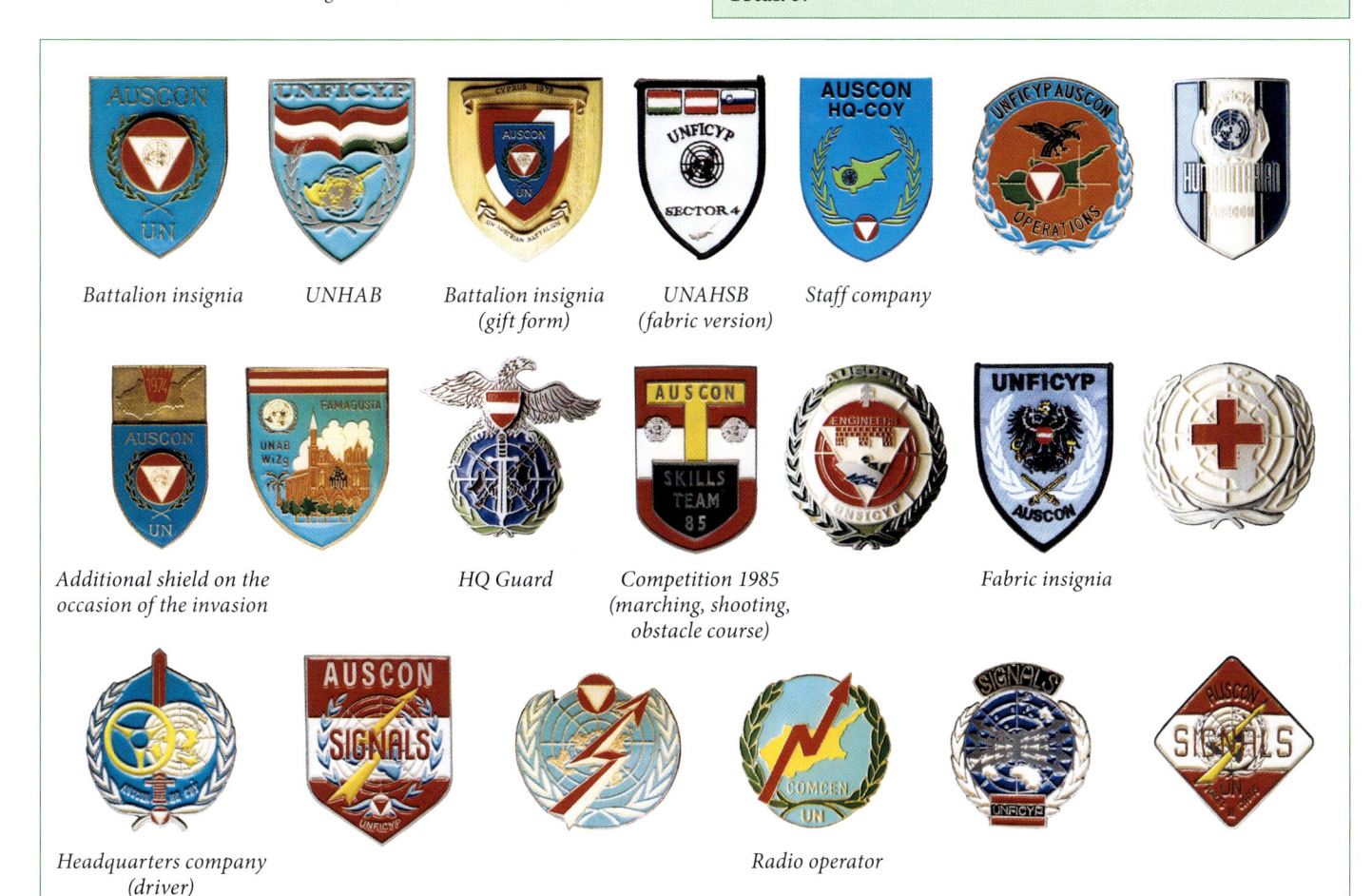

Battalion insignia — *UNHAB* — *Battalion insignia (gift form)* — *UNAHSB (fabric version)* — *Staff company*

Additional shield on the occasion of the invasion — *HQ Guard* — *Competition 1985 (marching, shooting, obstacle course)* — *Fabric insignia*

Headquarters company (driver) — *Radio operator*

UNFICYP insignia

United Nations Truce Supervision Organization (UNTSO)

Preliminary Events

In 1516 Palestine and Syria are incorporated into the Ottoman Empire. At 1900 around a half million people live in Palestine, of which 90% are Arabs and 10% Jews. Increased Jewish immigration from 1872 does not initially change this relationship seriously. The British Foreign Minister Lord Arthur Balfour delivers the following explanation in a letter to Baron Rothschild near the end of the 1st World War (1917):[62]

> *"The government of his majesty contemplates the establishment of a national homeland for the Jewish people in Palestine with goodwill and will do its best to facilitate the attainment of this goal, during which, it will of course be understood, nothing shall happen which could bring into question the civil and religious rights of the existing non-Jewish communities in Palestine or the rights and political status of the Jews in other nations."*

This explanation becomes the "Magna Carta" for the Zionist movement, however brings the British great complications, because the two goals formulated in it ("national Jewish homeland" and "preservation of the existing rights of the population there") prove to be hardly compatible. The cease-fire of Mudros on October 30th, 1918 puts an end to the Ottoman Empire. At the Conference of San Remo in the time from April 19th to 26th, 1920, Palestine and Iraq fall to Great Britain, Syria and Lebanon become mandates of France. Alternating privileges for Jews and Arabs lead to progressively worse situations. In 1936/37 the Peel Commission comes to the realization that the differences between Jews and Arabs are too great and Palestine must therefore be divided. The beginning stream of refugees as a result of the Jewish persecution in Germany and the fickleness of Great Britain lead to the ungovernability of Palestine.

After the UN Security Council of 1947, against the resistance of the Arabs, speaks out for the formation of a nation with Arabic and Jewish constituent republics and Jerusalem as a shared capital, renewed heavy fighting takes place between Jews and Arabs. On May 14th, 1948 the British government puts aside its Palestinian mandate; David Ben Gurion announces the state of Israel in Tel Aviv. On May 15th the regular armies of five Arabic states attack Israel; the first Arabic-Israeli war breaks out. The presence of UNO from August 1948 initially leads to a calming of the situation in Palestine. In 1949 the unrest flares up again. Israel expands its national territory in numerous offensives. The last offensive, "Horev", ends with a decisive defeat of Egypt. On February 24th, 1949, Israel and Egypt sign a cease-fire treaty, on March 23rd Israel and Lebanon, on April 3rd Israel and Jordan, and on July 20th, 1949 Israel and Syria. On October 29th, 1956 Israel attacks Egypt in an action agreed upon with France and England, and within a few days occupies the Gaza Strip and the Sinai Peninsula and pushes as far as the Suez Canal. In the "Six Day War" from October 5th to 10th, 1967 Israel makes preemptive strikes against Egypt, Jordan and Syria. Not until the achievement of all war goals (push to the Suez Canal, annexation of the West Bank and conquest of the Golan Heights) does Israel agree to the cease-fire call of the UNO. Further armed conflicts nevertheless follow: The War of Attrition in the years of 1968 to 1970 and the Yom Kippur War from October 6th to 25th, 1973. They are ended with cease-fire agreements. On September 17th, 1978 the Camp David agreement and on March 26th, 1976 the Israeli-Egyptian peace treaty are signed. A further important precondition for cooperative peace efforts is not achieved until the reciprocal recognition of Israel and the PLO by each other on September 9th, 1993 and the peace agreement between Israel and Jordan on October 26th, 1994. In the summer of 2006 the conflict between Israel and the Lebanese Hezbollah militia flares up again – six years after the withdrawal of the Israeli army from southern Lebanon.

International Reaction

After ongoing unrest between Arabs and Jews in Palestine, Great Britain finally calls for the UNO's mediation on February 14th, 1967. A special committee for Palestine, the **"UN Special Committee on Palestine" (UNSCOP)**, is established. The committee develops two proposals for solutions.

The first plans for a separation of Palestine into an Arabic and an Israeli section; Jerusalem is to receive international status. The second plan envisions a federal state with an Arabic and a Jewish section. According to this plan, Jerusalem would be envisioned as the capital.

Since the General Assembly decides for the separation of Palestine against the resistance of the Arabs on November 29th, 1947, new battles between Jews and Arabs take place. On April 17th, 1948, the Security Council takes up a resolution, in which both sections are called to a cease-fire. At the same time a cease-fire commission is established for Palestine. On May 14th, 1948, UNSCOP is dissolved. Great Britain puts aside its Palestinian mandate.

On May 29th, 1948, SC Resolution 50 (1948)[63] takes effect. In it, UN negotiator Count Bernadotte and the cease-fire commission are assigned the observation of the four-week cease-fire beginning

---

62 Quoted from Walter Laqueur: "The Path to the Nation of Israel – the History of Zionism", Vienna 1975.
63 Resolution of the Security Council of the United Nations.

on June 11th. With this, June 11th, 1948, is the official begin of the UNTSO deployment. The first contingent consists of 131 officers from Belgium, France, Sweden and the USA. By the end of August 572 men are already deployed. The mission of UNTSO encompasses the observation of the adherence to the cease-fire. The presence of UNTSO initially leads to a calming of tensions. On September 17th, 1948, Count Bernadotte and a French officer are murdered. Dr. Ralph J. Bunche is named his successor. After a renewed offensive by Israel Dr. Bunche succeeds in obtaining a unconditional cease-fire. On February 24th, 1949 the cease-fire treaty between Israel and Egypt and subsequently with the other Arabic nations is signed. After this the UNTSO headquarters are moved from Haifa to Jerusalem. In addition UNTSO sets up the so-called **"Mixed Armistice Commissions" (MAC)**. These commissions are responsible for the handling of the respective regional problems between Israel on one side and Egypt, Jordan, Lebanon and Syria on the other side.

After the Israel's renewed attacks in October 1956 (Suez Canal Crisis), UNO brings about a cease-fire and installs the **"United Nations Emergency Force" (UNEF)**. On March 8th, 1957, UNTSO is subordinated to UNEF I in Gaza and Sinai. Egypt is determined for war with Israel and forces the withdrawal of UNEF in May 1967. Without a realistic alternative, UN Secretary-General U Thant agrees to the withdrawal. During the hostilities in June 1967 the UNTSO headquarters falls between the fronts. On June 5th, 1967 the building is occupied by Israeli soldiers and the personnel are deported. Not until August 22nd can the building be reoccupied. The UNTSO area of operations is subsequently expanded to the Suez Canal and the Golan Heights. UNTSO also organizes the exchange of prisoners of war. Since Israel cancels its membership in the MACs, it is necessary to newly restructure UNTSO. Control centers with observation posts and liaison offices are established on the critical borders. These are the

- Kantara Control Center (KCC) on the Israeli side of the Suez Canal in Kantara, then later in Rabah, with observation posts along the Suez Canal, which are named after colors;
- Ismailia Control Center (ICC) on the Egyptian side of the Suez Canal in Ismailia, then later in Heliopolis/Cairo with observation posts along the Suez Canal, which are identified according to the English alphabet;
- Tiberias Control Center (TCC) on the Israeli side of the Golan Heights and
- Damascus Control Center (DCC) on the Syrian side of the Golan Heights.

The UNTSO observers are unarmed and perform their duties in pairs (two officers from different nations), with a liaison officer and a soldier ("handy boy") from the respective land in which they find themselves. This form of organization remains in existence until the Yom Kippur War (October 6th to 25th, 1973).

After the Yom Kippur War a further restructuring of UNTSO follows:
- Observer Group Sinai (OGS) on the Egyptian-Israeli border. This is composed of an Observer Group Egypt (OGE) and an Observer Group Jerusalem (OGJ). These are subordinate to the respective UNEF II contingents. After the Camp David peace agreement between Israel and Egypt on September 17th, 1978 UNTSO is represented through a few observers as the OGE in Cairo and at a few posts in Sinai. All UNTSO deployments in the Middle East are led from Jerusalem.
- Observer Group Golan (OGG) on the Syrian-Israeli border. This is composed of Observer Group Golan – Tiberias (OGG-T) on the Israeli side and Observer Group Golan – Damascus (OGG-D) on the Syrian side as well as Observer Detachment Damascus (ODD). OGG-T and OGG-D are deployed in the Area of Separation within the framework of UNDOF.
- Israel-Lebanon-Mixed Armistice Commission (ILMAC). This initially continues to exist on the Israeli-Lebanese border. From 1972 five outposts are constructed along the border as Observer Group Lebanon (OGL). These are assigned to UNIFIL since 1978. For further observation assignments, Observer Group Beirut (OGB) is stationed in Beirut in 1982 to observe the militant conflicts in the Lebanese capital.
- Gaza Strip. Here UNTSO has established a liaison office with the mission to take on the refugee problem.
- Jordan. Here a liaison office, besides representative duties, is to secure the connections to the government and army of Jordan.

On September 28th, 1995, in Washington D.C., the agreement prepared in secret talks (Oslo Conference) on the provisional self-government of the Palestinian West Bank and Gaza, occupied by Israelis, is signed. The implementation, which initially goes as planned, continually stalls after the elections in Israel in 1996. It is attempted to push the autonomy process for Palestine ahead with the Wye River agreement of October 23rd, 1998. Numerous incidents and domestic developments in Israel nevertheless continue to delay the carrying out of the agreed steps.

Decisive for the groupings is the fact that they always "move with" their respective cease-fire lines, and that UNTSO always succeeds in remaining in the mission area.

At this time UNTSO is composed as follows:
- Observer Group Golan (OGG),
- Observer Group Golan Tiberias (OGG-T),
- Observer Group Golan Damascus (OGG-D),
- Observer Detachment Damascus (ODD),
- Observer Group Lebanon (OGL).

Basis for deployment:	SC Resolution 50 (1948) of May 29th, 1948 (establishment of UNTSO);
	SC Resolution 54 (1948) of July 15th, 1948 (unconditional cease-fire);
	SC Resolution 73 (1949) of August 11th, 1949 (dispatch of UNTSO);
	SC Resolution 235 (1967) of June 11th, 1967; Consensus of July 10th, 1967 (S/8047);
	SC Resolution 339 (1973) of October 23rd, 1973.
Mission:	Observation organization to supervise the cease-fire of 1948 and the armistice of June 11th, 1949 in Palestine. From 1967 additional observation of the cease-fire on the Suez Canal and Golan Heights, cooperation with UNEF II, UNDOF and UNIFIL to support the missions there.
Duration of deployment:	June 11th, 1948 – to date.
Participating nations:	Argentina, Australia, Austria, Belgium, Burma (today Myanmar), Canada, Chile, China, Denmark, Estonia, Finland, France, Ireland, Italy, the Netherlands, Nepal, New Zealand, Norway, Slovenia, Soviet Union (today Russia), Sweden, Switzerland, USA. Military observers from UNTSO are also sent for the beginning phases of UNGOMAP, UNIIMOG, UNIKOM and UNPROFOR.
Strength:	Max. 300 military observers, high point in the year 1948 with 572 soldiers and 230 civilian employees, 153 military observers, 212 civilian employees (as of December 30th, 2000).
Headquarters:	Haifa, Jerusalem since 1949.
Commander:	The commander of the military observers of UNTSO carries the title "Chief of Staff", which in this context means "Chief of the Observation Staff".

Austrian Participation

Political Measures

In response to a petition of the UN Secretary-General of November 17th, 1967, the Austrian federal government decides on November 28th to dispatch 8 observation officers for the Suez Canal zone. On February 27th, 1968, a further petition to send an experienced medical assistant follows. On January 17th, 1973, the UN Secretary-General informs Austria that it is planned to expand the Austrian area of operations. For this a new ruling is necessary, which is made on March 13th. On October 24th, 1973, a further increase is requested. Thereupon the federal government decides on October 26th to establish an upper limit of 15 officers and at the same time to lengthen the deployment duration to twelve months. On March 12th, 1987, the next increase to up to 24 men takes place, after a corresponding decree of January 27th, 1987. In July 2000 the decision is taken to dispatch up to three representatives for a further six months.

Military Measures

On December 4th, 1967, the first 8 officers are set on the march to Jerusalem and deployed on both sides of the Canal after their arrival. On April 3rd, 1969, the contingent is increased by two officers. On April 24th, 1968, an additional medical noncommissioned officer (MedNCO) is deployed, on November 8th a 2nd and on October 13th, 1977, a 3rd MedNCO. These MedNCOs are deployed as medical assistants in Jerusalem and Beirut to treat the UN observers and there carry out duties which are normally reserved for doctors. As a result of their outstanding work they become "legends" among the blue helmets. In the time from May 7th, 1988 to March 24th, 1990, and again to April 5th, 1991, an officer each is transferred from UNTSO to UNGOMAP in Afghanistan and Pakistan. The Austrians continue to fulfill their duties on both sides of the Suez Canal and in the Gaza Strip as liaison officers to UNWRA (UN Relief and Works Agency). Beginning in 1973, the Austrians in the entire area of operations are entrusted with observer duties. During this periodically alternating compositions of workers take place in Cairo, Amman, Jerusalem, Damascus, Tiberias as well as in Naqoura and Beirut.

• Dispatch of Military Observers

Basis for deployment:	CM of November 28th, 1967, MC of November 30th, 1967 (dispatch);
	CM of January 27th, 1987, MC of February 25th, 1987 (dispatch until end of mission).
Mission:	Deployment as military observers; assumption of staff functions.
Appellation:	None.
Form of dispatch:	Until April 1997 according to the Foreign Deployment FCL 1965, from April 1997 according to the FCL-CSD 1997.
Area of operations:	Entire conflict area.
Duration of deployment:	December 4th, 1967 – to date.
Contingent strength:	Max. 14, currently 7.
	1 officer assigned duty with UNIT from June 26th, 1984 – October 28th, 1984,
	1 officer assigned duty with UNGOMAP/OSGAP from May 7th, 1988 – March 24th, 1990,
	1 officer assigned duty with UNGOMAP/OSGAP from May 7th, 1988 – April 5th, 1991,
	3 (as of January 1st, 2001).
Total:	299 (reporting day December 31st, 2009).

- **Dispatch of Medical Personnel**

Basis for deployment:	CM of March 19th, 1968, MC of April 23rd, 1968 (dispatch to end of mission).
Mission:	Medical duties for the treatment of the mission (as a result of UN-specific requirement, these go above the Austrian norms).
Appellation:	None.
Form of dispatch:	Foreign Deployment FCL 1965.
Area of operations:	HQ Jerusalem, Egypt, Jordan, Lebanon, Syria.
Duration of deployment:	April 24th, 1968 – March 16th, 1995.
Contingent strength:	3.
Total:	14.

Lieutenant Colonel Nikolaus Egger (left in the picture) is the 2003/2004 Chief of the Military Observers in Egypt.

I Had a Comrade

In the course of the hostilities four military observers, among them the Austrian Major Hans-Peter Lang, lose their lives in a direct attack by an Israeli fighter jet on the UN post in the vicinity of the town of Khiam on July 25th, 2006 at ca. 7:30 PM. At the event "Soldier of the Year 2007", at which special highlighted contributions from soldiers are honored, the "Special Award" is posthumously awarded to Major Hans-Peter Lang, who fell on July 25th, 2006 in southern Lebanon. Major General Mag. Christian Ségur-Cabanac presents his widow, Mrs. Rosemarie Lang, and his son, Georg Maximilian Lang, with the prize.

Medical Deployment in Biafra

In Nigeria a civil war occurs as a result of a secession attempt by the eastern region of Biafra. The deployment of the UNO is expected, but fails to emerge, since the African nations endeavor to involve only the "Organisation of African Unity" – OAU, but not, however, outsiders such as the UNO. The Eastern Bloc supports a similar understanding, since the Soviet influence on the OAU is greater than that on the UNO.

In 1968 the dispatch of an Austrian UN contingent, this time once more in the form of a field hospital, is again up for debate. It does not come to a deployment. Austria finally involves itself in another way: An semiofficial "Action Committee for Biafra", to which national (such as the Foreign and Defence Ministries) and non-national bodies (like Caritas and the Red Cross) belong, sends three small Austrian medical teams on the basis of a special leave to Biafra. The teams consist of a doctor and four medics each. Although their creation occurs through the Defence Ministry and the majority of the participants come from the armed forces, it is not, unlike all other UN deployments, an official campaign. The commander of the 1st team (November 7th, 1968 – March 23rd, 1969) and the 3rd team (March 24th, 1969 – September 24th, 1969) is Colonel med. Dr. Josef Mayer, the commander of the 2nd team (October 18th, 1969 – April 27th, 1970) is COL med. Dr. Herglotz. Both have already been able to gather experience with the Congo contingent. Dr. Mayer describes the "Biafra deployment" as a *"most difficult deployment under terrible conditions in a cauldron surrounded by Nigerian troops"*.[64]

---

64   Erwin A. Schmidl: "Blue Helmets, Red Cross", Innsbruck Researches into Modern History, Volume 13, Studienverlag, Innsbruck 1995.

United Nations Emergency Force II (UNEF II)

Preliminary Events

The observation deployment of UNTSO along the Suez Canal also continues during the "War of Attrition" between Israel and Egypt. On the Jewish day of atonement, the holiday of Yom Kippur (October 6th) in the year 1973, Egypt and Syria attack completely by surprise.[65] The Egyptians cross the Suez Canal and force their way to the Sinai Peninsula, the Syrians over the Golan Heights until almost into the Jordan Valley. After a general mobilization, Israeli troops succeed first in pushing the Syrians back over the Golan Heights and then attack the Egyptian troops on the Sinai peninsula. At one place the Israelis even succeed in crossing the Suez Canal and creating a beachhead on the west bank. Despite Security Resolution 338 the Israelis continue to push forward and finally close the entire 3rd Egyptian Army off on the east bank of the canal.

International Reaction

Since the surprising success of the Israelis means it is to be feared that they will march further, to Cairo, the UN Security Council passes Resolution 338, after which a cease-fire should have taken effect. However, Israel continues its attacks. In order to hinder a further escalation, SC Resolution 340 of October 25th, 1973 establishes a cease-fire. UN Secretary-General Dr. Kurt Waldheim is empowered to create a 7,000 man strong UN troop, which is now called the "(Second) United Nations Emergency Force (UNEF II)" after the "UN Emergency Force" of 1956 – 67. Since the only immediately accessible troops are on Cyprus, large parts of the contingents stationed there from Austria, Finland, Ireland and Sweden are already flown to Cairo on October 26th by the British Royal Air Force, within the framework of "Operation Dove". The mission of UNEF II reads, to occupy a buffer zone first on the west bank of the Suez Canal and from March 1974 also on the east bank, and through the construction of control posts to observe the adherence to the case-fire.

After the signing of the Camp David Accord and the conclusion of the peace treaty between Israel and Egypt on March 26th, 1979, the deployment of UNEF II ends on July 24th, 1979. In 1982 an international peacekeeping troop organized outside of UNO, the "Multinational Force and Observers (MFO)" is deployed in Sinai.

Basis for the deployment:	SC Resolution 338 (1973) of October 22nd, 1973; SC Resolution 340 (1973) of October 25th, 1973; SC Resolution 346 (1974) of April 8th, 1974.
Mission:	Observation of the cease-fire between Egypt and Israel and, after the agreements of January 18th, 1974 and September 4th, 1975, observation of the withdrawal of Egyptian and Israeli troops as well as monitoring of the buffer zones stipulated in these agreements.
Duration of deployment:	October 25th, 1973 – July 24th, 1979.
Participating nations:	Australia, Austria, Canada, Finland, Ghana, Indonesia, Ireland, Nepal, Panama, Peru, Poland, Senegal, Sweden.
Strength:	Max. 6,973 (in February 1974), at the last 4,031.
Headquarters:	Ismailia.

Austrian Participation

Political Measures

As a result of the petition from New York the federal government decides shortly before its ceremonial session on the occasion of the Austrian national holiday on October 26th, 1973, to shift a portion of its UNFICYP contingent to Egypt.

Military Measures

For the UNO troops on Cyprus, the demand to provide contingents for the new operation comes completely as a surprise in the night before October 26th. At 2:00 AM the battalion is informed. The distribution of the troops over around 60 small OPs makes informing them difficult. Nevertheless, still on the same day at 8:20 PM, a 42 man strong advance command can be flown with British transport planes from the NATO staging base Akrotiri to Cairo. Already two days later the main contingent follows with 205 Austrians, 60 vehicles and 214 t of provisions ("Operation Dove").

---

65 Horst Pleiner: "The October War 1973", Parts I – IV; Austrian Military Newspaper, Issues 3, 4, 5, and 6/1983, Ueberreuter Verlag, Vienna, 1983.

The briefing in the new area of operations takes place through Austrian officers of UNTSO. The Austrians move into their accommodations in the Cairo Military Academy. The Austrian contingent is initially deployed as the UNEF reserve and for the provisioning of the trapped 3rd Egyptian army. Furthermore the telegraph connection between the UNEF contingents and the UNEF headquarters in Ismailia is secured. Beginning in November, three positions are occupied southwest of Ismailia. Between November 8th and 14th the battalion is first expanded by 184 men and 60 t of equipment, by the middle of December a further 179 men follow. In January 1974 the command shifts to Ismailia, further, Positions 101 and 109 on the West Bank are occupied. Finally the withdrawal of the Israelis according to the agreement is observed from Kilometer Marker 101 from January 18th, 1974. In the middle of March 1974 the Austrians shift to Suez. There AUSBATT, as the Austrian battalion in the Middle East is called, observes a section of the buffer zone east of the Small Bitter Lake on both sides of the road to Giddi Pass. In the span of time between November 5th, 1973 and August 11th, 1975 Austria also provides staff personnel in UNEF HQ. Already by May 1974 Austria is informed that in the event of the accomplishment of a disengagement agreement between Israel and Syria, the transfer of the Austrian contingent to a new UN mission on the Golan Heights is planned. The transfer to Syria then takes place between June 3rd and 19th.

Basis for deployment:	CM of October 26th, 1973, MC of November 8th, 1974 (dispatch);
	CM of April 22nd, 1974, MC of May 3rd, 1974 (dispatch duration);
	CM of June 4th, 1974, MC of June 11th, 1974 (end).
Mission:	Occupation of the assigned sector of the buffer zone and accomplishment of the duties of the mission.
Appellation:	**Austrain Battalion (AUSBATT).**
Form of dispatch:	Foreign Deployment FCL 1965.
Area of operations:	Suez, road to Giddi Pass.
Duration of deployment:	October 26th, 1973 – June 2nd, 1974.
Contingent strength:	602 soldiers.
Total:	720 soldiers.
Commander:	Colonel Dr. Erich Weingerl.

"The endless caravan through the desert" – one could describe the bottom picture so. With 60 vehicles, the Austrian contingent shifts from Cyprus to Cairo. The insert picture shows an Austrian Steyr 680 M3 truck crossing a pontoon bridge over the Suez Canal in the course of a provisioning trip.

United Nations Disengagement Observer Force (UNDOF)

Preliminary Events

Syria belongs to the Ottoman Empire, and after the First World War is governed by France under the mandate of the League of Nations. In 1946, it becomes independent. The Golan Heights themselves are first governed by Great Britain, then since 1923, in exchange for Mosul, by the French. Because of their strategic position they have been the site of hostilities between Israel and Syria more than once since the withdrawal of the British from Palestine (1948). From the dominating Heights, the Israeli settlements in the Jordan Valley can easily be fired upon. In 1948, shortly after the creation of the nation of Israel, the Syrians push from the Golan Heights over the Jordan in this way, however withdraw again in 1949. In the Six Day War of 1967, Israel conquers large parts of the Golan; the Heights are developed as observation and early warning stations. In the Yom Kippur War of 1973 the Syrians succeed in a surprise attack until the Jordan Valley, which however subsequently comes to a halt as a result of a lack of supplies and air support.[66]

Israel succeeds in reconquering the entire Golan, including the dominating Mount Hermon, in an extremely short time after mobilization. The further advance can first be stopped 30 km before Damascus. On May 13th, 1974, a troop disengagement agreement takes place between Israel and Syria. However, this is only a ceasefire and not a peace treaty. In 1981 the Golan is annexed by Israel, which is however rejected by the UN General Assembly as illegal. In 1996 talks take place between Israel and Syria, but these initially remain unsuccessful.

In 1999 renewed talks between the two opponents begin. After the death of Hafez al Assad on June 17th, 2000, his son Bashar initially takes over the function of Secretary-General of the reigning Baath party, on June 25th he is elected president by the parliament.

International Reaction

After difficult negotiations initiated by the USA, Syria and Israel are successfully brought to signing a disengagement agreement. This takes place on May 31st, 1974 in Geneva. The agreement plans for Israel to return to the positions that it had already conquered in 1967. On the same day the Security Council enacts the creation of UNDOF[67] with Resolution 350. Between June 2nd and 5th, 1974, AUSBATT and the Peruvian battalion (PERBATT) are relieved by UNEF II and transferred to the Golan Heights. The disengagement agreement establishes an Alpha Line (A Line) in the west, which must not be crossed by Israelis, and a Bravo Line (B Line) in the east, which must not be crossed by Syrians. Between these two lies the demilitarized buffer zone (Area of Separation), which is observed by UNDOF. The A Line generally runs from around 20 km east of the Jordan Valley, and is so drawn that the hollow of Quneitra remains in Israeli possession. The importance of these Heights is underlined by Israel's establishment or upgrading of early warning and electronic surveillance stations. West of Quneitra the A Line is preceded by zone bordered by the A1 Line, which only Israeli military personnel must avoid. Outposts in the buffer zone and on the approach roads are operated by UNDOF. Between the outposts brisk patrolling activities take place. On both sides of the buffer zone is a 25 km broad zone (Area of Limitation), which is divided into three zones and in which the maximum number of soldiers, weapons and tanks is fixed. In the first zone, out to a distance of 10 km, only 6,000 men of the armed forces, with 75 tanks and 36 pieces of artillery are allowed to be stationed. In the adjoining zone, out to 20 km, the aggressors are allowed to maintain a further 450 tanks and 162 pieces of artillery, besides an unlimited number of soldiers. In the third zone, it is only forbidden to station anti-aircraft guns.

In July 2001, a new operational concept under the name **"Wild Mountain"** is developed by UNDOF. This plans for a reduction of the 30 constantly occupied positions by 2004, in exchange for an increased observation of the Area of Separation (AOS) by more mobile and flexible patrols.

As a result of the extremely tense situation in the Middle East, in July 2001 the area of the 1st company/AUSBATT is declared an area of emphasis, since an increased infiltration by Hezbollah activists is expected. Night patrols are therefore carried out with armored vehicles, without exception. In connection with the events of September 11th, 2001, "Phase One" is called in Syria, which means the implementation of certain security measures.

Under the leadership of Major General Mag. Wolfgang Jilke the UN troops move to a significantly more flexible deployment leadership. Infringements of the agreement are now not only reported, but attempts are made to actively advance against or prevent these infringements. Particular attention is also given to the increased appearance of smugglers in the UNO controlled zone, in that special mobile night patrols and new observation towers are established. The **"Barrel Project"** is a decisive improvement on the fulfillment of the mission. The UN observed zone is marked by clearly visible and raised signal barrels, in order to more quickly recognize infringements of the agreement. The barrels are placed by explosive ordnance disposal and engineering forces in sometimes heavily mined or difficult to reach terrain.

---

66 Horst Pleiner: "The October War of 1973"; Truppendienst, Volume 3/1983, Vienna 1983.
67 "On the Situation in the Middle East: The Deployment of UNDOF"; ÖMZ, Volume 4/1980, Vienna 1980.

Basis for deployment:	Troop disengagement agreement of Geneva on May 31st, 1974; SC Resolution 350 (1974) of May 31st, 1974; SC Resolution 1328 (2000) of November 27th, 2000 (extension).
Mission:	Observation of the troop separation agreement between Israel and Syria, above all through checks of the "Area of Limitation" and occupation of the "Area of Separation", and the agreed-upon troop withdrawal. Military observers from UNTSO are responsible for supporting the mission, in particular through observation of the troop reduction zones adjoining either side of the buffer zone. At times military observers are transferred to UNGOMAP.
Duration of deployment:	June 3rd, 1974 – to date.
Participating nations:	Austria, Canada, Croatia, Finland, Iran, Japan, Peru, the Phillippines, Poland, Slovakia.
Strength:	Max. 1,450; 1,047 (as of December 30th, 2009).
Headquarters:	Damascus until 1994, then Camp Faouar (near Amret al Faouar).
Force Commander:	December 15th, 1974 – July 15th, 1975 — Colonel GS Hannes Philipp (entrusted in the interim)
	July 16th, 1975 – April 20th, 1979 — Major General Hannes Philipp
	April 21st, 1979 – November 30th, 1979 — Colonel GS DI Günther Greindl (interim)
	December 1st, 1979 – February 25th, 1981 — Major General DI Günther Greindl
	February 26th, 1981 – June 30th, 1982 — Colonel GS Walter Schmitt (entrusted in the interim)
	September 3rd, 1988 – September 30th, 1991 — Major General Adolf Radauer
	February 22nd, 2007 – February 28th, 2010 — Major General Mag. Wolfgang Jilke

Austrian Participation

Political Measures

After the passing of Resolution 350, the UN Secretary-General directs a petition to the Austrian UN representative to agree to the shift of UNEF II from Egypt to Syria, which is also acceded to on the part of the federal government on June 4th, 1974.

Evacuation of UN Affiliates
The Council of Ministers decides on March 18th, 2003, as a result of the political developments in Iraq, to deploy up to 20 members of the UNDOF contingent to support the evacuation of UN affiliates in Syria through escorts.

Military Measures

The Austrian UNEF II contingent is immediately withdrawn from the buffer zone and shifted to Syria, together with the Peruvian contingent (PERBATT) within the framework of **"Operation Concorde"**. Before this, the section is transferred to the Senegalese and Ghanians. The troop already begins its march without an official Austrian resolution. However, the command is informed of its approval shortly before it reaches the 1st intermediate goal of Rabah (on the northern edge of the Sinai desert). With this, the worry of taking part in a UNO mission without legalization from their own government is taken from them. The transfer of the 179 men with 53 vehicles takes only four days (June 2nd to 5th). In total around 190,000 km are covered without accident. This is notable in view of the climate and the route (half of the road leads through the Sinai desert). The Austrian battalion (AUSBATT) occupies the northern part of the Golan since then. The battalion is accommodated between Mt. Hermon (2,814 m) and the Damascus-Quneitra road in a battalion camp and 19 permanent outposts with six branch outposts. Since 1974 the command and the headquarters company have been stationed first in Saassa (halfway between Quneitra and Damascus) with a Syrian tank battalion, and then in Camp Faouar with a Polish logistics unit. This camp must first be constructed. The water and electrical lines are laid, the sewer system put in order and the accommodations constructed out of pre-fabricated concrete pieces. Just before the end of the "disengagement operation", a tragic accident overshadows work in the camp: during the search for a crashed Iraqi pilot an Austrian patrol drives over a mine on June 25th, 1974. All four soldiers (MCPL Hans Hofer, CPL Helmut Sturm, LCPL Walter Neuhauser and PTE Alija Voloder) are killed. These are the first fallen soldiers which Austria has to mourn in a UN mission. In the following years still more Austrians die in mine and other accidents "in the service of peace". The 1st company observes Mount Hermon with their outposts, the 2nd company checks the area around the road Damascus-Quneitra, and the 3rd company is deployed between them. Poland moves a supply and engineering unit and Canada a logistics unit from UNEF II to UNDOF.

In July 1975 PERBATT is withdrawn and replaced by the Iranian battalion (IRANBATT) in August. The twelve positions of the Peruvians are taken over until the arrival of the Iranians, which places a 4th company (codename: Bedouin) for this purpose. IRANBATT takes over the section south of the main road from Khan Arnaba to Quneitra until the Jordanian border. Parts of IRANBATT are shifted to UNIFIL in southern Lebanon in 1978 and six of the positions previously held by them are taken over by

Headquarters of UNDOF (t.l.) and entrance to the Austrian headquarters (t.r.). The pictures show further AUSBATT outposts.

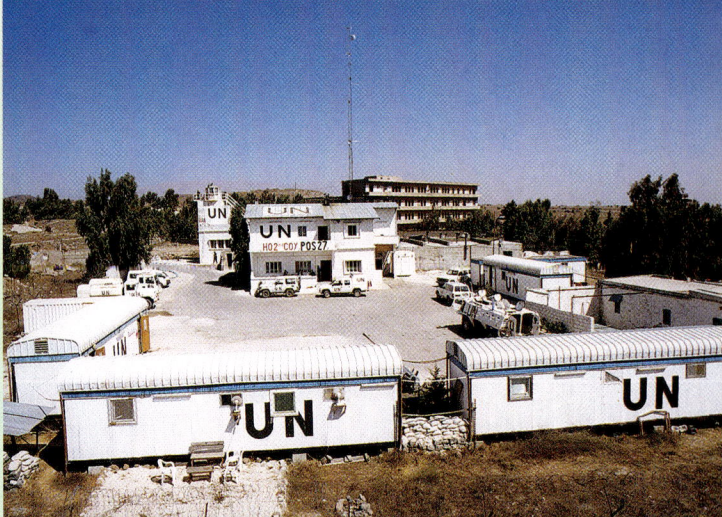

The soldiers are to fulfill their mission in all weathers and all times (t.l. and r.). Every movement must be correct, which demands intensive training and constant practice (m.). The dog as constant and faithful companion, whether on watch (b.r.), patrol (t.r.), or in the war on drugs. The extreme temperatures compel adaptations of the various types of uniforms. This can lead to strange combinations (b.l.). Seven soldiers in five different adjustments – that could be a record.

141

AUSBATT. At the end of March 1979 the Iranians are withdrawn to their own nation as a result of their revolution. So the 4th company is placed again in line with "Operation Fast Switch". This takes over the southern portion of the buffer zone as well until the arrival of the Finns. On September 17th, 1979 FINBATT takes over the southern portion. The Finnish government withdraws FINBATT in 1993. It is replaced with a Polish contingent (POLBATT), which fulfills duties in the Golan with AUSBATT to this day.

In September 1975 the Austrian Force Commander, Major General Hannes Philipp, succeeds in bringing about an important humanitarian project: an agreement between Israel and Syria makes contact for Druze families from the Israeli-occupied and Syrian areas possible. These families were torn apart by the war. These "family meetings" take place every two weeks.

Until the introduction of the Slovakian contingent in 1998 AUSBATT is deployed as follows: The 1st company is deployed in the north with heavy emphasis on Mt. Hermon. Furthermore, outpost "Position 12" at 1,750 m above sea level on the B Line is operated by the 1st Coy. Posn. 12 forms the starting point on the Arne road for the provisioning of soldiers deployed on the Hermon ridge. Besides the proven Pinzgauers, the 1st Coy also possesses two M113A1 armored personnel carriers and three Kässbohrer Pistenbullis for this provisioning. Further positions are Posn. 14 and 17 on the roads in the town of Hadar on the Syrian side as well as Posns. 10 and 16 on the road of Hadar-Majdel Chams. The outer post of 16A on the A Line by Majdel Chams is only occupied one day. Here the aforementioned family meetings take place. In addition, nine foot and two vehicular patrols are carried out. Notable for the time being is the special situation of the positions of the 1st company on Mt. Hermon. The highest Austrian point is in the direct vicinity of the summit. Wind speeds of 150 km/h, heavy snowfall and temperatures of up to negative 15 degrees Celsius make survival difficult. In the early times, when there are still no permanent accommodations, only the two somewhat lower-laying outposts of "South Hotel" (2,380 m) and "Base Hotel" (2,250 m) remain occupied. With the help of the **"UN Field Service"** (the logistics organization for UN deployments in the field), permanent accommodations are prepared in place of the tents. The foundations for these must be created by the Austrian contingent itself. Since the outposts are often cut off from the outer world for up to three weeks in the winter, they are already equipped with all necessary provisions in fall. A doctor is constantly deployed with the mountain company. The follow-up supplies take place with snow vehicles. The patrol activities are carried out on skis. Since the personal equipment is actually designed for the desert deployment of the 1973/74 troops deployed in Egypt, at first the appropriate winter clothing and alpine equipment must be sent after them. At the end of 1976 the high mountain outpost "Hotel" is also built on the highest observation point on Mount Hermon. In November it is dedicated and christened with the name "Edelweiss Hut".

The 3rd company observes the central section between the roads of Mazrat Beit Jinn and Massada as well as the area west of Khan Arnaba. A platoon occupies Posns. 33 (in the north, on the road to Massada) and 37 on the A Line southwest of Taranja. In addition the two outer posts 37A and 37B are occupied during the day. A further platoon established Posns. 30, 31, and 34 on B Line. The 3rd Coy furthermore carries out seven foot patrols and two vehicular patrols.

The southern section, including the road from Khan Arnaba to Quneitra, is observed by the 2nd company, in which their area of operations on the B Line demands only the Posns. 25 and 32, which lay west before Khan Arnaba. Posn. 20 is on the central street crossing within the strip, with outer postings 20A and 20B on the A Line near Hamidiye and northwards. Posns. 22 and 28 lay on the A Line north and south of Quneitra, where the latter of these is directly across from the Israeli checkpoint, the only crossing for UNDOF and UN personnel into Israel. The A1 Line west of Quneitra is observed from outer postings 22A, B, C, and D. The 2nd Coy additionally is to carry out four foot patrols and five with vehicles. A deployment group (infantry group with a transport and a communications vehicle) is ready at all times in every company. In addition to these positions, observation points are also occupied by observation officers, who above all are to provide observation of the area before the field. In the course of the new operational concept, a contribution for their own area of operations is developed for **"Wild Mountain"** by AUSBATT.

In the summer 2006 AUSCON is confronted with military conflicts lasting several weeks in Lebanon, despite the quiet situation on the Golan Heights.

After Poland announces that it will examine and, if necessary, withdraw their foreign deployments in the year 2008, the (Austrian) force commander decides to return currently POLBATT-held Position 22 to AUSBATT again on March 3rd, 2009. With this, the only outpost on Israeli-occupied territory comes into Austrian hands again after six years. At the same time, the freedom of operation as well as the continuity in the area of this important border crossing to Israel can be secured.

Slovakian Contingent (SLKCON)

On May 27th, 1998 a Slovakian infantry platoon (32 soldiers) takes over the duties of three outposts (Posns. 14, 31 and 33) in the area of the 3rd company and four functions in HQ (deputy company commander, doctor, ordnance officer, duty officer). On May 26th, 1999, the contingent is increased to 93 soldiers and takes over the duties of the 3rd Coy (the middle portion), parts of the headquarters company and two further staff functions (deputy battalion commander, duty officer) as well as a function in the HQ element (military police).

In June 1999 the anniversary of the placement of AUSBATT comes for the twenty-fifth time. Therefore a celebration takes place on May 17th, 1999, in the Van Swieten barracks in Vienna/Stammersdorf (the residence of the then-command for foreign deployments), during which besides the Austrian Defence Minister, his Slovakia counterpart, Dr. Pavel Kanis, also takes part. During this celebration both ministers also say farewell to a mixed Austrian-Slovakian relief contingent.

On June 6th, 2008, the ceremonial leave-taking of the Slovakian contingent takes place in Camp Faouar. The Slovakian contingent had finally occupied a total of five outposts (10, 16, 17, 30 and 31) with its soldiers in AUSBATT's troop disengagement zone.

Croatian Contingent (CROCON)

The Slovakian contingent is relieved by a Croatian contingent. The contingent has a strength of 95 soldiers and is deployed as a company within the framework of the Austrian battalion as follows:

- 76 soldiers in six positions with an area of responsibility of around 60 square kilometers in the northern area of separation;
- a group (eleven soldiers) in the framework of the intervention forces (Force HQ);
- eight soldiers in the UNDOF staff in staff functions (five officers and three noncommissioned officers).

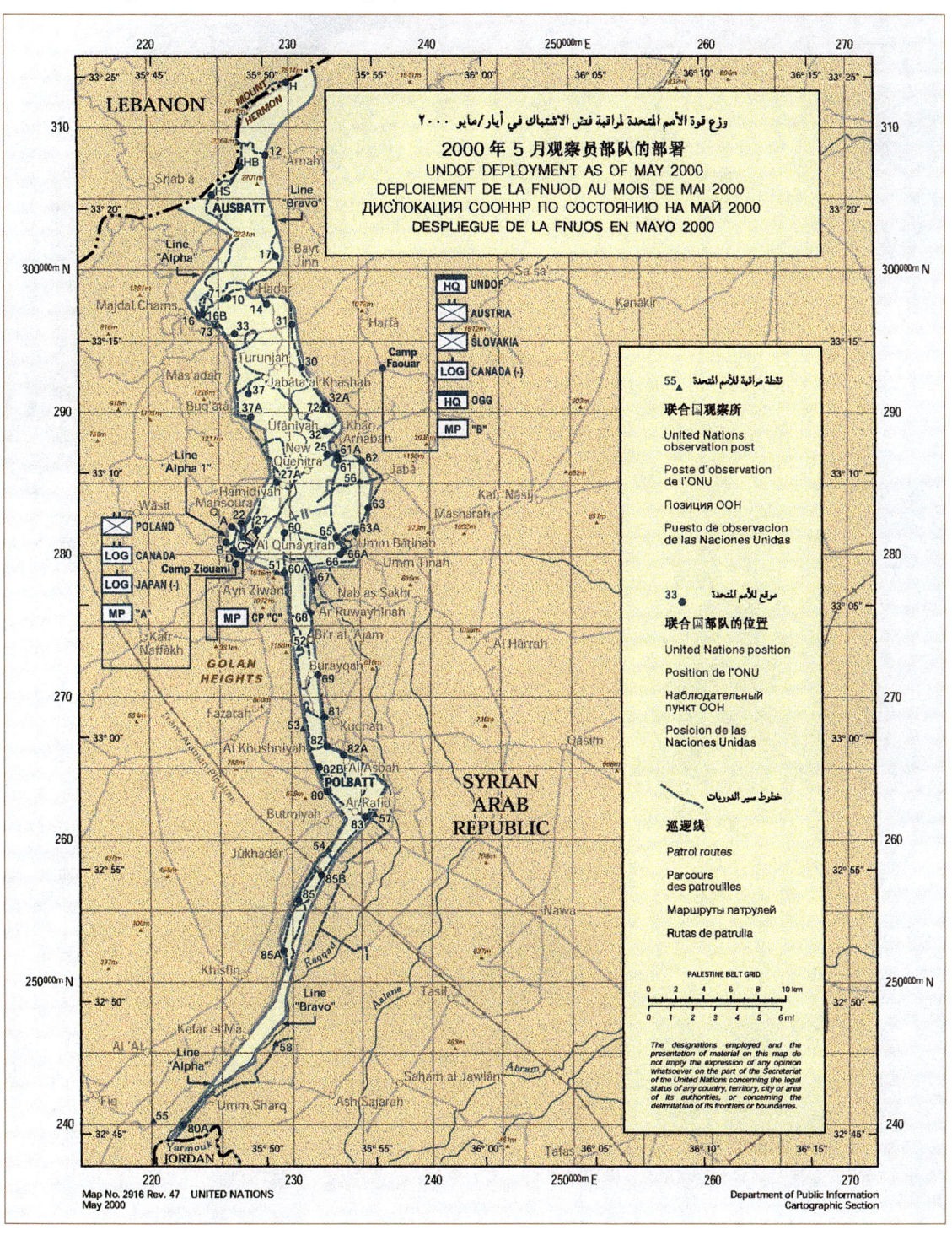

Mines – deadly danger at every step. Accordingly, great importance is afforded to training in recognizing and dealing with these weapons (t.l.). But weight is also laid on the traffic safety of vehicles. So the completeness and condition check belongs among self-evident activities even on a foreign deployment (t.r.). "Local workers" are not only a valuable workforce (m.r.), they are also employees and as such belong to the team. Accordingly, they are also given medical care from AUSBATT (m.l.). In their free time the soldiers also meet in the chapel for contemplation and prayer (b.l.) or use the superior snow conditions for a ski tour (b.r.). One can also find inner peace in this way.

The service on the Golan Heights is considered difficult and challenging above all because of the extreme weather conditions. In winter the high positions are often cut off from the outer world for days and completely dependent on themselves. Alpine experience is therefore a prerequisite for this service.

Basis for deployment:	CM of June 4th, 1974, MC of June 11th, 1974 (dispatch); CM of May 8th, 2001, MC of May 23rd, 2001 (strength of up to 373, up to five additional men for a short time, extension until December 31st, 2001).[68]	
Mission:	Fulfillment of the duties of the mission in the assigned sector.	
Appellation:	Austrian Battalion (AUSBATT/UNDOF).	
Form of dispatch:	Until April 1997 according to Foreign Deployment FCL 1965, from April 1997 according to the KSE FCL.	
Area of operations:	Northern section of the troop disengagement zone in the Golan Heights.	
Duration of deployment:	June 3rd, 1974 – to date.	
Contingent strength:	Up to 396.	
Total:	Around 50,000 (as of December 1st, 2009).	
Composition:	Battalion command (Camp Faour), headquarters company, 1st Company (Hermon Base, Hermon Hotel, Hermon South, Position 12), 2nd Company (Positions 27, 25, 32, 37), 3rd Company/CROCON (Position 10, 16, 17, 31, 30, 32A).	
National contingent commanders (NCC):		
	June 13th, 2001 – July 13th, 2002	Colonel GS Michael Sutter-Keller
	July 14th, 2002 – May 4th, 2003	Colonel Dr. Michael Kaes
	May 5th, 2003 – May 2004	Colonel Claus Amon (simultaneously COS)
	May 2004 – July 2004	Colonel Dr. Tassilo Pawlowski
	July 2004 – September 2005	Colonel GS Andreas Safranmüller (simultaneously COS)
	September 2005 – November 16th, 2006	Colonel GS Mag. Dr. Andreas Stuppka
	November 17th, 2006 – July 11th, 2007	Major (Lieutenant Colonel)[69] GS Mag. Rudolf Zauner
	July 12th, 2007 – January 27th, 2008	Major (Lieutenant Colonel) Robert Glanner
	January 28th, 2008 – February 2nd, 2009	Major (Lieutenant Colonel) Hans-Peter Hohlweg
	February 3rd, 2009 – July 2009	Lieutenant Colonel GS Mag. Rainer Winter
	July 2009 – February 14th, 2010	Lieutenant Colonel Armin Lehner MSD (simultaneously COS)
	February 15th, 2010 – January 10th, 2011	Lieutenant Colonel Karl Wolf MSD (simultaneously COS)
	January 11th, 2011 – to date	Colonel GS Mag. Martin Dorfer
Commanders:	May 9th, 1974 – August 30th, 1975	Lieutenant Colonel Franz Burgstaller
	August 31st, 1975 – December 12th, 1976	Lieutenant Colonel Hans Widhofner
	December 13th, 1976 – February 26th, 1978	Lieutenant Colonel Friedrich Ehrl
	February 27th, 1978 – May 20th, 1979	Lieutenant Colonel Arthur Klocker
	May 21st, 1979 – September 16th, 1980	Lieutenant Colonel Fridolin Gigacher
	September 17th, 1980 – September 7th, 1981	Lieutenant Colonel Nikolaus Horvath
	September 8th, 1981 – September 7th, 1982	Lieutenant Colonel Karl Stainer
	September 8th, 1982 – September 7th, 1983	Lieutenant Colonel Rudolf Löffler
	September 8th, 1983 – September 10th, 1984	Lieutenant Colonel Helfried Satter
	September 11th, 1984 – September 10th, 1985	Lieutenant Colonel Richard Wardein
	September 11th, 1985 – September 9th, 1986	Lieutenant Colonel Dieter Brell
	September 10th, 1986 – September 9th, 1987	Lieutenant Colonel Gerhard Sackl
	September 10th, 1987 – September 24th, 1988	Lieutenant Colonel Franz Gigler
	September 25th, 1988 – October 26th, 1989	Lieutenant Colonel Günther Winkler
	October 27th, 1989 – March 27th, 1991	Lieutenant Colonel Stefan Lehninger
	March 28th, 1991 – May 22nd, 1992	Lieutenant Colonel Maximilian Pacher-Theinburg
	May 23rd, 1992 – June 1st, 1993	Lieutenant Colonel Karl Schendl
	June 2nd, 1993 – May 27th, 1994	Lieutenant Colonel Andreas Kloss
	May 28th, 1994 – May 26th, 1995	Lieutenant Colonel Günter Bartunek
	May 27th, 1995 – May 20th, 1996	Lieutenant Colonel Josef Linder
	May 21st, 1996 – July 31st, 1997	Lieutenant Colonel Nikolaus Egger
	August 1st, 1997 – July 31st, 1998	Lieutenant Colonel GS Günther Ruderstaller
	August 1st, 1998 – August 2nd, 1999	Lieutenant Colonel Ernst Eder
	August 3rd, 1999 – October 6th, 2000	Lieutenant Colonel Silvio Kaiser
	October 7th, 2000 – October 26th, 2001	Lieutenant Colonel GS Stefan Thaller
	October 27th, 2001 – October 25th, 2002	Lieutenant Colonel Wolfgang Petermair
	October 26th, 2002 – May 4th, 2003	Lieutenant Colonel Ing. Siegmund Uray
	May 5th, 2003 – April 30th, 2004	Lieutenant Colonel Klaus Amon
	May 1st, 2004 – October 10th, 2004	Lieutenant Colonel Gerd Schrimpf
	October 11th, 2004 – November 15th, 2005	Lieutenant Colonel Herbert Pracher
	November 16th, 2005 – October 6th, 2007	Lieutenant Colonel Christian Friedhuber-Grubenthal
	October 7th, 2007 – January 27th, 2008	Lieutenant Colonel Robert Glanner
	January 28th, 2008 – February 2nd, 2009	Lieutenant Colonel Hans-Peter Hohlweg
	February 3rd, 2009 – February 14th, 2010	Lieutenant Colonel Armin Lehner
	February 15th, 2010 – February 6th, 2011	Lieutenant Colonel Karl Wolf MSD
	February 7th, 2011 – to date	Lieutenant Colonel Schiffbänker

---

68 Generally an extension must be approved again every six months by the Council of Ministers and the Main Committee of Parliament, since the agreement on Austrian participation is only ever extended for the duration of each UN mandate (and these mostly last six months).
69 For the duration of the foreign deployment.

Vehicle Equipage

Besides the normal equipage of 23 military vehicles, the Austrian contingent also has access to 86 UN vehicles. Especially mentionable are four APC[70] M113A1s and three APC SISUs.[71] The wheeled vehicles are primarily Japanese products from the firms of Toyota, Mitsubishi, Hyundai, and Nissan. In addition there are vehicles from Bedford, General Motors, Leyland, Mercedes, Opel, Renault, and Volvo.

Special Clothing

AUSBATT is clothed in the utility uniform/foreign deployment and the hunting calf shoes that belong with it, as well as the service uniform/UN (from Trevira). For the 1st Coy there is also the complete alpine equipage. Especially mentionable here are the plastic outer shoes, the protective glasses and the heat cells for the torso, hands and feet as well as the alpine overcoat with fur lining.

Since the new desert uniforms are identical to the American ones, the Austrian soldiers receive a sign over the left breast pocket on which "Austrian Army" is written in the Arabic language to avoid confusion. This well-meaning measure is a typical bureaucratic one, of course hardly anyone in this region can read.[72]

At the beginning of July 2002 AUSBATT is equipped with the light hot weather clothing (HWC) that is known worldwide since the Gulf War. Either the HWC shirt or a caramel-colored T-shirt with rank insignia and name tag is worn as the topmost piece of clothing. The soldiers of 1st Company on Mount Hermon receive an HWC field jacket for the summer as well as a result of the low temperatures predominating there. Light khaki-colored desert boots serve as the footgear. On patrol, on the other hand, well-tried canvas shoes in either black or black-green are still available. In the colder months, utility uniform 75 is still worn. In 2005 the already older utility uniform 75 will be replaced with uniform 03 in AUSBATT/UNDOF.

Maintenance of Ability

Particularly in a deployment such as this, leisure activities and the maintenance of ability have great importance. So, among other things, various competitions take place, during which the affiliates of the individual UN contingents can compare themselves in peaceful competition. Austria hosts the already legendary "AUSBATT March". In this march a total of 45 km with a vertical rise of 1980 m is to be covered. The march is not only conceived as a physical challenge, but should also offer the participants the opportunity to get to know the entire AUSBATT zone. Not only the soldiers challenge themselves, the force commander, some ambassadors and embassy affiliates take part in this "UN event". In 1999, 50 teams with 200 participants are at the starting line. 171 manage the route in blistering heat. Another athletic challenge is represented by the **"Enzian Run"** of 2nd Company, which is carried out twice a year.

Camaraderie

As a special symbol of unity after the deployment in the Golan, Catholic students who belong to the "Mittelschüler-Kartellverband (MKV)" (a high school student association) and to the „Österreichischer Cartellverband (ÖCV)" (the academic student association) found their own fraternity, the „Golania zu Arne". The mother-association is the „Theresiana im ÖCV". Theresiana is the academic student association at the Theresian Military Academy. At the annual conference in Brixen in 2000 a friendship agreement is made by the ÖCV.

> *"Austria's soldiers stand at their posts,*
> *Weapons in hand.*
> *For peace here in the Middle East,*
> *Far from our homeland.*
> *The sun burns high in the sky,*
> *No doubt in winter snow and ice.*
> *Duty is often no delight,*
> *For freedom we pay the price."*
>
> (Lad's verse e.V. Golania)

Radio Gecko

The "new ones" are greeted at the airport by those ready to fly home with loud calls of "Gecko! Gecko!"[73], whether they are on a UN deployment for the first time or they already wear a silver number, which indicates numerous foreign deployments, among their military decorations. Radio Gecko is founded in 1994 as a private organization and develops over time into an indispensable part of everyday life in camp. After marked beginning difficulties, the station receives a broadcast permit from the Syrian authorities in October 1995. The emcee team consists exclusively of volunteers, who devise the program in their free time, with much engagement and enthusiasm. This includes reports on novelties in the area of operations, visits from prominent people, music (over 30,000 titles are available) or also quiz shows.

---

70 Armored Personnel Carrier.
71 A Finnish product.
72 Since I have not mastered the Arabic language, I was previously of the opinion that this was the name of the wearer in Arabic. I thank Colonel Dr. Kurt Mitterer and Brigadier General ret. Mag. Wolfgang Fritsch for this information. The picture is from the Military History Museum in Salzburg.
73 The expression "Gecko" comes from the Cyprus deployment, where the "new rotation" is named after these lizards in their first months.

The volunteer fire department at AUSBATT is a special feature. The VFD has access to the most modern rescue equipment from Austria. For vehicles, a Cmd vehicle Toyota Station (t.l.) and a TLF M35 tank fire engine (t.r.) at the HQCoy, and a Renault Fire/Water tank fire engine (m.) at the 2nd Coy are available. Like at home, training and practice also have great importance here (b.l.), where it must be considered that the members of the AUSBATT FD change at least once a year and teamwork must therefore constantly be recoordinated.
In every rotation there is a special deployment: the fire department stands ready before the camp to "greet" the "new ones" with a powerful "Water march!" (b.r.).

Besides the vehicles that the armed forces are also equipped with in Austria, UNDOF/AUSBATT has access to a great number of vehicles which are only in the inventory overseas: Such as the tanker truck/Truck Fuel (t.l.) and the water tanker truck/Water 10,000 l (t.r.) from Leyland, the all-terrain armored truck/Fuel (m.l.) and the all-terrain truck of the type M35A1, the RG 32 patrol vehicle, a water tanker truck/10,000 l. Volvo FL10 (b.l.) and the Mercedes 2631 three-axle truck (b.r.).

The two APC M113A1 (t. and m.l.) and APC SISU XX-180 (m.r. and b.) armored personnel carriers available to AUSBATT are also a special feature. The M113 has an engine with 210 horsepower at 2,800 RPM, with outer measurements of 4,860 x 2,700 x 2,200 mm (L x W x H). The SISU's engine has a performance of 176 kilowatts at 2,500 RPM, and has outer measurements of 7,350 x 2,900 x 2,650 mm. While the M113 has already been deployed with AUSBATT since the beginning of UNDOF, AUSBATT has only had the SISU since October 1993. In the picture b.r. the various uniforms of AUSBATT can be clearly seen. The solders are wearing utility uniform 75, with the exception of the comrade pictured right, who is wearing the UN ticking instead.

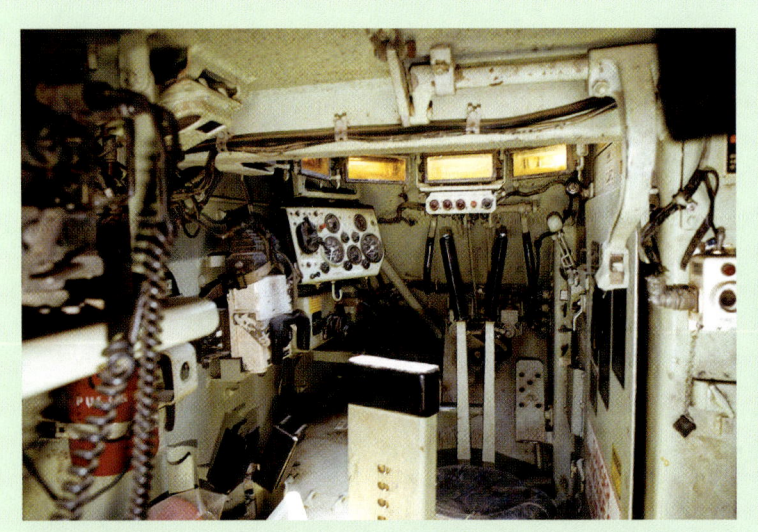

After three years of service, on March 1st, 2010, UNDOF Force Commander Major General Mag. Wolfgang Jilke hands over the command of the UN troops on the Golan to the Filipino Major General Natalio C. Ecarma (t.r.). For this, honor formations of all participating nations reported at the parade ground (t.l.). On February 26th, 1978, the camp church (in the picture t.l.) is ceremonially dedicated by the Apostolic Nuncio of Damascus, Archbishop Angelo Paroni. However, since time ate away at the church tower, replacing the old roof with a new one is unavoidable. As ever, the engineers of AUSBATT are on the spot for such assignments. No matter whether it is the bells, the windows, the prefabricated cross or the roof truss, everything must fit together. As a strictly religious Christian, Mr. Shahin provides his mobile crane for free, in order to lift the finished roof construct onto the tower. The renovation has a worthy conclusion with a celebratory ceremony from the Archbishop of Salzburg, Dr. Alois Kothgasser, and Military Superior Dr. Christian Rachlé (m.r.). On July 14th, 2008, 145 blue helmets from the 23 nations of the three UN missions in the Mediterranean zone (in Lebanon, in Golan and on Cyprus) open the traditional military parade on the Champs Elysées in Paris. Among them are also ten Austrians, who fulfill their duties for peace in the Golan Heights (b.r.). The picture b.l. shows the memorial for the four Austrian soldiers killed by a mine explosion on June 25th, 1974. In total 20 Austrians up to now have been killed or died while deployed in the Golan.

Feitl Club

On October 20th, 1980, the Carinthians among the officers celebrate their regional holiday in Golan in a special way with speeches, the regional anthem, Carinthian songs and a subsequent hearty traditional cold cheese and meat platter. Since only a few original Feitls (a special form of pocket knife) are available, only "VIPs" receive one. Lieutenant Colonel Nik Horvath and Major Ing. Günter Ganz decide as a result to found a "Feitl club". Requirement for membership: one must also carry the Feitl with him. If a member takes his Feitl out of his pocket, all other members must immediately do the same. Whoever does not have his Feitl with him must ring the "Horvath bell" and buy a round. Over time the proceedings are refined and, suitably for the deployment, named the "Feitl check".

Humanitarian Measures

On April 23rd, 1981, the "UO Feitl club" (the Feitl is a special form of pocket knife) is founded. The goal of this club is the financial support of the children's home and the foundling's home in Damascus. The ritual of the circle, consisting of 15 members, is notable: The "check" with the "Feitl" serves not only as a sign of recognition, in this way money also comes into the money box. If a member has forgotten his Feitl for whatever reason, then he must fetch it within two minutes, or else a financial donation must take place. Through this and other "practices", around US $2,000 come together yearly. New members are suggested half-yearly, must then submit to an "observation" and must finally be voted in by the majority.

Earthquake Deployment in Friuli

Preliminary Events

At the beginning of May 1976 a serious earthquake jolts the upper Italian region of Friuli. The effects can be felt in Carinthia as well, but cause only minor damages there. In Friuli itself numerous towns are totally destroyed.

Austrian Participation

Political Measures

The Italian military attaché in Vienna directs a petition from his government to Austria on May 9th, 1976, asking for the provision of equipment from Austrian military inventories as an aid contribution for the catastrophe zone. The Austrian federal government decides to accede to this request and commissions the Defence Ministry to begin appropriate measures.

International Reaction

International aid organizations participate in the aid measures to support the Italian authorities.

Military Measures

Transport columns with the necessary aid goods are immediately put together by the armed forces. Through an efficient and unbureaucratic cooperation of all responsible parties in Austria and Italy, the first aid column can already cross the Italian border on May 10th at 1:25 AM. On this and the next day, another six aid transports follow. Finally, three large tent cities are constructed in the area of Gemona.

Basis for deployment: CM Resolution.
Mission: Carrying out of aid transports.
Appellation: None.
Form of dispatch: Foreign Deployment FCL 1965.
Area of operations: Gemona.
Duration of deployment: May 9th, 1976 – May 11th, 1976.
Contingent strength: 273.
Total: 273.
Contribution: Construction of three tent cities; relinquishment of aid materials (tents, beds, blankets, mattresses, dishes and silverware) in the value of 10,300,000 AS.

Earthquake Deployment in Titograd

Preliminary Events

Heavy earthquakes shake the region on the southern Adria coast in April 1978.

International Reaction

International organizations participate in the aid measures to support the local authorities.

Austrian Participation
Political Measures

The federal government grants the request of the Styrian regional association of the Austrian Red Cross for air transport of aid goods from Graz-Thalerhof to Titograd, and commissions the Defence Ministry with the implementation.

Military Measures

The Defence Ministry deploys both transport planes of the type "Skyvan". The first flight is to take place on Easter Monday. For this, a "Skyvan" with tents shifts from Langenlebarn to Vienna. However, since the crew receives no diplomatic clearance, the aircraft must fly back to Langenlebarn on the same day. Finally, on the next day, the clearance is given and the first transport to Titograd can be carried out. There the crew's passports are immediately taken and only given back hours later. The aircraft returns on the same night to Graz, where it is immediately loaded for the next day. Afterward, daily flights between Graz and Titograd take place. With this, the air force shows that even with (extremely) limited possibilities, they can carry out purposeful missions abroad.

> **Basis for deployment:** Petition of the Austrian Red Cross.
> **Mission:** Air transport of aid goods.
> **Appellation:** None.
> **Form of dispatch:** Foreign Deployment FCL 1965.
> **Area of operations:** Titograd.
> **Duration of deployment:** April 16th, 1978 – April 25th, 1978.
> **Contribution:** In ten flights over 50 flight hours, 13 t of aid goods are transported.

Earthquake Deployment in Calabritto

Preliminary Events

On November 23rd, 1980 a heavy earthquake jolts the city of Naples and the surrounding region. By November 26th it is clear that the earthquake has caused extremely serious personal and material damages in an area the size of Lower and Upper Austria. On the morning of December 8th, an aftershock occurs.

International Reaction

Numerous international aid organization immediately take measures to come to the aid of the affected population. Among these are the Boy Scouts, who dispatch numerous aid groups to the region of the catastrophe.

Austrian Participation

A disaster relief platoon of the Viennese Boy Scouts, trained in disaster relief services at the NBC Defence School in Vienna on the weekends, decides to deploy and therefore petitions the Defence Ministry for personnel and material support.

Military Measures

Since 1972, Boy Scouts are trained in disaster relief services at the Engineer and NBC Defence Schools on the weekends. The Defence Ministry therefore unbureaucratically supports the Boy Scouts' plans: Engineers and aerial defence engineers who voluntarily report for the deployment receive special leave; the vehicles and equipment of the NBC Defence School are made available, provisions and monetary resources are gathered through donations. Since this is not an official deployment, a large amount of administrative work is created for immunizations, negotiations with employers, the Austrian Federal Railways and the insurance companies. The result of this is a delay of the move out, which finally takes place on December 4th.

At 9:00 PM the advance command leaves in an all-terrain vehicle. There are no breaks, the soldiers exchange turns driving. At 1:00 PM the team arrives in Rome, where it is cared for by the Austrian military attaché in Rome. After the arrival of the advance command in Caserta on December 6th at 10:00 AM the catastrophe platoon is assigned the town of Calabritto in the region of Avellino as their area of operations. The mayor of Calabritto requests the recovery of the buried, household goods, and cultural artifacts. On December 5th at 1:00 PM the contingent shifts 38 aid workers with three search dogs, rescue equipment, 9 special vehicles and aid goods by rail through Innsbruck into the area of operations. The aid goods, which were loaded in Vienna by soldiers of the Guard Battalion, fill 24 wagons which must be unloaded by the contingent at their end station. Initially, however, the train is "lost". In Italy no one knows of a special train from Austria. Not until the evening of December 7th is the train "found" in Battipaglia, on the other side of the (Italian) boot.[74] From there the catastrophe platoon moves by foot into the area of operations. After the construction of a base camp at the highway station Campagna, the actual recovery works begins the day after, on December 8th. Since the official coordination does not always function, the foreign experience and improvisational talent of the Austrians proves itself once again. It quickly spreads that the best help is to be found with the men "with the white helmets and the red-white-red stripes".

The recovery work itself proves to be exceptionally dangerous – sometimes even impossible – and demands a careful approach with safety always in mind. After initial orientation difficulties the dogs accomplish exceptional location successes; the disinfection and burial troop have their hands full. Although the withdrawal is planned for December 13th, it is petitioned through the "homeland staff" to obtain the agreement of employers for a "leave extension". After that, the deployment can be extended to December 16th.

On December 14th, a religious service is held in a temporarily constructed church, using the liturgical garments, utensils, and saints' statues rescued from the rubble.

On December 16th the withdrawal is begun. During this time it can only be made clear to the people with difficulty that their offered, often very valuable, presents cannot be accepted. However, they show the estimation that the Austrian soldiers and Boy Scouts have earned. On December 17th at 10:00 PM the special train leaves the catastrophe zone in the direction of Vienna. The S4 of the Air Defence Troop School is completely surprised when it can assure itself of the good condition, but above all of the completeness of its vehicles and equipment. This is supposedly not always the case during exercises in Austria. The soldiers participating in this deployment gather valuable experience in deployment tactics and cooperation with search dogs. It is therefore no coincidence that one of the participants is assigned as the deployment leader during the Armenian deployment in 1988.

Basis for deployment:	Volunteer.
Mission:	Clearance and recovery.
Appellation:	None.
Dispatch form:	Special leave.
Area of operations:	Calabritto.
Duration of deployment:	December 4th, 1980 – December 18th, 1980.
Contingent strength:	38 soldiers and three search dogs.
Total:	38 soldiers and three search dogs in area of operations, six soldiers in homeland staff.
Composition:	One catastrophe platoon.
Commander:	CPT Norbert Fürstenhofer.
Contribution:	In total 5,000 work hours are achieved. 37 buried people, numerous still living pets, 80 cubic meters of household goods, 27 valuable statues of saints and sacramental objects from three churches, as well as community and church documents, can be rescued. Within the framework of the deployment, 5,839 km are covered.

Donation Collection

As previously mentioned, monetary funds for the deployment are collected through donations. Furthermore, an extensive charity drive takes place throughout Austria, with the goal of building new houses for those people who have lost their property and possessions. Numerous Austrian firms arrive with material contributions, construction firms make workers and construction materials available. Within the armed forces collections are made as well. Among others, the currently running 9th General Staff Course, to which the author belongs, brought so much money together that a one-family home can be financed with it. Later, at the ceremonial dedication of the house, a plaque noting the donators will be attached.

---

74 Norbert Fürstenhofer: "Italian Diary", in "Spind, the Magazine for Duty and Leisure", Vol. 10, 2/81, No. 52.

United Nations Inspection Team in Iran and Iraq (UNIT)

United Nations Iran Iraq Military Observer Group (UNIIMOG)

Preliminary Events

A bitter war begins with Iraq's attack on Iran in September 1980, which goes down in history under the name of the **"Iran-Iraq War"**. The dispute between the two nations already flared up centuries ago over the Shatt al-Arab, the area around the mouth of the Euphrates. In an agreement from the year 1639 the river is already mentioned as a border line, and since then military hostilities occur again and again between the Ottoman and the Persian Empires, or later between Iraq and Iran. In the earlier agreement the entire river is granted to Iraq; Iran receives a guarantee of free shipping. In 1975 the Shah of Persia forces the center of the river to be established as the border, as is internationally customary. After the Islamic Revolution in Iran, the Iraqi president uses the occasion to declare the old Iraqi right to the Shatt al-Arab and demand the bordering areas back. The "Iran-Iraq War" begins, the Iranian revolutionary government declares it a **"Holy War"**, and the Iranian units actually succeed in stopping the Iraqi advance and even push forward into Iraqi territory. At the beginning of February 1985 Iraq declares that it will no longer hold itself to the agreement of June 12th, 1984, and will battle Iran to a proper cease-fire. The bombing attacks are subsequently taken up again. Iraq occupies the Al Faw peninsula. In fall 1987 the situation escalates further. The reciprocal attacks at sea lead to serious impairment of the civilian shipping. Iraq mines the Strait of Hormuz and the Persian Gulf and attacks civilian oil tankers. This also leads to serious discord between Iraq and the USA. In spring 1988 serious battles also take place. Iran wins the Al Faw peninsula back. Finally both nations accept SC Resolution 598. On August 20th, 1988, at 5:00 AM, the cease-fire takes effect; both aggressors hint that they are ready to let their weapons fall silent without delay.

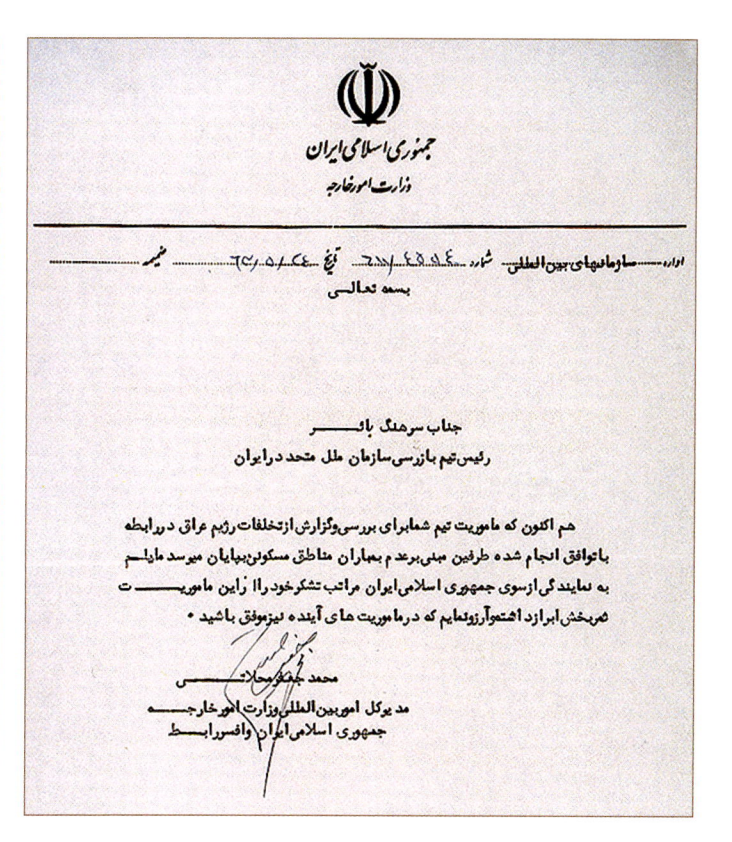

International Reaction

In 1980 UNO, the Gulf nations, various international associations and private initiatives already attempt to reach a cease-fire. On November 5th, 1980, the UN Security Council authorizes the Secretary-General to name a representative of UNO to visit both nations and lead talks to end the war. The visits take place, but do not lead to success. On June 12th, 1982, the Security Council passes Resolution 514, which demands an immediate cease-fire and the withdrawal of the respective troops to the internationally recognized borders. For the first time, the prospect of a dispatch of UNO troops is raised. On September 30th Resolution 522 is passed, which repeats Resolution 514 with all possible stridence. But further negotiations also remain unsuccessful. In May 1983 Iran petitions the Security Council to dispatch a commission to visit the Iranian territories in which Iraq has attacked civilian establishments. The commission determines there to be serious destruction in Iran, however only minor destruction in Iraq. On October 31st, 1983, the Security Council newly enacts a resolution (540) in which the infringement of international law is condemned. In it, the cessation of all hostilities as well as unchecked shipping in the Persian Gulf and the Strait of Hormuz is demanded. During an Iraqi attack on Iran at the end of February 1984 chemical weapons are also deployed. Iran petitions the UNO for the dispatch of a commission to investigate the gas attacks. A group of specialists visits Iran from March 13th to 19th. In a Security Council declaration of March 30th, the use of chemical weapons is condemned and compliance with the Geneva Conventions of 1925 is demanded. After Iraq attacks civilian establishments in Iran again on June 5th, 1984, during which hundreds of civilians die and serious destruction is cause, a call from the Secretary-General goes out to both nations to refrain from attacks on civilian targets. This call is accepted by both nations, and the Secretary-General is petitioned to take measures to investigate infringements of the agreement.

On June 12th, 1984, the agreement takes effect. At the ruling of the Secretary-General, within the framework of the **"United Nations Inspection Team in Iran and Iraq" (UNIT)**, two teams, one each for Iran and Iraq, are placed for observation. On June 16th, 1984, both nations are informed that the teams are ready for deployment and can be called upon from both aggressors at any time. The teams consists of three military observers and a civilian official of the UNO each. Initially only officers from Finland, Ireland, Austria and Sweden are accepted. The first team in Iran under the command of an Austrian begins its service on June 26th, 1984. The team in Iran is brought under the auspices of the **"United Nations Development Programme" (UNDP)** in Tehran, the team in Iraq under those of the **"United Nations Social and Economic Commision for Western Asia" (UNSECWA)**. From the beginning of 1985, only the team leader and the political advisors are in Tehran and Baghdad. The observers themselves carry out their duties with UNTSO in Damascus and Tiberias. From 1986, observers from Argentina, Australia, and New Zealand are also allowed to be deployed. In reality, however, only observers from Argentina take part in the inspections for three months. From April 1986, only the team leaders remain in the two capitals. The teams are very seldom deployed, since they are only allowed to act with the permission of the respective nation.

On July 20th, 1987, SC Resolution 598 is passed, in which the end of the battles on the Gulf is demanded and the basics of a plan for peace are laid out. UN Secretary-General Pérez de Cuéllar succeeds in establishing a cease-fire after intensive negotiations in Geneva and New York. Under the direction of the UNO, peace negotiations are taken up. At the same time, the UN Security Council passes Resolution 619 on August 9th, 1988, which has

UNIIMOG insignia

UNIT insignia

as its content the establishment of the **"United Nations Iran-Iraq Military Observer Group" (UNIIMOG)** as the successor organization to UNIT, and grants a mandate for six months for the time being. The mission of UNIIMOG is to test, observe, and confirm the cease-fire and the withdrawal behind internationally recognized borders. Furthermore, observing the return of prisoners of war belongs among its duties.

On August 9th, 1988, the advance command leaves Jerusalem for Iran, and reaches Tehran by way of Vienna and Istanbul on August 10th.

On August 15th the first contingent lands, on August 18th the transfer is completed. The Iranian side is divided into four sectors and maintains headquarters in Saqqez, Baktarah, Dezful and Ahwaz.

At the same time the contingents planned for Iraq shift and immediately begin with their work. For this the Iraqi territory is separated into three sectors: Sector North with HQ in Sulaymaniyah, Sector Central with HQ in Baqubah, and Sector South in Basra.

Two equally important headquarters are established in Tehran and Baghdad. The Force Commander of UNIIMOG alternates between a few days each in Iran and Iraq. The ca. 1,200 km long border is observed with mobile observation teams with all-terrain vehicles or helicopters, but also with boats and on the backs of donkeys (!). Each team consists of three monitors, a liaison officer, two guards, and in the immediate area of the front, an additional scout.

• United Nations Inspection Team in Iran and Iraq (UNIT)

Basis for deployment:	SC Resolution 514 (1982) of July 12th, 1982;
	SC Resolution 522 (1982) of September 20th, 1982;
	SC Resolution 540 (1983) of October 31st, 1983.
Mission:	Verification of accusations; observation of the agreements of the conflicting parties.
Duration of deployment:	June 26th, 1984 – August 15th, 1988.
Participating nations:	Argentina, Austria, Finland, Ireland, Sweden.
Headquarters:	Baghdad (UNIT/B) and Tehran (UNIT/T).
Strength:	Four military observers, two civilian UN officers from UNTSO.

Austrian Participation

Military Measures

From the beginning, Austria is one of the four nations (Argentina only participates for three months) who are accepted by both the conflicting parties to provide observers for inspection teams.

Austria supplies team leaders at times for both UNIT-Iran in Tehran as well as UNIT-Iraq in Baghdad:

Basis for deployment:	CM of June 19th, 1984, MC of June 27th, 1984 (dispatch of UNTSO).
Mission:	Deployment of observers for the observation of the cease-fire.
Form of dispatch:	Assignment of UNTSO.
Area of operations:	Iraqi-Iranian border area.
Duration of deployment:	June 26th, 1984 – August 15th, 1988.
Team leaders in Iran:	June 26th, 1984 – February 27th, 1985,
	June 30th, 1986 – December 21st, 1986,
	July 26th, 1988 – October 28th, 1988.
Team leaders in Iraq:	August 23rd, 1985 – February 25th, 1986,
	August 23rd, 1987 – March 3rd, 1988.
Contingent strength:	1.
Total:	5.

• United Nation Iran Iraq Military Observer Group (UNIIMOG)

International Reaction

Basis for deployment:	SC Resolution 598 (1987) of July 20th, 1987; SC Resolution 619 (1988) of August 9th, 1988 (dispatch of UNIIMOG).
Mission:	Observation of the armistice and the withdrawal of troops to the internationally recognized borders.
Duration of deployment:	August 20th, 1988 – February 28th, 1991.
Participating nations:	Argentina, Australia, Austria, Bangladesh, Canada, Denmark, Finland, Ghana, Hungary, India, Indonesia, Ireland, Italy, Kenya, Malaysia, New Zealand, Nigeria, Norway, Peru, Poland, Senegal, Sweden, Turkey, Uruguay, Yugoslavia, Zambia.
Headquarters:	Baghdad and Tehran.
Strength:	Max. 400 military observers, 300 civilian employees (1990), finally 114 military observers.

Austrian Participation

Political Measures

On August 10th, 1988, the UN Secretary-General petitions Austria to dispatch six officers (one in the rank of a Lieutenant Colonel and five with the rank of Major or Captain), whereupon the officers were to reach Baghdad by August 16th at the latest. The federal government also responds to this petition on August 16th. On September 13th, 1988, there is a further petition for the dispatch of four medical noncommissioned officers, of which two each should be deployed in Tehran and Baghdad as "medical assistants". In November 1989 two further officers are set on the march to UNIIMOG. On January 24th, 1990, the Council of Ministers decides on a further increase of four officers.

Military Measures

The first two officers are set on the march from the Defence Ministry so that they still arrive in Baghdad on August 16th, four more follow on August 26th. The Austrians are only deployed on the Iraqi side. The dispatch of the four medical officers is delayed as a result of organizational problems within the UNO. As a result, they first arrive in Tehran on December 21st and in Baghdad on December 23rd. The further observers can be punctually dispatched.

Basis for deployment:	CM of August 16th, 1988, MC of September 27th, 1988 (dispatch); CM of November 8th, 1988, MC of November 10th, 1988 (MedNCO); CM of January 24th, 1990 (increase); CM of July 30th, 1991 (end).
Mission:	Deployment as military observers; assumption of staff functions; medical care of mission affiliates.
Appellation:	None.
Form of dispatch:	Foreign Deployment FCL 1965.
Area of operations:	Border zone between Iraq and Iran.
Duration of deployment:	August 16th, 1988 – February 28th, 1991 (after the end of the mission a military observer remains until the discharge of his personal responsibilities until March 10th in line with the concluding forces of UNO in the area of operations).
Contingent strength:	Up to 17 (from which up to four are medical noncommissioned officers, two each in Iran and Iraq).
Total:	25.

United Nations Good Offices Mission in Afghanistan and Pakistan (UNGOMAP)

Office of the Secretary General in Afghanistan and Pakistan (OSGAP)

Preliminary Events

On December 25th, 1979, the USSR begins an intervention into Afghanistan. At this time point troops of the Afghan government, supported by Soviet units, face off against resistance groups of the Mujahideen. The Mujahideen operate partially on Pakistani territory, where they are also supplied with American weapons.

Despite the cease-fire of April 14th, 1988, and the troop withdrawal ordered therein, numerous attacks occur from the Mujahideen against the areas left by the Soviet troops. In response, the Soviets carry out an air attack against the rebel-occupied provincial capital of Maidan Shahr, which causes great damages.

International Reaction

In 1981, negotiations begin under the respective Deputy Secretary-General (initially Pérez de Cuéllar and then, after his election to Secretary-General, Diego Cordovez), which, after seven years of activity, can finally be brought to a successful close with the signing of an agreement by Afghanistan and Pakistan (with the USSR and the USA as guarantor powers) on April 14th, 1988, in Geneva. During these talks an understanding on the withdrawal of the Soviet troops is also achieved. The "Afghanistan agreement" includes four segments: a bilateral agreement on mutual relationships and non-interference, a bilateral agreement on the voluntary return of refugees, an declaration of the international borders and an agreement on the withdrawal of foreign troops. The last part also contains a formless agreement on the provision of observation by the United Nations. Since the signatories have no interest in an active role for the Security Council, the planned operation is only brought before them for agreement. At the end of October, the USSR nevertheless addresses the Security Council to discuss the situation after a withdrawal of Soviet troops. On October 31st, 1988, the Security Council acknowledges the report of the Secretary-General with Resolution 622. On April 25th the advance command of UNGOMAP reaches Islamabad, and on May 15th UNGOMAP begins its full activities as the agreement comes into effect. The core of UNGOMAP is formed by 50 observation officers from ten nations, 25 for each side. During the Soviet deployment three outer postings on the border to the USSR are established. UNGOMAP cares for around 31 million refugees from Afghanistan in field posts in Peshawar, Quetta, and Lahore. These are accommodated in a total of 341 refugee camps, from which ten apiece are then united into a so-called "refugee settlement" for easier administration. Besides the UN affiliates, around 12,000 Pakistanis are available to give care.

The observation of the troop withdrawal initially shows itself to be very problematic, since the Mujahideen carry out numerous attacks in the areas left by Soviet troops. In response, the Soviets carry out an air attack against the rebel-occupied provincial capital of Maidan Shahr, which causes great damages. After the completed withdrawal in spring 1989, the contingent is reduced to 40 observers.

On March 15th, 1990, UNGOMAP is transformed into the (smaller) **"Office of the Secretary-General for Afghanistan and Pakistan" (OSGAP)** as representatives of the UN Secretary-General. The mission of OSGAP is to gather and evaluate freely available information and to make suggestions for the achievement of a cease-fire and its observation, as well as to prepare for free elections. An officer who already participated in UNGOMAP is available for the senior military advisor in each country.

Nevertheless, OSGAP is also not able to end the conflicts and hostilities in Afghanistan; the mission expires in 1993. The government left behind by the Soviets in Islamabad cannot resist the underground fighters. In 1996 the Mujahideen take power and implement Islamic law particularly stringently. The hostilities also continue in 2001. The remaining UN aid programs must temporarily withdraw their workers from the land, in which (at the beginning of 2001) over a million people are in flight.

• United Nations Good Offices Mission in Afghanistan and Pakistan (UNGOMAP)

Basis for deployment:	Geneva Accords of April 14th, 1988; letter from the president of the SC to the Secretary-General of April 25th, 1988 (S/19836); SC Resolution 622 (1988) of October 31st, 1988; SC Resolution 647 (1990) of January 11th, 1990.
Mission:	Support of the representatives of the UN Secretary-General during "good offices" for the implementation of the provisions of the Geneva Accords; observation of the Soviet withdrawal; observation of compliance with the Accords and securing the return of Afghan refugees to the homeland. Since spring 1989 the UNO also maintains engineering teams (United Nations Mine Clearance Training Teams – UNMCTT) in the border area. These have the job of training the returning refugees in recognition, disposal, and deactivation of mines.
Duration of deployment:	May 15th, 1988 – March 15th, 1990.
Participating nations:	Austria, Canada, Denmark, Fiji, Finland, Ghana, Ireland, Nepal, Poland, Sweden.
Headquarters:	Kabul and Islamabad.
Strength:	Max. 50 military observers and 25 civilian workers temporarily assigned from UNTSO, UNDOF and UNIFIL.

Austrian Participation

Political Measures

On April 14th, 1988, during a meeting with the UN Secretary-General, the Austrian foreign minister declares Austria's general readiness to dispatch observers to UNGOMAP. The federal government decides on April 26th, 1988 to dispatch up to 5 observers for the duration of up to a year. On April 25th, 1989, the federal government decides on an extension of the mandate until January 15th, 1990 (end of the UN mandate). One day later Austria reduces its contingent from five to two officers, since UNO adopted none of the cost of the deployment in response to their commitment.

Because of the extension of the mandate for two months, a new decree of the Council of Ministers is also necessary. This takes place on January 24th, 1990. On March 15th, 1990, the withdrawal of the two officers ends participation in UNGOMAP.

Military Measures

Accordingly with the decree of the Council of Ministers, the armed forces dispatch 5 officers to UNGOMAP, 3 officers are deployed in Kabul, 2 in Islamabad. After the reduction three officers are repatriated. The two officers who were shifted from UNTSO to UNGOMAP at the beginning of May 1988 remain.

Basis for deployment:	CM of April 26th, 1988, MC of June 10th, 1988 (dispatch); CM of June 5th, 1990 (end).
Appellation:	None.
Mission:	Deployment as military observers.
Form of dispatch:	Initially reassignment from UNTSO, later according to Foreign Deployment FCL 1965.
Area of operations:	Border zone between Afghanistan and Pakistan.
Duration of deployment:	April 25th, 1988 – March 15th, 1990.
Contingent strength:	5 (2 in Islamabad, 3 in Kabul). 1 officer from UNTSO from May 7th, 1988 to March 24th, 1990. 1 officer from UNTSO from May 7th, 1988 to April 5th, 1991.
Total:	5.
Commander:	Colonel Günter Führer.

Duty room in Kabul (t.l.). "UN Permanent Presence" in Chaman, the border crossing between Pakistan and Afghanistan (t.r.). Major Sintler with an Afghani and a Pakistani officer (b.l.). The simple duty (and bed) room of a military advisor in Chaman (b.r.).

UNGOMAP insignia

- **Office of the Secretary-General for Afghanistan and Pakistan (OSGAP)**

Basis for deployment:	UNO Resolution 44/15 of November 1st, 1989.
Mission:	Consultation with the special deputy of the UN Secretary-General during the planning of a possible comprehensive peacekeeping operation in Afghanistan.
Duration of deployment:	March 16th, 1990 – September 1993.
Participating nations:	Austria, Canada, Denmark, Fiji, Finland, Ghana, Ireland, Nepal, Poland, Sweden.
Headquarters:	Islamabad.
Strength:	10 military observers.

Austrian Participation

Political Measures

The federal government agrees to the dispatch of an officer.

Military Measures

Austria sends an officer as a military adviser to HQ, who was assigned to duty from UNTSO to UNGOMAP and now carries out his duty at OSGAP.

Basis for deployment:	CM of March 20th, 1990, MC of April 26th, 1990 (dispatch), CM of January 12th, 1993 (end).
Mission:	Deployment as military adviser; assumption of staff functions as needed.
Appellation:	None.
Form of dispatch:	Assignment from UNOT/UNMOT, partially according to Foreign Deployment FCL 1965.
Area of operations:	Islamabad.
Duration of deployment:	March 16th, 1990 – May 5th, 1993.
Contingent strength:	1.
Total:	8.

Earthquake Deployment in Armenia

Preliminary Events

On December 7th, 1988, at 11:40 AM local time, an earthquake measuring 6.0 on the Richter scale jolts broad areas of the Soviet constituent republic of Armenia. The catastrophe occurs at a point in time in which the factories, office buildings and schools are in full operation. The region between the Black Sea and the Caspian Sea has been known since time immemorial as a classical earthquake area. It causes significant damage above all in the urban areas of Spitak, Leninakan and Kirowakan. Initial estimates speak of 40,000 dead, 12,000 wounded and more than 100,000 homeless. Spitak itself is 100%, the others half destroyed. In contrast to the practice of minimal information practiced by the Soviet Union up to this point, the Soviet government requests international aid in view of the extent of the destruction and the number of victims. This is also surely connected to the fact that the Soviet president is in New York at the same time to speak before the General Assembly. For the first time Soviet television transmits detailed hourly reports on the catastrophe.

International Reaction

The **"United Nations Disaster Relief Organization" (UNDRO)** in Geneva informs its member nations about the events in Armenia for the first time on December 8th at 1:42 PM. On the same day specialists from UNDRO arrive in Leninakan for a survey and constantly report on the situation. The "UNDRO Situation Report No. 2" informs all members on December 9th of the Soviet government's petition for international help, in which besides aid goods "search and rescue teams" are also requested.

Basis for deployment:	Call from UNDRO for aid contributions (search and rescue).
Mission:	Aid contribution after a catastrophic earthquake, in particular recovery of the buried in the assigned area of operations.
Duration of deployment:	December 10th, 1988 – December 20th, 1988.
Participating nations:	Austria, Canada, Denmark, Finland, France, Germany, Great Britain, Italy, Japan, Norway, Sweden and Switzerland (only Austria dispatches soldiers).
Headquarters:	Leninakan.

Austrian Participation

Political Measures

The Federal Ministry for Foreign Affairs (FMFA) makes contact with the Soviet ambassador in Vienna, Shikin, on December 9th, and immediately declares their readiness to dispatch aid forces. For the first time, the army command is commissioned to begin considerations for a deployment of parts of the armed forces, in particular rescue and recovery units of the NBC defence troop. The Austrian federal government accedes to the petition of the Soviet government on December 9th, and decides on the dispatch of a military contingent to assist in the catastrophe zone.

Military Measures

On December 9th (a gap day between the Feast of the Immaculate Conception and the weekend), the Army Command (AC) already takes all provident measures for an eventual deployment in Armenia. It is first thought to dispatch eight rescue and recovery groups as well as a field clinic. Since the military dogs are only trained for guard and security assignments, the absorption of parts of the Red Cross rescue dog brigade is brought into the plans as well. The concrete deployment order from the Defence Ministry arrives at 3:48 at Army Command (AC).[75] All details of the implementation, such as the issuance of a collective visa by the Soviet embassy and detailed information about the situation on the ground, are directly clarified with the diplomatic representatives of the USSR in Vienna. With regard to the transport of the large equipment and vehicles, it is assumed that the Soviet Union will provide the necessary air transport. This unfortunately proves to be an error. So the transport is carried out two Austrian Airlines aircraft of the type DC-9-80, at the cost of the Republic of Austria. This, however, means that taking along vehicles, including medical vehicles, must be foregone. As a result of the loading dimensions of the AUA aircraft, the large air compressors must be disassembled. Thanks to outstanding cooperation with AUA, this also occurs without a problem. Taking along explosive or fire-starting materials must also be foregone, so that from the beginning one deployment possibility (namely, rescue and recovery detonation) is eliminated. On December 10th, at 5:30 PM, the first aircraft starts, an hour later the second. 77 soldiers and ten dog trainers with their search dogs are flown to Armenia. An Austrian officer of Armenian heritage also belongs to the contingent as a translator (an indispensable requirement for an effective deployment in a foreign area). At the same time 28 tons of supplies, principally rescue equipment, medicines, replacement clothing, and provisions are brought into the area of operations.

On December 12th, a civilian group follows with a small vehicle and two cranes. While the equipment is extremely welcome, it quickly becomes apparent that the personnel has no experience or training; it therefore decides to return three days later.

On December 13th a further military command with T1000 radio teletype equipment arrives. This is made available from the FMFA at the request of the DM to secure the connection between the Austrian embassy in Moscow, the FMFA and the Austrian unit. In the written allotment they do not forget to suggest that *"the FMFA may assume that this piece of equipment will experience appropriate careful and experienced treatment as much as is feasible during the deployment in Armenia."* The further follow-up supply planned for this day proceeds less successfully, since the freight aircraft chartered for this from AEROFLOT flies to Leningrad instead of Leninakan with six tons of supplies. Regrettably, the transport cannot be "rerouted" for the duration of the entire deployment.

The Austrian defence attaché in Moscow can first respond to the instruction to immediately travel to the catastrophe zone to support the Austrians on December 15th, since he initially receives no authorization to travel into the earthquake zone from the responsible authorities in Moscow.

On December 14th, two rescue and recovery troops from the NBC Defence Platoon/Military Command Styria follow the contingent. With this, a total of 119 soldiers are deployed in Leninakan. The camp in Leninakan is made in the area of the polytechnic school, meanwhile the first positioning teams are set on the march.[76] As a result of the fact that according to military chemists, a stream in the mountain only 30 km away provides excellent water, the laborious construction of the drinking water preparation facilities brought along can be foregone. The urgent need for small vehicles for the transport of the rescue equipment to the recovery site is covered with the help of the Armenian church, since the local authorities are not able to help (a further proof of the necessity of

---

[75] Christian Ségur-Cabanac: "The Deployment of Rescue and Recovery Units of the Armed Forces in the Earthquake Zone of Armenia", Austrian Military Magazine, Volume 2/1989.

[76] Norbert Fürstenhofer: "The Armed Forces Helped in Armenia: A Report from the Commander of the Deployed Forces", Truppendienst, Volume 3/1989, Ueberreuter Verlag, Vienna 1989.

The damages are unimaginable (t.). Coffins everywhere one looks – our soldiers must also come to terms with that (b.l.). Federal Minister Dr. Robert Lichal greets the returning Austrians and accepts the Austrian flag which waved in Leninakan (b.r.). To the right is Colonel med. Dr. Schlögel, the medical leader of the contingent.

The pictures give an impression of the catastrophic damages. The Austrian soldiers must therefore look under every concrete block in order to possibly find some still living. The commander of the Austrian contingent, Colonel Fürstenhofer, in conversation with local officers (b.r.).

a person who has mastered the local language. Since the Austrian translation officer cannot be everywhere, he recruits multilingual students from the University of Jerewan, so that a translator is subsequently with every recovery troop). Since the local authorities are also not willing to coordinate the rescue measures, this is done by the commander of the Austrian contingent (OESTKON). The deployments each begin with a survey of the position of the buried and the questioning of people there. Afterwards clearance of the area of operations takes place and all engines are shut off to enable positioning. This is carried out first with dogs, then with positioning devices. Then the search through the elements of the rubble begins and is continued until the buried person is found. The actual recovery proves to be especially dangerous, since sliding materials endanger the victim and rescuer in the same way.

In the time from December 13th to 15th in Vienna the rescue and recovery groups of all military commands (134 soldiers) including equipment are all readied for an eventual reinforcement or relief of the Austrian aid contingent. However, this proves unnecessary. So the armed forces have once again proven, that contrary to the opinion of some malicious critics, it is also ready and able on Sundays and holidays to respond quickly and professionally to crises.

On December 17th, after handing over the tents, medical materials, and provisions to the population, the withdrawal is begun, which takes place in three lifts and ends on December 20th, at 2:00 PM, with a safe landing in Vienna-Schwechat. The contingent is greeted by Army Commander General Hannes Philipp with the following words: *"This contribution, brought under adverse conditions and in deployment around the clock, fills all Austrian soldiers with pride, and also finds unlimited recognition abroad, which was particularly articulated by high-ranking representatives of the Soviet Union more than once."* The last remark did not however hinder the Soviet Union from sending a bill for the return transport of OESTKON out of the earthquake region.

This deployment confirms that even world powers have only an inadequate supply of specialists in such a catastrophe and are dependent on worldwide help. The lack of appropriate personal air transport once again proves to be a serious disadvantage for the Austrian participation. With OESTKON the Austrian armed forces provide not only the best equipped, largest, and most successful deployment team, but also the team with the longest stay in the area of operations. This extensive deployment also experiences an important international echo. This is notably seen in an international evaluation of the Armenian aid, which takes place in line with a convention in May 1989 in the USA.

"**Call the Austrians**" is not only the most often used call for help in Armenia, it becomes the trademark of the humanitarian deployments of the Austrian armed forces. The deployment in Armenia leads to the establishment of an **"Austrian Armed Forces Disaster Relief Unit"** (AAFDRU)[77] on May 11th, 1990.

Basis for deployment:	CM of December 12th, 1988, MC of December 15th, 1988.
Mission:	Aid contribution after catastrophic earthquake; recovery of the buried.
Appellation:	**Austrian Contingent (OESTKONT/UNDRO[78]).**
Form of dispatch:	Foreign Deployment FCL 1965.
Area of operations:	Leninakan.
Duration of deployment:	December 10th, 1988 – December 20th, 1988.
Contingent strength:	119 soldiers.
Total:	123 soldiers, 13 dog trainers, three journalists.
Composition:	Command, logistics, medical, communications and repair units, five rescue and recovery groups, rescue dog group, press troop.
Commander:	Colonel Norbert Fürstenhofer (Commander of the NBC Defence School).
Contribution:	Around 35 rescue and recovery deployments, 70 survey and positioning deployments, 14 living and 65 dead recoveries, 400 treatments of locals, 60 treatments of contingent members, ten first aid assistances after living recoveries.

Also certainly notable in connection with the Austrian contingent's contribution is that during the withdrawal aid goods are always left in the area of operations, in order to further help the victims. In this concrete instance these are a ton of medical materials, four tons of provisions, a ton of clothing, 600 wool blankets, 140 sleeping bags, five heatable tents, five chemical toilets and 30 lamps. Naturally the burden of this must also be borne by the armed forces, a refund of these physical contributions brought by the military takes place in the rarest of cases. Although here cost sharing could be expected from the charitable institutions which collect for each catastrophe.

---

77 The name is altered to "Austrian Forces Disaster Relief Unit (AFDRU)" shortly thereafter.
78 UNDRO: United Nations Disaster Relief Organization.

United Nations Iraq – Kuwait Observation Mission (UNIKOM)

Preliminary Events

The extent of the Ottoman dominion stretches far into the Arabian Peninsula. Towards the end of the 19th century the Ottoman Empire attempts to expand its sphere of influence on land and over water into the Persian Gulf. Since this conflicts with the dominant role of the British in the Indian Ocean, they attempt to hinder the construction of Ottoman outposts through a row of contracts with local principalities on the Gulf. Among these is today's Kuwait, where the Al-Sabh family has been in power since 1752. However, the Emir is only a local ruler and from the point of view of the Ottoman Empire has no authority to conclude a protective treaty with Great Britain in 1899. Doubtless this is one reason for the 90-year dispute over the statehood of Kuwait. Kuwait takes a swift upturn after this treaty with the British. In 1913 the British prepare a treaty which is to establish the borders of Kuwait with Turkey and what would become Saudi Arabia; because of the outbreak of the First World War the signing does not take place. After its defeat in the First World War Turkey must accept the relinquishment of all its rights and claims outside of the borders established in the Treaty of Sevres on August 10th, 1920. The former provinces of Mossul, Baghdad and Basrah are combined into the Kingdom of Iraq. In 1922 the national borders between Kuwait, Iraq and Saudi Arabia are established at the Conference of Uqair under British chairmanship. In 1923 the national borders between Kuwait and Iraq are newly regulated and first confirmed in 1932 in a secret agreement. After the great oil wealth of Kuwait becomes known in the 1920's, Kuwait again takes a swift upturn. Despite the treaties, Iraq foments unrest in Kuwait and demands that Kuwait again become a part of Iraq, which feels itself as the successor to the Ottoman Empire.

After World War Two, Kuwait is released into independence from England on June 19th, 1961. Already six days later Iraq again demands Kuwait back. Kuwait calls for help from Great Britain; 48 hours later British troops land. After two months the British troops are replaced by troops from the Arab League; these leave the nation in spring 1963. On March 20th, 1973, Iraqi troops push into Kuwait, however withdraw again in April, without relinquishing their claims.

Over the many years it has become apparent in the Middle East that Iraq, under the leadership of Saddam Hussein, is building up a massive army. In July 1979 Hussein names three "historical goals necessary for survival" to the Revolutionary Command Council: destruction of Israel, establishment of a fair border between the Arabic nations and the Persians, and finally "the unification of all Arabs under the banner of socialism and rebirth". The Iran-Iraq War from 1980 to 1988 aims at the incorporation of the oil-rich Iranian province of Cuzestan and the Shatt al Arab. In this, Iraq is still supported (at least indirectly) by the western powers out of fear of a further expansion of Islamic fundamentalism. Iraq nevertheless does not succeed in reaching its war goals; the war is a complete failure. Heavy loss of life, most serious destruction across the nation, a national insolvency and exorbitant debts on the order of around 80 billion US dollars are all that remain. Nevertheless, the expansionist plans of Saddam Hussein go on. Shortly after the end of war, 1 million soldiers are again armed, the production of mid-range rockets ("Tammus" 2,000 km, "Al Abas" 900 km range) and of NBC weapons continues. Saddam Hussein presents his claim to predominance to the Arabic world and attempts to win control of Arabic crude oil policy and finances. During the Iran-Iraq War Kuwait contributes an enormous amount of financial support for Iraq. Nevertheless, in June 1990 renewed conflicts occur between Kuwait and Iraq over the use of Rumaila oil field in southern Iraq, of which a small portion reaches into Kuwait. Iraq accuses Kuwait of illegal exploitation. Furthermore, Saddam Hussein cannot pay back his credit.

On February 19th, 1990, Hussein demands the immediate withdrawal of American warships from the Persian Gulf. Furthermore, he threatens the deployment of binary chemical weapons, with which he could set half of Israel alight, if any action should be taken against Iraq. On July 16th, Hussein accuses Kuwait and the United Arab Emirates of exceeding the production limits set by OPEC and therefore keeping the crude oil price low. Furthermore, Iraq makes three demands to Kuwait: Reparations of $2.4 billion because of "stolen" oil reserves from Rumaila oil field; the cancellation of Iraqi "debts of honor" on the order of $15 billion from the last war and abandonment of the Kuwaiti islands Bubiyan and Warbah.

On August 2nd, 1990, Iraqi troops finally penetrate and occupy Kuwait. By August 31st, 100,000 men (with three elite tank divisions) are shifted to Kuwait. The Kuwaiti government flees to Saudi Arabia. On August 8th, 1990, Iraq annexes Kuwait and later declares it its 19th province. On August 16th, Iraq interns all the foreigners in Iraq in hotels and kidnaps many to "deploy" as "human shields" in strategically important facilities. By October Iraq gathers 350,000 men in Kuwait according to American information. Iraq subsequently rejects all SC resolutions and breaks off peace negotiations with the USA in December. Instead the armed forces in the south are increased to 500,000. On December 24th, Hussein threatens an attack against Israel, should international armed forces attack in the Gulf. On January 13th, Hussein reiterates to UN Secretary-General Pérez de Cuéllar that he is not ready to respond to the UN resolutions. On January 14th, the Iraqi "parliament" votes unanimously for war.

Already one day after the begin of Operation **"Desert Storm"** on January 17th, 1991, Iraq uses rockets against Israel. On January 25th, Iraq purposefully dumps around 1.7 million tons of oil into the Gulf and sets off a gigantic environmental disaster. On January 30th, an Iraqi land attack takes place on the Saudi border city of Khafji and other border areas. On February 22nd, Iraq accepts the Soviet plan for peace. This, however, is rejected by the allies, since the Soviet plan will only partially fulfill the UNO resolutions. Iraq, for its part, does not react to an ultimatum from the USA. At the begin of the land offensive Hussein answers by setting around 700 of the total 1,000 oil wells in Kuwait on fire.

On February 28th, a cease-fire takes effect. Between March 3rd and 6th, 1991, Iraq finally accepts UNO's armistice requirements. Unaffected by this, an extensive offensive starts against the Shiites, who are starting a large rebellion across the nation, and the Kurds operating in the north, who want to use the opportune moment for themselves. In the south the Shiites even succeed in bringing individual cities under their control. Thereupon, Hussein deploys poison gas and napalm against the rebelling Kurds. The following massacre of Shiites and Kurds leads to giant streams of refugees in the direction of Iran and Turkey. On April 24th, the Kurdish leaders do in fact come to an agreement with Baghdad on autonomy, however this never takes effect. Just the opposite, Iraq continues its actions against Shiite refugees in the Iraqi swamps in the south with all cruelty.

International Reaction

After Iraq's first threats against Kuwait, Egypt, Jordan and the USA attempt to intercede in numerous talks between July 19th and August 1st, 1990. Since this is unsuccessful, the USA shifts six battleships to the region and begins a military exercise with the United Arab Emirates. Already on the day of the invasion the UN Security Council condemns it with Resolution 660 and demands the immediate and unconditional withdrawal of all Iraqi troops as well as a cease-fire.

Hussein's quest for predominance leads King Fahd of Saudi Arabia to support the campaign by accepting Western troops into his country to operate against another Arab country, although this carries a high risk for his throne and the House of Fahd. For Cairo and Damascus this is another reason to take sides against the Iraqi annexation of Kuwait and dispatch troops to Saudi Arabia as part of an Arabian "peacekeeping force" to secure the Saudi border to Kuwait.

On August 6th, the UN Security Council passes sanctions against Iraq (Resolution 661). A trade embargo, from which foodstuffs in particular humanitarian cases and medicines are excluded, as well as a sea and air blockade, are to force Iraq to withdraw. The annexation of Kuwait on August 8th leads US president Bush to announce a dispatch of troops on the same day. On August 9th, Operation **"Desert Shield"** begins. The UN Security Council declares the annexation to be null and void in Resolution 662 on August 9th. The Arab League decides to dispatch a pan-Arabic troop for the protection of Saudi Arabia on August 10th. On August 18th, the UNO reacts to the Iraqi internment of all foreigners and demands that Iraq immediately release all foreigners in UNO Resolution 664. At their meeting in Helsinki on September 9th, Presidents Bush and Gorbachev demand Iraq's unconditional retreat from Kuwait. In the meantime the multinational troops receive reinforcements, among others from Great Britain, France, and Senegal. Further UN resolutions are passed almost weekly, to which Hussein always reacts only with small concessions (sometimes the release of hostages). On November 8th, the Russian government declares that a military deployment is no longer out of the question. On November 29th, the UNO's final demand for a withdrawal by January 15th takes place (Resolution 678). On December 3rd, the UN Human Rights Committee condemns Iraq's ongoing torture and mass executions. Finally, on January 16th, the final call to Hussein takes place.

Since all attempts to end the conflict without violence fail, the deployment of the allied forces under the leadership of the USA begins on January 17th, 1991, at 1:00 AM CET, as Operation **"Desert Storm"**[79], as a result of the UNO Resolution 678 (1990) of November 29th, 1990. By the end of January, 30,000 air deployments are flown, the mastery of the air is won in the briefest possible amount of time. The deployment of Iraqi SCUD missiles against Israel, which is not involved in the war, leads to the placement and first use of the US "Patriot" air defence system. On February 24th, 1991, 2:00 AM CET, **"Desert Sabre"**, the allied land offensive, begins. 25 nations with around 300,00 soldiers participate in these operations. After Kuwait is already freed on February 26th, a cease-fire takes effect on February 28th, 6:00 AM CET. President Bush, in agreement with the allies, orders the battles to cease, since Kuwait is freed and the opposing forces in the area of operation are destroyed. Between March 3rd and 6th armistice negotiations take place. Iraq agrees to all conditions. The armistice itself takes effect on April 12th, 1991; with this the Gulf War is over. Calling upon the Security Council resolutions, the allies start a "humanitarian intervention" in northern Iraq (Operation "Provide Comfort") for the humanitarian provisioning of the Kurdish refugees, which is supported by a massive deployment of air forces.

After the liberation of Kuwait, a demilitarized zone (DMZ) is created by the UN Security Council and its observation by a UN mission is decided upon. The DMZ has a length of around 200 km and a width of about 15 km (10 km of Iraqi and 5 km of Kuwaiti territory). The DMZ is separated into three sectors (southern, central and northern sectors). Each sector possesses a command and six permanent observation posts to observe traffic. Further, the observation of the estuary of Khawr Abd Allah falls to UNIKOM, which was established as the border between the two lands in a treaty from 1963. The estuary is around 40 km long.

On April 13th, 1991, MG DI Günther Greindl arrives with the UNIKOM advance command in Kuwait City. On April 22nd,

---

79 See "The Gulf War 1990/91", Truppendienst, Volume 1/92.

the transfer of numerous companies from UNIFIL out of south Lebanon and two companies from Cyprus begins by land and air. On April 28th, the security companies are ready for deployment. Towards the end of May the companies from Denmark, Fiji and Nepal are returned to Cyprus and Lebanon. The Austrian company follows to Cyprus on June 19th.

On December 27th, 1992, a serious air incident occurs in the southern **"no fly zone"**, in which an Iraqi MIG-25 is shot down by an American F-16. At the beginning of January Iraqi SA-2 and SA-3 batteries are placed in the same zone. The Americans demand that the Iraqis remove these batteries again. Parallel to this, Iraqi soldiers push onto Kuwaiti territory on December 10th, 1992, force their way into the armory under UNIKOM control in Unm Qasr and take munitions, weapons and anti-ship missiles of the Chinese "Silkworm" type. This type of robbery repeats itself on December 11th and January 13th, 1993. Since the UNO proves incapable of hindering such actions, a limited air attack from January 13th from American and British air forces takes place south of the 32nd line of latitude. The Iraqis continue their provocations, the allies answer with appropriate retaliations.

Basis for deployment:	SC Resolution 678 (1990) of November 29th, 1990 (ultimatum);
	SC Resolution 687 (1991) of April 3rd, 1991 (establishment of a demilitarized zone);
	SC Resolution 689 (1991) of April 9th, 1991 (creation of UNIKOM);
	SC Resolution 806 (1993) of February 5th, 1993 (reinforcement by one InfBn, authorization for the use of armed force).
Mission:	Surveillance of the Khawr Abd Allah estuary (with helicopters and airplanes) and a demilitarized zone along the Iraqi-Kuwaiti border according to the border lines established in the Iraqi-Kuwaiti protocol for the reestablishment of friendly relations of October 4th, 1963; prevention of border infringement through presence in the demilitarized zone and surveillance of the same; observation of hostile or potentially hostile actions of one nation against another.

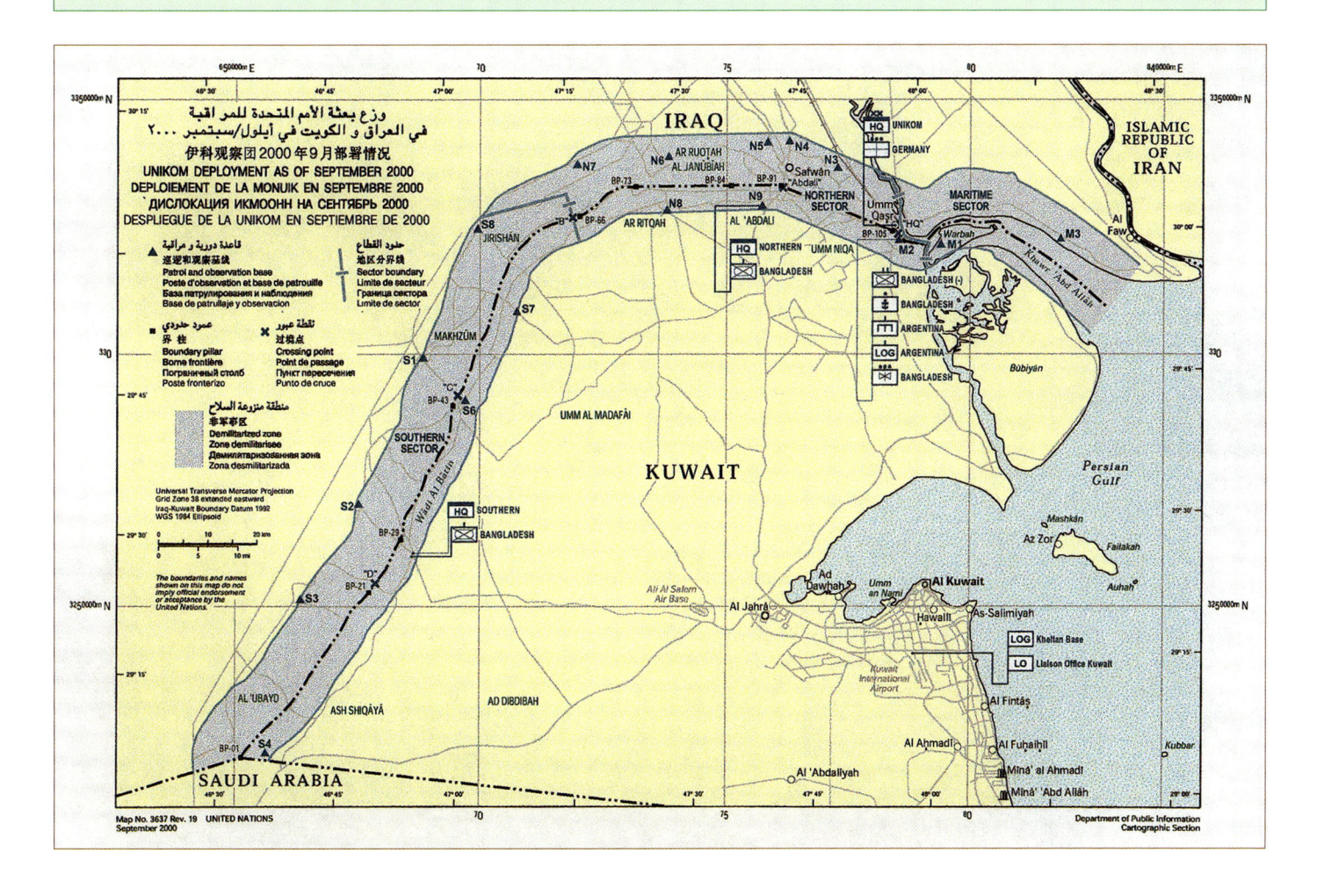

Duration of deployment:	April 9th, 1991 – October 6th, 2003.
Participating nations:	Argentina, Austria, Bangladesh, Canada, China, Denmark, Fiji, Finland, France, Germany, Ghana, Great Britain, Greece, Hungary, India, Indonesia, Ireland, Italy, Kenya, Malaysia, Nigeria, Norway, Pakistan, Poland, Romania, Russia, Sweden, Senegal, Singapore, Thailand, Turkey, Uruguay, USA, Venezuela.
Strength:	Originally 343. For the first six weeks 1,440 soldiers, since the end of 1991 around 1,160, of which 240 are (unarmed) military observers, minesweeping unit, logistics unit, infantry battalion, medical unit. In the first phase of the deployment five infantry companies from Cyprus (UNFICYP) and Lebanon (UNIFIL) are assigned for the security of UNIKOM, whose deployment ends at the end of June 1991; max. 1,187 including 254 military observers (as of February 28th, 1995); 1,310, of which 194 are military observers (as of December 30th, 2000).
Headquarters:	Umm Qasr, Iraq, since August 1992 Kuwait City.
Chief Military Observer:	May 1st, 1991 – July 11th, 1992: Major General DI Günther Greindl.
Chief of Staff:	1999: Brigadier General Helmut Fellner.

Austrian Participation

Political Measures

Initially the Austrians participate in the attempts to hinder the war. The Austrian Federal President personally intervenes with Saddam Hussein and achieves the unconditional release of the 100 Austrian hostages. This is initially condemned by the United Nations as "going it alone", however it subsequently leads to a row of prominent visits to Baghdad. Foreign Minister Dr. Alois Mock emphasizes the readiness at any time to dispatch UN troops, however Austria does not participate in the operations to liberate Kuwait and delays in allowing the transport of American recovery tanks through Austrian territory from Germany to Italy. On April 16th, 1991, the Council of Ministers responds to the UNO's petition for the dispatch of military observers and an infantry company; the experienced Austrian UN General Günther Greindl (previously Force Commander with UNDOF and UNFICYP) is named the first Commander ("Chief Observer") of UNIKOM.

Military Measures

The armed forces gather an infantry company from volunteers in Cyprus and hold them ready from April 20th, 1991, for a deployment in Kuwait. On April 25th, the advance command is dispatched, on April 26th and 27th, the main contingent follows with Swedish Hercules transports. Initially, the entire DMZ is planned as the area of operations for AUSCOY. However, the deployment is then changed to the guarding of an HQ and a field hospital. On June 1991, the company is returned to Cyprus.

• Dispatch of Military Observers

"The first 7 military observers leave Vienna for Saudi Arabia on April 22nd, 1991 in an AUA airplane. After an overnight stay in the Saudi Arabian capital Riyadh they continue to Kuwait with a C-160 of the French Air Force. The airport buildings lie in rubble or are completely burnt out. A French military bus brings the Austrians to the provisional HQ/UNIKOM, which is accommodated in the previous squash court of an otherwise destroyed SAS hotel. A few hours after arrival it goes, together with 9 military observers of various nationalities, to the some 120 km distant border region. Kuwait City offers a stunning picture: The streets are empty of people and strewn with wrecks, all businesses closed, the beaches mined, many houses destroyed or – especially along the coast – converted into artillery positions. Outside of the city they then go into the 'killing ground', a collection of 1,500 wrecked vehicles of all types. These vehicles were gunned down by the US Air Force shortly before the end of the war, to prevent their flight back to Iraq. The path is continued past burning oil wells, whose smoke darkens the sky, as well as giant tent camps, in which Iraqi refugees who no longer want to return to their homeland are accommodated. After going through numerous US checkpoints the future Outpost N3 is reached on Street Crossing 99. The Austrians live in just the same tent in which, a few weeks before, the cease-fire agreement was signed in the presence of US General Schwarzkopf. The following day the American flag is taken down in a celebratory ceremony, and the UN flag is raised by Austrian Major General D.I. Greindl.

The military observers are accommodated in an old, seriously tattered US tent, sleep on old US cots, and eat cold American field rations. A latrine and a wooden shower, as well a small generator, were also left behind by the Americans. These are the only 'luxuries'.

In the first days, the tanks of the withdrawing 3rd US Armored Division roll by day and night. Subsequently further outposts are constructed, which are each constantly occupied by five men, and which simultaneously serve as observation points as well as staging bases for the patrols, composed of two vehicles each. The typical day begins with waking up at 6:00 AM. After personal hygiene and breakfast they move on to cleaning and maintaining the vehicles, trash and waste must be burned. Then the patrols start on the path established by the outpost commanders, from which they first return in the evening. After dinner together the night patrols are on their way. Daily life is dictated by sandstorms, temperatures over 50 degrees Celsius in the tent, rats, scorpions, spiders and poisonous snakes. At times the wind carries the smoke from the burning oil wells directly to the outpost. Everything is covered with a fine, greasy film of oil as a result. A further danger comes from the mines and *armed munitions with which the area is strewn. In the middle of September the longed-for air-conditioning equipped trailers finally arriver. Each outpost receives four such trailers, in which besides the living rooms a work room for the duty officer, a kitchen, a pantry and a medical room are accommodated."*[80]

On March 17th, 2003, the mission is suspended because of the beginning of the Iraq war. The conclusion takes place on October 6th, 2003.

Basis for deployment: CM of April 16th, 1991, MC of April 18th, 1991 (disptatch).
Mission: Deployment as military observers; assumption of staff functions.
Appellation: None.
Form of dispatch: Until April 1997 according to the Dispatch FCL 1965, after April 1997 according to the FCL-CSD.
Area of operations: Umm Qasr.
Duration of deployment: April 22nd, 1991 – March 17th, 2003.
Contingent strength: Up to 7.
Total: 66.

Dispatch of an Infantry Company

To ensure the establishment of the UN mission, infantry divisions are temporarily needed. Austria participates with an infantry company, which is withdrawn from UNFICYP for the duration of the deployment.

Basis for deployment: CM of April 16th, 1991, MC of April 18th, 1991 (dispatch); CM of June 11th, 1991 (end).
Mission: Guarding the Sector HQ and the Norwegian field hospital in Umm Qasr.
Appellation: AUSCOY/UNIKOM.
Form of dispatch: Assignment from UNFICYP.
Area of operations: Umm Qasr.
Duration of deployment: April 25th, 1991 – June 23rd, 1991.
Contingent strength: 115.
Total: 115.
Commander: Major Erhard Moritz.

• Dispatch of a Medical Contingent

In a note of June 28th, 1993, the UN Secretary-General petitions Austria for the dispatch of a medical platoon with a strength of 35 men.

This petition has as its cause the fact that Norway announces the removal of its medical contingent in October of that year, and on the other hand the Security Council has decided in Resolution 806 to increase UNIKOM step by step by an infantry battalion. As it happens that the infantry battalion has its own medical care, a survey on the ground comes to the conclusion that a medical unit with a strength of twelve men would suffice. Therefore, on November 6th, an appropriate contingent is set on the march to Kuwait.

Basis for deployment:	CM of October 19th, 1993, MC of October 21st, 1993 (dispatch).
Mission:	Ensuring the medical care of UN personnel; operation of a stationary medical establishment in HQ; hygiene checks; evacuations from the air; immunizations.
Appellation:	AUSMED/UNIKOM.
Form of dispatch:	Dispatch FCL 1965.
Area of operations:	Umm Qasr.
Duration of deployment:	November 6th, 1993 – February 27th, 1995.
Contingent strength:	15 (including two doctors as well as six MedNCOs).
Total:	33.
Commanders:	October 31st, 1993 – November 8th, 1993 Lieutenant Colonel med. Dr. Hans Migglautsch
	November 8th, 1993 – February 5th, 1994 Colonel med. Dr. Wolfgang Mirtl
	February 6th, 1994 – June 5th, 1994 Colonel med. Dr. Markus Lechner
	June 6th, 1994 – July 17th, 1994 Lieutenant Colonel med. Dr. Eckart Breinl
	July 18th, 1994 – November 20th, 1994 Lieutenant Colonel med. Dr. Christian Lampersberger
	November 21st, 1994 – December 19th, 1994 Colonel med. Dr. Adolf Schöppl
	December 20th, 1994 – January 26th, 1995 Colonel med. Dr. Christian Kohnen-Zülzer
	January 27th, 1995 – February 27th, 1995 Lieutenant Colonel med. Dr. Hans-Peter Pölzbauer

---

80   Harald Gaß: "The Kuwait Crisis", Publication of the ARGE Militaria Austriaca Philatelia, privately published, Vienna 1991.

MG DI Günther Greindl, the Chief Military Observer, in conversation with US General Schwarzkopf, the Commander in Chief of the Allied Armed Forces (t.l.). Marking of the demilitarized zone between Kuwait and Iraq (t.r.). And the deadly danger of mines is everywhere (m.l. and r.).

UNMIK insignia

172

• Dispatch of a Logistics Element

The UNO subsequently petitions for the dispatch of a logistics contingent for 24 months. This dispatch is later extended to twelve months.

Basis for deployment:	CM of October 3rd, 1995, MC of November 7th, 1995 (dispatch).
Mission:	Ensuring the operation of vehicles; maintenance, recovery and repair of the vehicles of the mission; carrying out transport duties of all kinds (emphasis on fuel and water); provisioning of the observation points with the goods needed daily.
Appellation:	**AUSLOG/UNIKOM.**
Form of dispatch:	Until April 1997 according to the Dispatch FCL 1965, from April 1997 according to the FCL-CSD 1997.
Area of operations:	Umm Qasr.
Duration of deployment:	January 8th, 1996 – January 30th, 1999.
Contingent strength:	34.
Total:	195.
Commanders:	January 8th, 1996 – July 1996 Major Günter Maurer
	July 1996 – January 1997 Major Thomas Schuck
	January 1997 – July 1997 Major Walter Lohnegger
	July 1997 – January 1998 Major Eduard Schuster
	January 1998 – July 1998 Major Thomas Schuck
	July 1998 – January 30th, 1999 Major Günter Zippel
Contribution:	During the deployment all 182 vehicles of the mission are maintained in their own workshop and put in order.
Vehicle equipment:	30 (of which there are eight Iveco-Magirus tanker trucks, three 1.25 t HUMMV trucks, two Mack and two MB flatbed systems, five MAN trucks and numerous forklifts).

Maintenance of Contribution Abilities

The members of AUSLOG 4 show their team spirit, together with their professionalism and conditioning, not only through the maintenance and repair of the vehicles: On December 18th, 1997, they begin at 4:00 PM local time a murderous 200 km run at the so-called Border Marker 1 in the tri-national convergence of Iraq-Kuwait-Saudi Arabia. During this the Austrian flag is carried along the border running between Iraq and Kuwait. After a record time of only 14 hours and 25 minutes the soldiers reach their goal, Border Marker 106 at the Persian Gulf. With this outstanding accomplishment the Austrian UNO soldiers beat the previous American records by more than four (!) hours.

The "Wild Dog Motel" outpost. – In the desert the humor is obviously dry as well. Daily sandstorms, 50 degrees Celsius in the tent as well as any number of "hotel guests" such as rats, scorpions, spiders and poisonous snakes, provide constant distractions. In addition the wind carries the smoke from the burning oil wells directly into the outpost from time to time. Then day becomes night; everything one touches is covered with a fine, greasy film of oil. Then cleaning duty is announced again.[81]

---

81 Peter Hazdra: "Six Months with UNIKOM", in Visier, Volume 19/1992.

All 182 vehicles of the mission are maintained by AUSLOG/UNIKOM. Among these are also many vehicles which are not used in the armed forces. Meeting in the desert: an Austrian convoy with an armored Mack flatbed system and a dromedary (the vehicle in the background still has the insignia of the Danish contingent, the predecessor of AUSLOG/UNIKOM) (t.l.). Mercedes flatbed system (note Austrian insignia on the right front) with loaded shelter (t.r.). A shelter is lifted from a "Hino" truck with forklifts from Clark and Mitsubishi. Note the Austrian markings on the truck and the nickname "Hugo" on the Clark C500-Y50D forklift (m.l.). Finished UN outpost of shelters in the desert (m.r.). The State Secretary of the Austrian Foreign Ministry, Dr. Ferrero-Waldner, visits AUSLOG/UNIKOM and is briefed in mine clearance. In the background a 1.25 t HUMMV with Austrian markings (b.l.). This M936A2 crane truck is also in service wiht AUSLOG/UNIKOM (b.r.).

United Nations Austrian Field Hospital in Iran (UNAFHIR)

Preliminary Events

With around 20 million people, the Kurds are the largest ethnic group in the Middle East without their own nation. Their history reaches further than 3,000 years into the past, and because of the strategic importance of the area (border territory between Turkey and Iraq and between Iraq and Iran) constantly used as a buffer.[82] In 1975 Iraq recognizes the middle of the Shatt el Arab as the border to Iran in an agreement with Algeria, in exchange for which Iran ceases supporting the Kurds operating from Iranian territory. However, through this the Iraqi pogroms against the Kurdish minority are first made possible. Destruction, expulsion and deportation of hundreds of thousands of Kurds is the result. In late fall 1990 Jalal Talabani announces military resistance against Saddam Hussein. After the military defeat of Iraq in February 1991, the Iran-supported Shiites and the Kurds fighting for their autonomy start rebellions and unrest throughout the nation on March 4th. In the south, Hussein's Republican Guard succeeds in breaking the Shiite resistance. In the north, on the other hand, the Kurds initially succeed in conquering a few cities. Saddam Hussein deploys poison gas and napalm, above all in the north against the Kurds. As a result, massive streams of refugees enter Iran, who are seriously harmed by the weather conditions and the lack of foodstuffs. In total 1.5 million people are in flight towards Iran, 500,000 towards Turkey. In September 1991 new battles between Iraq and the Kurds break out. In the area of Orumiyeh, the Iranian authorities construct two refugee camps for over 60,000 people.

82　Norbert Sinn: "The Humanitarian Aid Contribution of the Austrian Armed Forces in Western Iran", ÖMZ, Volume 5/91.

International Reaction

US President Bush gives instructions on April 17th to construct protective camps for the Kurds in northern Iraq. The coalition forces, drawing on SC Resolution 688, establish a no-fly zone for the protection of the persecuted population against Iraqi military aircraft and protective zones for the Kurds in the north of Iraq. With this, the situation in Iraq itself stabilizes, however the support of the refugees in neighboring Iran represents a large problem. Austria, long active in aid for the Kurds, therefore decides to deploy a field hospital when a petition of the UN High Commissioner for Refugees, UNHCR, offers a formal basis for humanitarian aid.

Basis for deployment:	Petition of the UNHCR on April 19th, 1991, declaration of consent from the Islamic Republic of Iran of April 23rd, 1991.

Austrian Participation

Political Measures

The Austrian federal government immediately responds to the petition of the UN High Commissioner of Refugees, and after the declaration of consent from Iran, decides on the dispatch of a field hospital for humanitarian aid in the area of operations determined upon by the UNHCR. A cost of 70 million schillings is estimated for the deployment. In April 1991 a survey mission from the federal government and the community of Vienna visits the Iraqi border region in the area of Ziveh and Kirmanshar. The survey shows that the organization, construction and operation of a field hospital over a longer period of time is only possible through the armed forces. The city of Vienna offers the armed forces close cooperation, since the magistracy has already contributed significant preparatory work.

Military Measures

The first considerations in connection with the deployment are already made on April 17th. This is the first deployment of this type for the Austrian military. Special air-conditioned tents, which were previously not available, are immediately bought with the monetary allotment set aside for the military. The firm VOEST MCE provides four shelters free of charge, which can be adapted into two operations centers. On April 24th, the movement of a 300 bed reserve clinic from Medical Camp Eisenerz to Korneuburg is prepared, the transport itself takes place on April 30th. In order to gather the necessary, above all medically trained, personnel, an extensive advertising campaign is begun. Women are also invited to take part in this military deployment. The campaign produces over 2,000 volunteers with a few days, so that the selection can take place in peace and under the strict consideration of the desired activity profile. After the dispatch of the advance command on April 27th (12 soldiers, 8 t freight), the movement of the contingent takes place in two stages. The first part is transported to Iran from May 6th to 9th, the second part from May 13th to 27th. During this – once again – the lack of appropriate air transport is painfully noticeable. Chartering must be fallen back upon. This is made extremely difficult by the circumstantial bureaucracy in the target country. The crash of a Soviet IL-76 (which is deployed under similar conditions for Germany) on western Iranian territory makes the situation more difficult still. Finally a Bae-146 from the firm British Air Ferries is rented. The airlift is kept up between Vienna and Orumiyeh (a city in the western Iranian mountain country) for the entire duration of the deployment. In 41 provisioning flights a total of 600 tons are transported. In the first phase the capacity of the hospital equates with the operation of a clinic as well as that of a 100-bed station. At the same time a team of hygiene experts carry out first examinations on the spot. As a result of their reports, the 2nd construction stage is designed to fit the needs. In this phase the operation of the hospital is geared for the care of 300 stationary patients. The field hospital is construction at a height of ca. 1,600 m on a high plateau, which is surrounded by mountains from 3,000 to 4,000 m high. The field hospital is directly next to a refugee camp, in which 20,000 Kurds temporarily live.

Particularly mentionable is the medical care far from accustomed high-tech medicine. So improvisational talent is particularly called for here. *"At the children's station the little patients must often be respirated for hours by hand with Ambu breathing bags. For a little boy who had developed a hip fracture, the engineers build an 'extension'. This consists of a wooden frame and two stones. In the lack of an incubator a tin box is covered in black and heated in the sun to 35 degrees Celsius. On the other hand blood counts, for instance, must be counted by hand under a microscope. Differential blood counts can only be colored in the evenings or at night, since the colored dyes would evaporate in the high temperatures during the day."*[83]

The deployment doubtlessly represents an unusually high burden for all those involved. On the part of the host nation, as a result of the new identity as a religious state, attempts are made to influence the operation of the field hospital through constant restrictions. This leads to the fact that the guarded camp cannot be left and therefore contact cannot be made with the population. The connection with the homeland established by the Austrian

---

83 From a personal memoir from Dipl. Sr. Sabine Rhabek in "Rettungsdienst", Volume 15/1992.

postal service is a weak replacement. So the contingent is at least provided with three television sets and video recorders for distraction.

At the wish of the Iranian authorities the field hospital and the camp must be closed on July 31st. For this the contingent's vehicles must initially be moved on a land march to the loading dock on the Mediterranean coast. During this, a stretch of 1,100 km is covered in three days without a single accident. This is the largest march of a division of the armed forces abroad. The loading turns out to be very exciting. Bets are made between the soldiers about whether the hemp ropes with which the vehicles are hauled on board will hold. The ship transport also takes place under a bad star. Since war has meanwhile begun in Yugoslavia and the Danube has been blocked, the journey ends by the Iron Gate. There the ship with the Austrian vehicles is anchored. It takes months until the vehicles can be unloaded. This also takes place under difficult circumstances. Someone has meanwhile dismantled everything which was not nailed or screwed down, including the wheels. The mass of the medical personnel are returned to Austria in three rotation flights on July 20th, 23rd, and 25th. The military personnel remain another 10 days for deconstruction, packing and the return transport of materials by air from the area of operations.

Basis of deployment:	CM of April 23rd, 1991, MC of April 26th, 1991 (dispatch); CM of May 26th, 1992 (end).
Mission:	Securing of the medical care and the humanitarian aid and the Kurdish refugees.
Appellation:	**United Nations Austrian Field Hospital in Iran (UNAFHIR).**
Form of dispatch:	Dispatch FCL 1965.
Area of operations:	Orumi/Rezaiyeh near Orumiyeh (in the direct vicinity of the border to Iraq).
Duration of deployment:	May 7th, 1991 – July 31st, 1991.
Contingent strength:	280 (of which 180 medical personnel; the further team members are needed for the construction and maintenance of the camp).
Total:	590 (384 soldiers, 206 civilians (176 of which are women); of which 400 are medical experts (69 doctors).
Composition:	Divisions with bed stations: internal medicine, surgery, accident surgery, children's health (with a "milk bar" for dehydrated children), gynecology/midwifery; clinics: eyes, ears-nose-throat, tooth/mouth/jaw health, nutritional consultation; X-ray station with ultrasound; central laboratory; bacteriological-serological examination area; two air-conditioned operating rooms; dispensary.
Commanders:	Lieutenant Colonel Karl Schendl, Lieutenant Colonel Reisinger.
Medical Directors:	Colonel med. Dr. Robert Schlögl, Lieutenant Colonel Univ.-Prof. med. Dr. Meissner, Lieutenant Colonel med. Dr. Thomas M. Treu.
Contribution:	26,300 walk-in patients, 536 operations, 121 births, 900 X-ray and 900 ultrasound examinations, 7,000 immunizations. One can assume that around 1,000 lives, particularly children's, were saved by this deployment. Before the withdrawal the Iranian authorities are left medical technical equipment and medicines for the further mobile care of the refugees. During the deployment, a total 155,127 km are covered with accident by the 26 vehicles the contingent has access to.

Clothing of Female Members

In order not to injure the religious feelings of the natives, the female contingent members must conform to the Islamic clothing restrictions. Without further ado, special military bandannas are converted into head scarves and field utility pants are adapted for women. Furthermore, 15 chadors are created by the military clothing office, for which the appropriate black fabric must be found in a corresponding fabric store.

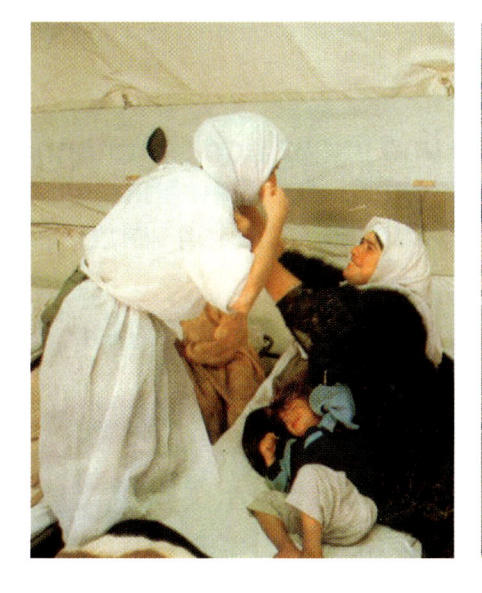

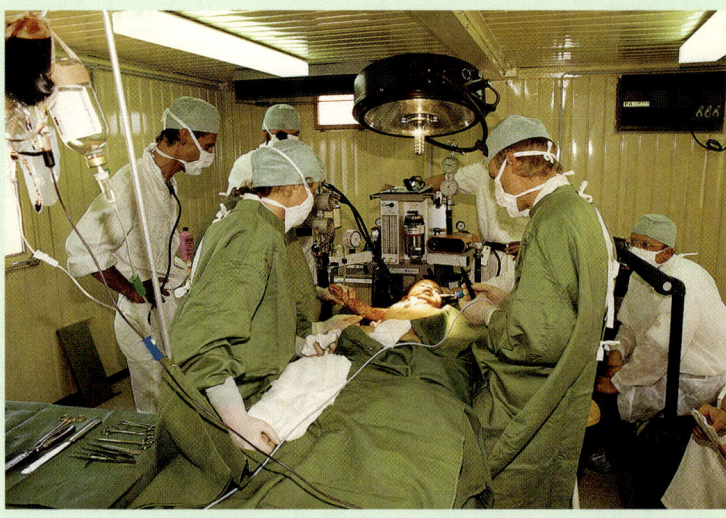

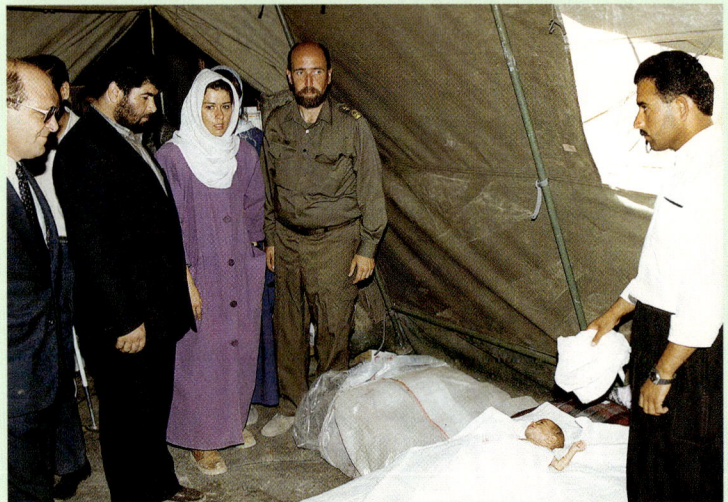

Flag ceremony at UNAFHIR. The female members of UNAFHIR (at the middle flagpole) wear their specially created "uniform" to comply with the Islamic clothing restrictions (t.l.). A look in the OP (t.r.). This is also everyday: Visitor and family visits. In the picture is the medical director MC LTC Dr. Treu (m.l.). The "Medhog", the UNAFHIR mascot (m.r.).
Naturally here, under the difficult hygienic conditions, especial value must be placed on cleanliness. This includes, even 1,000 km away from the homeland, washing machines (b.l.) and the daily "room sweep" (b.r.).

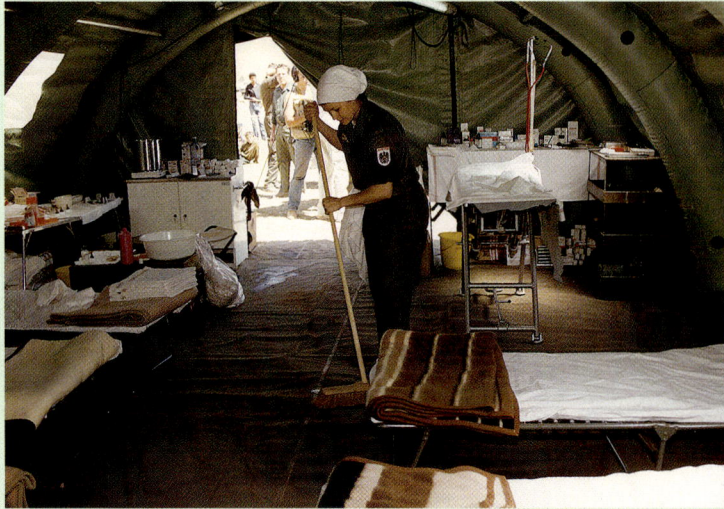

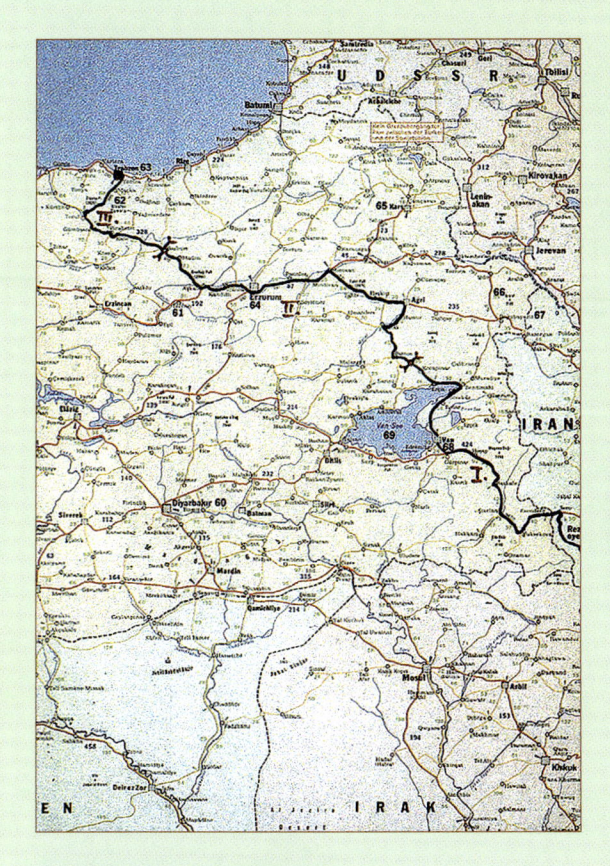

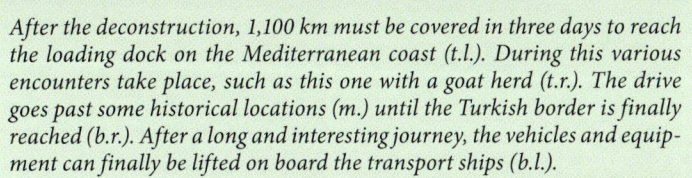

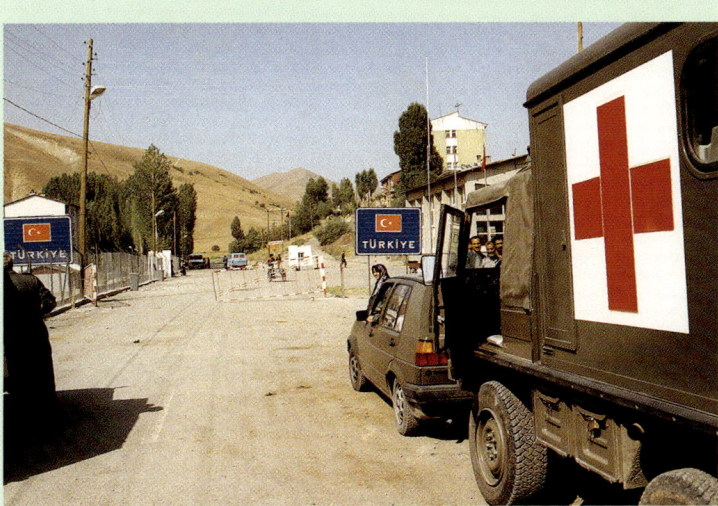

After the deconstruction, 1,100 km must be covered in three days to reach the loading dock on the Mediterranean coast (t.l.). During this various encounters take place, such as this one with a goat herd (t.r.). The drive goes past some historical locations (m.) until the Turkish border is finally reached (b.r.). After a long and interesting journey, the vehicles and equipment can finally be lifted on board the transport ships (b.l.).

United Nations Special Commission (UNSCOM)

United Nations Monitoring, Verification and Inspection Commission (UNMOVIC)

Preliminary Events

Iraq fires "Al Hussein" rockets at Israel, which is not involved in the war, already at the beginning of Operation "Desert Storm". Despite the ongoing armistice negotiations, Hussein deploys poison gas and napalm against rebellious Kurds on March 4th. And finally, after the war information about possible atom secrets comes to light. Iraq finally accepts the elimination of its weapons of mass destruction and their production sites as one of the armistice conditions. Nevertheless, Iraq attempts to hinder or at least delay the implementation of Resolution 678 in any way it can. In this Iraq also does not shy away from the temporary arrest of UN inspectors.

International Reaction

The UN Security Council decrees the destruction of the Iraqi weapons of mass destruction in April 1991 as a forced measure in connection with the Gulf War. A special commission collects the inventory and oversees the destruction. After this, the **"Baghdad Ongoing Monitoring and Verification Center" – BOMVC** is established in Baghdad from July 1993 as the 3rd phase. More than 8,000 bombs, grenades and missiles filled with chemical weapons or at least prepared for filling are destroyed by the UN inspectors. Of the suspected 400 hidden SCUD missiles, 54 are found and destroyed. UN experts find "important documents" about a secret nuclear weapons program while they work.

They are promptly arrested. The president of the UN Security Council issues an ultimatum in response, in which the experts must be released by September 24th, 11:00 PM CET. Iraq gives in to this demand.

On December 17th, 1998, the UN inspectors finally leave Iraq, after their work has been made impossible. In January 1999 UN Secretary-General Annan names the former head of the International Atomic Energy Agency, the Swede Hans Blix, as the one responsible for the new United Nations Monitoring and Verification Commission (UNMOVIC). The UN Security Council agreed upon this in Resolution 1284 in December 1999. Baghdad nevertheless refuses to work together with the UNO any longer. With

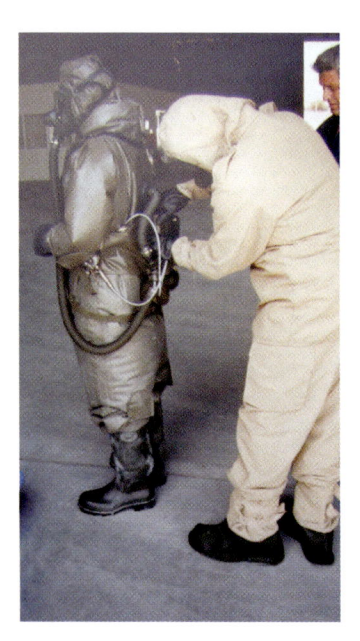

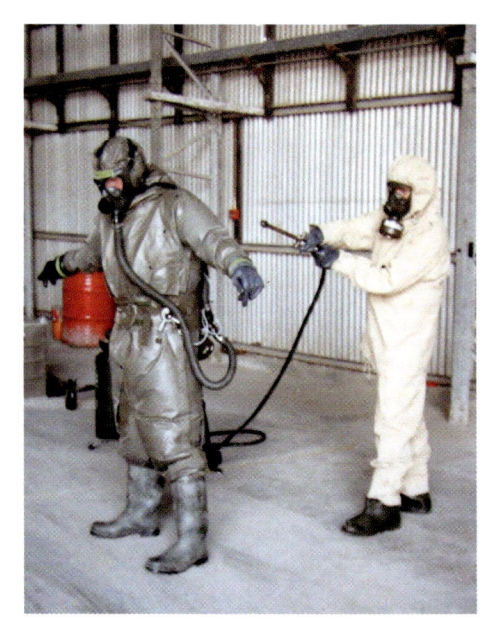

Donning the protective suit (l.). The recovery of a wounded person from his protective suit must also be practiced (m.). The highest level of concentration during the decontamination is called for after every deployment (r.).

this mission it is not a question of a standing troop, but of teams gathered of specialists appropriate to the case, which is also seen as a model for future armament inspection measures on the part of the UNO.[84]

• United Nations Special Commission (UNSCOM)

Basis for deployment:	SC Resolution 687 (1991) of April 3rd, 1991; SC Resolution 707 (1991) (surveillance with airplanes); SC Resolution 1284 (1999).
Mission:	Phase 1 and 2 (April 1991 – July 1994): Discovery of and supervision of the destruction of weapons of mass destruction, including chemical and biological weapons.
Phase 3:	(from July 18th, 1994): Long-term observation of compliance with the restrictions issued in the SC resolution through the "Baghdad Ongoing Monitory and Verification Center" (BOMVC) established in Baghdad for this purpose.
Duration of deployment:	August 1st, 1991 – February 29th, 2000 (since December 18th, 1998 suspended). The mission is taken over by UNMOVIC.
Participating nations:	Australia, Austria, Belgium, Canada, China, Czech Republic, Finland, France, Germany, Great Britain, Indonesia, Italy, Japan, the Netherlands, Nigeria, Norway, Poland, Russia, USA, Venezuela.
Strength:	Max. 180 specialists.
Headquarters:	Bahrain, from 1994 Baghdad. Evaluation centers exist in Bahrain and New York.

Austrian Participation

Political Measures

Austria shares responsibility for all of the UN Security Council resolutions from the beginning. Out of solidarity with the UN and for political security reasons the federal government furthermore decides to participate in all measures which are taken by UNSCOM.

Military Measures

Austria dispatches multiple experts in warfare agents and materials for individual assignments in line with the mission and also constantly participates with personnel for the observation center. The Austrian experts (chemists, biologists, data processing specialists, geometers, mine clearance specialists) help with the inventory and registration within the framework of international teams. The emphasis of these activities is first in the discovery and destruction of chemical and biological warfare agents, carried out by NBC officers and noncommissioned officers. Subsequently, verification from accredited experts from the militia is added. In addition the armed forces are represented by two experts in the UNO headquarters and through an advisor in the Commission.

Basis for deployment:	CM of July 2nd, 1991, MC of July 10th, 1991 (dispatch); CM of June 8th, 1999, MC of June 17th, 1991 (extension until June 20th, 2000).
Mission:	Inspection of the Iraqi declaration with regard to the quantity and type of the c-weapons and the facilities being used to produce them; opening of the c-weapons to take samples for later analysis; judgement of transportability to a possible destruction site; information gathering about the Iraqi c-weapons program; advice for the Commission and at UN headquarters.
Appellation:	None.
Form of dispatch:	Until April 1997 according to Dispatch FCL 1965; since April 1997 according to FCL-CSD 1997.
Area of operations:	Iraq.
Duration of deployment:	August 9th, 1991 – February 29th, 2000 (assumption of the mission by UNMOVIC).
Contingent strength:	Up to 8.
Total:	66.

---

84 Erwin A. Schmidl: "Blue Helmets, Red Cross", Studienverlag, Innsbruck 1995.

Verification

As a result of the participants' obligation to secrecy and the possibility of the endangerment of further participants, the concrete situation cannot be further discussed. This deployment should nevertheless be taken as an opportunity to elaborate further on the work of the inspectors.[85]

After Iraq complies with the SC Resolution with a declaration of the kind and type of the c-weapons, their location, number, as well as the condition of the facilities (undamaged, damaged, destroyed), commissions are formed by the UNO. In this, a compromise between optimum performance and international composition must be found. Commissions composed exclusively of one nationality have the advantage of the same language, training and equipment. However, they lack the international contacts necessary for the completion of the mission.

The commissions receive a continuous identification, such as UNSCOM 11/CW3 (UN Special Commission 11, Chemical Weapons 3). The composition of the commissions takes place in Bahrain. Here all administrative concerns are subsequently processed, such as the distribution of UN certificates, medical care (blood samples, distribution of pyridostigmine pills), briefing on the inspection sites, familiarization with the work procedures, and equipping other participants. Further, working procedures for even the most extreme situations are practiced. Finally the stay serves for acclimatization. Afterward the transfer to Baghdad takes place with numerous "Transall" transport airplanes from the German Air Force. From there the inspection teams are each brought with CH-53 transport helicopters to the inspection sites. The equipment is sent by land by relays separated by time.

The on-site inspections take place according to a scheme that remains the same and varies only depending on the condition of the facility and the stored munitions. The direct approach to the inspection target takes place in a convoy. A vehicle with Iraqi escorts drives at the point, then a bus with the inspectors follows, after that comes an equipment truck, a medical vehicle, a communications vehicle, and finally a water truck. The convoy stops at a safe distance from the target object. At first the terrain around the place is searched for unexploded bombs and chemical warfare agents and a decontamination area for makeshift detoxification constructed. Next secure approaches are established and possible dangers determined. After this the actual documentation of the C-munitions takes place. This is carried out while wearing protective gear (permeable protective suit, protective mask, gloves, overshoes). The taking of samples follows. For this the packing screws are opened by the Iraqis. Weapons which do not have this type of arrangement must be bored through in the field with the greatest possible security measures. The heavy protective suit is worn for this. A particular danger exists in this because of the serious excess pressure in the sun-heated munitions. The Iraqis deliberately store the munitions in the open, in order to eliminate danger from leaky points on the one hand, and on the other to "keep the UN inspectors away" from other areas. The opening of the munitions takes place in one movement, because the wear time of the protective suit is limited and the boring equipment can only be used once. There is basically no way to decontaminate a drill. Generally numerous samples are taken. One goes to the Iraqis, the others to various international laboratories. After every step of the work, a careful check for contamination takes place. Equipment and clothing that cannot be decontaminated is burned beside the campsite before leaving the inspection area. After the conclusion of the inspection the withdrawal to Baghdad occurs. There the appropriate final report is made.

• United Nations Monitoring, Verification and Inspection Mission (UNMOVIC)

Preliminary Events

After the suspension of UNSCOM forced by Iraq, the UN Security Council establishes three panels to consult on disarmament questions, humanitarian questions and questions of Kuwaiti prisoners of war and their property. In its report, the UN Security Council determines that a monitoring regime is still urgently necessary, and installs UNMOVIC for this.

International Reaction

As a result of the crisis between the UNO and the USA on one hand and Iraq on the other, after the end of the UN inspections in December 1998 the USA and Great Britain begin attacks on the north and south of Iraq. For this reason it is unknown when the newly formed UNMOVIC can take up its work.

Basis for deployment:	SC Resolution 1284 (1999) of December 17th, 1999.
Mission:	Detection and oversight of the disarmament of Iraq's weapons of mass destruction (biological and chemical weapons as well as ballistic missiles) (as with UNSCOM already); observation of compliance with the constraints established by UNO for Iraq in respect of the Iraqi weapons inventory.
Duration of deployment:	March 1st, 2000 – to date.
Headquarters:	Baghdad; evaluation center in UNHQ in New York.

---

85 Rudolf Müller: "Deployment in Iraq"; Truppendienst, Volume 3/1993, Vienna 1993.

Austrian Participation

Political Measures

The Council of Ministers takes all preparatory legal measures.

Military Measures

No measures are necessary on the part of the Defence Ministry at this time.

Basis for deployment:	CM of April 11th, 2000, MC of May 17th, 2000 (dispatch of up to four, for short periods of time up to ten experts until June 30th, 2001).
Mission:	Detection and supervision of the dearmament of Iraq's weapons of mass destruction (biological and chemical weapons as well as ballistic missiles) (as with UNSCOM already); observation of compliance with the constraints established by UNO for Iraq with respect to the Iraqi weapons inventory.
Appellation:	None.
Form of dispatch:	FCL-CSD 1997.
Area of operations:	Iraq.
Duration of deployment:	No dispatch since September 8th, 2000, an end is planned.

A UN inspection team at work (above). The Austrian inspectors (r.).

United Nations Guards Contingent in Iraq (UNGCI)

Preliminary Events

Serious unrest occurs in Iraq in connection with the "Gulf War" "Liberation of Kuwait". Both the Kurds in the north as well as the Shiites in the South attempt to initiate popular revolutions against Hussein. Despite the defeat in the Gulf War the Iraqi army is strong enough, however, to crush the uprisings. The result is an avalanche of refugees. After the allies threaten renewed attacks, the Iraqi government gives in and begins negotiations with the Kurds. A large part of the Kurds therefore return to their homeland. This subsequently leads to serious supply difficulties.

International Reaction

The coalition forces, drawing on SC Resolution 688, establish a no-fly zone for the protection of the persecuted population against Iraqi military aircraft and protective zones in the north of Iraq. The UNHCR agrees upon the implementation of humanitarian aid measures for the Kurdish population with Iraq, and after a large portion of the aid goods are "lost" at the beginning, the establishment of special protection for them. At the negotiation for this agreement the UNO is represented by the Coordinator for Baghdad, Brent Bernandner. The signing on April 18th, 1991 takes place with the Iraqi Foreign Minister and the executive delegate of the UNO for humanitarian operations, Prince Sadruddin Aga Khan. Since Iraq rejects the deployment of a defence troop for aid shipments, a "guard contingent" is formed of the UN guard personnel (normally deployed at the UN locations in New York, Geneva, Vienna and Nairobi) and brought to a status of 500 men through soldiers and policemen out of numerous nations. This troop is uniformly (without notation of the national origin) clothed in the blue uniforms of the UN guard personnel and equipped with Iraqi pistols.

Basis for deployment:	SC Resolution 688 (1991) of April 5th, 1991; agreement between Iraq and the UN of April 18th, 1991 (appendix to Document S/22663).
Mission:	Protection of the humanitarian aid contributions in the Kurdish settlement areas in the north in the "United Nations Sub-Offices and Humanitarian Centers – UNHUCs" decided upon in the agreement, and the Shiites in the south of the country; guarantee of appropriate medical care for the security forces stationed in northern Iraq, the UNHCR personnel, and improvement of the medical care of the Kurds cared for by UNHCR.
Duration of deployment:	June 1st, 1991 – to date (arrival of employees from June 18th).
Participating nations:	Austria, Czech Republic, Denmark, Fiji, Finland, Ghana, Greece, Poland, Slovakian Republic.
Strength:	Max. 500 men. Executive and security officials.
Headquarters:	Baghdad.

Austrian Participation

Political Measures

The federal government dispatches a total of 75 executive officials from July 13th, 1991 to September 19th, 1992 and from January 28th, 1993 to May 2nd, 1995 to guard and escort the UN aid transports as well as two medics from the Ministry of the Interior for personal medical care.

Military Measures

The armed forces dispatch a medical team to care for the mission.

Basis for deployment:	CM of September 10th, 1991, MC of September 17th, 1991.
Mission:	Medical care of the mission.
Appellation:	None.
Form of dispatch:	Dispatch FCL 1965.
Area of operations:	Baghdad.
Duration of deployment:	September 17th, 1991 – July 5th, 1992.
Contingent strength:	2 (1 military doctor and 1 medical noncommissioned officer).
Total:	4 (2 military doctors and 2 medical noncommissioned officers).

Misión de las Naciones Unidas para el Referéndum del Sáhara Occidental (MINURSO)

United Nations Mission for the Referendum in Western Sahara

Preliminary Events

From 1884 to February 26th, 1976, Spain is the colonial power in the Western Sahara. Already in the late phase of this dominance a conflict becomes apparent between Morocco and Mauritania over the ownership of a territory over over 250,000 square kilometers in the Western Sahara. In the course of secret negotiations between Spain, Morocco and Mauritania, an agreement is signed on November 14th, 1975, in which two thirds of the western Sahara, including its valuable resources, goes to Morocco and the remaining southern third is to fall to Mauritania.[86] Morocco bases its territorial claims on precolonial historical law as well as religious connections to the almost completely Sunni Muslim population. The liberation front **"Frente Popular para la Liberation de Saguia el-Hamra y de Rio de Oro" (Polisario)**, already founded in 1973, rises against this and announces the **"Democratic Arabic Republic of the Sahara" (DARS)** in February 1976, which also becomes a full member of the Organization for African Unity (OAU) in 1982. The "government" establishes its exile residence in the Algerian desert near Tindouf, where 165,000 people live in refugee camps. In 1975 over 150,000 Moroccans march in the "Green March" to take control of the Western Sahara. In 1979, after a change of power, Mauritania relinquishes the occupied territories, which are now controlled by Morocco in the same way. The extremely changeful and costly desert war, carried out from 1976 to 1991, brings the Polisario such great success as a result of its guerilla tactics that despite the strong numerical disadvantage, in the first seven years the area actually controlled by the Moroccan armed forces shrinks to an eighth. In 1980 Morocco alters its warfare tactics and begins the laborious construction of a defensive line, which by 1987 includes a system of earth and stone walls, mine fields, outposts and a thick network of electronic early warning systems of American origin with a total length of 2,500 km. Through the construction of a so-called "berm" Morocco is able to expand its sphere of control to 60% again, end the grueling war of attrition and cross into a static defence behind the berm. In 1981 King Hassan II agrees to a referendum. In it, the Western Sahara should vote on whether it should be an independent state as it formerly was a Spanish territory, or whether it should become a part of the Kingdom of Morocco. On August 30th, 1988, the so-called "reconciliation suggestions" are agreed upon (observation of a cease-fire, withdrawal of Morocco's and the Polisario's military divisions to predetermined positions, exchange of prisoners of war, release of political prisoners, voter identification, implementation of the referendum). The conflict continues, however. Not until 1991, after serious and costly battles, does a cease-fire occur on September 6th under UN mediation. In April 1993 the conflicting parties agree to the establishment of an "Identification Commission for the Referendum in Western Sahara" under the chairmanship of Erik Jensen (Malaysia). In 1997 the two conflicting parties, Morocco and the Polisario, managed by the UN special envoy for the Western Sahara, agree upon a code of behavior of the referendum. The Spanish census of 1974 recorded 74,000 "Saharauis" (the name for the inhabitants of this region). Nevertheless, in the past decades Morocco has settled over 170,000 Moroccans of supposedly Saharuani descent in the occupied territory and invested much in the resource-rich (above all in phospate) territory.

Although the Moroccan side has around 100,000 men and is overwhelmingly supported by the USA (and France) and the POLISARIO, with its 10,000 men in alliance with Algeria, can mostly fall back upon Soviet war materials, this conflict is less a question of a "classical" third-party war, but rather a power-politics conflict between two Arabic peoples.

International Reaction

In 1985 the UNO, in cooperation with the OAU, initiates an intermediary mission. In 1987 a UN delegation visits the Western Sahara for the first time. On August 30th, 1988 an initial peace plan ("The Settlement Proposals") is developed, which as the "Settlement Plan" is approved by the UN Security Council with SC Resolution 658 on June 27th, 1990. This also includes suggestions for a transitional UNO government and the establishment of MINURSO. On September 6th, 1991 UNO accomplishes a cease-fire between Morocco and the Polisario. However, the referendum is not able to be carried out due to lingering problems with recording those with a right to vote. Although the identification commission takes up its work in August 1994, it must realize at the end of

---

86 Gustav Gustenau: "On the Development of the Western Sahara Conflict"; ÖMZ, Volume 3/1998, Vienna 1998.

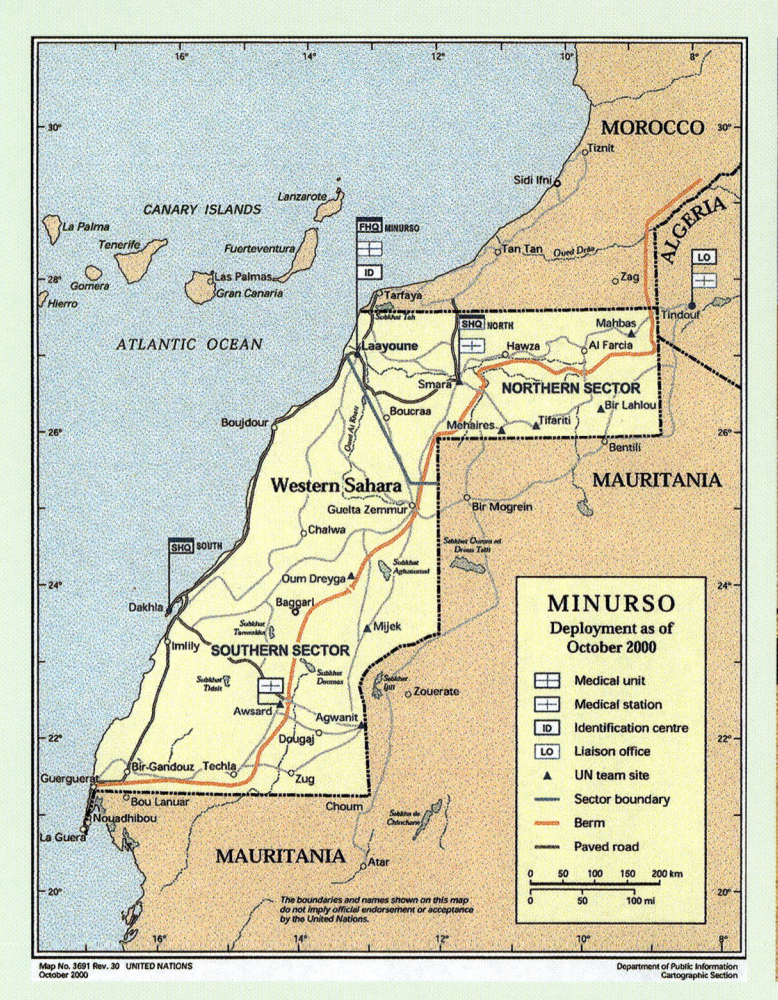

Satellite connection to UN HQ in New York (t.r.). "Siesta" in UN Camp (b.l.). Will the right measurements come out if the charming military doctor takes his blood pressure? At any rate LTC Baldia seems somewhat irritated, probably because of the disruption of his medical examination by the photographer (b.r.).

Caravan outpost of the Moroccan army. The embankment and trenches are part of the "occupational therapy" before the cease-fire, afterward forbidden and observed by UNO (t.l.). Abandoned tank platoon (t.r.) and refugee camp in the middle of the desert (m.l.). The provisioning of the UN posts takes place from the air (m.r.).
And this is how the daily life of the UN observer looks: Always left to themselves, they must overcome all situations, including changing tires (b.l.). "Rest over night" is the name of this camp. No trace of luxury, instead there are snakes and mosquitos (b.r.).

1995 that its continuation is made impossible by the insurmountable differences between the two conflicting parties. In May 1996 the identification is officially ceased and the military component reduced by 20% (from 288 to 230 men).

In March 1997 the UN Secretary-General starts a new initiative and names a personal envoy, the former US Foreign Minister James Baker. After a complex dance of negotiations, he seems to make a breakthrough in September 1997. During talks in Texas on September 16th, 1997, the still open questions regarding the referendum, the political responsibility of UNO during the transitional period as well as practical measures to complete the identification process are all clarified. The UN Security Council decides on October 20th, 1997 with Resolution 1,133 to call on the Secretary-General to bring the identification process to a conclusion by May 31st, 1998.

The United Nations begin in January 1998 with the registration of those with the right to vote. Simultaneously the Security Council approves the dispatch of an engineering unit for mine clearance. The registration process is given six months' time and serves as preparation for the planned referendum on December 7th, 1998, which up until this time has failed as a result of conflict over the number of those able to vote. The goal is the arrangement of a referendum in the area of the Western Sahara, in order to end the conflict between Morocco, which claims this area for itself, and the independence movement Polisario. In the referendum the inhabitants are to decide on their future (formation of a separate state or annexation by Morocco. In the end, however, ending the conflict, bringing the identification process to a close and arranging the vote are all unsuccessful.

MINURSO is therefore only deployed in a reduced form and with a limited mandate to observe the armistice. For this, observers are stationed in nine "Sub-Sector Commands" in the northern and southern sectors. Besides HQ in El Aaiún, two regional headquarters in Smara and Dakhla are established.

Basis for deployment:	SC Resolution 621 (1988) of September 20th, 1988; SC Resolution 658 (1990) of June 27th, 1990; SC Resolution 690 (1991) of April 29th, 1991; SC Resolution 973 (1995) of January 13th, 1995 (Identification Commission); SC Resolution 1324 (2000) of October 30th, 2000 (extension).
Mission:	Observation of the armistice and the cessation of hostilities. As a result of the reduced scope of the mission, the inspection of troop reductions, protection of returning refugees, observations of Moroccan troop withdrawal and demobilization of the Polisario ("liberation organization") cannot be fulfilled.
Duration of deployment:	September 5th, 1991 – to date.
Participating nations:	Argentina, Australia, Austria, Bangladesh, Belgium, Brazil, Canada, China, Croatia, Djibouti, Egypt, El Salvador, Finland, France, Germany, Ghana, Great Britain, Greece, Guinea, Hungary, Honduras, Ireland, Italy, Kenya, Korea, Malaysia, Mongolia, Nigeria, Norway, Pakistan, Peru, Poland, Portugal, USSR/Russia, Switzerland, Sri Lanka, Togo, Tunisia, Uruguay, USA, Venezuela, Yemen.
Strength:	Planned ca. 3,000 men (1,695 soldiers, 300 police, 900 – 1,000 civilian officials); 216 soldiers and 27 administrative personnel (as of December 31st, 2009).
Headquarters:	El Aaiún.
Chief Military Advisor:	August 6th, 1997 – October 31st, 1999: Major General Bernd S. Lubenik.

Austrian Participation

Political Measures

In response to a petition from UNO, the Council of Ministers decides to dispatch up to 15 men until the end of the mission. With the Council of Ministers resolution of February 10th, 1998, his decision is expanded to the dispatch of an infantry unit (ATCON/M) with a strength of up to 235 men for 8 months (however, this is never deployed).

In the time from July 2nd, 1993 – May 19th, 1997 25 executive officials are also dispatched. Notable in this is the assignment of the Austrian police officer Brigadier General Walter Fallmann as "CIVPOL Commissioner", with the rank of a police general, who commands the UN civilian police contingent in the time from January 3rd to July 28th, 1996. After this, Brigadier General Fallmann immediately becomes the CIVPOL Commissioner at the "United Nations Transitional Authority for Eastern Slavonia, Baranja and Western Sirmium – UNTAES" until January 15th, 1998.

Military Measures

As a result of the Council of Ministers resolution the armed forces prepare for the dispatch of an infantry company to the Western Sahara. It is at first planned to equip the unit with the "Pandur" armored personnel carrier introduced for UN deployments. Special uniforms are also created for this deployment, which are to be appropriate with the climactic conditions. This company is not deployed. Rather it is later dispatched to Kosovo. In June 2000 the plans for a possible dispatch are finally ceased (also in view of a possible deployment in Georgia).

Basis for deployment:	CM of August 13th, 1991, MC of September 17th, 1991 (dispatch);
	CM of June 8th, 1993, MC of June 17th, 1993 (dispatch of up to ten policemen);
	CM of February 10th, 1998, MC of March 10th, 1998 (dispatch of an infantry unit, not yet activated).
Mission:	Military observer, staff member.
Appellation:	None.
Form of dispatch:	Until April 1997 according to Dispatch FCL 1965, from April 1997 according to FCL-CSD 1997.
Area of operations:	HQ, North Sector and South Sector.
Duration of deployment:	September 19th, 1991 – to date.
Contingent strength:	Up to four military observers.
	3.
Total:	52 (as of December 31st, 2009).

Military Observers with MINURSO

UN military observers (UNMOs) are "maids of all work". They sometimes live in tents in ruins or old forts. The tents are in fact air conditioned and have their own electrical supply, but are designed for civilian needs and not tested for military goals in this area. UNMOs are to create the documentation of their patrols themselves, then carry out these patrols and then file the appropriate reports with HQ. These are all on military activities, such as troop movements, transfers of weapons and equipment, flyovers, forbidden construction activities, etc. Naturally the UNMOs must feed themselves and concern themselves with hygiene. During the observation work problems constantly occur with the native troops. The UNMOs are often denied access to the outposts in the desert. For this reason some patrols must also use a trick to gather information about the occupation of an outpost. Vehicle patrols approach the outpost from 2 sides. When the occupants then leave their quarters out of curiosity, the number of soldiers in this outposts can be exactly determined from a UN helicopter.

A patrol consists of two Nissans with two UNMOs each of differing nationalities. The commander sits in the 1st car, works the GPS as the navigator and stays in contact with HQ. The team carries provisions for two days (Compo rations) and 8 l of mineral water per man. Important for the vehicles are the reserve tires (the sharp-edged stones regularly cause flat tires) and 40 l of reserve diesel fuel per car. The MOs have cots with adequate distance from the ground (because of snakes, scorpions, and spiders) for the night.

For air transport and air reconnaissance, MINURSO has Romanian AN-26 and Mi-17s, Czech YAK-40s as well as Swiss Pilatus Porter and Twin Otters.

During their deployment the UNMOs must overcome a number of problems. Besides the aforementioned animals there are mines which were laid by the Moroccans over the past 25 years, and the climate (from December to February hot and dry without rain, between July and September temperatures between 45 and 56 degrees and sandstorms).

National Holiday in the Western Sahara

Naturally the national holiday plays a large role abroad as well, after all it offers the opportunity to present Austria especially well abroad. At MINURSO the celebrations already begin on the day before. The Force Commander (FC), MG Bernd Lubenik, hosts a reception in the red-white-red decorated ballroom of the UN headquarters in El Aaiún. As appetizers there are schnapps and Mozart balls. Accompanied by Austrian music, a menu is served, consisting of soup with semolina dumplings, veal goulash with gnocchi and a Sacher cake. This is cooked, and this is again so typical for Austria, by the wife and daughter of the FC. The two ladies are supported by "local workers". Beer and wine served with the meal, made available by Austrian firms and wine cultivators.

The national holiday itself begins with a military ceremony. After the flag ceremony the background of the national holiday and the meaning of the Austria colors are expounded upon. The high point is the "medal parade", the award of the UNO medal "In the Service of Peace". After this there is a "Viennese breakfast", to which the FC invites all UNCIVPOL affiliates and all civilian UNO personnel. There is cream cheese and apple strudel with Viennese coffee and whipped cream.

United Nations Advance Mission in Cambodia (UNAMIC)

United Nations Transitional Authority in Cambodia (UNTAC)

United Nations Military Liaison Team in Cambodia (UNMLT)

Preliminary Events

The dazzling high point in the history of Cambodia is the Kingdom of Angkor (802 – 1431 AD).[87] The centralized kingdom, based on the irrigated cultivation of rice, can nevertheless only be maintained through the most brutal methods of coercion.[88] In this the kings show characteristics of the Khmer, which have been preserved to this day. The overwhelmingly farming population is very bound to tradition and therefore not very open to revolutionary change. Beginning in the 14th century, numerous invasions from Siamese troops in the west lead to the fall of the kingdom. In 1431 Angkor Wat is taken over by the Siamese. Both Siam (from 1925 Thailand) as well as Vietnam annex parts of Cambodia, make the King of Cambodia a vassal and fight wars against each other on his territory. Furthermore, the Vietnamese carry out an intentional colonization of the eastern Cambodian provinces. The French finally hinder the total eradication of Cambodia with the establishment of a protectorate in 1863. During their 90-year presence they create a network of roads, open Cambodia to international trade, and bring many Vietnamese officials into the country, who prove to be hardworking and less corrupt. France also causes Siam to give annexed provinces of Cambodia back and makes Phnom Penh a blossoming French city. However, nothing changes the way of life of the common people. From 1941 to 1945 Cambodia is occupied by Japan.

After the end of the 2nd World War, resistance against French dominance begins to spring up, which forms into a guerilla group named "Khmer Issarak (Freed Khmer)". Nevertheless King Norodom Sihanouk succeeds in achieving the independence of his nation without extensive bloodshed – in contrast to Vietnam. The corruption, nepotism and oppression of the opposition lead to a strengthening of the Khmer Rouge (this term is created by Sihanouk for the Communists in the '60's). In addition to this there is the erosion of the Cambodian neutrality, since Sihanouk allows the Viet Cong and the North Vietnamese army the use of Cambodian territory as deployment, withdrawal, and provisioning territory (**"Ho Chi Minh trail"**). This last brings Sihanouk in conflict with the USA, whose policy in the 1950's was shaped by the Domino Theory. For the Nixon administration, therefore, a right-leaning military putsch in March 1970 is very convenient. While Sihanouk takes the lead of a Communist-dominated exile government (Governement Royal de l'Union National de Kampuchea), the new rulers under the leadership of General Lon Nol declare a republic in Phnom Penh. WIth this the land is finally drawn into the Second Indochina War. Gruesome massacres of Vietnamese cost the regime its final sympathizers; the Khmer Rouge, in contrast, achieve one success after another. On April 17th, 1976 – two weeks before the fall of Saigon – the Khmer Rouge move into Phnom Penh. The black-clothed fighters, closely following China, begin to radically alter the society (**"primitive Communism"**). Intellectuals are targeted for liquidation; millions of people driven from the cities to the land and forced to work in agricultural collectives. Sihanouk, returned to Phnom Penh as the nominal head of state, is forced to abdicate in 1976 and placed under house arrest.

These economic policies prove to be a complete failure, at least 1 million people are murdered. After the regime of the Khmer Rouge provokes numerous border incidents with the Socialist Republic of Vietnam, 14 divisions of the Vietnamese People's Army arrive for a major offensive on December 25th, 1978. The Khmer Rouge flee into the mountains. The Vietnamese attack causes outrage in the

---

87 Peter Hazdra: "Cambodias Rocky Road to Peace"; ÖMZ, Volume 6/1993, Vienna 1993.
88 Peter Hazdra: "The UNO Peacekeeping Operation in Cambodia – Preliminary Events, Concept, Progress and Critical Evaluation of the International Engagement"; Europ. Secondary School Writings, Volume XXXI/322, Peter Lang Verlag, Frankfurt/Main 1997.

West as well as in China. A condemnation in the Security Council fails, because of the Soviet Union's veto, however, the invasion itself is however condemned. The Khmer Rouge continue to take their United Nations chair, until this is vacated in 1982 for a newly founded resistance coalition under the leadership of Sihanouk (!).

The occupation itself is the beginning of long years of bitter civil war. On one side is the government established and supported by Vietnam, the "State of Cambodia (SOC)" under Prime Minister Hun Sen. The government troops, the "Cambodian People's Armed Forces" have around 125,000 armed men, in addition to 220,000 men in the militia. On the other side are three resistance groups, which in 1982 combine to form the extremely fragile exile government of the "Coalition Government of Democratic Kampuchea (CGDK)". These are the Khmer Rouge, who officially call themselves the "Party of Democratic Kampuchea (PDK)", the royalist group of the "Front Uni National pour un Cambodge Indépendant, Neutre, Pacifique et Coopératif (FUNCINPEC)" and the right-leaning and internally conflicted "Khmer People's National Liberation Front (KPNLF)", also called the Republicans.

On April 5th, 1989, Vietnam surprisingly announces the retreat of its occupation soldiers within six months. The stationing of troops is too expensive without Soviet help. According to Vietnamese reports, the withdrawal is concluded on September 26th, 1989.

On September 10th, 1990, the four Cambodian parties accept the framework set forth by UNO in its entirety and further decide to form the Supreme National Council (SNC) as the only legal and authorized institution during the transitional period. From December 21st – 23rd, 1990 the representatives of the SNC take part in a meeting with both chairmen of the Cambodia Conference (France and Indonesia).

UNTAC military deployment for electoral support

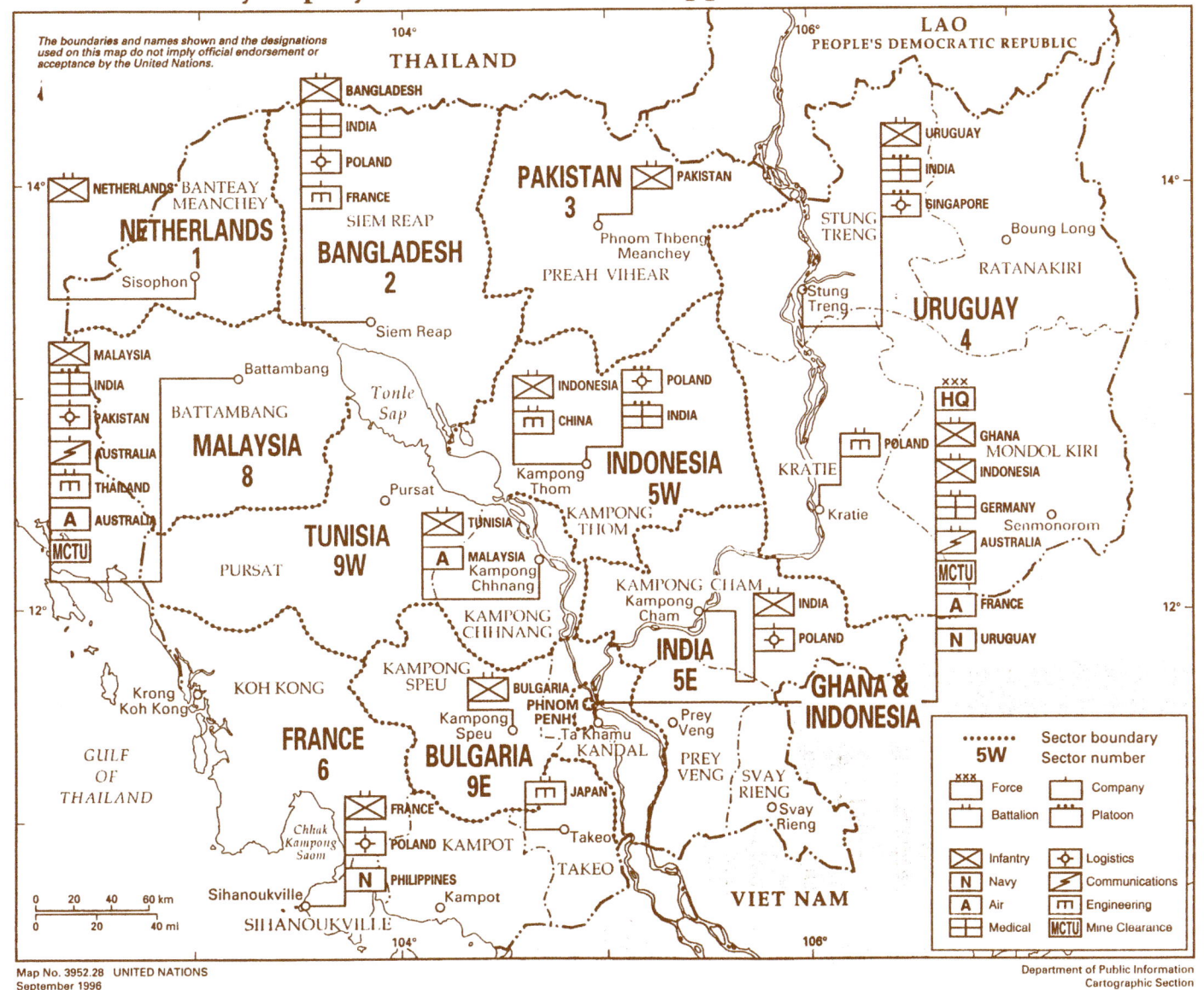

At this meeting there is agreement on most of the points of the agreement detailed by the UNO. In the middle of June 1991 Prince Norodom Sihanouk joins the SNC and also chairs it during the meeting from June 24th – 26th. In July the SNC elects him as the president of the SNC. At this meeting all remaining differences of opinion are put aside, so that nothing more stands in the way of the signing.

On October 23rd, 1991, at the Parisian Cambodia Conference, Cambodia signs the agreement with UNO on the complete political regulation of the Cambodian conflict. With this, Cambodia agrees to the creation of a transitional authority of the UN. Despite this, in some parts of Cambodia a resurgence of the civil war and banditry occurs. The bridges laboriously repaired by UNTAC engineers are blown up again by the Khmer Rouge. At the elections, which take place from May 23rd to 28th, 1992 despite the Khmer Rouge's threats to end them in a bloodbath, a number of surprises take place: Contrary to all prognoses the elections occur without incident and voter participation, at 90%, is unexpectedly high. The outcome is also surprising: FUNCINPEC wins the relative majority with 58 seats against the Cambodian People's Party (CPP) with 51, the Buddhist Liberal Democratic Party (BLDP) with 10 and the right-leaning splinter party MOLINKA with 1 seat. After a long tug-of-war, the four parties represented at the convention to create a constitution agree upon the formation of a provisional government under the joint chairmanship of Prince Norodom Ranariddh and Hun Sen. Right away in the inaugural session on June 14th, the constituent convention elects Prince Sihanouk as head of state and endows him with extensive (and not further defined) full powers "to rescue the land". In the same session the coup of 1970 is declared "null and void". In the following session it is decided to reintroduce the old flag and national hymn (from before 1970) and name the state "Cambodia" again. On September 21st, 1993, the constitutional convention enacts the new constitution by a large majority, which plans for the establishment of a constitutional monarchy. Three days later Sihanouk is elected as king.

International Reaction

The first endeavors for a peaceful solutions go all the way back to the year 1981, when a conference on Cambodia is held at the determination of the UN Secretary General. Subsequently the Secretary General makes his "good offices" available. After a personal visit to the crisis region he compiles 1985 the most important basic features for a comprehensive political solution. In August 1989 the **1st Parisian Cambodia Conference** is called under the chairmanship of France and Indonesia. Initially, no unity between the four Cambodian parties can be achieved. After the withdrawal of the Vietnamese the Australian Foreign Minister Gareth Evans brings movement to the negotiations with a new plan (**"Canberra Initiative"**). The central point is that the transitional government be placed from within the United Nations and not, as previously planned, from the factions of the civil war. The UN Secretary General dispatches numerous small missions to Cambodia, to sound out the need for a UN deployment.

Further endeavors take place on two levels: On one side regular encounters between the five standing members of the Security Council take place, on the other side informal meetings of civil war factions are held, mostly in Jakarta ("**Jakarta Informal Meetings**").

Between January and August 1990 the five standing members of the Security Council successfully work out the framework for comprehensive regulations at a row of high-ranking meetings. At the end of August the five standing members present an **"General Plan for a Comprehensive Political Regulation of the Cambodian Conflict"**, in which all the essential elements of the later peace agreement are already present. One of the core points is the establishment of a "Supreme National Council, SNC" from representatives of all civil war factions. However, haggling over the authority and composition of the SNC takes over a year. Finally it is determined that the SNC will not replace the government in Phnom Penh, but be placed at its side.

On November 26th, 1990, the five standing members and both chairmen agree on a text that includes three sections:

- General accord with detailed additions in respect to the planned mandate of the UNO's transitional authority in Cambodia (UNTAC), the military provisions during the transitional period, elections, the return of Cambodian refugees and exiles as well as the basis for a new constitution;
- Agreement on international guarantees;
- Explication of the reconstruction of Cambodia.

The agreement is unreservedly supported in UNO Resolution 718 (1991) on October 31st, 1991. Since the petition to the Security Council to establish UNTAC and provide it with an appopriate mandate is also included in the agreement, the UN Secretary General suggests the dispatch of the advance command UNAMIC as part of his "good offices". On October 16th, 1991, the Security Council approves the report of the Secretary General through the acceptance of Resolution 717 and decides to create UNAMIC immediately after the signing of the agreement.

On October 23rd, 1991, at the conclusion of the **2nd Parisian Cambodia Conference**, 18 nations and Cambodia sign the agreement for the comprehensive political regulation of the Cambodian conflict in the presence of the UN Secretary General. This agreement represents the high point of a decade-long negotiation process. The accord consists of four individual agreements:

- Last act of the Parisian Cambodian Conference;
- Agreement on comprehensive political regulation including central stipulations about the cease-fire and the demobilization in two phases;
- Agreement on the sovereignty, neutrality and national unity of Cambodia;
- Explication of the reestablishment and reconstruction of Cambodia.

On November 9th, 1991, UNAMIC begins its deployment. At the same time plans for UNTAC begin. The mission is led by a civilian liaison officer, who also keeps in constant contact with the SNC. UNAMIC consists of civilian and military liaison institutions. Australia provides a communications unit, France an air unit with four helicopters and a fixed-wing aircraft. The mission offers its "good offices", including the forwarding of messages between the parties or the planning of meeting between them. There is constant information for the protection of the population from injuries by mines or hidden bombs.

On February 19th, 1992, the UN Secretary General presents the Security Council with a suggest for the implementation of UNTAC. In Resolution 745 the **"United Nations Transitional Authority in Cambodia (UNTAC)"** is called into being for a maximum period of 18 months. UNTAC becomes the largest and most expensive UNO operation to date. Its responsibilities go far beyond classical "peacekeeping" and include broad areas of the civilian administration and reorganization of the police.

UNTAC consists of seven civilian (Administration for UNTAC, Human Rights, Elections, Civilian Administration, Repatriation, Rehabilitation, Civilian Police – CIVPOL) and one military component. CIVPOL is entrusted with the observation, support and training of the local police.

The numerically strongest component is the military one. The core element is twelve infantry battalions of 850 men each. In addition to this there are military and naval observers. As a result of the enactment of the constitution the gradual withdrawal of UNTAC personnel begins. Exceptions to this are the Mine Clearance Unit, which remains until the end of November, and parts of the military police and the medical component, which remain in the country until the end of the year.

The return of 365,000 refugees is to be counted as a success for UNTAC. On the other hand, UNTAC does not succeed in guaranteeing a lasting cease-fire and disarming the forces of the civil war factions. The slow arrival of the – difficult to access – civilian components and the too conciliatory stance of the mission leadership are recognized as fundamental weaknesses.

After the end of the United Nations transitional administration in Cambodia (UNTAC), isolated areas remain to be fulfilled from the Treaty of Paris of October 23rd, 1991. These are, among others, contact with the Cambodian government and army in questions of the security situation in Cambodia as well as existing military duties. The United Nations therefore establish the **"United Nations Military Mission Team (UNMLT)"** to fulfill these duties. UNMLT is not a direct successor mission to UNTAC, but should support the Cambodian government.

• United Nations Advance Mission in Cambodia (UNAMIC)

Basis for deployment:	UNO Resolution 717 (1991) of October 16th, 1991; UNO Resolution 718 (1991) of October 31st, 1991; UNO Resolution 728 (1992) of January 8th, 1992 (extension of the mandate of the mine clearance work).
Mission:	Preparatory mission for UNTAC to ease the communication between the parties of the conflict, secure the basis for the repatriation of Cambodian refugees; establishment of a mine training and clearance program.
Duration of deployment:	October 16th, 1991 – February 28th, 1992.
Participating nations:	Algeria, Argentina, Australia (communications), Austria, Bangladesh, Belgium, Canada, China, France (logistics), Germany (medical), Ghana, Great Britain, India, Indonesia, Ireland, Malaysia, the Netherlands, New Zealand (mine clearance training), Pakistan, Poland, Senegal, Soviet Union/Russia, Thailand (engineers), Tunisia, Uruguay, USA.
Strength:	Ca. 1,090 military observers and support troops.
Headquarters:	Phnom Penh.

Austrian Participation

Political Measures

The Council of Ministers responds to the UNO petition. Within the framework of UNTAC a contingent of the executive is also dispatched. In the time from July 2nd, 1992 to August 16th, 1993 a total of 31 executive officers fulfill duties.

Military Measures

The Defence Ministry plans to dispatch three military observers. However, since the working language of the advance mission is French, the choice of Austrian participants causes difficulties; numerous candidates fail the language test. Finally only two military observers are sent.

Headquarters of UNTAC in Phnom Penh (above). Outpost of UNTAC UN Observer Team 401 (below).

Identification card for UNTAC/APRONUC affiliates (t.l.). Pass for unimpeded transit through Thailand (m.l.). Instruction card for use of weapons by military observers (r.). The UNO disarmament of the various Cambodian armies and armed groups unfortunately occurs only in a very modest proportion (b.).

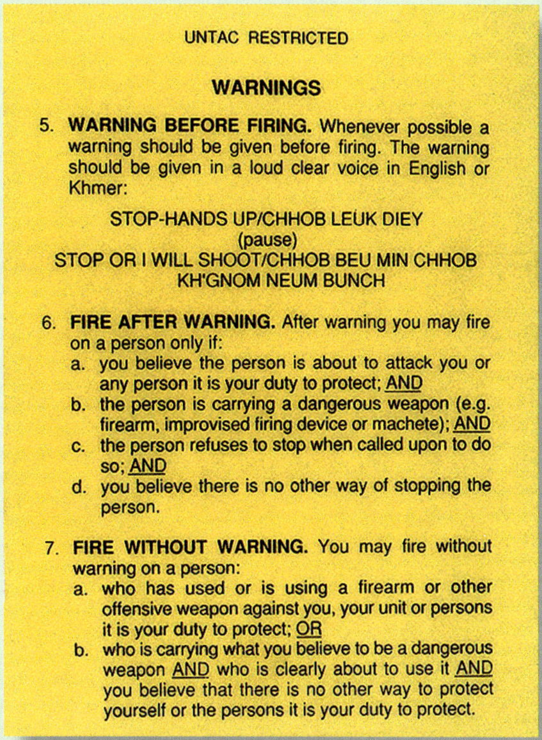

UNTAC RESTRICTED

WARNINGS

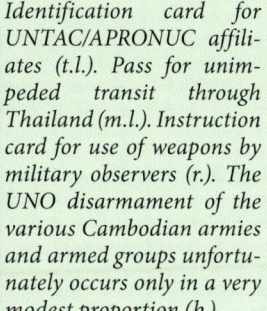

5. **WARNING BEFORE FIRING.** Whenever possible a warning should be given before firing. The warning should be given in a loud clear voice in English or Khmer:

   STOP-HANDS UP/CHHOB LEUK DIEY
   (pause)
   STOP OR I WILL SHOOT/CHHOB BEU MIN CHHOB KH'GNOM NEUM BUNCH

6. **FIRE AFTER WARNING.** After warning you may fire on a person only if:
   a. you believe the person is about to attack you or any person it is your duty to protect; AND
   b. the person is carrying a dangerous weapon (e.g. firearm, improvised firing device or machete; AND
   c. the person refuses to stop when called upon to do so; AND
   d. you believe there is no other way of stopping the person.

7. **FIRE WITHOUT WARNING.** You may fire without warning on a person:
   a. who has used or is using a firearm or other offensive weapon against you, your unit or persons it is your duty to protect; OR
   b. who is carrying what you believe to be a dangerous weapon AND who is clearly about to use it AND you believe that there is no other way to protect yourself or the persons it is your duty to protect.

Basis for deployment:	CM of November 12th, 1991, MC of November 13th, 1991 (dispatch).
Mission:	Deployment as military observers.
Appellation:	None.
Form of dispatch:	Dispatch FCL 1965.
Area of operations:	Cambodia.
Duration of deployment:	December 7th, 1991 – March 14th, 1992.
Contingent strength:	2.
Total:	2.

• United Nations Transitional Authority in Cambodia (UNTAC)

Basis for deployment:	SC Resolution 745 (1992) of February 28th, 1992; SC Resolution 860 (1993) of August 27th, 1993.
Mission:	Observation and verification of the cease-fire as well as the withdrawal of foreign troops; observation of the security units; inspection of all Cambodian facilities and institutions in the areas of reduction and reorganization of the police and foreign policy, defence, finance, public safety and information; return as well as settlement and reintegration of the Cambodian refugees; observation of compliance with human rights and the implementation of free and fair elections; observation of the disarmament and demobilization of the troops of the Cambodian parties.
Duration of deployment:	February 28th, 1991 – September 24th, 1993 (on March 15th, 1992 UNAMIC is incorporated into UNTAC; predecessor of UNMLT).
Participating nations:	Algeria, Argentina, Australia, Austria, Bangladesh, Belgium, Brunei, Bulgaria, Cameroon, Canada, Chile, China, Colombia, Egypt, Fiji, France, Germany, Ghana, Great Britain, Hungary, India, Indonesia, Ireland, Italy, Japan, Jordan, Kenya, Malaysia, Morocco, Namibia, Nepal, the Netherlands, New Zealand, Nigeria, Norway, Pakistan, the Phillippines, Poland, Russia, Senegal, Singapore, Sweden, Switzerland, Thailand, Tunisia, Uruguay, USA.
Strength:	Max. 15,991 soldiers (of which 485 military observers) and 3,359 policemen (in June 1993), 1,150 international civilian workers, 465 affiliates of the volunteer program of the United Nations and 4,830 local workers. In addition before and after the elections are tens of thousands of local workers. Besides the HQ, military observers, infantry forces, engineers, communications units and military police as well as a field hospital, a logistics division and a naval division (with 215 naval military observers) to observer the coast and internal waters belong to the military segment.
Headquarters:	Phnom Penh.

Austrian Participation

Political Measures

The federal government accedes to the UNO petition and decides to dispatch military observers and a police contingent to train and observe the local police, to protect the UN Election Commission and to observe the elections. Furthermore, the Federal Ministry for Foreign Affairs dispatches two officials in May 1993 to observe the elections.

Military Measures

As a result of the decision of the Council of Ministers, in addition to two observation officers a further 15 are set on the march. The 17 observers carry out duties at various observation posts spread throughout the entire country. From July 1993 the contingent is constantly reduced.

Basis for deployment:	CM of May 19th, 1992, MC of May 21st, 1992 (dispatch).
Mission:	Deployment as military observers and assumption of staff functions.
Appellation:	None.
Form of dispatch:	Dispatch FCL 1965.
Area of operations:	Cambodia, liaison officers in Bangkok, Hanoi and Laos.
Duration of deployment:	March 15th, 1991 – November 15th, 1993.
Contingent strength:	Continuing use of the two officers already deployed for UNAMIC. Dispatch of an addition 15 observation officers to the mission on May 25th, 1992. One officer is assigned to UNOMIL from October 31st, 1993 – October 4th, 1994.
Total:	17.

Military Observer Deployment

Hardly anyone can call to mind an image of the work methods of a military observer. Normally this is seen as a simple and well-paid job. Military observers are, however, in contrast to the members of the troop contingents, left to themselves and their foreign comrades and must organize their own stay. What this often means is shown in the following excerpt from the memoir of CPT Dr. Peter Hazdra:

"After a long flight and a night in Bangkok we, the 15 Austrian officers dispatched to UNTAC, reach the Cambodian capital of Phnom Penh. The first days pass with introductory lectures and administrative measures, identity cards are distributed, the UN driver's licenses filed and immunizations administered. Finally the Austrians are distributed among the deployment groups. The assignment is to be taken from a blackboard. After three days the members of Team 513 (one Austrian, Russian, Irish, Bulgarian, and Chinese each, and a Cambodian translator) find each other more through chance. The area of operations for Team 513 is a village named Phum Loveay in the central Cambodian province of Kompong Thom. It is not to be found on any map. Supposedly fighting is still going on there.

Before the decampment the equipment must still be gathered. There is no paper, but in exchange there are two packets of Tipp-ex; the map is procured at the market; it comes from the Vietnam War era. The movement initially takes place with an Mi-26 transport helicopter to Kompong Thom. Here there is also no clearer information on the area of operations. The overnight stay takes place with the Indonesian UN battalion which is responsible for this section. There everyone is warned of the danger of mines. Finally National Road 6 is taken to the area of operations. In any case, there is no village called Phum Loveay. The only jerkwater town far and wide is called Prolay, shelters ca. 400 inhabitants, the half of which are demoralized government soldiers, and lays exactly between the outposts of all four civil war factions. Quarters are taken up in a wooden shack. The mission to disarm and intern the 21st Brigade of the government troops cannot initially be thought of. It first takes 1 – 3 weeks to gather the necessary requirements to begin work. This includes the digging of a well and learning the national language, in order to at least make oneself halfway understood..."[89]

The report gives a small glimpse into the life and work of a military observer and shows the type of problems an observer must overcome. That all Austrian officers until now have very successfully fulfilled their duties is the outcome of personal engagement and outstanding training.

• United Nations Military Liaison team (UNMLT)

Basis for deployment:	SC Resolution 880 (1993) of November 3rd, 1993.
Mission:	Support of the government during the resolution of the remaining military issues of the Parisian Agreement.
Duration of deployment:	November 16th, 1993 – May 16th, 1994.
Participating nations:	Austria, Bangladesh, Belgium, China, France, Great Britain, India, Indonesia, Malaysia, New Zealand, Pakistan, Poland, Russia, Singapore, Thailand, Uruguay.
Strength:	Max. 20 military observers.
Headquarters:	Phnom Penh.

Austrian Participation

Basis for deployment: CM of November 16th, 1993, MC of December 3rd, 1993 (dispatch).
Mission: Deployment as military observers.
Appellation: None.
Form of dispatch: Dispatch FCL 1965.
Area of operations: Phnom Penh.
Duration of deployment: November 16th, 1993 – May 16th, 1994.
Contingent strength: 1 military observer (extension of the UNTAC mandate).
Total: 1 (UNAMIC, UNTAC and UNMLT total 25).

Brigadier General Loridan and some UN observers on the border to Vietnam.

---

89 Peter Hazdra: "The UNO Peacekeeping Operation in Cambodia – Preliminary Events, Concept, Progress and Critical Evaluation of the International Engagement"; Europ. Secondary School Writings, Volume XXXI/322, Peter Lang Verlag, Frankfurt/Main 1997.

United Nations Operation in Somalia I (UNOSOM I)

Preliminary Events

In the 19th century, the "Horn of Africa" slips into the sphere of interest of France (1884/85 Djibouti), Great Britain (1886 British Protectorate of Somaliland), Italy (1889 Italian Somaliland) and eastern-expanding Ethiopia. British and Italian Somaliland become independent on July 1st, 1960 and unite to become the Republic of Somalia. In the constitution of 1961 the goal is established of unifying the Somali people, divided by the borders of Ethiopia and Kenya into three parts, into one nation. After the murder of President Shermarke in 1969 and the army coup under General Mohamed Siad Barre, Somalia becomes a **"democratic republic with a socialist orientation"**. The USSR arms the nation and receives, among other things, harbor rights in Berbera in return. In 1976 Barre becomes president. As such, Barre supports the Western Somalian liberation front in Ogaden. In 1977 a political turn occurs and with it a break with the Soviet Union, above all because of their support for Ethiopia. Subsequently rebel movements develop against Barre; the two most important are the **"Somali National Movement – SNM"** and the **"United Somali Congress – USC"**. In December 1990 a state of emergency is declared. The SNM drives the troops of the meanwhile deposed president from the most important cities, the USA and Italy carry out extensive evacuations.

After the fall of the president, there are serious internal battles from 1991 among the Somalian factions under the leadership of powerful "warlords" in one of the poorest nations in the world. The USC supports the transitional president Ali Mahdi Mohamed, the SNM, which controls the north, rejects him and is supported in this by a third power, the **"Patriotic Movement of Somalia – SPM"**. At the beginning of February 1991 the USC rebels, victorious in Mogadishu, and the followers of the SPM, controlling the south, fight heavy battles against each other. On May 18th the SNM in the north declares its own republic. Rivalries between the president and the chief of the USC, General Mohamed Farah Aidid broaden the conflicts. The hostilities lead to increasing destabilization and to thousands of dead, millions of people without food are in serious danger of death. The battles hinder any targeted aid from UNO and represent a serious threat to the stability on the Horn of Africa. In April 1992 the deposed president Barre attempts to lead his bands of fighters to Mogadishu from the south, but is turned away 50 km from the city. Barre flees to Nigeria and then to Lagos. At the end of July 1992 General Aidid surprisingly agrees to the stationing of 500 Pakistani UN soldiers to secure aid efforts in Mogadishu, but later speaks out against further reinforcements. In September four civil war factions attempt to organize a peace conference in Cairo. The negotiations with the UNO are made more difficult by the fact that there are no legal authorities in Somalia. At the beginning of December 1992 Operation "Restore Hope" begins, the military deployment to secure the provisioning of the starving population in Somalia. Despite various agreements the clan chiefs do not let themselves be stopped from attacking allied troops or humanitarian facilities. On January 4th, under pressure from UNO, a conference in Addis Ababa finally takes place, in which 14 Somalian factions participate. Finally, after intensive negotiations in Mogadishu, interim president Mohamed and General Aidid separately sign the "Agreement on the Implementation of a Cease-fire" on March 3rd.

International Reaction

In cooperation with the Organization of African Unity (OAU), the League of Arab States (LAS), and the Organization of the Islamic Conference (OIC), the UNO pushes for a peaceful solution. Despite the dangerous situation, a group of high-ranking UNO officials leads talks at the beginning of January 1992 in Mogadishu. On January 23rd the Security Council, at the request of Somalia, calls in Resolution 733 (1992) for all parties to end hostilities. Further it is decided that all nations should immediately impose a general and comprehensive embargo on all deliveries of weapons and other military equipment to Somalia.

On January 31st the UNO Secretary General invites the LAS, OAU and OIC as well as interim president Mohamed and General Aidid to dispatch their representatives to New York to participate in deliberations from February 12th – 14th. The deliberations take place as planned. After the return of the joint delegation, Mohamed and Aidid separately sign the **"Agreement on the Implementation of a Cease-fire"** on March 3rd, in the presence of representatives from the UNO, LAS, OAU and OIC. At the same time the joint delegation carries out deliberations with both leading factions in the war and secures their agreement and support for a national reconciliation conference, to which all Somalian groups are invited. After the signing of the agreement a technical team from UNO arrives in Mogadishu in accordance with Resolution 746 (1992) of March 17th, in order to prepare the observation mechanism for the cease-fire. After negotiations with the team, on March 26th and 27th, Mohamed and Aidid sign a declaration of agreement on the mechanism for the observation of the cease-fire and agreements for the fair and effective distribution of humanitarian aid.

On April 21st, as a result of the report of the technical team, the Secretary General recommends the "United Nations Operation in Somalia (UNOSOM)". On April 24th the Security Council decides on the establishment of UNOSOM, in order to *"make an immedi-*

ate and effective end of hostilities, the maintenance of a cease-fire in the entire land to support the process of reconciliation and political settlement in Somalia, and the provision of humanitarian aid possible." In accordance with the agreement the cease-fire is observed by 50 military observers. These form mobile teams consisting of three observers with an all-terrain vehicle.

For the purpose of humanitarian aid and the observation of an agreement made between the national groupings, the UNO, with Resolution 794, authorizes the UN member states, in respect to Chapter VII of the UN charter, to "take all necessary measures to create secure conditions for humanitarian aid in Somalia as soon as possible" through a troop with a unified command. The first part of the "Unified Task Force (UNITAF)" formed for "Operation Restore Hope" under the leadership of the USA arrives on December 9th, 1992 in Somalia. This is a "secret" landing of US Marines. To their surprise the Marines initially find themselves confronted with hundreds of journalists who want to report on the landing. Next to this the observation mission of UNOSOM continues to exist, but de facto plays no further role. In total 26,000 American and 13,000 soldiers from other nations take part in the operation. Through them the food supply in parts of Somalia can be secured, although the battles are not yet ended. Not least because of the push of the new UN Secretary General Boutros Boutros-Ghali, UNITAF is replaced by the newer, larger UN operation UNOSOM II on May 4th, 1993. UNOSOM II is also a failure, however, and ends in March 1995.

The victims are the same everywhere – women, children and old people.

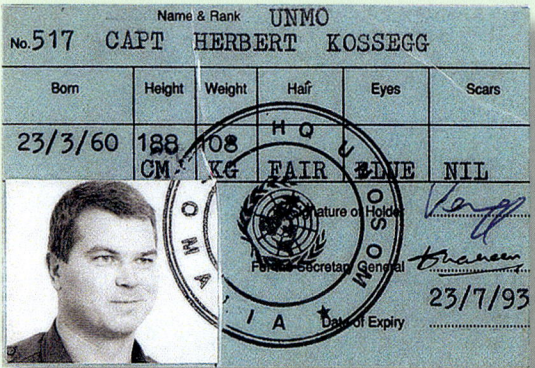

View of the UNO-SOM Camp (t.). Identification and driver's license of UNOSOM military observer CPT Herbert Kossegg (m.l. and r.). UNOSOM patrol (b.l.). Map of the area of operations (b.r.).

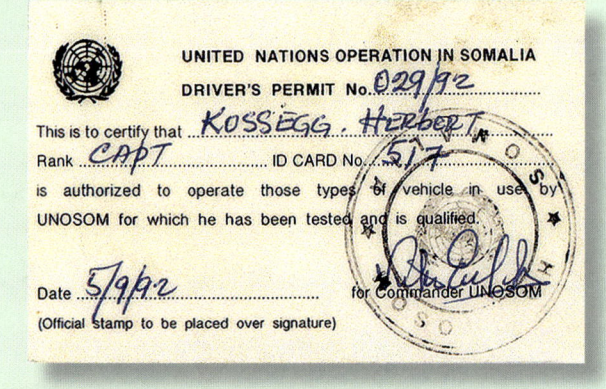

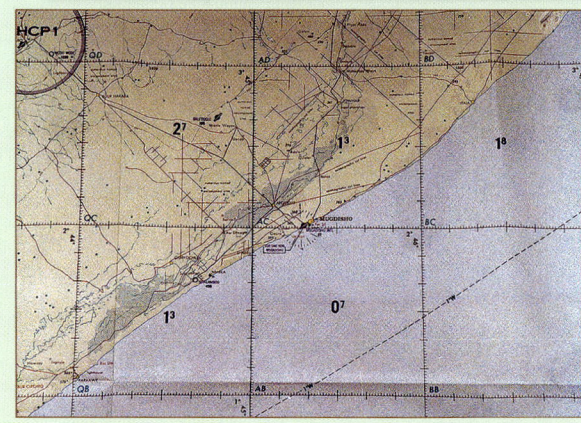

The MIG-21s are dragged out of the hangars by the US armed forces and "placed" in the desert to gain space for their own airplanes (t.l.). The UNOSOM Camp lies directly on the coast. From the living quarters one can watch the constant operations on land, water and in the air (t.r.). Tropical hat of a UNOSOM military observer (m.l.). Pakistani patrol (m.r.). After the end of UNOSOM CPT Kossegg is detached to the UN headquarters in New York. The picture (b.l.) shows CPT Kossegg and other MOs before the flight to New York. Identification for New York (b.r.).

201

Basis for deployment:	SC Resolution 733 (1992) of January 23rd, 1992 (embargo);
	SC Resolution 746 (1992) of March 17th (dispatch of a technical team);
	SC Resolution 751 (1992) of April 24th, 1992 (creation of UNOSOM);
	SC Resolution 767 (1992) of July 27th, 1992;
	SC Resolution 775 (1992) of August 28th, 1992;
	SC Resolution 794 (1992) of December 3rd, 1992 (deployment of UNITAF).
Mission:	Inspection of the cease-fire in Mogadishu; contact with the conflicting parties and cooperation with international aid organizations.
Duration of deployment:	July 3rd, 1992 – May 4th, 1993.
Participating nations:	Australia, Austria, Bangladesh, Belgium, Canada, Czech Republic, Egypt, Fiji, Finland, Indonesia, Jordan, Morocco, New Zealand, Norway, Pakistan, Slovakian Republic, Zimbabwe.
Strength:	50 military observers, 3,500 soldiers and up to 719 civilian employees are planned. 54 military observers. The increase of the contingent according to Resolution 775 does not take place.
Headquarters:	Mogadishu.

Austrian Participation

Political Measures

The federal government immediately responds to UNO's wish for the dispatch of military observers. The treatment of the petition for a dispatch of a mechanized infantry battalion, in contrast, occurs extremely controversially. Technical reorganizations of changes, such as the conversion of the vehicles for desert capabilities, is classified as possible on the part of the Defence Minister Dr. Fasslabend.

Foreign Minister Dr. Mock also supports such a deployment, since it accords with the foreign policy towards the UNO to that point, whereas a rejection would cause damage to Austria's international prestige. Federal President Dr. Klestil also expresses that participation would be a win for Austria. However the scales are tipped by Federal Chancellor Dr. Vranitzky, who denies his permission for the deployment with the reasoning that it is a "incalculable" risk for the soldiers. The echo from abroad is correspondingly negative.

Military Measures

All preparations for the dispatch of military observers are immediately taken on the part of the Federal Defence Ministry. After the petition of the UN Secretary General for the dispatch of troops, plans are also made for the dispatch of a mechanized infantry battalion. Major General DI Günther Greindl, who was already of service in Cyprus, in the Golan and in Kuwait, is assigned to this. Since, however, the deployment is denied from the political side, the preparations are cancelled again. Only the military observers are deployed, from which one is detached to the UN headquarters in New York in 1993.

Basis for deployment: CM of May 12th, 1992; MC of May 13th, 1992 (dispatch); CM of September 14th, 1993 (end).
Mission: Military observers; from time to time assumption of staff functions.
Appellation: None.
Form of dispatch: Dispatch FCL 1965.
Area of operations: Harbor of Mogadishu.
Duration of deployment: June 30th, 1991 – May 4th, 1993.
Contingent strength: 5 (from June 30th, 1991 – May 3rd, 1993). 1 in the planning staff for the mission in UNHQ in New York (from May 3rd – July 11th, 1993).
Total: 5.

CSCE/OSCE Spillover Mission to Skopje (CSCE/OSCE Skopje)[90]

Preliminary Events

Differences between the central government and the constituent republics as well as between individual constituent republics lead to the final collapse of the Yugoslavian nation in 1991.

International Reaction

Armed struggles subsequently take place in Slovenia, Croatia and Bosnia-Herzegovina, which are often accompanied by ethnically motivated violence. In other successor states numerous tensions exist, without an open war breaking out.

Basis of deployment:	Decision of the 16th Session of the Council of High Officials on November 18th, 1992.
Mission:	Avoidance of ethnic conflicts which could spill over into the territory of the Former Yugoslav Republic of Macedonia – FYROM; observation of sanctions and embargo against the previous constituent republic of Yugoslavia in cooperation with the EC/EU (leadership through the EU Coordination Office in Brussels).
Duration of deployment:	November 8th, 1991 – to date.
Participating nations:	Members of OSCE.
Strength:	Eight, in addition two from December 15th, 1992 who are assigned to the mission from the ECMM.
Headquarters:	Skopje.

Austrian Participation

Political Measures

The dispatch takes place as a result of the membership in the OSCE.

Military Measures

Basis for deployment:	Membership in OSCE.
Mission:	Fulfillment of the duties of the mission; establishment of communication lines.
Appellation:	None.
Form of dispatch:	Until April 1997 according to the Dispatch FCL 1965, from April 1997 according to the FCL-CSD 1997.
Area of operations:	Macedonia.
Duration of deployment:	November 27th, 1991 – May 31st, 1993, November 29th, 1994 – April 10th, 1995 one officer each; May 30th – June 3rd, 1994, January 31st – February 3rd, 1995 two noncommissioned officers each for the establishment of communication lines.
Contingent strength:	Up to 2.
Total:	7.

---

[90] The CSCE is renamed the OSCE in Budapest in December 1994.

United Nations Office in Tajikistan (UNOT)

United Nations Mission of Observers in Tajikistan (UNMOT)

Preliminary Events

Until the Communist division of the USSR by Stalin there is no national Tajik political structure.[91] Under the excuse of uniting all Tajiks in one nation, one of the largest ethnic shifts begins under Stalin. This is not, however, in order to realize a realistic political goal, but in order to play the ethnic groups against each other. So the structure of the national minorities is dictated by Stalin's settlement policies. In the 1930's "enemies of the people" of the most various heritage are exiles to Tajikistan. The linguistic and cultural variety of these mountain people in the difficult to access Pamir region has remained to this day. The Tajik language, which replaced Russian as the official language in 1990, belongs among the Iranian languages. In 1929 the Latin script replaces the Arabic, from 1940 the Cyrillic is forcibly introduced. The Muslim religion, alongside clan membership or the membership in a political party, becomes the only unifying force; the medieval clan structures are maintained and only artificially combined into a national structure, which as such is however rejected.

---

91 Gottfried Hoinig: "Hostage in Tajikistan – Reflections on a Life-changing Experience as a Military Observer"; in Armis et Litteris, Volume 3/1999, Wr. Neustadt 1999.

Tajikistan's independence on September 9th, 1991 in connection with the disintegration of the Soviet Union leads to religiously and ethnically motivated conflicts between the various ethnic groups, or alternatively between the Communists and the opposition. The reasons date from the time of Perestroika (1985 – 1991). In this time numerous informal groups develop which form political groups after the fall of the Soviet Union and the founding of the Commonwealth of Independent States (CIS). The conflicts finally lead to the deposition of President Nabiyev. In spring 1992 the opposition, initially supported by Afghanistan, gains the upper hand, the capital of Dushanbe is taken. Nevertheless, towards the end of the year, the government which reigns to this day is able to reconquer the city and bring the nation under its control with Russian and Uzbek support. After taking power there are serious persecutions; opposition leaders as well as journalists are murdered or placed under house arrest.

Although the hostilities cause more victims than for instance the conflicts in Bosnia, Abkhazia, or Nagorno-Karabakh, the world public initially takes no note of the events. In 1994, under the supervision of the UNO, a referendum to create a constitution takes place, combined with elections, from which Rahmon emerges as the president. The elections themselves take place under fear and intimidation with multiple voting and falsification of votes. The election laws are created so that neither the Islamic or the democratic opposition have the opportunity to put up their own candidates. The result of the "election success" is further brutality, oppression and exile.

On December 23th, 1996, the pro-Russian Tajik president Enomalii Rahmon and the leader of the Islamic rebels, Dr. Sayid Abdulloh Nuri, sign a basic agreement that regulates the preparations for a peace agreement in the presence of the Russian Prime Minister Viktor Chernomyrdin. Up to this point in time 30,000 dead and 500,000 refugees are to be complained of, who mostly flee into neighboring Afghanistan and there cause a humanitarian catastrophe.

International Reaction

At the invitation of the government the UN Secretary General dispatches a mission of good offices (UNOT) on October 29th, 1992, which is supported by the **"United Nations Military Observers in Tajikistan" (UNMOT)** from January 21st, 1993. At the request of the government in Dushambe, the Foreign Minister of the CSCE/OSCE decides on December 1st in Rome to dispatch a mission to Tajikistan to intercede between the government and the opposition and guarantee the protection of human rights. On April 26th, 1993 the Secretary General names a special envoy, who can subsequently lead talks between the parties in the conflict. In April 1994 further talks take place in Moscow and in July 1994 in Tehran. These finally lead to a temporary cease-fire and to the formation of a mixed implementation commission. Not until the continuation of the Tehran negotiations on September 18th, 1994 does the signing of a definitive cease-fire agreement take place, through which the conditions for the dispatch of UN observers are created. With the approval of the government, Russian border troops are deployed on the Afghani-Tajik border and peacekeeping troops from the Commonwealth of Independent States (CIS) are deployed in the interior of the country. In October the first 16 observers from, among others, Belgium and Austria arrive in the area of operations in the Pamir mountains. On December 17th the **"United Nations Mission of Observers in Tajikistan" (UNMOT)** takes up its work. The UN mission ends in May 2000 when a political consensus on the future of the nation is reached.

Basis for deployment:	Approval of the Security Council from April 29th, 1993 on the decision of the Secretary General of the UN to dispatch a special envoy to Tajikistan; SC Resolution 968 (1994) of December 16th, 1994; SC Resolution 1274 (1999) of November 12th, 1999 (extension of the mandate until May 15th, 2000).
Mission:	Support of the UNO special envoy for the achievement of a cease-fire, with the development of suggestions for an international observation mission, with the determination of a negotiation position between the parties in the conflict and the winning of possible support from the neighboring nations; cooperation with the OSCE mission and the peacekeeping troops of the CIS; political contacts to secure the humanitarian air measures of the international community.
Duration of deployment:	December 4th, 1994 – May 15th, 2000.
Participating nations:	Austria, Bangladesh, Bulgaria, Denmark, Hungary, Jordan (Chief Military Observer), Poland, Switzerland (two military observers, two doctors, one medic), Ukraine, Uruguay.
Strength:	Up to 44 military observers and 44 civilian workers.
Headquarters:	Dushanbe.

Austrian Participation

Political Measures

The federal government accedes to the UNO's petition and decides on the dispatch of military observers as well as, from May 26th, 1998 – May 31st, 1999, an executive official to advise the local executive.

Military Measures

The UNMOT deployment is fundamentally different from other observation missions. Since there is no demilitarized zone for the UN observers in Tajikistan, the work must necessarily lie in one of the zones of influence of the conflicting parties. This forces an extremely delicate implementation of the mission, in order to not come under suspicion of espionage for the respective other side. The teams must survey the military, humanitarian, political and economic situation. Negotiations with the local parties must be held. As a part of this it must be determined who shot first in a conflict and which weapons were used for this. Finally the teams must provide for the (unarmed) escort of refugee convoys from UNHCR.

The military observers fulfill their duties at headquarters as well as at so-called "team sites" (TS), which are established according to necessity in especially sensitive sections. Each team is assigned an "area of responsibility" (AOR), within which their duties as observers are carried out. The occupation takes place internationally, in which at least four officers of varying nationalities as well as a Tajik translator each form a team.

Besides the military team leader a "political affairs officer" (a civilian official with UNO) also belongs to the teams. This person is to carry out the political evaluation. Since Major Hafner's team has no such official, this duty must also be fulfilled by the Austrian officer. The mission does not have its own logistics. The teams must therefore provide for themselves (this includes, among other things, the repair of the vehicles). This mission therefore places the highest demands on all affiliates in all areas.

Basis for deployment:	CM of January 12th, 1993, MC of January 21st, 1993 (dispatch).
Mission:	Military observers, assumption of staff functions as needed.
Appellation:	None.
Form of dispatch:	**UNOT** Assignment from UNTSO.
	UNMOT until April 1997 according to the Dispatch FCL 1965, from April 1997 according to the FCL-CSD 1997.
Area of operations:	Tajikistan, with the exception of the autonomous northern area of Khujand (Leninabad), only accessible from Uzbekistan.
Duration of deployment:	**UNOT** January 21st, 1993 – May 5th, 1993 and August 3rd, 1993 – December 16th, 1994;
	UNMOT December 17th, 1994 – May 15th, 2000.
Contingent strength:	**UNOT** 1; **UNMOT** up to 5. After the conclusion of the mandate 1 MB remains at the request of UNO for concluding work until July 31st, 2000.
Total:	**UNOT** 2; **UNMOT** 23.

Hostage Taking

That UN soldiers do not always have the protection due to them and that (almost all) UN deployments can be dangerous, is proven by the report of Gottfried Hoinig, who was even taken hostage as a military observer with UNMOT. He reports:[92]

"As a result of a stubborn case of diarrhea, HQ decides to evacuate me to Dushanbe, in which case the transport is to be carried out by air. The UN flight, however, is bound to the approval of the conflicting parties, and this is denied by the UTO. So the team, which consists of a doctor, two military observers, and a Tajik translator, is set on the march to Garm by land. There treatment is carried out by a Swiss military doctor. On the next morning, it was February 4th, 1997, we left early in order to be able to cover the 200 km long way back in one day. Near Obigarm (ca. 80 km east of Dushanbe) we stumbled into an ambush of the Bakhrom group, who took us hostage. Among other things, they demanded in exchange for our freedom that the governments of Tajikistan and Russia open a corridor between Afghanistan and Tajikistan to make possible the unhindered entry of the Mujahideen fighting in Afghanistan, and their weapons. This demand seemed so unsatisfiable that we had to fear the worst. The Bakhom group also displayed their determination for us: So, poorly clothed, we had to lay in the snow while the hostage takers shot around themselves as if mad. In such moments control over escalating feelings is vital. Had one of us lost their nerve and, for instance, sprung up, it would have been our certain death. I do not shy away from the observation that religious people find it easier to remain calm in a situation in which one by necessity begins to come to terms with the end of one's own life. Luckily, after days of hoping, giving up and hoping again, we came away with only a scare. Since the UNO did partially give in to some demands, we were let go after eight days. At this point the acting commander, COL Jan A., must be thanked, who probably saved the lives of the team with the professionalism with which he worked in the crisis staff. The first psychological pressure was taken from us after arriving in UNO headquarters by the presence of negotiation specialists flown in from Scotland Yard during our captivity, who worked in cooperation with the UN crisis staff. A military psychiatrist was also sent to Tashkent on the part of the Swiss Army, in order to give the freed hostages professional aftercare."

Unfortunately this is not the only incident during the mission: On September 18th, 1995, Austrian Lieutenant Colonel Wolf Sponner, who leads the observation group in Kurgun-Tyube, loses his life. On December 16th, 1996, a UN convoy is taken prisoner, on August 23rd, 1997, a UNMOT helicopter is shot at, the pilot only manages an emergency landing with difficulty.

---

92 Gottfried Hoinig: "Hostage in Tajikistan".

United Nations Observer Mission in Liberia (UNOMIL)

Preliminary Events

The basis of the conflict in this African nation is also the battle between clans for domination. In addition to this there is the special confrontation between the native population and freed slaves who settled here from the US and ruled the nation as "black colonists" for more than 100 years. In 1989 a civil war is set off by rebels. After numerous failed attempts, a cease-fire is successfully reached in the Cotonou agreement on July 25th, 1993. In accordance with this agreement the civil war parties form a cease-fire commission, with whose work the UNO observers cooperate. In the transitional period the national authority is wielded by a national council in which all the parties of the civil war are represented. Parliamentary and presidential elections are planned for six months (February/March 1994) after the signing of the agreement at the latest. The renewed outbreak of hostilities between Liberian splinter groups nevertheless makes the implementation impossible. Not until the elections, taking place on July 19th, 1997, does the transition to a peaceful state seem possible; with this the deployment of the UN observers also ends.

International Reaction

The UNO establishes UNOMIL in order to observe the cease-fire of July 25th, 1993, at the request of the civil war parties, in cooperation with the Economic Community of West African States (ECOWAS) and the "ECOWAS Cease-Fire Monitoring Group (ECOWOG)" peacekeeping troops deployed by them in Liberia since 1990. While ECOMOG is primarily responsible for the implementation of the agreement with regard to content, UNOMIL's duty is to observe the implementation. In the following months a row of further agreements takes place. The election, delayed as a result of the continuing violent conflicts, can finally be carried out under the observation of UNOMIL. With this the main goal of UNOMIL has been achieved. The mandate can therefore be allowed to run out on September 30th.

Basis for deployment:	Cotonou Agreement of July 25th, 1993; SC Resolution 856 (1993) of August 10th, 1993; SC Resolution 866 (1993) of September 22nd, 1993.
Mission:	Observation of cease-fire, the housing, disarmament and demobilization of the combatants and the weapons embargo; observation of the election process as well as humanitarian aid activities; reporting on human rights violations; information for the ECOMOG (ECOWAS Cease-Fire Monitoring Group).
Duration of deployment:	September 22nd, 1993 – September 30th, 1997.
Participating nations:	Austria, Bangladesh, Belgium, Brazil, China, Congo, Czech Republic, Egypt, Guinea Bissau, Hungary, India, Jordan, Kenya, Malaysia, the Netherlands, Pakistan, Poland, Russia, Slovakian Republic, Sweden, Uruguay.
Strength:	303 military observers, 45 construction engineers, 20 medics.
Headquarters:	Monrovia.

Austrian Participation

Political Measures

The federal government decides to dispatch up to ten officers.

Military Measures

On September 3rd, 1993 an officer from UNTAC is detached as a member of the advance commando for UNO.

Basis for deployment:	CM of October 19th, 1993, MC of October 21st, 1993 (dispatch).
Mission:	Military observer.
Appellation:	None.
Form of dispatch:	Dispatch FCL 1965.
Area of operations:	Liberia.
Duration of deployment:	October 30th, 1993 – November 4th, 1994.
Contingent strength:	Eleven military observers (of which one colonel in a leadership position), one assigned from UNTAC from October 31st, 1993 – October 4th, 1994, one assigned to UNAMIR from July 28th, 1994 – November 18th, 1994.
Total:	11.

UNOMIL patrol before their "office". While an officer relays the latest information over the radio, his comrade gets to turn his attentions to the care of their vehicle.

United Nations Assistance Mission in Rwanda (UNAMIR)

Preliminary Events

For centuries a conflict between the Hutu and Tutsi ethnic groups swells in the thickly settled areas of the large lakes. The Hutu, a farming Bantu people, migrate to the region from the west starting from the 7th century. Beginning in the 15th century, the Tutsi, who are counted among the Nilotic peoples and live off cattle herding, push from the Horn of Africa into the Great Lakes region. They subdue the Hutu, but nevertheless remain a minority (15%). The area of the current states of Rwanda and Burundi are initially part of the German colony of East Africa and then administrated by Belgium as an area under the mandate of the League of Nations. During this the colonial administration leans on the dominion of the Tutsi elite and strengthens the tensions, above all when a clear demarcation of the until then only loosely defined groups is carried out on the basis of their acquired rights. Not until the end of the 1950's do the Belgians begin to push democratization with the inclusion of the Hutus. In 1959, for the first time, serious riots and massacres of the Tutsi occur, who then subsequently flee by the tens of thousands into the neighboring lands of Uganda, Zaire, Burundi and Tanzania. In Rwanda the first elections in 1961 end with the overwhelming victory of the Hutu, while in neighboring Burundi the Tutsi maintain their claim to power. On July 1st, 1962, Rwanda and Burundi become independent. With the exception of a few attempted coups from the Tutsi and subsequent revenge acts of the Hutu, both nations remain quiet. Starting in 1973 the fortunes of Rwanda are guided by President Juvenal Habyarimana after a bloodless coup.

On October 1st, 1990, the latent conflict receives a fully new dimension. On this day the newly-founded rebel organization, which calls itself the **"Rwandese Patriotic Front (RPF)"**, pushes from the north into Rwandan territory. The RPF recruits primarily from the Tutsi which fled Rwanda in 1959 in the course of the violent riots and now see the chance to return to their homeland. With this a civil war begins between the RPF and the Hutu-dominated regime of President Juvenal Habyarimana in Kigali. Neither party succeeds in decisive territorial gains during the hostilities. In contrast there are significant changes on the political level: The poor economic situation and the international pressure force the previously absolutist governing President to introduce a democratization process. The establishment of a coalition government with the inclusion of all (Hutu) opposition parties follows. A line of summation is to be drawn under the armed conflicts and a settlement found with the RPF with the **Arusha Peace Agreement** (Tanzania) of August 4th, 1993. The agreement envisages the withdrawal of all foreign troops, the formation of a transitional government with the inclusion of the RPF as well as the establishment of a demilitarized zone (DMZ) controlled by UN peacekeeping troops. Towards the end of the year UNAMIR takes up its duties, the peace process itself nevertheless comes to a standstill. It is not even possible to conclude the first phase – establishment of a transitional government – until April 1994. Immediately after a renewed SC Resolution on April 5th, 1994, the regional heads of state meet in Tanzania in order to consul on a way out of the crisis. The meeting ends without a result. On the flight back on April 7th, 1994, the presidents of Rwanda and Burundi, both Hutus, lose their lives in a plane crash. Three Burundi ministers, the chief of staff of the Rwandan army, as well as the crew of French officers die with them. The situation escalates and a brutal civil war begins. In the same night of the crash, the presidential guard begins to murder members of the Tutsi minority and opposition Hutu politicians. Among the first victims are Prime Minister Agathe Uwilingiyimana (a Hutu held to be friendly to Tutsis) and ten Belgian UN soldiers who were placed for her protection. The police and civilian militias join the conflicting parties, which subsequently spread a reign of terror over the land. Among others, these are the militia of the presidential party, the so-called **"Interahamwe" (The Unified Attackers)** as well as those of the still more radical Hutu party the **"Coalition pour la Defence de la Republique" (CDR)**. The militias operate with unimaginable brutality. Women, children, priests or nuns are indiscriminately dismembered. The army and police watch inactively. The cities are strewn with corpses. These are transported away by clearance commands consisting of convicts and hastily buried in mass graves. Over a half million people die, millions flee over the border.

At the same time an interim regime consisting only of Hutu hardliners constitutes itself on April 8th, 1994, which is not recognized by RPF. Likewise on April 8th the Tutsi intervene in the battles with the goal of ending the massacres and bringing the responsible parties before a court. In the following days the RPF troops quickly succeed at winning ground. At the beginning of May they control the entire northern and eastern parts of the nation, Kigali is surrounded, the airport must be closed because of the heavy bombardments. All UNAMIR attempts to declare the airport a neutral zone are rejected. The Tutsi behave with relative discipline, however, the forward push of the RPF sets off the largest wave of refugees the world has ever seen (UNHCR report). Three million Hutus lose their settlement areas. On July 17th, 1994, the RPF troops in the north push to the Zaire border. With this they control the entire country – with the exception of a "Humanitarian Protected Zone" (established with SC Resolution 929 on June 22nd, 1994 for the creation of stable conditions for humanitarian aid) established by France and its African allies in the southwest. On July 18th, 1994, the RPF leadership declares a one-sided cease-fire.[93]

On March 8th, 1996, the Rwandan government demands the withdrawal of all UN forces.

International Reaction

On October 5th, 1993, the UN Security Council decides on the creation of the **"United Nations Assistance Mission for Rwanda" (UNAMIR)**. The divisions arriving at the end of 1993 suffer from an acute lack of vehicles for the transport of refugees and aid goods. The peace process continually runs into delays. The international community reacts with irritation and extends the mandate in its resolution of April 5th, 1994 by only four months (instead of six) and only under the condition that the transitional institutions be established with six weeks. The following **Tanzania Summit Meeting** ends unsuccessfully as well. In May, at the urging of the High Commissioner for Human Rights, first established as the result of the UNO Human Rights Conference of the previous year in Vienna, the UN Human Rights Commission concerns itself with the massacres. There are efforts during this to detect the ones behind it, bring them before a tribunal and punish them. The UN troops themselves cannot intervene to prevent the massacres as a result of their limited mandate. At this point a soldier must make the serious accusation of irresponsibility to the responsible UN politicians. It is irresponsible to deploy soldiers for the protection of the population and then not give them the possibility of intervention. With this the soldiers are brought in an unimaginable moral conflict, and that leads to hate from the despairing population for the UN soldiers, who do not (cannot) understand their inaction and so make them enemies.

On April 8th French and Belgian paratroopers land in Kigali, in order to evacuate foreign citizens by air in cooperation with UNAMIR. Further foreigners form auto convoys, which, escorted by UNAMIR personnel, escape to the neighboring countries by land. Attempts to take Rwandan citizens on the way fail as a rule; whoever is recognized as a native has no chance of survival. Sub-

---

93 Peter Hazdra: "Rwanda – Political and Military Developments"; ÖMZ, Volume 3/1995, Vienna 1995.

sequently the civilian UN workers, the 60 civilian police and the Belgian UN contingent (as a result of the murder of ten Belgian soldiers) are flown to Nairobi with Belgian, Spanish and Canadian transport planes. On the political level further options for UNAMIR are considered. The consensus is to expand the mission of UNAMIR to mediate between the conflict parties and support the humanitarian aid. UNAMIR still does not receive an authorization to hinder the massacres by force.

In the time from June 23rd to August 22nd, 1994, **"Operation Turquoise"** takes place under French leadership. Around 2,300 men participate in it. The goal of the operation is the protection of refugees and the formation of a safe zone in West Rwanda. UNAMIR itself is reduced to 270 men (1 infantry company and military observers) and a small political-administrative staff. This leads to heavy criticism, above all from African states, since UNO simultaneously agrees to the dispatch of 6,000 blue helmets to Bosnia. As a result of this criticism, as well as that of many NGOs and the awareness of ever more gruesome details, the UN Secretary General is caused to take a new initiative.

Secretary General Boutros Boutros Ghali and most of the African states demand at least 5,500 men, who were to be deployed across the entire nation in numerous security zones. The USA, in contrast, speaks out for a smaller contingent, which would form a protective zone for refugees only along the Rwandan border. After long discussions the UN Security Council decides on the dispatch of up to 5,500 men in numerous phases, including five partly mechanized infantry battalions. In the 1st phase, however, only the evacuated military observers are brought back and the Ghanian battalion brought to full strength. Further, the UN Security Council places an arms embargo against Rwanda.

Initially, the planned stationing of around 5,500 blue helmets is nevertheless significantly delayed. The cause is, among other things, the demand of the African contingent for full equipage, motorization and armament through the UNO. The procurements then also take much time. In order to make swift aid possible, Western nations step in: Australia sends a field hospital, Canada a transport unit and England a transport unit, an engineering unit and a medical unit (the last, however, is withdrawn again at the end of November). America again ensures the establishment and maintenance of a humanitarian aid bridge (**"Operation Support Hope"**). A part of the equipment is handed over from the withdrawing contingents to the African UNAMIR troops. Not until November 1994 does UNAMIR II reach its planned strength. For tactical reasons, Rwanda is partitioned into six sectors, in which the forces can be deployed according to the picture of the threat. UNAMIR is subsequently unsuccessful at reestablishing peace.

Besides the military deployment, the humanitarian aid also begins. In September 1994, besides the UN special organizations (such as UNHCR, UNDP, UNICEF, etc.) over 100 NGOs are also registered. Here vehement criticism is also necessary. 100 NGOs work completely without coordination, need 100 staffs, 100 personal communications networks, etc., and follow only their own interests. Here, like all other humanitarian deployments, there is acute need to act. The UN special representative for Rwanda presents an expansive program for normalization. The UN Secretary General petitions for 435 million dollars for humanitarian aid. In the middle of January 1995 a renewed call for over 1.4 billion dollars follows, while Prime Minister Faustin Twagiramungu petitions for a further 764 million dollars for reconstruction. In the course of time attempts are made to find new development strategies, such as the "Help for Self-help" drive. The genocide itself remains unresolved.

Duration of deployment:	UNO Resolution 872 (1993) of October 5th, 1993;
	UNO Resolution 909 (1994) of April 5th, 1994;
	UNO Resolution 912 (1994) of April 21st, 1994;
	UNO Resolution 918 (1994) of May 17th, 1994;
	UNO Resolution 1029 (1995) of December 12th, 1995.
Mission:	Observation of the Arusha peace agreement; observation of the return settlement of refugees; observation of the police and gendarmerie activities; preparation for general elections; humanitarian aid. Since December 1994 also protection of the personnel of the criminal tribunal and the military observers.
Duration of deployment:	October 5th, 1993 – March 8th, 1996 (+ six weeks for withdrawal).
Participating nations:	Argentina, Australia, Austria, Bangladesh, Belgium, Brazil, Canada, Chad, Congo, Djibouti, Egypt, Ethiopia, Fiji, Germany, Ghana, Great Britain, Guinea, Guinea-Bissau, Guyana, India, Indonesia, Jordan, Kenya, Malawi, Mali, the Netherlands, Niger, Nigeria, Pakistan, Poland, Romania, Russia, Senegal, Slovakia, Slovenia, Spain, Switzerland, Togo, Tunisia, Uruguay, Zambia, Zimbabwe.
Strength:	5,200 soldiers, 350 military observers, 120 police, 376 civilian workers.
Headquarters:	Kigali.

Austrian Participation

Political Measures

The CM accedes to the UNO's petition for participation in the observation mission. Furthermore a police contingent in the strength of 20 executive officials is also dispatched from December 25th, 1993 – April 25th, 1994 (CM of December 21st, 1993, MC of January 20th, 1994) for the training and observation of the local gendarmerie and community police, to support the election commission and for other occurring police duties. Since Austria is offered the function of a **Police Commissioner**, the FMI decides to entrust Colonel Bliem with this duty. COL Bliem moves on December 25th, 1993 to the area of operations. While the deployment of CIVPOL ends on April 23rd, 1994, the military observers remain in the area of operations until the end of UNAMIR.

Military Measures

Five military observers are initially sent from the MoD on December 10th, 1993, 10 more follow on January 21st, 1994.

Basis for deployment:	CM of November 16th, 1993, MC of December 3rd, 1993 (dispatch).
Mission:	Military observer; assumption of staff functions from time to time.
Appellation:	None.
Form of dispatch:	Dispatch FCL 1965.
Area of operations:	Rwanda, Burundi, Tanzania, Uganda, Zaire.
Duration of deployment:	December 10th, 1993 – April 19th, 1996.
Contingent strength:	5 (until January 1994), 15 (from January 1994). 1 officer assigned from UNOMIL from July 28th, 1994 – November 18th, 1994. At the petition of the **Department for Humanitarian Affairs (DHA)** in Geneva a radio specialist each is assigned to Kigali in the time from April 20th, 1994 – May 18th, 1994 for the establishment of a radio network for the non-military deployment forces of UNO and for communication with the headquarters in Geneva, and in the time from July 3rd, 1994 – July 26th, 1994 to Nairobi for the organization of the provisioning of refugees.
Total:	30.
Contribution:	An example of the personal contribution the Austrian soldiers abroad are able to bring, even in deadly peril, is shown in the following extract from a letter of thanks:

During the civil war the orphanages of Kigali are also supplied with nourishment and water by UN soldiers (in the picture is Major Peter Hazdra with a sister of the "Missionaries of Charity", of the later legendary Mother Teresa).

"Most honored Mr. Federal Minister...

...On April 7th, 1994, around 7:00 PM, Rwandan militia and armed civilians forced their way into the "EDELWEISS" hotel in GISENYI in line with a planned deportation campaign, which also affected Mrs. NOEL, owner of the hotel, her two children, and her family, all of Tutsi heritage. The armed men took as many members of this family as they could discover and murdered them at the graveyard near the airport.

The hotel was plundered and set on fire, and they expressed the plan to go back and prepare the same fate for the owner and her two children.

Aware of these conditions, I alerted the Rwandan and Belgian authorities to take measures in order to take these people to safety. Admittedly without result, because the Belgians had no instructions and did not want to take any measures. Here it should be noted that Mrs. Patricia NOEL is the widow of the dead Mr. NOEL, a Belgian, and, like her children, has the same citizenship.

I made telephonic contact with Major UNGER, in which we exchanged information and opinions about measures to do with these events. After I explained to him the dramatic situation in which this family had fallen, the Major recognized my despair and started out, despite having to overcome many searches and the difficult dealings with the militias, to search for these people in their haven, in order to bring them to relative safety in Hotel Meridien.

(Nevertheless) over the course of the day the Rwandan militias forced their way into the hotel despite the presence of the regular Rwandan army, where they murdered the entire reception personnel with machetes and firearms.

Major UNGER was in the hall, where he was gruffly questioned, attacked and (even) threatened with death. The militia accused him of concerning himself with the refugees over the level of his authority. His papers and money were confiscated and he was ordered to lie on the ground. In the given situation the order to lie down means the threat of imminent death! With outstanding courage he asserted himself over these bandits, negotiated and concerned himself with the other families..."

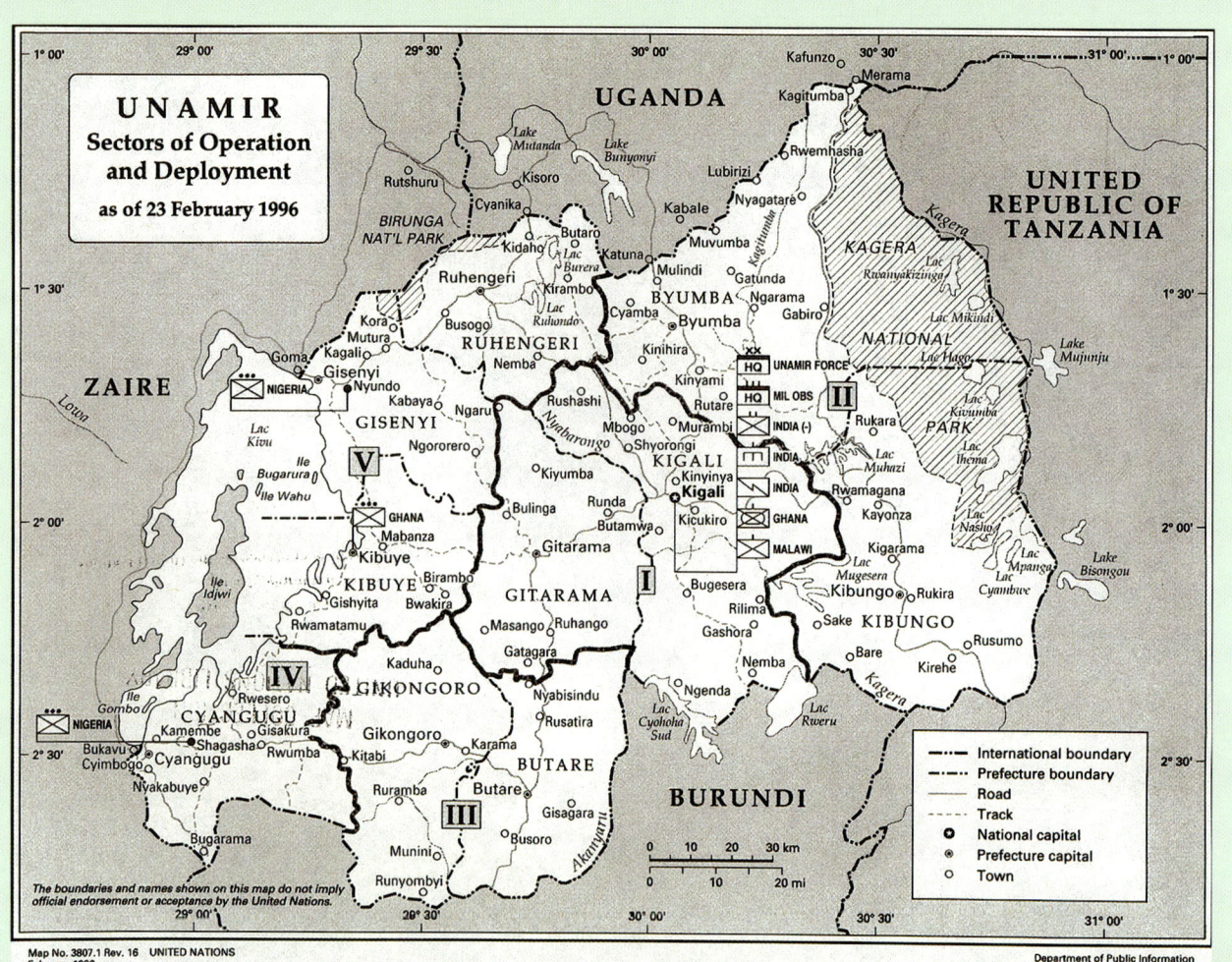

The UN deployment in Rwanda is also not very successful due to the lack of motivation from the community of states. In the picture (b.l.) is Austrian UN observer Major Peter Hazdra with comrades from Zimbabwe and Toto, in 1994. Major Hazdra's identification as an affiliate of UNAMIR/MINUAR (m. and r.b.).

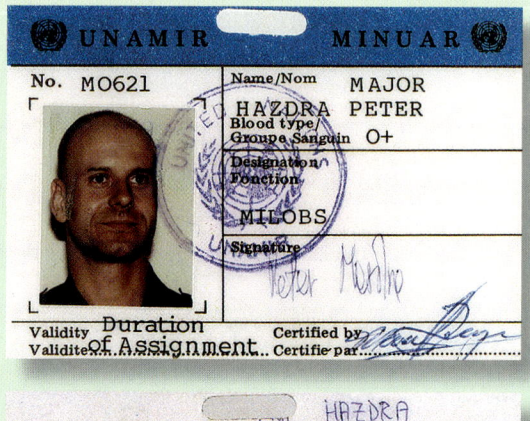

CSCE/OSCE Mission to Nagorno-Karabakh

Preliminary Events

As a result of the settlement history of the Transcaucasus there are recurring social tensions between the Turkish-speaking, Muslim Azeri and the Christian Armenians. The around 4,400 square kilometer large Armenian enclave of Nagorno (Highland)-Karabakh, which lies in Azerbaijani territory, is especially affected by this. After the dissolution of the USSR and international acceptance of Azerbaijan and Armenia as independent states, as well as their entry into the CSCE in January 1992, the tensions between the Armenian inhabitants of the Nagorno-Karabakh enclave and Azerbaijan escalate into an armed conflict.

At this time around 50,000 Azeris and 150,000 Armenians live in this area. Already on December 10th, 1991, the Karabakh Armenians declare their independence. The armed forces of Nagorno-Karabakh subsequently occupy around 17,000 square kilometers (20%) of the total Azerbaijani territory, above all between the enclave and Armenia. In the year 1994, under the mediation of Russia, which militarily supports Armenia, a cease-fire agreement is signed; up to this point in time 40,000 people have already lost their lives, 1 million become refugees. In November 1998 Azerbaijan rejects OSCE's suggestion to solve the still swelling conflict, which envisions a "shared" state. The Azerbaijani government continues to favor an earlier OSCE suggestion, which grants the region of Nagorno-Karabakh the "highest possible" level of autonomy within Azerbaijan. On October 27th, 1999, a group of five armed persons cause a bloodbath in Armenia's parliament with the slogan "This is a coup", in which Prime Minister Sargsyan and seven members of parliament are shot. On October 28th the rebels surrender.

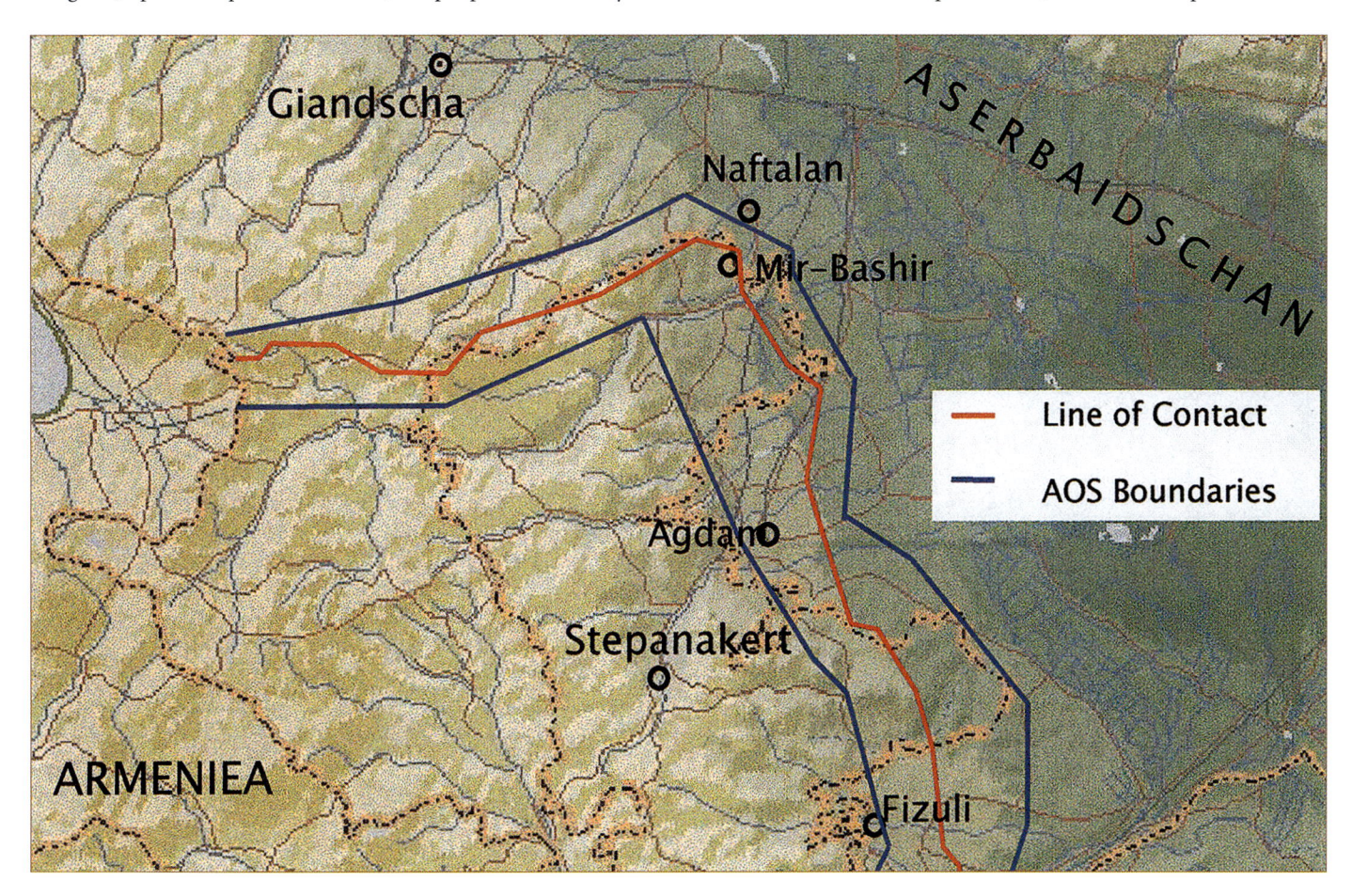

In view of their shared Muslim beliefs, Turkey and Iran seem to be natural allies of Azerbaijan. With Iran, in which, like in Azerbaijan, the Shiite persuasion predominates, the relationship is nevertheless not unproblematic. The southern part of Azerbaijan belongs to Iran since the Russian-Persian treaty of 1828, in which around ten million Azeri live. Since the takeover of power by the nationalistic people's front in Azerbaijan, both sides dream of the reunification of the Azeri people. This means that despite the religious connection, Iran must fear a too powerful Azerbaijan. Therefore their readiness to help is limited, in order to not provoke a new conflict on their own territory, called forth by the possible reunification of all Azeri. Turkey's role as mediator comes into question for numerous reasons. First, through its position as a NATO member and secondly because of the genocide against Armenians in 1915 and previous partisanship for Azerbaijan. It is certain that for Turkey only a solution which secures the territorial integrity of Azerbaijan can be considered. Turkey accuses Armenia from the beginning of disturbing the peace in this region and even threatens Armenia with a military intervention. The Russian Federation itself is hardly in a position to play the unbiased mediator. As the legal successor to the USSR it is charged with having already been incapable of resolving the conflict. Furthermore the members of the Commonwealth of Independent States (CIS) harbor the suspicion that Russia could misuse its position as peacekeeping nation for a pro-Armenian policy. The Russian Federation thereafter disavows a pure "CIS peacekeeping mission" and agrees to participation in line with an OSCE peacekeeping mission. The participation of Russian soldiers could, however, provoke terrorist activities on the part of Azerbaijani nationalists and therefore endanger the success of an OSCE mission. Since, however, neither Turkey or Iran can afford a war and Russia is connected through Chechnya, the deployment of OSCE troops is in the interests of everyone and is massively supported by all three of the nations named. The fact also cannot be overlooked that Azerbaijan and Georgia orient themselves to the West and NATO, as the Azerbaijani Foreign Minister Guliyev expresses it, while Armenia remains Russia's only strategic partner in the southern Caucasus.

A prerequisite for peace is the release of the territory occupied by Yerevan. In addition the Azerbaijani president Heidar Aliyev demands that the refugees be able to return to their homeland. A complete political solution must also include the regulation of the possibility of connection between Armenia and Nagorno-Karabakh and between Azerbaijan and Nakhchivan.

"Azerbaijan! We are all ready to sacrifice ourselves for you! We are all able to fight for you!" (from the national hymn of Azerbaijan)

International Reaction

A sub-group of the CSCE, the so-called **"Minsk Group"**, initially engages themselves for a political solution. They suggest a time schedule in 1993 which is to form the basis for numerous measures for conflict resolution in the form of a step-by-step process. Among these are the withdrawal of Armenian troops from the occupied areas, the repair of the communications and transport infrastructures, exchange of prisoners, unrestricted access for international aid organizations in the affected areas, as well as the signing of a cease-fire observed by CSCE. This plan is not accepted by the conflicting parties. Nevertheless a cease-fire is signed in 1994 through Russian mediation attempts. In September 1994 the involved nations begin to evaluate the possibilities for the establishment of peacekeeping troops in line with Chapter 3 of the Helsinki Document of 1992. In order to further intensify the peace efforts, the OSCE chairman names a **"personal representative"** for the conflict in 1995. **"Field assistants"** do the preliminary work for him. The field assistants are alternately deployed in Baku, Yerevan, and Stepanakert (Nagorno-Karabakh) from 1995.

Efforts of the co-chairmen Finland and Russia to reach agreements between the conflicting parties fail in 1996. At the OSCE summit in Lisbon in 1996 the Swiss OSCE chairman regrets that Armenia does not agree to the principles brought in by all OSCE member states for the solution of the conflict. In 1997 the OSCE chairman decides to expand the number of co-chairmen by one representative each from France and the USA. The co-chairmen work out a new peace plan in 1997. However, this causes a crisis in Armenia, in consequence of which the president resigns at the beginning of 1998.

The peace plan envisions the largest possible autonomy of Highland Karabakh within the Azerbaijani national union. In 1999 there are increased infringements of the cease-fire; the most serious military conflict happens on June 14th.

On the part of the OSCE, the dispatch of officers to survey for the stationing of observers (verification) is decided upon. At the time the OSCE considers the deployment of OSCE peacekeeping troops to the extent of some 775 men (minimum variation) to 4,400 men (maximum variation). This means that in the most extreme case 4,200 soldiers and 200 observers would be available for an area of 17,000 square kilometers (for comparison: NATO has access to over 50,000 men for 11,000 square kilometers in Kosovo and already complains of a lack of personnel with that).

Furthermore, the Austrian Foreign Minister Dr. Wolfgang Schüssel and, after the formation of the government in February 2000, Dr. Benita Ferrero-Waldner, who function as the acting council chairpersons in the OSCE in the year 2000, endeavor to find a solution for the conflict. Dr. Schüssel expands on this at the assumption of the chairmanship from the Norwegian foreign minister on January 1st, 2000: *"Southern Europe and the Caucasus also remain important areas of focus for the OSCE during the Austrian chairmanship."*

On June 28th, 2000, the debate on the acceptance of the Caucasus republic in the pan-European federation begins in the Council of Europe in Strasbourg. On April 3rd, 2001, the Minsk group meets once again. The crisis is also introduced in the CFSP.

Basis for deployment:	Deployment according to the preparatory conference in Rome.
Mission:	Personal representation of the OSCE chairman.
Duration of deployment:	December 3rd, 1991 – to date.
Participating nations:	Austria, Belarus, Germany, Great Britain, the Netherlands, Poland, Switzerland, Ukraine.
Strength:	5 (a pers. representative and four field assistants).
Headquarters:	Tbilisi (for political reasons the HQ is established in Georgia).

Austrian Participation

Political Measures

The political measures are limited to active cooperation in the OSCE. During the chairmanship in 2000 the consultations are increased. Austria endeavors with this to make a decisive step towards conflict resolution. The federal government agrees to the dispatch of up to twelve military observers in 1992 and an alpine special operations company in 1994. This agreement is updated again during the chairmanship in 2000. In view of the Minsk Group talks taken up again in April 2001 the question of the dispatch of a company is repeatedly brought up on the part of the Foreign Ministry.

Military Measures

Initially in the time from 1993 to 1995 1 officer is placed with the "Initial Planning Group" (IOPG) and the **"High Level Planning Group" (HLPG)** respectively. In view of the Austrian chairmanship in the year 2000 an increased engagement on the part of the Defence Ministry is also assumed by the armed forces. Therefore all preparatory measures are taken in order to be able to take part in an eventual peacekeeping deployment. A survey command is held ready from the middle of 2000. The expectation is for the deployment of forces in the strength of about an alpine mobile infantry company. Since the Austrian chairmanship endeavors to be optimally prepared for the deployment, the personal representative of the sitting chairman for this conflict, Ambassador Andrzej Kasprzyk (Poland) meets repeatedly with representatives of the Defence Ministry in Vienna. The deployment itself, however, requires an agreement between the conflicting parties as well as an OSCE mandate with clearly defined military instructions including a strict time schedule. The fact that many people in the crisis area speak German is notable, there are also German newspapers. This will certainly be helpful during a possible deployment of Austrian soldiers.

As a result of the many-sided engagement of the armed forces and the high costs that a first deployment in a new area of operation would bring with it (around 1 billion ATS/72,700,000 Euros), the new request of the FMFA of April 2001 for the dispatch of an alpine special operations company cannot be acceded to.

Basis for deployment: Membership with OSCE.
Mission: Survey for later participation; military observer.
Appellation: None.
Form of dispatch: At present in the form of business trips abroad.
Area of operations: Nagorno-Karabakh.
Duration of deployment: In the sections of time between February 28th, 1994 – March 8th, 1994, April 15th, 1994 – April 21st, 1994, May 29th, 1994 – June 21st, 1994, August 23rd – August 29th, 1994, September 7th, 1994 – September 11th, 1994 and August 29th, 1995 – September 6th, 1995 Colonel Norbert Baldia is surveying in the area of operations; September 23rd, 1995 – June 30th, 1996 (deployment as "field assistant"); in October 2000 in the course of the Austrian OSCE presidency a deployment of 1 monitor each for both sides of the "line of contact" (LOC) takes place.
Contingent strength: 1 (in October 2000: 2).
Total: 2.

This picture was taken on the occasion of taking up contact between the OSCE Field Representative for Nagorno-Karabakh, Colonel Norbert Baldia, with his Austrian comrade Lieutenant Colonel Ernst Deu, who serves duty at the same time as the UN liaison officer in Tbilisi (November 1995).

The president of Azerbaijan, Heidar Aliyev, greets the Austrian OSCE observer Colonel Baldia (t.l.) Colonel Baldia wears the OSCE band on his right bicep. Colonel Baldia at the negotiations (t.r.). OSCE monitoring during the Austrian OSCE presidency in October 2000 on the "line of contact (LOC)" in the area of Ter Ter (m.l.). A Mitsubishi Station Car with the appropriate labeling in English and Cyrillic serves as the patrol vehicle (m.r.).

The duty is carried out in the most various of adjustments according to the weather situation. Sometimes the old battle uniform does it (b.l.). Note the yellow beret and the OSCE identification on the right bicep. The newest adjustment already encompasses the new helmet with the yellow (OSCE) cover and the flak jacket for battle uniform 75 (b.r.).

Work room (t.l.) and identification of Colonel Baldia. Invitation to a reception from the Georgian president Shevardnadze (b.). Parking tag for the reception (t.r.). Visa from the unrecognized Republic of Nagorno-Karabakh in Colonel Baldia's passport (r.).

Mr. Norbert Baldia

PRESIDENT OF GEORGIA and Mrs. NANULI SHEVARDNADZE
request the pleasure of Your company at the Reception on the occasion of the Inauguration on November 26, 1995 at 19.00 hrs.

«Krtsanisi» State Residence, house N 2.

Please have this invitation with you.

CSCE/OSCE Mission to Georgia

Preliminary Events

The ethnic divisions of Georgia are like a mosaic. Around 5.4 million inhabitants can be separated into ca. 70 groups. 70% are ethnic Georgians, 8% Armenians, 6.3% Russians, 5.7% Azeris, 3% Ossetians, 2.4% Adjarians, and 1.8% Abkhazians. Following the dissolution of the USSR the highest Soviet of Georgia already enacts constitutional amendments to strengthen the Georgian sovereignty in 1989. In 1991 Georgia declares its independence. There are conflicts with South Ossetia and Abkhazia. These are on the question of autonomy or independence. South Ossetia does not accept a CSCE suggestion in which it would be promised a broad-ranging autonomy within Georgia. On January 19th, 1992, South Ossetia declares its independence and demands a union with the Russian North Ossetia. Nevertheless, the conflict stagnates. The cease-fire between Georgia and South Ossetia holds thanks to Russian peacekeeping troops. Trust grows between the ethnic groups in connection with the 7th sitting of the Unified Commission for the Regulation of the South Ossetian Conflict on February 13th, 1997 in Russian Vladikavkaz, in which the representatives of Russia, North and South Ossetia and the OSCE take part. The control points of the peacekeeping troops along the cease-fire border can be noticeably reduced. The return of refugees is also eased.

The Abkhazian leadership again rejects a strengthened engagement of the OSCE (only one OSCE representative is a standing member in the UN Human Rights Office in Sukhumi; so the OSCE is at least represented in this conflict region). The armed incidents increase above all in the southern province of Gali with the uncontrolled return of Georgians driven out from there in a threatening magnitude. The situation is intensified through their endangerment by minefields. Furthermore, armed clashes occur between Georgian partisans and Abkhazian bands. Despite all efforts of the UNO and the OSCE Abkhazia is not ready to give up its nationalist and separatist principles for a pragmatic solution.

International Reaction

During the Helsinki Council of Ministers meeting on March 24th, 1992 the nation is officially accepted into the CSCE; three months later it becomes a member of UNO. During this the UNO intercedes clearly for the preservation of the territorial integrity and sovereignty of Georgia over South Ossetia and Abkhazia.

The CSCE mission is called into life with the goal of encouraging the negotiations between the conflicting parties in Georgia towards a peaceful resolution of the conflict. The mandate, which besides the promotion of the democratic legal national structure in Georgia initially also stretches over the conflicts in South Ossetia and Abkhazia, is also expanded at the request of Georgia through an act of the Standing Council on December 15th, 1999 to the observation of the border between Georgia and the Russian Federation/Chechnya, in order to prevent a spillover of the conflict after the melting of the snow. For this mission civilian and unarmed observers with military expertise are deployed. The number of the observers is increased for this from 15 to 42 (although it must be determined that for a consistent observation at least 1,500 men would be necessary). The leadership of the border observation operation is carried out from the HQ in Tbilisi, operations near the border are carried out from three team bases in Shatili (1,460 m), Girevi/Kebulo (2,030 m) and Omalo (1,860 m).

While the mission in the South Ossetia conflict succeeds in bringing both parties back to the negotiation table and creating a basically positive negotiation climate, the process in the Abkhazia conflict comes to a halt. Here neither the UNO nor the C/OSCE are able to create mutual trust.

The problem in South Ossetia and Abkhazia has model characteristics for the entire area. Although this is a locally limited ethnic conflict, escalation could turn this into a conflagration. For the CSCE/OSCE not only the security of the region, but their own believability as crisis managers is at stake.

Basis for deployment:	Decision of the Standing Council of November 6th, 1992 (17th CSO meeting), decision of the Standing Council of December 15th, 1999 (expansion of the mandate).
Mission:	Conflict resolution; observation of human rights as well as development of democracy and a free news media; securing of the return of refugees; since December 1999 additionally the observation of the border to the Republic of Chechnya.
Duration of deployment:	December 3rd, 1991 – to date.
Participating nations:	Austria, Azerbaijan, Estonia, Germany, Great Britain, Hungary, Lithuania, Moldavia, Poland, Romania, Russia, Slovakia, Sweden, Ukraine, USA.
Strength:	42.
Headquarters:	Tbilisi.

Austrian Participation

Political Measures

The Main Committee of Parliament approves a request of Foreign Minister Dr. Ferrero-Waldner for the dispatch of a military observer to the OSCE evaluation mission in Tbilisi in February 2000. The mission works independently of UNOMIG, with which up to six observation officers from Austria are deployed. Since the OSCE confers the leadership of the mission on the dispatched officer, the Main Committee decides on the dispatch of a further officer.

Military Measures

As a result of the OSCE decision to expand the mission to the observation of the border to Chechnya, Brigadier General Lubenik is initially dispatched to Tbilisi for preparation for this deployment to the border in the time from February 25th to March 3rd, 2000.

Major General[94] Lubenik then takes over the command of the (civilian) observers on June 1st, 2000. Since the majority of the observers have no alpine experience at the beginning of the mission, an alpine experienced Austrian officer is assigned as "Chief Training Officer" at the request of Major General Lubenik. Furthermore, tents, alpine backpacks, sleeping bags, and alpine equipment are brought into the area of operations.

Not until an in-depth training with the ski touring equipment, walking with crampons and the recognition and evaluation of alpine dangers in winter can the mission also be carried out in winter.

A helicopter of the type MI-8 as well as numerous UAZ and Lada Niva all-terrain vehicles are available for the mission. Communication takes place over CAPSAT satellite telephones.

Basis for deployment:	CM of February 15th, 2000, MC of February 16th, 2000 (dispatch until April 20th, 2000); CM of November 30th, 2001 (end of mission); CM of August 29th, 2008, MC of September 5th, 2008 (renewed dispatch).
Mission:	Observation of compliance with human rights (1994/95); construction of a communications connections; border observation (1999 – to date).
Appellation:	None.
Form of dispatch:	Until April 1997 according to the Dispatch FCL 1965, from April 1997 according to the FCL-CSD 1997.
Area of operations:	Area of border to Chechnya.
Duration of deployment:	May 14th, 1994 – September 15th, 2001 (with interruptions); September 8th, 2008 – June 28th, 2009.
Contingent strength:	1 – 3. In the time from May 14th, 1994 – May 18th, 1994, August 23rd, 1995 – October 9th, 1995 and 1996 two noncommissioned officers each are with the CSCE mission for the construction of the SAT-C data transfer and navigation system.
Total:	5.
Head of Mission:	September 24th, 1994 – June 30th, 1995, Brigadier General Mag. Simon Palmisano; June 1st, 2000 – August 31st, 2001, Major General Bernd S. Lubenik.

This deployment takes place under especially difficult conditions: In the border area there is almost no infrastructure. The road network consists only of unfortified roads, when that, which are partially unpassable through mud and landslides. The entire area of operations is therefore only reachable with helicopters until the end of June. The accommodations are more than spartan. The house in Shatili has only cold running water, the house in Omalo has only water from its own well and in Girevi there is only a tent with water from the nearest stream. The observer teams must plan all logistical measures far in advance, since foodstuffs etc. can only be procured in Tbilisi. The provisioning and relief itself takes place with an OSCE helicopter and is very dependent on the weather.

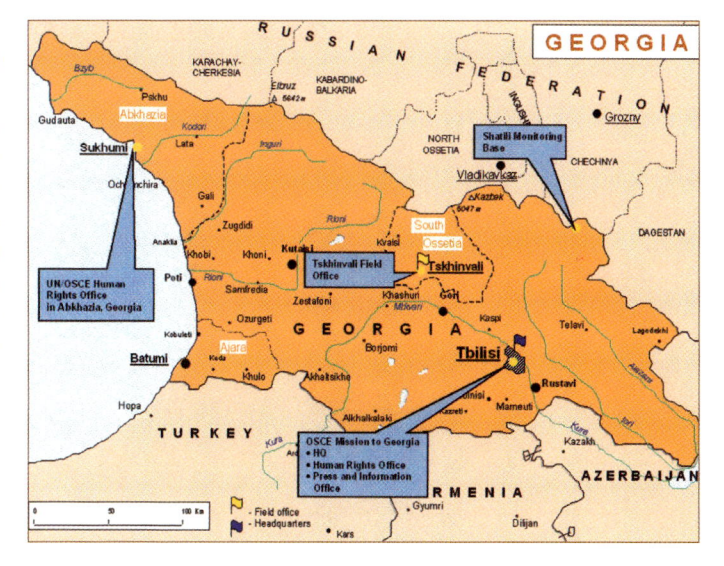

---

94 Rank for use abroad.

United Nations Observer Mission in Georgia (UNOMIG)

Preliminary Events

The conflict in Georgia on the secession of the constituent republic of Abkhazia on the coast of the Black Sea leads to the intervention of Georgian troops in summer 1992. In the following civil war over 100,000 people are killed and the Georgian troops are driven from Abkhazia. Two cease-fire agreements from September 3rd, 1992 and July 27th, 1993 are each broken after a short amount of time. Not until the Moscow Agreement on May 14th, 1994 does it lead to a longer-lasting relaxation of tensions. The border is now formed by the Inguri river. However, the situation worsens as a result of the lack of an effective executive, which leads to lawlessness. Countless violent acts of a criminal nature are caused by the dismal economic situation. It is also attempted to "come into money" from UNO, considered "rich", through provoked traffic accidents.

Georgia's march into South Ossetia in August 2008 leads to a massive military deployment of the Russian Federation, which ends with an occupation of South Ossetia, Abkhazia, as well as parts of Georgia.

International Reaction

The members of the UN mission work together with the CIS peace-keeping forces. The deployment of the observers is unarmed. This is seen as the "strongest weapon" of the UNO, since a man without a weapon cannot be considered an enemy. Nevertheless, the UN observers are guarded by a 25-man professional security troop and a part of the presidential guard of the internationally unrecognized Abkhazian "president" Ardzindba.

As a result of the new apportionment of forces as well as the fully displaced geographic order of the original mandate in the area a back mandate or alternatively an adaptation of the mandate for both military observers takes place. The mission is ended on June 15th, 2009.

Basis for deployment:	SC Resolution 849 (1993) of July 9th, 1993; SC Resolution 854 (1993) of August 6th, 1993; SC Resolution 858 (1993) of August 24th, 1993; SC Resolution 1311 (2000) of July 28th, 2000 (extension).
Mission:	Observation of compliance with the cease-fire agreement with special consideration of the situation in Sukhumi.
Duration of deployment:	August 24th, 1993 – June 15th, 2009.

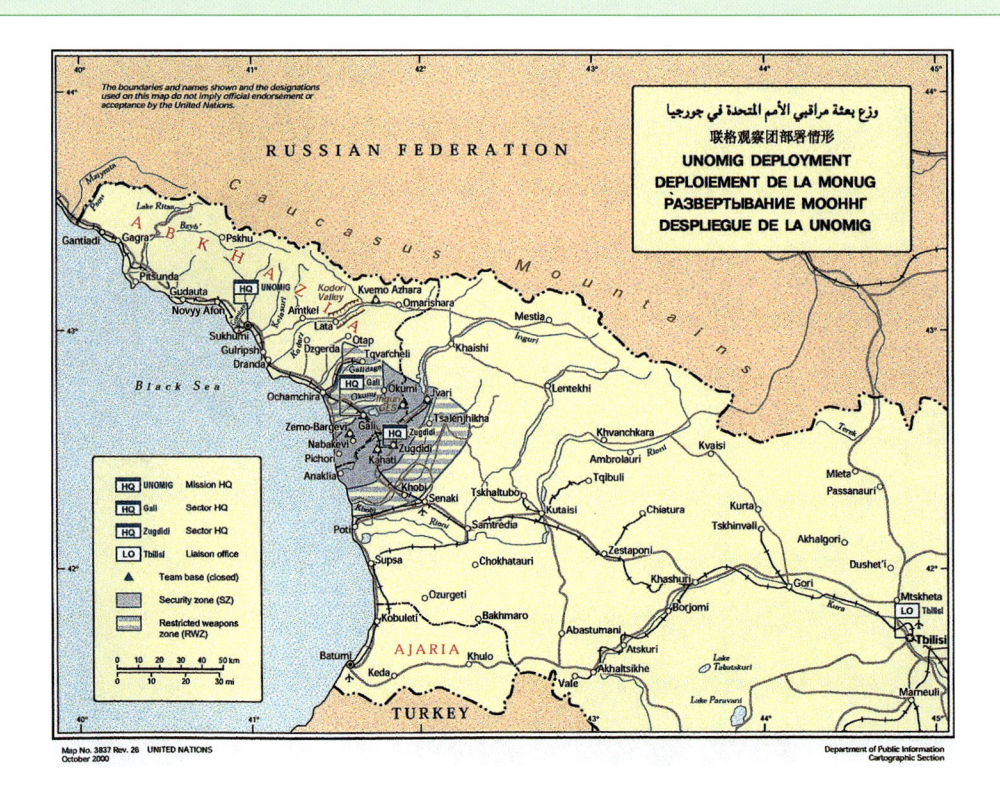

Participating nations:	Albania, Austria, Bangladesh, Canada, Croatia, Cuba, Czech Republic, Denmark, Egypt, France, Germany, Ghana, Great Britain, Greece, Hungary, Indonesia, Jordan, Korea, Lithuania, Moldavia, Mongolia, Nepal, Nigeria, Pakistan, the Phillippines, Poland, Romania, Russian Federation, Sweden, Switzerland, Turkey, Ukraine, Uruguay, USA, Yemen.
Strength:	Up to 150 military observers, 64 international and 75 local civilian workers; 150 military observers (as of December 31st, 2009).
Headquarters:	Sukhumi.

Austrian Participation

Political Measures

The Council of Ministers decides on the dispatch of up to three officers.

Basis for deployment:	CM of August 24th, 1993, MC of September 24th, 1993 (dispatch), CM of December 5th, 2000, MC of December 15th, 2000 (extension for a year).
Mission:	Military observers; from time to time assumption of staff functions.
Appellation:	None.
Form of dispatch:	Until April 1997 according to the Dispatch FCL 1965, after April 1997 according to the FCL-CSD 1997.
Area of operations:	Sukhumi.
Duration of deployment:	July 14th, 1994 – June 15th, 2009 (return by July 7th, 2009).
Contingent strength:	3.
Total:	54.
Note:	From September 8th, 2008, an officer is in the country as a "Military Monitoring Officer" in line with the **"OSCE Mission in Georgia"** (see page 370).

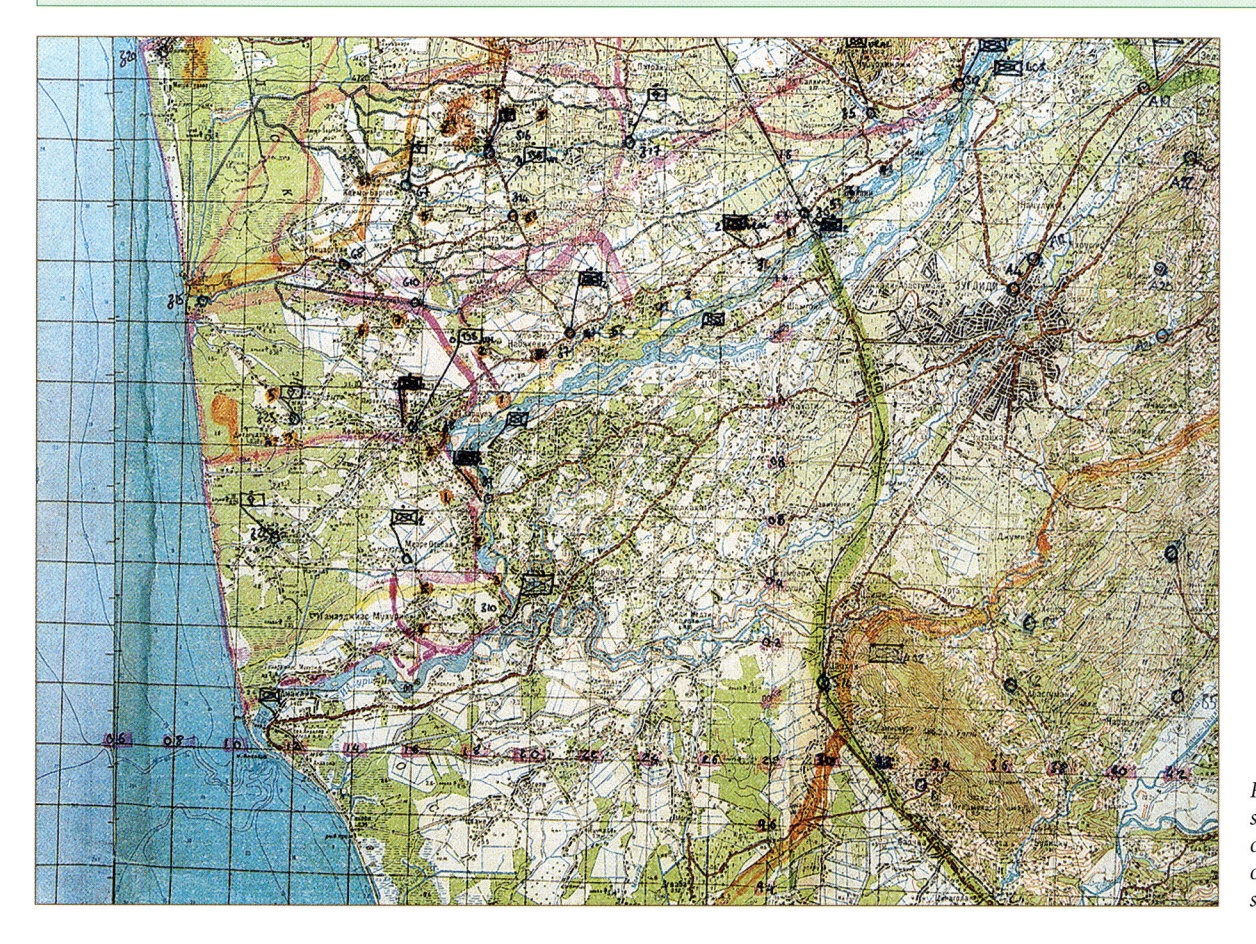

Picture of a Russian military map of the area of operations at the scale of 1:100,000.

United Nations Observer Mission in South Africa (UNOMSA)

Preliminary Events

The National Party, which comes to power in South Africa in 1948, attempts to preserve the "racial separation" ("apartheid") previously customary in all colonies. This policy, grounded in a claim to the separate development of the various cultures, leads in practice above all to discrimination and suppression against the non-white populations. In 1961 the South African Union resigns from the Commonwealth and becomes a republic.

In view of the increasing national protests against apartheid South Africa is ever more isolated. Internal unrests (1976, 1984 on) and sanctions from outside contribute to the change of the policies of the South African government. In 1990 the new South African president F. W. de Klerk releases opposition politician Nelson Mandela, imprisoned since 1962, who had become a symbol of the resistance. The peace process in the nation moves forward (not without hindrances). In 1994 the first free elections for South Africans of all ethnic groups take place. The African National Congress (ANC) gains almost two thirds of the mandate; Mandela becomes president, de Klerk vice-president.

International Reaction

The UNO – active since the 1960's in the South African question – supports the peace process from 1992 through the dispatch of an initially small civilian observer mission. In the preparation phase for the elections on April 27th, 1994 this mission is initially increased to 500 and then – during the elections – to over 2,200 observers, who are also to coordinate the deployment of observers from the EU, the Commonwealth and the Organization of African Unity (OAU). After the elections the UN deployment ends in June 1994.

Basis for deployment:	SC Resolution 772 (1992) of August 17th, 1992, SC Resolution 894 (1994) of January 14th, 1994.
Mission:	Supervision and support of the peace process, then support of the South African authorities during the preparation for the elections in April 1994; during the elections election observation and observation of the vote counts.
Duration of deployment:	September 11th, 1991 – June 27th, 1994.
Strength:	Up to 2,200 observers.
Headquarters:	Johannesburg.

Austrian Participation

Political Measures

At the request of the UNO, in January 1994 the Foreign Ministry initially nominates six Austrians who seem suited for the mission in view of the elections, because of their previous experience as election observers or as South Africa experts. During the elections themselves 20 Austrians are dispatched.

Military Measures

On the basis of the "Old Boys Network", the Command for International Deployments supports the preparation of some observers.

Mission:	Support of the peace process and the preparation for the elections; election observation and observation of the vote counts.
Appellation:	None.
Form of dispatch:	Nomination through the Federal Ministry for External Affairs. The dispatch itself takes place on leave through the Austrian service positions through the UNO. For the short-term observers in April the dispatch takes place through the FMEA on the basis of special leave.
Area of operations:	Distributed in UNOMSA teams throughout South Africa.
Duration of deployment:	February 1st, 1994 – May 1st, 1994.
Total:	Among the 25 Austrian observers are three members of the MoD.
Contribution:	The presence of the UN observers eases the preparation and implementation of the elections and so contributes to the peaceful development in South Africa. As in most such cases, the international presence already long before the elections is more important than the presence of numerous election observers during the elections themselves, after all it depends on the formation of trust.

United Nations Mission in Haiti (UNMIH)

Preliminary Events

After its discovery by Christopher Columbus in the year 1492, the island is settled by the Spanish motherland, later however as a result of a treaty ceded to France. Since the natives, the so-called "Arawaks", are not equal to the heavy physical labor on the sugar-cane plantations, the French colonial masters begin to settle African slaves from Benin and the Ivory Coast. After bloody revolts the slaves gain their freedom in 1804; the first "black republic" is declared. Following this revolution uneasy times rule in Haiti for almost 200 years now. Dictators and presidents "for life" are constantly exchanged and plunge the land in poverty and suffering.

After the dictatorship of the Duval brothers and the national instability connected with it, the elections on February 7th, 1991, form a start for a democratic development. Jean Bertrand Aristide is elected the president of Haiti in a democratic election. But his tenure also does not last long. A military coup under General Cedras destroys this hope on September 30th, 1991. The **Governor's Island Accord** (New York City), concluded on July 3rd, 1993, between the elected and meanwhile living in exile President Aristide and General Cedras remains ineffective, despite diplomatic support, UN sanctions and UN missions (MICIVIH, UNMIH). On November 11th, 1993, the landing of UN troops is prevented. In October 1994 a restoration of the constitutional government takes place under the pressure of an international troop authorized by UNO. Despite some logistical problems democratic parliamentary elections can be carried out in the summer of 1995. On December 17th the presidential elections are successfully carried out and on February 7th, 1996 an orderly transfer of power to the new president takes place.

International Reaction

After the signing of the Governor's Island Accord the mission is originally established in order to implement it. Subsequently the mandate is expanded to the effect that UNMIH is to help with the modernization of the armed forces and the establishment of the local police. As a result of the lack of readiness to cooperate the mission cannot be fulfilled.

After all attempts to calm the situation have failed, it comes to the intervention of a multinational force on September 19th, 1994, which is authorized by the Security Council and lead by America, in order to create the basic requirements for the deployment of the UN mission and to end the flight of thousands of "boat people" in the direction of Miami. UNMIH takes up its actual duties in full measure on March 31st, 1995.

In the following years the support of UNO continues under various appellations in a reduced capacity, where above all the police support plays a large role. During the 2000 elections the previous president Aristide again comes to power.

Basis for deployment:	SC Resolution 46/7 of October 11th, 1991;
	SC Resolution 862 (1993) of August 31st, 1993;
	SC Resolution 867 (1993) of September 23rd, 1993;
	SC Resolution 940 (1994) of July 31st, 1994;
	SC Resolution 975 (1995) of January 30th, 1995.
Mission:	Development of armed forces and a police organization.
Duration of deployment:	September 23rd, 1993 – June 30th, 1996.
Participating nations:	Algeria, Antigua and Barbuda, Argentina, Austria, Bahamas, Bangladesh, Barbados, Belize, Benin, Canada, Djibouti, France, Guatemala, Guinea-Bissau, Guyana, Honduras, India, Ireland, Jamaica, Jordan, Mali, Nepal, New Zealand, the Netherlands, Pakistan, the Phillippines, Russia, St. Kitts & Nevis, St. Lucia, Suriname, Tobago, Togo, Trinidad, Tunisia, USA.
Strength:	Max. 6,000 soldiers, 900 civilian police, 230 international and 200 local workers; 6,065 soldiers, 847 police, supported by up to 160 civilian workers (status of June 30th, 1995); reduction after the elections on December 17th, 1995 to 14.
Headquarters:	Port-au-Prince.

Austrian Participation

Political Measures

The federal government decides to support Haiti through the construction of a police academy. The Ministry of the Interior is commissioned with the implementation. In total, 21 executive officials are placed in Haiti in the time between March 6th, 1995 – February 7th, 1996. In the first phase contact with local police forces is maintained in order to ascertain that they use their executive power according to the laws. Furthermore they have the assignment of establishing a local security system and preparing for the elections.

Military Measures

The Defence Ministry accedes to a petition from the UNO for the dispatch of a doctor for the medical care of UNMIH. The battalion doctor from AUSCON/UNFICYP is dispatched.

Basis for deployment:	CM of November 15th, 1994, MC of November 18th, 1994 (dispatch).
Mission:	Planning and preparation of the medical care of UNMIH.
Appellation:	None.
Form of dispatch:	Dispatch FCL 1965.
Area of operations:	Port-au-Prince.
Duration of deployment:	October 13th, 1994 – December 11th, 1994 and February 22nd – March 11th, 1995.
Contingent strength:	1 doctor.
Total:	1.

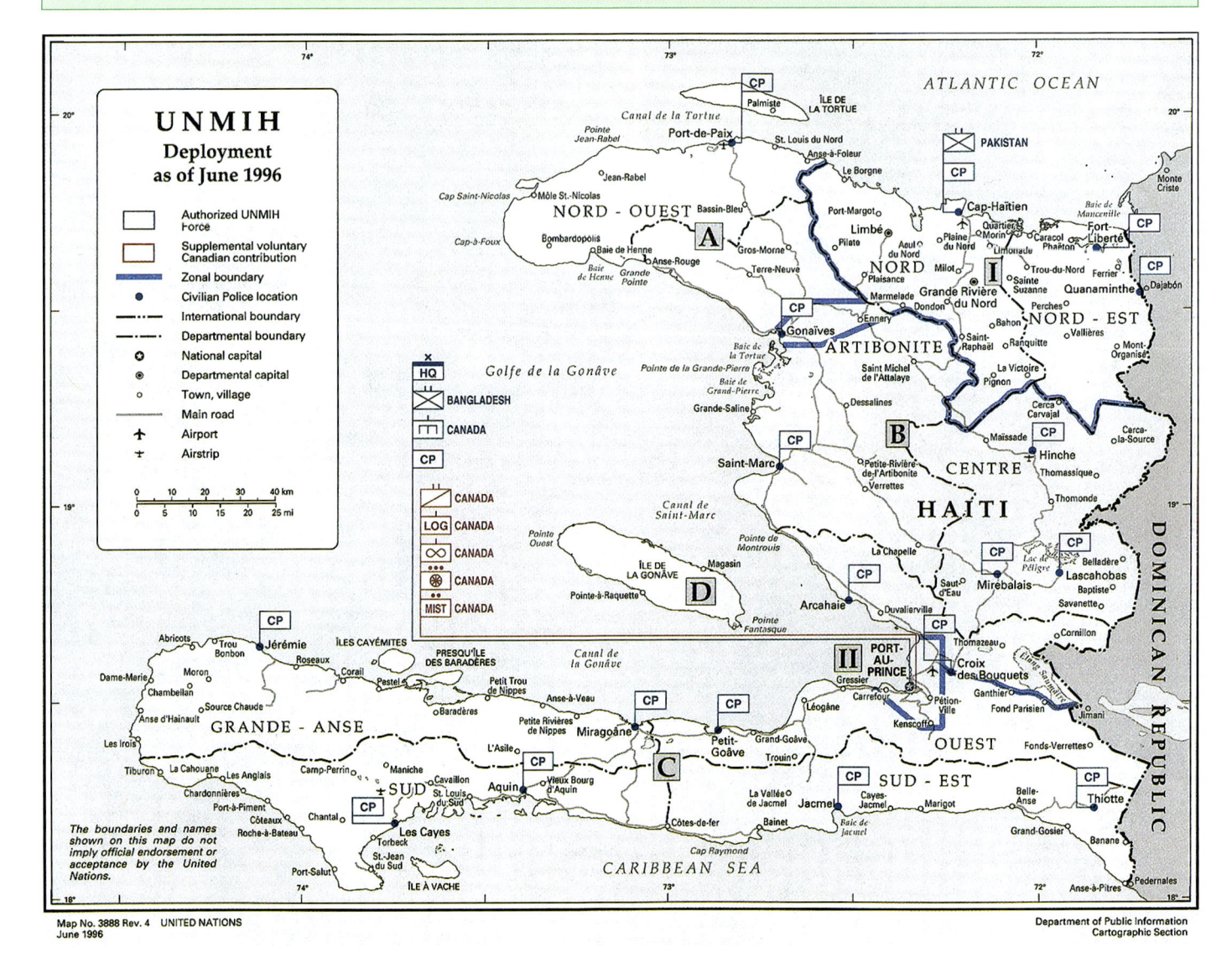

European Community Monitoring Mission in former Yugoslavia (ECMM)

European Union Monitoring Mission in former Yugoslavia (EUMM)[95]

Preliminary Events

Differences between the central government and the constituent republics as well as between the individual constituent republics lead to the final collapse of the Yugoslavian government in 1991. Subsequently, armed battles take place in Slovenia (1991), Croatia (1991 – 1995), Bosnia-Herzegovina (1992 – 1995) and Kosovo (1998 – 1999), which are often accompanied with ethnically motivated violence. In other successor states the are also many tensions, without it nevertheless coming to the outbreak of open war.

International Reaction

The mission implemented by the European Union is to contribute to the solution of the bloody conflict between the ethnic groups in the former constituent republics of Yugoslavia. The foundations for this are the **"Brioni Accord"** of July 7th, 1991 between the European Community (EC), represented by the "Troika" (Luxembourg, the Netherlands, Portugal) and the 6 successor states (Bosnia-Herzegovnia, Croatia, Macedonia, Montenegro, Serbia, Slovenia), the ministers' meeting of the European Political Cooperation (EPC – predecessor of the CFSP) which is concluded on July 10th in the Hague, and the Memorandum of Understanding (MOU) between the EC and Yugoslavian federal government, Slovenia and Croatia, signed on July 31st, 1991 in Belgrade. Further MOU's are concluded with Albania, Bulgaria, and Hungary. In October 1991 the mandate of the ECMM is expanded. The ECMM is assigned to observe the cease-fire in Croatia and to prevent hostilities in Bosnia-Herzegovina. In the 1st year of the mission the original mandate is limited to a purely military assignment of tasks. After the assumption of this function by the **"United Nations Protection Force" (UNPROFOR)** in 1992 the mission is defined anew. It now encompasses cooperation on long-term peaceful solution to all conflicts in the former Yugoslavia. The practical implementation of the Dayton Peace Accord continues to run into unforeseeable and sometimes unsurmountable obstacles. Difficulties are caused above all by the return of refugees, the incorporation of the remaining Serbs and the hindrance of mutual acts of revenge. A further problem develops from the necessary support in reconstruction of the cities and villages destroyed by the war. As a result of the **Amsterdam Accord** taking effect on April 1st, 1999, the next exchange of the chairmanship from Germany to Finland on July 1st, 1999 is announced as the basis for a "cooperative action" within the framework of the Common Foreign and Security Policy (CFSP). This is implemented by an act of the EU parliament in June 1999. The mission is therefore active on a new legal basis since July 1st, 1999, with the same goals as before. The name of the mission – ECMM – goes back to the time before the creation of the European Union. While the deployment of unarmed observers to observe the withdrawal of Yugoslavian troops out of Slovenia in summer 1991 is successful, the EC observers are fairly powerless in view of the wars that break out then in Croatia and in 1992 in Bosnia-Herzegovina. A withdrawal, however, would have sent the wrong signal. Subsequently the observers, called "ice cream sellers" because of their clothing, exert themselves for local mediation, prisoner exchanges, etc., and support the "United Nations Protection Force (UNPROFOR)" deployed from 1992. Not until the stabilization of the situation through the provisions of the Dayton peace treaty do new possibilities develop: The EU observers support the peace process and the reconstruction, above all through the gathering of information, and with this supply the basis for the activities of the EU in this area.

The headquarters (HQ ECMM) leads and provisions the regional centers (RCs) in Belgrade, Sarajevo, Tirana and Zagreb. These in turn lead and care for the coordination centers (CCs) through which the work of numerous field teams is coordinated. These teams are normally composed of two observers, a translator and a driver. The main mission of the teams is the observation of their assigned area. In this every change in the status quo is to be reported in the form of "daily reports", "special reports" or "briefings". In addition to this there is the information exchange with SFOR, OSCE, the International Police Task Force, UNHCR, and the NGOs.

---

[95] The renaming takes place on December 22nd, 2000 according to GZ 2000/811/CFSP.

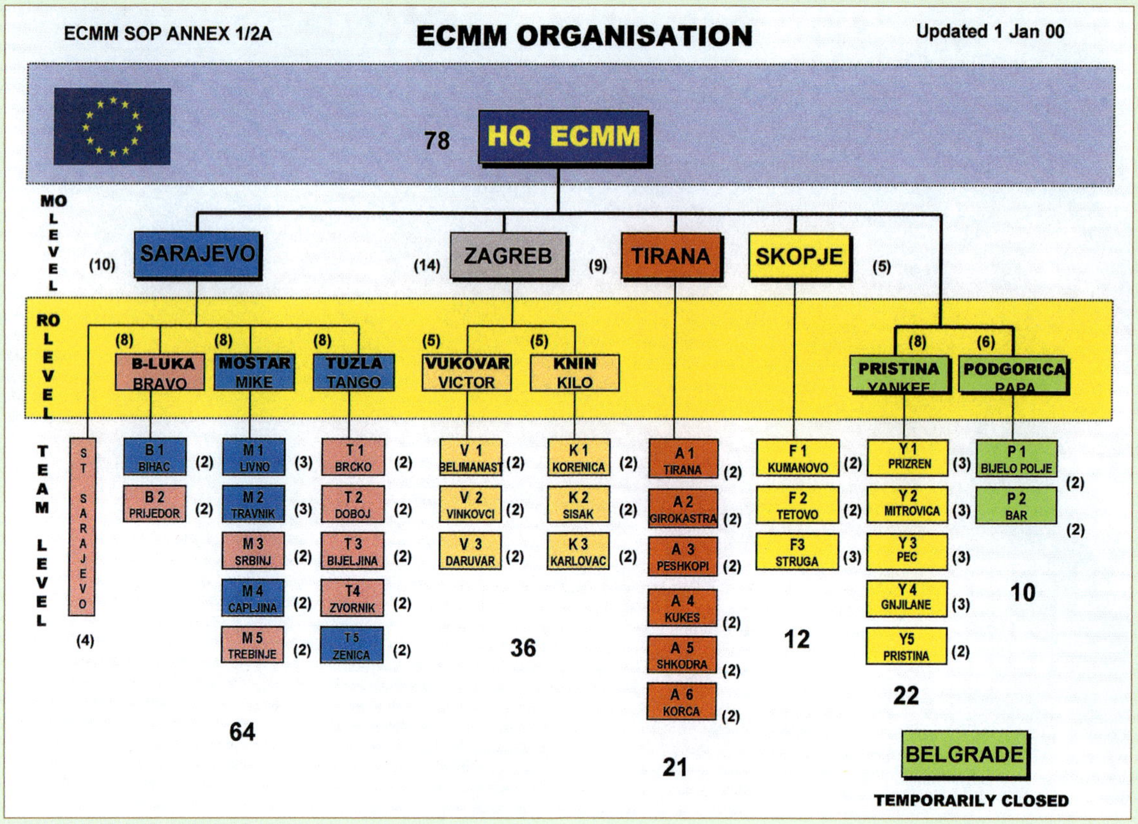

ECMM SOP ANNEX 1/2A
ECMM ORGANISATION
Updated 1 Jan 00
78
HQ ECMM
MO LEVEL
SARAJEVO (10)
(14) ZAGREB
(9) TIRANA
SKOPJE
(5)
RO LEVEL
(8) B-LUKA BRAVO
(8) MOSTAR MIKE
(8) TUZLA TANGO
(5) VUKOVAR VICTOR
(5) KNIN KILO
(8) PRISTINA YANKEE
(6) PODGORICA PAPA
TEAM LEVEL
S T SARAJEVO (4)
B 1 BIHAC (2)
B 2 PRIJEDOR (2)
M 1 LIVNO (3)
M 2 TRAVNIK (3)
M 3 SRBINJ (2)
M 4 CAPLJINA (2)
M 5 TREBINJE (2)
T 1 BRCKO (2)
T 2 DOBOJ (2)
T 3 BIJELJINA (2)
T4 ZVORNIK (2)
T5 ZENICA (2)
64
V 1 BELIMANAST (2)
V 2 VINKOVCI (2)
V 3 DARUVAR (2)
K 1 KORENICA (2)
K 2 SISAK (2)
K 3 KARLOVAC (2)
36
A 1 TIRANA (2)
A 2 GIROKASTRA (2)
A 3 PESHKOPI (2)
A 4 KUKES (2)
A 5 SHKODRA (2)
A 6 KORCA (2)
21
F 1 KUMANOVO (2)
F 2 TETOVO (2)
F3 STRUGA (3)
12
Y 1 PRIZREN (3)
Y 2 MITROVICA (3)
Y 3 PEC (3)
Y 4 GNJILANE (3)
Y5 PRISTINA (2)
22
P 1 BIJELO POLJE (2)
P 2 BAR (2)
10
BELGRADE
TEMPORARILY CLOSED

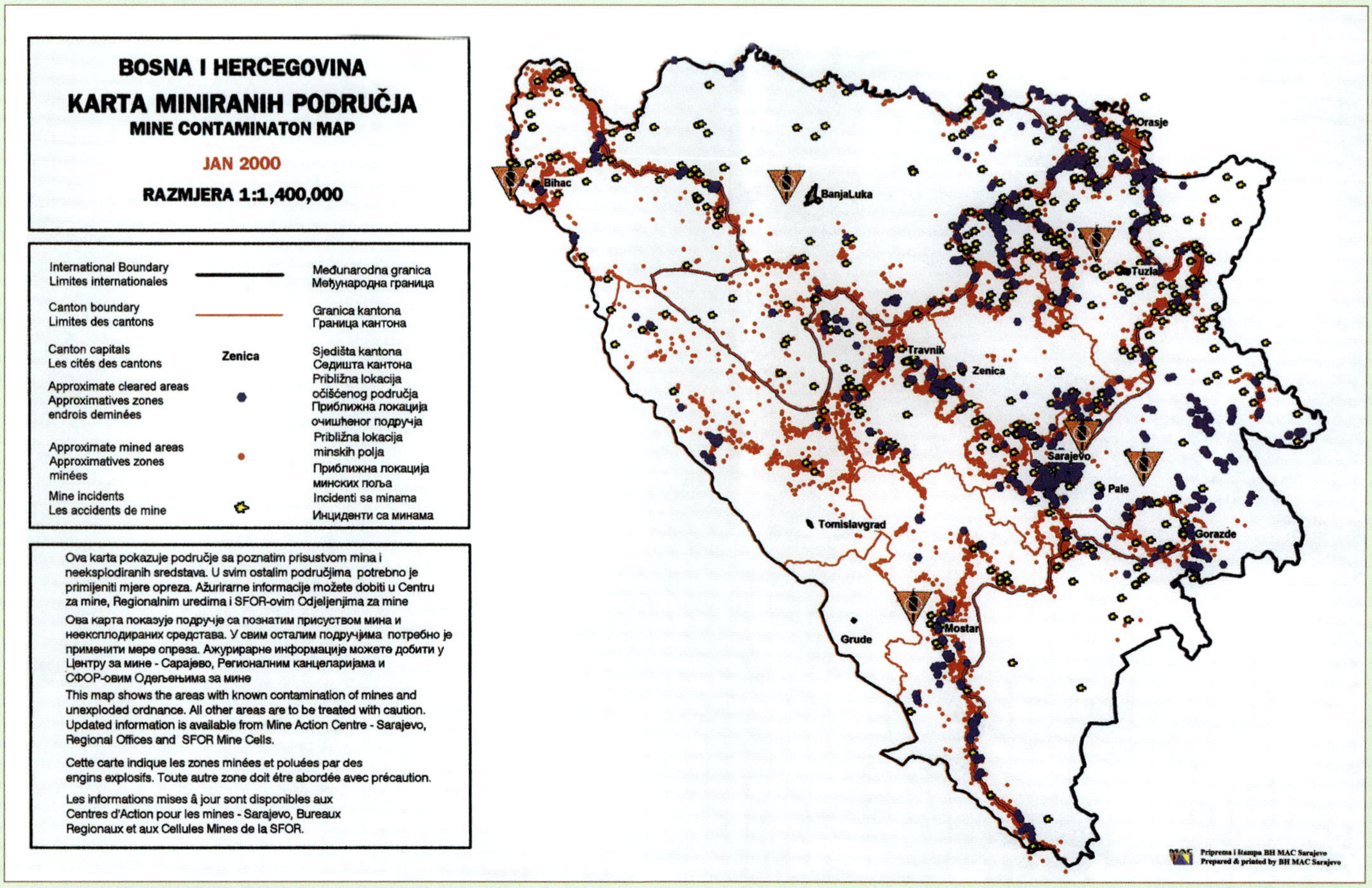

BOSNA I HERCEGOVINA
KARTA MINIRANIH PODRUČJA
MINE CONTAMINATON MAP
JAN 2000
RAZMJERA 1:1,400,000
International Boundary Limites internationales
Međunarodna granica Међународна граница
Canton boundary Limites des cantons
Granica kantona Граница кантона
Canton capitals Les cités des cantons
Zenica
Sjedišta kantona Седишта кантона
Approximate cleared areas Approximatives zones endrois deminées
Približna lokacija očišćenog područja Приближна локација очишћеног подручја
Approximate mined areas Approximatives zones minées
Približna lokacija minskih polja Приближна локација минских поља
Mine incidents Les accidents de mine
Incidenti sa minama Инциденти са минама
Ova karta pokazuje područje sa poznatim prisustvom mina i neeksplodiranih sredstava. U svim ostalim područjima potrebno je primijeniti mjere opreza. Ažurirane informacije možete dobiti u Centru za mine, Regionalnim uredima i SFOR-ovim Odjeljenjima za mine
Ова карта показује подручје са познатим присуством мина и неексплодираних средстава. У свим осталим подручјима потребно је применити мере опреза. Ажуриране информације можете добити у Центру за мине - Сарајево, Регионалним канцеларијама и СФОР-овим Одељењима за мине
This map shows the areas with known contamination of mines and unexploded ordnance. All other areas are to be treated with caution. Updated information is available from Mine Action Centre - Sarajevo, Regional Offices and SFOR Mine Cells.
Cette carte indique les zones minées et poluées par des engins explosifs. Toute autre zone doit être abordée avec précaution.
Les informations mises à jour sont disponibles aux Centres d'Action pour les mines - Sarajevo, Bureaux Regionaux et aux Cellules Mines de la SFOR.
Bihac
BanjaLuka
Orasje
Tuzla
Travnik
Zenica
Sarajevo
Pale
Gorazde
Tomislavgrad
Grude
Mostar
Priprema i štampa BH MAC Sarajevo
Prepared & printed by BH MAC Sarajevo

Basis for deployment:	Brioni Agreement of July 7th, 1991; MOU with Slovenia and Croatia of September 1st, 1991; MOU with Bosnia and Herzegovina of October 1st, 1991; Vance Owen Plan of January 2nd, 1992; MOU with Bulgaria of September 18th, 1992; MOU with Hungary of December 9th, 1992; MOU with Albania of December 12th, 1992; MOU with the OSCE of December 21st, 1995.
Mission:	Originally only observation of the cease-fire agreed upon between the parties in Slovenia and the withdrawal of the Yugoslavian army out of Slovenia; later the mission is expanded to Croatia and Bosnia-Herzegovina and finally even to Albania, Bulgaria, Macedonia and Kosovo. With the Dayton Peace Accord, however, Bosnia-Herzegovina crystallizes as the clear-cut point of emphasis. This is accommodated with the shift of the headquarters from Zagreb to Sarajevo. In 1998 the ECMM is increasingly engaged in the blazing conflict in Kosovo and organizes the first observer teams before the arrival of the OSCE observers.
Duration of deployment:	July 7th, 1991 – to date.
Participating nations:	All 15 member states of the EU (Austria, Belgium, Denmark, Finland, France, Germany, Greece, Great Britain, Ireland, Italy, Luxembourg, the Netherlands, Portugal, Spain, Sweden) as well as Canada (until 1993), the Czech Republic (before 1993 CSFR), Poland, Norway, the Slovakian Republic.
Strength:	Up to 330 diplomats, officers and noncommissioned officers in 43 teams, 140 military observers (as of December 31st, 2000).
Headquarters:	Zagreb, from June 27th, 1997 Sarajevo.

Austrian Participation

Political Measures

Although Austria does not initially participate in the ECMM, it dispatches some observers from the beginning of its EU membership.[96] These and other personnel are partially dispatched from the FMFA, partially from the MoD (similarly to military observers), but have exclusively non-military duties. Since the ECMM is led by the foreign ministry of each country that has the EU chairmanship, the ECMM is subordinate to the Federal Ministry for Foreign Affairs in Vienna in the second half of 1998.

This is traditionally connected to the assumption of the largest part of the leadership functions on various levels. An effective leadership of the ECMM during the presidency is therefore of crucial importance for its total assessment by the members.

Military Measures

On the part of the MoD, it is only necessary to secure the required number of observers. Furthermore a medical team, consisting of two military doctors and two medical noncommissioned officers, is dispatched to provide medical care. In the second half of the year 1998 the MoD organizes a strengthened contingent of up to 70 people in the ECMM headquarters. Among these are counted staff functions, logistics experts, military observers, mechanics, drivers, data processing and radio experts and office personnel. Since the ECMM is not a military but a civilian mission, the affiliates fulfill their duties unarmed, in white uniforms without rank insignia.

Basis for deployment:	CM of June 25th, 1999, MC of July 7th, 1999 (dispatch of up to three diplomats and up to 15 military observers); CM of December 12th, 2000, MC of December 15th, 2000 (dispatch of up to seven officers until July 31st, 2001).
Mission:	Deployment as monitors, assumption of staff functions as needed; during the EU presidency (2nd half of year 1998) and in the six months prior and post to it (Troika) leadership functions as well; medical care of the mission.
Appellation:	None.
Form of dispatch:	Up to the FCL-CSD takes effect, without a special act, since it is a cooperative EU action. After the FCL-CSD takes effect, according to this.
Area of operations:	Bosnia-Herzegovina.
Duration of deployment:	March 6th, 1995 – December 22nd, 2000 (ECMM); December 23rd, 2000 – March 30th, 2008 (EUMM).
Contingent strength:	Four officers, one noncommissioned officer (until September 18th, 1997); from September 19th the contingent is step by step expanded to 67 soldiers in view of the assumption of the EU presidency in the 2nd half of 1998 and reduced again by July 1999; in addition two military doctors and two medical noncommissioned officers. 6 (as of January 1st, 2001). In connection with the transfer of the humanitarian burral of war victims from the ECMM to the Office of the High Representative (OHR), the noncommissioned officer who fulfilled these duties with ECMM is temporarily transferred to the OHR in fall 1998.
Total:	121 (ECMM), 146 (EUMM).

---

96 Austria becomes a member of the European Union on January 1st, 1995.

Activities as Monitor

The fieldwork of individual observer teams is limited to their assigned responsibility areas. As a rule these areas are contiguous with the borders of cantons or communities and have an expanse of around 2,500 square kilometers. The teams consist of two observers which come from two different countries, a native translator and a native driver. An all-terrain vehicle and fitting communication equipment are the most important parts of the gear. Numerous teams are gathered together by a Coordinating Center (CC). Numerous CCs are in turn coordinated into a Regional Center (RC). The members of the ECMM wear white clothing, however no rank insignias, in order to be recognizable as non-combatants in case of a conflict.

On December 15th, 1995, the Security Council installs the office of the **"High Representative"** with Resolution 1031, with the goal of implementing the Dayton Agreement in the civilian area. The instrument for this is the **"Office of the High Representative"**, an institution similar to a government in its composition and which is to fulfill its duties in the crisis area. The Austrian diplomat Dr. Wolfgang Petritsch is entrusted with this function. Among his duties are the establishment of a unified currency, the return of refugees and the organization of the reconstruction. One of the duties, however, is also the discovery of missing persons. In Bosnia-Herzegovina alone there are around 30,000 people, around 22,000 Muslims, 4,000 – 5,000 Serbs and 1,000 – 3,000 Croats. The majority of these people were murdered in the course of ethnic "cleansings" during the previous wars. The problem: They lie in the territory of their one-time war enemies. On April 19th, 1998, an Austrian noncommissioned officer, Warrant Officer I Werner Zofal, is deployed in Mostar as **"Head of the Office of Missing Persons and Exhumations"**. His first and, because of the mistrust and hostility, most difficult duty, is to move the representatives of all the ethnic groups to work together. After intensive negotiations Croats, Muslims and Serbs search for Muslim and Croat victims on Serbian soil. WO I Zofal describes how the deployment takes place as follows:

"A Bosnian returnee tells the Bosnian police that in the area of Rogatica 36 Muslim villagers were murdered by Serbian Chetniks; he himself survived only by chance. The police send a report to the Bosnia-Herzegovina Ministry of the Interior. From there it goes further to the OHR and they further commission WO I Zofal to investigate and solve the case. In the course of the investigations the Serbian side must be negotiated with as well as with the members of the Bosnian Commission for Missing Persons. Then he goes on to the crime scene with the witnesses and representatives of all parties as well as a protective escort of the Federal Mine Action Team (FedMAC). After it is determined that the area is free of mines, a first report is sent to OHR and then the course of events for the recovery of the victims is organized. For this a metal detector is often necessary. If the victims are found, they are recovered. While still on the site, pathologists attempt to determine the cause of death and identity. Afterwards the dead are packed in "body bags" and laid in a refrigerated truck. The column returns to Bosnia, the dead are brought to the pathologist and examined again. Afterwards the victims are laid in zinc coffins, which are welded shut and laid in wooden crates serving as outer coverings. Only after this are they given over to their relatives for burial. This complicated procedure is necessary so that it is possible to open the coffins even years later for evidence. Finally reports are composed for the OHR and the highest prosecutor of the International Tribunal for War Crimes. 1,700 victims are recovered in this way from May to December 1998 in Bosnia-Herzegovina, two and a half times as many as in both the previous years."

WO I Zofal's success can be easily gathered from the letters of thanks that the president of the Republic of Bosnia-Herzegovina, Alija Izetbegovic, directs to Federal President Dr. Thomas Klestil on November 20th, 1998, in which he says among other things: *"... Mr. Zofal is one of the most commendable people for the discovery and exhumation of more than 450 victims in West Herzegovnia and in the area of Rogatica. These are areas which were fully inaccessible for our experts before his arrival..."*

During its EU Council chairmanship Austria provides around 70 men for the EU observation mission in Southeast Europe in the second half of the year of 1998. In the picture Colonel Fridolin Gigacher as EU observer (also called "ice cream seller" because of the typical white clothing) during the delivery of a report by satellite telephone.

United Nations Disaster Assessment and Coordination Mission in Laos (UNDAC/Laos)

Preliminary Events

In the middle of September 1995 Laos is devastated by a disastrous tidal wave. 39 districts are affected, 62,000 ha. of farmland are destroyed, 200,000 people die, 400,000 are homeless.

International Reaction

An UNDAC[97] team is immediately alerted through the United Nations Office for the Coordination of Humanitarian Affairs (UN-OCHA) to coordinate the disaster relief and set on the march to Laos.

Austrian Reaction

At the request of UN-OCHA the urgent dispatch of an UNDAC catastrophe expert to Thailand takes place for the duration of up to three weeks by the Federal Ministers of the Interior and Defence, authorized in case of urgency according to Sec. 1 para. 1 sub-para. c in connection with Sec. 2 para. 3 FCL-CSD.

> **Basis for deployment:** International request for aid from the Laotian government.
> **Mission:** Coordination of disaster relief.
> **Duration of deployment:** September 16th, 1995 – September 24th, 1995.
> **Participating nations:** Austria, DHA[98], Great Britain, Sweden.
> **Strength:** 4.
> **Headquarters:**
> **Austrian Expert:** M. Lechner.

---

[97] **UNDAC:** The improvement of the coordination of humanitarian aid is established by the General Assembly of the United Nations with UN Resolution No. 62/182 of February 14th, 1992, wherein the installation of a "stand-by capacity" of disaster relief experts is to be seen as a crucial component. At the time 67 nations, including the Republic of Austria, and 16 international organizations hold experts ready for any type of deployment in national "UNDAC Stand-by Teams". The MoD participates in the Austrian "UNDAC Stand-by Team" through the preliminary, continuing and extension training, equipage and maintenance of a maximum of five catastrophe experts from all military specialties.
The deployment of an UNDAC Team takes place during larger natural, environmental and technical catastrophes (such as earthquakes, floods, tidal waves, tropical storms, volcanic eruptions, refugee movements, chemical accidents, etc., including the consequences resulting from them) and basically serves to survey and subsequently to coordinate an international search and rescue deployment in the affected area. An UNDAC team is subordinate during the fulfillment of its duties to the instructions of the Secretary General of the United Nations. In accordance the Agreement on the Privileges and Immunities of the United Nations, FLG I No. 126/57, Article VI, Section 22, the member of an UNDAC team counts as an "expert on mission" and enjoys the UN privileges and immunities established therein for the duration of the deployment, including the travel time.
The dispatch of an Austrian UNDAC expert to a deployment in a catastrophe zone basically takes place according to Sec. 1 para. 1 sub-para. c in connection with Sec. 2 (2) FCL-CSD. The deployment to exercises and training measures takes place according to Sec. 1 para. 1 sub-para. d in connection with Sec. 2 (3) FCL-CSD.
[98] **DHA:** United Nations Department of Humanitarian Affairs.

Peace Implementation Force (IFOR)

Peace Stabilization Force (SFOR)[99]

Preliminary Events

Differences between the central government and the constituent republics as well as between the individual constituent republics lead to the final collapse of the Yugoslavian government in 1991. Subsequently, armed battles take place in Slovenia, Croatia, Bosnia-Herzegovina, which are often accompanied with ethnically motivated violence. After the Dayton – Paris Agreement of 1995 the Bosnia and Herzegovina develop into a factual international protectorate.

International Reaction

After the UN deployment, as of 1992 with a limited mandate, cannot end the battles in Bosnia-Herzegovina, the international community, with strong participation of the USA, takes a new approach in 1995: The county is newly organized on three levels – a national state, which consists of both "entities" the Republic of Srpska and a Bosnia-Croatian federation, which for its part is again composed of a Bosnian-Muslim and a Croatian section. A strong international presence is to implement peaceful development. The military component is realized as a "Peace Implementation Force" (American identification **"Joint Endeavor"**) from NATO and the partnership for peace, while the police are provided by the UNO. The EU and OSCE are responsible for the various duties of reconstruction and human rights. The international "High Representative" of the United Nations is to concern himself with the (difficult) coordination of the various components.

On December 15th, 1995, the deployment of IFOR is authorized by SC Resolution 1031. With this IFOR becomes a UNO-authorized mission with a coercive nature, whose mission also includes the armed implementation of its mission ("peace enforcement"). On December 6th NATO also invites Austria to participate in IFOR through a note from NATO Secretary General Sergio Ballanzino. IFOR is limited in time to a year. Since a further military presence in Bosnia-Herzegovina seems necessary, it is extended at the end of 1996 on a smaller scale as a "stabilization force" (American identification **"Joint Guard"** and from 1998 **"Joint Forge"**).

Basis for deployment:	Dayton Agreement (skeleton agreement for peace in Bosnia and Herzegovina, ratified on November 21st, 1995 in Dayton/Ohio; signed on December 14th, 1995 in Paris); SC Resolution 1031 (1995) of December 15th, 1995 (authorization of IFOR); SC Resolution 1088 (1996) of December 12th, 1996 (authorization of SFOR); SC Resolution 1174 (1998) of June 15th, 1998 (extension of the SFOR mandate); SC Resolution 1147 (1999) of June 18th, 1999; SC Resolution 1305 (2000) of June 21st, 2000 (extension until June 19th, 2001).
Mission:	Observation of the marking of the troop division zone between the conflicting parties and troop withdrawal out of the zone; establishment of air sovereignty and the sovereignty over the most important lines of movement in the area of operations; establishment of a mixed military commission for the observation of the peace accord; establishment of secure conditions for the implementation of non-military duties; support of humanitarian aid through UNHCR and other international organizations; observation of the clearance of minefields.
Duration of deployment:	IFOR: December 16th, 1995 – December 19th, 1996 (transitional phase for SFOR until February 3rd, 1997). SFOR I: December 20th, 1996 – June 19th, 1998; SFOR II: June 20th, 1998 – December 1st, 2004.
Participating nations:	16 NATO countries (Belgium, Canada, Denmark, France, Germany, Great Britain, Greece, Iceland, Italy, Luxembourg, the Netherlands, Norway, Portugal, Spain, Turkey, USA), 13 PfP countries (Albania, Austria, Czech Republic, Estonia, Finland, Hungary, Latvia, Lithuania, Poland, Romania, Russia, Sweden, Ukraine) as well as Egypt, Jordan, Malaysia, Morocco.
Strength:	IFOR: 60,000; SFOR I: 34,000; SFOR II: 31,000; 22,400 (as of December 31st, 2000).
Headquarters:	Sarajevo.

---

[99] The renaming takes place on December 20th, 1996.

The first impressions are frightening – and this is not far from home (t.l.). An Austrian soldier in front of an advertisement for the 1984 Olympic Games – memories of better times? The survey team finds a one-time factory, which seems to be ideally (?) suited for the accommodations of the Austrian IFOR contingent (m.l. and r.). An SFOR patrol leaves the BELUGA camp (b.).

Austrian Participation

Political Measures

The Austrian desire to secure a lasting peace in the geographically close region of Bosnia-Herzegovina and the prerequisite invitation from NATO on October 20th, 1995, in line with the "partnership for peace", are the bases for the Austrian federal government to consider participation. An appropriate act is passed on December 12th. On December 15th, 1995, the Main Committee of Parliament approves of the dispatch of a reinforced troop unit as well as engineers to the multinational peacekeeping troops in Bosnia. At the same time the MC approves a draft of the federal government concerning the granting of "rights and privileges" to NATO to achieve a quick and frictionless transit of the IFOR units through Austria. Austria indicates, however, that the dispatched unit will not take part in coercive measures. This is also accepted by NATO. On December 16th the Austrian ambassador in Brussels hands over an appropriate answering note. Federal President Dr. Thomas Klestil greets this measure and expresses his pleasure that in Austria the thought of European solidarity has finally also prevailed in overcoming war. At the release of 316 noncommissioned officers from active service, taking place later that same day, the federal president literally remarks: *"We cannot stand to one side when the greatest human tragedy in Europe in the postwar era is to be overcome. I am sure that the little Austrian troop to Bosnia will once more display the high training standard of our peacekeeping soldiers to the eyes of the world."* In line with the political preparations for the IFOR dispatch, the American defence minister, William Perry, comes to Vienna for talks on November 23rd, 1995. There he makes his case for "A new American-Austrian dialogue on security, in the interest of peace and stability in Europe."

On January 16th, 1996, the Council of Ministers approves the text of the agreement with NATO, which was determined in an exchange of letters between the NATO Secretary General and the Austrian Foreign Minister. Within these, among other things, it says: *"Austria participates in the multinational peacekeeping operation in Bosnia (IFOR) for the duration of a year, with a strengthened transport unit and engineers with a total strength of up to 300 men. The duration of the deployment can be extended by a mutual understanding."* The Council of Ministers further approves an exchange of letters in which it is determined that Austria must cover all the costs which the deployment of the Austrian contingent incurs itself.

The Austrian deployment in line with IFOR opens new dimension for the armed forces. During a meeting with his Swedish counterpart, Defence Minister Dr. Werner Fasslabend sees the ability to overcome the situation in Bosnia-Herzegovina as one of the *"decisive factors for future European security policy, in which Austria will fully participate."* And after the meeting of the General Chiefs of Staff in Brussels, the GTI declares:[100] *"The joint deployment of NATO troops and soldiers from PfP countries has brought the various military structures closer together. The pressure of the joint deployment of IFOR troops has brought a much quicker accommodation with regards to **"interoperability"**, the usage of comparable terms, maps or computer programs, than was expected. Only months ago it would have been unimaginable for the highest military men from countries such as Russia, Albania, Austria and America to "equally and freely" exchange their views. The Austrian troops have earned the highest praise for their deployment in Bosnia."*

This deployment is an Austrian one under NATO command. The military, but above all its soldiers, can compare themselves directly to their comrades from NATO countries for the first time – and do not need to fear the comparison. Everywhere and at all times, the lack of equipment is replaced by knowledge and skill, motivation and improvisational talent.

Military Measures

On November 27th, 1995, the General Troop Inspector, General Karl Majcen, shares with the Supreme Allied Commander Europe (SACEUR) General George A. Joulwan that in the case of an invitation to participate in IFOR, Austria would consider the participation of a reinforced transport company. On February 9th, 1996, the Austrian GTI and the Belgian General Chief of Staff, Vice Admiral W. Herteler, sign an agreement on cooperation within the transport battalion ("Memorandum of Understanding – MOU") as well as supplemental technical agreements.

---

100 APA report of April 24th, 1996.

• Transport Unit

On February 1st at 6:00 AM the transfer of a 68 man advance command with 22 vehicles begins a land march to Visoko. The soldiers' assignment is the construction of a camp in the onetime factory hall of the Vitex company.

Until the day of the movement, February 15th, 1996, a mission-oriented training takes place through CoyCmdI for the volunteers, 2/3s of whom come from the militia and reserves. The previously staggered cadre training is under the leadership of Section III of the MoD, which leans upon the CmdIE for this. The trucks are reinforced against bullets and mines. Flak jackets and battle helmets are quickly procured from France for the soldiers, after all, the safety of the soldiers has the highest priority besides the efficiency of the deployment.

The transport company is initially deployed from the location of Visoko (30 km northwest of Sarajevo) within the limits of a transport battalion under Belgian command, together with forces from Belgium (until March 31st, 1997), Luxembourg, and Greece throughout the area of operations. The battalion is identified as the **"BELUGA group"** (Belgium, Luxembourg, Greece, Austria) and is directly subordinate to the **"Allied Rapid Reaction Corps – AARC"**.

As a result of the reported workload a reduction of the TrspCoy to two groups of trucks (twelve vehicles) and one group of dump trucks (six vehicles) takes place during the 1st rotation. After the reduction of the Belgian contingent the battalion is led by Greece. On June 20th, 1998 the Belgian and Luxembourgian contingents are withdrawn, in place of them a Bulgarian transport platoon arrives, equipped with 10t trucks in order to maintain a roughly similar transport capacity. The battalion is renamed **"HELBA Group"** (Hellenic, Bulgaria, Austria). Within a short amount of time transports for international aid organizations are carried out besides the purely military transport assignments. So during the "Seeds for Peace" action both the Red Cross and Caritas are also cooperated with. An additional duty consists of the repair of bridges and streets. It is determined in the course of a workload inspection that the platoon equipped with heavy trucks is not utilized more than 50%. In the course of the next rotation the 6th contingent is therefore reduced by this platoon and its necessary leadership and support elements. Afterwards the transport company consists only of two transport platoons.

In the course of the reduction of NATO troops from 34,000 to 20,000 men a further decrease of the Austrian contingent also takes place. After the further reduction of a platoon with twelve trucks/dump trucks and the reorganization connected with it takes place in February, the new (9th) contingent takes up its duties on March 1st, 2000, in the new structure. However, the changes reach deeper: The Austrians leave their previous quarters in Camp HELBA in Visoko and occupy their new outpost in **Rajlovac**, around 5 km northwest of Sarajevo. This international camp mostly houses German soldiers. The barracks in Rajlovac were constructed in 1904 by the Austrian Imperial Army as a cavalry barracks. Since the frontline in 1992 ran directly next to the barracks, the building was seriously damaged in places. The space made available to the Austrian is adapted in February by 24 engineers of the Engineering Troop School of the armed forces. The experiences from Kosovo, where the Austrian battalion is dependent on cooperation with a German brigade (Operational Control), now also come into play in Bosnia. AUSLOG/SFOR is now subordinate to a German logistical battalion within the framework of MNB(SE) and cooperates with the German army in a mixed transport company.

In the spring of 2000 the decision is made to end participation in SFOR for efficiency reasons. The closing ceremony for the end of the SFOR deployment takes place on February 27th, 2001, in Rajlovac and on March 15th in Vienna in the Van Swieten barracks. 40 soldiers are dispatched to Bosnia from the beginning of January to the end of April 2001 to dismantle the infrastructural establishments.

Basis for deployment:	CM of November 28th, 1995 (basic participation in IFOR);
	CM of December 12th, 1995, MC of December 15th, 1995 (dispatch);
	CM of January 16th, 1996 (approval of the agreement with NATO);
	CM of October 23rd, 1996 (basic participation in SFOR);
	CM of January 28th, 1997, MC of January 30th, 1997 (extension of the dispatch begun with IFOR);
	CM of May 18th, 1999, MC of May 25th, 1999 (dispatch of up to 185 soldiers until June 30th, 2000);
	CM of June 6th, 2000, MC of June 14th, 2000 (end in February 2001, conclusion of the dismantling by April 2001 with the possibility of temporarily increasing by up to 100 men for this purpose).
Mission:	Transport of people and goods on the corps level, humanitarian aid.
Appellation:	**AUSLOG/IFOR** or **AUSLOG/SFOR**.
Form of dispatch:	Until April 1997 according to the Dispatch FCL 1965; after April 1997 according to the FCL-CSD.
Area of operations:	Visoko (30 km northwest of Sarajevo); from March 2000 Rajlovac (5 km northwest of Sarajevo).
Duration of deployment:	IFOR: February 14th, 1996 – January 31st, 1997;
	SFOR: February 1st, 1997 – March 14th, 2001 (farewell in Götzendorf: March 16th).
Contingent strength:	Initially 290 men and 100 vehicles, then a reduction to 240 men, in October 1999 a reduction to 185, in February 2000 finally to 54 men (four officers carry out duties in NATO HQ) and 25 vehicles.
Total:	501 (IFOR); 1,537 (SFOR).

> **Composition:**
> **AUSLOG 1:** Leadership section (the staff officers as well as the officers sent to international commands are included in this. So a Lieutenant Colonel is in the HQ in Sarajevo as "Senior Logistics Operations Officer", a Major is at HQ/ARRC in Kiseljak, a Captain as "Liaison Officer Logistics" in Split, a Captain and two noncommissioned officers in the staff of the "Corps Transport Battalion").
> **Logistic Base** (a form of headquarters company) with camp command (this is responsible for accommodation in a total of 68 highly modern, air conditioned and heated tents), staff platoon, logistics platoon with fuel group, field kitchen group, "National Support Element (NSE)" (this element, consisting of 82 people, is responsible for the procurement of the necessary provisions from Austria as well as the removal of no longer necessary or repairable equipment), psychological care group and medical group and repair platoon.
> **Transport company** (two TrspPls with 48 6t AAF dump trucks, a TrspPl with 24 10t AAF heavy trucks with loading cranes).
> **Engineering platoon** (with a strength of 25 men for three months for the construction of the camp).
> **AUSLOG 2:**
> Reduction to 42 dump trucks and twelve heavy trucks with a total transport capacity of 370 t, addition of five armored Puch Gs.
> **AUSLOG 6:**
> Leadership section; LogBase with six AAF dump trucks, two heavy trucks with flatbeds, a crane, two FAGO busses and two tanks for their own provisioning; two TrspPls with 18 dumptrucks each.
> **AUSLOG 9:**
> Leadership section, LogBase and a TrspPl.
> **Commanders:**
>
> | | |
> |---|---|
> | January 30th, 1996 – August 20th, 1996 | Lieutenant Colonel Josef Kienberger |
> | August 21st, 1996 – February 17th, 1997 | Lieutenant Colonel Friedrich Scheibler |
> | February 18th, 1997 – December 15th, 1997 | Lieutenant Colonel Thomas Rapatz |
> | December 16th, 1997 – November 30th, 1998 | Lieutenant Colonel Egbert Mayr |
> | December 1st, 1998 – August 10th, 1999 | Lieutenant Colonel Klaus Amon |
> | August 11th, 1999 – February 14th, 2000 | Lieutenant Colonel Franz Horvath |
> | February 15th, 2000 – August 16th, 2000 | Lieutenant Colonel Alfred Oswald |
> | August 17th, 2000 – March 16th, 2001 | Lieutenant Colonel Dietmar Foditsch |

Contribution

In the first four years 10,300,000 km are covered on partially risky roads, during which 470,000 tons, from gravel to seeds, are transported. The impressive 150,000 km driving distance per at-fault accident must be pointed out (for comparison: In Austria this driving distance is "only" around 100,000 km per at-fault accident). This performance is proof of outstanding training, attention to duty, but also the fact that the soldiers on a deployment act with more responsibility. In Austria, in contrast, accidents as a result of sloppiness or inattention come to the fore.

Vehicle Equipage

At the begin of the deployment the contingent has 20 Puch Gs. Beyond the transport company, the fuel troop has access to two tanker trucks of 15,000 l, and for the pickup of the fuel from the UA army's tank camp, 30,000 l tank tractor trailer. Three tractors with snowblowers are ready for snow clearance in the camp. Three dump trucks in each transport platoon are additionally equipped with hydraulic dozer blades for the opening of provisioning roads for transports. The command of the transport company has two pivot loaders for the loading of bulk goods. Two busses serve the transport of persons.

In order the improve the orientation of the transport platoons or with the command vehicles, the vehicles possess a **Global Positioning System (GPS)**. With this navigation system and the use of the newest shortwave radio equipment, the secure leadership of the transports is assured.

Protective Equipment

During this deployment the security and protection of the soldiers is acknowledged as an especial area of focus. So the soldiers in the platoons receive an advanced model of flak jacket and Kevlar combat helmets. The flak jackets conform the latest technological developments. they offer protection from flak and under specific circumstances also protection from direct shots from light infantry weapons. The combat helmet is significantly lighter than the usual steel helmet and at the same time offers a far higher level of protection.

The trucks are "reinforced" against mine explosions and bullets. This **reinforcement** occurs through a comprehensive protection of the driver's cabin. Sheets of steel, 15-layer Kevlar and so-called "spoil liners", a combination of various materials that prevent fragmentation, which are attached to the bottom of the vehicles, are used. In addition, the driver's cabin is secured with a protective grate over the windscreen and the side windows. A fitting contract for equipage including all this work is made with the Steyr firm. The costs for these measures run to 44 million ATS (3.2 mil. Euros!).

The trucks are "reinforced" against mine explosions and bullets. This reinforcement occurs through a comprehensive protection of the driver's cabin. Sheets of steel, 15-layer Kevlar and so-called "spoil liners", a combination of various materials that prevent fragmentation, which are attached to the bottom of the vehicles, are used. In addition, the driver's cabin is secured with a protective grate over the windscreen and the side windows. Note the red-white-red insignia on the license plate. This is stuck over "BH" (for Bundesheer, or armed forces) in order to avoid confusion with "Bosnia-Herzegovina". Some Puch Gs are also provided with protection. These vehicles can be recognized through the black mudguards in the front and back (m.).

Cooperation functions outstandingly between the Austrian IFOR/SFOR contingent and the comrades from the Austrian police contingent of the **"WEU Unified Police Force Mostar – UPFM"** *(while the administration in Mostar takes place through the EU, the police are subordinate to the WUE). So joint staff meetings for mutual information are constantly carried out. In the middle of the picture (t.) Gendarmery Captain Reinhold Hubegger, Cdr of the Austrian police contingent, in conversation with the 1st Cdr/AUSLOG/IFOR, LTC Günther Kienberger (2. from l.) and a delegation of the MoD from Vienna. The police carry out their duties armed. Note the sleeve insignia of the WEU police (t.). The picture was taken on the destroyed bridge in Mostar. The soldiers help where they can (m.l. and r.). A special focus is placed on the care of the children. So a school can be reconstructed and furnished with Austrian help (b.l.) and soldiers even take over the occasional hour of instruction in their (meager) free time (b.r.).*

236

Fire Prevention

Austria is one of the first countries to respond to a NATO request for the dispatch of a complete military firefighting unit. Specialists from all provinces are drawn together for this deployment and undergo a two week deployment-specific technical training. For this the Vienna General Hospital's fire brigade's breathing protection training compound is used under the expert counsel of the on-duty team. The practical training in various damaged areas takes place at the Tritol works in Großmittel. The fire prevention platoon is led as a separate partial unit from AUSLOG/SFOR and is assigned to the **"Fire Fighting Marshall/SFOR"**.

After reaching the area of operations the infrastructure for a fire station must first be produced, since no advance work was contributed on the part of the Cmd/SFOR. In zero degree temperatures and under heavy snowfall a complete winter-proof **fire station** is constructed with the help of AUSLOG according to plans from the firefighting platoons PlCmdr, consisting of an operations trailer, a living trailer, storage room and a garage tent for the vehicles.

As a result of the complete roofing of the area it is possible to carry out all storage and maintenance work without hindrance from the weather. The actual fire fighting already begins two days after the arrival at the camp. The minimum personnel strength makes work hours of 110 – 120 hours necessary to assure 24-hour readiness for operation. Meanwhile the average time from alert until the arrival at the place of operations in Camp Butmir is two minutes (!). In reality, however, besides the camp three additional SFOR building complexes are cared for in the center of Sarajevo, and numerous national camps within the framework of regular fire safety inspections. The main focus is preventative fire safety. Much importance is placed on the **training** of extinguishing assistants in the camps. An operational plan is prepared for every property, in order to be able to proceed efficiently in case of deployment. Furthermore, the technical training for a local firefighting troop is organized and carried out with the help of translators. For this the necessary training materials and rules are also translated into the national language by interpreters. A further focus is laid on environmental protection, which is still a foreign concept for many other armies. So during occasional floods of the gas stations a deployment with oil-binding materials occurs. The professional work of the firefighting platoon leads to their great acceptance by the population, but also by the members of at least 46 nations which are accommodated in camp.

Basis for deployment:	CM of September 3rd, 1998, MC of September 15th, 1998.
Mission:	Firefighting service in HQ/SFOR in Sarajevo.
Appellation:	**Fire Protection Team (unofficial: Austrian Fire Brigade).**
Form of dispatch:	FCL-CSD 1997.
Area of operations:	Camp Butmir near Sarajevo.
Duration of deployment:	October 15th, 1998 – May 15th, 1999.
Contingent strength:	14 (from April 5th).
Total:	14.
Composition:	1st – 3rd Firefighting Troops.
Commander:	WO I Erwin Bachinger.

Equipment

Besides a Puch G Cmd truck and two TLF 4000 tank fire engines, various special firefighting tools belong to the equipment, such as the new pulse firefighting tool IFEX 3000. The personal protective gear of the personnel conforms to the high standards of a civilian firefighting team.

Maintenance of Ability

A meaningful use of free time plays an important role in such deployments. So the soldiers construct their own climbing wall on their own initiative. The necessary climbing shoes are provided by sports consultants from the Carinthian provincial government.

Mine Danger

In Bosnia the mines still lead to serious accidents. In the years between 1996 – 1999 around 1,200 mine explosions are counted, around 40% of these are deadly; in 20% of the cases children are the victims. 19,000 minefields with roughly a million miles are identified in Bosnia. The yearly costs for clearance are estimated at 280 million schillings. Austrian soldiers also participate in the information of the population on the mine danger.

Homeland Customs Abroad

On December 5th, 2000, the Austrian contingent receives a legendary visit from their homeland. Around 8:00 PM the Krampus from Carinthia emerges in Café Amadeus, submerged in red light and decorated in red and black for this purpose. Certainly two and half meters tall, with a terrifying mask and loud ringing bells, he jumps through the crowd. Numerous guests from the most diverse nations accept the invitation of the commander of AUSLOG 10/SFOR, who brought this Austrian custom into the camp. The ancient tradition is, however, markedly different from province to province, or even from valley to valley. The mask used is brought specially from Glainach in Carinthia.

Franz Ferdinand Memorial

On June 28th, 1914, the Austrian heir to the throne Franz Ferdinand and his wife Sophie lose their lives in an assassination near the Latin Bridge in Sarajevo. In the year 1917 a monument is built on the site of the assassination, which is removed again after the establishment of the Soviet state. In its place a "footprint" of the murderer Gavrilo Princip is put into the ground, the bridge is named after him. Shortly after Bosnia-Herzegovina's independence the "footprint" is removed. At the initiative of the Austrian ambassador in Sarajevo, Dr. Gerhard Jandl, the monument is established in its original place again by AUSLOG/SFOR. This should also emphasize that the Austrian period (1878 – 1918) is experiencing a renaissance in Bosnia-Herzegovina.

• Staff Duty

In connection with the end of the dispatch of AUSLOG the Council of Ministers decides on the stay or further dispatch of initially up to four staff members, the personnel limit is expanded to up to 10 in 2004.

> **Basis for deployment:** CM of December 4th, 2000, MC of December 15th, 2000; CM of November 18th, MC of December 9th, 2004 (up to 10 staff members).
> **Mission:** Staff duty.
> **Form of dispatch:** FCL-CSD.
> **Area of operations:** Sarajevo (Camp Butmir).
> **Duration of deployment:** January 1st, 2001 – December 1st, 2004.
> **Contingent strength:** 2.
> **Total:** 6.

• Infantry Contingent[101]

At the NATO summit in Istanbul in early summer 2004 the end of the NATO-led SFOR at the end of the year and the transition to the EU-led EUFOR mission is prepared. The assumption of a NATO mission in the Balkans as a European responsibility has – although on a much smaller scale – taken place in spring 2003 in Macedonia with the European operation "CONCORDIA", and successfully at that. This transfer was a further sign of the normalization of the total area, but also a direct result of the EU's progress in the development of its Common Foreign and Security Policy.

The European Union newly evaluates the situation against the background of the expected assumption of the NATO mission in Bosnia-Herzegovina at the end of 2004. This leads to the dispatch of a further Austrian contingent to the area of operations at the end of June 2004, initially still under SFOR command. The decision to dispatch an infantry contingent in the strength of up to 150 people is made in the Council of Ministers in March. The members of the staff are nevertheless included in this total.

The Austrian presidency in the Central European Nations Cooperation (CENCOOP) in the year 2003 can be used during the preparation for AUCON/SFOR. CENCOOP was founded on the Austrian initiative in 1997 and includes the countries of Austria, Croatia, Hungary, Romania, Slovakia, Slovenia, and Switzerland and serves as a platform for the exchange of experience and cooperation. In the four meetings of the planning staff at International Operations Command in 2003 in Graz, the joint participation of Austria, Slovenia, Hungary and Romania in the SFOR Italian-led **Multinational Specialized Unit Regiment (MSU-Rgt)** is agreed upon and enacted at the CENCOOP Defence Ministers' meeting on October 24th, 2003 in Graz. With this, the Austrian Defence Minister can already report this consolidated contribution on the political level at the EAPC on December 2nd, 2003. In addition preliminary discussions are led with Italy as lead nation of the MSU-Rgt. on the necessary composition, capability parameters, time requirements, and cooperation in the areas of training and logistics. The MSU is deployed throughout Bosnia and directly led by SFOR as a reserve.

At the end of 2004, in case of a crisis in Bosnia, the dispatch strength is raised by up to a further 100 people, who are sent within the framework of KFOR. The number of people is subsequently raised to up to 150 people (of which 50 are from KFOR). At the same time it is decided to raise the dispatch strength of KFOR in case of a security need by up to a further 100 people, who are dispatched within the framework of SFOR or are planned to be dispatched for the purpose. Essentially the goal is to be able to move forces quickly from Kosovo to Bosnia or the reverse in case of a crisis, or alternatively to be able to quickly move forces which are being held ready for one of these deployments in Austria into the area of operations. With this the legal requirements for a swift military procedure and so for military flexibility are secured.

On December 1st, 2004, the NATO-led operation SFOR ends. On December 2nd, 2004, the European Union takes over the mission under the appellation **European Union Military Operation in Bosnia and Herzegovina (EUFOR/ALTHEA)**. Only the command relationships are changed for the Austrian contingent.

---

101   This section is based among other things on an article from Brigadier General Mag. Günter Ruderstaller in the magazine "Truppendienst".

Identification for affiliates of IFOR and SFOR (t.). In order to make themselves understood to the natives, the soldiers receive cards with the most important expressions in both languages (m.).

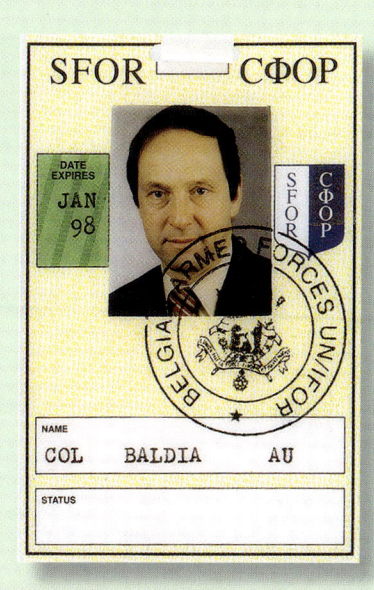

humanitarna pomoc	humanitäre Hilfe
namještaj	Möbel
hrana	Nahrung
odijelo, odjeca	Kleidung
obuca / cipele	Schuhe
mješovita roba	gemischte Waren
kutija	Schachtel
paket	Paket
paleta	Palette
šljunak	Schotter
pijesak	Sand
kamenolom	Schottergrube
gradjevinski materijal	Baumaterial
drvo	Holz
kovina / metal	Metall
ulica	Gasse/Straße
put	Weg

Zovem se... / Moje ime je... / Ja sam... - Ich heiße... / Mein Name ist... / Ich bin...

Ja sam od austrijskog kontingenta SFOR-a u Visokom. - Ich bin vom österreichischen SFOR-Kontingent in Visoko.

Gdje mogu naci gospodina / gospodju ...? - Wo finde ich Herrn / Frau ...?

Gdje cemo tovariti / istovariti? - Wo ist die Lade- / Entladestelle?

Imate li ...? - Haben Sie ...?

Ima li ovdje ljudi, koji mogu pomoci tovariti / istovariti? - Gibt es hier Leute, die beim Laden / Entladen helfen können?

Gdje mozemo ovdje okrenuti kamionom / prikolicom? - Wo können wir hier mit einem LKW / mit Anhänger wenden?

IFOR/SFOR insignia

"Austrian Firebrigade" insignia

Austria is one of the first countries to respond to a NATO request for the dispatch of a complete military firefighting unit (t.l.). Much importance is placed on the training of extinguishing assistants in the camps (m.r.).
In zero degree temperatures and under heavy snowfall a complete winter-proof fire station is constructed with the help of AUSLOG according to plans from the firefighting platoons PlCmdr, consisting of an operations trailer, a living trailer, storage room and a garage tent for the vehicles (m.l.). The firefighters have the most modern equipment, including an impulse extinguisher for an incipient fire (b.r.) and a foam pipe for liquid fires (b.l.).

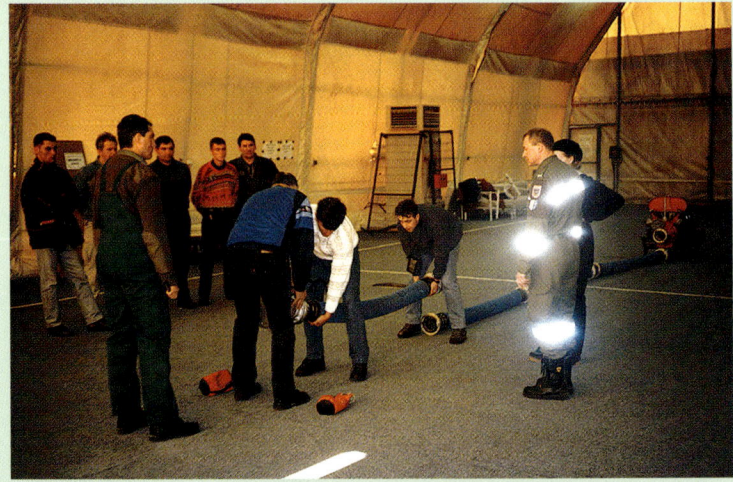

> **Basis for deployment:** CM of March 2nd, 2004, MC of March 17th, 2004; CM of Septmber 27th, 2004, MC of November 3rd, 2004.
> **Mission:** Support of the SFOR troops as well as the civilian authorities in the maintenance of public order and safety.
> **Appellation:** Austrian Contingent (AUCON/SFOR).
> **Form of dispatch:** FCL-CSD.
> **Area of operations:** Camp Butmir.
> **Duration of deployment:** June 27th, 2004 – December 1st, 2004.
> **Contingent strength:** 135.
> **Composition:** Infantry company with supplemental leaderships, special duty, information gathering and logistics elements.
> **Commander:** Lieutenant Colonel Klaus Eisenbach.

"These Crazy Austrian Engineers"

After a long and strenuous train ride the Austrian AUCON1/SFOR contingent arrives in Sarajevo in the night of June 28th, 2004. Thanks to the preparation of the advance commander under the leadership of Major Hannes Krainz and the capable support of the "National Representative" with SFOR, Major Erwin Kauer, Camp Butmir and the MSU Camp (the Multinational Specialized Unit Camp) can be occupied immediately. The MSU camp will be the quarters for most of the Austrians in the next months. The office building, renovated in record time by Austrian engineers and ICT (information and communication technology) personnel, receives much praise. The speed and professionalism brought to the renovation is noticed by the other nations living in the camp: So there are numerous requests to "borrow these crazy Austrian engineers" as needed.

AUCON/SFOR carries out its duty within the framework of the Multinational Specialized Unit (MSU) in Bosnia-Herzegovina. The contingent is part of an Italian-led battalion in the area of operations. Among its main duties are above all the support of the SFOR troops as well as the civilian authorities in the maintenance of the public order and safety. The mission includes patrols with "Pandur" armored personnel carriers, information gathering, deployments during demonstrations and unrest to return safety and order in close cooperation with the Bosnia-Herzegovina police forces, the support of the return of refugees and cooperation with the implementation of the laws.

Special Observation Squad

This element of the Austrian Command's special deployment unit works closely with an Italian "maneuver unit". Besides the Austrian soldiers and the Italian carabinieri, Slovenian and Hungarian partial units belong to the squad.

Military Police

In order to best conform to the police-like duties of the Multinational Specialized Unit, Puch G 300 GD LF-FMs are equipped with sturdy construction and light bars, search and work headlights, signal antennae and reinforced panels. The military police personnel and station equipment supplement this equipage. In addition to crowd and riot control equipment, automatic weapons with rubber bullets are taken into the material organization as non-deadly weapons, including the appropriate use and safety requirements.

Liaison Observation Team

At the beginning of 2004 "Liaison Observation Teams" (LOT) are established in SFOR as elements of the so-called "deterrent presence". These teams make a better view of the situation as well higher flexibility and reaction capability from SFOR possible, despite numerous reductions of troop strength and the thinning of the forces. An LOT is composed by eight to ten soldiers, led by an officer and accommodated in a rented civilian house in a town. From this house they keep in intensive contact with the authorities and the population, above all for the achievement of an authentic, current picture of the situation. Predecessors of LOT were already used in the European Union Monitoring Mission – albeit as unarmed observers there – as well as in Macedonia as "Field Liaison Teams" of NATO and later the EU.

Civilian-Military Cooperation

The CIMIC team of AUCON/SFOR pursues a double goal: First the support of humanitarian aid projects such as the "Farmers Helping Farmers" action of the Salzburg provincial councilwoman Doraja Eberle. Besides this the CIMIC team attempts to contribute to the development of economic cooperation between Austrian and the area of operation. Previous intensive cooperation in the area of finance and insurance economics as well as in the construction and supply markets offer a good basis for this. But the international troops themselves are also a meaningful economic factor in the area of operations. The first visible signs of this goal are joint events of AUCON/SFOR with the Austrian Foreign Economic Center in Bosnia and Herzegovina. The initially unbureaucratic institutionalization of this cooperation leads to the installation of a **CIMIC Center Austria** in the vicinity of the International Operations Command in Graz.

United Nations Disaster Assessment and Coordination Mission in Africa (UNDAC/Africa)

Preliminary Events

Violence between numerous ethnicities dominates this region since 1993, to the the exclusion of the world public. After the genocide of the Tutsi in Rwanda in 1994, refugee camps emerge in the east of the Congo, then still called Zaire, where many of the génocidaires responsible for the ethnic cleansing and members of the former Rwandan army FAR stay. The hard core of the Hutu involved in the genocide soon begin to carry out attacks on Rwanda from Zaire, in order to overthrow the meanwhile newly formed government again. Between 1994 and 1996 after the Rwandan genocide, ca. 2.5 million Rwandan Hutu refugees are in North and South Kivu. They are cared for by numerous international organization. In 1996 the situation escalates through attacks on the Tutsi by the Hutu militias, sometimes with the participation of soldiers from Zaire. Many hundreds of people are already killed in spring 1996, a further 250,000 driven away.

On April 6th, 1994, the airplane carrying the Rwandan and Burundian presidents is shot during its preparation for landing in the Rwandan capital of Kigali. In the crash that follows, both lose their lives. After the assassination a civil war with devastating consequences breaks out. Already by the end of April there are 200,000 deaths. With the war in 1996 the region changes to a ghost town overnight. As could be expected, the UNO (UNHCR) loses all control over the largest refugee camp in the world. A large number of refugees use this situation to return to their homeland in Rwanda. The hardliners, responsible for the genocide in Rwanda, distribute and hide themselves in the huge forests of the Congo, occupy and control large parts of the province. They murder and massacre at will, the streets are filled with Rwandan and Congolese military and militias. After taking the capital, Kigali, RPF troops begin to drive out the Rwandan army and Hutu civilians. By the middle of July an estimated 1.2 million Rwandans flee over the border to Zaire from the advancing troops of the RPF and establish huge refugee camps around the city of Goma.

International Reaction

In June 1996 the last UN soldier leaves the country. All other organizations withdraw their workers from the region by the end of 1996. As a result of the terrible refugee disaster the United Nations and the European Union participate in renewed international efforts to overcome the results of the Rwandan tragedy, especially the serious humanitarian crisis, the acute refugee problem as well as the regional process of reconstruction.

Through the United Nations Office for the Coordination of Humanitarian Affairs (UN-OCHA), an UNDAC team is immediately alerted and set on the march to coordinate the disaster relief.

Basis for deployment: Alert through UN-OCHA.
Mission: Assessment and coordination of the aid forces.
Duration of the deployment: December 14th, 1996 – January 9th, 1997.
Participating nations: Austria, DHA[102], Finland, Great Britain, Switzerland.
Strength: 6.
Austrian expert: Major Rudolf Müller.

Austrian Reaction

Political Measures

An urgent dispatch of an UNDAC disaster relief expert from the military to Rwanda for up to three weeks takes place through the Federal Ministers for Foreign Affairs, Finance, the Interior and Defence, licensed according to Sec. 2 para. 5 of the FCL-CSD in the case of urgency.

---

102 United Nations Department of Humanitarian Affairs.

Misión de Verificacion de las Naciones Unidas en Guatemala (MINUGUA)

English Appellation: United Nations Verification Mission in Guatemala.

Spanish Appellation: Misión de Verificacion de las Naciones Unidas en Guatemala.

The appellations are determined in connection the with change of mandate (although keeping the abbreviation) on April 1st, 1997. Before they were:

English: United Nations Mission for the Verification of Human Rights (and of Compliance with the Commitments of the Comprehensive Agreements on Human Rights) in Guatemala.

Spanish: Misión de las Naciones Unidas para la Verificacion de los Derechos Humanos (y del Cumplimiento de los Compromisos del Acuerdo Global sobre Derechos Humanos) en Guatemala.

Preliminary Events

In 1994 the Guatemalan government and the resistance movement "Unidad Revolucionaria Nacional Guatemalteca" (URNG) agree to negotiations for the end of the as yet longest conflict in Latin America. A 36-year conflict ends on December 29th, 1996, with the signing of an agreement on an effective and lasting peace by the government of Guatemala and the URNG.

International Reaction

After partial agreements on human rights and the creation of a schedule of peace in March 1994 as well as repatriation and the formation of a commission for the punishment of human rights abuses in June 1994, MINUGUA takes over the observation of the human rights situation from November 1994. Agreements follow on the rights of natives in March 1995, on economic issues in May 1996 and on the role of the executive and the army in September 1996. On December 4th, 1996, a cease-fire agreement is signed, in which constitutional and election law reforms and the reintegration of the URNG are also regulated. On December 29th, 1996 the concluding peace treaty is finally signed in Oslo.

Basis for deployment:	SC Resolution 48/267 of September 19th, 1994; SC Resolution 1094 (1997) of January 20th, 1997.
Mission:	Verification of all agreements, in particular the cease-fire agreement of December 4th, 1996.
Duration of deployment:	November 23rd, 1994 – to date.
Participating nations:	Austria, France, Germany, Great Britain, Italy, Luxembourg, the Netherlands, Portugal, Spain.
Headquarters:	Guatemala City.
Strength:	Since March 3rd, 1997: 155 military observers and medical personnel.

Austrian Participation

Military Measures

Political Measures

The federal government decides on the dispatch of a medical contingent.

Basis for deployment:	CM of January 28th, 1997, MC of January 30th, 1997.
Mission:	Medical care of the mission.
Form of dispatch:	Until April 1997 according to the Dispatch FCL 1965, after April according to the FCL-CSD 1997.
Area of operations:	Guatemala City.
Duration of deployment:	February 14th, 1997 – May 18th, 1997.
Contingent strength:	3.
Total:	3.

United Nations Disaster Assessment and Coordination Mission in Malawi (UNDAC/Malawi)

Preliminary Events

In January 1997 in Malawi/Southeastern Africa, the river Shire is dammed by the unusually high waters of the Zambezi, causing it to overflow its banks. The result is a flood catastrophe. The government estimates that 400,000 people have lost their goods and chattels and urgently need help. Subsequently the deployment of an UNDAC team is called for.

International Reaction

At the petition of the Malawian government, an UNDAC team is dispatched through DHA/Geneva.

> **Basis for deployment:** SC Resolution 48/47 of January 31st, 1997[103].
> **Mission:** Determine the concrete factual need for aid.
> **Duration of deployment:** February 18th, 1997 – March 3rd, 1997.
> **Participating nations:** Austria, Denmark, DHA[104] (Sweden), Norway.
> **Strength:** 4.
> **Headquarters:** Lilongwe; advanced HQ in Blantyre.
> **Austrian expert:** Colonel of the General Staff Herbert Bauer.

Austrian Reaction
Political Measures

The federal government decides on the dispatch of a catastrophe manager through a foreign business trip assignment for the initial duration of three weeks. The deployment takes place in civilian clothes, the diplomatic immunity is secured by the UN. The costs for travel and the stay are carried entirely by the DHA.

Military Measures

Colonel of the General Staff Herbert Bauer, who was already involved in the establishment of the UNDAC team in 1993 and was integrated into the first respective training in Geneva, is dispatched on the part of the Defence Minister. Since the dispatch modalities at this time are still somewhat unclarifed, there is no dispatch according to the Dispatch Act.

Bauer flies through London (gathering point for the team) to Nairobi and further to Lilongwe. After a first meeting with Malawian governmental authorities, representatives of the EU and UN organizations, the team separates. Colonel GS Bauer moves to Blantyre with his Danish colleague and leads a two-day assessment with a helicopter from the Malawian armed forces. Assessment results are gathered in the area between Blantyre and the southernmost point of the national border between Malawi and Mozambique. With the help of conversations carried out with the authorities during stopovers, as well as the comparison of the data provided by the authorities with their own visual impressions, the team realizes that of the 400,000 people who live in the affected area, ca. 100,000 need aid immediately. The damages are classified in the following categories: Harvest destroyed/seeds in the huts intact – harvest and huts with seeds destroyed – only huts with seeds destroyed. The need for temporary housing or delivery of food and seeds is processed according to categories and passed on to the Desk Officer of the DHA in Geneva through satellite data transfers according to the basics of deployment for UNDAC. In addition, the destroyed/interrupted bridges and train connections are reported through assessments with wheeled vehicles in supplement to the assessment from the air. In a stay in the affected area one must be especially careful of snakes and crocodiles, who are swept into the inhabited areas through the floodwaters and have already tasted civilian victims. Besides the government authorities, cooperation is particularly intensive with the UN organizations already represented in the nation (UNDP, WFP, UNICEF, UNHCR, etc.). The team at the site is subordinate to the UNDP and is supported with vehicles from UNICEF, including local drivers and VHF radio equipment. After the disclosure of a definitive assessment result to the local UNDP representative and the DHA center in Geneva, according to the principles of deployment used for UNDAC, the next job of distributing aid goods is assumed by the local UN organizations. As one of the duties not covered by the mandate, a discussion between the Malawian authorities and the diplomatic representative of Mozambique is escorted, during which the accommodations and the support of the specified 20,000 Mozambican national affiliates in the south of Malawi is discussed.[105]

---

103 UN System of the "Coordination of Humanitarian Emergency Assistance".
104 United Nations Department of Humanitarian Affairs.
105 From the concluding report of COL GS Herbert Bauer.

United Nations Mine Action Center in Bosnia and Herzegovina (UNMAC/BiH)

International Reaction

In compliance with a peace treaty signed on December 14th, 1995 by Bosnia and Herzegovina, Croatia and the Federal Republic of Yugoslavia (Serbia and Montenegro), the UN Security Council establishes a headquarters of the **"United Nations Mission in Bosnia and Herzegovina" (UNMIBH)** on December 21st, 1995. In line with UNMIBH, a program for the removal of explosive ordnance is initiated through the (then) **"Department for Humanitarian Affairs" (DHA)**. This is implemented by the United Nations Mine Action Center (UNMAC).

Basis for deployment:	SC Resolution 46/182 of December 19th, 1992; SC Resolution 47/168 of December 22nd, 1992; SC Resolution 48/57 of December 14th, 1993; SC Resolution 38/139 of December 20th, 1994.
Mission:	Development of an infrastructure for the removal of explosive ordnance through the training of local specialists; support of the explosive ordnance removal organizations of the government; fostering of an awareness of the existing dangers of explosive ordnance in the population.
Duration of deployment:	May 20th, 1996 – December 31st, 1997.
Participating nations:	Austria, Canada, France, the Netherlands, Norway.
Headquarters:	Sarajevo.
Strength:	30.

Austrian Participation

Political Measures

The federal government initially decides on the dispatch of executive officials in line with the **"United Nations International Police Task Force (UNIPTF)"** on February 6th, 1996, for the training of the local Croatian police, preparation for elections and to secure international aid transports. Subsequently the petition for the dispatch of specialists in explosive ordnance removal is acceded to.

Military Measures

Basis for deployment:	CM of February 25th, 1997, MC of February 27th, 1997 (dispatch).
Mission:	Training of specialists for explosive ordnance removal.
Form of dispatch:	Until April 1997 according the Dispatch FCL 1995; after April according the FCL-CSD 1997.
Area of operations:	Bosnia-Herzegovina.
Duration of deployment:	April 17th, 1997 – December 31st, 1997.
Contingent strength:	4.
Total:	4.

General

Legal questions must initially be clarified for the dispatch decided upon in June 1998 (CM of June 3rd, 1998, MC of June 17th, 1998) of up to four experts for up to a year, at the very latest until June 13th, 1999. Although this takes place by September, the experts are not called upon by the project leading United Nations Office for Project Services (UNOPS) – the dispatch is therefore not carried out.

Multinational Protection Force in Albania (MPF)

Italian Appellation: Forza Multinazionale di Protezione (FMP)

Preliminary Events

Internal unrest, which exacerbates into conflicts between the government and the opposition, leads to a quickening disintegration of national structures of order in spring 1997. The essential causative element for the final collapse of order and the supply system is the collapse of a pyramid scheme for which almost all the people in the country have often deposited the entirety of their money in the hope of a quick win. The following anarchy divides the nation into the South (opposition forces) and the North (government forces) and leads to strong streams of refugees, in particular to Italy by sea. Neither the army nor the police stands in the way of the unrest and looting. The Albanian government petitions the United Nations and the OSCE for help with the reestablishment of normal conditions in the nation, in particular however with the implementation of advance parliamentary elections. With the support of international organization, these finally take place under the protection of the multinational troops on June 29th and July 6th. The General Secretary of the Socialist Party, Rexhep Mejdani, comes out the victor at the polls. He therefore assumes office as the successor to Sali Berisha, who resigned on July 23rd. The state of emergency in effect since March is declared over.

International Reaction

The UNO Security Council identifies the situation in Albania *"as threatening to the peace and security of the region"* in its Resolution 1101 and embraces the offer of some member nations to form a multinational security troop. The mission of this troop is to be to ease the humanitarian aid for Albania and to create secure conditions for the international organizations. The inclusion of the UNO

In 1997 Austria participates in the mission led by Italy to protect the camp in Tirana with a guard company.

occurs at the demand of Russia and against the stated wishes of Albania and Italy, who fear a veto from China and therefore support a deployment of international troops with an UNO mandate. Russia prevails with its opinion that a deployment of force or coercion must only take place with an UNO mandate, however. With this, Russia wishes to prevent a precedent for future crisis situations and emphasize its own position of power.

The dispatch takes place within the framework of a comprehensive international engagement in and for Albania, in which namely the OSCE, the EU and the Council of Europe participate. The OSCE supports the reestablishment of public safety and the areas of democratization, human rights and the media with word and deed, the EU humanitarian and economic aid. The overall coordination is conferred on Dr. Franz Vranitzky in his role as the personal representative of the acting chairman of the OSCE. This resolution precedes a decision of the OSCE which determines that such a protective troop is to carry out its assistance in accordance with the OSCE principles and the bylaws of the United Nation. In this act it is also explicitly declared that this is an official petition of Albania as an OSCE member to a group of nations to be of assistance in the solution of a security problem. NATO eliminates a NATO operation as a result of the chaotic situation in the nation and the lack of military goals for a deployment, however embraces the activities of the neighboring nations and agrees to nonmilitary support such as with logistics. The WEU also renounces a military deployment and so follows the example of NATO. The Albanian crisis so becomes a test case for European security policy. The Security Council confers the leadership of the organization and command of the multinational protection force (MPF) on Italy. In Italy the Senate votes with a large majority for the deployment in Albania on April 8th, 1997. On April 18th Italy begins to shift the III. Corps (HQ/MPF) to Tirana. Subsequently Italy concludes a "memorandum of understanding (MOU)" with Albania on April 23rd for all participating nations, which regulates the stay of the MPF in Albania.

"Operation Alba" begins on April 14th and occurs in three phases. In Phase 1 Italian special forces land at the airport in Tirana to secure it. Teams and equipment are unloaded in the harbor of Durres from Italian and Spanish landing craft. Further units are placed in the harbor city of Vlora. The landing is secured on the coast by the Italian "Vittorio Veneto" cruiser. In the 2nd phase the advance on the capital of Tirana takes place. In the 3rd phase the security troops occupy other important cities like Shkoder, Saranda or Berat. The operation should be concluded one month after the elections in Albania, set for the end of June.

Basis for deployment:	Act of the Standing Council of the OSCE No. PC.DEC/160 of March 27th, 1997; SC 1101 (1997) of March 28th, 1997.
Mission:	Securing humanitarian aid deliveries.
Duration of deployment:	April 12th, 1997 – August 12th, 1997.
Participating nations:	Austria, Denmark, France, Greece, Italy (lead nation), Romania, Spain, Turkey.
Headquarters:	Tirana (Don Bosco School).
Strength:	6,360.

Military Operations within the Framework of the Mission

"Alba" ("Sunrise"): Protection of humanitarian aid measures.
MPF: SC Resolution 1101 (1997).

Austrian Participation

Political Measures

Austria immediately declares its readiness to prepare an infantry unit for MPF in the strength of 115 men. This includes two guard platoons besides the staff and logistics units. Engineer forces can also be added in the beginning phase. In order to create the legal requirements, the Federal Constitutional Law on Cooperation and Solidarity When Deploying Units or Individuals Abroad (FCL-CSD), then in parliamentary debate, takes effect on April 24th, 1997 (after this deployment is not only possible within the framework of international organizations, but also within the framework of the OSCE, EU, and the NATO partnership for peace). The costs are estimated at around 20 million schillings. With regard to the budget, it is declared that factually proven extra costs which emerge from the deployment will be compensated for by the MoD by an overspending law.

Military Measures

The transfer of ATCON partially takes place by rail through the Italian harbor of Brindisi. Further transport then takes place through the Italian navy to the port of Durres. The rest of the contingent is shifted with a civilian fleet airplane. After arrival the tent camp is established on the football field of the newly constructed Don Bosco School. Since the location of HQ/OSCE is not yet determined, ATCON is initially assigned to secure the Italian-Austrian camp. Six days later the assignment is expanded to secure HQ/OSCE, now established in the ambassadors' quarter. The situation in the location of the camp subsequently escalates. The camp is shot at. One of the sandbag positions occupied by Austrian soldiers is put under aimed fire. When shots are fired over the camp falling projectiles strike through the walls of the tents. For this reason ATCON shifts to established accommodations. These lay at the northeast edge of the city of Tirana at the foot of the local mountain in a newly built apartment complex. At this time ATCON is also assigned to secure the civilian-military coordination center (CIMIC) in Don Bosco School. During the decisive elections on June 29th and July 6th the transport of election observers takes place. For this six drivers with Puch Gs are provided by ATCON. During the elections it is also applied to protect the computer center established by OSCE in Hotel "Tirana" for the counting of the election results.

The major problem with dissolving the entire MPF is the transport capacity of the available ferries, airplanes and helicopters. So parts of the team and the equipment must initially be taken after a long wait by ferry to Italy. The remaining team is finally brought to Venice with a Boeing 747 from the Italian armed forces.

The train is then taken to Austria. The vehicles go to Croatia by ferry and from there to Klagenfurt by rail.

At this point the outstanding cooperation with the Rogner hotel directorship in Tirana must be particularly mentioned, which contributed much to the success of the operation.

Basis for deployment:	CM of April 15th, 1997 (readiness for participation), CM of April 22nd, 1997, MC of April 22nd, 1997 (dispatch).
Mission:	Stationary guard and security duties in Tirana within the framework of the 1st Italian carabinieri-paratrooper regiment according to the instructions of COMALBA. Securing of HQ/OSCE, CIMIC and the election observers; escort of the federal minister and the General Troop Inspector during their visits; escort of important persons and provisioning trips.
Appellation:	**Austrian Contingent/Multinational Protection Force (ATCON/MPF).**
Form of dispatch:	FCL-CSD 1997.
Area of operations:	Tirana.
Duration of deployment:	April 24th, 1997 – July 20th, 1997 (July 27th – conclusion of the withdrawal, eight soldiers still remain a few days to take part in the official farewell).
Contingent strength:	115 (a liaison officer with the planning staff in Rome and four officers in staff functions with the Cmd of the III Corps, which leads the operation).
Total:	125.
Composition:	Company command, expert group (translators, liaison officers), command group, logistics group (medical, maintenance, and field kitchen troops), I and II guard platoons (platoon troop with anti-tank guns, four guard groups). The fact that the soldiers of the company during this deployment are organized in elements of the peace structure especially proves itself of value; company leadership through the Special Operations Forces Training Center, I. Platoon through the 7th Infantry Regiment, II. Platoon through the 6th Infantry Regiment.
Commander:	Captain (Major for the duration of the mission) Heinz Assmann.
Contributions:	Securing the sea ports of Durres and Vlore and the airport of Tirana. Only through this is the transition of aid goods possible. In connection with this over 300 escorts are carried out for humanitarian convoys. Over 200 security patrols and more than 100 street reconnaissance missions are carried out by day and night and therefore raise the level of security on the streets (as a consequence of this the curfew can be shortened by three hours). The contingent carries out over 1,200 aid measures of the most varied types for the international community. Further, over 400 OSCE election observers are guarded and escorted. Finally 20 NBC inspections are carried out in the most varied regions of Albania.

In the pictures the vehicles of the Austrian contingent can be seen. Left a medical Pinzgauer. The vehicle is already in Austria again. The inscription AMPF in the rear area of the shelter can only dimly be seen. The connection to the homeland is secured by radio (r.).

Austrian Humanitarian Contingent/Poland (ATHUM/PL)

Preliminary Events

Long-lasting rainfall across broad sections of Europe lead to grave supply and medical problems. Among these is the urgent need for drinking water due to the unsuitability or impurification of wells and springs and the acute danger of epidemics. In Poland alone 230,000 hectares of land and 245 cities and villages are flooded by the high waters, 50 people are killed, around 70,000 people must be evacuated. The Polish government sends a request for international assistance on the Department for Humanitarian Affairs (DHA) in Geneva on July 16th, 1997.

International Reaction

The DHA informs all members on July 16th through "Situation Report No. 3/Poland Floods/Disaster Update" and requests the dispatch of water purification equipment. An UNDAC assessment team is simultaneously dispatched to the flood area.

Basis for deployment:	DHA Situation Report No. 3 of July 16th, 1997.

Austrian Participation

Political Measures

Immediately after the floods become known, the Austrian Foreign Ministry sends the Polish Foreign Ministry an offer of help on July 25th, 1997. Before this, as a result of a request from the Czech government on July 21st, 1997, the decision is taken on the part of the federal government on July 24th to send a regiment of the same type (ATHUM/CZ) for flood relief in the Czech Republic. Since the Czech government answered on the same evening that the situation had abated and help would no longer be required, the Polish request can be answered. The Polish government accepts Austria's offer of help with a note on July 31st.

Military Measures

The military's new NBC defence concept envisions an additional service area besides detectioin, de-radiating, disinfection and decontamination as well as rescue and recovery work: Drinking water purification (until 1997 this was the duty of the medical troop). With this a contingent is available for the deployment in Poland which also receives its "baptism by fire" in this deploy-

The "battle post" of ATHUM/PL is established in a Polish school (l.). The flood makes it necessary to carry out assessment and communications travel with inflatable boats (r.). From this one sees what one must think of during the composition of the equipment.

ment. On the evening on July 29th the assessment team drives to Wrocław in order to create the requirements for the deployment. Three drinking water purifications systems (WPE) are seen as necessary. On August 2nd ATHUM/PL arrives in the area of operations at 1:30 AM after a sixteen hour drive with 33 soldiers and 18 vehicles and immediately begins work. The reduction of the team strength from originally 55 to now only 40 soldiers leads to a high physical and psychological pressure. The connection to the homeland takes place with GSM and satellite telephones. The return of the floods and the BC danger increasing with the weather situation demands a mission expansion of ATHUM/PL carried out on-site by the duty supervisors, with the goal of implementing the necessary water analyses. On August 8th, therefore, an additional water analysis group consisting of parts of the NBC Defence School and the field laboratory element of the Office for Defence Technology (ODT) are set on the march. Since an increase of the contingent is not allowed, four soldiers must make their way home. Since the situation in Poland is stabilized, the withdrawal can begin on August 28th. On August 29th at 3:00 PM the contingent arrives in the Wilhelm barracks in Vienna again.

Basis for deployment:	Urgent dispatch according to Sec. 1 no. 1 subsec. b in connection with Sec. 2 para. 5 FCL-CSD through the Federal Chancellor, Foreign and Defence Minister on July 31st, 1997; report to the CM and MC on July 31st, 1997; acceptance through the FG on August 19th, 1997, debate by the MC on August 26th, 1997; bilateral agreement between Poland and Austria.
Mission:	Securing the provision of drinking water through the operation of drinking water purification systems; clearance and decontamination of water withdrawal systems; analysis of the available water resources in the area of operation for hazards.
Appellation:	**Austrian Humanitarian Contingent/Poland (ATHUM/PL).**
Form of dispatch:	FCL-CSD 1997.
Area of operations:	Nova-Sol.
Duration of deployment:	August 1st, 1997 – August 29th, 1997.
Contingent strength:	40.
Total:	44.
Composition:	Command with logistics group, medical and field kitchen group, NBC Group/Clearance and Recovery with rescue, firefighting, and recovery troops; NBC Group/Decontamination with persons, arms, and equipment decontamination troops; NBC Group/WPE with two water purification and water provisioning troops each; water analysis group.
Commander:	Captain Otto Strele.
Contribution:	850,000 liters of drinking water. Around 6,000 people are supplied with 660,000 liters. Decontamination of 18,300 square meters in 21 locations, three pump deployments with a total of 120 cubic meters of water pumped out.

Water Analysis

During the deployment of ATHUM/PL, the **mobile component of the NBC field laboratory** is also deployed. This is in a special vehicle, which is not generally known. This is a vehicle of the type "Noriker". This vehicle is a prototype in which the construction of a VW LT box truck is placed on a Steyr chassis. In the vehicle is all the equipment of a field laboratory element of the Office for Defence Technology (ODT). This includes a mobile mass spectrometer (MM-1) and a gas-phase chromatograph. The springs in the area of Nova-Sol are inspected by the team. High values of pesticides or the byproducts of pesticides which multiply exceed the allowed levels according to the EU drinking water regulations are detected in a total of 23 springs. As a result of these findings the springs are pumped dry and purified with high doses of calcium hypochlorite. The following inspection produces contaminant levels only at the normal level.

As a result of the experiences had in Poland the problems called forth by a non-optimal adaptation of the equipment are immediately rectified through the purchase of pieces of equipment.

Fueling of a vehicle of the Austrian contingent by the Polish armed forces.

OSCE Mission to Bosnia and Herzegovina (OSCE/BiH)

Preliminary Events

Serbs, Bosniaks (Muslims) and Croats have become entangled in armed conflicts in Bosnia and Herzegovina over numerous years. The armed hostilities between Muslims and Croats are ended in 1994 with the Washington Agreement. This initiates the founding of the "Federation of Bosnia and Herzegovina" and leads, when only theoretically, to the founding of the United Armed Forces of the Federation, consisting of the (Muslim) "Armija of Bosnia and Herzegovina" and the "Croatian Defence Council (HVO)". In contrast to them are the Serbs, with their own army, supported by the "Federal Republic of Yugoslavia (FRY)".

The appendix of the "General Framework of Peace Agreement" from Dayton founds the legal constitutional basis for Bosnia Herzegovina, including the division of responsibilities between the (relatively weak) central government and the two entities, but also envisions areas which are to be implemented and realized by international organizations.

International Reaction

In the "General Framework of Peace Agreement", initialed in Dayton/Ohio on November 21st, 1995 and signed in Paris on December 14th, 1995 for the settlement of the armed conflict in the former Yugoslavia, the OSCE is also called on for cooperation.

Basis for deployment:	Decision of the OSCE Council of Ministers of December 8th, 1995 in Budapest (this also includes the fusion of the OSCE mission in Sarajevo, going on since 1994).
Mission:	Observation of the preparation and implementation of free and fair elections as well as compliance with human rights, the creation of regional stability through trust and security forming measures and regional armament control measures.
Duration of deployment:	December 18th, 1995 – to date.
Participating nations:	All members of the OSCE.
Strength:	150, during the elections up to 2,800.
Headquarters:	Sarajevo.

Austrian Participation

Political Measures

The federal government decides on the dispatch of up to two officers.

Military Measures

The MoD initially dispatches two officers. At the instruction of the GTI the dispatch strength is reduced by one officer from September 26th, 2000.

Basis for deployment:	CM of February 10th, 1998; MC of March 10th, 1998.
Mission:	One officer serves duty in the Implementation Section/Department for Regional Stabilization in the area of Trust Building Measures/Armament Inspection; one officer works as Senior Operations Officer.
Appellation:	None.
Form of dispatch:	FCL-CSD 1997.
Area of operations:	Sarajevo.
Duration of deployment:	April 21st, 1998 – December 31st, 2003.
Contingent strength:	Up to 2; 2.

Unusual Episode[106]

As a result of a request for support with the implementation of a seminar on the topic "Democratic Control of Armed Forces" from August 24th – 26th at the National Defence Academy, its commander, General Ernest König, invites the defence ministers of the "Federation BiH" and the "Republika Srpska", the chiefs of the general staffs of both armies, as well as other high-ranking politicians and military members, to Vienna.

The international tribunal in The Hague simultaneously issues an international warrant for the arrest of Colonel General Momir Tailic, the Chief of the General Staff of the army of the "Republika Srpska", and sends this to the Austrian federal government with a request for execution.

Since every UN member nation is obligated to implement this in its territory on the basis of UN Security Council Resolution 827 (1993) of May 27th, 1993, under Chapter VII of the UN charter, General Talic is arrested on August 25th, 1999, at 10:30 AM by the state police in the Chancellery of the Commander of the DA, a complete surprise for all those affected. The Defence Minister of the Republika Srpska leaves the seminar and Austria with his entourage in protest. To this day it is not clear who gave the international tribunal information on the seminar and the participation of the General.

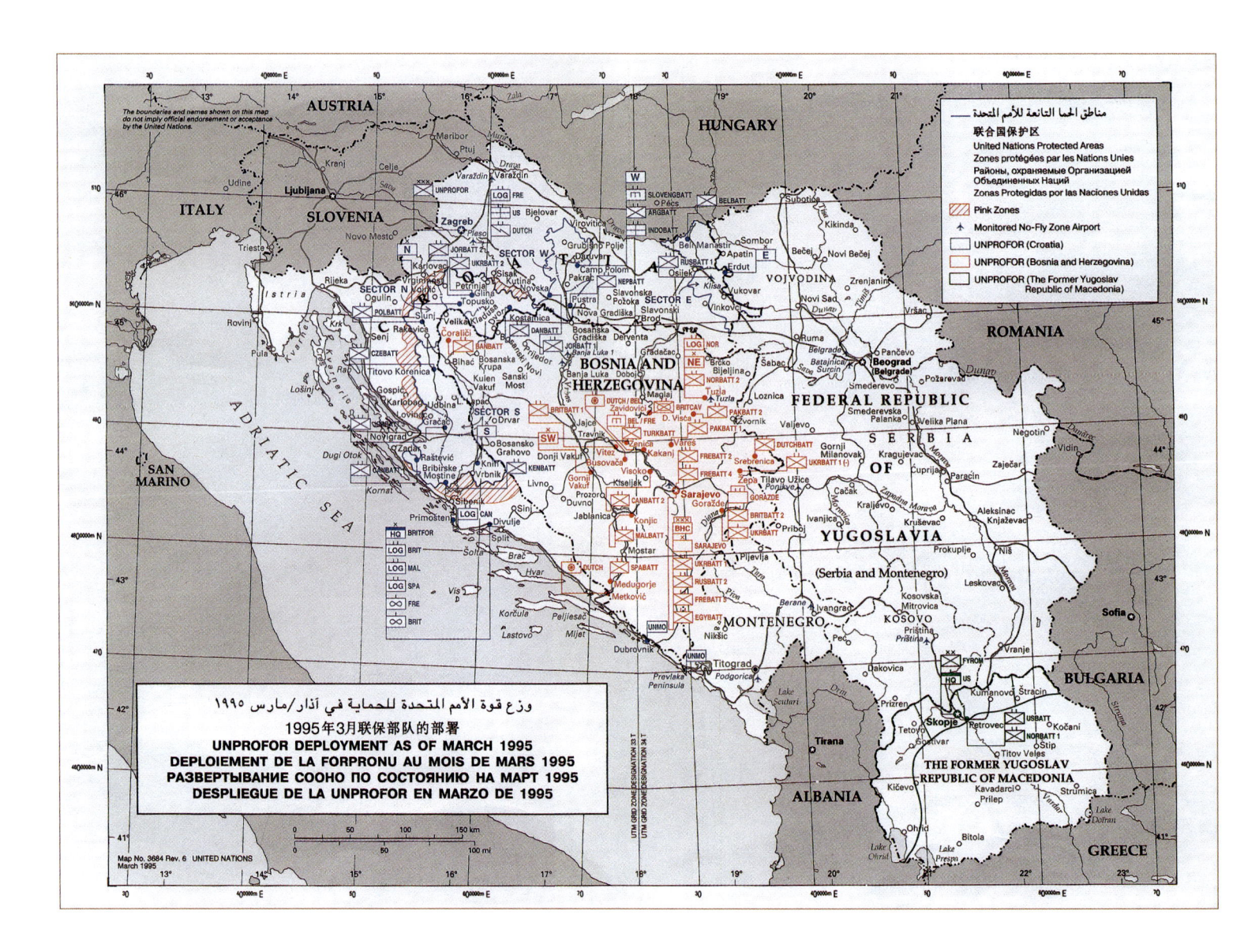

---

106 From a report from LTC Dunichand Thakur, at the time Training and Strategy Coordinator as an Austrian affiliate of the OSCE mission, who as the organizer of the seminar was temporarily under suspicion of passing on information.

United Nations Disaster Assessment and Coordination Mission in Afghanistan (UNDAC/Afghanistan)

Preliminary Events

In February and at the end of May 1998, Afghanistan is devastated by the most disastrous earthquakes of the decade. In the province of Thaker the earthquake claims 5,000 human lives on May 30th, 1998; around 70,000 become homeless. Long-lasting rainfall also destroys their few belongings and the stores of foodstuffs.

International Reaction

An UNDAC team is immediately formed, which coordinates the aid measures. The following report of an Austrian UNDAC member describes the way this unfolds concretely.[107] The report clearly shows how swiftly the UNO can react here. However it also shows under what conditions this type of deployment functions. Here not only technical competence, but also skill in persuasion, initiative and talent in improvisation are demanded from every affiliate. Lieutenant Colonel Ing. Feigl is an air operations expert.

"It was Friday, June 5th, 1998, when I unsuspectingly left Neusiedl am See to take part in a UN event in England. I landed at 10:30 AM in London and waited on other participants, who were to arrive at 2:30 PM. When it was time, a Dane came to me and told me that he and I would not participate in the planned event, but must fly to Islamabad/Pakistan at 4:30 PM on the next day, in order to lead the way for relief measures for Afghanistan, which had been devastated by earthquakes. The Red Cross had already begun with the provisioning of the victims in the meantime. A crushing scarcity of large helicopters as well as fuel, foodstuffs, medicines and tents nevertheless dominated. With this information we were brought to the Tajik capital in a Russian airplane which carries out UNO connecting flights. From there we were immediately arrested by members of the border guard, because at this point we naturally had no visa for Tajikistan. After a long back and forth we received confirmation that our passports would be retained for the duration of our stay. The situation in the area also presented itself as extremely irregular. At the time the Pakistani population was wallowing in a war euphoria and celebrated its first successful atom bomb test, which had taken place not long ago. Five days later and after many tough negotiations with the Tajik Defence Ministry and the airport authorities, we finally prevailed in getting a large Russian helicopter deployed for supply flights on June 12th. So more than 1,000 tons of aid goods could be transported from Peshawar into the earthquake zone by my return flight on June 18th. The return flight to Vienna lasted eight hours, but eight hours before that were necessary to overcome the Russian bureaucracy."

> **Basis for deployment:** Alert through UN-OCHA.
> **Mission:** Assessment and coordination of the relief forces.
> **Duration of deployment:** June 5th, 1998 – June 18th, 1998.
> **Participating nations:** Australia, Austria, Denmark, Finland, Great Britain, Norway, OCHA, Sweden, Switzerland.
> **Strength:** 15.
> **Headquarters:** Islamabad, Peshawar.
> **Austrian expert:** Lieutenant Colonel Ing. Heinz Feigl.

Austrian Reaction

Political Measures

The urgent dispatch of an UNDAC military disaster relief expert to Pakistan for the duration of up to two weeks takes place through the Federal Ministers of the Interior and Defence, licensed according to Sec. 2 para. 5 FCL-CSD in cases of urgency.

---

107 Heinz Feigl: "With the Stepchild of World History – On a Disaster Deployment in Afghanistan", Blue Helmet News 2/99, Vienna 1999.

Austrian Humanitarian Contingent/Croatia (ATHUM/CRO)

Preliminary Events

Beginning on August 5th, 1998, serious conflagrations rage in Dalmatia between Sibenik and Dubrovnik, on the Peljesac Peninsula, on the islands of Korcula and Lastovo as well as in other areas of the Dalmatian coast. On August 6th the Croatian authorities in Dubrovnik petition the SFOR command for help. The Republic of Croatia requests further international support in firefighting on August 12th, 1998, as a result of the worsening of the situation.

International Reaction

The command of SFOR immediately provides helicopters for survey and transport flights for the wounded. On August 7th a deployment staff is formed to coordinate with the Croatian authorities. On August 12th German CNH-53 helicopters are also deployed for the first time. These have the ability to transport and dump 5 t of water as outer weight. At the same time a tactical command post is established on the island of Korcula. On August 14th a French fire department is deployed on board a French "Cougar" helicopter.

Austrian Participation

Political Measures

The Federal Chancellor, Foreign and Defence Ministers decide on the urgent dispatch of four helicopters equipped for firefighting flights with up to 30 men crews and technical personnel to Ploce in accordance with the FCL-CSD.

Military Measures

After the first information in the evening of August 11th, the flight division provides the immediate deployment and flight readiness of two helicopters each (Agusta Bell AB-212s) of the 1st and 3rd Flight Regiments as part of the Prepared Units (PREUNIT). These craft have special outer load-bearing hooks for water containers to fight fires. Such containers have a carrying capacity of 1,000 l and are seawater compatible, which means that the gathering of water can also take place from the sea. The MoD distributes co-flight approval for both fire department specialists who are responsible for the technical care of the large fire-fighting buckets provided from the provincial fire department divisions. Notable is the fact that all necessary volunteers for duty are present within 60 minutes despite the coming weekend and holiday time.

The advance command moves on Aguust 13th at 2:45 PM in one of the two Skyvans. After numerous stopovers and an accidental arrest, the advance command arrives on the Dalmatian coast on the evening of August 13th, the helicopters follow on the next day. The technical maintenance infrastructure is secured through a complete workshop, which is brought to the area of operations with a shelter vehicle by land. The land march is escorted by Croatian police from the national border. Subsequently firefighting deployments are flown from 6:00 AM to 8:00 PM. During this time they cooperate with the French Special Firefighting Troop of the UISC-7 (Brignoles). On August 17th at 11:00 AM the deployment readiness is lifted, at 2:00 PM the Austrian contingent begins their withdrawal.

The armed forces have a broad range of experience with firefighting flights and have contributed aid in many opportunities in the past, lastly during the large forest fire in Carinthia in May 1998, and cooperated with the local fire fighters. The participation in the relief action in Croatia with firefighting helicopters is the 1st deployment of the air armed forces abroad. Great appreciation is shown by the Croatian Defence Minister, Dr. Andrija Hebrang, and the French Commander of the Special Forces, who emphasizes above all the flight skills of the helicopter pilots at the farewell.

Basis for deployment: Agreement between Croatia and Austria; urgent dispatch according to Sec. 1 no. 1 subsec. b in connection with Sec. 2 para. 5 FCL-CSD by the Federal Chancellor, the Foreign and the Defence Ministers on August 13th, 1998; report to the federal government and the Main Committee on August 13th, 1998; acknowledgement by the FG on August 20th, 1998, MC on September 15th, 1998.

Mission: Support of the fight against the conflagration from the air with large firefighting buckets according to the assignment of the deployment leadership.

Appellation: None.

Form of dispatch: FCL-CSD 1997.

Area of operations: Korcula island.

Duration of deployment: August 13th, 1998 – August 17th, 1998.

Contingent strength: 28 (+ 2 civilian fire department experts for technical care of the large firefighting buckets).

Total: 28 (Cdr, deployment NCO, 14 pilots, 11 technicians, 1 doctor).

Composition: 4 Bell AB-212 helicopters, 1 Short Skyvan SH-7 transport airplane, 1 technical shelter truck.

Commander: Colonel Peter Rinderhofer (commander of the 1st Flight Regiment).

Contribution: In three days in around 50 flight hours 119 people and 277,000 kg (of which around 200,000 l of firefighting water) of freight are transported.

OSCE Kosovo Verification Mission (KVM)

OSCE Task Force for Kosovo (TFK)

Preliminary Events

A demonstration of Albanian students dissolved by Serbian police in Pristina in November 1997 is the cause of new tensions between the ethnic groups in Kosovo. In March 1998 attacks of Albanian underground fighters on Serbian police stations in Kosovo lead to drastic retaliation actions through the militarily organized Serbian special police. During these, entire villages are set afire. Strong streams of refugees occur.

International Reaction

After threats of NATO air attacks to prevent a further worsening of the humanitarian situation and the establishment of sanctions on the part of UNO, negotiations take place between Holbrooke and Milosevic on May 1998. The result is an agreement signed by the OSCE chairman Geremek and Milosevic, in which the deployment of an unarmed verification troop on October 13th, 1998 is finally agreeed upon. After the transfer of the mission to Kosovo three areas are formed: an organization core for the administration and planning of the future return to Kosovo, Deployment Group Albania to support the UNHCR; Deployment Group Macedonia to support the UNHCR.

The verifiers are to observe the partial withdrawal of Serbian military and security forces (the upper border of the forces in Kosovo is declared 25,000) and work to establish trust in the implementation of political measures. In addition in a separate agreement with NATO the observation of the agreed-upon measures (withdrawal of troops, return to the garrisons, stationing of inspection forces) through unarmed reconnaissance flights by air during the deployment is agreed upon. The **"Kosovo Air Verification Mission"** (on the basis of SC Resolution 1199 (1998), American appellation "Eagle Eye") takes place over a 25 km wide security zone on the border of Kosovo to Serbia. The deployment coordination occurs through the **"Kosovo Verification Coordination Center" (KVCC)** established by NATO in Kumanovo (FYROM).

Since an agreement cannot be reached on the stationing of armed security forces in Kosovo, military forces in the strength of around 2,300 soldiers under French command are stationed from November 1998 in Macedonia for protection within a limited amount of time or for the evacuation of the verifiers in danger or under threat (Operation "Determined (Joint) Guarantor"). The troops receive the appellation **"Extraction Force – EFOR"** – also called "XFOR" – (rescue troops to the KVM). Germany, France and the Netherlands provide contingents for this. In view of the peacekeeping troops planned for Kosovo (KFOR), these forces are strengthened to 4,500 from February 25th, 1999, and to 10,000 soldiers in March (which subsequently provide the core of the around 19,000 soldier strong forces which form the beginning of the march into Kosovo). The stationing takes place against the stated wishes of Belgrade.

As a result of the renewed acts of violence, above all caused by the diverse paramilitaries ("Seslj Band", "Arkan Tiger"), the OSCE feels forced to withdraw the verifiers from Kosovo in March 1999. The closed and unpublicized withdrawal of the OSCE team on March 20th, which had grown to 1,300 verifiers, not only signals the final failure of this mission (despite great engagement only a few local successes take place, such as the exchange of prisoners), but also enables the beginning of the NATO air war against Yugoslavia ("Allied Force").

Basis for deployment:	Agreement in Belgrade of October 13th, 1998; act of the Standing Council of the OSCE No. PC. DEC/263 of October 25th, 1998; SC 1199 (1998) of September 23rd, 1998.
Mission:	Verification of the cease-fire; observation of troop movements in, into, and out of Kosovo; observation of roadblocks and border controls.
Duration of deployment:	November 17th, 1998 – June 9th, 1999. Because of the threatening Serbian attacks activity nevertheless ceases on March 20th, the verifiers are evacuated to Macedonia. In the time from March 26th – April 3rd all 1,400 verifiers return home.
Participating nations:	All OSCE members.
Headquarters:	Pristina.
Strength:	Planned max. 2000, however only around 1,400 are deployed.

Austrian Participation

Political Measures

The Council of Ministers immediately accedes to the request of the OSCE and decides to dispatch observers, provided by the armed forces (up to 13), the executive (7) and from the civilian field (2).

Military Measures

Basis for deployment: CM of November 5th, 1998, MC of November 10th, 1998.
Mission: Verification.
Form of dispatch: FCL-CSD 1997.
Area of operations: Kosovo.
Duration of deployment: December 29th, 1998 – June 7th, 1999, June 8th, 1999 – June 30th, 1999 as "Task Force Kosovo" (successor to OMIK).
Contingent strength: 14 (KVM); 2 (TFK).

Albanian Force (AFOR)

Preliminary Events

As a result of the systematic displacement of the Albanian population in Kosovo and the increase of the refugee streams to Albania, the Albanian Prime Minister turns to the Austrian federal chancellor during Holy Week with the request for help overcoming the catastrophic refugee situation. At this point in time around 1.5 million people who previously lived in Kosovo are in flight. An estimated 430,000 refugees live in Albania.

International Reaction

On April 1st, 1999, a call for regional humanitarian aid and support for the refugees from Kosovo who are staying in Albania and Macedonia goes out from the UNHCR to all UN member nations. A request is also sent from UNHCR to NATO for the coordination of this humanitarian support.

The **"Euro-Atlantic Disaster Response Coordination Center (EADRCC)"**, which has existed since June 1998 within the framework of NATO and the PfP, supports the "United Nations High Commission for Refugees (UNHCR)", which also leads the humanitarian aid for refugees in Albania. The deployment takes place within the framework of "Operation Allied Harbour" through the "Allied Mobile Force/Land (AMF/L)" of NATIO in cooperation with the **"Office for Coordination of Humanitarian Affairs (UN/OCHA)"**, which operates an **"air operations cell"** in Tirana.

Basis for deployment:	Request of UNHCR to NATO; SC Resolution 1239 (1999) of May 14th, 1999, decision of the North Atlantic Council of June 16th, 1999 (deployment of AFOR).
Mission:	Humanitarian aid for the displaced people from Kosovo in Albania.
Duration of deployment:	April 16th, 1999 – August 31st, 1999.
Participating nations:	Albania, Austria, Belgium, Canada, the Czech Republic, Denmark, France, Germany, Greece, Great Britain, Italy, Lithuania, Luxembourg, the Netherlands, Norway, Poland, Portugal, Romania, the Slovak Republic, Turkey, the United Arab Emirates, the USA.
Headquarters:	Plepa (near Durres).
Strength:	8,000.

Already a few hours after the alert the loading and movement of the first parts of ATHUM/ALBA can be begun in line with the largest humanitarian aid action yet in the history of the armed forces. The main contingent uses a Belgian C-130 among others (t.l.). Immediately after the arrival of the contingent the construction of the "Austria Camp", for up to 5,000, later 7,000 displaced persons, is begun (t.r.). Note the red-white-red armband of the caterpillar driver and the identification on the caterpillar bulldozer. This is how Shkodër looks to our soldiers (b.).

Austrian Participation

Political Measures

The federal chancellor explains in a speech to parliament on April 7th, 1999, that *"the package of measures for displaced persons from Kosovo to the total extent of ca. 500 million schillings can be seen as a visible sign of international solidarity from the armed forces… Up to 400 members of the armed forces are dispatched for the duration of up to two months for the time being… The unit has the mission of supporting the aid measures for displaced persons in Albania. In particular through the support of the aid contributions in Austria Camp."*

With this, Austria reacts immediately to the petition of UNHCR in a concentrated action of national and non-national organizations, through the construction of a refugee camp (Austria Camp) in cooperation with the armed forces, Caritas, the Maltese Hospital Service and the Austrian Red Cross. A payment of 260 million schillings is approved for the proven additional costs of the deployment in personnel and materials.

Military Measures

The military contingent is reported to the Euro-Atlantic Catastrophe Coordination Center with the instruction that it is dispatched for the construction and operation of a refugee camp, and ordered to the humanitarian aid forces coordinated by NATO in Albania. The Red Cross provides 3,000 tent spaces, Caritas 1,600 and the Maltese Hospital Service 500 tent places. The entire camp has access to a shared kitchen, which is operated by the armed forces and the Red Cross. The civilian personnel, mainly doctors and medics, are incorporated into the military contingent and provided with the field uniform with sovereignty insignia and personal protection gear, in order to ease the leadership of the contingent through a unified image.

The question of whether these personnel are combatants or camp followers does not come up, since the deployment is under the aegis of the UNHCR. The Austrian soldiers are equipped with their originally planned hand or fist weapons and battle portion of munition for the purpose of personal protection and emergency aid. Albania and Austria ratify the **"NATO Partnership for the Peaceful Status of Forces Agreement" (NATO-Pfp-SOFA)**. After this the Austrian provisions of law, such as guard duty regulations, count for Austrian contingent members in Albania as well.

The largest humanitarian aid action in the history of the armed forces begins without the possibility of comprehensive planning. On Holy Saturday the Provincial Deployment Center commissions the International Deployment Command to gather a survey command for aid deployment. At the same time the advertisement for volunteers begins. Already on April 4th the survey command takes off with one of the two "transport planes" of the armed forces of the type Short SC-7 "Skyvan" in the direction of Albania. A refused flyover approval from Greece, technical problems with the aircraft, two necessary stopovers to refuel in Rimini and Pescara, and the refusal of Albanian customs officials to allow the survey command to enter are the first difficulties with this mission. Besides this there are difficulties with the rental of private transport airplanes, since as a result of the humanitarian catastrophe situation in the Balkans a noticeable scarcity of the air transport capacity on the free market can be determined and the prices rise as a result of the rising demand.

On April 6th the move of the first guard and security sections takes place with a C-160 "Transal" transport airplane of the German Air Force. On April 10th the transfer of the contingent in its full extent begins. During this they initially lean on a C-130 Hercules transport aircraft of the Belgian Air Force, a French 6-160 "Transal" and an Ilyushin-76 from a Ukrainian transport firm, rented for the month. From April 8th an L-100-30 transport aircraft (civilian version of the "Hercules") from a private South African air transport firm is also available. With the Ilyushin (40 t freight capacity), ca. 475 t. freight in 24 flights is transported, predominantly from Linz/Hörsching. The Hercules (22 t freight capacity) can be operated from Langenlebarn Military Airfield, through which land taxes can be saved. In total 2,600 people and 1,000 t of freight are transported in 85 lifts between Austrian and Albania with the transport airplanes. On April 13th, 220 men with over 2,100 t of freight, including 70 vehicles, engineering machines and containers, move to Koper/Slovenia with three special military trains and then further with ferries to Durres/Albania. Two further special military trains follow on April 14th to Rijeka/Croatia; these transport 35 containers, further trucks (including refrigerated trucks and decontamination vehicles) and heavy equipment with over 1,700 t. The field hospital is transferred to the area of operations in two phases. On April 18th, 350 soldiers with 100 vehicles, 22 tractor-drawn trailers, 18 coolant aggregates, seven electrical aggregates, 80 trailers, four water purification systems, 150 tents and 5,000 t of material are in the area of operations (this is in fact 10 times what was deployed in Iran in 1991 with UNAFHIR).

The entire operation has the pressure of high expectations from the population from the beginning. Practically every news report begins with the "latest report" from Albania. The ORF reports constantly through its own satellite emission truck in the area of operation.

On April 8th the commander of the advance command, after numerous failures, reports having found a suitable place for the construction of the **"Austria Camp"** near the northern Albanian city of Shkodër. This is a former airfield with a size of around 15 ha. This size ratio was previously calculated for a camp with a capacity of up to 5,000 people. Expansion possibilities are present. At first the construction is hindered through the uncoordinated activity of individual aid organizations, the lack of a national authority and the increase of organized crime. From the beginning, great value is placed on an unimpeachable hygienic condition. Further the guard is given great attention. Not insignificant thanks are due to the professional deployment of the soldiers from the Special Operations Forces Training Center in Wiener Neustadt and the 25th Infantry Battalion (airborn) out of Klagenfurt for the great success of this deployment. So the first 150 persons displaced by war can move into a safe and clean camp on April 17th.

One of the main problems at the location is **ensuring drinking water** for the full operation as well ensuring the removal of human waste. Practically all other camps have failed at this problem (and the faulty guard). In contrast, Austria contracts the boring of four springs with a depth of 16 – 35 m from local firms. With these the daily need of ca. 200,000 l can be covered without a problem. The water is prepared to Austrian norms and permanently observed through laboratory examinations in Austria. The water purification is carried out by specialists from the AFDRU.

The **power supply** is initially provided by generators. The camp is subsequently fully electrified and lighted by a donation of the EVN as well as the Viennese City Works in line with the "Neighbors in Need" campaign. With this the connection to the public electrical network also succeeds, with the simultaneous securing of a generator supply in case of electrical blackouts.

The **military field hospital** represents a special contribution within the framework of Austria Camp. It excites high international interest through its medical apparatus equipage and the high standard of the medical personnel. As a result of the special structure of those displaced by war, especial value is placed on the care of women (half of them are pregnant), children and the old. The field hospital is supplemented with a surgical and an internal medicine station as well as an X-ray diagnosis on the most modern level with a satellite connection to the university clinic in Innsbruck. A further point of emphasis is the psychological care of the largely traumatized displaced persons. It is attempted, with the help of translators, to help with the processing of the suffered experiences.

A large challenge is presented, as previously mentioned, by the **security** in and around the camp. The insecurity of the environment (organized crime, tribal feud, blood revenge, etc.) make a strict guard necessary. This initially applies to the so-called "Chicken Farm", a one-time deteriorated factory area near Shkodër which is used as the interim storage for the military vehicles and trailers in the beginning. Only the demonstrative determination of the soldiers with the red berets is to be thanked that the storage is preserved from attacks or looting. All persons who want to enter Austria Camp are also searched by the soldiers for weapons, munitions, or smuggled goods, among other things. In contrast, a serious accident occurs on July 5th in the course of the dismantling of the camp for displaced persons run by the German Maltese, which is directly next to the Austria Camp: Local inhabitants attempt, partially through the use of violence, to loot the camp. A massive use of weapons takes place through the special police. Stray bullets and ricochets must also be noted in Austria Camp and a child is harmed. On July 9th a firefight takes place, in which Austrian guards are targeted under fire. They return fire and hit four Albanians; two are captured, given first aid in the Austrian field hospital and then brought under cover to Shkodër. This incident moves the MoD to immediate reinforcement measures for the guard and security forces for the orderly dismantling of the camp and a secure return to Austria. The camp is dismantled according to plan in the time from July 14th – 31st, and the personnel is returned to Austria by transport on land, in the air, and by sea.

How highly the deployment of Austrian soldiers is recognized by domestic and foreign organizations is shown by a special honor conferred on the commander of the Austrian contingent in Albania, Colonel Nikolaus Egger: He is awarded the highest distinction each can give from the Maltese Hospital Service of Austria as well as the Austrian Red Cross for his activities within the framework of ATHUM/ALBA. These are the golden medal of honor on a band of the Maltese Hospital Service and the 1st class service cross of the Red Cross.

Basis for deployment:	Urgent dispatch according to Sec. 1 no. 1 subsec. b in connection with Sec. 2 para. 5 FCL-CSD through the federal chancellor, foreign, interior and defence ministers on April 5th, 1999; report to the federal government and the main committee according to FCL-CSD on April 5th, 1999; CM of April 7th, 1999, MC of April 13th, 1999.
Mission:	Construction of an "Austria Camp" for up to 5,000, later up to 7,000 displaced persons and care of these persons; construction and operation of a field hospital; guard of their own establishments; securing of transport and connective flights to support the Austrian aid measures.
Appellation:	**Austrian Humanitarian Contingent for Albania (ATHUM/ALBA).**
Form of dispatch:	FCL-CSD 1997.
Area of operations:	Shkodër.
Duration of deployment:	April 5th, 1999 – August 6th, 1999.
Contingent strength:	703.
Total:	703.
Composition:	Command, headquarters company (including a guard and security and protection of persons platoon and a hygiene and drinking water purification platoon), construction/engineering company, field hospital, transport helicopter element.
Commanders:	April 12th, 1999 – June 18th, 1999: Colonel Nikolaus Egger,
	June 19th, 1999 – August 1st, 1999: Colonel Gerd Rieszland.
Contributions:	In 80 workdays more than 23,400 treatments (only 652 of these are dispensed to contingent members) are carried out in the field hospital. This includes a child nutrition program with 11,188 treatments and an immunization program with 8,428 immunizations, besides ambulatory and stationary cases. Further, 1,711 laboratory tests and 32 emergency doctor cases are carried out. More than 5,200 people as well as 125 t of freight are transported in 1,000 flight hours by the helicopter element.

The picture (t.l.) clearly shows the huge extent of the military field hospital and "Austria Camp". Austria's flag waves, visible from afar, over the field hospital (t.r.).

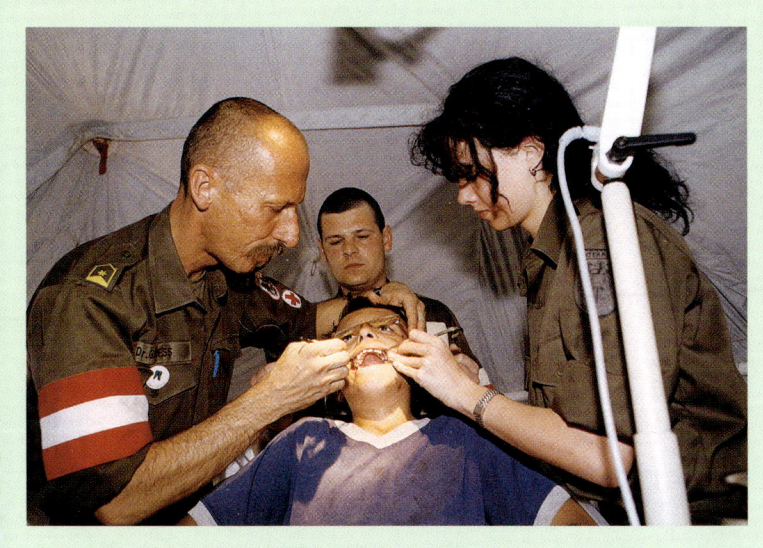

Besides the operation of the field hospital and the treatment of the patients (t.l.), the security of the camp and the operation of a water purification system (t.r.) count among the duties. For the better evaluation of X-rays a satellite connection is maintained with the university clinic in Innsbruck (m.l.). The necessary transports take place with AB-212s of the Austrian flight elements (m.r.). The worst threat for the population comes from the 100,000's of mines which were indiscriminately laid. Their own EOD team of the Military Logistics School informs the population of the dangers (b.l.). For especially complicated operations the patient is flown to Austria. In the picture (b.r.) a small Albanian can be seen who, after a successful intervention, visibly looks forward to the trip home with the C-130.

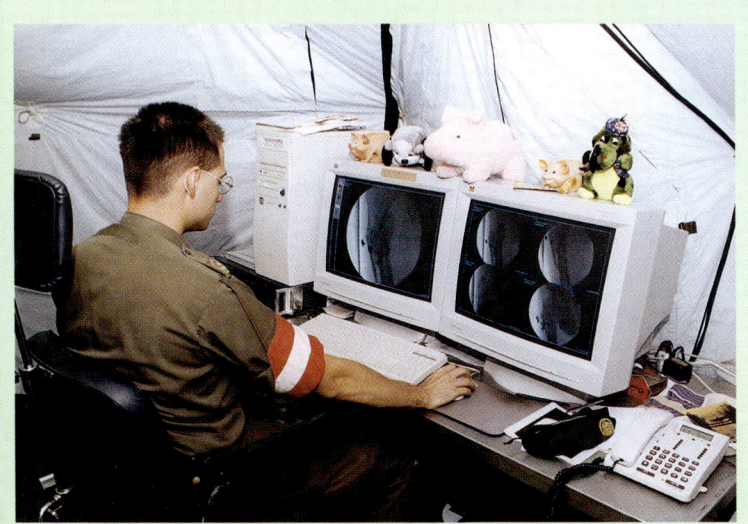

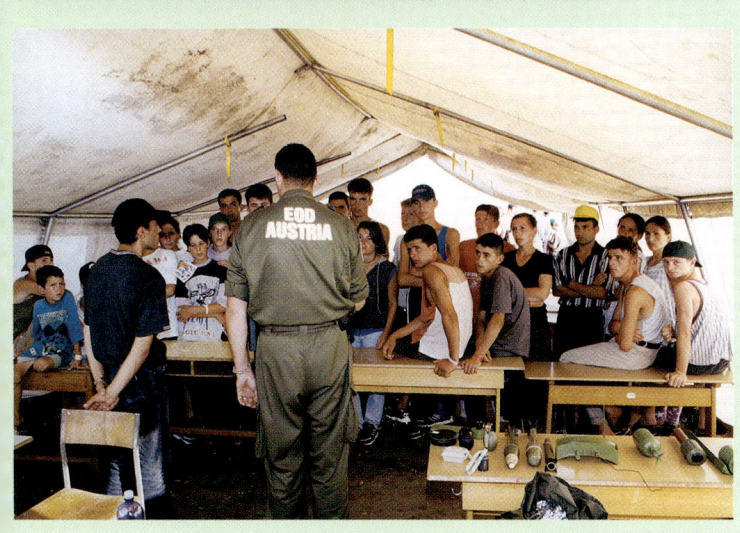

Engineer Company VOREIN Deployed for the First Time

The 112 man strong engineer company VOREIN[108] moves in April to the area of operations in three parts after a significantly reduced formation time. Already six days after the beginning of formation, the first advance command flies out on April 12th, two days later a significant reinforcement follows through half an engineer platoon. The mass of the engineer company – 60 vehicles and heavy engineering equipment as well as large quantities of construction materials and necessary gear – follows immediately by land with rail transport to Koper/Slovenia. From there it continues by ferry until the Albanian harbor in Durres, from whence another 80 km must be overcome in a march through the streets to the actual camp in Shkodër. The engineer company consists of roughly equal parts of soldiers from active service, the militia, and the reserves. The formation takes place through the VOREIN system at the Engineer Troop School in Klosterneuburg, which also provides five percent of the total cadre.

Among the main duties of the company are the construction of the camp, making lines and areas of movement in the immediate vicinity of the camp passable and usable, and supplying water.

Military Psychologist Service

The Austrian soldiers are accompanied by military psychologists for the first time while deployed on ATHUM/ALBA. The duty of the psychologists is the

- psychological decision-making support for the military leadership (for instance cooperation on projects and working groups, composition of position papers and certificates, presentation activities, etc.);
- personnel selection (for instance selection of qualified leadership personnel, of military pilots and volunteers); basics of military psychology (for instance development and evaluation of psychological procedures, research activities, etc.);
- critical incident stress management (for instance the development and relaying of special stress debriefing procedures and techniques for psychological help from comrades, etc.);
- examination and repair of the psychological and military deployment readiness (for instance carrying out the functions of clinical psychologists, training of psychologists for deployment in field clinics, duty with the Help Line service, etc.).

This excerpt from a situation report from the ATHUM/ALBA command to the provincial deployment center in Austria shoes that the Austrian security measures are given such great meaning for good reason.

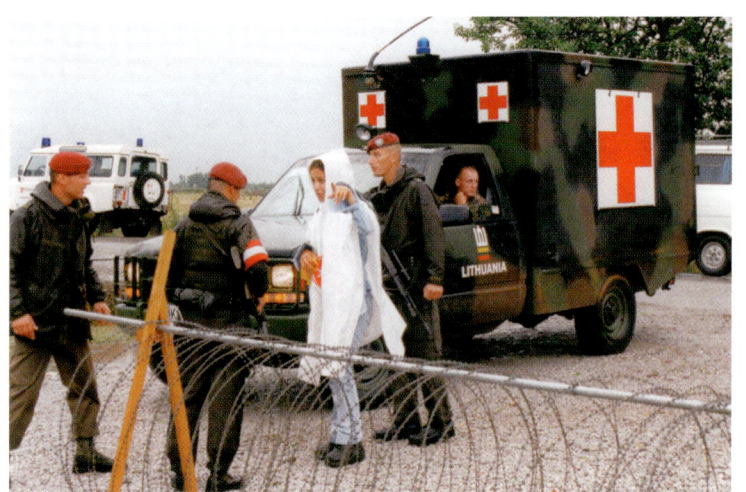

---

108 VOREIN (Prepared Units) are small divisions (battalions), units (companies) or partial units (platoons) which are formed for deployments abroad. Their modular composition and their deployment concept makes it possible to hold contingents ready in line with the "stand by arrangements" for international deployments.

Western European Union Demining Assistance Mission in Croatia (WEUDAM)

Preliminary Events

In the course of the violent conflicts between Croatia and the rest of Yugoslavia large areas of Croatia are mined. Furthermore, the population is endangered by unexploded munitions.

International Reaction

The EU Council decides to carry out a joint action for the support of the mine clearance in Croatia on November 9th, 1998 (on the basis of Art. 3 of the treaty on the EU in the summary of the Treaty of Maastricht). This is connected (on the basis of Art. 4 Sec. 2 of the EU treaty) with the petition to the WEU to carry out this action. The Standing Council of the WEU decides to implement the operation under Swedish leadership. The WEU concludes a memorandum of understanding (MOU) with Croatia for this purpose on April 22nd in Brussels.

Basis for deployment:	EU Council of November 9th, 1998, Standing Council of the WEU of January 22nd, 1999, MOU of April 22nd, 1999.
Mission:	Explosive ordnance clearance.
Duration of deployment:	May 10th, 1999 – to date.
Participating nations:	Austria, Belgium, Bulgaria, Finland, France, Germany, Italy, Sweden.
Headquarters:	Sisak.
Strength:	9.

Austrian Participation

Political Measures

The Council of Ministers decides on the dispatch of up to two experts until May 10th, 2000 or until twelve months after dispatch.

Military Measures

Basis for deployment:	CM of March 23rd, 1999, MC of April 13th, 1999.
Mission:	Instruction and consultation on explosive ordnance disposal; cartographic data collection with the use of the Global Positioning System (GPS).
Appellation:	None.
Form of dispatch:	FCL-CSD 1997.
Area of operations:	Croatia.
Duration of deployment:	May 10th, 1999 – February 10th, 2000.
Contingent strength:	One expert on explosive ordnance disposal.
Total:	2.

United Nations Assistance Mission in East Timor (UNAMET)

Preliminary Events

After the withdrawal of the Portuguese colonial troops in the year 1974 there are serious clashes between both freedom movements, the "Frente Revolucionaria de Timor Teste Interdependente (FRETILIN)" and the "Uniao Democratica Timorese (UDT)". After an attempted coup in 1975 the Democratic People's Republic of Timor is founded. In December 1975 Indonesia intervenes. The annexation, which succeeds in 1976, leads to a long-lasting guerilla war. President Suharto rejects attempts at negotiation and mediation. In 1994 direct talks between the government and the opposition take place. In 1995 Portugal suggests a referendum. During the following conflict resolution talks Austria receives an important role. On January 27th, 1999, the new president Habibie announces that he will grant the East Timorese the right of self-determination. This leads to first acts of violence. The violence is driven further when an agreement is signed between Portugal and Indonesia which envisions the withdrawal of Indonesian troops. This agreement is signed on May 5th, 1999. In the further preparatory phase for the referendum on August 8th there are brutal attacks from various militias in order to intimidate potential voters.

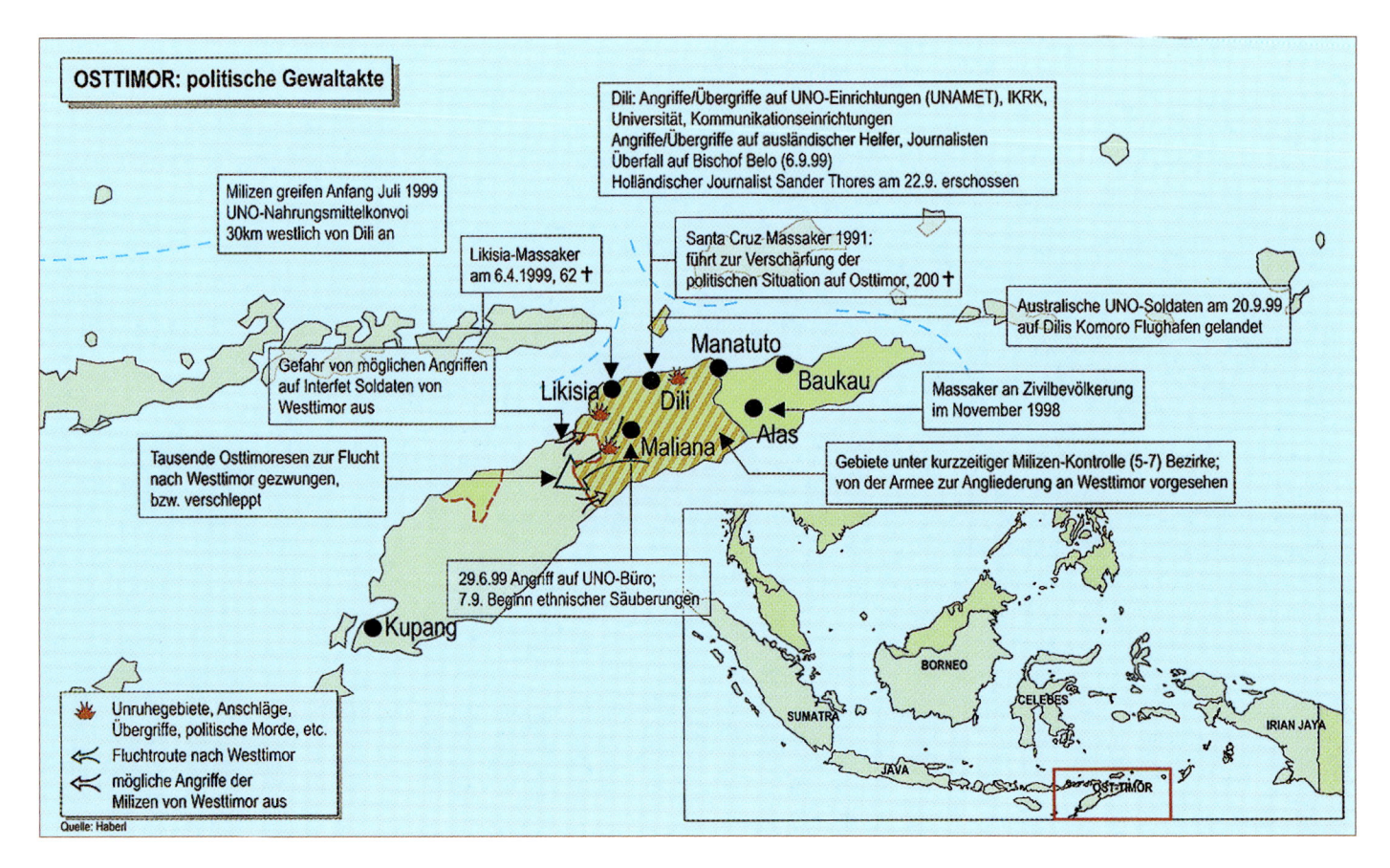

In the referendum finally carried out on August 30th, 1999, the independence of East Timor is preferred with 78.5% agreement (final result according to UNAMET). Immediately afterwards there are massive acts of violence. These are an expression of an unclear political division of responsibilities between the political and military worlds after the collapse of the old state apparatus, as well as the latent readiness for violence of the militant communities within the various Indonesian ethnic groups. In this phase of upheaval it is easy for Indonesia to fan the flames of organized ethnic violence. On September 7th, 1999, a state of emergency must finally be declared. The tensions between the military and the political world increase. President Habibie cannot, however, do without the support of the army if he wants to guard his chances of reelection in October 1999. So he must allow the army a certain amount of freedom in East Timor politics. So it later becomes clear that the army at no time planned to release East Timor into independence. On the contrary, preparations are made under the codename Operasi Sapu Jagad (Operation Last Dance) with the goal of murdering prominent supporters of independence and intimidating and terrorizing the population. The acts of violence do not stop even for UN soldiers or foreign journalists. So after the referendum there are attacks on UNAMET and IKRK establishments; a Dutch journalist is shot on September 22nd. Nevertheless Indonesia withdraws around 20,000 soldiers and police by the end of September 1999; in conformity with the agreement, only two battalions remain with ca. 1,500 men.

International Reaction

In the forefront of the referendum, there are political efforts on the part of the UN mission to curtail the violence in order to ensure the implementation of the mission. Among other things, the dismissal of the officer most responsible for East Timor, General Zacky Anwar Makarim (a specialist in covert operations) is demanded. The army has even worked out a plan, which in the case of independence envisions annexing the five most fruitful provinces of West Timor in order to marginalize the rest economically (the line of attack of the militias makes an understanding with the military public).

In order to end the battles, an international intervention troop, the **"International Force in East Timor" (INTERFET)** under Australian command, according to Chapter VII of the UN charter is established and deployed in East Timor, after the presentation of an agreement from the Indonesian government on September 12th. In the resolution the Security Council declares that *"the current situation in East Timor represents a threat to peace and safety"*. INTERFET is to reestablish peace and safety in East Timor and protect and support the UN mission UNAMET in the implementation of its duties. The deployment of the Australians represents a temporary end point in the ambivalent Australian-Indonesian relationship. This is the result of the loudly announced Australian criticism of the Indonesian East Timor policy, although in the years before, Australia, in contrast to many other nations, rejected the East Timor referendum out of political concern for a good relationship with Jakarta and its own economic interests.

After Habibie makes it known that he wants to allow East Timor to decide its own future, an opportunity arises for Australia to free itself of the international taint of supporting a repressive violent regime. Canberra therefore expresses its support for a UN mission early (April 1999). Australia can also pay back a historical debt from the Second World War to East Timor with its engagement. At the time the East Timorese, with great sacrifice, helped to hinder the Japanese "leap" into Darwin in northern Australia. On May 5th, 1999, the Foreign Ministers of Portugal and Indonesia, Jaime Gama and Ali Alatas, together with UNO Secretary General Kofi Annan, sign the agreement on the self-determination of East Timor in New York.

On September 20th, 1999, the control of the half of the island is transferred to INTERFET under the Australian commander General Peter Cosgrove. On October 26th, 1999, UNO takes over the transitional government. Representatives of UNO determine by helicopter flights that three fourths of all provincial cities are destroyed. Approximately 400,000 people have lost their housing. UNO runs into bitter international criticism, since this destruction took place under the eyes of 900 unarmed UNO workers.

The deployment of German soldiers within the framework of INTERFET is also notable. The German Foreign Minister, Dr. Joschka Fischer, justifies this step based on the reinforcement of UNO and the dependability of Germany. It is to be guessed that the intention behind this was rather to document that Germany deserves a place as a standing member in the Security Council. The mission of INTERFET is transferred in February 2000 to the **"United Nations Transitional Authority in Eastern Timor" (UNTAET)**.

Basis for deployment:	SC Resolution 1246 (1999) of June 11th, 1999;
	SC Resolution 1264 (1999) of September 15th, 1999 (deployment of INTERFET).
Mission:	Preparation and support of the referendum on the independence of East Timor.
Duration of deployment:	June 11th, 1999 – November 30th, 1999 (afterwards taken over by UNTAET).
Participating nations:	Argentina, Australia, Austria, Bangladesh, Bolivia, Canada, China, Denmark, Egypt, Fiji, France, Gambia, Ghana, Great Britain, Ireland, Jordan, Kenya, Republic of Korea, Malaysia, Mozambique, Nepal, New Zealand, Niger, Norway, Pakistan, Papua New Guinea, the Phillippines, Portugal, Russia, Senegal, Singapore, Spain, Sri Lanka, Sweden, Thailand, Turkey, USA, Uruguay, Zambia, Zimbabwe.
Strength:	241 international workers, 420 UN workers, 4,000 local workers, 280 executive officials, military observers.
Headquarters:	Dili.

Austrian Participation

Political Measures

The federal government accedes to the request of the UN and decides to dispatch up to 50 executive officials and up to 10 military experts. In May 2000 the dispatch of a further 20 executive officials to the **"United Nations Transitional Authority in East Timor" (UNTAET)**, the successor organization to UNAMET, is decided upon. The contingent takes up its duties on December 1st, 1999.

Basis for deployment:	CM of June 8th, 1999, MC of June 17th, 1999 (dispatch); MC of May 17th, 2000 (increase by a further 20 executive officials until December 31st, 2000 and extension of the original mandate until July 10th, 2001).
Mission:	Observation of the military forces in view of an orderly implementation of the referendum.
Appellation:	None.
Form of dispatch:	FCL-CSD 1997.
Area of operations:	East Timor.
Duration of deployment:	June 29th, 1999 – November 30th, 1999.
Contingent strength:	4.
Total:	4.

OSCE Mission to Kosovo (OMIK)

Preliminary Events

See KVM.

International Reaction

From the beginning of June 1999, after negotiations, the decision is made on June 9th and 10th on the basis of the peace plan of the G-8 nations (the seven leading industrial nations and Russia) to end the armed conflict and establish a transitional government under the aegis of the United Nations.

The OSCE mission succeeds the KVM or the **"Task Force for Kosovo" (TFK)**[109] and forms an independent part of UNMIK.

Basis for deployment:	SC 1244 (1999) of June 10th, 1999; Decision 305 of the Standing Council of the OSCE of July 1st, 1999.
Mission:	Construction of a police school and training of the justice and administrative personnel; promotion of civilian societal structures, political parties and local media; implementation and observation of free elections; protection of human rights; fulfillment of other duties in accordance with SC Resolution 1244.
Duration of deployment:	July 1st, 1999 – to date.
Participating nations:	OSCE members.
Strength:	Up to 700, during the implementation of elections temporarily more.
Headquarters:	Pristina.

Austrian Participation

Political Measures

The Council of Ministers decides on the dispatch of up to 20 civilian experts and up to five military logistical experts until July 31st, 2000.

Military Measures

The MoD dispatches two logistical experts.

Basis for deployment:	CM of July 13th, 1999, MC of July 13th, 1999.
Mission:	Securing of logistics and the internal organization of the mission; support during the establishment of the governmental structure.
Appellation:	None.
Form of dispatch:	FCL-CSD 1997.
Area of operations:	Kosovo.
Duration of deployment:	July 1st, 1999 – December 31st, 1999.
Contingent strength:	2.
Total:	4.

---

[109] Appellation of the mission from June 8th to June 30th, 1999.

Kosovo International Security Force (KFOR)

Preliminary Events

In the middle ages Kosovo is the center of the empire of the Serbian czars from the House of Nemanjić, which nevertheless collapses after a short time. A milestone and the foundation of the Serbian mythos is represented by the **Battle of Kosovo (Kosovo Polje)** on June 28th, 1389, which is the starting point of the 500-year Ottoman domination in this area. Both leaders fall in this battle, the Serbian Prince Lazar as well as Sultan Murad. Lazar's son Stefan recognizes the superior Ottoman authority. Prince George Kastriot "Skanderbeg" (1443 – 1468) defends himself against the Turks in northern Albania. His Byzantinian double eagle flag later becomes a national symbol for Albania. In 1453 the Ottomans conquer Constantinople and push forward again into the Balkans. In 1455 Kosovo becomes Ottoman, in 1459 the rest of Serbia as well. In 1689 and 1737 Austrian imperial troops advance into the area of Kosovo, but must withdraw again without success, during which large parts of the Serbian population flee into Habsburg territory. In 1878 after the Russian-Turkish War there is a new order established through the Congress of Berlin. Serbia and Montenegro become formally independent (de facto this has long been the case), Austria-Hungary occupies Bosnia-Herzegovina. 1878 also becomes the starting point for the Albanian nationalist movement. After the Balkan War of 1912/13 the European powers force the creation of Albania in roughly its modern borders as a neutral state, while Kosovo, despite a meanwhile large Albanian percentage of the population, falls to Serbia.

With the foundation of the South Slavic Kingdom in 1918 Kosovo becomes a part of Yugoslavia. In 1948 Kosovo receives autonomous status under Tito as a part of the Socialist Federal Republic of Yugoslavia (SFRY). In 1968 this autonomous status is expanded; Kosovo is renamed the **Socialist Autonomous Province of Kosovo**. Kosovo sends members to the federal parliament and a representative into the executive committee of the SFRY. It receives its own assembly (parliament), an executive committee (head of province) and an executive council (government). From 1981 serious conflicts occur between Serbs and Albanian nationalists, who demand a separate Kosovar republic. The country is constantly shaken by demonstrations and violent riots, although the government in Belgrade attempts to end the civil war-like situation with the held of the federal police. Since the conflicts increase, the Yugoslavian President Milosevic cancels Kosovo's autonomy in 1990. The crisis comes to a point. At this point in time the population consists of 87% Albanians and 9% Serbs. These possess the leadership functions in all public offices and national industries, besides all significant political offices.

While the efforts of the Albanian Kosovans for more rights initially have a completely peaceful character, the Albanian liberation army, **Ushtria Clirimtare e Kosoves (UCK)**, is founded at the end of the 1990's. With this, the "battle for liberation" takes on a new dimension. The "brigades" of the UCK consist of 100 to 500 fighters, who have partially gathered military experience in Yugoslavia and partially abroad. The UCK is led by former Yugoslavian officers who show outstanding experience in guerrilla warfare. The Serbian measures against the UCK are sometimes very brutally carried out, so there are displacement campaigns along the main connection streets in Kosovo. After deployments in the UCK strongholds of the Llap, Shala and Drenica regions, the UCK, which represents an instrument of terror and separatism for the Serbs, loses its base and backing. At the high point of the operation the number of people who have been driven or fled from their homes runs to around 300,000; up to 50,000 camp in the open air. Despite participation in negotiations in Rambouillet and Paris from March 15th – 19th, 1999, the Serbs continue the operation against the UCK and the civilian population. At the end of March the operation is in full swing, after further forces had been added. The battles spread to the Drenica region, in which the starting point of the UCK's battle in spring 1998 was the massacre of the Jahari clan by Serbs. After this the emphasis shifts to the area of Pec-Djakovica. The number of displaced persons climbs dramatically. In July and August Serbian troops smash the UCK core area with the center of Malisevo. The number of refugees rises to 265,000. On October 4th the Yugoslavian defence council declares its intention to defend against NATO attacks "by all means".

On October 13th, 1998, the **Holbrooke Milosevic Agreement** takes place. Milosevic partially gives in and allows the OSCE verification mission. Nevertheless a new massacre takes place on January 15th, 1999, during which this time 45 people are murdered in Racak. At the Kosovo conference in Rambouillet (February 6th – 23rd, 1999) and Paris (March 15th – 19th, 1999) the peace plan of the contact group is accepted by the Albanian, however not by the Serbian delegation. On March 22nd Milosevic causes the last interim mediation attempts of US negotiator Holbrooke to fail once again. One day later, on March 24th, 1999, shortly before the 50th anniversary of NATO existence, NATO Secretary General Solana distributes the **1st NATO deployment order.** 79 days of ever more intensive air battles, the emergence of the land deployment and the increasing success of the UCK finally lead to a capitulation from the Serbian government. On June 3rd, after negotiations between Milosevic and the Finnish President Ahtisaari, the Yugoslavian government and the Serbian parliament accept the international peace plan for Kosovo under clearly worse conditions than the Treaty of Rambouillet would have offered. On June 5th negotiations begin between NATO and the Serbian security forces about the Serbian withdrawal out of Kosovo. On June 9th the **"military-technical agreement"** is signed on the orderly and observed withdrawal of the Serbs as well as the stationing of the KFOR peacekeeping troop under the leadership of NATO.

On June 20th, 1999, the Yugoslavian battle and security forces conclude their troop withdrawal. Nevertheless there are signs that paramilitary forces have been left behind. On June 21st (K-Day) the UCK signed the **demilitarization agreement** with NATO. Besides the acceptance of the authority of KFOR, this includes the cessation of hostilities, the clearance of positions and the surrender of weapons to NATO. This should be concluded within 90 days of the signing. Furthermore, the UCK is forbidden to appear in uniform or wear the UCK insignia. All foreign advisors must immediately leave the nation. Here it is also certain that weapons are held back in secret caches.

Until the end of June 1999, despite all warnings of mine dangers, 400,000 refugees return to Kosovo, one month later it is already 700,000 (ca. 95%). All across Kosovo bloody battles go on under the eyes of the KFOR soldiers. Now the Serbs are displaced, arson and looting takes place through Kosovars. By the end of August, 180,000 Serbs leave Kosovo out of fear of revenge actions by the ethnically Albanian population. Members of the UCK appear publicly armed despite the ban on weapons and so attempt to cause a "legalization" of these circumstances.

On September 21st, 1999 (T-Day), the UCK is dissolved, parts are transferred into the **"Kosovo Protection Corps (PKPC)"**, in Albanian "Trpat Mbrojtese Kosoves (TMK)". This is a multiethnic civilian protection troop with the following duties:

- Provision of support for catastrophe and accidents;
- Search and rescue deployments;
- Humanitarian aid provision;
- Demining services;
- Reestablishment of the infrastructure.

International Reaction

In its Resolution 1160/1998 of March 31st, 1998, the UN Security Council calls for the authorities in Belgrade and the leaders of the Kosovar-Albanian ethnic group to immediately and unconditionally take up a sensible dialogue. On June 8th, 1998, the EU decides to freeze Yugoslavian foreign credits. Two days later the USA joins the EU sanctions. On June 15th NATO carries out the air maneuver **"Determined Falcon"** in Macedonia and Albania. On September 23rd the UN Security Council demands an immediate cease-fire in its Resolution 1199 (1998). The Serbian government is threatened with "further" measures. On September 24th NATO passes the **"activation warning"**. On October 12th NATO distributes the **"activation order"**, in which a believable potential threat is made possible by the collection of 430 fighter jets in Italy, and makes its readiness for air operations against Yugoslavia known. After the intensification of the conflict between the Serbs and Kosovar-Albanians the deployment of the OSCE mission KVM takes place in December 1998 in line with diplomatic reconciliation attempts, and from February 7th, 1999, on the basis of a 10-point plan, negotiations take place under the leadership of the EU in French Rambouillet near Paris. There are differences regarding a possible intervention between the Balkan contact group and the UN Security Council. This strengthens Milosevic in his hardline policies. The resulting refugee movements speed up the process of forming opinions within NATO. NATO threatens military air attacks in case peaceful reconciliation fails, in accordance with the condemnation of human rights violations by the UN in Resolution 1199 (1998). On March 23rd NATO Secretary General Solana distributes the deployment order for Operation **"Allied Force"**, on the next day NATO air attacks begin against military targets in Serbia. However there are drastic limitations made by the political leadership, which lead to additional work and expense for NATO troops which must not be underestimated:

- No losses on their own side;
- As few losses as possible among the civilian population in the target zone;
- As little collateral damage (damage to surroundings) as possible; and
- A short, limited war.

The air forces of 13 NATO nations participate in this operation, at the beginning of the attacks 430 airplanes (the USA provides 245 of these) are deployed. With the exception of the bombers and reconnaissance airplanes, all the aircraft initially start towards Italy. Besides the air fleet, cruise missiles are also deployed, which are sent from American (USS Phillippine, USS Sea, USS Gonzales, USS Norfolk) and British (HMS Splendid) submarines. France sends the aircraft carrier Foch to have a further base for aircraft available. The USA deploys its aircraft carrier the USS Theodore Roosevelt and England deploys its aircraft carrier the HMS Invincible. In total 20 ships are involved. The increasing scarcity of space on land and in the air leads to the redirection of the US reinforcements to outposts in Germany. So a further twelve F-117A stealth bombers operate from Spangdahlem from the middle of April. The first deployment of American B-2 bombers occurs directly from the USA. The number of airplanes rises over the course of the operation to 900 (a further increase to 1,100 was in fact prepared, but no longer carried out), the number of the daily deployments climbs from 300 at the beginning to 800 in the final phase. Refueling planes are also stationed in Hungary in order to be able to lower costs by shortening distances.

Also to be counted among Operation "Allied Force" is the contingent called "Task Force HAWK", consisting of 5,500 men, 22 "Apache" combat helicopters and 18 repeating rocket launcher systems. Despite pressure from General Clark, however, these forces are not released, although they would have been dependent on cooperation with ground troops for a successful deployment.

On the other hand, the "Allied Force" is accompanied by the "US Special Operation Command (SOCOM)" in Kosovo territory and by US special airplanes to send radio programs and to light targets.

The wave of refugees, unpredictable in its intensity, causes NATO to carry out a purely humanitarian aid operation already a few days after the begin of attacks, which demands further resources. After an intensive collaboration with UNHCR is started and aid measures already begin on April 1st, SACEUR General Clark orders Operation **Allied Harbour**" on April 16th. The commander of **"Allied Command Europe Mobile Force/Land" – AMF(L)** is assigned with the implementation.

Already on February 12th, 1998, NATO preemptively decides on the establishment of a peacekeeping troop with a strength of 28,000 – 32,000 men. Participation is also to be open to the members of the Partnership for Peace (PfP), who already form the parameters of this with the **"Extraction Force"** standing in Macedonia. For this reason, this contingent is also increased to 10,000 men. On June 9th and 10th, 1999, as a result of a peace plan of the G8 nations (the 7 leading industrial nations and Russia), a decision takes place through which the armed conflict is ended and the deployment of KFOR established. KFOR is to ensure the creation and maintenance of a safe environment for the entire population of Kosovo. The deployment is authorized with Resolution 1244 (1999) on the part of UNO. On June 11th the NATO council gives the activation order for Operation "Joint Guardian" for KFOR, which is under the command of the **"Allied Land Forces Central Europe (LANDCENT)"** until October 8th, 1999, and then under the **"Allied Command Europe Rapid Reaction Corps (ARRC)"**.

On June 12th, 1999, a British and a Spanish brigade march at the forefront of the NATO troops from Macedonia to Kosovo. Operation **"Joint Guardian"** begins.

The basic duties of KFOR consist of
- Establishment of a security presence in Kosovo;
- Inspection and enforcement of the agreements;
- Establishment of a secure environment as an prerequisite for international aid and the establishment of a transitional government and
- Provision of aid with the goal of a self-sustaining secure environment that allows the transfer of responsibility for the public safety to civilian organizations.

To accomplish this agreement, Kosovo is divided into five sectors, in each of which a multinational brigade operates under the responsibility of a lead nation. The German brigade, to which the Austrian contingent also belongs, operates in the south. A special problem is represented by the integration of a Russian contingent, which provides irritation on the part of the alliance through the surprise stationing of a small advance division of 200 paratroopers from SFOR at the airport in Pristina. Moscow insists on its own sector, which however is rejected by NATO as well as the Kosovar-Albanian population. In the beginning of July NATO prevails, the Russian contingent, with a strength of 3,616 men, is divided between the American, German and French sectors.

The growing organized crime (OC) makes KFOR and UNMIK's efforts to establish a stable security situation increasingly difficult. Since only 2,052 police are stationed from UNMIK/CIV-POL until spring 2000, the deployment of KFOR soldiers is also necessary for the maintenance of public peace and safety ("constablization").

In April 2000 the **Euro Corps**, of the Allied Rapid Reaction Corps (ARRC), takes over the leadership of KFOR. The responsibility ends on October 17th, 2000.

Basis for deployment:	National peace plan of June 3rd, 1999; military-technical agreement between NATO and Yugoslavia on the Yugoslavian troop withdrawal from Kosovo of June 9th, 1999 in Kumanovo (Macedonia); UNO Resolution 1244 (1999) of June 10th, 1999.
Mission:	Securing of the return to refugees in Kosovo; establishment and maintenance of a secure living environment in Kosovo.
Duration of deployment:	June 10th, 1999 – to date.
Participating nations:	The 19 NATO members (Belgium, Canada, the Czech Republic, Denmark, France, Germany, Great Britain, Greece, Hungary, Iceland, Italy, Luxembourg, the Netherlands, Norway, Poland, Portugal, Spain, Turkey, the USA), 12 PfP nations (Austria, Azerbaijan, Finland, Georgia, Ireland, Lithuania, Russia, Slovakia, Slovenia, Sweden, Switzerland, Ukraine) as well as Argentina, Jordan, Morocco and the United Arab Emirates.
Strength:	Initially 57,000; subsequent reduction to 43,000.
Headquarters:	Pristina.
Commander/MNTF S:	May 29th, 2008 – November 26th, 2008 Brigadier General Mag. Robert Prader November 27th, 2008 – May 28th, 2009 Brigadier General Mag. Thomas Starlinger
Chief of Staff:	May 25th, 2004 – November 11th, 2004 Colonel GS Christian Platzer May 18th, 2009 – November 27th, 2009 Colonel GS Mag. Johann Jamnig

Military Operations under the Framework of the Mission

"Joint Guardian": Implementation of the agreements between NATO and Yugoslavia; NATO PfP; SC Resolution 1244 (1999).

Austrian Participation

Political Measures

Already on February 15th, 1999, NATO directs a request to Austria as a PfP nation with regard to a possible participation in the multinational peacekeeping troop **"Kosovo Force" (KFOR)**. Subsequently, the Council of Ministers makes a basic resolution for participation in such a deployment on March 9th, since similarly to its IFOR/SFOR deployment, it is authorized by the UNO. The Austrian contingent is to be "dependent on cooperation" with the responsible KFOR command (so-called "operational control") and, in line with the VOREIN concept, to fulfill observation, security, protection and support duties. On June 15th the CM decides on the financing of the participation of the armed forces in the Kosovo mission. This takes place through a over-budget law, in which 366 million schillings are made available "for factually proven extra costs". The CM act of June 25th initially envisions an infantry contingent with armored personnel carriers of up to 450 men (in the first month up to 500 men) within the framework of the German brigade. Further, participation in the **"United Nations Interim Administration Mission in Kosovo" (UNMIK)** is decided upon. The necessary size of the contingent to fulfill its duties then forces the MoD to apply for an increase of up to 490 men, to cover an urgently needed peak demand up to 540 men. This is acceded to on November 23rd, 1999. Furthermore, on April 28th, 2000, it is also decided to match the spectrum of the Austrian unit's duties to those of KFOR (the debate and decision in the MC take place on June 14th, 2000). In particular this deals with the possibility of defence measures during attacks on KFOR forces and against armed persons who do not obey KFOR orders as well as the possibility of preventive measures for a deployment. Until then the Austrian contingent was not allowed to participate in violent measures for the defence of peace. The limited reaction possibility had also led to a higher risk for Austrian soldiers. The need for a stronger participation had also been shown by the events in Kosovska Mitrovica.

In October 2000, the Council of Ministers decides on a further extension by a year and an upper limit of 560 people. Through this up to 20 Officers/NCOs can be dispatched to COM/KFOR or to HQ/MNB(S) or to a temporary necessary camp construction command as needed without an additional CM act.

Military Measures

On June 23rd, 1999, two liaison officers take up to their duties in Prizren as staff members of the (GE)BrigCmd of the **"Multinational Brigade South" (MNB/S)** and for the preparation of the deployment of AUCON/KFOR. On June 30th talks take place with the Swiss General Staff with regards to the integration of SWISSCOY. On July 3rd both officers in Prizren are reinforced by 1 Ofc. and 1 NCO in the CIMIC area. On July 14th talks take place with the Slovakian General Staff with regards to the integration of SLOVCON. On July 19th the battalion commander, the assessment command, and seven Puch Gs move into the area of operations for a briefing at Cmd/MNB(S). On July 26th all the staff officers and staff noncommissioned officers assigned to HQ KFOR and HQ MNB(S), the assessment command for the construction of the camp, the air deployment as well as 20 administrative assistants all take part in the specific training for the area of operations. The movement itself is delayed, since no final assignment of the forces is available because of the behavior of the Russians. Finally the deployment plan is presented, the Austrian survey command becomes active and finds a suitable place for the camp in a rubber factory in Suva Reka. On August 18th it is time: Parts of the **"Camp Construction/KFOR"** contingent (in total 173 men with heavy engineering equipment, wheeled vehicles and Pandurs) move into the area of operations with an IL-76, an L100/30 on August 21st, as well as an IL-76 and L100/30 each on August 22nd and 23rd, and construct a tent camp there in the factory hall. On August 19th the advance command of SWISSCOY arrives in the area of operations, and on September 10th the main contingent of SLOVCON.

Through the assignment of the 2nd Russian Battalion in the German brigade's sector in the area of Orahovac, the Dutch battalion is assigned a new area of responsibility north of Prizren, including Suva Reka and Musutiste. Because of this, the deployment in AUCON's area must also be newly evaluated. Nevertheless, the camp in Suva Reca can be constructed. In the time from September 14th – 16th, the certification of AUCON/KFOR takes place through German officers in Strass in the 17th Infantry Battalion.

On September 17th, the loading of the trains begins in Leibnitz. The 2nd partial contingent initially shifts vehicles and equipment for this from Leibnitz to Koper. There it is loaded onto a ferry and taken to Saloniki. The team moves with an airplane. After the unloading they march by land to Suva Reka. At the same time the camp construction element moves back to Austria. The personnel of the 1st partial contingent already move on September 21st by air on board a rented South African C-130 to Saloniki. On September 23rd, the 1st and on October 10th, the 2nd partial contingent of AUCON/KFOR arrive in the area of operations after a forced march without stopping through Greece and Macedonia. The first deployment duties in line with MNB(S) must already be taken up on September 25th. On October 6th SWISSCOY arrives.

On October 8th, 1999, AUCON/KFOR takes over the full responsibility (Transfer of Authority – TOA) in the area of responsibility – AOR as **"Task Force Dulje"**.

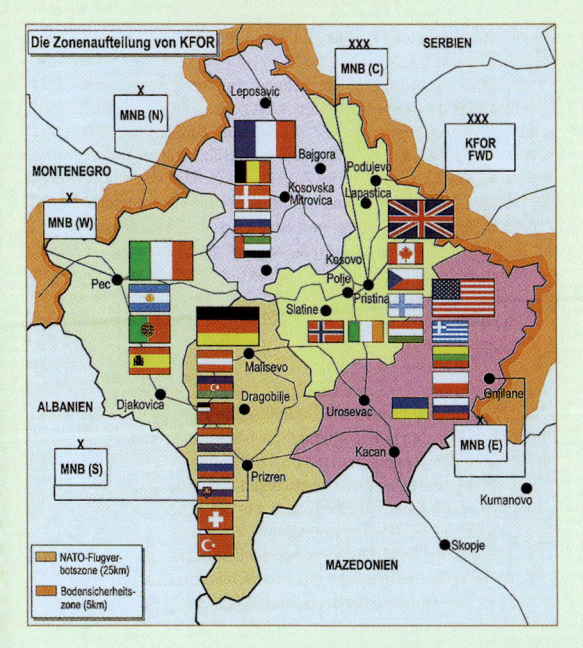

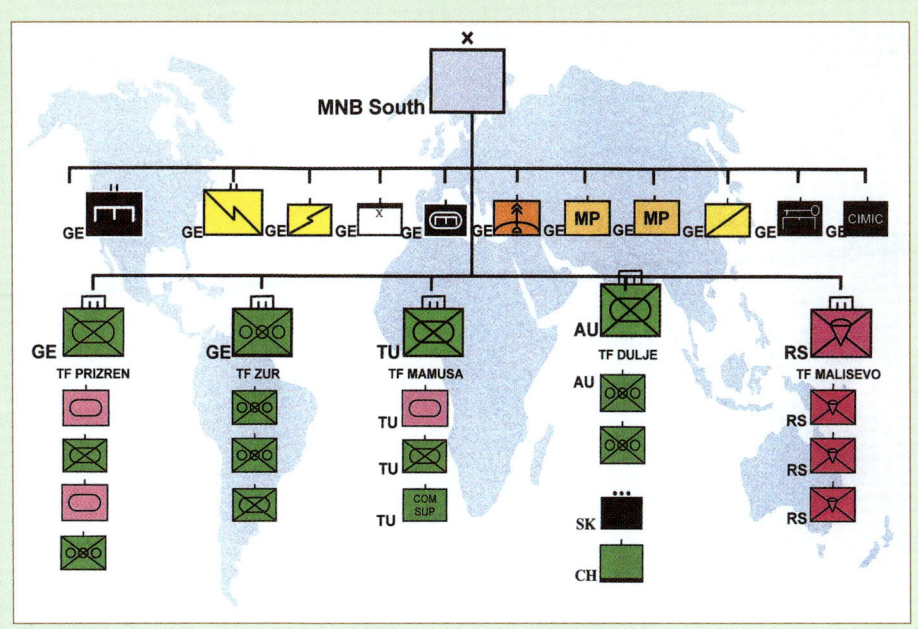

The 1st KFOR contingent is loaded in Langenlebarn in rented airplanes and on the train in the 19th Viennese district.

Their duties consist of:

- Implementation of patrols in its own AOR;
- Occupation of check points;
- Securing of escorts and protection for UNMIK, UN money transports, VIP visits, etc.;
- Support of transports of the (GE) EngBn;
- Protection arrangements for the civilian police;
- Holding open the lines of movement in its own AOR with emphasis on the Suva Reka – Stimlje road as well as
- Disposal of explosive ordnance;
- In addition assignments in line with the reserve deployment of parts of the MNB(S) must be fulfilled.

After the extension of the area of responsibility (AOR) in April 2000 this now stretches over 600 (before 350) square kilometers in partially impassable mountain regions with heights of up to 1,200 m. Around 70,000 inhabitants live in 81 villages. Above all the number of inhabitants in Suva Reka has increased by leaps and bounds. The duties, however, remain unchanged with the same means.

The AUCON soldiers fulfill more than just the function of **military security** in a destroyed region in their deployment. The battalion is the **police, emergency medical services, fire departments, road maintenance and contact person in every situation.** Through this multifaceted work the soldiers enjoy the full trust of the population and give them a feeling of security just through their presence. Together with Austrian aid organizations, the soldiers also ensure the most comprehensive and fair distribution of the aid goods coming from Austria.

Austrian soldiers are deployed four times in the year 2000 alone outside of their own area of responsibility for **crisis management:**

Since the area of Mitrovica in the French sector constantly represents hot spot number 1, a regular reinforcement of the "Multinational Brigade North (MNB/N)" is necessary. For this an armInfPl in line with a Turkish-German-French company under German command and a French battalion for provisions are assigned for deployment. In line with this routine an armored infantry platoon from Task Force Dulje is also to be placed to guard the camp for 96 hours from February 5th. An armInfPl under the command of the German company is planned for this in February 2000. All preparations have been made, when a serious incident occurs of February 3rd. An UNHCR bus occupied by Serbs is shot by anti-tank guns. One day later there are serious riots, during which two Serbs and an Albanian are killed. The HQ in Pristina therefore increases the KFOR presence in the city in order to make the transport of illegal weapons and explosive ordnance more difficult. So the company initially prepared to secure the camp receives the assignment of taking up inspections on one of the two bridges over the Sitnica. The checkpoint is occupied under the most difficult conditions (thickest fog with a visibility of 10 m). Despite the most stringent inspections, from engine to trunk, no incidents occur. A few Austrian soldiers are only greeted with a thumb pointed downwards. This is however the result of the fact that the soldiers wear French flak jackets and so are taken for French. After they make themselves known as Austrians, the behavior immediately changes as a result of their good reputation. Incidentally, the mine search equipment proves itself during the search of female persons.

In April the American eastern sector is temporarily "Hot Spot No. 1". Problems with Serbian and Albanian inhabitants on the Kosovar side and open conflicts in Presevoltal overpower the forces in the area. Twelve injured Americans and a Serb shot in self-defence by a Swede prove how difficult the situation is. On April 7th the new Austrian contingent is asked if the Austrians are in a position to place a new company. The question can be positively answered. And so an armInfCoy is deployed in Gniljane from April 9th – April 18th, 2000 as a KFOR reserve. The duties are similar to those in February in Mitrovica. During inspection activities at the checkpoint the Austrians then succeed in making the big "catch": Potato chips are officially loaded in a small bus with a Serbian license plate and two Albanian occupants. The soldiers notice, however, that the vehicle is sitting far too low for such a load. During the inspection the soldiers make the largest illegal weapons discovery yet. Besides hand armaments, anti-tank weapons and the munition belonging to them, 77 TM-A5 tank mines and 44 hand grenades are also secured. The careful examination of the vehicle however also brings to light that the suspension is reinforced and further customization has been done. This is enough proof for the already long-suspected weapons smuggling. The deployment is even officially praised in Brussels, which is by no means a matter of course. It can be considered an even greater recognition that this deployment to reinforce the US contingent was even mentioned with praise on April 11th in the "Stars and Stripes", the magazine of the US armed forces, published worldwide. This deployment can be seen as a model deployment for the transfer to another brigade, since a closed company was drawn upon for the first time for this.

One deployment shapes up politically to be especially sensitive: In the middle of the time of the EU boycott against Austria, the Belgian battalion under French command is to be reinforced from August 8th – 18th. In the area of Kosovska Mitrovica there is a lead foundry which scoffs at all environmental regulations. Because of the blockade raised by the UNMIK, unrest among the workers is feared. The French commander makes this area his emphasis. A Belgian company is assigned as a reserve. In the area of operations a reinforced company of AUCON moves in. The company is reinforced by a German platoon with a "Fuchs" armored personnel carrier and a "Luchs" reconnaissance group as well as Swiss medical, communications and provisions units. Smuggling must be suppressed in an area inhabited almost exclusively by Serbs with a long border with Serbia, 2,000 m above sea level. The cooperation between the four nations shapes up without any notable problems. On August 18th the company is relieved by a German company from the ZUR task force. This in turn is reinforced with a platoon of the 1st Armored Infantry Company.

When Russian soldiers are fired upon, platoon strength forces from AUCON are deployed in the Russian AOR, among other things to guard the Russian camp, but also in order to patrol with Russian and German solders. Through this they can demonstrate to the population that the KFOR mission is a concern of the international community and no wedge can be forced between the contingents.

The camp is constructed in a rubber factory in Suva Reka through engineers especially transferred into the area of operations for this.

KFOR insignia

273

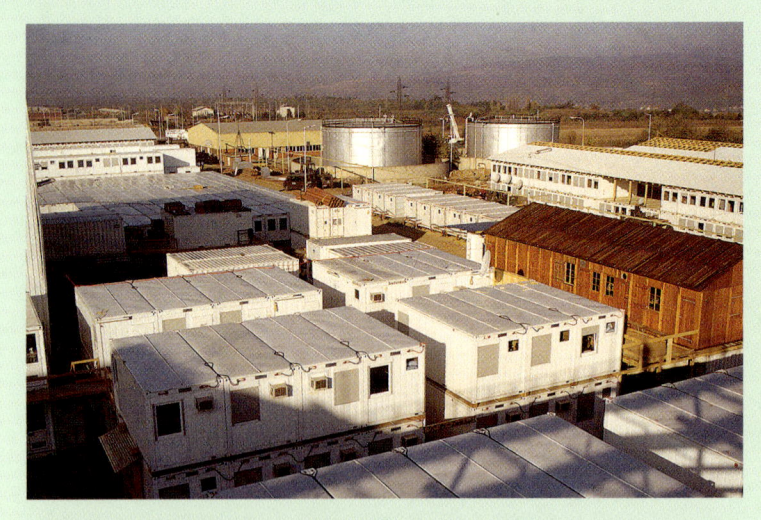

"Camp Casablanca" with its white shelters (t.l.). Rainbow over the tent city (t.r.).
Staff meeting in one of the Drash tents (m.l.). Austrian KFOR soldiers also guard UNMIK headquarters in Suva Reka (m.r.). The most modern communication equipment is available for the connection to HQ and the homeland (b.l.). The cell phone must serve for very private conversations. And one can also determine how far it is to the homeland at the same time (b.r.).

But Austrian KFOR soldiers also prove themselves in other areas: During their withdrawal the Serbs took all the keys to the office safes with them. However, all records are in these **safes**, for instance on land tenure. At the request of the mayor the detonation experts open the steel boxes with a regulated charge. The main duty of these specialists, however, is in the battle against the 100,000s of **mines** laid by Serbs in buildings as well as in fields and meadows. In addition there are also thousands of unexploded bombs of all calibers, not only from the Serbs but from the NATO bombardment. Five years are needed in order to remove only 50%. However mines and heat also make the cultivation of the fields impossible. Aid with foodstuffs, which is in the hands of SLOVCON, must therefore be extended for an indeterminate period.

The EOD teams' "safe crackers" open the steel boxes with linear cutter charges at the angles of the door and the bolts. The locks are broken above all with hollow charges. Just about everything is found, such as UCK passes, dinars, jewelry, documents, weapons, munitions, etc. (WO I Scherz).

The following example should illustrate how outstandingly the **international cooperation** functions: An Austrian vehicle falls around 40 m in a traffic accident in March 2000. The drivers loses his life, the passenger is seriously injured. Despite the acute danger of mines he is recovered by Albanians, Polish soldiers provide first aid, an American military doctor operates on the captain, German soldiers spontaneously donate blood. Afterwards the patient is brought to Macedonia by a US helicopter.

On the other hand incidents can occur which are unforeseeable and prove the danger of the deployment: Two Austrian soldiers, including the NCC, who travelled to support the Austrian team are hurt during the European handball final in Macedonia in May 2000. As a consequence it must be ordered that soldiers can only go out in threes and in civilian clothes (none are present!). In fall 2000 the number of officers at HQ-KFOR is increased to twelve and those with the MNB(S) staff to eight.

At the beginning of winter 2000 the power plant in Pristina is partially taken offline. Not only the drinking water supply is affected, but also the functioning capacity of the health care center in Suva Reka. Subsequently there are increased aid requests to AUCON, which together with the Samaritan Alliance of Austria can often be complied with.

The war crimes trial, beginning in Prizren on January 22nd, 2001 (planned duration until January 28th), has repercussions for AUCON/KFOR. The criminal defence lawyers are to be accommodated securely in Camp Casablanca. Increased security measures are taken around the camp. On court days a platoon with **"riot control equipment"** is held in readiness for an alert. Finally a special forces troop with a helicopter is also ready during the phase moving to or from the courtroom.

The international discussion on the supposed danger of enriched uranium (EU) leads to intensive inspections with the Austrians as well. As with all other contingents – as expected – no raised radioactivity levels can be measured.

In March 2001 parts of the contingent (Austrian National Intelligence Cell – AUNIC, Brigade Staff/AUCON) move from the Progres military camp to the Prizren military camp. In addition a construction command in the strength of ten men is formed by the Pioneer Troop School and dispatched to Kosovo on March 8th.

Expansion of the Area of Responsibility 2002
At the beginning of June 2002 the Swiss-Austrian Task Force Dulje's area of responsibility is enlarged from 407 square kilometers to 565 square kilometers by the withdrawal of the Russian contingent from the area of Malishevo. Since the security situation in Kosovo is noticeably better and the merge of the multinational Brigades South and West into MNB (SW) is planned for the beginning of December, the German leadership decides on a renewed expansion of the area of operations. This takes place within the framework of a ceremonial celebration on Saturday, November 2nd,

2002 in Orahovac. At this event the commander of the Task Force Dulja, Lieutenant Colonel Norbert Pallan, receives the key for **Area of Responsibility** (AOR)[110] ZUR. With this the area of operations grows by another 45% to 960 square kilometers. These region is separated into three regional districts, namely Orahovac, Malishevo and Suva Reka. In total around 210,000 people live in this area, of which there are 1,350 Kosovar-Serbs as well as 330 Roma and members of other ethnic groups. This drastic enlargement of the area of responsibility leads to the fact that the duties assigned to the battalion can no longer be carried out with the forces available at the time. Therefore the Task Force Dulje is assigned a German mechanized infantry company for tactical assignments. So in the future one sees German, Swiss and Austrian soldiers on patrol together. Notable in this context is that Austria, as the only non-NATO member, is responsible for its own area of responsibility.

Under American Command
On July 27th, 2003, for the first time in the history of the 2nd Republic, an Austrian company is placed with the US Army, concretely to the Task Force 1-111 Infantry of the US National Guard, which in turn represents one of the battalions of the US Multinational Brigade East in Kosovo. The armored company, predominately recruited from Tyroleans and Vorarlbergers, relieves a French company after a three-day overlap and orientation into the terrain. For the Austrians this is a major challenge. The company is given a hearty farewell from Camp Casablanca with trumpets and best wishes from the staff of Task Force Dulje.

Reinforcement 2004
Defence Minister Günther Platter decides, after consultations with the General Staff on March 19th, 2004, to reinforce the military contingent in Kosovo by around 90 men. The soldiers are to relieve the around 500 man strong military contingent in Kosovo. Through the reduction of the German army in Kosovo, Task Force Dulje is assigned an additional German company in the rotation in April 2004. This is combined with the enlargement of the task force's area of responsibility (AOR). This causes a changed picture of the situation from AUCON 10 for Austria, as leading nation of Task Force Dulje. From April 2004 the task force consists of the Austrian headquarters company, two armored Austrian infantry companies, two German armored infantry companies and a Swiss company.

Transformation 2006
The division of the Multinational Brigade South West (MNB SW) into the "Multinational Task Force West" (MNTF W) and the **"Multinational Task Force South" (MNTF S)**, into which the mass of the Austrian contingent is integrated since the transformation in May 2006, brings significant changes for AUCON/KFOR as well: Besides the retention of occupancy in the KFOR headquarters, the participation in the MNTF S headquarters is seriously increased. The Austrian participation in the multinational logistic unit (MNLU), the assumption of the role of framework nation (FN) in the area of the liaison and monitoring teams (LMT), and from fall 2006 also participation in the multinational reconnaissance company, all represent new challenges. The mass of AUCON serves within the framework of the **Maneuver Battalion (MAN BN) Dulje** in position in Suva Reka (Camp Casablanca), one of three MAN BNs of the MNTF S. The MAN BN Dulje includes, besides the AUT headquarters company and two AUT deployment companies, a Swiss deployment company and is deployed in heavy concentrations in three districts (so-called municipalities).

New KFOR Structure 2010
As a result of the constant improvement of the security situation in Kosovo, the Kosovo Force can take on a new structure on February 1st, 2010. The mass of the heavy forces is returned step by step to their homelands. At the same time more value is laid on mobility. The "Multinational Task Force South" is changed into **"Multinational Battle Group South (MNBG S)"**. Deployment companies take the place of the previous deployment battalion. This means a structural change for the Austrian contingent as well: The Dulje deployment battalion is dissolved and changed into the **Austrian National Element (AUNE)**; the 1st (Austrian) and the 3rd (Swiss) company are now directly led by MNBG S. Parallel to this, the situational awareness structures are so developed that the possibility exists for the transfer to a civilian mission by 2011.

Basis for deployment:	CM of March 9th, 1999 and of June 15th, 1999 (basic agreement to participation); CM of June 25th, 1999, MC of July 1st, 1999 (dispatch).
Mission:	Fulfillment of duties according to the Austrian participation on the basis of the participation requirements agreed upon in the Operational Plan "Joint Guardian" of NATO from June 9th, 1999 within the framework of the Task Force Tulje, which belongs to the Multi National Brigade MNB (S) led by Germany: patrol activities; observation of inspection points; escort protection; humanitarian aid. SWISSCOY operates provisioning establishments, supports the construction of the infrastructure and the CIMIC projects and secures the guard of Camp "Casablanca" in rotation with other forces. SLOVCON supports the infrastructure construction and carries out demining.
Appellation:	**Austrian Contingent (AUCON/KFOR)** (until January 31st, 2010); **Austrian National Element (AUNE/KFOR)** (from February 1st, 2010).
Form of dispatch:	FCL-CSD.

---

110 Area of responsibility.

Area of operations:	Suva-Reka, furthermore Austrians are also deployed in the divided city Kosovska Mitrovica and in Gniljane as well as border observation duties on the Macedonian and Albanian borders.	
Duration of deployment:	July 2nd, 1999 – to date.	
Contingent strength:	488 Austrians, 140 Swiss, 40 Slovaks.	
Total:	10,000 (as of December 31st, 2010).	
Composition (as of 2009):	Contingent command, battalion command with the headquarters company, armored infantry company with "Pandurs", logistics company (Swiss), engineering platoon (Slovakia), air element MEDEVAC, national reconnaissance cell (NRC), national counter intelligence element, CIMIC element.	
Contingent commanders:	August 16th, 1999 – April 4th, 2000	Colonel GS Karl Pernitsch (1)
	April 5th, 2000 – September 19th, 2000	Colonel GS Johann Luif (2)
	September 20th, 2000 – April 7th, 2001	Colonel GS Alois Frühwirth
	April 8th, 2001 – October 8th, 2001	Colonel GS Helmut Habermayer (4)
	October 9th, 2001 – April 8th, 2002	Colonel GS Robert Brieger (5)
	April 9th, 2002 – October 7th, 2002	Colonel GS Karl-Heinz Wiedner (6)
	October 8th, 2002 – April 2003	Colonel GS Reinhard Schöberl[111] (7)
	April 2003 – October 29th, 2003	Colonel GS Michael Janisch (8)
	October 30th, 2003 – April 6th, 2004	Colonel GS Gerhard Weiner (9)
	April 7th, 2004 – November 10th, 2004	Colonel GS Christian Platzer (10)
	November 11th, 2004 – May 10th, 2005	Colonel GS Franz Hollerer (11)
	May 11th, 2005 – November 9th, 2005	Colonel GS Markus Koller (12)
	November 10th, 2005 – April 27th, 2006	Colonel GS Dr. Karl Schmidseder (13)
	April 28th, 2006 – November 20th, 2006	Colonel GS Horst Hofer (14)
	November 21st, 2006 – February 2007	Colonel GS Peter Deckenbacher (15)
	February 2007 – July 2007	Colonel GS Norbert Gehart (16)
	July 2007 – January 29th, 2008	Brigadier General Reinhard Schöberl (16)
	January 30th, 2008 – May 2008	Colonel GS Mag. Jürgen Wörgötter (17)
	May 2008 – November 2008	Brigadier General Mag. Robert Prader (18)
	November 2008 – May 27th, 2009	Brigadier General Mag. Thomas Starlinger (19)
	May 27th, 2009 – July 20th, 2009	Brigadier General Mag. Bernhard Christiner[112] (21)
	July 20th, 2009 – January 27th, 2010	Brigadier General MMag. Norbert Huber (21)
	January 28th, 2010 – May 19th, 2010	Colonel GS MMag. Jürgen Ortner (22)
	May 20th, 2010 – September 17th, 2010	Colonel GS MMag. Klaus Anderle (22)
	September 18th, 2010 – May, 2011	Colonel GS Mag. Riener (23)
	May, 2011 – to date	Colonel GS MMag. Dr. Andreas Stupka (24)
Commanders:	July 2nd, 1999 – July 31st, 1999	Lieutenant Colonel GS Mag. Karl Schmidseder
	August 1st, 1999 – August 15th, 1999	Major GS Wolfgang Luttenberger
	August 16th, 1999 – April 4th, 2000	Lieutenant Colonel Hans Tomaschitz (AUCON 1)
	April 5th, 2000 – October 7th, 2000	Lieutenant Colonel Johann Hornung (AUCON 2)
	October 8th, 2000 – April 7th, 2001	Lieutenant Colonel Herbert Pachinger (AUCON 3)
	April 8th, 2001 – October 8th, 2001	Lieutenant Colonel Ernst Konzett (AUCON 4)
	October 9th, 2001 – April 6th, 2002	Lieutenant Colonel Emmerich Bauer (AUCON 5)
	April 7th, 2002 – October 7th, 2002	Lieutenant Colonel Franz Langthaler (AUCON 6)
	October 8th, 2002 – April 2003	Lieutenant Colonel Norbert Pallan (AUCON 7)
	April 2003 – October 17th, 2003	Lieutenant Colonel Josef Hartl (AUCON 8)
	October 18th, 2003 – April 6th, 2004	Lieutenant Colonel Anton Willmann (AUCON 9)
	April 7th, 2004 – October 2004	Lieutenant Colonel Wolfgang Kaufmann (AUCON 10)
	October 2004 – April 18th, 2005	Lieutenant Colonel Franz Baumgartner (AUCON 11)
	April 19th, 2005 – October 8th, 2005	Lieutenant Colonel Ferdinand Klinser (AUCON 12)
	October 9th, 2005 – April 5th, 2006	Lieutenant Colonel Reinhard Kunert (AUCON 13)
	April 8th, 2006 – October 14th, 2006	Lieutenant Colonel Herbert Pachinger (AUCON 14)
	October 15th, 2006 – March 31st, 2007	Lieutenant Colonel Bernd Aschauer (AUCON 15)
	April 1st, 2007 – October 13th, 2007	Lieutenant Colonel Ronald Schmied (AUCON 16)
	October 14th, 2007 – March 29th, 2008	Lieutenant Colonel Volkmar Ertl (AUCON 17)
	March 30th, 2008 – September 27th, 2008	Lieutenant Colonel Hans-Otto Hrbek (AUCON 18)
	September 28th, 2008 – April 6th, 2009	Lieutenant Colonel Manfred Hofer (AUCON 19)[113]
	April 7th, 2009 – October 2nd, 2009	Lieutenant Colonel Ulfried Khom (AUCON 20)
	October 3rd, 2009 – March 23rd, 2010	Lieutenant Colonel Johann Gaiswinkler (AUCON 21)
	March 24th, 2010 – October, 2010	Major Alfred Steingreß (AUNE 22)
	October, 2010 – March 28th, 2011	Lieutenant Colonel Daniel Handej MSD (23)
	March 29th, 2011 – to date	Lieutenant Colonel Reinhard Bacher MSD (24)

111 Simultaneously DCOS (Deputy Chief of Staff).
112 Prior to this BG Chistiner is Deputy Chief of Staff since January 21st, 2009.
113 The first military contingent abroad which consists entirely of professional soldiers from cadre presence units (see Task Force 18).

Preparation for Deployment[114]

The takeover of the area of responsibility of the Multinational Task Force South (MNTF S) in Kosovo by Brigadier General Mag. Robert Prader on May 29th, 2008 is preceded by almost a year of preparation and planning. The first step in spring 2007 is the formation of a planning staff for the formation and training of the **"Maneuver Battalion Dulje" (ManBn Dulje)** and the staff of the MNTF S. Initially the 14th Tank Battalion in Wels is chosen as a kind of godparent unit for ManBn Dulje and simultaneously is assigned with the advertisement for personnel. At the conclusion of the planning phase the brigade commander moves into Kosovo at the beginning of September 2007 with the planned key personnel. The goal of this fact finding mission is to test the basics worked out in the planning phase in the area of operations and to get a first picture of the situation on site.

To secure the necessary foreign language knowledge for the foreign deployment, the foreign language training regularly carried out since 2004 at the brigade command is intensified by two trainers from the Armed Forces Language Institute. The emphasis lies on holding situation reports, the preparation of order contributions, as well as the operation of the reporting system. A three-day intensive seminar for immediate preparation for the multinational staff framework exercise **"Cooperative Longbow (COLW)"** in Albania rounds off this training segment.

During the staff framework exercise COLW in Albania the staff officers and noncommissioned officers planned for the MNTF S Command at this time can first be assigned and exercised in the appropriate functions in the framework of the multinational exercise staff. The experience won by all exercise participants in the framework of the multinational staff work stands in the foreground as the training goal.

In June 2007 the 3rd Tank Artillery Battalion (3rd TkArtBn) is given the responsibility for the training of ManBn Dulje. With this, a constant training situation until transfer into the area of operations is created. The deployment preparation is infrastructurally benefited by the fact that special training establishments for peace support operations, such as the company outpost on Toten Berg, the checkpoint at the town entrance after Steinbach as well as the village of Steinbach itself have been available at Allentsteig Military Training Ground for quite some time. The Liechtenstein Barracks are established as a camp for two deployment companies, a headquarters company with its infrastructural establishments, the battalion command post as well as all of the elements directly led by the MNTFs. Besides the individual command posts, accommodations, garages, workshops, care facilities, the camp exit is also adapted with trailers, concrete elements, sandbags and post stands so that this delicate area conforms to a multinational deployment and a possible escalating threat situation.

In order to optimally implement a deployment preparation, the area of operations is "transferred" to the military training ground, in which the border communities of Allentsteig, Göpfritz, and Pölla are included with which to represent the civilian environment and the daily life. Kosovar government areas, villages, cultural sites, major supply lines, and KFOR establishments are assigned and determined on the training map. So the special protected property of the Zociste cloister is in Steinbach, Velika Hoca is in Bernschlag, Orahovac is in Allentsteig and Musutiste in Merkenbrechts.

The training map is supplemented with information on the mine situation as well as wayside points as the communication system. In order to realistically represent the temporal situation as well as the physical situation, the constant deployment rhythm is simulated as realistically as possible, during which the assumption of the Operational Reserve Force (ORF) of the 24th Infantry Battalion as a third deployment element has positive results, since in ManBn Dulje the SWISSCOY carries out its duty as a third company.

Parallel to the deployment-specific training on the level of the individual soldier, the half-platoon, the platoon, and the company, the key personnel of the battalion staff and the company command are challenged by the duties actually carried out in leadership proceedings and in the giving of orders: These concern the evacuation of a liaison monitoring team from Orahovac (the Allentsteig movie theater), the protection of the special protected property the Zociste cloister (Steinbach) by all means and possibilities, the implementation of a go and see visit in Musutishte (Merkenbrechts) and the reinforcement of a neighboring MNTF with company strength forces.

The concluding deployment preparation in the Deployment Preparation Center in Götzendorf serves for the teaching and adjustment of training topics in the areas of mine dangers, general dangers in the area of operations, nation and people, first aid for oneself and comrades, general social, defence and legal compensation issues, and family care.[115]

Task Force 18

In year 2007 the armed forces expand the cadre presence units (CPU) by a battalion command (BnCmd) as well as a headquarters company (HQCoy), which are placed in addition to the present infantry forces. Task Force 18 (TF18), with a seat of the command in the 18th Infantry Battalion in St. Michael, consists of cadre presence companies of the 17th, 24th and 25th Infantry Battalions as well as parts of the headquarters company of the 18th and 19th Infantry Battalions. From these sections a cadre presence battalion is formed for the first time in the history of the armed forces. This has its first practical test in the "Pacemaker07" and "Pacemaker08" exercises in Allentsteig, where Task Force 18 is put under a NATO evaluation, which comes out positive for the battalion.

A further assignment of the TF18 is the formation of the Maneuver Battalion "Dulje" in the 19th Austrian KFOR contingent (AUCON19/KFOR). Primarily trained and held ready for first deployments, the mass of Task Force 18 carries out a six-month deployment in Kosovo according to the phased plan of the KPE soldiers. The soldiers also discharge the contractual obligation of all cadre presence soldiers for at least six months use abroad during their three year commitment.

---

114 On the example of the 4th Mechanized Infantry Brigade.
115 Gerhard Bojtos, Reinhard Lemp: "Leadership of the MNTF S – A Year of Deployment Preparation with the 4th Mechanized Infantry Brigade".

Air Element

On January 9th, 2003, two Austrian helicopters of the type Agusta Bell AB-212 land at Airfield Toplicane after a total flight time of nine hours and 29 minutes, in order to take up their duty in Multinational Brigade South West. The arrival is appropriately ceremonially staged for the event. A full complement of two armored infantry platoons of the 1st and the 2nd company stand to receive them at Airfield Spalier. This is the first time in the history of the 2nd Republic that an Austrian air element is deployed with a peace support operation.

At the end of May 2008, in the course of taking over the command of the Multinational Task Force South (MNTF S) by Brigadier General Mag. Robert Prader, a reinforcement of the mixed military air division (Air Aviation Battalion "Mercury" – AAVN Bn "Mercury", a multinational helicopter unit) takes place in Toplicane with Austrian Air Forces. For the first time Austrian SA-316B Alouette III connection helicopters and S-70A "Black Hawk" transport helicopters are deployed with KFOR, which relieve the previously used Agusta Bell 212s.[116] The "Mercury" multinational helicopter division is commanded by an officer of the German Army and has a total of 14 helicopters from three nations available. The largest proportion (eight Agusta Bell 205 transport helicopters) are provided by Germany and the second largest (four helicopters) by Austria. Switzerland participates with two "Super Puma" transport helicopters.

The Austrian helicopters cover a broad spectrum of duties: The Alouette III carries out people and freight transports as well as reconnaissance and surveillance flights by day and night (the pilots wear night vision goggles for that). The "Black Hawk" primarily serves for troop transports by day and night. It can carry 12 passengers or ten crowd and riot control forces (CRC forces)[117] with equipment as well as outer or inner weight transports of larger breadth, but also carry out firefighting deployments. All deployments of the Austrian helicopters go through the multinational command of Task Force South. 431 people are transported in 201 flight hours with the Alouette III; both S70 "Black Hawks" bring it to 3,110 people and 16.5 t in 172 flight hours.

With the end of the Austrian brigade leadership the Alouette III and Black Hawks are returned to Austria and replaced by AB-212s.

S-70A "Black Hawk" transport helicopters (t.l., Gunter Pusch). On December 31st, 2008, the opening of the first helicopter hangar takes place. In the new maintenance hall, two "Black Hawks" have place at the same time. Inside the helicopters are protected from the weather. Because of its form the hangar is named "Moby Dick" by the soldiers (t.r. Rosenblattl). An Agusta Bell AB-212 (b.l.) over Orahovac (WO I Alfred Sattmann) and an Alouette III connection helicopter (b.r.).

---

116 The Alouette III already flew in the EUFOR mission in Bosnia; this is the premier deployment of the "Black Hawk".
117 These forces are deployed in case of a demonstration, unrest or similar things.

Daily life at AUSCON/KFOR: Patrol activities in the city (l.) and in the country (b.). In the picture below KFOR forces can be seen before an action against smugglers. The leadership of the deployment takes place from the AUSCON/KFOR commander from a German helicopter.

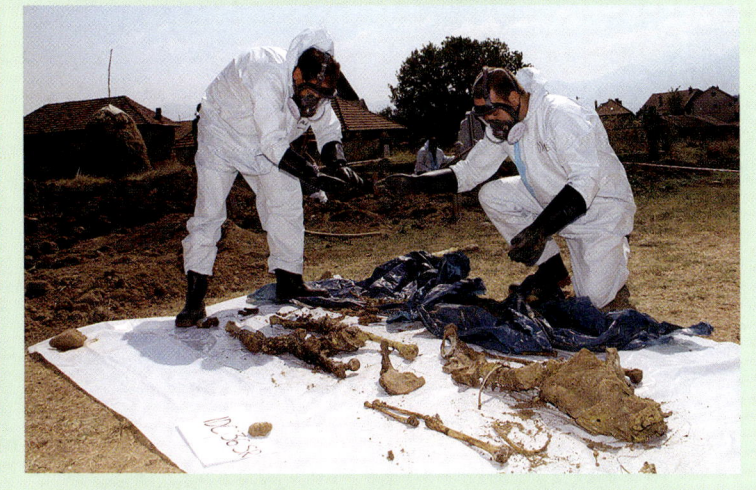

The Austrian soldiers attempt to immediately adapt to the circumstances everywhere: So some Pandur crews craft themselves protection from the blistering sun out of corrugated iron sheeting for their stationary inspection activities (t.l.). Special helmets with protective visors are distributed for the use of the heavy machine gun (t.r.). Unthinkable not long ago: Austrian soldiers protect a Russian camp in Kijevo from attacks by the local population (m.l.). Everyday sadness: Forensic examinations must be carried out for the UNO war criminals tribunal, which includes exhumations (m.r.). The maintenance and repair has a very special meaning while deployed (b.).

Vehicles

AUCON/KFOR is the first division abroad which has access to **"Pandur" armored personnel carriers**. Besides the 27 "Pandurs", around 100 further wheeled vehicles as well as 28 trailers are in use. The armored personnel carriers are equipped with mine search and night vision equipment; besides this PAR66/79 anti-tank weapons are carried along. The MG gunner has a helmet with a protective visor (see page 280 and 281). In addition, there is another Pandur in a medical specification (m.l.).

In fall 2004 tanks are deployed abroad for the first time with the transfer of four **"Kürassier A2"** light tanks (m.r.). With this reinforcement, riots in the course of the elections in October 2004 are to be preemptively hindered.[118]

At the end of November 2005 seven **all-protected transport vehicles (APTV) "Dingo 2"** follow (b.l.). The Dingo covers the essential requirements which come up for troops in international deployment with its configuration, efficiency and equipage. Although this is not a battle vehicle, its mobility, protection and equipage allow it to transport soldiers in an unsecured area. Predominantly reconnaissance and surveillance duties are to be executed with the new vehicle in obstructed but also in open terrain.

The Dingo has the most modern communication equipment such as a satellite telephone, radio and GPS. A 7.62 mm machine gun is available as the weapon on board. The Dingo offers protection from the effects of mines, shrapnel as well as shots from small arms weapons. Besides its function as a team transporter (three man basic crew and five further people), the Dingo is deployed as a troop vehicle with mission appropriate equipment and armament.

Within the framework of the Kosovo contingent the following deployment possibilities emerge: Protection of areas and properties, protection of transports, establishment and operation of inspection points, deployment during civilian unrest and evacuations. Finally AUCON/KFOR also receives a **Nissan "Pathfinder"** for the military police (b.r.) to test.

---

118   Major General Christian Ségur-Cabanac in a press conference.

Stop! – Military Police!

The armed forces first participate in the international military police element within the framework of the Kosovo deployment. As already during the SFOR deployment, Austria places the **Deputy Provost Marshall (DPM)** in Kosovo and furthermore the commander of the multinational MP station in Suva Reka. Among the international duties of the military police are order duty, traffic duty, personal protection, uprising duty, security police duty and cooperation with the local police. In addition to this is the protection of their own troops as a national duty.[119] "Watch out, radar!" also incidentally applies in Kosovo (see picture).

Personal Protection (Close Protection Team – CPT)

When Brigadier General Mag. Robert Prader takes over the command of the Multinational Task Force South the question of the personal protection of the commander arises, since according to international norms the commander of a brigade is seen as a "good worthy of protection".

The implementation of personal protection for a constant protectee abroad hardly differs in the essentials from the work in the usual environment in Austria, where protectees are basically only temporarily to be protected as guests of the Federal Ministry of Defence. With the assumption of the function of commander of the MNF N by the Austrians, the personal bodyguards are deployed abroad for a longer period of time for the first time. The protocollary leadership of the visit program in Kosovo is in the hands of the military assistants of the commander of the Multinational Task Force South. An exact timetable of the departure and arrival times is coordinated with the CPT, since each driving or flying time must be calculated into the timetable. The strength and equipment of the CPT varies according to the level of endangerment of the protectee. The commander of MNTF S keeps his appointments in most cases with the aid of a helicopter, where one of two close protectors are along in the aircraft. The rest of the team moves with vehicles to the site of the appointment, in order as far as possible to secure a back-up with the vehicles at the onset of bad weather or the technical failure of the helicopter. Here there are no differences from a deployment in Austria. In contrast to Austria, where deployments are only carried out in civilian clothing, the CPs in Kosovo are generally out in uniform. The P 80 pistol as well as the assault rifle 77 and/or the P 90 pistol belong to the constant equipment of the CPT abroad. On some occasions bodyguards are also equipped with all-purpose shotguns, sniper rifles, or similar. The CPT is connected with each other by the team radios, which are optionally equipped with a so-called "bodyguard kit" or with an inductive headset.[120]

"Combat Camera Team" (CCT)

The Combat Camera Team is the national media element for the support of the staff of the Multinational Task Force South in Kosovo under the command of Brigadier General Mag. Robert Prader. Two Austrian soldiers are responsible for taking pictures in the area of operations and their archiving. This team serves to create information on operations of the MNTF S, exercises, deployments and activities, during and after military maneuvers and in emergencies. All these events are documented with photos, viewed and made available to the HQ MNTF S and its divisions as well as the HQ KFOR. From the late afternoon the departments can access a file for 24 hours, take pictures for their purpose and use them in their area. After 24 hours everything is saved in an archive and on CDs.

A picture says more than a thousand words, and a short Powerpoint presentation, underlined with music, or a short video, give a more realistic representation of an event than any briefing. Checkpoints, the training of KFOR troops, high-ranking officers under supervision, religious events, the discovery of UXOs and their destruction by the EOD team, ongoing aid measures for and among the population in Kosovo are preserved in pictures and sound. The CCT drives to the battalions in the MNTF S's area of operations and records the progressive, professional work of the soldiers in pictures, whether guard posts, cooks, mechanics or firemen, and many others more. Sometimes it patrols along roads, paths or in isolated towns and captures interesting details with its cameras. "Is the street passable – especially in summer after heavy rainfall or in winter after heavy snowfall? How is the situation in the area of operations? How do the Kosovar-Albanians and Kosovar-Serbs really live? What has changed in Kosovo up to now? Which new assignments will be carried out by the deployed KFOR armed forces in Kosovo in the future? What happens now, today, tomorrow?" These are some of the many questions that one asks every day in Kosovo. These are also the questions of the Combat Camera Team of the MNTF S for their internal planning. It is evaluated where information is still to be gathered daily. This assignment is also fulfilled through the CCT in the area of responsibility of the MNTF S.[121]

---

119 Richard Prenter: "50 Years of Military Patrols".
120 Joachim Meier, Michael Barthou: "Military Personal Protection in Kosovo".
121 Klaus Prader: "Combat Camera Team" (CCT) – Eyes and Ears of the Multinational Task Force South in Kosovo.

Engineer Element

The Slovakian Engineer Element (SLOVENGCON) ends its participation with AUCON/KFOR on February 28th, 2002. The reason is the formation of a joint Czech-Slovakian division within the framework of KFOR. These duties are fulfilled by an Austrian engineer division from April 1st, 2002, which is composed of the following parts:

- Technical engineer group within the framework of the camp operation platoon,
- Explosive ordnance clearance and disposal platoon within the framework of the headquarters company/AUCON with a platoon troop,
- Explosive ordnance disposal troop,
- Mine clearance group,
- Technical mine clearance group.

Protection

One day the Austrian explosive ordnance remover Warrant Officer 1 Josef Scherz enters the hospital ward of Camp Casablanca and demands 100 condoms there. The on-duty Swiss military doctor looks at him uncomprehendingly and only succinctly remarks that these are not available to the Swiss contingent. As a result of the questioning faces of all those present, WO I Scherz (for whom this was very serious) finds it necessary to "enlighten" the Swiss medical personnel: With the radio remote control, munitions can also be shot, in order for instance to set off an explosion. WO I Scherz has discovered by experimentation that shooting with condoms filled with water achieves a great effect. Incidentally, after a written request the desired "munitions" are allotted to them through the Austrian supply route, no questions asked.

For the technical mine clearance group, two parts of the mine clearance system "Bozena 3" are obtained (which was also deployed by SLOVENGCON). This is a remote controlled (reach up to 500 m) de-mining vehicle, equipped for surface mine clearance through the detonation or destruction of all kinds of mines. The operation is carried out by an operator in an armored cabin, which is loaded onto a vehicle (Steyr 12M18).

In Kosovo death or amputation lurks from mines as well. The mine clearance center of the Military Logistics School endeavors not only to discover and clear mines, but also to educate the population. The most modern equipment, like the robot above, is available for clearance.

Deployment of Military Dog Trainers

Inspections are generally carried out only at so-called "checkpoints". AUCON also operates some of these checkpoints and participates in the international "Checkpoint Echo", which lies between the capital, Pristina, and the second largest city, Prizren. The soldier inspect people and vehicles for illegal weapons and drugs, among other things. This checkpoint is passed by around 5,000 vehicles daily. Therefore dog trainers with their dogs are brought in from time to time as reinforcement. The dogs, who belong to the military dog echelon in Kaisersteinbruch, are trained guard, explosives and drug search dogs. The training for this lasts four months.

Espionage

The KFOR troops see themselves confronted with expansive espionage activities from the Serbs as well as the Kosovar-Albanians. It must be assumed that the largest part of the "local workers" (who fulfill translation duties, kitchen and cleaning work as well as construction activities within and outside of the camp) perform espionage activities. Nearly every action carried out by KFOR troops is already known from the beginning. So for instance in summer 2000 the deployment of a brigade to search for UCK and current TMK secret weapons caches across Kosovo is already announced on the internet 48 hours before. Under such conditions the mission represents an even more sensitive assignment. The "National Intelligence Cell (NIC)", which is integrated into the KFOR contingent, also receives great importance because of this.

Election Support

On October 28th, 2000, the first free community elections in Kosovo are held. The election observation falls to the OSCE mission, the guard is carried out by UNMIK, UNCIVPOL and KPS (Kosovo Police Service). AUCON/KFOR holds a "mobile crisis intervention team" ready in cooperation with the contingent psychologist, which in case of unrest or tumult would intervene in order to hinder disruptions of the election process. This is the Austrian "way of understanding". The transport of the election urns takes place on the day after the election with AMT "Pandur" from AUCON. The fact that the elections in the region of Suva Reka are the quietest and safest in all of Kosovo is thanks to the engagement of the Austrians and their good relationship with the civilian population.

On November 15th, 2009 the occupants of Kosovo elect the new political leadership of the municipalities. In the Austrian Deployment Battalion Bulje's area of responsibility the municipal leaders of Suharekë, Rahovec and Malishevo are elected. For the young nation of Kosovo these elections are a test in the questions of democracy and freedom of opinion. For the soldiers of the armed forces the ballots mean heightened deployment readiness.

Even when the situation in their deployment area is quiet, first tensions between the ethnic groups cannot be totally discounted. The Austrian soldiers are trained to separate conflicting parties during possible demonstrations or unrest, in order to hinder worse transgressions. The prerequisite for the success of so-called crowd and riot control deployments (CRC) is that the deployed forces reach the hot spots quickly and are optimally coordinated even under especially difficult conditions. Should conflicts come to light, bad and overcrowded streets can quickly lead to soldiers of the KFOR troop being hindered and their deployments then delayed. For this reason the Deployment Battalion Dulje also trains cooperation with helicopters as preparation for the elections. Difficulties develop during such air transports above all through the fact that the soldiers bring along extensive extra equipment: Protective shields, elbow and shin guards, combat helmets as well as batons for clearance and coercion (see page 290).

Aid Contribution

A special institution of the Austrians is the so-called **"5 x 5 Tour"**, which is always held on Sundays. During this, five vehicles drive from Camp Casablanca near Suva Reka, the "homeland" of the Austrians, to five different villages in the area and bring aid goods as well as things worth knowing. So there is, for instance, instruction in recognizing mines. The special thing about this project is that above all those soldiers come into action who otherwise must spend most of their time in camp as a result of their functions as cook or typist and so do not see much of the area of operations. Another Austrian idea is to carry out the **"Mayor Conference",** in which 66 of the 68 local leaders of the district of Suva Reka take part and have the opportunity to articulate their worries and needs.

Various projects for reconstruction are led through an Austrian officer who carries out the **CIMIC (civilian military cooperation)** agenda in HQ. So under his leadership Slovakian engineers are requested to at least temporarily reestablish the infrastructure in the 43 villages that lie in the Austrian sector. The situation of the children is (as all over the world where war and poverty dominate) especially bad. **"Children off the streets"** is therefore a particular concern. Just these "streets" lead through extremely mined areas. Fitting places are leveled and therefore the preconditions established for the construction of playground and sports fields. Naturally, money is also needed for this. A charity drive from famous athletes, well-known sports companies and the Austrian Military Sports Division (AMSD) is called to life by government official Kurt Ahammer from the bureau of the TrnB (the author presided over this bureau as bureau director for many years). The same goes for the **"1 schilling schoolbus drive"**. This is meant to say that if every Viennese schoolchild only donated 1 schilling, all the children in Kosovo could be brought to their often faraway schools by bus. A bus pass costs 7 ATS with a monthly income of 500 ATS. The award of a travel expense grant is dependent on success in school and the distance from the domicile to the school. With the help of the Youth Red Cross and many schoolchildren from Austria, around 120,000 ATS can be collected. The payment to the schoolchildren takes place later, so that misuse can be hindered. The press and information service of the city of Vienna support this drive with advertisements, in cooperation with the daily newspaper the Kurier and the international radio project of ORF.

In the time after Christmas, special activities take place; after all, donations from the homeland have to be brought to the affected population. Especially notable during this is the aid organization "Mother Teresa" (this is an international aid organization which has a liaison person in every town). The needy are initially recognized through this organization and the military patrols. These are then systematically provided with clothing and toys. At Christmas 1999, for instance, leftovers from the care of refugees in the parishes of Steinakirchen and Fischlhama are brought for distribution. These were previously brought into the area of operations with three tractor-trailers together with windowsills, door frames, and other aid goods from private freighters, and there given over to AUCON. The Muslims do not celebrate Christmas. However, presents are traditionally exchanged among friends to celebrate the change of the year. Therefore the handover deliberately takes place during this time which is so symbolic for the Kosovars.

In order to master the environmental pollution, every support for the individual communities, such as construction of a sports field, is made dependent on the previous cleanup of the surrounding area, for educational reasons.

Since the beginning of the deployment the commanders have been aware of the use of **munitions with enriched uranium cores** by NATO. Austrian NBC defence personnel therefore carry out regular measurements with German colleagues. The result is, to general relief, that only the natural environmental radiation can be determined. During measurements in May 2000 parts of the planned air detection system are tested in a deployment from a vehicle by the specialists of the NBC Defence School. Furthermore ca. 10,700 UXO's (unexploded ordnance) and ca. 200 mines are destroyed by the EOD team. Further more over 6,000 soldiers are taught about the dangers in the area of operation in the form of mine awareness trainings.

But two individual **road maintenance staffs** are also established by the Austrian soldiers. The Ministry of the Interior and Lower Austrian provincial government have six used civilian winter service vehicles available. With these, snow clearance is secured in the AUCON area of responsibility. The revitalization of the vehicles takes place in line with a project from the company ÖAF with resources from the EU. The vehicles are generally overhauled by Bosnian and later Kosovar-Albanian people displaced by war. The transfer of the vehicles takes place on November 18th, 1999 through military volunteers. Natives are trained as drivers in the area of operation. On August 21st eleven utility vehicles (four trucks for street repair, a garbage truck, two fire trucks as well as some busses for the transport of invalids and the handicapped) follow, which are provided by the province of the Tyrol. These vehicles are also prepared by refugees from Kosovo and Iran in Fieberbrunn (district of Kitzbühel). After the transfer of the road maintenance staffs to the local stations the road maintenance staffs continue to be under Austrian patronage. Through this, the cleaning of the most important streets for patrol activities and provisioning is also ensured. The vehicles from the Tyrol are also deployed under the supervision of the armed forces.

Drinking Water Purification

Another important CIMIC project is **drinking water purification.** The well water contains germs of all kinds as a result of the pollution deliberately caused by the Serbs (besides trash, the springs contain corpses, animal cadavers and mines). Therefore the well purification becomes very important. WO I Tagger leads this project, and by the end of July 2000 can already mark down 440 purified springs. Furthermore, the natives are given the necessary know-how and the technical equipment is left to them.

But the **EOD team** secures the water supply as well: May 24th, 2007. Like almost every other day, a farmer from Balince gathers water from his eight meter deep well. Nevertheless the water level has sunk almost to the bottom through the dryness, and so the clip of a grenade comes to view. Since the farmer already pulled uniform pieces from the well shortly after the war, he informs the Kosovo Police Service about his find. They alert the Austrian EOD team (explosive ordnance disposal team), which immediately sets off. After a first sounding the clearance of the well is begun. For this a man from the team rappels into the maximum one meter broad well. The floor of the well is searched with a metal detector. The detector is nevertheless irritated by scrap iron and other impurities and so a further painstaking sounding must be done by hand. Within a few minutes an M75 hand grenade is discovered in 40 cm of muddy water, which was already pulled, but never went off. The unexploded bomb is carefully drawn up in a bucket to the surface to be defused. The explosives experts, protected with Kevlar vests and protective helmets, can only remove the detonator of the safe to handle grenade and so make it safe to transport. A further search in the well results in the remains of four exploded hand grenades. These were probably thrown in the well during the war in order to make it unusable as drinking water. After the Austrian de-miners have also disposed of the last contaminants, the farmer thanks the Austrians very heartily for securing his drinking water supply.[122]

---

122 Report of Warrant Officer I Josef Scherz.

"Camp Casablanca"

The camp, which got its name thanks to the white trailers of which it is composed, is on a one-time factory site in Suva Reka, 20 km north of Prizren. The camp is established in August and September 1999 by a 170 man strong construction contingent (engineer company) and is best equipped for the winter with its 700 (!) climate-controlled trailers (the trailers in fact represent a value of around 50 mill. schillings). In order to bring the large number of trailers into the area of operations, contracts are made with civilian Austrian freighters. The camp has its own power plant and generators, with which it can secure its own electrical and water supply. The Austrian Mineral Oil Administration (OMV) drives two bore holes to a depth of more than 80 m for the water supply. The camp is completely equipped: Besides the accommodations, there is its own medical area, work and storage rooms, the kitchens and leisure rooms. Its own transmitter mast, constructed by TELEKOM, makes it possible for the soldiers to stay in contact with their homeland – for Austrian domestic prices! The Austrian camp, in which around 1,500 soldiers from other nations are also accommodated, is also a significant economic factor for the region. So 40 local workers are constantly employed in the camp.

The **guard and the water purification** are in the hands of SWISSCOY, among others. For this it has fort guards, military police and engineers deployed. Further Swiss soldiers are dispatched outside of the camp to rebuild the school and hospitals. The members of SWISSCOY are only partially armed. Only the fort guards, military police and officers carry their personal weapons. All others wear their weapons only outside of the camp for self-defence. This is compromise which had to be made in Switzerland as a requirement for international participation. Naturally the soldiers are more than unhappy with this solution, since they are of course dependent on the protection of soldiers from other contingents.

For the provisions around 250 kg of meat and sausage per day and 24,000 l of mineral water and 20,000 l of fruit juice per month are necessary. To secure these amounts a foodstuffs transport from Austria takes place every 14 days. The deep frozen foods and meat, etc., is delivered in two containers. The vegetables are bought in the area, three local bakers deliver ca. 130 kg of bread per day.

Amusements in Free Time

Since the soldiers are not allowed to spend their free time outside of Camp "Casablanca", this is fittingly embellished upon with help from Austrian firms. So the KFOR members stationed here have many leisure opportunities available. For physical training there is a climbing wall, a soccer field, beach volleyball and tennis courts and a sauna. A 20 x 12 m large pool officially called a "firefighting pond" serves as a swimming pool. There is music or film at an open air theater. Besides the community restaurant there are three other restaurants such as the "Chalet Suisse", "Stuppis Bay", or the "Austrian Courtyard".

The establishment of the **Barbara Chapel** in Camp Casablanca represents a special kind of cooperation in line with D-A-CH: For this chapel, whose construction goes back to the initiative of Austrian soldiers, the Austrians establish the foundation and the bottom walls, the Swiss lay down the nave and the Germans build the bell tower. After a call from the Austrian daily newspaper "Täglich Alles" for the readers to donate a figure of Saint Barbara, to whom the chapel is consecrated, there are numerous spontaneous reactions. One reader, the artist Wilhelm T. Gönner from Enns, even carves a figure especially for this purpose from a 400 year old tree trunk. This figure now watches over the soldiers in the new chapel. The Austrian military chaplain Gerhard Hatzmann founds its own international church choir, the "Suva Reka Gospel Singers". Besides this there is also the brass band "Casablanca Buam" (Austrians and Germans), which plays at ceremonial occasions.

Naturally such a deployment brings with it many visits. The federal president, members of the federal government and the provincial governments, journalists and many other people from public life would like to make an impression of the contribution of the Austrian soldiers on-site.

In July 2000 **top athletes** from the armed forces visit their comrades in Kosovo. Among them are world-class skiers Benni Raich and Pepi Strobl, biathlon vice-world champion Ludwig Gredler, Mario Stecher (silver medal at the nordic combination), Christoph Bieler and Judo fighter Sabrina Filzmoser. The athletic soldiers view all the Austrian facilities, naturally including the athletic fields and climbing wall inaugurated in May 2000. At the conclusion they distribute balls and sports uniforms to the schoolchildren in Suva Reka.

During this visit the top military athletes are confronted with the suffering of the children. The idea emerges to establish an athletic facility. This idea is implemented by the Austrian Military Sports Association under the sole management of its Secretary General, RegR Kurt Ahammer. During a charity drive, in which the AMSA participates as well as sports associations as well as prominent companies, 480,000 ATS are gathered. With this money, a multi-purpose sports facility is constructed in three months' construction time by KFOR soldiers and local firms and handed over to the affected population. The local representatives, top military athletes Sieber, Richter-Libiseller and Herczig and well-known Austrian sports journalists, who are flown to Suva Reka in the 250th Casa flight, take part in the celebration. The campaign goes down in history as the **(Sports Facility) Miracle of Suva Reka**.

Care of Loved Ones

For soldiers in the area of operations, the fulfillment of their duties is the first priority. Nevertheless the duties to be mastered abroad can only be fulfilled with difficulty without a functioning familial network. Soldiers abroad can hardly or only with difficulty be supported by their families. Therefore well-functioning networks (friends, family...) are important in order to minimize additional stress factors (for instance unresolved family problems, conflicts with partners or comrades, daily work and responsibilities...), so that the capacity and deployment readiness of the soldiers is not influenced by such additional burdens. Only when their heads are clear are the soldiers in the position to make good contributions. For this purpose a care group for loved ones is called into life by the commander of the 4th Mechanized Infantry Brigade. Their duty is to comprehensively inform and advise the loved ones of those soldiers who are planned for a deployment abroad at an early stage, and – when necessary – to be available around the clock as a first contact person. The care group consists of experienced noncommissioned officers of the brigade and in case of need is reinforced by peers[123], the brigade psychologist, an educator and the military chaplain.

The protection of cultural goods is also among the duties of KFOR (t.l.). Sister Johanna, the "angel of Kosovo", visits Kosovo in spring 2008 in order to track the progress of her many projects for reconciliation in the Balkans, together with Maria Hauser Seibl-Sauper, the sister of the famous "Stanglwirt" in Kitzbühel and one of her major sponsors. Sister Johanna enjoys in Kosovo a high degree of popularity. For years she has been one of the most engaged fighters in the battle against need and poverty in this nation. The engaged nun has worked with soldiers of the civilian-military cooperative (CIMIC) in Austria-led Multinational Task Force South's area of responsibility in almost all the aid projects which have benefited the population of Kosovo in the past. The children are the future of the young Republic of Kosovo and she especially contributes valuable work with the soldiers in the education sector, from kindergartens to extension schools up to career training. The crowning conclusion of the visit is the celebration of Sister Johanna's birthday, to which numerous well-wishers come (t.r.). In July 2004 the charming Austrian pop singer Christina Stürmer visits "Camp Casablanca" with her band and excites hundreds of pacifiers there. As spartanly accommodated as the soldiers, she accompanies the peacekeepers on their patrols, sees the land destroyed by unrest and observes, among other things, the military experts defusing mines (b.l.). During the farewell to Colonel GS Horst Hofer as NCC on November 24th, 2006, the commander of the Maneuver Battalion Dulje, Lieutenant Colonel Bernd Aschauer, causes a Swiss honor platoon to form up, whom he himself had earlier taught the Austrian presentation of arms. During his speech Aschauer points out that besides Colonel Hofer, there is only one other person who has a "Swiss Guards"[124] (b.r.).

---

123 Psychosocial first care givers.
124 Naturally the Pope is meant.

For the maintenance of battle readiness and free time amusement, expansive sports facilities are constructed on their own initiative (t.l.). Naturally it is also attempted to economize during this. So materials cleared for the sports facilities are then used for an urgently necessary 3 m high protective wall. It is a big concern for the Austrian soldiers to keep the children off the streets and productively amused. This includes not only personal conversation (t.r.), but also athletic care. The picture m.l. shows soldiers and children at the opening of a sports facilities for the youth. A further point of focus within the framework of CIMIC is the purification of the wells (m.r.). Visits of all kinds from the homeland give a feeling of connection and bring variety into hard daily life: Whether from superiors (in the picture b.l. is BG Höfler, the commander of the International Deployments Command, surrounded by members of personal protection of the Special Operations Forces Training Center), who form a personal image of the situation or famous musicians (in the picture b.r. the beloved "Stoakogler"), who do not pass up the chance to play for our KFOR soldiers.

• Operational Reserve Force (AUCON DEU-ORF)

In the course of the many international deployments of NATO and EU there are always unforeseen escalations in the area of operations. In order to combat these forces to master these unforeseen situational developments are held ready in European homelands. In general these forces are called **"Over the Horizon Forces" (OTHF)** and essentially represent reserves on a strategic level. For the Joint Operation Area (JOA) of the Balkans, battalion-strength forces are held ready as Operational Reserve Forces (ORF) in half-year alternations for the two deployments which remain since the middle of the 1990's, EUFOR/ALTHEA and KFOR. The ORF forces are basically subordinate to the authority of the respective operation commander, transfer within the framework of the preparation for deployment to the **"Stand by Phase"** (functional in the area of operations within 14 days) and after the establishment of deployment readiness are held on call in the "Ready Phase" (functional in the area of operations within four days) in their home postings. In line with deployment exercises to achieve deployment readiness (operational rehearsals) of various levels, battalion commanders with their staff, then company commanders and finally the entire troop are briefed in the specific factors of the area of operations. In the course of this transfer actual deployments often occur, such as during the elections in 2009.

The Council of Ministers decides on the participation of the armed forces in the operative reserve forces by holding up to 230 people in readiness for security crises in the duration of up to three months each for KFOR and EUFOR/ALTHEA.

The contribution of the armed forces consists at its core of an infantry company with Pandur armored personnel carriers as well as national divisions to the extent of 170 soldiers. Depending on the situation and assignment, this contingent can be increased to up to 230 soldiers at any time. The contingent is incorporated into the German battalion and carries out deployment preparations with them as well as the following deployments. As a result of the given swift movement times, the Pandur armored personnel carriers planned for the ORF company are stored with AUCON/KFOR.

Basis for deployment: CM of June 13th, 2007, MC of June 19th, 2007.
Mission: Support of KFOR and EUFOR/ALTHEA during worsening of the security situation in the area of operations.
Appellation: AUCON/ORF.
Form of dispatch: FCL-CSD.
Area of operations: Bosnia and Herzegovina, Kosovo.
Contingent strength: 170.
Composition: Command, staff personnel,
  infantry company ("Pandur" armored personnel carriers),
  EOD team,
  medical element,
  military police element,
  logistical element.

Elections in Kosovo

On November 15th, 2009, the occupants of Kosovo elect the new political leadership of the municipalities. In the Austrian Deployment Battalion Bulje's area of responsibility the municipal leaders of Suharekë, Rahovec and Malishevo are elected. For the young nation of Kosovo these elections are a test in the questions of democracy and freedom of opinion.

For the soldiers of the armed forces the ballots mean heightened deployment readiness. Even when the situation in their deployment area is quiet, first tensions between the ethnic groups cannot be totally discounted. For reinforcement **AUCON 4/ORF** is transferred to Kosovo. The Austrian soldiers are trained to separate conflicting parties during possible demonstrations or unrest, in order to hinder worse transgressions. The prerequisite for the success of so-called crowd and riot control deployments (CRC) is that the deployed forces reach the hot spots quickly and are optimally coordinated even under especially difficult conditions.

Should conflicts come to light, bad and overcrowded streets can quickly lead to soldiers of the KFOR troop being hindered and their deployments then delayed. For this reason the Deployment Battalion Dulje also trains cooperation with helicopters as preparation for the elections. Difficulties develop during such air transports above all through the fact that the soldiers bring along extensive extra equipment: Protective shields, elbow and shin guards, combat helmets as well as batons for clearance and coercion.

Rapid response forces during "boarding training" with an AB-212 (photo WO I Alfred Sattmann).

United Nations Interim Administration Mission in Kosovo (UNMIK)

Preliminary Events

On June 20th, 1999, the Yugoslavian armed and security forces concluded their withdrawal out of Kosovo. However, there is evidence that the Serbs have left paramilitary forces behind. These are probably to maintain a climate of violence in Kosovo through attacks and ambushes. With this, the Yugoslavia government's argument that KFOR is not in a position to maintain security in Kosovo is to be supported. For this purpose Yugoslavia also introduces a request to the United Nations in the 26th week of the year to be allowed to return security forces to Kosovo.

On June 21st, 1999, the UCK signed the demilitarization agreement with the NATO. In it, the UCK pledges itself to recognize the authority of KFOR, cease all hostilities and clear its positions. Further, the agreement regulates the turnover of weapons. Within 30 days all foreign advisors or other non-Kosovars who have fought on the side of the UCK are to leave the nation.

The security situation is nevertheless extremely critical and marked by the collapse of the local order. There are lootings, revenge acts and violence throughout the entire province. The flight of Serbs out of Kosovo continues. Conversely, around 590,000 Kosovars return to their homeland by July 1999. The biggest danger for those returning home is the uncontrolled mining which was carried out by the Serbs before leaving the nation. In total, 425 minefields are found, booby traps and NATO unexploded ordnance represent further dangers.

International Reaction

After negotiations at the beginning of June 1999, the decision is made on the basis of the peace plan of the G-8 nations (the seven leading industrial nations and Russia) on June 9th and 10th to end the armed conflicts and to establish a transitional government under the aegis of the United Nations. In paragraph 11 of the SC resolution the decision is made to establish a civilian transitional government under the aegis of UNO, in close cooperation with the EU and the OSCE. UNMIK is to take over the duties of administration, police and justice and observe the return of the 100,000 refugees. Furthermore, a special representative of the UN Secretary General is ordered with the rank of an under secretary general.

In his office a military liaison bureau is also established. It remains problematic that KFOR, led by NATO, is not subordinate to UNMIK, but organized parallel to it. Because of this there are constant misunderstandings during the cooperation of the military and civilian elements of the international presence.

UNMIK police patrol passes an Austrian checkpoint.

Basis for deployment:	Agreement between the Federal Republic of Yugoslavia and NATO of June 9th, 1999, SC Resolution 1244 (1999) of June 10th, 1999.
Mission:	Securing of a transitional administration in Kosovo including the fulfillment of the duties of the police and justice department; observation of the return of refugees; support with reconstruction.
Duration of deployment:	July 4th, 1999 – August 31st, 2009.
Participating nations:	Austria, Belgium, Canada, Denmark, Finland, Hungary, Ireland, Italy, Kenya, Malaysia, Malawi, Nepal, New Zealand, Norway, Pakistan, Poland, Spain, Russia, Ukraine, USA, Zambia.
Strength:	Up to 3,000 police officials and up to 60 military liaison officers (MLOs). 2,745 police officials and 40 unarmed MLOs (as of December 31st, 2000).
Headquarters:	Pristina.

Austrian Participation

Political Measures

It is decided by the federal government to dispatch up to 20 executive officials and up to ten military liaison officers.

Military Measures

The MoD accepts the decision of the CM and dispatches two officers.

Basis for deployment:	CM of June 25th, 1999, MC of July 1st, 1999 (dispatch of up to 50 executive officials); CM of July 13th, 1999, MC of July 27th, 1999 (dispatch of up to ten soldiers); CM of April 11th, 2000, MC of May 17th, 2000 (reinforcement of executive contingent by 20 officials); CM of May 8th, 2001, MC of May 23rd, 2001 (extension until July 10th, 2002).
Mission:	Ensuring of coordination and liaison services (MLO) to the military deployment forces and civilian UN structures in Kosovo; winning the trust of the involved parties.
Appellation:	None.
Form of dispatch:	FCL-CSD 1997.
Area of operations:	Kosovo.
Duration of deployment:	July 20th, 1999 – August 9th, 2002.
Contingent strength:	2.
Total:	6.

Organization

In every district (the deployment zone of a brigade) a team in the strength of four soldiers works under the leadership of a "chief military liaison officer". The liaison teams in Belgrade and Tirana cannot be activated.

The biggest danger for those returning home is the uncontrolled mining of the terrain. In the picture one of the devilish anti-person mines, a so-called "booby trap" can be seen (UN Photo/R. Chalasani).

Austrian Forces Disaster Relief Unit/Turkey 1 (AFDRU/TU 1)

Preliminary Events

On August 17th, 1999, at 3:15 AM local time, an earthquake with a strength of 7.4 on the Richter scale jolts Turkey. The epicenter lies in the industrial city of Izmit around 100 km east of Istanbul. The extent is initially completely underestimated by the Turkish government. Early reports speak of 2,000 dead and more than 11,000 wounded. But already shortly afterward the agencies report more than 4,000 dead and over 20,000 wounded, according to UN reports there are even 40,000 dead, more than 70,000 wounded and over 200,000 homeless to complain of. The earthquake is the most serious in this country since 1939. Because of the collapse of many supply and disposal systems, there is the greatest danger of the outbreak of epidemics. The high number of dead and seriously wounded results from the poor construction conditions and the fact that above all poorer regions are affected. Around the middle of the day on August 17th the largest refinery in Turkey, in Izmit, goes up in flames. On the same day the Turkish government hands over a request for aid to the "United Nations Office for the Coordination of Humanitarian Affairs (UN/OCHA)" for the urgent provision of rescue equipment of all kinds and search dogs.

International Reaction

Already in the morning hours of August 17th the international disaster relief begins. UN/OCHA dispatches a team to survey the catastrophe area. By the afternoon of August 18th, 1,055 helpers from 19 nations arrive in Turkey. Among others, the dog trainers of the Austrian Red Cross, who are already deployed on August 18th, manage to recover 20 people alive. The fire in the refinery can be successfully brought under control by firefighting planes from Germany, France, Greece and Israel on August 19th.

Basis for deployment: UN/OCHA situation report.

And again an Ilyushin takes our contingent abroad. The photo shows the landing in Turkey.

Austrian Participation

Political Measures

An urgent dispatch takes place through the Minister of Defence.

Military Measures

Initially an AFDRU alert exercise is ordered by the MoD in order to be able to react quickly to a fitting request for aid from Turkey. The request for aid arrives at 3:00 PM. With a drastic shortening of the procedures the readiness to march can be achieved on the same day (!) at 12:00 AM. The movement of the contingent takes place on August 18th at 4:40 AM with a Boeing 737 from Lauda Air. The equipment (20 t) follows at 5:06 AM with a civilian L-100-30 "Hercules" rented by the armed forces from Schwechat airport. In a 2nd lift on August 19th, provisions and medical supplies for a 14 day deployment, a water purification system, a decontamination element as well as further medical and tent equipment is added. The further transport of AFDRU/TU takes place through the Turkish army. The follow-up supply takes place through Ammerer Air, since the IL-76 and L-100 are needed for the advance and construction commands for KFOR.

The first liaison contact is made after landing with the "local emergency management authorities (LEMA)". Afterwards the camp is constructed on an fenced-in sports field. At 5:00 PM the search and rescue deployment begins. Already by 6:45 PM the first living recovery is made. The work takes place under the greatest strain and the dangers resulting from a number of aftershocks.

In the lack of a fitting efficient institution for the coordination of the international search and rescue team in the area of Yalova, an **"on site operation and coordination center (OSOCC)"** is established and lead by AFDRU/TU according to UN/OCHA guidelines. This staff offers advice and help to all deployed organizations, maintains a constantly updated map of the damage situation, points out damaged areas and maintains contact with the UN institutions and LEMA.

On August 24th the authorities release the entire catastrophe area for total clearance; the buried are then officially considered dead. After the local authorities then begin to carry away the collapsed buildings, the deployment of AFRDU is concluded on August 24th and the withdrawal is begun. This takes place on August 25th with two flights on the rented Ilyushin IL-76.

Basis for deployment:	Urgent dispatch according to Sec. 1 no. 1 subsec. c in connection with Sec. 2 para. 2 FCL-CSD through the Federal Minister of Defence on August 17th, 1999; report to the CM according to Sec. 2 para. 2 of the FCL-CSD; acknowledgement of the CM of September 7th, 1999 (an act of the MC can fall away according to the FCL-CSD).
Mission:	Search and recovery of the buried with the use of search dogs and special equipment.
Appellation:	Austrian Forces Disaster Relief Unit/Turkey (AFDRU/TU).
Form of dispatch:	FCL-CSD 1997.
Area of operations:	Yalova (north of Bursa on the coast of the Marmara Sea, 160 km from Istanbul).
Duration of deployment:	August 18th, 1999 – August 25th, 1999.
Contingent strength:	67 (including an emergency doctor from the Innsbruck Military Hospital and communications specialists from the Communications Staff and 12 dog trainers with twelve search dogs).
Total:	67.
Composition:	Commander, command group (chemist, structural engineer, translator, situation cartographer, liaison officer), logistics group, medical group (including an emergency medical team from the Innsbruck Military Hospital) for first aid on the people freed from the rubble as well as care of the contingent, 1st – 2nd Clearance and Recovery Sections (in the CaRSecs twelve dog trainers from the Austrian Rescue Dog Brigade and the Vienna Professional Fire Department are incorporated).
Commander:	Captain Otto Strele.
Contribution:	Twelve living recoveries, of which four are in their own area (the recovery of an almost unharmed girl succeeds only after 24 hours of work); 40,000 people can be provided with drinking water.

Equipment

The contingent has a Puch G and two motorcycles, protective clothing (heavy protective suit and overgarment), pneumatic pillows (to lift heavy loads up to 24 t), electrical excavation equipment (rock drill, percussion drill), breathing protection apparatus, sound ranging equipment, rappelling and climbing equipment, leakproof pillow kits (to seal open gas lines and containers), deco-jet trailer (for decontamination), drinking water purification system, lifting tools, coolant and electricity generators and more.

The two motorcycles are a big help: So a connection can quickly be made between the local duty posts and the Red Cross (page 294). And the Drash tents prove themselves once more, since only a few soldiers are needed for their construction (top). The Austrian camp is established on a sports field. The extent of the destruction is unimaginable, the work of the soldiers is life-threatening (middle). Captain med. Dr. Sylvia-Carolina Sperandio, one of the two first female military doctors in the armed forces, also belongs to the contingent (b.l.). In the picture bottom right a member of AFDRU in a protective suit with breathing protection apparatus can be seen.

Austrian Humanitarian Contingent/Turkey (ATHUM/TU)

Preliminary Events

The **"Euro-Atlantic Disaster Response Coordination Center (EADRCC)"** tallies up the terrifying sum of the disastrous earthquake in Turkey: 18,000 dead, 35,000 missing, 42,200 wounded and 200,000 homeless. The Turkish NATO delegation reports the losses on September 1st as 14,202 dead, 25,254 wounded and 73,679 destroyed buildings. One day later a new "official" sum comes out from the national crisis management: 14,559 dead, 24,093 wounded and 94,466 destroyed houses. After the phase of the searches, the phase of reconstruction begins on August 25th. For this a request goes out from the Turkish government for the provision of portable toilets, hygiene, medical and decontamination materials as well as water purification systems, among other things.

International Reaction

On the side of the EADRCC, in agreement with the UN/OCHA, all NATO members and their partners are called upon to provide aid. 13 international field hospitals and 32 partially mobile doctor teams are provided for medical care alone. In the first phase of aid 35,000 tents are constructed. The European Investment Bank provides 1 million euros as immediate help for urgently necessary construction work.

Austrian Participation

Political Measures

Immediately after the aid request is made public, the Federal Chancellor, Foreign, Finance, and Defence Ministers decide as a result of the urgency on the dispatch of 60 members of the armed forces with four drinking water purification systems and a water tank vehicles for the duration of up to a month from the beginning of the deployment. The costs are estimated at 10 million öS. The material costs are refunded to the armed forces from the general budget.

Military Measures

Already on August 23st (at this point AFDRU/TU is still in the area of operation in Turkey), the preparations are begun for the dispatch of a military contingent for water purification. On August 28th and 29th, 60 soldiers, four drinking water purification systems and around 85 t of equipment and materials for a one-month deployment are brought to Turkey in an Ilyushin IL-76 in five lifts. In addition a portion of the necessary equipment is taken over on site from AFDRU/TU. The weekly follow-up supply takes place with an L 100-30 "Hercules" rented from Safair. Shortly after landing the construction of the camp is begun. The drinking water purification itself begins on August 30th. The distribution is carried out by the Turkish army. The Austrian medical element is only dispatched for the care of the contingent itself, at the instruction of the Turkish authorities. The medics only help out in emergency cases. Since the local authorities are able to provide the population a suitable water supply again, the deployment can be ended. On September 21st the camp is closed in a public ceremony. Between September 23rd and 25th, ATHUM/TU withdraws to the homeland in six lifts with an IL-76.

Basis for deployment:	Urgent deployment according to Sec. 1 no. 1 subsec. c in connection with Sec. 2 para. 2 FCL-CSD through the Federal Chancellor, the Foreign, Financial, and Defence Ministers on August 26th, 1999; report to the CM and MC according to Sec. 5 para. 5 FCL-CSD on August 31st, 1999; acknowledgment through the CM on September 7th, 1999.
Mission:	Securing of the drinking water supply in the assigned area of operation.
Appellation:	**Austrian Humanitarian Contingent/Turkey (ATHUM/TU).**
Form of dispatch:	FCL-CSD 1997.
Area of operations:	Yalova.
Duration of deployment:	August 28th, 1999 – September 25th, 1999.
Contingent strength:	60.
Composition:	Commander, command group, logistics group (MedTrp, Field Mess Trp, DocTrp), 1st NBCDefGrp (FieldLab, RescueTrp, RecTrp, Firefighting Truck Trp, DecoTrp), 2nd – 3rd NBC DefTrp (2 DWPTrp each).
Commander:	First Lieutenant (Lieutenant Colonel for the duration of the mission) Martin Beck.
Contribution:	Around 120,000 l of drinking water are produced daily, 50,000 – 90,000 l are given out to the population, the rest are filled in tanks. Furthermore 50 – 140 Turkish patients are treated in clinics daily.
Equipment:	6 large trucks, 1 firefighting truck, 1 medical Pinzgauer, 1 clearance and recovery Pinzgauer, 2 Puch Gs, 2 motorcycles, 2 drinking water purification systems, 1 field kitchen trailer. The team is equipped with the desert clothing created for MINURSO.

Multinational Search and Rescue Unit/Taiwan (S+R/TW)

Preliminary Events

On the evening of September 20th, 1999, a serious earthquake with a strength of 7.6 takes place in Taiwan, on the following day an aftershock with a strength of 6.8 on the Richter scale takes place. A further serious aftershock takes place again on September 26th. The epicenter lies around 12.5 km west of Nantou. Around 2,200 people are killed in the earthquake, many thousands wounded, and around 30,000 buildings are destroyed.

International Reaction

As a result of the many victims and daunting damages, the United Nations Office for the Coordination of Humanitarian Affairs (UN/OCHA) requests the dispatch of United Nations Disaster Assessment and Coordination (UNDAC) – as well as search and rescue (SAR) – teams. Great Britain, Japan, Russia, Switzerland and the United States immediately report their readiness to help. Incomprehensibly, the Taiwanese government subsequently lays down upper limits for foreign aid forces. German immediately provides 25 members of the technical relief organization and Switzerland 42 members of the Swiss Rescue Chain. Together with the 10 Austrians they form a **trinational unit (D-A-CH)**. Financial support from the World Bank cannot take place, since Taiwan is not a member. Instead, the Chinese Red Cross offers aid for the first time in its history of the Taiwanese earthquake victims. This aid encompasses $100,000 US in cash and aid goods for around $80,000 US.

> **Basis for deployment:** UN/OCHA Situation Report No. 2 and No. 3 of September 21st, 1999.
> **Mission:** Search and recovery of the buried with the use of search dogs and special equipment.
> **Duration of deployment:** September 21st, 1999 – September 29th, 1999.
> **Participating nations:** Austria, Germany, Japan, Korea, Russia, Singapore, Switzerland, USA.
> **Headquarters:** Nantou (140 km southeast of Taipei).
> **Strength:** 77.

Austrian Participation

Political Measures

An urgent dispatch takes place through the Federal Minister of Defence.

Military Measures

After the arrival of the first reports on the earthquake, in view of the expected request for aid, a test alert of AFDRU is set off in order to secure its readiness at any time. This takes place despite the simultaneously occurring deployment within the framework of ATHUM/TU. After the arrival of the request, a 36 man strong search and rescue unit is initially formed and gathered together in the NBC Defence School on September 21st. Following the measures of the Taiwanese government, the mission is then changed to the dispatch of ten experts from the rescue and recovery service (with emphasis on the areas of acoustic detection and structural analysis) and the emergency medical area. On September 22nd these ten men travel to Switzerland with an AUA airline flight, where they are integrated into the joint German-Swiss-Austrian contingent. One sees how quickly this all proceeds from the fact that the necessary immunization for Taiwan against Japanese encephalitis is no longer possible in Austria and therefore carried out by the medical emergency services in Zurich through Swiss Tropical Institute. From Switzerland, the contingent travels to Taiwan on a chartered airplane with 15 search dogs and 16 tons of special equipment. The team is independently provisioned for 14 days. The Austrian team arrives on September 23rd, 1999, 4:30 AM local time, in the area of operation in Ufong and establishes their base camp in Wufeng. The deployment itself is carried out by mixed D-A-CH teams.

> **Basis for deployment:** Urgent dispatch according to Sec. 1 no. 1 subsec. c in connection with Sec. 2 para. 2 FCL-CSD through the Federal Minister of Defence on September 21st, 1999; report of the Defence Minister to the CM on September 28th, 1999 (an act of the MC can fall away according to the FCL-CSM).
> **Mission:** Search and rescue duties within the framework of a trinational unit.
> **Appellation: Austrian Forces Disaster Relief Unit / Taiwan (AFDRU/TW). Form of dispatch:** FCL-CSD.
> **Area of operations:** Region of Taichung, ca. 140 km south of Taipei.
> **Duration of deployment:** September 22nd, 1999 – September 29th, 1999. **Contingent strength:** 10.
> **Composition:** Commander, NBC defence officer/clearance and recovery, NBC defence officer/structural engineer, medical troop (doctor, MedNCO), five NBC defence noncommissioned officers/clearance and recovery.
> **Commander:** Captain Otto Strele.
> **Contribution:** Through the "Joint Contingent", 18 buried people can be located and 13 people recovered only dead. It is also possible for the AFDRU team to cooperate with a Korean rescue team on a live recovery. So a six-year-old boy, who was trapped for around 90 hours in the rubble, can be rescued.

Austrian Forces Disaster Relief Unit/Turkey 2 (AFDRU/TU2)

Preliminary Events

On the evening of November 12th, 1999 (5:57 PM CET), there is a new earthquake with a strength of 7.1 on the Richter scale and the epicenter in Düzce in the province of Gerede, around 100 km east of Izmit.

Around 550 people are killed during this and 3,300 are wounded, 715 buildings are completely destroyed. 80,000 people are directly affected by the effects of this earthquake, which is comparable in strength to the one in August. Immediately after the earthquake the Turkish government requests aid.

International Reaction

UN/OCHA immediately dispatches an UNDAC team to support the local authorities and aid forces. Offers of help come in from many lands. Even Greece, which exists in a certain tense relationship with Turkey, immediately offers support. In order to gain an impression of the extent of such an international aid drive, Situation Report No. 7 of November 18th is cited.

This publishes the following numbers: 18,801 tents (of which 1,000 are winterproof), 200,631 blankets, 433 doctors, 100 certified nurses, 1,051 medics, 20,337 beds, 467 medical vehicles, 195 other vehicles, three medical airplanes, 28 helicopters, 61 portable toilets, 336 portable shower cabins, 235 electrical generators, 4,980 coffins (unfortunately, this must also be considered).

Basis for deployment: UN/OCHA Situation Report No. 1 of November 13th, 1999.
Mission: Search and recovery of the buried with the use of search dogs and special equipments.
Duration of deployment: November 13th, 1999 – November 21st, 1999.
Participating nations: Algeria, Armenia, Austria, Belgium, Bulgaria, Czech Republic, Denmark, Egypt, Finland, France, Germany, Great Britain, Greece, Hungary, Israel, Italy, Kyrgyzstan, the Netherlands, Poland, Romania, Russia, Slovakian Republic, Slovenia, South Africa, Spain, Sweden, Switzerland, Ukraine, USA.
Headquarters: Düzce.
Strength: 12,265 people and 152 search dogs.

Austrian Participation

Political Measures

An urgent dispatch takes place through the Federal Minister of Defence.

Military Measures

In this case as well an alert exercise for AFDRU is ordered immediately after the earthquake becomes known, in order to be able to react quickly in view of a possible international request for help. 250 volunteers report at the first call, 162 are called in and 113 finally chosen for the deployment. On November 13th, 58 men travel with 30 t of equipment and provisions to Istanbul with a C-130 "Hercules" from Saf-Air and an additional two Lockheed L-188 "Elektras" from Amerer Air. On November 14th, a further 55 soldiers follow with the C-130 and 20 t equipment with both L-188. The AFDRU team is already expected at the airport by a Turkish businessman, who was already most helpful for AFDRU 1. This time again he can provide valuable help with the search and determination of the area for the camp. After the landing and establishment of contact with the "on site operations cooperation center (OSOCC)", two CaRTrps immediately begin the deployment. The other two first unload the aircraft. The lack of maps makes the work more difficult, so initially the search is begun in the immediate surroundings. Thanks to the timing of the earthquake, few people were in the buildings and therefore far fewer dead and wounded are to be complained of than was the case in August. Since international aid troops are working at practically all the damaged areas already, their own mission is changed so that they are now supported by AFDRU with personnel and materials. On November 15th, a clearance and recovery troop each relieve the Israeli and the Bulgarian teams. A shopping center represents the largest area of damage, which has completely collapsed in on itself and in which at least 20 people are supposed to be. This damaged area finally occupies all four CaRTrps in shifts until almost the end of the deployment. Since it relatively soon becomes clear that further live recoveries can no longer be counted on, the contingent travels home on November 21st and 22nd with two lifts each on an L-100 (landing in Schwechat) and an IL-76 (landing at the airfield in Langenlebarn/Lower Austria).

Basis for deployment:	Urgent dispatch according to Sec. 1 no. 1 subsec. c in connection with Sec. 2 para. 2 FCL-CSD through the Federal Minister of Defence on November 13th, 1999; report to the CM on November 16th, 1999; acknowledgement of the CM on November 16th, 1999.
Mission:	Search and recovery of the buried with the use of search dogs and special equipment.
Appellation:	**Austrian Forces Disaster Relief Unit/Turkey 2 (AFDRU/TU2).**
Form of dispatch:	FCL-CSD 1997.
Area of operations:	Düzce.
Duration of deployment:	November 13th, 1999 – November 21st, 1999.
Contingent strength:	113 soldiers, search dog team from the Austrian Red Cross (twelve men, ten dogs) and the Austrian mountain rescue (31 men and dogs).
Total:	113.
Composition:	Commander, command group (chemist, structural engineer, translation troop, signal corps, NBC defence and hygiene troop), supply staff (SupplyGrp, MedGrp, Field Mess Trp, MTrp), 1st – 4th clearance and recovery section (rescue troop, support troop, recovery troop).
Commander:	First Lieutenant (Lieutenant Colonel for the duration of the mission) Markus Bock.
Contribution:	One live recovery in cooperation with other teams, a birth, three recoveries of the dead, 150 walk-in treatments.

Goods for Sale to the Army

During this deployment an aspect should also be further looked into which cannot be forgotten in an undertaking of this type: goods for sale to the army. Even when the team's supplies are secured, certain daily need articles or additional individual "sweeteners" are needed.

Since the time and possibility is often lacking for procurement "on site", they must be taken along during the move out. The sales can then take place during the deployment at individual prices.

In order to form an impression of their extent and number, the assortment of goods for sale to the soldiers taken along for ATHUM/TU2 is represented as following (in relation to a contingent strength of 113 soldiers):

Shampoo	40	bottles	Shaving cream	100	cans
One-use razors	100	pieces	Chips	200	packets
Pretzels	200	packets	Cheese wheels	200	packets
Snack mix	200	packets	Peanuts	200	packets
Salted pistachios	200	packets	Salted almonds	200	packets
Crackers	200	packets	Sour sweets	200	packets
Cough drops	200	packets	Red Bull	2000	cans
Coca Cola	2000	cans	Iso Star	2000	cans
Cigarettes	400	packs	Light cigarettes	400	packs

During the participation of female soldiers or civilian workers an appropriate offering of monthly hygiene is added.

The "Slow" Austrians

Yalova, Thursday, 5:20 PM. Warrant Officer I Hölbling, commander of a rescue and recovery troop, remembers:

"The three-story building was so pressed together that the roofs of the levels lay above each other 50 cm apart at best. We knew that there must nevertheless still be life in there, and we had to get in there, no matter the cost. But the earth was constantly shaken by the jolts of the aftershocks. Never mind, we fought 18 meters ahead, centimeter by centimeter. Four men worked with pneumatic drills, hydraulics, etc. One stood outside and watched to see if anything moved, and then called us back out immediately with a megaphone. We had to clear the damage site six times this way. Around 9:30 PM, after four hours, we finally came upon a boy of around nine years, who was only mildly injured, but seriously shocked and exhausted. Locals had told us: 'He must be lying behind a radiator.' I slid on my belly into a hollow, really kicked at the radiator and reached behind it. Then my hand was grabbed and squeezed tight. It was an indescribable feeling. We recovered the boy, gave him first *aid and transferred him to the Red Crescent. But his sister must still have been somewhere in there, we could clearly hear knocking. The situation was dramatic. We had to work from the peak of the ruins, so practically from the third story, through concrete, roofing and iron down to the ground level. At 3:00 AM the earth shook again so strongly that we had to stop for three hours, time for a small breather. On Friday at 7:30 AM it finally continued. We made our first verbal contact with Sevcan, the 14-year-old sister. In one place it was only possible to go further when we worked our way through a couch pressed between two layers of concrete. The steel springs had to be individually separated. Near 11:00 AM the Turks became rebellious; we worked too slowly for them. Their displeasure became ever stronger. Suddenly five large wheel loaders arrived and began to rummage wildly about in the rubble. This would have subsequently led to the girl's certain death. I succeeded in convincing a police officer of the madness of this plan. Finally a large contingent of police managed to push the furious crowd back. At 3:15 PM, after 20 hours of painstaking and dangerous work, it was time, I already had the girl by the hand. Then came the alarm from outside: "Everyone out!" But then it went very quickly. We carried Sevcan, who was doing well, out. Outside the mood changed: A thousand-head crowd cheered for us and clapped. At once the "slow" Austrians were heroes".*

The report comes from the 1st earthquake deployment in Turkey (ATHUM/TU) in September 1999 (see page 293 ff).

United Nations Disaster Assessment and Coordination Mission in Mozambique I/II (UNDAC/MZB I/II)

Preliminary Events

In December 1999 heavy rainfall comes down on Mozambique and the neighboring nations whose rivers feed from the rivers of Mozambique. In February 2000 unusually strong rainfall floods the south of the country. In addition the country is also devastated by cyclones "Connie", "Hudah" and "Eline". At the beginning of the flooding over 300,000 people are affected by the catastrophe. The government of Mozambique petitions the UN Office for the Coordination of Humanitarian Affairs (UN-OCHA) for international aid.

After the heavy flooding in February 2000 in the south of the country (UNDAC/MZB II), central Mozambique is affected by devastating masses of water at the beginning of March. Further flooding emerges through the opening of the embankment dams in order to prevent their bursting. According to the report of the National Institute for Catastrophe Management (Instituto Nacional de Gestão de Calamidades – INGC) of March 21st, 2000, 4.5 million people are threatened by the floods, in which 650,000 people must leave their homes, 699 people meet death. The government of Mozambique again requests international aid from UN-OCHA.

International Reaction

A five-person UNDAC team, to which an Austrian officer also belongs, is immediately alarmed and set on the march to the catastrophe zone by UN-OCHA. Besides the assessment, the total coordination of the newly established catastrophe protections division of Mozambique (Instituto Nacional de Gestão de Calamidades – INGC) falls to the UNDAC team. Fur this purpose, a coordination center is opened and operated in the INGC building in the capital of Maputo. Coordination meetings of originally ca. 30 people up to more than 150 participants (including the foreign minister) are carried out daily with a strict agenda and clear time limits. A system of "sector meetings" is also introduced by the UNDAC team wherever a national and an international organization together take over the coordination of a sector. So for instance the Ministry of Health and the World Health Organization (WHO) are responsible for the health issues. Through this the times of the joint coordination meetings can be drastically reduced, or alternatively the course for continuation after the withdrawal of the UNDAC team can be set. At the beginning of this catastrophe only four helicopters are available to rescue people. An UNDAC team is then shifted to assessment in the direct area of operations.

At the end of February another UNDAC team is dispatched. The Colonel of the director's office Mag. Hirschmugl, newly placed by Austria, establishes and operates a local on site operations coordination center (OSOCC) with a 2nd UNDAC member in central Mozambique for the complete coordination in an area the size of ca. four provinces. After CNN coverage of a birth in the trees the urgently needed helicopters are finally provided by the international community. Finally 147 national and international organizations as well as 40 airplanes, 51 helicopters (daily costs for kerosene in central Mozambique ca. 100,000 euros) and 140 boats must be coordinated in total. Once more the problems are shown that occur when far too many aid organizations make their way there without consultation, before it is even clear what is needed where in what capacity. 87 camps with a capacity between 100 – 60,000 people are constructed by the deployed air organizations, ca. 35 t of foodstuffs are distributed to the affected daily.

Basis for deployment:	Alert through UN-OCHA.
Mission:	Assessment and coordination of international aid.
Duration of deployment:	February 10th, 2000 – February 24th, 2000 (UNDAC/MZB I);
	February 28th, 2000 – March 13th, 2000 (UNDAC/MZB II).
Participating nations:	Austria, Great Britain, OCHA, Zambia (UNDAC/MZB I);
	Austria, Great Britain, Finland, Norway, WHO, Zambia (UNDAC/MZB II).
Strength:	5.
Headquarters:	Maputo/INGC Building and Assessment in the south of Mozambique (UNDAC/MZB I);
	Maputo/INGC Building, Beira/Central Mozambique (OSOCC) (UNDAC/MZB II).
Austrian expert:	Colonel Mag. Alois A. Hirschmugl.
Duration of deployment:	February 10th, 2000 – February 24th, 2000.

Austrian Reaction

Political Measures

The Federal Minister of Defence orders the dispatch of a disaster relief expert in the course of a foreign business trip. Since no insurance protection is given, the dispatched officer must insure himself!

Austrian Humanitarian Contingent for Mozambique (ATHUM/MOC)

Preliminary Events

A flood and cyclone catastrophe breaks over the south and southeast of Africa at the beginning of February 2000. Parts of South Africa, Botswana and Zimbabwe are devastated. Nevertheless, the worst affected is Mozambique (by area, it is around ten times as large as Austria). 11,000 cubic meters of water per second fall for weeks in the main river, the Limpopo, alone, and destroy entire cities and villages. 1,000 dead and 100,000s of homeless are the result. Almost all flee if they still can. Many save themselves on roofs or in trees (many from them are there recovered and rescued by South African helicopter pilots). No sooner has the rainfall stopped, but hundreds of thousands return to their homeland to rebuild their houses. However, they are surprised by the new onset of rainfall. While 350,000 people were affected by the first rainfall, the number subsequently climbs to 950,000. The rainfall makes aid flights practically impossible. Initially only a few helicopters are even available, which were dispatched from South Africa to provide aid. Not until later can the number be raised to 51.

International Reaction

UN Secretary General Kofi Annan calls for the international community to send Mozambique all thinkable aid. The American Secretary of State Madeleine Albright not only immediately announces US aid, but also calls for the US Congress to make more money available for foreign aid. The US Department of Treasury plans to release Mozambique from debt in the amount of $5.7 billion US.

Basis for deployment:	OCHA-Geneva Request Situation Report of March 4th, 2000.
Mission:	Drinking water purification.
Duration of deployment:	March 17th – April 19th, 2000.
Participating nations:	Austria, Germany, Switzerland.
Strength:	Unknown.

Austrian Participation

Political Measures

As a result of the request for aid from UN/OCHA on February 10th, 2000, an officer is dispatched to the five-person multinational team for coordination of the catastrophe deployment. Because of the urgency resulting from the situation in the catastrophe zone, the federal government decides on the dispatch of a military contingent to supply drinking water on March 7th, 2000, with regard to the federal constitutional law on cooperation and solidarity during the dispatch of units and individuals.

Military Measures

The personnel and material formation takes place in two phases: In the 1st phase (3/6 – 3/10) the personnel selection takes place (including reserve personnel), the medical examinations and immunizations as well as briefings on the local conditions (domestic situation, culture, climate). Further the technical equipage of the contingent in the area of the formation staff/AFDRU is determined. In Phase 2 the final personnel assignments are made, the equipment (total 90 t) is loaded onto pallets, the move is made to Schwechat Airport and everything is loaded into four Ilyushin-76 airplanes chartered in Ukraine.

On March 10th, a four-person advance command leaves Austria in a plane from a civilian airline. The advance command immediately takes up with the nation and international deployment leaderships, with the Swiss chargé d'affaires as well as the representatives of the "Swiss Disaster Relief Unit" and the "German Technical Relief Organization" (the planned cooperation of the joint disaster relief D-A-CH – Germany, Austria, Switzerland – does not occur, since the German forces are deployed 400 km away). Instead there is an outstanding cooperation with the Swiss forces. The advance command also prepares the unloading of the airplanes and the reception and a press conference in the presence of the Mozambican minister responsible for the entire deployment.

On March 16th, the movement takes place, the contingent lands in Maputo on March 17th. There, after unloading by hand with the help of American soldiers and African pathfinders (technical unloading help is lacking), a temporary camp is established. On the same day a second flight takes place to Samora Marchel of a DWP element with helicopters from the US Air Force in two lifts. Already on March 18th the production and distribution of drinking water can begin. The rest of the contingent is transferred to the Airfield/Chibuto between March 18th and 20th with the support of the German Air Force, in twelve lifts with C-160s and the USAF (six lifts with CH-53s). There too the unloading must take place by hand. The base camp is constructed on the airfield. On March 21st the base camp as well as the reinforced DWPGrp placed near the refugee camp of Samora Machel are both fully functioning. An examination of the produced drinking water and the formal notified authorization of the distribution takes place through the authorities responsible for water distribution (DANN). With this, the rejection of purified water and the gathering of water from the contaminated Limpopo river can be prevented.

At a distance of more than 8,300 km, this is the furthest deployment of Austrian soldiers from Austria yet in the history of the armed forces. The large distance also demands the full independence of the contingent for supplies over a period of four weeks. So no foodstuffs can be bought from the country besides a daily requirement of bread! Bringing along a large quantity of "bottled water" for the time before and after the production of drinking water is also decisive for accomplishing the mission because of the high water needs of each individual due to the climactic influence.

The soldiers are confronted with great heat, high humidity, tropical rainfall as well as the danger of being bitten by snakes or stung by scorpions during this deployment and must accept great personal privation. Above all the poverty and need with which the soldiers are directly confronted represents a fully new experience for many. On the other hand, the great joy of the affected population at the deployment of the armed forces represents a strong motivation and causes their own worries and problems to be forgotten. According to UNO estimates two million land mines are placed in Mozambique. These are swept away by the rushing rivers and so form a constant danger. Therefore an EOD team is also with ATHUM/MOC for mine clearance.

The communications connection to the homeland takes place by satellite telephone. The connection between the contingent command and the liaison officers in Maputo goes over mobile telephones procured in the country. Within the contingent contact is maintained over AN/PRC-77.

Besides the simple purification of water there are also a number of other unplanned activities: So at the mission station of the Austrian Caritas, the defective water pump is repaired and the water containers cleaned with pressure washers. After a call from UNICEF, two water purification systems donated by Norway, which have stood in Xai-Xai for two weeks but could not be deployed as a result of a lack of knowledge (!), are built and set in operation by the liaison officers of the Austrian contingent. Further, a cooperation takes place with the German Maltese Aid Service. This was initially on the search for a suitable area of operations for its highly qualified tropical medic. ATHUM/MOC offers them the use of the infrastructure of the Austrian camp and with regard to the secured drinking water supply at the Samora Machel refugee camp, to take over the medical care on side. Finally as a result of the personal initiative of some soldiers, an elementary school with three makeshift classrooms for 60 children each is constructed in Samora Machel. After a charity drive among the soldiers the children can also be provided with notebooks, books, and writing utensils. In the time from April 2nd to 7th, four Mozambican officers are briefed in the use of the DPS. As a result of the precarious situation in the "Fidel Castro" and "O.M.M. Centro Experimental" refugee camps, a "water bridge" is maintained for two consecutive weeks over a distance of 80 km.

The dismantling and withdrawal begin on April 9th. Since the USAF as well as the German Army have already ended their deployments at the end of March, the return of the no longer necessary equipment takes place in cooperation with the Joint Logistic Operation Cell/UN (JLOC) and the contingent of the South African Air Force (SAAF) with "Buffalo" on one side and a "Casa" on the other. During this the wheeled vehicles, including the Med-Pinzgauers, are flown as outer weights in nets with SAAF helicopters to a road. From there on a land march takes place over 200 km to Maputo. In order to ease the loading activities, a tractor with hydraulics is converted into a field loading device with the help of two metal prongs.

The preparations for the withdrawal represent a large problem. Since it was naturally ordered to bring the WPS back to Austria (the military only has these systems, there is no budget for a new procurement), they must be completely cleaned before loading. So in the last days before the flight home no more drinking water can be produced. A measure which is absolutely necessary for the maintenance of deployment readiness, but calls up no understanding from the population. Not until three weeks after the withdrawal of ATHUM/MOC can a high-quality water supply be secured for the victims again by the installation of two wells in the region. The boring of the wells goes back to an initiative of the two Austrian liaison officers in Chibuto, who bring this about with the local authorities through a donation from the Maltese Aid Service.

Since the flight home is delayed by two days, this time is used for recovery. The closed return (except for the advance command, which has a return ticket) takes place on April 17th from Maputo through Johannesburg to Vienna. The advance command follows on April 19th with a commercial flight from Lauda Air.

Basis for deployment:	Urgent dispatch according to Sec. 1 no. 1 subsec. b in connection with Sec. 2 para. 2 FCL-CSD through the Federal Chancellor, Foreign, Finance and Defence Ministers on March 7th, 2000.
Mission:	Drinking water purification, de-mining duty, emergency medical care.
Appellation:	**Austrian Humanitarian Contingent for Mozambique (ATHUM/MOC).**
Form of dispatch:	FCL-CSD 1997.
Area of operations:	Chibuto and Samora Machel (Province of Xai-Xai).
Duration of deployment:	March 16th, 2000 – April 19th, 2000 (advance command from March 10th).
Contingent strength:	64.
Composition:	Contingent command, command group (signal team, DocTrp), specialist group (liaison officer, field laboratory, clearance, recovery and decontamination specialists), technical support group (EODTrp, EngTrp), supply staff (SupplyGrp, MTrp, Field Mess Trp, MedGrp), 1st and 2nd drinking water purification groups.
Commander:	Lieutenant Colonel Michael Schuster.
Contribution:	3,300,000 l drinking water.

The drinking water purification system is constructed near the Samora Machel refugee camp (t.l.). Naturally the quality of the water is constantly tested in their own laboratory (t.r.). The examination of the produced water and its release according to orders takes place through the authorities responsible for water distribution. Further, local officers are briefed in the usage of the WPS (m.l.) Besides the production of drinking water the reactivation of the village well is also a focus (m.r.). Seemingly other inhabitants of the country are also interested in our water, or perhaps more in our soldiers? (b.l.). However all dangers and struggles are quickly forgotten in view of the thankfulness for help (in the photo b.r. from a Caritas sister, who heartily bids farewell to the soldiers who repaired her own water purification system).

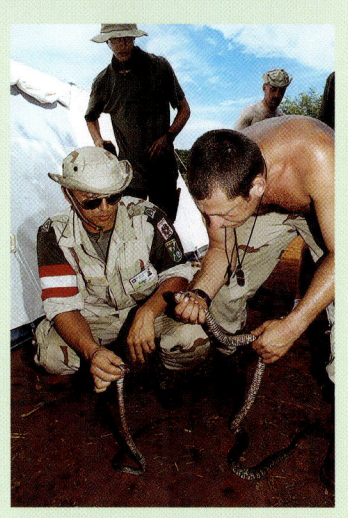

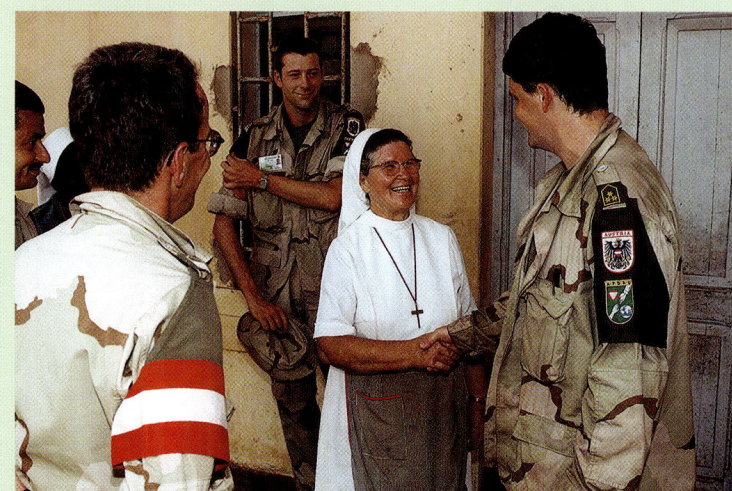

The "airport" from Chibuto in Mozambique. Faith in God belongs in every deployment – here it is especially tested.

Office of the High Representative for Bosnia and Herzegovina (OHR/BiH)

International Reaction

A "high representative" is dispatched to coordinate the measures of the Dayton Agreement. Since 2000, the Austrian diplomat Dr. Wolfgang Petritsch (before the Austrian ambassador in Belgrade and EU special ambassador during the Ramouillet negotiations of the settlement of the Kosovo crisis in 1999) fulfills this function.

Basis for deployment:	Dayton Agreement of November 21st, 1995, ratified in Paris on December 14th, 1999; SC Resolution 1031 (1995) of December 15th, 1995; SC Resolution 1088 (1996).
Mission:	Implementation of the civilian goals of Dayton.
Duration of deployment:	December 21st, 1995 – to date.
Participating nations:	Members of the EU, Sweden, Switzerland, Norway (no national dispatches; the recruitment takes place individually through the OHR).
Headquarters:	Sarajevo.

Austrian Participation

Political Measures

During the Austria EU chairmanship in the 2nd half of 1998, a noncommissioned officer initially dispatched to ECMM is temporarily moved to OHR, in order to now carry out the duties of the humanitarian return of the war victims, which he had previously fulfilled at ECMM, at OHR. In May 2000 the decision is then made to accede to the request of the OHR for the dispatch of an officer to the Military Cell and once again a noncommissioned officer for Humanitarian and Refugees Affairs to carry out the humanitarian war victims' return. In view of the fact that the Austrian diplomat Dr. Wolfgang Petritsch resigns his function as **High Representative for Bosnia and Herzegovina** at the end of April 2002, the dispatch of both Austrian soldiers is also ended.

Military Measures

Basis for deployment: CM of May 14th, 2000, MC of May 17th, 2000 (dispatch of up to two military experts until July 31st, 2002).
Mission: Military advisor to the High Representative, support of the Office for Missing Persons.
Appellation: None.
Form of dispatch: FCL-CSD 1997.
Area of operations: Sarajevo.
Duration of deployment: July 1st, 2000 – July 31st, 2002.
Contingent strength: 2 (1 officer, 1 NCO).
Total: 3.

United Nations Mission in Ethiopia and Eritrea (UNMEE)

Preliminary Events

Eritrea is initially an Italian colony. After the Second World War it is administrated by Great Britain under a UN mandate. In the year 1950 the decision is made by the UN General Assembly that Eritrea and Ethiopia should be combined into a federation. For this a new constitution is created, which includes the following points: The government of Ethiopia is also to be seen as that of the federation; the Emperor is represented in Eritrea through a governor-general. The Ethiopian sovereignty only applies in the areas of defence, foreign and domestic trade between the two nations, foreign and interstate communication as well as the administration of harbors. The legislative and executive branches are regulated by regional governments. In 1952 Eritrea becomes an autonomous region under the Ethiopian crown. In 1962 Eritrea is annexed by Ethiopia, but subsequently, above all after the end of the Ethiopian empire and in view of the chaotic developments under the Communist dictatorship of Mengistus, there are efforts for the independence of Eritrea again; extended hostilities occur. In 1993 Eritrea finally becomes independent after the death of Mengistus. However there is continual conflict over the demarcation of the border, which still stems from colonial times. For Ethiopia the loss of Eritrea (which before the Italian colonial period had belonged to the empire) brings the problem that it now has no access to the sea. The termination of the monetary union by Eritrea in November 1997 leads to further tensions.

The conflict about the Eritrean border, with a 400 square kilometer area around the city of Badme, determined by England, Italy and Ethiopia in 1903, finally leads on to the outbreak of a border war on May 12th, 1998, which is briefly interrupted by a ceasefire at the beginning of the rainy season on August 3rd. On February 4th, 1999, heavy fighting breaks out anew. On February 28th, 1999, both countries agree to a peace plan from the OAU, but the Ethiopian Army begins again with military advances in the western and central sections of the front on May 11th, 2000. The Ethiopians achieve their greatest successes at the Mereb front sector from Telozie to the Mereb river in the Badme sector. The Eritrean units can be surrounded and overrun on the Badme front with a few days. Around a week later there are serious and finally decisive hostilities on the Zela Ambessa-Egala front. On May 23rd the Ethiopian Premier Meles Zenawi declares that the war could be ended with a day. In reality, Zela Ambessa is reconquered on May 24th, the Eritrean independence day. The Ethiopian Army celebrates a "blitzkrieg". Shocked by the partially crushing defeat, on May 25th Eritrea declares itself ready for a complete withdrawal of its troops from the areas conquered in 1998, as called for by the plan from the Organization of African Unity (OAU). Ethiopia nevertheless still continues its air attacks on May 28th and 29th against facilities in the area of Eritrea's most important harbor, Massawa, and the air force base of Asmara. These however gain no decisive value. The following days, however, are marked by local combat and contradictory statements about the end of the war. On June 14th Ethiopia announces the reconquering of the area of Tesseney in western Eritrea. This area has the greatest importance for Eritrea's agricultural production. For Ethiopia it is especially a question of hindering its agricultural use as long as possible by laying land mines. Ethiopia's systematic destruction in this area reaches from the destruction of factory sites to the looting of apartments and also does not stop at air attacks on refugee and reception camps. The focal point of the Ethiopian advances lies in Assab, the onetime most important supply harbor for Ethiopia, at the same time one of the causes of the bilateral conflict. After the Eritrean troops, as called for by the OAU, have withdrawn from this section of the front, the Ethiopian army breaks the agreement and SC Resolutions 1297 and 1298 (on respecting national sovereignty rights) and advances into this area.

Despite the continuation of the hostilities, both parties in the war meet on June 5th, 2000, in Algeria with the mediation of the OAU for pre-talks. The efforts to settle the war-like conflicts lasting since 1998 culminated on June 18th, 2000, in the conclusion of an agreement regarding the cessation of hostilities. This is signed by both foreign ministers Seyoum Misfin and Haile Waldensaye under the aegis of the Algerian president Abdul Aziz Butaflika in his capacity as OAU chairman and the American special envoy Anthony Lake. Nevertheless, the Eritrean Foreign Ministry still reports in the beginning of July that Ethiopian troops make 25 villages and towns within the buffer zone uninhabitable. By the peace treaty of December 12th, 2000, 100,000 people lose their lives, 1.3 million are forced to flee.

International Reaction

Already a few hours after the outbreak of hostilities, the UN Security Council demands the cessation of all hostilities within 72 hours on May 13th, 2000. On May 17th the Security Council enacts a twelve-month weapons embargo against both parties in the war, which however has no effect. The call of the OAU on May 14th initially also has no effect.

After the failure of the mediation attempt the UNO attempts to initiate the talks process again through a high-ranking special mission under the leadership of the American UNO ambassador Richard Holbrooke. Both parties, however, continue to show themselves unready to compromise. Limited by the harsh stance of the Ethiopian government, which first agrees to talks on a peace plan

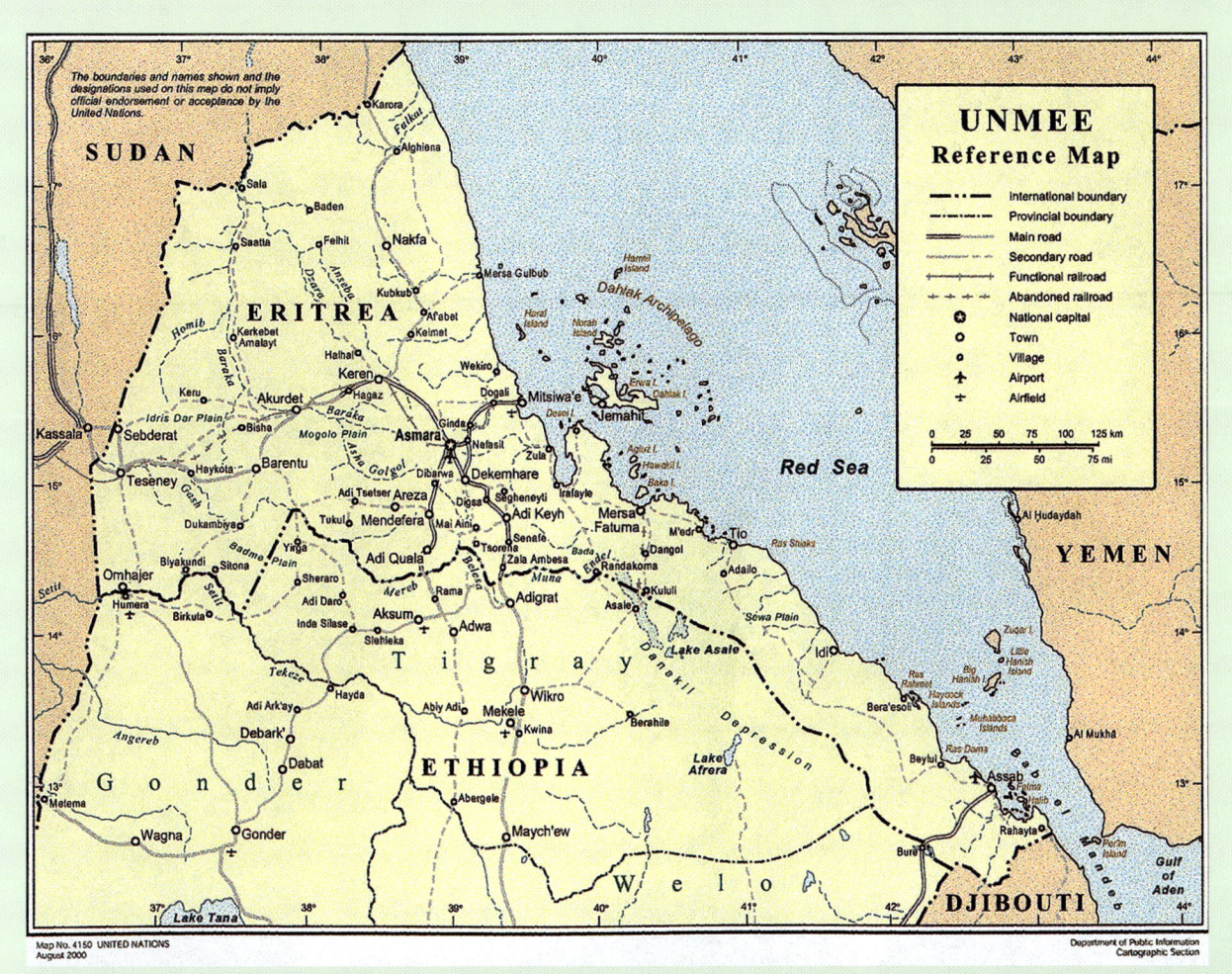

Headquarters (b.).

on June 11th, a continuation of the talks first takes place after the consent of the parliament.

The agreement signed on June 18th in Algeria finally represents the first decisive step to the reestablishment of peace between the two countries. This agreement envisions the establishment of a 25 km long buffer zone ("Temporary Security Zone – TSZ") along the entire border, from which the Eritrean army is to withdraw and in which the Ethiopian army may remain until two weeks after the UNO troops arrive. Subsequently a lasting, so-called "comprehensive peace agreement" is to be negotiated. In this the borders are to be newly demarcated with support from the colonial contract and international law. Continuing talks begin for practical implementation on June 21st. At the same time, however, painstaking measures begin to reconstruct the infrastructure, to fight the threatening famine as well as to solve the problem of the war refugees.

In order to make a rash implementation of the agreement possible, the UN Secretary General suggests to the Security Council in his S/2000/643 report of June 30th, 2000 to establish a group of military observers for the preparation of a peacekeeping operation in Ethiopia and Eritrea. The Security Council agrees to the suggestion on July 31st, 2000 in Resolution 1312. The Security Council establishes the extent with up to 100 military observers as well as the necessary civilian personnel. The mission is initially to carry out its activities until January 31st, 2001 with a view to the planned peacekeeping operation. On September 15th the Security Council establishes the extent of the mission as 4,200 (troops, military observers, and civilian personnel).

On December 6th, 2000, UN Secretary General Kofi Annan officially declares the war between the neighboring states on the Horn of Africa ended. On December 12th the peace agreement is signed in Algiers.

Basis for deployment:	SC Resolution 1298 (2000) of May 17th, 2000; SC Resolution 1308 (2000) of July 17th, 2000; SC Resolution 1312 (2000) of July 31st, 2000 (dispatch); SC Resolution 1320 (2000) of September 15th, 2000 (extent and duration).
Mission:	Establishment and maintenance of a connection to both parties in the conflict; implementation of the mission on the instructions of the UN Secretary General through visits to the military headquarters and establishments in the entire area of operations; establishment of a mechanism for the verification of the cessation of hostilities; observation and verification of a withdrawal of Ethiopian troops from positions that were taken after June 6th, 2000; observation of the temporary 920 km long security zone (TSZ); preparation for the creation of the military coordination committee envisioned in the agreement; coordination and support of a mine clearance program within the TSZ; help with the planning of a future peacekeeping operation.
Duration of deployment:	August 1st, 2000 – July 31st, 2008 (expiration of mandate).
Participating nations:	Algeria, Austria, Bangladesh, Canada, China, Finland, Ghana, India, Italy, Jordan, Kenya, Malaysia, Nepal, the Netherlands, Norway, Peru, Poland, Romania, Spain, Sweden, Switzerland, Tanzania, Tunisia, Ukraine, Uruguay, Zambia.
Strength:	4,200 (troops, military observers, civilian workers).
Headquarters:	Addis Ababa (Ethiopia) and Asmara (Eritrea).

Austrian Participation

Political Measures

At the request of the Secretary of the United Nations, the federal government decides on the dispatch of up to nine staff members within the framework of the "Standby High Readiness Brigade" (SHIRBRIG) for up to six months. Since it subsequently becomes apparent that the military staff of the mission is to be formed without the addition of the SHIRBRIG staff, the federal government decides to respond to the petition for a dispatch under the altered conditions as well. Since the deployment is extended by a year on the part of UNO, however, the maximum dispatch strength is limited to five officers, in order to ensure that the total costs of the dispatch remain unchanged. In addition it is decided to dispatch up to five military observers.

Military Measures

After Admiral Tegetthoff's expedition in 1857, the mission of Austrian Imperial observers at the court of Emperor Menelik II, and the deployment of Austrian volunteers during the Italian invasion in Abyssinia in 1936, Austrian soldiers are again in the Horn of Africa – this time, however, on a peaceful mission.

Initially the dispatch of three military observers takes place. The three military observers are stationed in the inhospitable area of the front. Their daily situation reports ("SITREPS") show that the behavior of both conflicting parties is still influenced by mistrust and aggression. Proof of this is the constant construction of positions and fortifications, the renewed laying of mines and the limitations of the freedom of movement of the UNMEE soldiers.

A petition comes from the UNO to Austria to occupy the following positions in HQ/UNMEE:

- Senior Staff Officer Operations (Operations Cell),
- Administration Officer,
- Logistic Operations Officer,
- Transport/Movement Control Officer,
- Operations Clerk.

Accordingly, four officers and a noncommissioned officer are named for the dispatch within the framework of SHIRBRIG for the duration of one year by the MoD (also according to the act of the Council of Ministers). The five soldiers initially travel to Copenhagen with a commercial flight on November 13th, 2000 for briefing and training specific to the deployment, and from there on November 23rd further to Asmara, Eritrea, to the area of operations. The five soldiers initially fulfill their duties in HQ/UNMEE. Their mission is to ensure the integration of new staff members and the movement of international troops. The soldiers are armed with StG 77 and P 80s. The deployment is made more difficult by the extreme climatic and geographical conditions (central highlands 2,400 m above sea level, and Danakil Depression at -116 m).

Basis for deployment:	CM of August 8th, 2000 (dispatch); CM of September 5th, 2000, MC of September 18th, 2000 (dispatch of up to five military observers until September 30th, 2001 and up to five staff members until November 30th, 2001).
Mission:	Establishment of a connection to the parties in the conflict; observation of the cessation of hostilities; assistance with the planning and establishment of a future peacekeeping mission.
Appellation:	None.
Form of dispatch:	FCL-CSD.
Area of operations:	September 18th, 2000 – July 31st, 2008 (military observers); September 27th, 2003 – September 6th, 2006 (leader of CIMIC).
Contingent strength:	2 – 3.

Medical Care

Especially during the deployment of military observers, who move in a larger area of operations, it is important to plan the medical care looking ahead. So in this concrete case the dispatch instructions envision the following:

"*Teams of doctors in Barentu, Adrigrat and a third place. With street transportation until Medevac. Field hospital (Level II) in Asmara, evacuation there directly from the accident site or from, among other things, a med-facility with med-helicopter. Evacuation to the homeland, when this is medically possible, with a commercial flight, in other cases with the doctors' clinic."*

Uniforms

During this deployment the Austrians (as already in Mozambique) wear US desert uniforms, which prove themselves outstandingly.

South-East European Regional Arms Control Verification and Implementation Assistance Center (RACVIAC)

Preliminary Events

The new order in the Southeast European area leads to structure and stabilization problems in many affected nations, which calls for the adjustment of long-term measures and support. The Stability Pact for Southeast Europe, concluded on EU initiative, is to strengthen the participating nations in the region in their endeavors to promote peace, democracy, respect for human rights and economic well-being.

International Reaction

Initially the RACVIAC is founded as the first project within the framework of the "Quickstart List" of the Stability Pact of June 10th, 1999, under the aegis of "Worktable III – Security Questions". It is to help create an atmosphere of trust and security in which transparency, openness and predictability in the area of military security are improved, as well as cooperation and a broad security dialogue between the participating nations.

The RACVIAC wants to support the OSCE in the fulfillment of its mandate in line with the Dayton Peace Agreement with regard to the creation of trust and security as well as the promotion of cooperation and good neighborly relationships, and for its part has no influence on existing national rights and duties beyond the various armament monitoring treaties and agreements.

Basis for deployment:	Stability Pact for Southeast Europe of June 10th, 1999; Act of the Standing Council PC.DEC/306 of July 1st, 1999.
Mission:	Humanitarian aid; election support; promotion of human rights; disposal of explosive ordnance.
Duration of deployment:	October 20th, 2000 (mission establishment from July 10th, 2000) – to date.
Participating nations:	Albania, Austria, Bosnia-Herzegovina, Bulgaria, Croatia, France, Great Britain, Greece, Germany, Hungary, Italy, Macedonia/FYROM, the Netherlands, Romania, Russia, Slovenia, Turkey, United States of America.
Strength:	30 employees.
Headquarters:	Rakitje near Zagreb.
Director:	September 9th, 2002 – October 8th, 2004: Brigadier General Johann Pucher.

Austrian Participation

In spring 2002, Austria is invited to take over the function of the director of the RACVIAC which is alternately occupied by the participating nations for two years each, starting in September 2002. As a result of the security and military-political emphasis in the Southeastern European area, this offer is accepted.

Military Measures

Basis for deployment: CM of September 12th, 2000, MC of September 18th, 2000.
Mission: Cooperation in the maintenance of order and safety in Kosovo.
Form of dispatch: FCL-CSD.
Area of operations: Rakitje.
Duration of deployment: October 2nd, 2000 – to date.
Contingent strength: 1 (until May 31st, 2001: 2) staff officer.
Total: 8.

United Nations Military Observer Group in India and Pakistan (UNMOGIP)

Preliminary Events

With the end of the British occupation and declaration of independence of India and Pakistan, a conflict occurs in 1947 over possession of the province of Jammu and Kashmir. In 1949 both countries agree to the establishment of a cease-fire line. In 1965 hostilities occur over the use of the Indus, the East Pakistan question and the ownership of Kashmir. Since 1972 India no longer cooperates with the mission, which since then can only develop its activities from the Pakistani side. In 1998 both countries undertake atomic bomb tests. India accuses Pakistan of supporting the Muslim militias fighting in the Indian part of Kashmir for annexation by Pakistan. The battles take place for the most part on the Siachen Glacier 5,500 – 7,000 m above sea level (!).

International Reaction

Starting in 1948, the United Nations attempts to mediate. With Resolution 39 (1948) on January 20th, 1948, the **"United Nations Commission for India and Pakistan (UNCIP)"** is established for this purpose. UNMOGIP is installed to support UNCIP with Resolution 47 (1948). In July 1949 a cease-fire line between the province claimed and occupied by India and Pakistan is able to be established. The cease-fire agreement takes effect on January 1st, 1949. After the end of UNCIP 1951, UNMOGIP is continued as an independent observer mission. Since new hostilities occur in 1965, UNMOGIP is reinforced with Resolution 210 (1965). At the end of 1971 the battles flare up again. In July 1972 a monitoring line is established which is largely identical with the previous line. A final settlement of the conflict also cannot be accomplished during the ongoing summit talks (last in June 2001).

The events of September 11th, 2001, the terrorist attacks themselves and the following attacks of the USA on targets in Afghanistan, pull this region into the center of the world public's interest. The tense situation in Kashmir escalates once more. India and Pakistan put their troops on raised alert readiness and carry out massive troop marches along the joint border.

Basis for deployment:	SC Resolution 47 (1948) of April 21st, 1948 (additional dispatch of military observers to UNCIP); SC Resolution 91 (1951) of March 30th, 1951 (UNMOGIP).
Mission:	Observation of the cease-fire line.
Duration of deployment:	January 1st, 1949 – to date.
Participating nations:	Austria, Australia, Belgium, Canada, Denmark, Ecuador, Finland, Italy, Republic of Korea, Mexico, New Zealand, Norway, Sweden, Uruguay.
Strength:	45 military observers, 70 civilian workers (of which 43 local workers).
Headquarters:	Srinagar, Indian-Kashmiri capital (summer half of the year), Rawalpindi, Northern Pakistan (winter half of the year).
Chief Military Observer:	August 15th, 2001 – August 31st, 2002: Major General Hermann K. Loidolt.

Austrian Participation

As a result of an announcement from UNO, Brigadier General Hermann K. Loidolt, previously representative office director in the MoD, volunteers for the function of chief military observer (CMO)/UNMOGIP.

After a hearing in New York, BG Loidolt is appointed the leader of UNMOGIP by UN Secretary General Kofi Annan.

Since this deployment takes place in accordance with Sec. 39 a of the Official Service Law (assignment of duty to an international organization), no further political or legal measures are necessary. BG Loidolt takes up his duties on August 15th, 2001, for the duration of the duty assignment he carries the international rank of his function, Major General. With this, MG Loidolt is the highest-ranking Austrian officer on a foreign deployment at the time.

Reception of MG Loidolt by an Indian honor formation in the Indian-Kashmiri capital of Srinagar. Note the stripes down MG Loidolt's pants and the general's pennant on the vehicle (picture t.l.). The entire UNMOGIP crew on October 31st, 2001 in Srinagar (picture t.r.).

Every November 1st the flag is raised in Rawalpindi, where the HQ is in the winter half of the year (picture m.l.). At a UN border crossing point between India and Pakistan (picture m.r.).

In a village near the line of control – LOC (picture b.l.). The South Korean observers after the medal parade (picture b.r.).

International Security Assistance Force (ISAF)

Preliminary Events

The mountainous character of Afghanistan initially helps the country to preserve its independence. In the 1st century AD Buddhism arrives in the country, in the 9th century the majority of Afghanistan is incorporated into the Islamic area. In the 10th – 12th centuries a distinct nation emerges for the first time under the Ghaznavids and Ghurids, who are ravaged by Ghengis Khan in the 13th and 14th centuries. In the 16th and 17th centuries Afghanistan is divided between Persia and the Indian Mogul kingdom.

The national history of Afghanistan first begins in 1747, when Ahmed Shah Durrani, the founder of the eponymous dynasty in Kandahar, announces himself as the Emir of Afghanistan. After the death of his son Timur the kingdom declines, however remains a nation. Not until the 19th century are rules from the Barakzai tribe able to stabilize the situation in the country. At the high point of European imperialism, after two wars against Great Britain (1838 – 1842 and 1878 – 1881), Afghanistan becomes a buffer state between British India and Russia. After costly battles, Great Britain concludes the Duran Agreement with Emir Abd Ur-Rachman, which establishes a certain British domination in return for payments. In a British-Russian agreement from 1907, both world powers accept Afghanistan's independence. Afghanistan behaves neutrally during both world wars. In 1921 Emir Aman Ullah (he becomes king in 1926) manages to assert the full independence of his country. His efforts to implement internal reforms leads to his fall in 1929 as a result of strong resistance, especially from the Islamic clergy. His successor, King Nadir Shah, invalidates most reforms, nevertheless he transforms the kingdom into a constitutional monarchy. After his murder in 1933 Mohammed Sahir Shah takes the throne. In 1964 Afghanistan receives a modern constitution for the first time. Mohammed Zahir Shah is overthrown by his cousin Mohammed Daud Khan in 1973. Mohammed Daud declares a republic, makes himself president and rules the land dictatorially.

In 1978 a coup takes place through the Communist "Democratic People's Party" under M. N. Taraki. The resistance of the Islamic-traditionally oriented population rises against his attempts to subject the traditional societal structures to an extensive reorganization, which finally climaxes in an armed rebellion. In September 1979 Taraki is overthrown and murdered. Two months later his successor Amin is also executed. The new national and party chief is B. Karmal. At the same time, Soviet troops march into the country, supposedly at the request of the government. Resistance forms against the regime and the occupation forces, strengthened by American and Pakistani aid. Over five million Afghans flee to Pakistan and Iran. In 1986 Najibullah takes over from Karmal.

In April 1988 an agreement is concluded between Afghanistan and Pakistan (with the USA and the USSR as guarantor powers), which envisions mutual uninvolvement and the return of all refugees. Subsequently the withdrawal of Soviet troops takes place by February 1989. Since the resistance groups, the "Mujahideen", are not allowed to take part in the negotiations, they form an exile government and continue their fight against Najibullah's government, which ends in his overthrow in 1992. The new national president is B. Rabbani.

Bloody conflicts between the various Mujahideen groups hostile to each other lead to further destabilization. In 1994 the radical Taliban intervenes in the civil war and brings large parts of Afghanistan under its control. The previous president Najibullah is publicly executed, his successor Rabbani flees Kabul. The militias supporting him are only able to assert themselves against the Taliban in the northeast. For its part, the Taliban founds a strict Islamic religious state, the Islamic Emirate of Afghanistan, and introduces Sharia. Mullah Mohammed Omar has himself declared the "Ruler of the Faithful". The destruction of cultural goods from pre-Islamic times, including the two world-famous monumental Buddha statues of Bamiyan (125 km west of Kabul) from the 5th century AD, calls forth the protests of the entire world. The support of the Islamic extremist and multimillionaire Osama bin Laden, who is held responsible for most of the terrorist attacks, leads to conflict with the USA.

This escalates on September 11th, 2001, when the most serious terrorist attack yet in history takes place: Islamic suicide bombers use three previously hijacked and fully occupied civilian planes as flying bombs against the World Trade Center (WTC) in New York and the Pentagon in Washington. The two towers of the WTC collapse in on themselves shortly afterward. Thousands of dead are to be mourned. This act of terrorism is not only seen as an attack on the military and economic nerve center of the leading western power, it is in fact an attack on the entire civilized world.

International Reaction[125]

Initially the USA reacts militarily to the most brutal terrorist attack yet on America through a worldwide alert of their armed forces. Parallel to this a broad and expansive longterm strategy is begun:

---

125 "September 11th: Terrorist Attack on our World", in: Our Security Europe, Newsletter of the Austrian Institute for European Security Police, Issue 3/01, Maria Enzersdorf 2001.

Immediately after arrival in Kabul, the Austrian contingent moves to "Camp Warehouse" (t.). The service begins with a flag parade. Austria's flag now also waves in Afghanistan (m.r.). The 24-hour forced pause on the Turkish Black Sea coast offers time for conversation with natives (b.r.). Here the foreign experience of most members of ISAF is shown once again. Our soldiers are, thanks to intensive language training, in a position to form contact everywhere. The picture b.l. shows the Austrian soldiers with the German comrades (in the camouflage field uniform) during the jointly preparatory training in Germany. The soldiers are equipped with "police personal protection equipment" during deployment against demonstrators (see page 321 as well). In the background vehicles of the German Feldjäger (roughly equivalent to our military police) can be seen.

in the shortest amount of time President George W. Bush is able to forge a worldwide political alliance against terrorism, in which all members and partners of NATO, all EU members, but also Russia (President Putin makes, among other things, the use of airports in Uzbekistan possible for American jet fighters) and China, India and Japan as well as some Islamic nations, such as Pakistan, participate. President Bush makes it clear during this that the enemy is not to be seen as Islam, but the terrorist network[126] of radical fundamentalist Islamists[127]. The goals of the following American military operation in Afghanistan, in which British special forces are also involved, are the elimination of the Saudi millionaire Osama bin Laden, who is seen as the manipulator of the terror, and the destruction of the alliance between the Taliban[128] and Al-Qaida[129], in order to deprive the Islamic terror network[130] of its territorial foundation in Afghanistan. There is also a broad cooperation between intelligence agencies and police authorities on an international level in line with the War on Terror. Furthermore, measures are take to suppress illegal financial transactions and close illegal accounts.

The troops of the Northern Alliance initially operate on the ground with the support of the American Air Force. On November 29th the USA begins the largest ground operation yet. 1,000 US Marines establish an outpost in the area of Kandahar. All caves and tunnels are searched in the area between the capital of Kabul and the Khyber Pass on the border to Pakistan. More than 40 possible research sites for weapons of mass destruction are found by the US soldiers. On December 7th, two months after the beginning of the war, the last bastion of the Taliban falls in Kandahar. The fighters surrender or flee. A Pashtun tribal council takes over the control of the city. After the victory over the Taliban the anti-terror campaign in Afghanistan concentrates on the hunt for Bin Laden and his followers. They are supposed to be in the expansive labyrinth of bunkers, tunnels and caves of Tora-Bora, near the Afghan city of Jalalabad. The mountain fortress is in a mountain range 4,000 m above sea level, is driven up to 350 m deep in the fock and offers space for up to 2,000 people. On December 18th Tora-Bora also falls under the cooperation of American and British special forces.

The representatives of the Northern Alliance, the Afghan tribes and the previous king, who still enjoys great prestige in the country, come together on the Petersberg near Bonn with the help of the United Nations to lead the way to a new political order in Afghanistan. At this Afghanistan Conference the representatives of the most important Afghan tribes and ethnic groups agree on December 5th, 2001 in the Bonn Agreement to an interim government under the Pashtun leader Hamid Karzai. After six months the traditional "Large Assembly" (**"Loya Jirga"**) is to appoint a transitional government which officiates for 18 months. Parallel to this a constitution is drawn up and free elections prepared. A UN protection troop is to secure the peace process. This last is endorsed once more in a note from the foreign minister of the provisional Afghan government to the president of the UN Security Council on December 19th.

On December 13th, 2001, the USA publicizes a video in which Bin Laden confesses to being one of the responsible parties for the terrorist attacks. The European Council embraces in Laeken the Bonn Agreement in its session on December 14th and 15th, 2001 and calls on all Afghan groups to implement it. It declares its obligation to take part in all the endeavors of the United Nations.

The UN Security Council, in its resolution of December 20th, 2001 with reference to Chapter VII of the Articles of the United Nations, authorizes the creation of the International Security Assistance Force (ISAF) to support the Afghan interim authorities in the maintenance of safety in Kabul and its surroundings for a duration of six months, in order to make the activities of the interim authorities and UN personnel in a secure environment possible and to provide for the formation of a new gender-sensitive, multi-ethnic, representatively composed national government. Among the duties of ISAF are the securing of the Kabul – Bagram (airport 56 m north of Kabul) line of movement, property protection, patrol activities, support with the installation of new security institutions, planning of the subsequent operations to disengage ISAF or if necessary for its reinforcement.

The political situation remains fragile, particularly as the composition of the Afghan government does not conform to the ethnic spectrum (so the prime minister is Pashtun, the ministers are recruited from the United Front). One not unimportant factor for

---

126 The worldwide terrorist network exists since the beginning of the 1990's. Cells and groups exist in more than 70 countries in Asia, Africa, Europe and America. The main characteristic is their amorphous organization. The various conspirator cells function largely autonomously and do not know each other. The terrorists of today use the possibilities of modern information technology to their fullest extent (so on September 13th, two computer hackers are able to break into the homepage of the Taliban. A wanted poster of Bin Laden is put on the start page. Through the concentrated attack on their homepage the Taliban is forced to take it off the internet. With this they lose the possibility of making contact with the "sleepers" that exist worldwide) and have access to the most modern conventional weapons.
127 The current Islamic fundamentalism has its basic religious roots in Wahhabism. The Wahhabi sect is founded in the 18th century in Saudi Arabia as a reaction against the beginning westernization. An essential characteristic of the current representatives is therefore the basic rejection of the open western, in their view decadent social system, its values and principles such as pluralism, the separation of church and state, democracy and rule of law. Every method, including violence and terrorism, is right in order to reach its goal, the Islamization of the western world. The religious terrorist sees the use of violence as a duty commanded by God. Terrorism receives a transcendental dimension in this way, the death or execution of the terrorist for Allah's cause is interpreted as a martyr's death.
128 Bin Laden creates the territorial basis for his activities with the takeover of power of the Taliban regime in Kabul.
129 Al-Qaida ("The Basis") is a terrorist organization founded by Osama bin Laden at the end of the 1980's, which has made its goal the overthrown on "un-Islamic regimes" in Islamic countries, the establishment of a pan-Islamic worldwide caliphate and the expulsion of all non-Muslims from these countries. Al-Qaida finances and recruits above all Sunni extremists in numerous training camps in Afghanistan. The financial capital springs among other things from the flourishing narcotics trade, which according to UN reports brings in around 8 billion US dollars yearly.
130 Among others this includes Al Jihad in Egypt and Somalia, Harakut ul-Mujahideen (Pakistan and Kashmir), Asbet al-Ansar (Lebanon), the GIA (Algeria), the Islamic Battle Group (Libya), the Abu Sayyaf group (in the Philippines), HAMAS (Palestine) and the Chechnyan Mujahideen.

insecurity is the Uzbek General Dostum, who could not assert his goals during the negotiations in Bonn, but now belongs to the government as representative defence minister. In addition the Shiite minority of the Hazara located in Kabul (and supported by Iran) creates a potential for conflict, since they are disadvantaged during the distribution of aid goods. So 1,000 men must be drawn together for their protection in the area of Kabul alone. In addition in Kabul there is the danger of mines, emerging epidemics, rising criminality (including the drug problem), shootings (often caused by the improper use of weapons), high numbers of traffic accidents and cultural and religious conflicts (blood revenge). Outside of Kabul battles on the clan borders, highway robbery, etc., is the order of the day.

On January 4th, 2002 an internationally accepted status of forces agreement (SOFA) for the stay in the area of operations is made between ISAF and the Afghan interim authorities. In it, among other things, the observation of the Islamic rules by foreign troops (such as alcohol consumption and sexual relationships between male and female soldiers) is regulated. In the night before the 11th of January, all 17 participating nations sign the agreement on the Afghanistan mission.

Among the most difficult duties of ISAF is the deactivation and/or the destruction of rockets and grenades. During this there is a serious accident, in which two German and three Danish specialists lose their lives on March 6th, 2002.

On June 20th, 2002, the command of ISAF is transferred in a celebratory ceremony from Great Britain to Turkey in the presence of the Afghan president. It must particularly be noted that Turkey is the only Muslim country among the 18 participating nations.

In the spring and summer of the year 2002 there are increased incidents and explosions. In September 2002 the USA and Great Britain call for an extension of the mandate with the goal of stabilizing the region in connection with the preparations for a renewed military deployment in Iraq to overthrow Saddam Hussein.

Basis for deployment:	SC Act 1373 (2001) of September 28th, 2001 (international endeavors for protection and the combat of terrorism after the terrorist attacks of September 11th);
	SC Act 1378 (2001) of November 14th, 2001 (establishment of a transitional government);
	SC Act 1383 (2001) of December 6th, 2001 (acknowledgment of the Bonn Agreement);
	SC Act 1386 (2001) of December 20th, 2001 (creation of ISAF, acknowledgment of the British leadership).
Mission:	Support of the Afghan interim authorities with the maintenance of security in Kabul and its surroundings, in order to make possible the activities of the interim authorities and the UN personnel in a safe environment.
Duration of deployment:	January 11th, 2002 – to date.
Participating nations:	Austria, Belgium, Bulgaria, Denmark, France, Germany, Great Britain (lead nation until April 20th, 2002), Greece, Italy, the Netherlands, New Zealand, Norway, Portugal, Romania, Spain, Sweden and Turkey.
Headquarters:	Kabul.
Strength:	4,500.

Austrian Reaction

Political Measures

After various consultation and the basic declaration of intent to participate in the international peacekeeping troop, the Council of Ministers initially decides on January 8th, 2002, on the dispatch of up to 75 people, consisting of one each of infantry, logistics, support and staff elements for the duration of six months within the framework of the German contingent (together with Danes and Dutch). With regard to the extent of the personnel the Council of Ministers acceded to the wish of the Defence Ministry for the first time, in that this was set somewhat higher from the beginning. With this, a new act of the Council of Ministers must not be added, as previously done for a necessary reinforcement of even only a few people. This always led to a time delay in the past and with that led to limited freedom of action. The Council of Ministers likewise enacts a special funding (this was previously highlighted by Federal Minister Scheibner and General Troop Inspector Pleiner as a prerequisite for a dispatch, since the current budget makes a further foreign dispatch no long possible). Budget resources in the amount of 4.5 million Euros are to be held ready by the Minister of Finance for the military deployment for the duration of six months. 1.7 mill. Euros fall to the personnel costs, 2.8 mill. Euros are planned for the material costs (necessary investments, operational costs, air transport and the like). In addition the federal government declares itself ready to contribute 5.5 mill. Euros to finance civilian aid on the occasion of the Afghanistan Reconstruction Conference taking place in Tokyo on January 21st and 22nd.

It is notable that the Main Committee of Parliament enacts a resolution unanimously for the first time, in connection with the deployment of the armed forces on January 17th, 2002.

Military Measures

While the decision-making process goes on at the international level, the first plans are already being introduced in the Defence Ministry. After clarification with the federal government and with the understanding of the GTI, the federal minister declares on December 21st that Austria will already participate in the 1st phase of ISAF with platoon-strength security forces. Shortly before New Years', LTC GS Dr. Schmidseder is initially set on the march as a liaison officer to Berlin and South Cerney (GB) and then to Kabul, in order to make contact with the local military commands and civilian authorities and carry out a first assessment for the dispatch of an Austrian contingent. A liaison officer each is dispatched to the Deployment Leadership Command (DepLdCmd) in Potsdam and to the Permanent Joint Headquarters (PJHQ) in Northwood (GB). On January 8th an international advance command, to which an Austrian officer also belongs, travels from Dutch Eindhoven to Trabzon in Turkey. As a result of the weather situation, the further flight to Kabul can only take place two days later. On January 11th the German advance command, to which two Austrian officers also belong, arrives in Kabul. Among other things, the assessment and preparation of accommodations falls to the advance command. This is on the site of a former factory, 10 km away from Kabul, on the road to Jalalabad, and receives the name "Camp Warehouse". Initially eight tents are planned for the Austrian soldiers. The connection to the homeland takes place over a satellite telephone system constructed by the German armed forces.

Since the Austrian contingent is under German command, the pre-graded deployment preparation ("force integration training – FIT") is carried out in Germany. The air transport into the area of operations also takes place from Germany. The German armed forces, lacking sufficient air transportation space of its own, must fall back on the same Ukrainian Tupolev transport airplanes which have already flown for Austria a number of times.

The farewell to the contingent takes place on January 18th in ceremonial form in Wiener Neustadt. Afterwards the contingent travels to Hammelburg in Germany for training. On January 28th the trailers with the equipment follow. On February 1st, 2002 the transfer of the contingent into the area of operations takes place.

A deployment under the most extreme conditions awaits the soldiers, caused by battles between the clans, the acute danger of mines and the most dismal hygienic conditions. The "camp" in which the Austrians are accommodated develops on a one-time industrial site on the northeastern edge of Kabul. Initially there are neither firm accommodations, nor electricity, heat or water. Since the connections exist, after the transport of the appropriate trailers after a few weeks there is already a noticeable relaxation of tension in this area. This is all the more urgent since leave from the camp in free time cannot be granted for security reasons. In order to underline their peaceful deployment, the deployed soldiers do not wear combat helmets; the safeties are also on their weapons. In exchange all soldiers are equipped with a bulletproof vest.

The Austrian soldiers are assigned Districts 9 and 10. Besides patrol activities, the training of the local police also falls to the soldiers. The patrols are carried out together, they consist of one Austrian soldier, one Afghan policeman and one translator each. It takes some time until all of them win the necessary trust among each other.

On February 15th, 2002 there is a serious incident at the front during a football game between a Kabul assortment and ISAF: Instead of the 30,000 people which the stadium can contain, somewhat more than 15,000 additional people attempt to break through the barriers. The entrances are secured by the ISAF soldiers, among them also the Austrians. Inexplicably fanatics begin to hurl stones at the ISAF soldiers, during which some soldiers are also hurt. The soccer match is the first large sporting event ever. This match is to be a symbol for a peaceful future (the stadium was previously used by the Taliban as an execution site). The riots during this certainly represent a drop of bitterness, however they cannot cause a break in the ongoing peace process.

On March 30th the CIMIC team, the air transport element and the medical element are transferred to Afghanistan.

Unfortunately the situation in Kabul worsens in April. The constantly increasing attacks on ISAF members even force the MoD to transport on April 4th four Pandur wheeled armored vehicles through Cologne to Kabul with an Antonov, so that the AUCON/ISAF patrols can be carried out safely at night as well. On April 7th the most serious incident yet occurs: In the early morning two rocket attacks on Camp "Warehouse" occur, which – thank God – cause no damage to people. Shortly afterward 151 rockets of Chinese origin are secured during a raid. Besides this a large number of grenades, detonators, munitions and mines are discovered. On April 12th British ISAF soldiers are shot at by members of the Afghan security forces. The Austrian contingent is equipped with armored Puch Gs and "Bill" 2000 anti-tank guided weapons.

For the Grand Assembly, the Loya Jirga, taking place in the time from June 10th to 16th, during which 1,500 delegates meet in Kabul to elect a new transitional government, tents are put up by ISAF and accommodations, dining and recreational halls repaired again. Furthermore the Afghan National Guard is prepared for deployment and supported with the security measures.

For the command transfer carried out on July 17th, the police officers of the 9th district are invited for the first time to the guard and security movements. The emphasis of the Austrian activities lies in this district. The cooperation with the local authorities functions so outstandingly that the celebration is taken as an occasion to especially honor these officers and the translators.

On July 23rd, 2002, at 7:00 PM local time in Kabul, the transfer of command from ISAF 1 to ISAF 2 takes place. During this the air transport element is no longer reoccupied. On August 24th WO I Striednig is honored with the German lifesaving medal for the rescue of an Afghan who fell into a 30 m deep well.

In September 2002 it is decided to confer the deployment medal introduced in Austria on the members of ISAF 1 and 2.

Basis for deployment:	CM of January 8th, 2002, MC of January 17th, 2002 (dispatch); CM of December 15th, 2002, MC of December 22nd, 2002 (dispatch of staff members).
Mission:	Securing of buildings in Kabul and the road from Kabul to Bagram airport; staff duty.
Appellation:	**AUCON/ISAF.**
Form of dispatch:	FCL-CSD.
Area of operations:	Kabul, Bagram.
Duration of deployment:	February 1st, 2002 to December 20th, 2002.
Contingent strength:	Up to 71.
Total:	104.
Composition:	Staff element, guard and security platoon, national reconnaissance cell, air transport element, CIMIC experts (civilian-military cooperation), medical experts. Four "Pandur" armored personnel carriers, 19 Puch Gs.
Commander:	February 1st, 2002 – April 28th, 2002 Lieutenant Colonel GS Roman Horak (G3/Ops and NCC15); April 29th, 2002 – July 14th, 2002 Lieutenant Colonel GS Philipp Eder (return on July 25th); July 15th, 2002 – December 20th, 2002 Lieutenant Colonel GS Thomas Heinold.
Contributions:	480 military deployments (368 patrols in Kabul and surroundings, 40 guard deployments in Camp Warehouse, 26 deployments as reserve deployment forces in the German battalion, 31 deployments within the framework of intervention forces of ISAF, nine guard deployments at the Kabul airport, four guard deployments at the ISAF central munitions warehouse. The medical element cares for more than 900 people, of which more than 80 at the intensive care station. Almost 130 Afghans are among the patients, predominantly children.

The patrols take place on foot (t.l.) or are motorized (t.r.). They are always accompanied by a Kabul "policeman" and a translator. Before a football match there are initially small riots. A minor injury is quickly treated and soon forgotten (b.l.). The service of an air traffic controller at Kabul International Airport is a special experience (b.r.).

• Civil-Military Cooperation – CIMIC

CIMIC's work on foreign deployment is decidedly different from their work in Austria. Abroad CIMIC generally determines the cooperations between the military, national authorities, executive organs and other organizations, such as the Red Cross, the UNO or other NGOs (nongovernmental organizations). At ISAF concretely, it is a question for the support of the reconstruction of the civilian infrastructure, such as the construction or renovation of childcare centers, schools, hospitals and police stations. During this, finance plans are also created, calls for bids organized and construction progress monitored. Furthermore immediate measures are carried out, such as the distribution of foodstuffs or school supplies. These projects are largely financed by the German federal government; but also through Austrian national, raised by the economy, or totally private donation money. Besides their military security service, the soldiers implement 23 reconstruction projects with their German comrades, with a total value of more than 1 million US dollars. These include the Sawari Sangari and Tahey Maskan school projects including well construction, with a volume of around 180,000 US dollars and the Stara, Shirin Gol, Wasir Abad, Ariana, and Malalai childcare center projects, with a total volume of more than 130,000 US dollars. The International Deployments Command is able to collect a large high figure of donation money in line with the Mörbisch Lake Festival for a CIMIC project in Kabul. This is the renovation of the Ariana childcare center by the AUCON soldiers.

• Staff Service

Basis for deployment: CM of December 15th, 2002, MC of December 22nd, 2002.
Appellation: ISAF.
Form of dispatch: FCL-CSD.
Area of operations: Kabul.
Duration of deployment: December 21st, 2002 – August 5th, 2003 and March 17th, 2004 – to date.
Contingent strength: 3 – 5.

Air Traffic Controller[131]

At the request of NATO, Austria places air traffic officers as air traffic controllers from February 2005 until the end of 2007 at Kabul International Airport (KAIA)[132]. The main duty of the 1,600 soldiers dispatched here from 28 nations is to ensure the smooth operation of flights from the airport and during this to support the civilian airport as best as possible. Under ISAF responsibility the runway is also renewed, navigation lights, an instrument landing system (ILS), a VOR (VHF omni-directional radio beacon) as well as a TACAN (military omni-directional radio beacon) are installed. The financial coverage comes from the World Bank. Two Foreign Legion companies are responsible for external security. Internal security is achieved by cement walls and numerous rows of hescobastions (anti-shrapnel walls), which are guarded by a Belgian company. Since thousands of mines are still laid in the entire area of the airport and its nearest surrounding, there is close cooperation between EOD teams from the Czechs (LAGUNA) and the United Nations (UNMACA).

From the beginning, every air traffic controller is confronted with the immense amount of air traffic. The flight statistics at KAIA for 2004 show 39,104 flight movements. This is made more difficult by cooperation with the Afghan workers, who also carry out their activities in the tower and with whom the parking positions of the Afghan national airline flights and the other civilian aircraft must be coordinated. During flights of the Afghan Army's Antonovs, MI-17 and MI-24 helicopters, the pilots' lack of English knowledge makes a careful discussion with an Afghan liaison officer necessary. Nevertheless, he only faultily translates the instructions into Afghan, which leads to accordingly risky flight maneuvers. In the monitored zone, German military drone flights (LUNA and ALADIN) also take place. These flights need clearance from air traffic control. Therefore, during planned flights two liaison officers of the German armed forces are always in the tower. The largest problem, however, lies in the management. The time windows of the aircraft often do not agree. Many aircraft have no flight plans at all. There is no planning in advance with respect to the parking of the aircraft. Pilots must wait hours for a shuttle or unloading. In bad weather visibility conditions there are extreme delays, since aircraft are only allowed to take off when the approaching aircraft are already on the ground. As a controller one must be prepared for practically anything: So pilots approach the airport at their own risk despite the worst weather figures and then lose their way in the air while searching for the runway. Or they report themselves as south and downwind, but then emerge to the northeast in a right crosswind, do not manage the landing and then swerve in front of the nose of another aircraft without warning.

The deployment in Afghanistan also means an immense broadening of the horizon in all areas for the air traffic controller. The professional challenge is in the possibility of working at an international airport and during this controlling aircraft such as the B-747, AN-124, Il-76, F-16 or Apache.

---

131 Excerpt from a personal report from Major Rudolf Peschl.
132 Before the abbreviation was KIA, but this was changed, since KIA stands for "killed in action".

ISAF II

To support the parliamentary and provincial elections on September 18th, the United Nations Security Council decides on the extension of the ISAF mandate from the area of Kabul to all of Afghanistan with Resolution 1563 (2004) of September 17th, 2004. This reinforcement of the (at the time around 8,500 people strong) deployed forces in Afghanistan should include around 3,500 people in total. The ISAF mandate consists of the support of the Afghan government in the establishment and preservation of internal security and human rights, the delivery of humanitarian aid goods and the regulated return of refugees.

The federal government decides on the dispatch of an infantry contingent in the strength of up to 100 members of the armed forces until October 31st, 2004, at the latest. The basis for this is formed by German-Austrian technical discussions at the ministerial level in March of this year. An advance command and AUNIC are pre-staged on July 18th from Linz to Cologne and from there transferred to Termes in Uzbekistan with German military Airbus. From there a further flight takes place on July 20th to Kunduz. On Tuesday, August 2nd, 2005, the first portion of the Austrian AUCON3/ISAF contingent lands in Afghanistan. The American C-17 touches down at the Kabul airport at 6:30 AM local time. After the reception and unloading of the plane it's on to "Camp Warehouse", where the headquarters of the German brigade is. On Wednesday, August 10th, 2005, the Austrian ISAF contingent moves into its area of operations in the north of Afghanistan, for which 400 km of paths through partially bizarre terrain must be overcome. The actual deployed element of the contingent is formed by the mass of **Task Force 6**, a cadre presence unit from the Absam, Lienz and Bludesch garrisons, which are deployed as an armored infantry/protective company in the northern region of Afghanistan after a short dispatch preparation.

The duty of creating stable basic parameters for the elections on September 18th is central to the mission. For this, the armed forces place a reinforcement company with the German Battalion. The infantry parts have the following duties: Securing the airports in Kunduz and Feyzabad, securing transports and temporary outposts (substations) outside of Camp Kunduz, securing of freedom of movement along the main lines of movement, implementation of patrols including verbal reconnaissance, assessment for evacuation operations and checkpoints, readiness to take over the security and defence of the camp, deployment as a Quick Response Force (QRF) for evacuations in cooperation with the military police (MP), Explosive Ordnance Disposal (EOD) experts and Medical Evacuation (MEDEVAC).

A further goal of the deployment is to support the Afghan central government with the reconstruction of security and social structures in the northeastern region. Together with eight partner nations, the Austrians engage themselves in the PRT – provincial reconstruction team Kinduz. This team is led by the German armed forces. The pressure on the soldiers is high, with heat by day (up to 45 degrees Celsius) and night (under 0 degrees Celsius), dust, impassable terrain and extremely long patrols as well as the "personal constriction" of individual soldiers. The Austrian contingent is accommodated in trailers in the newly constructed part of Camp Kunduz. The low construction is a part of the protection for the troops against unguided missiles, since the containers are removed from direct sight by the surrounding houses. Shots fired at camps with these weapons is a latent threat in Afghanistan. Logistically, and with regard to leadership support, the Austrian contingent leans primarily on the facilities of the German armed forces. The soldiers are deployed twelve hours daily on average. In total 75,000 km are driven without accident- a tour de force of the dispatched drivers above all, but also for the assigned commanders.

Basis for deployment:	CM of June 7th, 2005, MC of June 10th, 2005.
Mission:	Securing the elections, help with reconstruction.
Appellation:	AUCON 3/ISAF.
Form of dispatch:	FCL-CSD.
Area of operations:	Provinces of Kunduz, Takhar and Badakhshan.
Duration of deployment:	July 18th, 2005 – November 11th, 2005.
Contingent commander:	Lieutenant Colonel Johannes Eisner.
Commander:	Captain Bernd Rott.
Contingent strength:	93.
Vehicle equipage:	Twelve "Pandur" armored personnel carriers, a medical "Pandur" with emergency medical equipment and six all-protected transport vehicles (APTV) "Dingo 2".

Hot Weather Clothing

A raised body temperature affects health, ability and with that also combat readiness. The clothing in areas of operation with high temperatures must therefore fulfill various criteria: Wicking away of sweat to external layers with the maintenance of a dry layer on the skin, maintenance of a suitable microclimate on the surface of the skin through good air circulation, protection from overheating in direct sun, wearability and little effort to clean.

The new "Dingo" protected vehicles and the tried-and-true armored "Pandur" are unloaded in a few minutes (t.l.). The most narrow places must be overcome again and again on the march to the camp (t.r.).

After a long march through the desert (m.l.) the convoy arrives in "Camp Warehouse" (m.r.). Lieutenant General Mag. Christian Ségur-Cabanac, Director General Operations, forms a personal impression of the situation in the Austrian area of operations in Kunduz (b.l.). Austrian soldiers in the new "personal police protection equipment" after an alert. In the background three "Pandurs" (b.r.).

European Union Mission in FYROM "Concordia"

Preliminary Events

In Macedonia there are increased attacks from the so-called Albanian Liberation Army, a separatist and militaristic group which strives for the annexation of the Albanian settlement areas in Macedonia by Kosovo. The danger is that the unrest caused by the actions of this group could lead to civil war, and consequently to the dissolution of the Macedonian state. Under pressure from the European Union and the USA, the representatives of both major Slavic and both major Albanian parties in the countries decide to hold talks on how to solve the ethnic conflict between the Macedonian majority and the Albanian minority. With the help of international mediators, a framework agreement is decided upon on August 13th, 2001, in Ohrid, which among other things envisions a decentralization of the administration, a new demarcation of the community borders and further possibilities for use of the Albanian language in the administration. The agreement itself is not legally binding. Rather, the changes envisioned must be translated into effective law by acts of the Macedonian parliament. This process, however, is always torpedoed.

International Reaction

On March 31st, 2003, the EU introduces its first military crisis management operation, Operation "Concordia", into the former Yugoslavian republic of Macedonia. "Concordia" relieves the **NATO Operation "Allied Harmony"**. The goal of the operation is to contribute to the creation of a stable environment, in order to put the government of the previous Yugoslavian republic of Macedonia into a position to implement the **Framework Agreement of Ohrid** of August 13th, 2001. This framework agreement is an agreement concluded between the two major Slavic and the two major Albanian parties of Macedonia, which is to secure a suitable representation of the Albanian minority in politics and administration. The occasion for the conclusion of the agreement is attacks of the so-called **Albanian Liberation Army** in Macedonia, which strives for the annexation of the Albanian settlement areas in Macedonia by Kosovo.

In line with Operation "Concordia", the so-called **"Berlin Plus"** agreements come into use, according to which the EU can lean on the planning capacities and command structure of NATO. In this respect, "Concordia" is not only the first EU-led military deployment, but also the first step to a "not only institutional, but also operative-practical foundation of the Strategic Partnership between EU and NATO".[133] After a transitional phase from December 16th – 31st, 2003, the mission is transferred to the EU police mission EUPOL/PROXIMA.

Basis for deployment: SC Resolution 1371 (2003); FAC/CFSP. Action 2003/92/CFSP of January 27th, 2003.
Mission: Observation of the Ohrid Framework Agreement in the former Yugoslavian Republic of Macedonia.
Duration of deployment: March 31st, 2003 – December 15th, 2003.
Participating nations: 27 (of which 13 EU countries).
Strength: Around 400.
Headquarters: Skopje.

Austrian Reaction

Political Measures

The federal government decides on the dispatch of up to ten members of the armed forces for the duration of up to six months. The Austrian contingent consists of up to three staff members (Light Field Liaison Team) and an Explosive Ordnance Disposal Team (EODT).

Military Measures

Basis for deployment: CM of March 11th, 2003, MC of March 18th, 2003 (dispatch of up to 10 people); CM of August 12th, 2003, MC of September 24th, 2003 (dispatch of up to 15 people).
Mission: Advising member of the local administration and EUFOR, explosive ordnance disposal, education of the local population.
Appellation: Austrian Contingent (AUCON).
Form of dispatch: FCL-CSD.
Area of operation: Northern Macedonia.
Duration of deployment: March 25th, 2003 – December 15th, 2003.
Contingent strength: 11.
Composition: 3 staff members, EOD team.
Commander: Lieutenant Colonel Harald Menzel, Warrant Officer I Josef Scherz (EOD team).

---

133 Reinhard C. Meier-Walser: "The Global Security Policy Profile of the European Union".

A Killer Job – Explosive Ordnance Disposal[134]

Among the duties of this mission under French command is a presence in conflict threatened areas such as Tetovo and Kumanovo, advising the local authorities on security concerns and the support of international observers. After the shift into the area of operations, activities are taken up on April 1st. The special demands of an explosive ordnance disposal team, such as expanded storage capacity for equipment, explosive agents, and munitions and for the remote-controlled manipulator (EOD manipulator vehicle) make it necessary to station the team in the Norwegian-led camp "Banski Rid" south of Skopje. However, this stationing has the advantage that it makes communication and coordination with the Italian EOD team easier. For the first time, the Austrian EOD team has a "Pandur" available as a deployment vehicle. This measure results from the analysis of the threat in the area of operations as well as the requirements of the lead nation.

The main area of operations in the northern part of Macedonia extends from the Albanian border area around Gostivar in the west to the eastern border area to Serbia in the area of Kumanovo. In this problematic section of terrain there were numerous mine accidents with deadly consequences. In March 2003 a Polish patrol and in June a convoy of Macedonian border police drove onto mines. With these accidents there was the justified suspicion that these mines or explosive devices were newly laid, since these routes had been driven numerous times in the days before without incident. The mission of the explosive ordnance disposal team includes the destruction of unexploded objects (UXOs) and booby traps when these limit the mobility of EUFOR; the rescue of injured EUFOR members from areas contaminated by explosive ordnance, and the examination of helicopter landing areas in the EUFOR area of operations. The assignments must be very exactly planned in the very mountainous border area to Kosovo, with height differences of more than 2,000 m. Information on the local political situation in the villages is as important as the newest mine maps in the planned lines of movement. It is often necessary to make contact with local leaders of Albanian descent, in order to not take the "wrong" (newly mined) road to the next town.

Furthermore the Austrian EOD team carries out a **mine awareness training** for 22 light field liaison teams from Germany, Finland, France, Norway, Austria, Poland, Portugal, Turkey, Sweden and Spain as well as heavy field liaison teams from Italy and France, for the Macedonian armed forces and for civilians.

Mine Awareness Training (MAT) with Finnish soldiers in Erebino (above). Training of German soldiers in reading mine maps (right).

---

134 Josef Scherz: "A Killer Job – Explosive Ordnance Disposal", in Truppendienst, Vol. 2/2006.

United Nations Mission in Côte d'Ivoire (MINUCI)

Preliminary Events

In September 2002 an ethnically, socially and religiously motivated conflict breaks out in Côte d'Ivoire, which leads not only to civil war-like hostilities but also to massive consequences for the entire coastal region of West Africa. According to governmental reports, 3,000 people are killed. Estimates go up to a million refugees. The cause of the civil war is a mutiny of one-time officers, who are enraged over their dismissal. This mutiny develops into a rebellion within a short time, which other groups join, and which soon includes among its demands the resignation of President Gbagbo, the end of ethnic discrimination and the organization of new elections. The conflict leads to a division of the country into a northern part controlled by rebels and a south controlled by the government.

International Reaction

Already shortly after the beginning of the crisis, French and UN armed forces manage the separation of the armed parties in the conflict and a reduction of the battles. The United Nations Security Council unanimously approves the dispatch of 76 unarmed officers to Côte d'Ivoire. Together with French and additional West African soldiers, they are to see to security and order. In MINUCI a civilian and a military component support each other with the guarantee of stability and the observation of the implementation of the Linas-Marcoussis Agreement of January 24th, 2003. Initially the military component deployed is 26 officers, whose main task consists of the observation of the situation and advising the UN Security Council's Special Envoy, Albert Tevoedjré. MINUCI leads into the **United Nations Operation in Côte d'Ivoire (UNOCI)** on April 4th, 2004.

Basis for deployment:	SC Resolution 1479 (2003) of May 13th, 2003.
Mission:	Observation of the situation and advising the UN Special Envoy.
Duration of deployment:	May 15th, 2003 – April 4th, 2004.
Participating nations:	Austria, Bangladesh, Benin, Brazil, Gambia, Ghana, India, Ireland, Jordan, Kenya, Moldova, Nepal, Nigeria, Pakistan, Paraguay, Poland, Romania, Russia, Senegal, Tunisia, Uruguay.
Strength:	76.
Headquarters:	Yamoussoukrois.

Austrian Reaction

Political Measures

The federal government decides on the dispatch of a member of the armed forces as Deputy Chief Military Liaison Officer (DCMLO).

Military Measures

Dispatch of a staff officer as representative director.

Basis for deployment:	CM of June 11th, 2003, MC of June 16th, 2003.
Mission:	Observation of the situation and advising of the UN Special Envoy.
Form of dispatch:	FCL-CSD.
Area of operations:	Ivory Coast.
Duration of deployment:	June 16th, 2003 – May 5th, 2004 (one month transitional phase).
Contingent strength:	1.

United Nations Disaster Assessment and Coordination Mission in Algeria (UNDAC/Algeria)

Preliminary Events

On the evening of May 21st, 2003, the strongest earthquake in two decades, with a strength of 6.8 on the Richter scale, jolts Algeria. The effects of the seismic shock can even be detected on the Mediterranean island of Mallorca. According to reports from the authorities, the earthquake immediately costs almost 1,500 people their lives, around 7,000 are wounded, many more are still missing. Those most seriously affected are the region around the capital, Algiers, in the north of the country, and the administrative district of Boumerdés, around 30 kilometers east of that. The infrastructure completely collapses in broad sections, roads and paths are still blocked, telephone lines and the electricity supply are disrupted. A hospital is also destroyed. In other clinics the doctors and nursing personnel desperately exert themselves for the victims, whose numbers rise without an end. People must often be treated in the open air, since the hospitals are overflowing. On May 22nd, 2003 the government of Algeria petitions the United Nations for humanitarian aid.

International Reaction

UN-OCHA dispatches an UNDAC team to Algeria immediately to coordinate 38 teams (of which 20 are international) with 220 search dogs.

Basis for deployment:	Alert through UNDAC.
Mission:	Coordination of the rescue teams and rescue measures.
Duration of deployment:	May 22nd, 2003 – June 3rd, 2003.
Participating nations:	Austria, Great Britain, OCHA, Russia, Sweden.
Strength:	8.
Headquarters:	Bourmerdès.
Austrian expert:	Brigadier General Mag. Alois A. Hirschmugl.

Austrian Reaction

On May 22nd, 2003, the urgent dispatch of an UNDAC disaster relief expert to Algeria occurs according to Sec. 1 para. 1 c FCL-CSD for up to three weeks through the Federal Minister of Defence empowered by the urgency case.

Austrian Forces Disaster Relief Unit Algeria (AFDRU/AG)

Preliminary Events

On the evening of May 21st, 2003, the strongest earthquake in two decades, with a strength of 6.8 on the Richter scale, jolts Algeria. The effects of the seismic shock can even be detected on the Mediterranean island of Mallorca. According to reports from the authorities, the earthquake immediately costs almost 1,500 people their lives, around 7,000 are wounded, many more are still missing. Those most seriously affected are the region around the capital, Algiers, in the north of the country, and the administrative district of Boumerdès, around 30 kilometers east of that.

International Reaction

At Algeria's request, experts and search dog echelons are sent from many countries into the earthquake zone of the North African country.

Austrian Reaction
Political Measures

The Defence Minister, according to Sec. 1 para. 1 sub-para. c FCL-CSD, orders an urgent dispatch of a disaster relief expert (UNDAC) as well as a search and rescue unit with a strength of 39 members of the armed forces to provide aid after the earthquake in Algeria for the duration of up to two weeks.

Military Measures

> **Basis for deployment:** Instruction of the minister of May 22nd, 2003; CM of May 27th, 2003, MC of (acknowledgment).
> **Mission:** Search and rescue service.
> **Appellation:** AFDUR/AG.
> **Form of dispatch:** FCL-CSD.
> **Area of operations:** Bourmerdès.
> **Duration of deployment:** May 23rd, 2003 – May 29th, 2003.
> **Contingent strength:** 39.
> **Composition:** Command, a rescue and recovery group as well as eight dog trainers.
> **Commander:** Lieutenant Colonel Bernd Bergner.

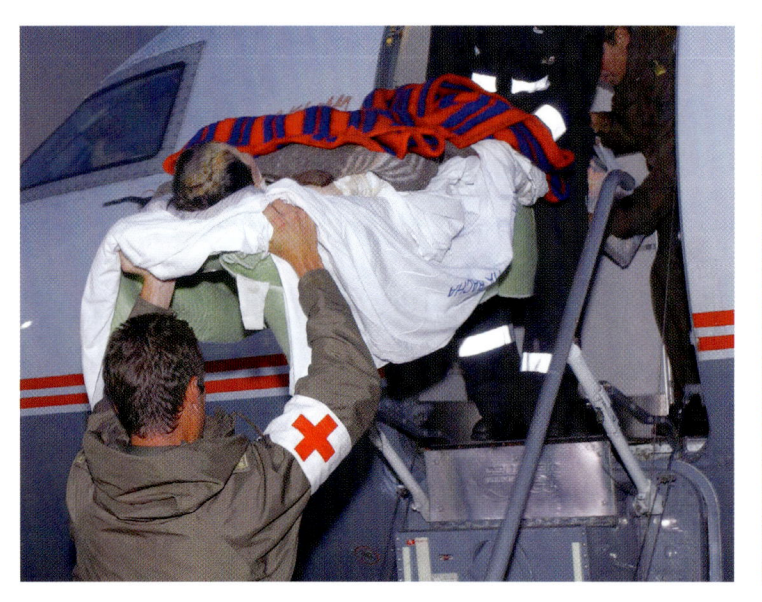

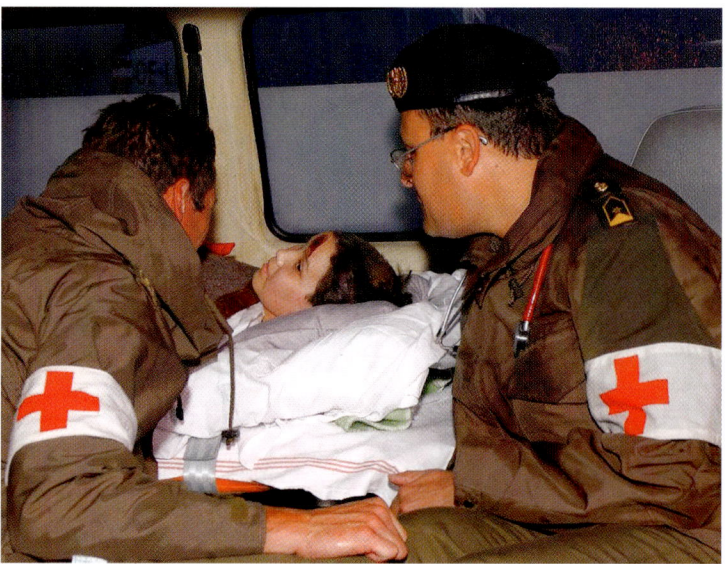

On the flight home a seriously wounded eleven-year-old girl is also on board. Little Ilhem Bouchakour lost both arms during the earthquake. In addition, the girl becomes a full orphan during the catastrophe. Military doctors have taken the helpless girl into their midst. "With these injuries Ilhem would have had hardly a chance of survival in the catastrophe zone," military doctor Dr. Martin Cappy says at the landing. The armed forces, Foreign Minister, Ministry of the Interior and the region of Salzburg unbureaucratically make this relief operation possible. A military helicopter transports little Ilhem further to Salzburg. Military doctors accompany the girl with a medical vehicle until the Hospital of the Merciful Brothers, where she is operated on by specialists. The costs of the treatment are taken over by the region of Salzburg. A social worker from Algeria attends to the child, since she understands no word of German.

European Union Military Operation in the Democratic Republic of the Congo "Artemis"

Preliminary Events

In May 2003 serious fighting breaks out in the province of Ituri in the east of the Democratic Republic of the Congo between the Hema and Lendu ethnic groups. In order to suppress these, the Ugandan 1st Infantry Division was previously stationed in this area. After their withdrawal the battles flare up again. Besides mass executions, the looting of a hospital and the warehouse stock of international aid organizations, these battles lead to a dramatic worsening of the humanitarian situation and to ca. 500,000 (domestic) displaced persons.

International Reaction

The Secretary General of the United Nations initially unofficially petitions the French president to test if a dispatch of military forces would be possible, with which the UN battalion of the United Nations from Uruguay could be supported. On May 30th, 2003, the Security Council of the United Nations issue the mandate for the EU mission. The goal of the operation is the stabilization of the security conditions and the improvement of the humanitarian situation in the Democratic Republic of the Congo (Bunia, Ituri Region). "Artemis" is the first deployment in which NATO resources are not fallen back upon. In this mission France acts as the so-called "framework nation" (the nation which provides the leadership and the essential parts of the multinational forces).

After an extremely short preparation time the first landing and deployment of the Special Forces Task Group takes place on June 5th. In the first phase decisive parts of the terrain, beginning with the airport, are brought under their own control. In the second phase the peacekeeping troops take the local militia's maneuvering room by securing possible lines of approach, the imposition of a weapons ban as well as permanent and irregular patrols around the clock. The militias finally cease their battles within the city and withdraw to the periphery. On July 12th the MONUC[135] reinforcements begin to flow in, and in a further phase, beginning on August 15th, their continual relief through Task Force 2 (MONUC reinforcements) takes place.

The main field headquarters are initially in Entebbe as a result of the lacking infrastructure in Bunia. In the course of the mission there is then a division of duties: The deployment leadership henceforth takes place in the Forward Field Headquarters (Fwd FHQ) in Bunia; the Main FHQ in Entebbe deals primarily with the deployment support.

The mission is transferred to the **United Nations Organization Mission in the Congo (MONUC)** by Resolution of the United Nations Security Council on September 15th, 2003.

Basis for deployment: SC Resolution 1484 (2003) of May 30th, 2003; FAC/CFSP. Action 2003/423/CFSP of June 5th, 2003; SC Resolution 1501 (2003) of August 26th, 2003 (transfer to MONUC by September 15th, 2003).
Mission: Support of the UN mission MONUC in the Democratic Republic of the Congo.
Duration of deployment: June 12th, 2003 – September 15th, 2003.
Participating nations: Austria, Belgium, Brazil, Canada, Cyprus, France, Germany, Great Britain, Greece, Hungary, Italy, Ireland, the Netherlands, Portugal, Spain, South Africa.
Strength: 2,000.
Headquarters: Paris (Operational Headquarters); Entebbe (Forward Headquarters in Bunia).

Austrian Reaction

Political Measures

The Council of Ministers decides on the dispatch of up to three people.

Military Measures

Basis for deployment: CM Circulat. B-6/13 of June 13th, 2002, MC of June 16th, 2003.
Mission: Staff service.
Form of dispatch: FCL-CSD.
Area of operations: Entebbe, Bunia, Kampala and Bombo.
Duration of deployment: June 9th, 2003 – September 1st, 2003 (dismantling by September 15th).
Contingent strength: 3 (1 in Paris, 2 in Congo).

---

135 United Nations Organization Mission in the Congo.

United Nations Disaster Assessment and Coordination Mission in Iran (UNDAC/Iran)

Preliminary Events

On December 26th, 2003, at 1:57 AM local time, there is an earthquake of 6.7 on the Richter scale in Iran. The consequences are ca. 34,000 dead, over 30,000 wounded, of which 10,000 are among the critically wounded. 80% of the houses in Bam are destroyed, 70,000 people are homeless.

International Reaction

UN-OCHA calls an UNDAC team, which also has an Austrian officer in Brigadier General Dr. Alois A. Hirschmugl, into the catastrophe region and petitions all members for the urgent dispatch of search and rescue teams. BG Dr. Hirschmugl is already picked up by a helicopter from the Ministry of the Interior and brought to the airport two hours after the alert. From there the further transfer takes place together with members of the International Rescue Dogs Organization (IRO) with a Lear jet to the area of operations. BG Dr. Hirschmugl is commissioned with the direction of the **"Reception Center"**, an essential coordination site. This establishment is the central place of reception and coordination for the multinational aid deployment in Iran. Among its duties are the first briefing on the situation [updated information is provided by the UNDAC team, which operates the **"On Site Operations Coordination Center (OSOCC)"** in Bam and also carries out surveys], support in customs/visa issues (these formalities were generally interrupted somewhat later by the Iranian government), the organization of further transport to Bam through busses, trucks, helicopters or C-130 transport airplanes (the unloading and reloading is extremely well supported by the Iranian military), the organization of the fueling of aircraft, the provision of weather reports, the making of contacts with the territorial authorities on the governmental levels, the Ministry of Health, the airport operation society, the immigration office and the information center for the international and national media.

In total the deployment of 61 international teams (of which 38 are US rescue and recovery teams), but also individual people, is to be coordinated. In addition there are 20,000 Iranian volunteer helpers. 1,400 airplane landings are completed with aid, rescue, and recovery goods. The further distribution of the aid goods takes place through the Iranian Red Crescent. Eight people can be rescued alive. From December 30th, 2003, the Reception center also serves as the **"Departure Center"** and as such supports the teams flying away during their checking out (customs/immigration office).

> **Basis for deployment:** Alert by UN-OCHA.
> **Mission:** Assessment and coordination of the aid forces.
> **Duration of deployment:** December 26th, 2003 – January 9th, 2004.
> **Participating nations:** Austria, Denmark, Estonia, Great Britain, Russia, Sweden, Switzerland, WHO.
> **Strength:** 11.
> **Headquarters:** Kerman Airport.
> **Austrian expert:** Brigadier General Mag. Dr. Alois A. Hirschmugl.
> **Duration of dispatch:** December 26th, 2003 – January 2nd, 2004.

Austrian Reaction

On December 26th, 2003, the instruction for the dispatch of an UNDAC military disaster relief expert to Iran for the duration of up to three weeks takes place through the Federal Ministers of the Interior and Defence, authorized in case of urgency according to Sec. 1 no. 1 subsec. c FCL-CSD.

Bam before and after the earthquake (Source: Recovery Project of Bam's Cultural Heritage. The professor for the planning of loadbearing structures from the Technical University of Dresden helps with the reconstruction of the destroyed citadel of Bam).

Austrian Forces Disaster Relief Unit Iran (AFDRU/Iran)

Preliminary Events

On December 26th, 2003, at 1:56 AM UTC (5:26 AM local time), the citadel and a large part of the city Bam are devastated by an earthquake. Its strength is 6.6 on the Momentum-Magnitude scale. 70% of the modern city Bam is destroyed. The quake officially claims 30,000 people, according to the reports of the inhabitants of Bam it is 60,000. Bam lies in the area of the edge of the Eurasian Plate, which the Arabic Plate moves towards at ca. 3 cm per year. Through this massive tensions arise underground, which are released from time to time through earthquakes.

International Reaction

The United Nations petition all member nations for immediate humanitarian aid.

Austrian Reaction
Political Measures

On December 27th the order is given by the Federal Ministers for the Interior and Defence, authorized by the urgency case according to Sec. 2 FCL-CSD, for the dispatch of a disaster relief unit in the strength of up to 120 soldiers of the AFDRU (Austrian Forces Disaster Relief Unit), 16 men of the special unit SARUV (Search and Rescue Unit Vorarlberg), as well as dog trainers and search dogs of the dog echelon of the Vienna Provincial Firefighting Association and the Volunteer Fire Department of Kapfenberg/Styria.

Great praise for the professional service of the Austrian troops comes from international organizations, and the Iranian authorities also express their thanks. At the request of UNO and Iran the Austrian armed forces continue their rescue and search duties in Bam until December 31st, 2003. The withdrawal of the team and equipment to Austria takes place from January 1st, 2004. At the airport the contingent is received by Foreign Minister Dr. Ursula Plassnik.

Military Measures

Not even 20 hours pass from the time of the alert to the flight out, which, in view of the Christmas holidays and the arrival of the contingent members from almost all provinces, represents a sensational achievement.

The contingent consists predominantly of soldiers from the NBC Defence Company of the Military Command of Styria, the Military Commands of Upper Austria, Carinthia, Salzburg and Lower Austria, the NBC Defence School, Military Hospital 2 in Innsbruck as well as the civilian dog trainers from the Vienna Provincial Firefighting Association, the Volunteer Fire Department of Kapfenberg, the Austrian Dog Union and the Austrian Rescue Dog Brigade.

Basis for deployment: Instruction of the federal minister of December 27th, 2003.
Mission: Clearance and recovery.
Appellation: Austrian Forces Disaster Relief Unit Iran (AFDRU/IRAN).
Form of dispatch: FCL-CSD.
Area of operations: Bam.
Duration of deployment: December 27th, 2003 – January 2nd, 2004.
Contingent strength: 120.
Composition: Four rescue and recovery troops with search dogs.
Commander: Lieutenant Colonel Michael Paulewicz.
Contribution: By the early morning of December 29th, 2003 20 earthquake victims, regrettably already dead, can be recovered from the rubble.

United Nations Assistance Mission in Afghanistan (UNAMA)

Preliminary Events

The rules for the election in Afghanistan in June 2002 are established by the Special Independent Commission for the Convening of the Emergency Loya Jirga[136] with its 20 Afghan members, in cooperation with the United Nations. From June 12th through 19th, 2002, a Loya Jirga is held on the campus of the Polytechnic High School of Kabul. Its 1,670 delegates elect Hamid Karzai as the president of the transitional government of Afghanistan. On January 4th, 2004, a Loya Jirga to establish a constitution is held. The 502 delegates enact a constitution worked out by a nine-person commission.

International Reaction

UNAMA is a political mission. The process across the country and outside of the country among the refugees is already organized and observed by 50 UNAMA workers and further international observers during the election preparations in April 2002. Furthermore, the duty of UNAMA is to accompany the presidential election on October 9th, 2004, and the parliamentary elections on September 18th, 2005. Both elections are organized by a commission formed of Afghans and representatives of the United nations. For the parliamentary elections there is additionally a media commission, which observes the access of the candidates to the media, and an electoral complaints commission, which is to examine complaints on the elections.

The UNAMA coordinates the endeavors of the other UN organizations (like the UNHCR) in close cooperation with international aid organizations. In cooperation with the Afghan transitional government more than 1 million refugees are supported in their return to Afghanistan. UNAMA also has a central role in the coordination of the reconstruction of war-devastated Afghanistan and organizes, among other things, the distribution of foodstuffs, seeds and fertilizer. In addition the mission aids in the establishment of catastrophe protection in the country, repeatedly destroyed by earthquakes.

Basis for deployment:	SC Resolution 1401 (2002) of March 28th, 2002; SC Resolution 1536 (2004) of March 26th, 2004.
Mission:	Securing of the elections and support with the endeavors for national reconciliation, coordination of the international humanitarian aid.
Duration of deployment:	March 28th, 2002 – to date.
Participating countries:	17.
Strength:	20.
Headquarters:	Kabul.

Austrian Reaction

Political Measures

The federal government decides on the dispatch of a staff officer to Afghanistan as a leading military adviser, as needed in service also in the liaison offices of the mission in Iran (Tehran) and in Pakistan (Islamabad). In September 2004 the additional dispatch of up to two military observers is decided upon.

Military Measures

Basis for deployment:	CM of June 8th, 2004, MC of June 15th, 2004; CM of September 27th, 2004, MC of November 3rd, 2004 (military observers).
Form of dispatch:	FCL-CSD.
Area of operations:	Kabul (HQ ISAF).
Duration of deployment:	June 16th, 2004 – June 30th, 2006 (senior adviser). November 3rd, 2004 – September 28th, 2006 (military observer).
Contingent strength:	2.

---

136 The Loya Jirga is the grand assembly, which is held up to this day in Afghanistan (but also in Uzbekistan, Turkmenistan and Mongolia), which is held to clear up the large national and ethnic questions (Wikipedia).

United Nations Disaster Assessment and Coordination Mission in Bangladesh (UNDAC/Bangladesh)

Preliminary Events

In July 2004 Bangladesh is devastated by one of the worst flooding catastrophes of the last century. An area of around 21,000 square kilometers is flooded. 33 million people are affected, which means around 6.5 million families. 700 dead are to be mourned, ca. 70,000 fall ill to gastroenteritis, another ca. 12 – 14,000 are added daily. Fever, cholera, skin illnesses and malaria worsen the situation. The groundwater is contaminated by arsenic, 2.6 million hectares of crops are destroyed, 60,000 km of roads, 5,300 bridges and 3,000 dams are destroyed.

International Reaction

UN-OCHA alerts the UNDAC teams, in order to coordinate the international aid. UNO attempts to collect aid supplies for 33 million people.

> **Basis for deployment:** Alert through UN-OCHA.
> **Mission:** Coordination of the aid deployment.
> **Duration of the deployment:** July 29th, 2004 – August 12th, 2004.
> **Strength:** 7.
> **Headquarters:** Dakar.
> **Austrian expert:** Brigadier General Dr. Alois A. Hirschmugl.

Austrian Reaction

The urgent dispatch of a UNDAC disaster relief expert for the duration of up to three weeks to Bangladesh takes place through the Federal Minister of Defence, authorized by the urgency case according to Sec. 1 no. 1 subsec. c FCL-CSD.

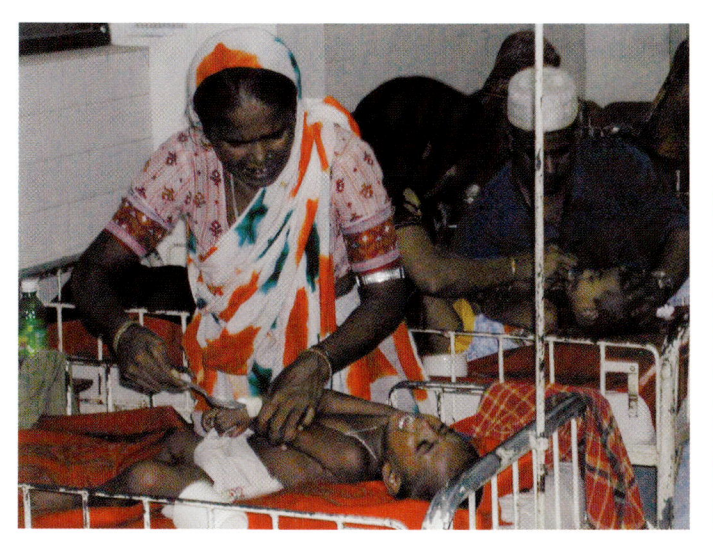

After the destructive storms there are wide-ranging floods. The survey of the catastrophe area is also one of the duties of the UNDAC team. Numerous urgent care hospitals are established through international organizations to be able to comprehensively treat the affected population.

International Humanitarian and Disaster Relief for Beslan/Ossetia (Hum/Beslan)

Preliminary Events

On September 1st, 2004, at 9:30 AM local time, a group of at least 33 heavily armed people storm Middle School No. 1, in which schoolchildren in the age of seven to eighteen years are taught, and take 1,127 hostages, including many children. The attackers are partially masked and heavily armed, some even with belts of explosives for suicide bombings. Women are also among the attackers (so-called Smertnizy – black widows). After an exchange of shots with the police, the attackers occupy the school building. During the occupation, numerous explosions are heard in the school building, during which the first hostages are supposed to be killed.

On September 3rd, at around 12:30 PM local time, there are hour-long firefights, in the course of which the Russian special forces of the Ministry of the Interior, "Alfa" and "Wympel", storm the school building. Russian militaries fire tanks at the school building, which can only be brought under control after many hours. In the course of the fighting the ceiling of the gymnasium collapses, this costs more hostages their lives. According to official reports, 704 people are wounded, including more than 200 children, during the obviously unplanned storming. In total 394 dead are to be recorded. 27 hostage takers are killed (including two women), one hostage taker is taken alive, two further are killed by the military during their capture (Wikipedia).

International Reaction

After the violent end of the hostage situation in Beslan, around 700 people, some critically wounded, are dependent on medical aid, and many of the affected must be further cared for over a longer period of time. Nevertheless, the materials necessary for this are lacking; a comprehensive and long-term medical care of so many victims cannot be accomplished by the resources of the region alone. Therefore international aid is immediately deployed.

Austrian Reaction

Military Measures

Defence Minister Günther Platter immediately orders the flight of one of the three Austrian military C-130 "Hercules" transport planes from the Linz-Hörsching airport to Beslan in Russia. "The people in Beslan have had traumatic experiences. Our C-130 delivers aid goods to the region. A flight which brings hope," the minister comments. The aid goods are medicines, painkillers, bandage materials, IV bags, antibiotics and mobile laboratory equipment. The pilot of the plane, Captain Joachim Eder, and the 18 men of the crew are received by the Russian authorities of open arms. The military loading team gives the air delivery to a delegation of the Russian health authorities. The return of the aircraft takes place on September 9th.

Basis for deployment: Instruction of the Federal Minister of Defence.
Mission: Transport of supply goods after the terrorist attack in Beslan.
Appellation: Austrian contingent (OESKON).
Form of dispatch: Foreign business trip.
Area of operations: Vladikavkaz, airport of Beslan.
Duration of deployment: September 7th, 2004 – September 9th, 2004.
Contingent strength: 18.
Composition: Commander, crew of C-130, photographer/Armed Forces Photo and Video Production Service, three loading personnel.
Commander: Lieutenant Colonel Rudolf Ebenberger.
Contribution: Nine tons of medical aid goods.

European Union Military Operation in Bosnia and Herzegovina "ALTHEA"[137] (European Union Force in Bosnia and Herzegovina)

Preliminary Events

Despite all the endeavors after the Paris Protocol, Bosnia-Herzegovina still remains divided into three (ethnically determined) parts as a result of the war. All political levels of the land are dominated by nationally oriented forces, which in contradiction to the **Dayton Agreement** hinder the coalescence of the ethnically torn nation of Bosnia-Herzegovina. Above all the problems of the return of refugees and the displaced as well as the establishment of the political institutions of the Bosniak-Croatian Federation and the Bosnian national government continue to remain unsolved.

International Reaction

Immediately after the signing of the Dayton Agreement on Novemeber 21st, 1995, the United Nations begins its longest and most ambitious peacekeeping mission yet in Bosnia-Herzegovina. Besides the international armed forces, which secure the implementation of the military agreements, the **Office of the High Representative** serves as the central coordination site for the civilian reconstruction. The United Nations are assigned to the return of refugees, the OSCE to the implementation of elections. More than 600 international governmental and non-governmental organizations (NGOs) cooperate on the reconstruction and the consolidation of peace in and around Bosnia-Herzegovina.

On December 1st, 2004, the extremely successful **NATO Operation "SFOR"** ends. This began in 1996 with 60,000 soldiers; at the end of SFOR only 7,000 soldiers are still in the area of operations. 80 percent of these SFOR troops continue to remain there, now nevertheless as EUFOR troops under the high command of the European Union. The mission rests on a mandate of the UN Security Council. The assignment also continues to be the stabilization of the military aspects of the peace agreement, the hindrance of violent riots and the maintenance of the security and order in agreement with Appendixes 1A and 2 of the Dayton Agreement and the creation of a safe and secured environment, so that the core duties according to the Mission Implementation Plan of the Office of the High Representative (OHR) and the Stabilization and Association Process (SAP) can be fulfilled. The "secure environment" is an essential requirement so that Bosnia-Herzegovina can realize its efforts towards the long-term goal of EU membership. The prospect of EU admission has become the most important motor for reforms in Southeast Europe.

The transition from the NATO-led operation to a mission led by the EU is prepared at the NATO summit in Istanbul in early summer 2004. This transfer is also to be seen as a further sign of the normalization throughout the entire region, but also as a direct consequence of the advances of the EU in the development of its joint foreign and security policy. The EUFOR "ALTHEA" operation is formed on the basis of the **"Berlin Plus" Agreement**, which regulates NATO support for EU-led operations. Because in order to avoid double structures, the EU falls back on the materials and abilities of NATO. The supreme commander of the entire operation, as usual with "Berlin Plus" operations, is the representative NATO supreme commander for Europe (Deputy SACEUR). NATO continues to play a weighty role in Bosnia-Herzegovina, especially as this country is also to receive the prospect of later membership in the North Atlantic organization. Military and civilian teams of experts from NATO help the local government with the reform of its defence sector and prepare for the membership of the country in the NATO Partnership for Peace. The ca. 200 soldier strong NATO troops are in the same terrain and in the same buildings as the headquarters of EUFOR.

At the beginning of July Brussels dispatches an EU planning team (EUPT) to Bosnia to prepare for the operation and to secure a smooth transition form SFOR to EUFOR. This team subsequently includes specialists from all basic leadership areas and consists of a total of 18 officers from numerous member states of the EU. The first member of EUPT and simultaneously the first soldier from EUFOR in the area of operations is the Austrian Colonel of the Management Service Dr. Michael Pesendorfer, who immediately takes up his work as legal advisor and simultaneously as representative commander of the EUPT. Austria is represented in the planning team with a total of two officers and one noncommissioned officer and with this provides almost a fifth of the personnel. The main duties of the EUPT are the planning of the future HQ of EUFOR in view of personnel and infrastructure, the separation of duties between the future EUFOR and the future NATO HQ Sarajevo as well as the securing of an advance "initial operational capability" for the EUFOR headquarters from October 1st, 2004. The EUPT is absorbed into the growing staff of EUFOR in the middle of October 2004.

With the acceptance of the reorganization "Transition Step 1" for the reduction of the military forces in EUFOR in the middle

---

[137] Althea: "The Healer" – Greek goddess of the healing arts.

of 2007, the structure of the Task Forces is replaced with a **"Situational Awareness Matrix"** (observation structure with intervention forces). EUFOR now only has a **Maneuver Battalion,** two **Integrated Police Units** and five **Regional Coordination Centers (RCC)** with subordinate **Liaison and Observation Teams (LOT)** in varying strengths.

The reduction forces the placement of quickly recallable operative reserves in their respective homelands. Three **"Operational Reserve Forces Battalions" (ORF BN)** are formed for both Balkan missions. One of the three battalions is also always in "ready" status, which means that it is to be ready for deployment in the area of operations within seven days. The other two battalions are on "stand by" status; this means deployment readiness within 14 days. The rotations take place every six months.

On June 27th, 2007 an era ends for the soldiers of the international peacekeeping troop in Bosnia: Camp Eagle Base is transferred to the Bosnian government in a celebratory ceremony. With this, "Multi National Task Force North" also ends.

On December 4th, 2009, Major General Mag. Bernhard Bair assumes the command of the EUFOR forces in Bosnia and Herzegovina for a year. With this, an Austrian officer leads a peacekeeping mission of the European Union for the first time. EUFOR "ALTHEA" has around 2,00 soldiers from 25 nations at the time; ca. 100 of them come from Austria. The appointment of Bair as Commander of the EUFOR forces in Bosnia and Herzegovina also speaks to the high position of the soldiers of the Austrian armed forces in Europe.

Basis for deployment:	SC Resolution 1575 (2004); EU-Council/J. Action 2004/803/CFSP of November 22nd, 2004.	
Mission:	Stabilization of the military aspects of the peace agreement, hindrance of violent riots, maintenance of safety and order.	
Duration of deployment:	December 2nd, 2004 – to date.	
Participating nations:	33 (reduced to 25 by 2007).	
Strength:	7,000 (reduced to 2,000 by 2007).	
Headquarters:	Camp BUTMIR on the grounds of the Sarajevo airport.	
COMEUFOR[138]:	December 4th, 2009 – to date	Major General Mag. Bernhard Bair;
CO/MNTF N:	November 30th, 2005 – May 27th, 2006	Brigadier General Mag. Karl Pronhagl;
	May 28th, 2006 – December 1st, 2006	Brigadier General Mag. Rudolf Striedinger.

Major General Mag. Bernhard Bair accepts the flag from the hands of the Force Commander. In the right of the picture is the previous commander, the Italian Major General Stefano Castagnotto (picture left). On November 30th, 2005, with Brigadier General Mag. Karl Pronhagl, an Austrian officer becomes commander of a multinational brigade for the first time (right picture).

---

138 COMEUFOR: Commanding Officer.

Austrian Reaction

Political Measures

The Council of Ministers, with the agreement of parliament, decides on the continuation of SFOR and the further dispatch of an infantry contingent in the strength of up to 300 people as well as up to ten staff members within the framework of the infantry contingent. Of the up to 300 people, up to 50 are used from the KFOR contingent. The maximum total status of both contingents may amount to 850. Up to 100 people can be deployed to the respective other contingent for reinforcement during security risks for a duration of up to three months.

In June 2007 the federal government decides on the dispatch of up to 230 members of the armed forces within the framework of the ORF battalion (operative reserve forces)[139] led by Germany. In October 2007 the Council of Ministers decides on the extension of the dispatch of now only up to 150 members of the armed forces (with an additional up to 250 for the maximum duration of three months in case of crisis as well as up to 250 for the ORF battalion on demand). With the decision for the further continuation of the dispatch of the contingent, the Council of Ministers also decides in October 2009 on a heightening of the contingent to up to 190 members of the armed forces. The planned reinforcements in case of need remain.

Military Measures

Assumption of the Command of the Multinational Task Force North (MNTF-N)

In December 2005, in addition to its existing duties, Austria assumes command of the Multinational Task Force North (MNTF-N) in Tuzla for the duration of a year. This is a visible sign of the special responsibility which Austria has during its EU presidency in the first half of the year 2006. Soldiers from Belgium, Estonia, Finland, Greece, Ireland, Lithuania, Austria, Poland, Portugal, Slovenia, Sweden, the Czech Republic and Turkey are subordinate to the Command. New duties are connected with the assumption of the command by the armed forces. International administrative duties must especially be mastered, such as the assumption of the infrastructure of other nations (for instance the halls constructed by the Americans, which are used as hangars for the "Alouette IIIs") and the entrance into various contracts with property owners and service providers, with all the costs and risks associated with them. With the leadership of MNTF-N, Austria provides not only the commander, but also the political adviser, the legal adviser, the head of the Visitors and Observer Bureau, the G2, the Commander of the Tactical Operation Center (TOC), a staff officer for the helicopter element, the Chief Medical Officer (at this time the highest position on a foreign deployment occupied by a woman), a quartermaster, a CIMIC officer (Civil Military Cooperation) and a military chaplain. Further, the representative G6 as well as some staff officers and noncommissioned officers in the G2, information, operations, media and logistics areas are members of the Austrian armed forces. Beyond this there are a total of three further officers in NATO-HQ Sarajevo, in the EU Staff Group with SHAPE (in Mons/Belgium) and in the EU Command Element Naples/Italy, which are equally directly involved in the operative leadership of the forces in the area of operations. Austria further provides the framework for a so-called Composite Company to lead the Liaison and Observation Teams and Verification Teams (LOT) with two Austrian LOTs (beyond which 1 AUT LOT is dispatched with MNTF NW in the area of Banja Luka). As a result of the numerical limitation to 300 members of the armed forces, the guard and security company must be reduced to a platoon.

The shift of the emphasis of the Austrian armed forces in Bosnia from Sarajevo to Tuzla also leads to the fact that a **National Intelligence Liaison Office (NILO)** is formed in Tuzla, because the **Austrian National Intelligence Cell (AUNIC)** and the **Counterintelligence (CI) Element** must be left in Camp Butmir because of their ties to the NIC community there. The Austrian Task Force Commander is nevertheless to have access to the information from his intelligence service. For the national logistics, a logistics element is created during the shift of emphasis to Tuzla to coordinate with Sarajevo. All other national elements remain essentially unchanged.

Consequences of the Restructuring for AUCON

From the middle of 2007, AUCON is present with a portion of staff in the headquarters of EUFOR, with an officer in the NATO headquarters, a small CIMIC team and national intelligence services in Sarajevo. The mass of the contingent is further in Tuzla in rented civilian infrastructure. The contingent is reduced from nearly 300 to around 110 soldiers. Austria leads the **Regional Coordination Centers 4 (RCC 4)** with ten subordinate **Liaison and Observation Teams (LOT).** Three of these (Tuzla, Bratunac and Vlasenica) are overseen by Austrians. The RCC 4 encompasses the entire northeast of Bosnia and Herzegovina with ca. 7,000 square kilometers and 1 million inhabitants. Furthermore a **Field Humit Team (FHT)** is brought in by Austria. This is ceased and returned in the middle of 2009. Their own provisioning takes place through the **Austrian National Element (AUNE).**

Operational Reserve (ORF)[140]

As a result of the limited resource situation, after intensive negotiations with Germany, an Austrian contribution to the multinational operative deployment forces is determined for both Balkan missions, EUFOR-Althea and KFOR, in order to shore up the claim to the leadership of Task Force South in Kosovo, in order to send a visible signal of participation in valuable reserves forces out of solidarity, and in order to be able to gather first experiences with a

---

139 Operative reserve forces for ALTHEA and KFOR. They are held ready at their home stations, the short-term movement into the area of operations is secured.
140 See KFOR, page 290.

view to a future engagement within the framework of the EU Battle Group. The political authorization takes place through the Council of Ministers in June 2007. The Austrian portion of the ORF battalion led by Germany is mostly soldiers from standing cadre units and is ready from September 1st, 2007. As a result of the requisite quick movement times the "Pandur" armored personnel carries envisioned for the ORF company are already stored with AUCON/KFOR. The first "Ready" phase begins according to plan in the middle of 2008.

Basis for deployment:	CM of November 9th, 2004, MC of November 17th, 2004.	
	CM of June 13th, 2007, MC of June 19th, 2007 (dispatch of up to 230 people for the ORF battalion).	
Mission:	Maintenance of safety and order.	
Appellation:	**Austrian Contingent (AUCON).**	
Form of dispatch:	FCL-CSD 1997. **Area of operations:** Sarajevo, Tuzla.	
Duration of deployment:	December 2nd, 2004 – to date.	
Contingent strength:	280 – 300 (until the end of 2007); 110 – 121 (from the beginning of 2008); 151 (from the beginning of 2009)[141];	
	4 (in Naples and Brussels). **Total:** 1,500.	
Composition:	Reconnaissance company; guard and security company (reduced to a guard and security platoon within the framework of a multinational guard and security company in 2005); helicopter element (December 15th, 2005 – December 1st, 2006 and from September 15th, 2009).	
Commander AUCON:	December 2nd, 2004 – March 9th, 2005	Lieutenant Colonel Klaus Eisenbach (1)
Contingent Commander (NCC):	March 9th, 2005 – July 27th, 2005	Lieutenant Colonel GS Mag. Christian Habersatter
NCC/Chief of staff (COS):	July 28th, 2005 – November 30th, 2005	Lieutenant Colonel GS Mag. Martin Jawurek
	December 2nd, 2006 – July 4th, 2007	Colonel GS Mag. Friedrich Schrötter
NCC/Chief of current affairs:	July 5th, 2007 – December 5th, 2007	Colonel GS Mag. Bruno Hofbauer
	December 6th, 2007 – October 25th, 2008	Colonel GS Ing. MMag. Günther Rozenits
	October 26th, 2008 – May 16th, 2009	Colonel GS Mag. Hermann Lattacher
	May 17th, 2009 – December 3rd, 2009	Colonel GS Dr. Peter Vorhofer
	December 4th, 2009 – June 4th, 2010	Colonel GS Mag. Josef Holzer
	June 5th, 2010 – to date	Colonel GS Mag. Johann Lattacher

Helicopter Element

Three **SA.316B "Alouette III"** helicopters are dispatched to Tuzla to support the Austrian commander of MNTF N for the time from December 15th, 2005 until December 1st, 2006. The main duty of the helicopter element consists of the implementation of connection and transport flights with two helicopters. Furthermore, reconnaissance flights also take place with the reconnaissance company (RECCE-COY). Beyond this the helicopter element is also assigned to transport medically stable patients who are accompanied by emergency medical technicians to a hospital (Casual Evacuation – CASEVAC). Since according to the deployment plan none of the three "Alouette IIIs" in Tuzla are equipped for MEDEVAC deployments (Medical Evacuation), these duties are carried out by the two US Army UH-60A "Black Hawk" transport helicopters stationed at the airfield in Tuzla.

During the decision on the type of helicopter, the choice is made for the "Alouette III" helicopter because it is the least maintenance intensive and can be operated with the least logistical effort. For further deployments abroad, the "Alouette IIIs", which were previously not planned for international operations, are retrofitted. Kevlar shrapnel protection mats are procured for two helicopters. Furthermore, six helicopters receive lighting sets for night vision goggles (NVGs); additionally one set serves as a general reserve. With these the implementation of missions at night is possible. Furthermore a loading exercise takes place in Hörsching, in which two fully equipped "Alouette IIIs" are loaded into a C-130 "Hercules" within a few hours.

On September 15th, 2009, two transport helicopters of the type **S-70 "Black Hawk"** land in Camp Butmir. The Austrian helicopter teams have the assignment of supporting the EUFOR soldiers with transport and other deployments in the area of operations. After a two-week development and training phase the two Austrian helicopter teams replace the Swiss helicopter crews, who end their deployment on October 1st, 2009. Since both helicopter types have similar ability parameters and deployment spectrums, the transport duties can be continued without a problem.

In connection with the occupation of the position of Force Commander of EUFOR by Major General Mag. Bernhard Bair, three additional "Alouette III" helicopters for medical evacuations (MEDEVAC) are placed for the support of COM EUFOR, besides additional staff personnel.

---

141 On June 1st, 2010, the Council of Ministers decides on an increase of up to 400 people from July 2010.

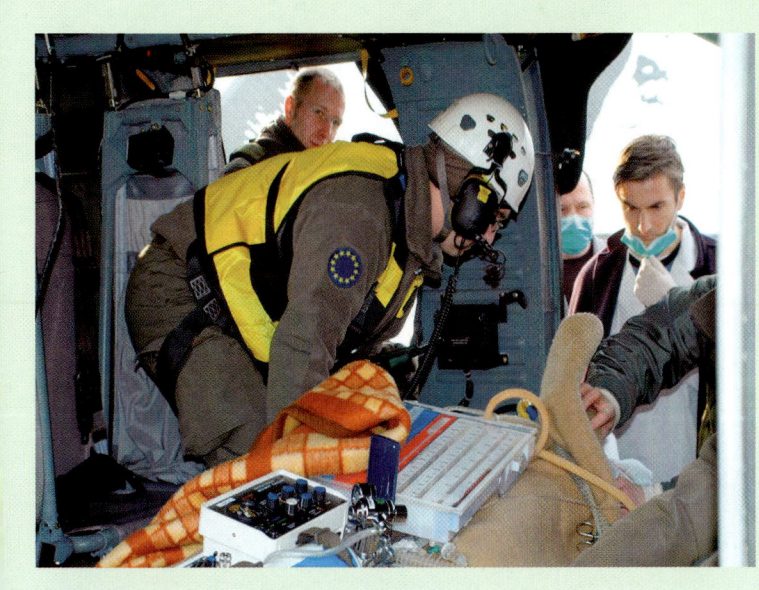

After a despairing call for help from the mayor of Bihac on February 2nd, 2010, Austrian soldiers rescue a seriously wounded 21-year-old Bosnian, who was seriously injured weeks ago in a traffic accident. Her condition in the hospital in Bihac dramatically worsens, so that an immediate transfer to Sarajevo represents her only chance of survival. An Austrian S-70 "Black Hawk" helicopter with an emergency doctor on board starts immediately from Camp Butmir and transfers the critically wounded patient from the Kosevo clinic in Bihac to Sarajevo (Photo Jauk, Galli).

Impressions of Camp Butmir. Soldiers from the Austrian EUFOR contingent work hand in hand with comrades from other countries at the camp on the grounds of the airport in Sarajevo. The pictures were taken between August 2006 and December 2008. The camp from the air, below the "International Police Unit" (Photo Johann Hermann). Since June 2004, Austrian soldiers serve in the Integrated Police Unit (IPU), a military police regiment that provides safety and order in Bosnia-Herzegovina. The military police support the local executive forces, are in constant contact with the population, patrol the streets and search for illegal weapons (for the protection of the military police, their faces have been made unidentifiable) (b.r.).

The direct responsibility for the part of Camp Eagle in which the forces of the European Union are deployed is connected to the command of MNTF (N). The Director of Joint Command and Control Staff of the Austrian armed forces, Major General Mag. Christian Ségur-Cabanac, therefore meets the director of the Finnish Office of Military Policy, Major General Holma Hekki, to sign the appropriate contracts which formally make Austria the owner of the barracks. In addition an agreement for the support of the Austrian section with communications and intelligence systems is signed (t.l.). The 15th of February 2008 is probably the coldest day of February in Bosnia – and one of the most important for the "Austrian National Element", the Austrian camp in Tuzla: The camp receives a new name. The new nameplate is attached to the gate with the excited participation of members of the Austrian contingent (t.r.).

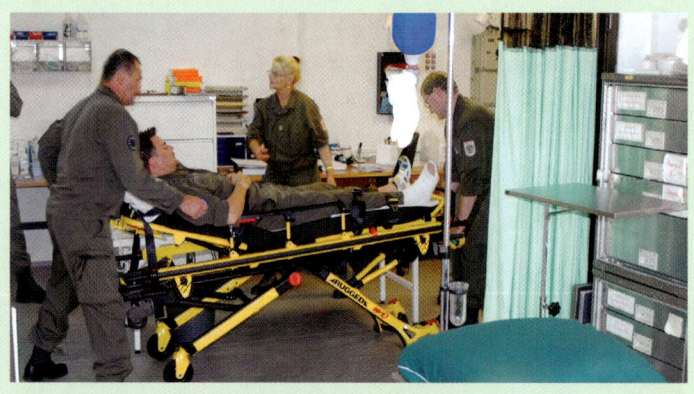

Since July 2007 around 50 EUFOR soldiers find good working and living conditions in the new "Camp AUNE" (Austrian National Element) (m.l.). A wounded soldier is brought into the emergency room. There the first diagnosis takes place through the military doctor (m.r.). Many Austrian soldiers serve abroad. During this, however, they do not forget where they come from and which traditions are lived out at home in Austria. So for instance the soldiers of the "Austrian National Element" raise a maypole in Camp Edelweiß. Since felling evergreen trees is not looked upon kindly in Bosnia because of the low concentration of evergreens, the soldiers use a birch (b.l.). Likewise, the traditional christmas market takes place in Camp Butmir at the beginning of December. The American and German armies, together with the Austrian armed forces, are the event organizers. During this there is a performance of the local children's home choir. Physical well-being is also attended to with hot spiced wine, coffee, tea and cookies. The net profit benefits charitable establishments in Sarajevo (b.r.).

CIMIC Projects[142]

Two of the **"Community Assistance for Reconstruction and Development Projects"** chosen and sponsored by the **"European Commission to Bosnia and Herzegovina"** are taken over by the Austrian CIMIC group. These are above all attended to by Major Ing. Horny, dispatched to the CIMIC group. He is responsible for planning, filing, construction supervision and the examination of factual correctness. In the years 2006 and 2007 there is a general renovation of the schools of Potocari. The extent of the construction includes the roof, a new heating system, insulation, electrical installation, exchange of windows as well as the renewal of the exterior and interior facade. 150,000 Euros are used for this. At the time of the renovation the school attends to ca. 65 schoolchildren; the return of families with school age children is expected after the repairs. At the same time the **clinic in Vlasenica** is renovated. The extent of the construction is identical with that of the school. The investment here runs to 95,000 Euros. In this clinic ca. 50,000 people, who live in 181 villages in the region, are cared for by eleven doctors of various specialties. Both projects are concluded in the middle of April 2007. The properties are officially turned over to the responsible communities on April 19th, 2007 in the presence of local dignitaries and EUFOR representatives, the Austrian ambassador in Sarajevo, representatives of the press and CIMIC workers.

The soldiers deployed in the **"Liaison and Observation Teams"** are in constant contact with the public institutions and the population of Bosnia. In the furthest sense these teams have the function of seismographs, who recognize, note and evaluate all the mood changes in the population.

The organization of the Salzburg provincial minister Doraja Eberle, **"Farmers Helping Farmers" (FHF)**, has been active in the former Yugoslavia since 1992. Since 2005 FHF transports are also carried out by the armed forces from Austria to Bosnia. In the area of operations the FHF is supported with personnel and vehicles during the distribution of aid goods such as foodstuffs, clothing, seeds or agricultural equipment. Since 2007 transports of civilian aid goods can no longer be carried out by the armed forces as a result of restrictions from Bosnian authorities and EUFOR. Cooperation with local representatives and/or support with the distribution nevertheless continues as before. Between 2005 and 2007 around 200 tons are transported by the armed forces, the value of the contributions made by the armed forces adds up to 47,000 Euros.

On March 17th, 2010, the Guards, in cooperation with the Vienna Rotary Club, hosts the spring concert of the Guards Band in the Viennese Hofburg. The net profit, with a sum of 15,029 Euros, is handed over to Mrs. Annemarie Kury, the initiator of the **"Koraci Nade – Steps of Hope"** project, on May 21st, 2010, in line with the guards' tradition day in the Maria Theresia Barracks (picture middle right). The goal of the project is to build a handicapped-accessible day center for children with multiple handicaps in a central site in Tuzla. Currently around 100 children with multiple handicaps receive the necessary therapies, their parents are strengthened in their efors for the children and their rights, and receive professional training.

Individual "FHF" houses emerged in the mountains of Bratunac (Photo H. Pendl) (t.l.). The commander of the Guards, LTC Stefan Kirchebner MSD, handing over the profit of the concert to Mrs. Annemarie Kury (t.r.). On the occasion of the conclusion of renovation work on Kulin – Ban Primary School in Visoko, the school hosts a celebration in cooperation with the community of Visoko (b.l.). "Bring children in need joy with Christmas presents!" With the help of the "Round Table" organization, around 4,000 presents from Austria stack up in the armed forces camp. Presents are given to the children in school as well (b.r.).

---

142 Dominik Horn: "CIMIC Projects in the Balkans".

Austrian Rescue Team/Thailand – Administrative Assistance Team

Preliminary Events

After the serious seaquake off the west coast of Sumatra on December 26th, 2004, at 12:58 AM (GMT), with a strength of 9.0 on the Richter scale, and a further quake of that strength near the Great Nicobar Islands, devastating tsunamis develop, which destroy the livelihoods of the coastal inhabitants of India, Thailand, Sri Lanka, Indonesia, Malaysia, Burma and the Maldives within a few minutes. The consequences are 300,000 dead and 1,656,650 homeless.

The worst affected is the island nation of Sri Lanka. The floodwaves hit the land of the coastal regions from Kankasanrurai to Negombo with a speed of up to 960 km/h and a height of 15 m and more. The power of the giant wave costs over 11,000 people their lives, further hundred thousands lose their homes. The earthquake is designated as the strongest of the last 50 years.

International Reaction

As a result of a request for help on the part of the government of Thailand, an extensive international aid campaign begins.

Austrian Reaction

Political Measures

The federal government decides on the dispatch of an UNDAC military catastrophe expert to Thailand and an Austrian Forces Disaster Relief Unit to Sri Lanka. As the result of a call for assistance on the part of the Federal Ministry for Foreign Affairs (FMFA), military specialists are additionally assigned to them. The consulate in Phuket (point of emphasis) and the embassy in Bangkok are to be supported in the areas of staff work, identification and/or search for missing Austrians, construction of an IT communications infrastructure, forensic examinations, DNA sampling, medical examinations and psychosocial care, together with representatives of the FMFA, the Federal Ministry of the Interior, the Search and Rescue Unit Vorarlberg (SARUV) and the Austrian Red Cross. The military teams are composed of staff personnel, catastrophe management and IT experts as well as medical and psychological personnel.

Military Measures

Six experts for catastrophe deployments and military medics already make their way to Thailand on December 28th, 2004. The members of the armed forces fly around 11:00 PM through Bangkok into the catastrophe zone of Phuket. The experts support the representatives of Austrian authority in Phuket with the collection and return of Austrian tourists. Beyond this the doctors are to concern themselves with wounded Austrians and prepare them for the transport back home.

On December 29th, 2004, another aid team from Austria leaves for Sri Lanka. The mixed "Austrian Rescue Team" consists of specialists of the Ministry for the Interior and the armed forces. The disaster relief specialists, doctors and psychologists arrive on the morning of December 30th in Colombo and there immediately begin their work. Like the team already on site, the eleven new helpers are to support the Austrian authorities in Sri Lanka. Their most important duty is to find the Austrians still missing, to help them and to prepare their safe return home.

Basis for deployment: Call for assistance from the FMFA.
Mission: Support of the Austrian consulate in Phuket as well as the embassy in Bangkok.
Appellation: Austrian Rescue Team (ART), subsequently **Administrative Assistance Team (AAT).**
Form of dispatch: Business trip abroad (BTA).
Area of operations: Phuket and Bangkok.
Duration of deployment: December 28th, 2004 – May 2005.
Contingent strength: 6.
Total: 36.

United Nations Disaster Assessment and Coordination Mission in Thailand (UNDAC/Thailand)

International Reaction

The **UN Office for the Coordination of Humanitarian Affairs (UN-OCHA)** carries out an UNDAC alert immediately after the catastrophe becomes known and dispatches UNDAC teams to Indonesia, Sri Lanka and Thailand as well as on the Maldives and Seychelles. As a result of the dimensions the UN-OCHA decides to bring in **Military Civil Defence Assets (MCDA)** and **UN Civil Military Coordination Officers (CMC)** in addition to the UNDAC teams. On December 31st, 2004 a personal request on the part of UN/OCHA/GENEVA comes to BG Dr. Alois A. Hirschmugl, if he would be available for an UNDAC deployment with a duration of 10 – 14 days if the need arose, since an experienced UNDAC member with a military background and a rank of at least Colonel or Brigadier General is necessary for the establishment of a regional civilian-military coordination site for Southeast Asia at the JTF 536 to overcome the tsunami catastrophe. MCDA are first deployed when the civilian institutions are no longer in the position to overcome the effects of the catastrophe without them. For this a regional UN CMC cell is established at the command post of the deployed US Joint Task Force 536 (later Combined Support Force 536) in U-Tapao in Thailand. 1,267 aid deployments are brought in through military forces within the framework of this operation. In addition a **"Combined Coordination Cell (CCC)"**, which organizes the coordination of humanitarian aid, is additionally established by the Americans.

The MCDA project is tested for the first time in a deployment encompassing numerous nations within the framework of this deployment (hence the necessary high rank). The main mission consists of the establishment of a connection between civilian and military organizations in HQ/JTF 536 in U-Tapao for the entire region of Southeast Asia. This includes meetings between the UN Regional Coordinator (GPC), the commanding General of the JTF 536, the director of the Combined Coordination Cell (CCC) and the responsible UN bureaus, in order to discuss planned UN activities in connection with the military support activities of the CFG 536 in the affected region of Southeast Asia. The Austrian UNDAC experts furthermore keep constant contact with the AFDRU contingent in Galle/Sri Lanka. From January 15th, 2005, Austrian Major Joseph Reiterer, placed on leave for service with MCDU/OCHA, is dispatched by UN OCHA/MCDU as a UN Civil Military Coordination Officer (UN CMCO) to Banda Aceh to coordinate in Indonesia.

The deployment is the largest military aid operation in Southeast Asia, in which military forces from 35 nations participate with 30,000 soldiers, 41 ships, 43 airplanes and 75 helicopters. The largest contingent is provided by the USA, with 18,000 soldiers and all thinkable resources (including aircraft carriers, hospital ships, satellites, landing boats).

Basis for deployment: Alert through UN-OCHA.
Mission: Coordination of the aid measures.
Duration of deployment: December 26th, 2004 – January 14th, 2005.
Participating nations: 18.
Strength: 44 UNDAC team members from 18 countries and 11 MCDA officers from four international organizations.
Headquarters: U-Tapao (200 km south of Bangkok) at the site of the Combined Support Force (CSF 536) of the US Pacific fleet.
Austrian expert: Brigadier General Dr. Alois A. Hirschmugl.
Duration of deployment: January 3rd, 2005 – January 14th, 2005.

Austrian Reaction

On January 2nd, 2005 the urgent dispatch of an UNDAC catastrophe expert to Thailand takes place for the duration of up to three weeks through the Ministers for Foreign Affairs, Finance, the Interior and Defence authorized by the urgency case according to Sec. 1 no. 1 subsec. c FCL-CSD.

Austrian Forces Disaster Relief Unit in Sri Lanka (AFDRU/Sri Lanka)

Austrian Reaction

Initially a military transport team moves to Sri Lanka on January 3rd to implement the transport and handover of aid goods.

In order the help the many thousands of victims of the tsunami catastrophe, among them also numerous Austrians, the Austrian armed forces finally dispatch an AFDRU unit (Austrian Forces Disaster Relief Unit) into the catastrophe region. The 80 solders are to secure the drinking water supply for the population in the especially hard-hit area around the city Galle.

Basis for deployment:	Order of the minister of January 2nd, 2005; CM of January 25th, 2005, MC of January 26th, 2005 (acknowledgement).
Mission:	Drinking water purification and distribution.
Appellation:	**Austrian Contingent (AUSCON).**
Form of dispatch:	FCL-CSD 1997.
Area of operations:	Galle, Thailand, Geneva.
Duration of deployment:	January 3rd, 2005 – January 7th, 2005 (transport team); January 4th, 2005 – February 16th (aid contingent/drinking water purification).
Contingent strength:	109.
Composition:	Two crews for C-130 Hercules transport airplane, transport team, four drinking water purification troops.
Commander:	Major Markus Bock.
Contribution:	Transport of aid goods with C-130; two million liters of drinking water are purified by the military experts.

At the farewell to the aid troop the governor of the region and the Minister for Handicrafts and Technical Education in Sri Lanka especially emphasize the contributions of the Austrians. Austria sets the standard for water purification and distribution. Especially in the difficult to reach area of the crisis zone, the Austrians with their all-terrain Pinzgauers are the only ones in the position to supply the people living there with drinking water.

The Austrian Camp Elephant Lodge (b.l.). Even on a deployment there must be time for this: Major Markus Bock congratulates Warrant Officer I Walter Opelz on his birthday (b.r.).

Humanitarian Aid Contribution in Albania (HUM/ALB)

Preliminary Events

Similarly to Austria, large parts of Albania also suffer from extreme weather conditions in spring 2005: heavy snowfall cuts numerous settlements off from their surroundings, the inhabitants are no longer reachable by land.

International Reaction

For this reason, NATO petitions the nations of KFOR stationed in Kosovo for humanitarian aid. Parts of the Albanian army, who are already in an assistance deployment, support the measures. In total around 44 tons of foodstuffs are transported into seven villages south of Kukes. Since the planned actions go beyond the KFOR area of responsibility, the troop-providing nations must individually agree to the undertaking. After the green light from Germany, Italy, Switzerland and Austria, the Multinational Brigade Southwest, MNB (SW), is commissioned with an aid deployment.

Thereupon a survey team from the brigade starts on February 10th in order to create the prerequisites for the multinational aid deployment. On the morning of February 11th an advance command establishes the necessary infrastructure on the ground, around mid-day the first helicopters are able to start with the aid goods. The foodstuffs, provided by Albania, are unloaded in the main square of Kukes with the support of the Albanian army. So valuable aid can be contributed to the Albanian population until the early evening.

On Saturday at 9:30 AM the airlift is taken up again. In total on both days 32 tons of foodstuffs can be transported in 44 flights with seven helicopters from Germany, Italy, Switzerland and Austria. The air fleet is supported on land by 68 KFOR soldiers and seven vehicles.

Basis for deployment: Request of the Albanian government and NATO.
Mission: Aid contribution from the air for the population cut off by snow.
Duration of deployment: February 10th, 2005 – February 12th, 2005.
Participating nations: Austria, Germany, Italy, Switzerland.

Austrian Reaction
Political Measures

At the order of the Federal Minister of Defence, authorized according to Sec. 2 para. 5 FCL-CSD in case of urgency, the urgent dispatch of an aid contingent in the strength of up to ten men and two transport helicopters from the Austrian KFOR contingent takes place for a humanitarian deployment in Albania.

Military Measures

Two transport helicopters of the type Agusta Bell AB-212 are immediately transferred to the area of operations by the Austrian KFOR command.

Basis for deployment: Order of the minister of February 4th, 2005; CM of February 15th, 2005, MC of February 15th, 2005 (acknowledgement).
Mission: Humanitarian aid contribution after extreme snowfall.
Appellation: Austrian Contingent (OESKON).
Form of dispatch: FCL-CSD.
Area of operation: Border area with KOSOVO.
Duration of deployment: February 10th, 2005 – February 12th, 2005.
Contingent strength: 10 (helicopter crews, support personnel).
Composition: 2 Agusta Bell AB-212 transport helicopters.
Contribution: In four transports 2,150 kg of flour, sugar and oil are flown into the villages of Kalis, Bushtrice and Shkinak in total.

African Union Mission in Sudan (AMIS II)

Preliminary Events

After a civil war lasting almost 20 years, a humanitarian cease-fire agreement takes place in spring 2004 between the two conflicting parties.

International Reaction

The **African Union (AU)** decides on May 28th, 2004, in Darfur to deploy an observation mission to observe compliance with this **N'Djamena Ceasefire Agreement** of April 8th, 2004 (AMIS). On October 20th, 2004, the Peace and Security Council of the African Union decides on an expansion of the AMIS observation mission, whose mandate now includes the support of trust-building measures, the protection of the civilian population and humanitarian operations and the observation of the compliance of all the agreements signed by the parties since the N'Djamena Humanitarian Ceasefire Agreement (AMIS II). The United Nations Security Council calls on the international community to prepare itself for a long-lasting engagement in its Resolution 1547 on June 11th, 2004. In its Resolution 1556 of July 30th, 2004, the United Nations Security Council approves the dispatch of international observers in the Darfur region in Sudan under the leadership of the AU, and calls on its member nations to reinforce the international observer team under the leadership of the AU; during this the already offered contributions, above all from the European Union, are embraced.

To support the operation AMIS II of the African Union, the EU Council for Foreign Affairs decides on July 18th, 2005, on an operation which is to participate in practical support in the military as well as the police area. On June 19th, 2007, the mission transitions into the **African Union Mission in Somalia (AMISOM)**.

Basis for deployment: SC Resolution 1556 (2004) of July 30th, 2004; FAC/CFSP. Action/2005/557/CFSP of July 18th, 2005.
Mission: The civilian part is essentially composed of the support of the police components of AMIS II (in particular advice and training), the military component includes logistical support (planning support as well as technical support, including the coordination structure), the provision of military observers, the training of African troops with whom AMIS II is increased, the implementation of transports as well as, at the request of the AU, support in the area of airspace surveillance.
Duration of deployment: December 22nd, 2000 – December 31st, 2007.
Participating nations: 11.
Strength: 6,300.
Headquarters: Addis Ababa.

Austrian Reaction

Political Measures

The Austrian federal government initially decides on the dispatch of a "legal expert". In December the additional dispatch of up to five staff officers to support the EU mission takes place.

Military Measures

Basis for deployment: CM of January 21st, 2005, MC of January 26th, 2005 (legal expert). CM of June 6th, 2007, MC of June 19th, 2007 (follow-up mission AMISOM)[143].
Mission: Support of the police components of AMIS II in the areas of advice and training, planning support, military observers.
Form of dispatch: FCL-CSD.
Area of operations: Addis Ababa.
Duration of deployment: March 3rd, 2005 – June 19th, 2007 (legal expert).
Contingent strength: 1.
Total: 4.

---

143 This is nevertheless not sent.

United Nations Mission in Sudan (UNMIS)

Preliminary Events

After 20 years of civil war, the government of Sudan and the South Sudanese People's Liberation Movement (SPLM/A) conclude the **Naivasha Peace Treaty** on January 9th, 2005, in Kenya. With this the war of secession in Southern Sudan is ended. Besides the disarmament of the rebels and their integration in the regular army, the peace treaty envisions a referendum in the year 2011, during which it is to be decided if the South remains within the territory of the nation as a whole. Independently of this the humanitarian disaster in the western region of Darfur continues.

International Reaction

UNMIS initially appears as the leader of the negotiations for the international community. Subsequently the support of the implementation of the peace agreement, including the observation of the cease-fire; the support of the return of the refugees and/or displaced persons; humanitarian aid; the support of measures for explosive ordnance disposal; the support of endeavors to comply with human rights and for the personal safety of the inhabitants, in particular especially endangered groups such as returnees, women, children; the implementation of all necessary measures for the protection of United Nations personnel and institutions as well as help for civilian persons in cases of immediately threatening violence (Chapter VII of the articles of the United Nations) all fall to the mission. UNMIS is the longest mission within the framework of the Standby High Readiness Brigade (SHIRBRIG).[144]

Basis for deployment:	SC Resolution 1590 (2005) of March 24th, 2005.
Mission:	Observation of the peace agreement, humanitarian aid.
Duration of deployment:	April 2005 – to date.
Participating nations:	49.
Strength:	10,000 soldiers (including up to 750 military observers), around 700 policemen.
Headquarters:	Khartoum.

Austrian Reaction

Political Measures

The Council of Ministers decides on the dispatch of up to five staff members in line with SHIRBRIG.

Military Measures

Basis for deployment:	CM of April 5th, 2005, MC of April 6th, 2005.
Mission:	Staff service.
Form of dispatch:	FCL-CSD.
Area of operations:	Khartoum, south and southeast of Sudan.
Duration of deployment:	April 24th, 2005 – September 30th, 2006.
Contingent strength:	2.
Total:	4.

---

144 SHIRBRIG is founded by Austria, Canada, the Netherlands, Norway, Poland and Sweden on December 15th, 1996 on the initiative of Denmark. Up to 4,500 soldiers from 14 member states (Austria, Canada, Denmark, Finland, Ireland, Italy, Lithuania, Norway, the Netherlands, Poland, Romania, Slovenia, Spain and Sweden) are held ready for the United Nations in line with SHIRBRIG. The multinational brigade takes part in five UN deployments in the African area. After twelve successful years SHIRBRIG ends its activities on June 30th, 2009, since the members are involved in many various missions.

European Union Monitoring Mission in Aceh (EU-AMM)

Preliminary Events

In the Indonesian province of Aceh, a decade-long bloody civil war takes place, which claims over 10,000 human lives. Life in Aceh is marked by the guerilla war of the Aceh Movement for a Free Aceh (Gerakan Aceh Merdeka – GAM) against the Indonesian army, which leads to many human rights violations and murders on both sides. On August 15th, 2005, a peace agreement is signed in Helsinki between the Indonesian central government and the GAM. The contractually fixed agreement on the renunciation of violence is also mostly complied with in practice. The rebels are to hand over all of their 850 weapons to the Aceh Monitoring Mission by January 27th, 2006. Among these are automatic weapons, munitions and a rocket launcher. The weapons are destroyed by AMM. In return 1,800 GAM fighters and sympathizers are released from prison and amnestied. On December 11th, 2006, democratic elections for governor can be carried out for the first time.

International Reaction

The mission of the AMM, an observer mission placed by the EU and the ASEAN countries (Association of Southeast Asian Nations), is the observation of the demobilization and reintegration of the GAM fighters, observation of their surrender of weapons and/or the disablement of the surrendered weapons, observation of the partial withdrawal of Indonesian security forces not regularly stationed in Aceh, observation of the human rights situation as well as the addressing of conflicts between the parties in the conflict during the implementation of the Memorandum of Understanding (MoU) from Helsinki.

Basis for deployment:	EU Council/J. Action 2005/643/CFSP of September 9th, 2005.
Mission:	Observation of the demobilization.
Duration of deployment:	September 15th, 2005 – December 15th, 2006.
Participating nations:	EU members, ASEA members, Brunei, Malaysia, the Phillippines, Singapore, Thailand.
Strength:	125 EU and 93 ASEAN observers; 29 EU and seven ASEAN observers (until end of mission).
Headquarters:	Banda (provincial capital of Aceh).

Austrian Reaction
Political Measures

The Council of Ministers decides on the dispatch of up to two members of the armed forces and the Foreign Ministry each as observers to the province of Aceh in Indonesia. The observers fulfill their duties unarmed. The dispatch is cancelled on March 16th, 2006.

Military Measures

Basis for deployment:	CM of August 30th, 2005, MC September 7th, 2005.
Mission:	Supervision of demobilization and surrender of weapons as well as observation of the partial withdrawal of the Indonesian armed forces and the human rights situation.
Form of dispatch:	FCL-CSD.
Area of operations:	Banda Aceh.
Duration of deployment:	September 15th, 2005 – September 15th, 2006 (cancelled from March 16th, 2006).
Contingent strength:	1.

Austrian Forces Disaster Relief Unit in Pakistan (AFDRU/PAK)

Preliminary Events

On October 8th, 2005, at 8:50 AM local time (3:50 AM UTC), there is an earthquake in the area of Kashmir administrated by Pakistan. The epicenter is near Muzaffarabad, around 100 kilometers north of the capital Islamabad. In the affected area, the Indian plate pushes into the Asian continent with a speed of around eight centimeters per year. The quake, with a strength of 7.6 on the Richter scale, develops at a depth of 10 kilometers under the surface of the earth and causes destruction in North Pakistan, in Afghanistan, and in North India. More than a dozen aftershocks continually cause panic in the population. The authorities fear that more than 40,000 dead are to be mourned. Along a ca. 100 kilometer break practically all the buildings are destroyed. Many villages in the Kashmir mountains can hardly be reached, the roads are buried or have slid away. Thousands of people wait urgently for help, they are in danger of freezing, starving or becoming ill from contaminated water. After a week the official victim count is corrected to 73,000 dead and 70,000 critically wounded. Around three million people are homeless.

International Reaction

Many countries, international organizations and NGOs[145] offer the region aid in the form of money, foodstuffs, medical equipment, tents and blankets. Rescue and recovery teams with helicopters and rescue dogs are sent to the region from various parts of the world; the United Nations call for the collection of donations, in order to collect at least $US 272 million for the people in the region. Cuba counts as one of the largest direct supporters, which according to a SPIEGEL report from December 8th sends 789 doctors to the region and with this even exceeds the number of the Pakistani doctors (around 500).

Austrian Reaction

Political Measures

On October 12th, at the request of Pakistan, a Minister Committee decides on the urgent dispatch of up to 70 people for drinking water purification.

Military Measures

The disaster relief forces fly from Vienna-Schwechat Airport to Islamabad on October 13th, 2005, with two Ilyushin transporters and a passenger aircraft. The aid contingent remains in contact with home over a satellite connection. The latest reports from the area of operations arrive daily in the Situation Center in Graz.

> **Basis for deployment:** Order of the minister of October 12th, 2005; CM of December 18th, MC of October 20th, 2005 (acknowledgement).
> **Mission:** Provision of drinking water for the population.
> **Appellation: AFDRU/PAK.**
> **Form of dispatch:** FCL-CSD.
> **Area of operations:** Muzaffarabad (in north Pakistan).
> **Duration of deployment:** October 13th, 2005 – December 7th, 2005.
> **Contingent strength:** 65 (of which three are women).
> **Composition:** Four drinking water purification troops.
> **Commander:** Lieutenant Colonel Friedrich Aflenzer.
> **Contribution:** 4,876,270 liters of drinking water.

Not Everyone is Equal
In accordance with the treaty the contingent carries no weapons. Only the Americans arrive with their entire arsenal – and must then allow themselves to be disarmed by the Pakistanis. During an encounter with a US General the Austrian commander greets him out of courtesy. When the General sees the pistol on the Austrian's belt, he flies into a rage. After all, he had to surrender his weapon earlier. With a "disarming" smile the Austrian officer attempts to make it clear to the General that there are simply small differences between the USA and Austria. Which, he leaves discreetly unmentioned.

"The water is flowing!"
In Pakistan the soldiers of the armed forces operation four drinking water purification systems. With the four systems brought along, the helpers are in the position to be able to produce up to 120,000 liters of drinking water per day. With this the Austrians can supply 40,000 people with pure drinking water per day. After the arrival in Islamabad a truck convoy must initially be organized. The Pakistani army proves to be extremely cooperative, a helicopter for assessments is even made available to the contingent com-

---

145 Non-governmental organizations.

mander. The next two days the military convoy must fight for hours over narrow, partially buried mountain paths to its area of operations. And although rain and hail make the work difficult, the soldiers begin the construction of their 70 ton equipment as quickly as possible. On October 17th Lieutenant Colonel Friedrich Aflenzer is able to report: "The water is flowing!" Meanwhile, the demand for clean drinking water climbs constantly. In order to keep an overview of the situation, the soldiers concentrate on the most important distribution points and deliver above all to hospitals and larger tent camps. The "Pinzgauers" brought along show their value during this, since AFDRU has the only drinking water purification system with a distribution system. Plastic tanks are mounted on the "Pinzgauer" vehicles, with which it is possible to reach even out-of-the-way camps. In the center of Muzaffarabad the large tank in the mosque is filled, so that they can cook for 7,000 people there. But the international aid forces' helicopter landing pad is also supplied. Furthermore water analyses are carried out, wells reactivated and the local authorities are supported with the reestablishment of the destroyed infrastructure. Five all-terrain Pinzgauer vehicles, two motorcycles, a repair car as well as a medical Pinzgauer allow for independence in the area of operations.

Alert!

Numerous organizations begin with the drinking water purification at the same time. But soon there are alert reports of massive gastroenteritis ailments and the first cases of cholera at the Medical Meetings in the UNO deployment center. It is striking, though, that in the camps with around 40,000 people who are supplied by the Austrians, not a single case of illness is to be noted. Finally the Austrian contingent doctor, Major med. Dr. Andreas Kaltenbacher, the decision makers from UNO and the WHO (World Health Organization) are able to represent the presumed connection between the water quality and the cases of illness in an extremely engaged report. During this Kaltenbacher draws upon experience data from the deployment in Mozambique. General Dr. Malik, the highest ranking medical officer of Pakistan, thereupon causes water samples to be taken from all the organizations who deliver drinking water. The result makes the Austrians "world champions": Their water qualities lies far above the standards called for by the WHO. While the German Technical Relief Organization (TRO), the Canadian army and Caritas deliver useable water, the systems of numerous nongovernmental organizations (NGOs) must be immediately closed. They contented themselves with adding chlorine tablets to the seriously contaminated river water – and with this actually delivered "poison" as "drinking water".

Subsequently there are numerous excursions by the Pakistani decision makers, the UNO and the WHO to the Austrian camp. The systems are studied and photographed. Dr. Malik declares the Austrians to be the quasi highest water authorities of the region. The small field laboratory of First Lieutenant Michael Eichhübl and veterinary doctor Katharina Faukal especially delights the dignitaries. From then on no water tank vehicle is allowed to drive to the people without previously being approved by the Austrians. Two days later there is not a single new cholera case; the cases of gastroenteritis also swiftly fade. With Austrian help the public water supply system is repaired again. The Austrians soon enjoy a legendary reputation in the basin. It gets around to even the last Pakistani that the soldiers with the one-tone green battle uniforms are those with the good water.

On December 2nd the drinking water production is ceased. Before this representatives of a British NGO are briefed on the places to be supplied. General Dr. Malik has the drinking water system and the analysis program explained to him once more. The analysis tent is donated to a nearby school and constructed by the NBC group. Until then classes had taken place in the open air.

The AFDRU deployment in Pakistan is the most spectacular international one yet. The Austrian know-how succeeds in hindering a beginning cholera epidemic in the catastrophe area[146].

An Interesting Encounter

In the middle of Muzaffarabad – a partially fundamentalist dominated region – there is the Catholic Father Elias with his tiny church community. Elias is likewise buried by the quake and rescued. The AFDRU soldiers are put on Elias' trail by Brigadier General Herman Loidolt. Loidolt came to know and appreciate the active Father during his deployment as Commander of the United Nations Military Observer Group in India and Pakistan (UNMOGIP). After arduous researches Pater Elias can in fact be located. The camp pastor, Military Deacon Franz Auer, honors the occasion with a joint mass in the mess tent, in which AFDRU soldiers, Pakistani Catholics, and friendly Muslims take part.

Armed Forces Aid Goods for Earthquake Victims in Pakistan

On November 30th a total of 55 tons of aid goods from military inventories are loaded for transport to Pakistan. 12,000 field sweaters, 1,000 field blankets, a large number of tents, bedrolls and box cookers are to preserve the survivors of the devastating earthquake from death of cold. Besides this the armed forces donate 33 field kitchen stoves, with which 200 people each can be cooked for. The majority of the aid goods are transported by rail from the military logistics center in St. Johann in Tyrol to the arsenal in Vienna. Further loads come by truck from the military warehouse in Klosterneuburg. In the arsenal itself the consolidation of the materials takes place and the further transport to Vienna-Schwechat Airport. For the last stage on Austrian soil, three semitrailers, at 30 tons, and a further 24 trucks are deployed. A civilian Boeing 747 made available by NATO finally brings the aid delivery to Islamabad.

---

146 From a report by "Kurier" editor Lieutenant Colonel Wilhelm Theuretsbacher.

After intensive study of the map with comradely support (t.l.), it's on the adventurous way to the area of operations with rented "local" trucks (t.r.). There the water purification system is established in a Pakistani army area directly on the banks of the river in the vicinity of an SOS Children's Village (m.l.). It is a seemingly attractive picture with a beautiful mountain river, a picturesque backdrop of mountains with Himalaya cliffs and a historical fort site. A deceptive picture: The river water has meanwhile been contaminated by 300,000 earthquake victims and on the edge of the camp the first mass grave is sited. EU Foreign Commissioner Dr. Benita Ferrero-Waldner also convinces herself of the professionalism of the troops in the course of the donator's conference in Islamabad. A situation as much an honor as it is nerve-wracking: The AFDRU soldiers must positively "smuggle" the high-ranking politician through the boiling pot of Muzaffarabad with two Pinzgauers (m.r.). A woman suffering from great pains in her feet is cared for by Captain med. Dr. Andrea Maierhofer. First Lieutenant veterinarian Mag. Katharina Faukal assists her (b.l.). But the population tested by suffering is also helped outside of "official" service whenever possible (b.r.).

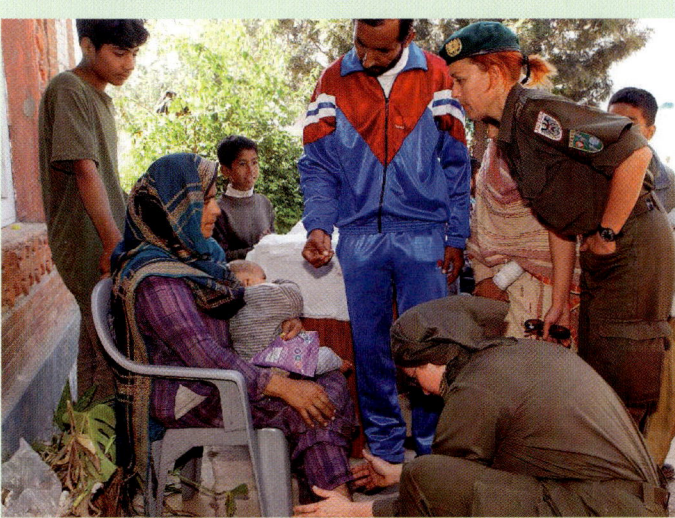

European Border Assistance Mission for the Rafah Crossing Point (EU-BAM Rafah)

Preliminary Events

As a result of the Israeli withdrawal from the Gaza Strip, the necessity arises to open the Rafah border crossing, in order to open an access point for the 1.4 million inhabitants to the outer world. In line with their peace negotiations the Israeli government and the Palestinian autonomous authorities unite on an agreement on freedom of movement and access, which is signed on November 15th, 2005. The European Union (EU) is asked by the parties involved to actively observe the handling of the personal and goods traffic on the Ramah border crossing. After the elections for the Palestinian legislative council won by Hamas on January 25th, 2006, the Palestinian elite unit Force 17, which is directly subordinate to the Palestinian president, takes over protection of EU-BAM Rafah.

International Reaction

The EU mission serves to support the border protection on the international Rafah border crossing from the Gaza Strip to Egypt. The goal of EU-BAM Rafah is to provide a third-party presence at the Rafah border crossing. Through this, in cooperation with the measures of the community to establish institutions, a contribution is to be made to the opening of the Rafah border crossing and to the formation of trust between the Israeli government and the Palestinian authorities. Since the border crossing is closed on June 9th, the EU cancels the mission on June 15th, 2007. On July 7th, 2007, the EU decides to leave the mission as a whole in a constant state of readiness, nevertheless to reduce the personnel strength.

Basis for deployment:	FAC/CFSP. Action 2005/889/CFSP of November 25th, 2005.
Mission:	Support (training, equipage and technical support) of the Palestinian autonomous authorities during the establishment of their capabilities for border protection and customs; evaluation of the procedures used by the Palestinian autonomous authorities; at any doubt with regard to compliance with the applicable agreements and regulations by the Palestinian border protection and customs employees to demand that persons, baggage, vehicles or wares are newly examined or evaluated; promotion of Israel-Palestinian trust building and cooperation; cooperation during the establishment of institutional capacities among the Palestinian autonomous authorities to secure trans-border cooperation.
Duration of deployment:	November 25th, 2005 – to date.
Participating nations:	Austria, Belgium, Denmark, England, Estonia, Finland, France, Germany, Greece, Italy, Lithuania, Luxembourg, the Netherlands, Portugal, Romania, Spain, Sweden.
Strength:	89.

Austrian Reaction
Political Measures

The federal government decides on the dispatch of up to two members of the armed forces and up to two customs officials to the Rafah border station as security experts, during which duty-related stays in the Palestinian areas, Israel and/or Egypt could be necessary. In addition the dispatch of two policemen takes place.

Military Measures

Basis for deployment:	CM of December 6th, 2005, MC of December 13th, 2005.
Mission:	**Support of border surveillance.**
Form of dispatch:	FCL-CSD.
Area of operations:	Rafah border crossing.
Duration of deployment:	December 13th, 2005 – December 31st, 2006.
Contingent strength:	2.

European Union Disaster Assessment and Coordination Team in Indonesia (EUDAC/Indonesia)

Preliminary Events

On May 27th, 2006, 3:20 PM local time (10:20 AM CEST), an earthquake with a strength of 6.3 on the Richter scale jolts the Indonesian island of Java and causes a tsunami. The epicenter of the earthquake is around 15 kilometers deep in the Indian Ocean, circa 360 kilometers south of Jakarta. The earthquake claims over 6,000 dead and 15,000 wounded; around 60,000 houses are destroyed and 200,000 people homeless. An additional threat develops from the Merapi volcano, tending to erupt.

International Reaction

The UN Office for Humanitarian Affairs (UNOCHA) dispatches an UNDAC team in order to organize aid as soon as possible. Furthermore an EUDAC team is dispatched to Indonesia on the part of the European Commission.

On November 3rd, 2004, the European Commission and the United Nations Office for the Coordination of Humanitarian Affairs agree to an intensification of their cooperation in the area of disaster relief, in order to better serve the needs of the victims. The agreement is to ensure efficient cooperation in the cases in which both organizations help or support aid contributions in a land devastated by a manmade or natural disaster. The goal is to maximize the use of resources and avoid redundancies. The commission has access to two instruments for disaster relief: The Office of the European Commission for Humanitarian Aid (ECHO), through which measures for immediate aid and for support are implemented, and the Community Process for Catastrophe Protection, which mainly coordinates the aid for countries within and outside of the EU for catastrophe protection cases. UNOCHA receives great importance during the leadership and coordination of the emergency aid measures of the international community in accordance with the global mandate entrusted to it by the General Assembly of the United Nations. For this UNOCHA operates an integrated emergency deployment system, which supervises, assumes and coordinates the international aid measures after natural disasters and complex emergency situations.

Basis for deployment: Alert by the EU/Monitoring and Information Center (MIC).
Mission: Assessment and coordination.
Duration of deployment: May 29th, 2006 – June 6th, 2006.
Strength: 1 UNDAC team, 1 EUDAC team.
Headquarters: Yogyakarta.
Austrian expert: Brigadier General Dr. Alois A. Hirschmugl.

Austrian Reaction

On May 29th, 2006, the urgent dispatch of an UNDAC disaster relief expert to Indonesia/Java for up to three weeks within the framework of an EU coordination team takes place through the Federal Ministers for Foreign Affairs, Finance, the Interior and Defence, authorized by the urgency case according to Sec. 1 no. 1 subsec. c in connection with Sec. 2 FCL-CSD (acknowledgement by CM on June 1st, 2006, by MC on June 14th, 2006).

Austrian Humanitarian Mission Cyprus (ATHUM Cyprus)

Preliminary Events

In July and August 2006, as a result of the effects of the lasting hostilities between the Israeli armed forces and Hamas in southern Lebanon, foreign nationals are also endangered. As a result of the reports of further flight movements by sea to Cyprus, the urgent need develops to bring further Austrian nationals as well as citizens of other nations to safety in line with humanitarian aid.

International Reaction

Numerous armed forces therefore begin with the immediate evacuation of foreign nationals, including Austrians.

Austrian Reaction

Political Measures

Only a few days after the beginning of the Israeli offensive against southern Lebanon and the begin of the refugee waves, it becomes clear that Austrians are among the EU citizens seeking help. The Foreign Ministry acts immediately and requests support from the armed forces.

Military Measures

Dispatch of a C-130K "Hercules" transport airplane including capacities for medical first aid and psychological care to Larnaca on Cyprus.[147] The evacuation is supported by the Austrian staff sections of UNFICYP.

> **Basis for deployment:** Petition of the Foreign Ministry.
> **Mission:** Evacuation of Austrian citizens and the citizens of friendly nations.
> **Form of dispatch:** FCL-CSD.
> **Area of operations:** Larnaca/Cyprus.
> **Duration of deployment:** June 17th, 2006 – June 22nd, 2006.
> **Contingent strength:** 7.
> **Composition:** 1 C-130K "Hercules" transport airplane, med-team (1 doctor, 1 medic, 1 psychologist).
> **Contribution:** 125 people (of which 77 are Austrian) are flown from Larnaca to Vienna in three flights.

After the men, women and children manage the passage to Cypriot Limassol on Wednesday night, they are received at the harbor directly by UNFICYP members. The military team brings the group to Larnaca, 70 kilometers away, without further delays, where they are initially cared for. Then they return home with a military "Hercules".

---

147 As a result of the destruction of the airport in Beirut and because of the lack of personal protection equipment for the "Hercules", no evacuation can be carried out in the direct area of the crisis.

European Union Forces in the Democratic Republic of the Congo (EUFOR RD Congo)

Preliminary Events

Although the nation has some of the largest natural treasures in Africa, it is one of the poorest in the world. Many of the nation's resources are exploited by the neighboring countries. The main cause of the instability is more than 30 years of mismanagement and corruption by the Mobutu regime, followed by serious war-like hostilities until the present day. At the beginning of the 1990's the economy totally collapses. Since 1996 the Congo war is carried out on the territory of the Democratic Republic of the Congo. This is often divided into the First Congo War from 1996 to 1997 and the Second Congo War since 1998, which is also sometimes called the Great War of Africa. The causes of the war are many. The main cause is the refugee camps in the east of the Congo, then still called Zaire, which emerge after the genocide of the Tutsi in Rwanda in 1994. The reason for the second phase of the conflict must mainly be the exploitation of resources. On February 18th, 2006, the new constitution is put into effect by President Joseph Kabila. On July 30th, 2006, the first free and democratic elections in over 40 years take place in the Congo.

International Reaction

The United Nations has already accompanied the Democratic Republic of the Congo (COD) on its way to a sovereign democracy since 1999, with the **MONUC (United Nations Organization Mission in the Democratic Republic of the Congo)**, which consists of around 16,000 soldiers and is therefore the biggest UN peacekeeping mission yet. However in the extremely critical phase of the presidential elections, besides the parliamentary and provincial elections, further military support is needed to secure the election process. Since a reinforcement of the MONUC troops proves unrealizable, the UN requests military support from the European Union on December 27th, 2005.

In a mutual understanding between New York and Brussels, the first military assessment missions begin in January 2006. On the basis of these, an "option paper" is produced on February 9th, 2006, which points to the basic possibilities and conditions of a European military operation in the Congo. Taking this paper as a basis, the actual mission, the "Initiating Military Directive" is formulated in cooperation between Brussels and Potsdam, so between the political and military leadership.

The EU mission takes place in complement to the already existing European missions in the region, such as EUSEC RD Congo (advising and support mission to promote the reform of the security sector) and EUPOL Kinshasa (support mission in line with the training of the Congolese police).

For the first time in European history, a European headquarters, EU OHQ (European Union Operation Headquarters) is operated in Potsdam according to EU guidelines for Operation EUFOR RD Congo. In Kinshasa a Force Headquarters (FHQ) is established. The operational reserve forces which are held ready in Gabon and France are also subordinate to the first of these.

The deployment phase of the operation begins with the elections on July 30th, 2006. During this time the presence, military strength, and the professional, determined and constantly friendly appearance of the EUFOR soldiers is an essential guarantee for the success of the deployment. The reconnaissance elements provide a detailed picture of the situation day and night, the troops are unrestrictedly fit for action at night and air mobile and constantly present in the media as well as on the main roads and in the slums. Furthermore, Operation EUFOR RD Congo is continually accompanied by civilian measures. Projects in the area of civil-military cooperation contribute to the reception of positive feedback. With the social equality and equal treatment of women as a systematic component of the entire operation, the trust and respect of the Congolese, especially the female part of the population, can be won. With this the operation contributes decisively to the securing of the election process.

The EU mandate for the mission ends on November 30th, 2006. The mass of the FHQ personnel withdraws to Paris on December 7th, 2006, the day after the inauguration of President Joseph Kabila. The return of the forces lasts until January 10th. On February 27th the European Council declares the official end of the operation; on the same date the FHQ in Postdam is deactivated.

Basis for deployment: SC Resolution 1671 (2006) of April 25th, 2006, EU Council/J. Action 2006/319/CFSP of April 27th, 2006.

Mission: Support of MONUC for the duration of the elections; protection of the civilian population against physical violence; protection of Kinshasa airport; evacuation of Persons with Designated Special Status (PDSS).

Duration of deployment: April 2006 – February 27th, 2007.

Participating nations: 21.

Strength: 2,400.

Headquarters: Operational Headquarters (OHQ) in Postdam/German; Force Headquarters (FHQ) in Kinshasa/Congo.

Austrian Reaction

Political Measures

At the request of the EU the federal government decides on the dispatch of up to ten members of the armed forces as staff officers within the framework of the EU mission to support the UNO mission in the Democratic Republic of the Congo (MONUC).

Military Measures

The armed forces dispatch two officers to the FHQ in Potsdam and three officers to the FHQ in Kinshasa. The latter occupy the posts of J9 (leader of the 9th Staff Division Civil-Military Cooperation – CIMIC), J35/ROE (deployment leadership and deployment planning with regard to the rules of engagement) as well as J35/PSYOPS (deployment leadership and deployment planning with regard to psychological operations).

> **Basis for deployment:** CM of May 4th, 2006, MC of May 11th, 2006.
> **Form of dispatch:** FCL-CSD.
> **Area of operations:** Potsdam, Kinshasa.
> **Duration of deployment:** July 13th, 2006 – December 31st, 2006.
> **Contingent strength:** 5.
> **Composition:** Three staff officers in Force Headquarters, two staff officers in Operational Headquarters.

United Nations Office for West Africa (UNOWA)

Preliminary Events

West Africa includes 15 nations with more than 250 million inhabitants in an area of 5,000,000 square kilometers. The leading African oil producer, Nigeria, and the Ivory Coast, the world's largest cocoa producers, lie in this area. All the countries are members of the Economic Community of West African States – ECOWAS. While some countries of this subregion have found a way towards peaceful development, others are devastated by serious conflicts and instabilities, which are ethnically, culturally, and historically based and often expand beyond their borders.

International Reaction

The United Nations therefore maintain peacekeeping missions in the Ivory Coast, Guinea-Bissau, Liberia and Sierra Leone, which work for political and economic stabilization as well as compliance with human rights and for humanitarian aid.

> **Basis for deployment:** Directive of the UN Secretary General of October 25th, 2004 in agreement with the UN Security Council.
> **Mission:** Promotion of the United Nations contributions for peace and safety in the subregion of West Africa.
> **Duration of deployment:** April 7th, 2004 – to date.
> **Headquarters:** Dakar.

Austrian Reaction

Political Measures

The federal government decides on the dispatch of a member of the armed forces as a deputy military adviser in the UNO Office for West Africa. According to the application of the Foreign Ministry, stays in the entire subregion of West Africa (Senegal, Gambia, Guinea-Bissau, Guinea, Sierra Leone, Liberia, Côte d'Ivoire, Burkina Faso, Ghana, Togo, Benin, Niger, Nigeria and Cameroon) as well as in the UNO offices in Geneva and New York as needed are planned during this deployment. The duties of the military adviser encompass advising the UNO Secretary General's Special Representative with regard to military aspects of UNOWA, the connection to other UNO operations and to armed forces in the subregion as well as advising the International Commission for the Bakassi Conflict (border conflict between Cameroon and Nigeria over the Bakassi peninsula).

Military Measures

> **Basis for deployment:** CM of June 29th, 2006, MC of July 11th, 2006.
> **Mission:** Advising of the UN Special Representative.
> **Form of dispatch:** FCL-CSD.
> **Area of operations:** Dakar.
> **Duration of deployment:** July 15th, 2006 – July 14th, 2009 (rotational relief).
> **Contingent strength:** 1.
> **Total:** 3.

United Nations Political Mission in Nepal (UNMIN)

Preliminary Events

After a ten year long conflict between the monarchical regime and the Maoists, after weeklong mass demonstrations, the representative of the SPA (Seven Party Alliance) and the Maoists sign a cease-fire at the end of May 2006. In connection with this the king is removed and the parliament put back into power.

With the support of the United Nations, the SPA and the Maoists agree on November 21st, 2006 on a "Comprehensive Peace Accord" which envisions the disarmament of the Maoists, the formation of a transitional government, a transitional constitution and new elections, among other things. The disarmament and return to the barracks of the Maoists is a prerequisite for the further implementation of the peace treaty. For this an "Agreement on Monitoring of the Management of Arms and Armies" is signed on November 28th, 2006.

The peace process initially goes only slowly. However, the situation soon changes again. On May 30th, 2008, the era of the Shah Dynasty ends in Nepal after 240 years. The political parties in the young Republic of Nepal thereupon enter into a bitter power struggle with each other. Nepal's Maoists finally proclaim the first autonomous federal states and call for a general strike on December 18th, 2009.

International Reaction

UNMIN supports the implementation of the agreement concluded upon between the government of Nepal and the Communist Party of Nepal. Although there is a row of positive developments, there are nevertheless some delays, in particular during the elections, which take place on April 10th, 2008, after being postponed twice. At the beginning of 2009, UN Secretary General Ban Ki Moon determines that there have been no steps forward in key elements of the peace process, such as the integration and rehabilitation of former Maoist guerrillas or the development of a new constitution. The Security Council therefore decides on the reinforced continuation of the mission.

Basis for deployment:	Res/SC 1740 (2007) of January 31st, 2007; Res/SC 1864 (2009) of January 23rd, 2009.
Mission:	Supervision of the cease-fire as well as support of the election preparations.
Duration of deployment:	January 23rd, 2007 – to date.
Participating nations:	18.
Strength:	72.
Headquarters:	Kathmandu (International Convention Center, New Baneshwor).

Compliance with the cease-fire and the surrender of weapons is supervised by the Austrian military experts.

Austrian Reaction

Political Measures

In February 2009, the federal government accedes to the petition of the Federal Ministry for European and International Affairs for the renewed dispatch of two members of the armed forces as military experts and a further five members of the armed forces for preparatory and supportive activities within the framework of the political mission of UNO in Nepal.

Military Measures

Basis for deployment:	CM of February 21st, 2007, MC of March 6th, 2007; CM of February 17th, 2009, MC of February 26th, 2009 (renewed dispatch).
Mission:	Supervision of the disarmament and military forces as well as election observations.
Form of dispatch:	FCL-CSD.
Area of operations:	Kathmandu.
Duration of deployment:	April 1st, 2007 – December 31st, 2008 (UNMIN 1). April 8th, 2009 – to date (UNMIN 2).
Contingent strength:	2.
Total:	4.

Crisis Support Team (KST)

Preliminary Events

It happens ever more often that Austrian citizens are victims of the elements, political conflicts or abductions. Until now one could always hope that these people would be rescued in the course of evacuations or hostage rescues by third nations.

Political Measures

Under the leadership of the Federal Ministry for European and International Affairs (FMEIA), therefore, suitable preparations have been made for a few years for an independent approach in case of provocation. As a collective national measure the diplomatic institutions in particularly sensitive regions are subjected to constant examination. This includes the holding of evidence of Austrians abroad with an address (reachability), occupation (for the possible need of specialists), summary lists, as son on. As a result of the clear division of duties, protection within representations of Austria abroad (embassy, consulate) falls to the special deployment command of the executive, "Cobra", while measures outside fall to the special deployment forces of the armed forces (evacuation, rescue, personal protection during transport, etc.). All measures take place in close coordination with the appropriate institutions of the European Union.

Military Measures

The armed forces support FMEIA by the placement of military experts from the armed forces leadership command, the special forces, the military intelligence bureau and the military geographical institute. At the order of and in coordination with FMEIA, these crisis support teams are dispatched to representations of Austria abroad, in order be able to support them with:

- The preparation of contingency plans (KST 1),
- The evaluation of the military situation with military expertise on site during critical developments (KST 2),
- As needed with the planning and implementation of military deployments, such as evacuation operations (KST 3).

KST 1 takes place within the framework of a business trip abroad (BTA), KST 2 and 3 in accordance with FCL-CSD.

European Union Security Sector Reform Mission in the Democratic Republic of the Congo (EUSEC RD Congo)

Preliminary Events

Murders, sexual violence, forced recruitment of children and forced labor, but also sickness and malnutrition make the conflict in the east of the Democratic Republic of the Congo (DR Congo) into one of the most deadly since the Second World War. Although the regions is not lacking in ceasefire agreements, despite military operations of the United Nations and the European Union (EU) and numerous diplomatic initiatives, the Region of Great Lakes and in particular the eastern part of the DR Congo is in a conflict between the Congolese army (**Forces Armées de la République Démocratique du Congo – FARDC**) and the Hutu militias (**Forces Démocratiques pour la Libération du Rwanda – FDLR**) and the resistance movement (**Lord's Resistance Army – LRA**).

In April 2005 the government of the Democratic Republic of the Congo asks the European Union for support in connection with the reform of the security sector. On July 30th, 2006 the inhabitants of the Congo, the third largest African nation, elect a parliament and president for the first time in over 45 years.

International Reaction

In the time before and after the elections the European Union makes an important contribution to peace and stability in the region in an extremely sensitive phase with Operation "EUFOR RD Congo" The around 17,000 members of the **United Nations Organization Mission in the Congo (MONUC)** further accompany the democratization process, while the EU supports the establishment of a sovereign national authority in the Democratic Republic of the Congo as before with its projects EUSEC RD and EUPOL Kinshasa (support mission in line with the training of the Congolese police). The political integration of the various regional groups as well as support with the restructuring and reestablishment of the Congolese army stand in the forefront. The mission is directly and supportively at the side of the Congolese security authorities with concrete projects. Essential factors are compliance with human rights, humanitarian international law as well as engagement for the rights of women and against the use of child soldiers.

Basis for deployment: FAC/CFSP. Action 2005/355/CFSP of May 2nd, 2005; FAC/CFSP. Action 2007/406/CFSP of June 12th, 2007 (police mission).
Mission: Advice and support of the security reform in the Democratic Republic of the Congo.
Duration of deployment: June 8th, 2005 – to date.
Strength: 60.
Headquarters: Kinshasa.

Austrian Reaction

Political Measures

The Council of Ministers decides on the dispatch of up to two members of the armed forces as military experts in the field office.

Military Measures

Basis for deployment: CM of June 6th, 2007, MC of June 19th, 2007.
Mission: Advice and support of the security reform in the Democratic Republic of the Congo.
Form of dispatch: FCL-CSD.
Area of operations: Kinshasa.
Duration of deployment: August 6th, 2007 – to date.
Contingent strength: 2.

European Union Disaster Assistance and Coordination in Peru (EUDAC/Peru)

Preliminary Events

On August 15th, 2007, a very serious earthquake occurs on the coast of Peru. The earthquake begins at 11:40 PM UTC (6:40 PM local time), lasts around two minutes and reaches a strength of 7.5 on the Richter scale. The hypocenter is around 150 km southeast of Lima at a depth of around 30 km. More than 600 people are killed and over 1,600 wounded by the earthquake. The districts of Ica, Pisco, Lima and Huancavelica are the worst affection. The affected regions are cut off from their electricity supply and communications, supplies of drinking water and food are only possible by air transport because of the destruction of the main traffic routes. Looting makes the deployment of aid forces more difficult. More that 85,000 houses are destroyed by the earthquake. Especially tragic is the collapse of a church in Ica during a Catholic mass on the occasion of Ascension Day: 17 people lose their lives, over 70 suffer injuries when it collapses. Subsequently there are over 70 noted aftershocks, one even with a strength of 7.9. Wounded who cannot be cared for in the local hospitals are flown from the airport in Pisco by an air bridge to Lima. As a result of the strength of the shaking, tsunami warnings are called for Peru, Ecuador, Chile and Colombia.

International Reaction

The European Commission requests the dispatch of an Austrian UNDAC expert within the framework of a mission of the EU Monitoring and Information Center (EUMIC).

After traveling to Lima assessments are carried out on August 21st, 2007 with a vehicle in Chichen Alta, ca. 150 km south of Lima. On August 22nd the team, which consists of a seismologist and two doctors, travels from Lima with a Boeing 200-737 from the Peruvian air force to Pisco, where all aid forces are accommodated at the airbase of the Peruvian Air Force for security reasons. Here further coordination meeting take place. As a result of the weather situation, however, no further assessment from the air can take place. A return flight of the team to Lima is only possible after the personal intervention of one of the responsible parties from the Peruvian Air Force with a civilian airline. On August 23rd a debriefing takes place in the course of a teleconference with EUMIC, on August 24th the final conclusion briefing of EUMIC and ECHO with all workers of the resident delegations under the leadership of the EU ambassador.

Basis for deployment: EU Council/Joint Action/CFSP/2007.
Mission: Assessment and evaluation for a catastrophe deployment.
Duration of deployment: August 19th, 2007 – August 28th, 2007.
Strength: 3.
Area of operations: Chichen Alta, Pisco.
Austrian expert: Lieutenant Colonel med. Dr. Sylvia-Carolina Sperandio.
Duration of deployment: August 19th, 2007 – August 28th, 2007.

Austrian Reaction

The Defence Minister orders the dispatch of a catastrophe expert to Peru within the framework of an EU assessment and coordination team on August 17th, 2007, in accordance with Sec. 1 no. 1 subsec. c in connection with Sec. 2 FCL-CSD (acknowledgment by the Council of Ministers on August 29th, 2007).

LTC med. Dr. Sperandio (b, center of picture) with her UNDAC colleagues during the discussion with local representatives.

Austrian Humanitarian Contingent in Greece (ATHUM/GR)

Preliminary Events

In August 2007 devastating forest and steppe fires rage across broad sections of Greece. 64 people lose their lives, many more are injured. The extent of the destruction is so large that people speak of it as the most serious natural disaster in human memory.

International Reaction

Numerous EU countries participate in an extensive international aid campaign with firefighting and military forces as well as with special firefighting plans and helicopters.

Austrian Reaction
Political Measures

On August 27th, 2007, a Committee of Ministers (Federal Ministers for the Interior and Defence), in accordance with Sec. 1 no. 1 subsec. b in connection with Sec. 2 para. 5 FCL-CSD, decide on the urgent dispatch of a total of 35 members of the armed forces and other people (fire department members) who have declared themselves ready to participate in contributions to fighting the forest fires in Greece.

Military Measures

In order to help the deployed Greek forces, the Austrian military dispatches two Agusta Bell AB-212 transport helicopters from Linz/Hörsching and three Pilatus PC-6 "Turbo Porter" transport airplanes from Langenlebarn on August 27th, which take part in the firefighting. Further personnel, including three members of the Upper Austrian Fire Department, and the necessary equipment is brought from Linz/Hörsching to the Greek airfield of Elefsina in the vicinity of Athens with a military Lockheed C-130 "Hercules" transport airplane.

The helicopters and airplanes of the armed forces already begin their first deployments in Greece on the next day. The Austrian forces are assigned the island of Euboea, which is especially affected by the fire's blaze, as their area of operations. While the two helicopters and two PC-6s are deployed to fight the fire, the third PC-6 is used for transport and survey flights. The C-130 "Hercules" fulfills additional transport assignments with its six-person crew. Early in Tuesday afternoon the airplanes start from Elefsina to the island, on which the fires rage particularly strongly. Already in the first 24 hours around 100,000 liters of water are transported into the fire zone with both helicopters and the airplanes.

On the following day the contingent of the armed forces moves its outpost from Elefsina to Tatoi, through which the flight time to the fire zone is halved and an even more effective deployment of forces made possible. Already by the afternoon of August 29th the deployed Austrian forces, together with further international aid forces, succeed in containing the forest fires in the south of the island of Euboea; around 3 PM the pilots report that the fires there are under control. In the days afterward, the Austrian forces support the firefighting work in the central and northern parts of the island.

On August 31st the three PC-6s withdraw to Austria, while both AB-212s are deployed a further day to support the Swedish aid contingent. Their withdrawal to Linz/Hörsching takes place on September 1st together with the C-130 "Hercules".

Basis for deployment:	Order of the minister of August 27th, 2007; CM of August 29th, 2007, MC of September 27th, 2007 (acknowledgement).
Mission:	Forest fire fighting.
Appellation:	ATHUM/GR.
Form of dispatch:	FCL-CSD 1997.
Area of operations:	Island of Euboea, Military Airbase TATOI (20 km north of Athens).
Duration of deployment:	August 27th, 2007 – September 1st, 2007.
Contingent strength:	35 (26 soldiers, C-130 crew, three fire department members).
Commander:	Colonel Gerold Doblhammer.
Aircraft:	Two Agusta Bell AB-212 transport helicopters, three Pilatus PC-6 "Turbo Porter" transport airplanes, a Lockheed C-130 "Hercules" transport airplane.
Contribution:	In firefighting deployments lasting a total of 120 flight hours, 220,000 liters of water are dropped onto the burning areas.

A military C-130 "Hercules" starts from Hörsching in the direction of Greece. The airplane transports equipment necessary for the firefighting deployment and 20 specialists from the armed forces (t.l.). One of the two AB-212s takes off from the outpost at the Elefsia military airbase to pick up water. The helicopters can refill their water tanks directly from the sea after every deployment flight. The external firefighting container holds 1,000 liters (t.r.).

View from the cockpit of the AB-212 on the hotspot of the fire (m.l.). The water container is emptied above the fire's hotspot (m.r.). Both PC-6s are equipped with internal 800 liter tanks to fight fires (b.l.). For the refill of firefighting water they must fly back to the outpost. The thanks for the affected population is expressed in many ways (b.r.): THANKS.

European Union Force "Tchad/Republique Centralafricaine" (EUFOR/TCHAD/RCA)

Preliminary Events

Since 2003 the people in the southern region of Darfur suffer under the armed conflicts between rebel movements and the central government in Khartoum. In the battles against the rebels the government supports above all local riding militias. These militias do not go up against rebels, but also against the civilian population with inhuman harshness. The United Nations assume that these battles have caused around 250,000 dead and 2.5 million refugees. In Chad, there are about 256,000 refugees from Western Sudan and 180,000 IDPs in camps. The picture to the right shows such a camp from the perspective of a helicopter crew (Czech Defence Ministry).

International Reaction

In the eastern border area of Chad, military observers fulfill since 2007 their duties within the framework of the mission of MINURCAT together with policemen to stabilize the borders and the respective areas in the interior. In summer 2007 it nevertheless becomes clear that this mixed force will neither reach the necessary strength nor the corresponding structures to fulfill the mission.

In order to help the many refugees, the United Nations and many nongovernmental organizations also engage themselves in Chad. In July 2007 first talks begin within the body of the European Union on a possible EU mission in Chad. On September 25th, 2007 the United Nations Security Council authorizes the mission in the east of Chad and in the northeast of the Central African Republic. On November 9th and 14th troop placement conferences take place for EUFOR Tchad in Brussels. On December 19th a further troop placement conference takes place in Brussels on the EUFOR deployment for the protection of refugees. On January 11th, 2008 the member nations of the European Union agree on the military equipment still needed for the humanitarian EUFOR mission in Chad. On March 15th, 2008 the interim operational capability (IOC) of the mission is reached. With this the one year duration of the mandate begins in accordance with the resolution of the UN Security Council, in which the multinational presence in the CAR and in Chad, including the UN mission MINURCAT and that of an EU transitional mission, is authorized for the duration of a year after the achievement of operational capability. The full operational capability (FOC) is given as September 15th.

On March 15th, 2009 the mission is taken over by the **UN Mission in the Central African Republic and Chad 2 (MINURCAT 2)**.

Basis for deployment:	SC Resolution 1778 (2007) of September 25th, 2007; EU Council/Joint Action 2007/677/CFSP of October 15th, 2007.
Mission:	Protection of refugees, improvement of the general security situation to secure humanitarian aid provision, protection of persons, institutions and equipment of UNO.
Duration of deployment:	January 30th, 2008 – March 15th, 2009.
Area of operations:	Chad and the Central African Republic, border areas to Sudan in the east of Chad.
Participating nations:	Albania, Austria, Belgium, Bulgaria, Croatia, Cyprus, the Czech Republic, Finland, France, Germany, Great Britain, Greece, Hungary, Ireland, Italy, Lithuania, Luxembourg, the Netherlands, Poland, Portugal, Romania, Slovakia, Slovenia, Spain, Sweden.
Strength:	2,732.
Headquarters:	Mont Valérien near Paris (operational headquarters); N'Djamena (rear force headquarters); Abéché (field headquarters).

Austrian Reaction

Political Measures

From July 2007 Austria is already pushing for the UN mandate to include clear framework requirement and an exit strategy by Foreign Minister Dr. Ursula Plassnik. Between October 3rd and 5th, 2007, Defence Minister Mag. Norbert Darabos travels with experts from the Defence Ministry and Foreign Ministry to Chad, in order to personally form an impression of the situation on site. On October 10th, the Council of Ministers decides on the political support of the EU bridging mission in Chad. On the same day the general staff of the Defence Minister is assigned to work out a concept for a substantial Austrian contribution to the EU bridging mission in the extent of around a company, which above all includes aspects of security and a humanitarian dimension. On November 7th, 2007, the dispatch of up to 170 members of the armed forces as well as up to 50 members for the construction and dismantling of the camp is unanimously enacted by the Council of Ministers.

Military Measures

The preparations for the military Chad mission begin in December: Around 160 Austrian soldiers prepare for the humanitarian aid deployment in Chad in the Deployment Preparation Center (DPC) in Götzendorf (LA). The move of the contingent, which is ready for deployment from the middle of December, fails because of the fact that the international mission cannot be started as a result of grave deficits above all in the areas of medical care and air transport despite the promises of some participating nations.

On January 30th, 2008, the Austrian advance command travels to N'Djamena. The deployment immediately begins "heatedly": At the beginning of February the rebels push as far as the center of the capital of Chad and enters partly serious battles with the government troops, which also claim numerous victims. The Austrian advance command is at this time in Hotel Kempinski and holds its position there, the Austrian soldiers nevertheless are not entangled in the hostilities. On February 5th, the advance command occupies Camp Kossei in the direct vicinity of the EUFOR headquarters. Within the shortest amount of time a connection to Austria is established. Special beds with mosquito nets even make it possible to spend a quiet night in the open air.

On February 25th, the advance command moves to Camp Europe of the EUFOR forces, in oder to establish the communication and leadership center there and to prepare the reception of further Austrian forces. Camp Europe, however, only serves as a temporary camp until the move to Abéché, which takes place in March. Only the "National Support Element", which is responsible for the provisioning of the contingent in the area of operations, remains in N'Djamena. On February 26th, a further 50 soldiers of the special forces, engineers, doctors, medics and logistical specialists, take off from Vogler airbase in Linz-Hörsching for N'Djamena with a chartered Boeing 737. In addition transport airplanes with the vehicles (special vehicles, trucks, emergency medical vehicles), engineering equipment, material for camp construction, tents, supplies of provisions and drinking water and the like (in total over 900 tons) land in the capital of Chad.

On March 4th, a further 70 Austrian soldiers – special forces, engineers and logistical specialists – land at the airport in N'Djamena. On March 10th, the main part of the contingent travels into the actual area of operations, Abéché, around 800 kilometers away. The soldiers use the first days in Abéché for making contact with nongovernmental organizations and UN institutions such as the OCHA (Organization for Coordination of Humanitarian Aid), among other things. The workers of such organizations usually have current information on the area of operations. Among the most important measures in a new area of operations is also to introduce themselves to the civilian population as well as to make their intentions and the goals of the military mission known. This takes place, insofar as the language barriers can be overcome, in personal conversations. Already by the middle of March 2008, the initial deployment readiness can be provided.

Basis for deployment:	CM of November 7th, 2007, MC of November 9th, 2007.
Mission:	Protection of refugee camps, patrol activities, personal protection
Appellation:	AUCON Tchad/RCA.
Form of dispatch:	FCL-CSD.
Area of operations:	Abéché.
Duration of deployment:	January 30th, 2008 – March 15th, 2009.
Contingent strength:	160 (4 of which are in Paris).
Total:	740.
Composition:	Staff personnel in OHQ and FHQ; contingent command with leadership and logistical elements, reconnaissance element and medical element with three emergency medical teams; special forces, support element, camp construction element.
Commander:	January 30th, 2008 – June 21st, 2008 Colonel GS Mag. Heinz Assmann (AUCON 1);
	June 21st, 2008 – November 10th, 2008 Colonel GS Mag. Horst Hofer (AUCON 2);
	November 11th, 2008 – February 16th, 2009 Colonel GS Mag. Peter Hofer (AUCON 3);
	February 16th, 2009 – March 15th, 2009 Colonel GS Mag. Manfred Hanzl (AUCON 4).

On March 10th the majority of the contingent travels to the actual area of operations, Abéché, around 800 kilometers away (t.l. and t.r.). Sandstorms and torrential rains often arise from one moment to another (m.r.). Protection from these caprices of the weather must then be created with "lightning speed" (m.l. and b.l.). Encounter with the governmental soldiers of Chad (b.r.).

363

The "Shade"[148]

At the end of January 2008, the advance command of the Austrian engineers travels to the area of operations. On February 26th the first construction command follows and immediately begins with the construction of the DRASH tents (Deployable Rapid Assembly Shelter) in Camp Europe in N'Djamena. These tents are to accommodate parts of the NIC (National Intelligence Cell) and the NSE (National Support Element) as well as a transit area (accommodations for additionally arriving soldiers and/or units who need accommodates for the day of the arrival/departure from N'Djamena). During this shade receives priority because of the expected temperatures of 55 degrees Celsius (or more) in the shade in the area of operations. Already during the preparation for the deployment the Austrian camp is planned in detail by a small group of engineers with deployment experience. During the joint deliberations the idea of shading the camp area emerges, since every reduction of the temperature in the work and accommodation tents raises the deployment ability of the soldiers (and the efficiency of the cooling equipment). The load-bearing construction is formed by individual stands from water supply pipes, which are bound together with steel cables and into ground anchors with tension belts. Over this the camouflage nets usual in the armed forces are laid over them and secured. The system works like a Faraday cage (the electricity flows around the object and not through it) and so offers all the soldiers and equipment under it protection against lightning strikes. Through the shade the air in the tents is around 15 degrees Celsius cooler than the surrounding temperature. This is soon spread around by the EUFOR soldiers and leads to unbounded admiration (also to many visits) by the members of other nations.

After a few days the engineers move from Abéché in the east of Chad to the area of the ONDR (Office Nationale du Développement Rural) for the planning and preparation of an advance field camp (picture below). This "temporary camp" is necessary, since the preparatory work for the actual **Camp Stars** is not yet finished. The area of ONDR is an area rented by EUFOR on the edge of the city of Abéché, which is planned for Austrian, French, Belgian, Finnish and Irish forces. French tents (without shade or air conditioning) serve as accommodations, in which at midday 50 degrees Celsius and more are measured. Temperatures in which a stay in the interior of the tent is not really restful. The main duty of the first engineers in Abéché consists of the planning of the Austrian contingents' camp area under great time pressure, since the mass of the Austrian contingent is already on the march over land. Within a week the tents are ready to be moved into. The camp receives large international attention.

The work in Camp Stars, in which the Austrian contingent is to be permanently accommodated, can first be begun in the middle of June. Above all in order to be protected from the high water levels which can reach up to 40 cm during the rainy season, podiums are constructed for the DRASH tents. These consist of individual elements (2 x 1 m) which can be coupled with each other with adjustable telescoping legs (picture). They are a further modularly usable system, which in connection with the shade also provides protection against damp on the ground during the rainy season, but also against unwelcome animal "visitors" during the dry season. Furthermore an Austrian mobile full biological sewage treatment plant is procured. The usable water won by in this way is used as flushing water for WC facilities in the medical containers as well as washing water for vehicles. It also serves for the greening of untilled spaces, a measure against the enormous production of dust during the dry season. Finally the condensed water from the air conditioning equipment is gathered and fed into the usable water cycle. This brings up to 1,200 liters of additional useable water per day! In total the engineers use around 900 camouflage nets from Austria for shade. Furthermore 3,000 square meters of podiums are constructed, 600 square meters of them are equipped with plates of grating for the possibility of water drainage. In the middle of July, **Camp Neptun** within Camp Stars is "ready for move in" for the accommodation of the Austrian and initially also the Swedish contingent. It is proven once more that Austrian soldiers see the construction of field camps differently than other nations. From the Austrian point of view, a field camp is never "finished"! The "Austrian standard" is initially "ogled" by other countries, finally though admired. After all, a field camp counts as one of the most important infrastructural requirements for the success of every foreign deployment, from the structural measures to the "force protection" (measures for their own protection, for instance against enemy weapons fire) to the design of the "recreation area". The Austrian part of Camp Stars is finally renamed Camp Schönbrunn. The newly established construction company of the 3rd EngBn in Melk has passed its first "baptism of fire" with flying colors.

---

148 Excerpt from the experience report of Captain Mag. (FH) Bernhard Weingartmann (Commander of the Engineering Construction Company) and First Lieutenant Mag. (FH) Sandra Rumplmair (Commander of the planning and survey group).

By June 25th, 2008 the Austrian EUFOR contingent moves: From the ONDR camp the soldiers move into Camp Stars. There they initially find accommodation in Belgian tents (t.r.) and begin with the construction of work tents and social areas. 60 trailers, 2,000 camouflage nets, 70 so-called Drash tents, 1,750 tent stakes and untold numbers of sandbags are shifted, mounted, set up, driven in and filled by the 40 engineers from Melk. And that in temperatures between 40 and 50 degrees in the shade. In addition the extremely hard ground makes the work more difficult for soldiers, above all while driving in tent stakes and the meter long ground nails (page 364). The Austrian part of the multinational Camp Stars receives the name Camp Neptun. This part of the camp receives this name during the rainy season, when it is important to keep the soldiers' accommodations dry. In the vehicle workshop the vehicles are maintained and repaired (m.l.). The soldiers of the armed forces contingent can rest in camp and prepare for their work. The Guereda outpost (m.r.). After the fiftieth takeoff and landing of the C-130 "Hercules" transport airplane in Chad, Captain Bernd Staudacher, the pilot of the jubilee flight, and his team are received within the framework of a small celebration in Abéché (b.l.). December 24th with 35 degrees Celsius: At a Christmas celebration presents are given to the Austrian peacekeeping soldiers in Chad. The Christmas tree also cannot be lacking (b.r.).

Special Forces Task Group

Within the framework of the deployed forces, a proportionally high number of special operations forces is planned, which is led by the Combined Joint Special Operations Component Command (CJSOCC), directly subordinate to FHQ. Their special ability to persevere enables the special forces to be deployed around the entire EUFOR area of responsibility. The mission of the special operations forces in the first phase of this EUFOR deployment is to "unlock" these areas for the troops that follow. This includes the survey of the road network as well as reconnaissance of the area of operations, in order to receive a detailed impression of the situation. Furthermore the soldiers demonstratively show their presence, in order to frighten off armed groups. Further on in the deployment the special operations forces are the "eyes and ears" of EUFOR. Through their observations and perceptions create the prerequisites for a secure surrounding for the refugee camp. With the special forces Task Group (TG), AUCON offers an essential contribution to the duties of surveillance, supervision and the securing of large areas as well as specialized reconnaissance.

From April to October 2008 the Austrian contingent commander, Colonel GS Mag. Heinz Assmmann, is entrusted with the leadership of the "Special Operations Component Command (SOCC)", the command over all EUFOR special operations forces. The transfer of command takes place on April 14th, 2008 by the EUFOR commander in Chad, Brigadier General Jean-Philippe Ganascia (t.l.). Parachute jumps are also part of the duties of the SOF in Chad (t.r.). Reconnaissance troop (b.l.) and Forward Operation Post (b.r.).

Medical Care

The Austrian contingent provides three emergency medical teams, who secure the general medical and emergency medical care. For further care there are international field hospitals. The contribution of Austria in the area of the inspection of foodstuffs and drinking water hygiene, which is secured by the Austrian team for the entire European deployment, is highly valued.

"**Operation Nicole**", the EUFOR soldiers call the deployment of the Italian field hospital in Abéché. Within the framework of "Task Force Ippocrate" the Austrian dentist, Captain med. Dr. Elisabeth Engl treats the local population, civilian workers and EUFOR soldiers with her Italian team in the dental walk-in clinic, which is equipment with the most modern tools and furnished at the most current technological state (for example with the help of digital X-rays). The spectrum of treatments ranges from fillings and root canals through the re-cementing of crowns to the removal of wisdom teeth. During this communication takes place in German, English, French, Italian, and with the help of a translator also in Arabic. In the first months the dentist team cares for 99 EUFOR soldiers, as well as 43 female and 99 male natives. In the course of their activities Dr. Engl sees a little girl with swollen cheeks in the triage tent of the military hospital. The doctor realizes that the girl must be immediately helped. On the same day she begins treatment with antibiotics. At the beginning of treatment the girl can hardly open her mouth, her eyes are completely swollen. Kaltuma can see nothing and take no nourishment. The entire personnel of the Italian field hospital touchingly concerns themselves with the girl, Dr. Engl finally carried out an operation with the Italian team, which is a complete success. During this the Austrian Captain med. Dr. Christian Chiochirca, who fulfills his service in this mission in the MEDEVAC ("medical evacuation") helicopter of the French armed forces, functions as anesthesiologist.

Even the distribution of medicines to the population (t.l.) must take place under the watchful eyes of the SOF (t.r.). A military doctor cares for a man who was just the victim of an attack by a band of robbers (b.l.). Obviously one is gladly treated by this Eng(e)l – "angel" (b.r.).

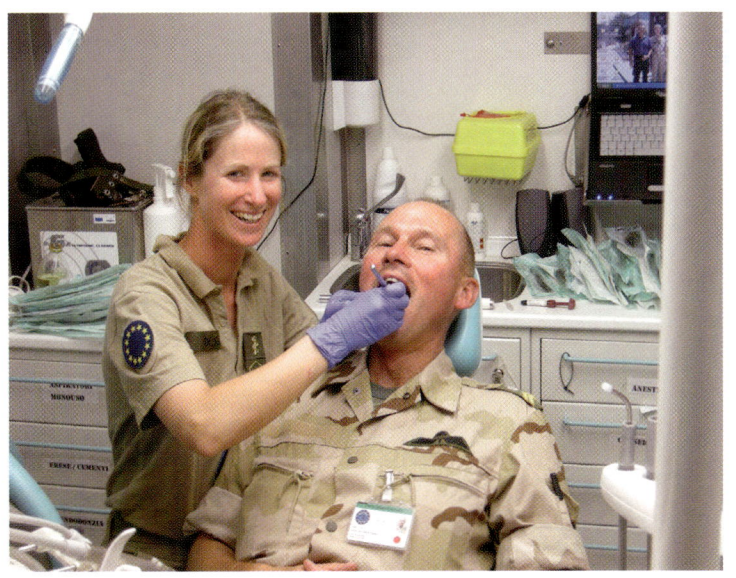

Language Primer

The linguistic situation in Chad represents a great challenge for the Austrian soldiers. The official languages in the deployment country are Chadian, (Chadian-)Arabic and French. Furthermore there are over 100 languages and dialects which are above all used by the rural population and the refugees. Because of the linguistic situation and/or linguistic variety in this country, the written form of the language is not always useful. Therefore, besides the most important phrases and words in Chadian-Arabic and French (in cooperation with the special forces), illustrations for nonverbal communication must be available. For this purpose, a language primer is created to provide "helpful communicative ability" through the Language Institute of the Austrian Armed Forces. With this communication help all soldiers are in the position to make themselves understood in emergency situations even without effective knowledge of the language. The "visual communication primer" is made of rip and water resistance paper, so that it can be worn on the person in every weather. Furthermore a more extensive "French for Chad language primer" is made available from the Language Institute for cooperation of Austrian leadership and logistics sections with the French troops.

"Sand Viper"

The deployment of the special forces in Chad also represents a test of the vehicle of the Austrian special operations forces, the Puch G SOF "Sand Viper" (in which SOF stands for Special Operations Forces). This is the Puch G 290GD all-terrain truck introduced into the Austrian armed forces, which is adapted for the requirements and needs of the Austrian special operations forces in the central Africa area of operations. For this a project group is initially formed from members of the special forces and the bureau for vehicle and equipment technology, which defines the capabilities for a so-called "Light Reconnaissance Vehicle" (LRV) on the basis of the Puch G. These are based above all on the experience of the special forces from deployments in Afghanistan in 2002, 2005 and 2006/07. Immediately after this the construction of a prototype is begun in Zwölfaxing. The vehicle receives a gun mount from the area of the driver and passenger to the rear to hold the primary and secondary armament (a 7.62 mm machine gun 74 each) as well as various modules such as radios or additional equipment. A turning ring is mounted for the primary weapon, which comes from discarded "Jaguar" armored antitank vehicle. Parts of the vehicle not necessary for the deployment are dismantled and replaced by new modules, including the seat for the gunner on board, for which the folding seat system of the "Ulan" armored infantry fighting vehicle finds a use.

A general overhaul as well as increased efficiency and a modification of the vehicle type as well as the painting of the vehicle in a camouflage scheme suitable for the area of operations all occur through the Magna/Steyr company. Magna/Steyr also adapts the vehicle's electrical system (camouflage for battle operations) so that driving in battle is possible without the emission of visible light.

As an additional camouflage possibility, the Habernig compnay construction two mountable rapid camouflage nets on the vehicle according to sketches of the special forces. The driver receives a slidable panel for his protection. On the front side of the vehicle two infrared headlights are included for driving during deployments with LUCIE night vision goggles. In addition there are holder for the three 77A2 "Kommando" assault rifles of the crew during the drive, for the reserve belts of the machine guns as well as ordnance pockets for blinding instruments or smoke grenades. For driving on desert roads and in the desert climate, "Goodrich Mud Terrain" tires are procured and filled with the sealant "Air Seal". This makes the tires drivable in emergencies after shots of up to a caliber of 7.62 mm (and perhaps even further). For communication the vehicle receives TFF-41 digital VHF hand radio equipment as well as a KFF-46 VHF radio equipment set including equipment and antenna holders. For operation over large distances there is a portable TFF1-0 shortwave system in the back of the vehicle. The shortwave operation is also possible while driving. Every vehicle is equipped with a Global Positioning System (GPS). Already on December 21st, 2007, the special forces in Zwölfaxing receive the first six finished Puch G SOF "Sand Vipers". In a record time of three months it is possible to reequip a tested vehicle type of the Austrian armed forces for the demands of the deployment in central Africa.

The first vehicles reach the area of operations by air transport with the transfer of the special forces. Subsequently the Puch G SOF "Sand Vipers" prove themselves capable and dependable. It also becomes clear that they must not fear comparison with the battle and reconnaissance vehicles used by other special operations forces in the area of operations. On the contrary: It proves to have be absolutely correct to have chosen a vehicle which needs no optimized vehicle electronics.

The first experiences in the area of operations form the basis for a further modification of the vehicle: There is a need for vehicles with heavy armament. Therefore some vehicles are equipped with a rotating assembly from the A1 Saurer armored vehicle, which carries a gun mount for a 12.7 mm extra heavy machine gun as the primary weapon. For easy distinction these vehicles are now called "Sand Viper" IIs. The first Puch G SOF "Sand Viper" IIs travel for deployment in Africa on July 10th, 2008.

United Nations Disaster Assessment and Coordination Mission in Albania (UNDAC/Albania)

Preliminary Events

During work in a munitions warehouse in Gerdec, 15 km from Tirana, there is an accident of unusual extent as a result of uncontrolled explosions on March 15th, 2008, at 11:30 AM. Official sources speak of an explosion of a thousand artillery grenades and an explosive quantity of ca. 7,000 kg. The explosion kills 24 people, critically wounds ca. 300 more, destroys 308 buildings and seriously damages another 3,835. 4,000 people must be evacuated and accommodated in public buildings.

International Reaction

UN-OCHA alerts the UNDAC teams. A petition for the dispatch of Brigadier General Dr. Alois A. Hirschmugl arrives in Austria on March 19th, 2008 on ca. 1:30 AM via text message. With Brigadier General Dr. Alois A. Hirschmugl, who can look back on long years of experience as an UNDAC member and has concluded a team leader training, an Austrian is appointed as the leader of a multinational UNDAC team for the first time. Immediately after the arrival in Tirana on March 20th a meeting takes place with the Resident Coordinator of the United Nations (official representative of the UN Secretary General), Mrs. Gülden Türkos-Cosslett and the very helpful United Nations Country Team. In Albania, as in seven other countries, the project "One United Nations" is running – this means that all UN organizations in Albania work together under one leadership, one program and a budget. This functions very well in Albania and represents an immense relief in case of a disaster. During this meeting the implementation of the first assessment and establishment of a total picture of the situation, the assessment of the environmental endangerment, the taking of samples and suggestions for protective measures and the support of the government with the coordination of the necessary measures are all determined.

The damage assessment generates the following results: The reconstruction costs for the houses (without the damaged infrastructure) are assumed to be ca. 17 million Euros. Nevertheless the largest problem are the still existing 100,000 tons of old munitions which are still to be disposed of or destroyed. The financial cost will add up to (roughly estimated) 50 million Euros. Ca. 9.2 million Euros are needed for environmental protection measures in Gerdec (Vore).

At the concluding briefing on April 1st, 2008, during which the ambassadors of Austria, the Czech Republic, Denmark, France, Germany, Great Britain, Hungary, Italy, the Netherlands, Poland, Spain, Sweden, Switzerland, the USA, but also the European Delegation, the European Commission, the World Bank, USAID, the OSCE, the Italian Military Delegation of Experts, the US Army as well as UNDP, UNDSS, WHO, UNICEF and IOM are present, the participants are informed by Brigadier General Dr. Hirschmugl of all middle and long-term results. In connection with this there is also an "update" on their donations or planned undertakings.

Basis for deployment: Alert through UN-OCHA.
Mission: Assessment and coordination of disaster relief.
Duration of deployment: March 20th, 2008 – April 3rd, 2008.
Participants: Austria, Denmark, Estonia, Great Britain, India, Italy, Sweden.
Strength: 7.
Area of operations: Gerdec, ca. 15 km from Tirana.
Headquarters: Tirana.
Austrian expert: Brigadier General Dr. Alois A. Hirschmugl.

Deployment meeting between Brigadier General Dr. Hirschmugl and Albanian officers.

Austrian Reaction

On March 19th, 2008 the urgent dispatch of an UNDAC catastrophe expert to Albania takes place for the duration of up to three weeks through the Federal Minister of Defence authorized by the urgency case according to Sec. 1 no. 1 subsec. c FCL-CSD.

OSCE Mission to Georgia (OSCE/GEO)

Preliminary Events

Georgia's march into South Ossetia in August 2008 leads to a massive military deployment of the Russian Federation and to the occupation of South Ossetia, Abkhazia as well as parts of Georgia by Russian troops.

International Reaction

The OSCE mission in Georgia is active since 1992. Around 200 workers with the organization, including eight military observers, are in the country. Their mission is to reach a peaceful solution of the conflict between Georgia and the renegade region of South Ossetia. The main activities of this mission, besides the peaceful conflict resolution, are the strengthening of democracy, human rights and freedom of press, help with the economic development of the country and cooperation with international organizations, such as the United Nations. These are present with the UNOMIG (United Nations Observer Mission in Georgia) mission in the region of Abkhazia in the northeast of Georgia.

A full new division of forces in the region takes place in August 2008 through the war between Russia and Georgia. This forces the OSCE to adapt its mandate. As a consequence the OSCE dispatches 28 additional observers to the region, in order to observe the ceasefire mediated by the European Union. They are to be stationed in an area in the neighborhood of South Ossetia. Besides this the OSCE attempts to mediate talks between representatives of Russia and Georgia. The observers must also ensure that there is no looting during the withdrawal and that the ceasefire is complied with. The withdrawal of the Russian troops itself takes place "sluggishly".

The Organization for Security and Cooperation in Europe (OSCE) must conclude its mission in Georgia on January 1st, 2009, since the Russian OSCE ambassador speaks out against an extension of the mandate in Vienna on December 22nd, 2008, although all other ambassadors of the 56 member countries in total have already agreement to the proposal.

> **Basis for deployment:** OSCE Council Act PC.DEC/831/08 of December 21st, 2007.
> **Mission:** Support of a peaceful regulation of the conflict over South Ossetia on the basis of the 104th OSCE Geo-ceasefire agreement.
> **Duration of deployment:** 1999 – June 15th, 2009.
> **Strength:** 160.
> **Headquarters:** Tbilisi, Tskinvali (regional office).

Austrian Reaction

Political Measures

At the request of the Organization for Security and Cooperation (OSCE) and as a result of the report to the Council of Ministers made by Foreign Minister Dr. Ursula Plassnik, the Council of Ministers decides to dispatch another five members of the armed forces as military observers to Georgia in addition to the previous four civilian observers.

Military Measures

Dispatch of Major[149] Mag. (FH) Bernhard Urach as a Military Monitoring Observer (MMO). The military expert carries out his duties unarmed.

> **Basis for deployment:** CM of August 29th, 2008; MC of September 5th, 2008.
> **Mission:** Observation of the withdrawal of heavy equipment out of the demilitarized zone.
> **Form of dispatch:** FCL-CSD.
> **Duration of deployment:** September 8th, 2008 – June 28th, 2009.
> **Contingent strength:** 1.

The OSCE also observes the withdrawal of the Russian troops (OSCE/David Khizanishvili).

---

149 Temporary rank for the duration of the dispatch.

United Nations Mission in the Central African Republic and Chad II (MINURCAT II)

Preliminary Events

Despite the Tripoli agreement signed between Sudan and Chad on February 8th, 2006 and the N'Djamena agreement on July 26th, 2006, through which the relationship between the two nations was to be bettered, a row of bloody conflicts takes place, in which besides regular forces various rebel groups are involved. In May 2009 there are renewed heavy battles between government troops and rebels of the Union of Resistance Forces (UFR) in the east of Chad. The UFR rebels are on the move from East Chad to the interior and according to their own reports want to eventually take N'Djamena. The Chadian government accuses the neighboring country of the Sudan of supporting the rebels and pushing into Chad with its own troops.

International Reaction

On March 15th, 2009, the UN MINURCAT mission relieves the largest independent mission of the European union so far in the Central African Republic and in Chad. Their core duties are the same as those of the EU mission. In addition to military components a civilian as well as a group of UN military observers and 300 UN police are added.

Austrian Reaction

Political Measures

Austria initially dispatches two staff officers as liaison officers. In February 2009, the decision is made to continue the engagement of the Austrian armed forces in Chad. Since UN contingents normally have no access to special operations forces, the Austrian contribution is newly assessed and agreed upon with the UNO. The political option falls to the benefit of the dispatch of a logistics contingent in the strength of up to 130 members of the armed forces until March 15th, 2010 and the dispatch of a construction and dismantling contingent in the strength of up to 50 members for the duration of up to three months.

Military Measures

The new mandate is composed of a logistics contingent, which is responsible for the transport of provisions for the UN troops. During this **"rehatting" personnel** (the personnel deployed with EUFOR/Chad/CAR are made subordinate to MINURCAT and remain in the area of operations until the beginning of the MINURCAT mission) is fallen back upon. The contingent has Steyr 12M18s for transportation as well as Puch G "Sand Vipers" and APTV "Dingos" to cover the transports. The contingent has commodities for the individual battalion and company outposts in the area of operations that are up to two days's journey away from base camp.

Basis for deployment:	SC Resolution 1834 (2008) of September 24th, 2008; SC Resolution 1861 (2009) of January 14th, 2009.
Mission:	Protection of civilian personnel, in particular of refugees and internally displaced persons; improvement of the general security situation, in order to ease humanitarian aid contributions; support of the basic requirements for the long-term civilian reconstruction and of measures which are necessary for the voluntary return of refugees and displaced persons; protection of personnel, institutions and equipment of UNO.
Duration of deployment:	September 25th, 2007 – to date.
Participating nations:	Albania, Austria, Bangladesh, Bolivia, Brazil, Croatia, Ecuador, Egypt, Ethiopia, Finland, France, Gabon, Gambia, Ghana, Greece, Ireland, Italy, Jordan, Kenya, Kyrgyzstan, Malawi, Mali, Namibia, Nepal, Nigeria, Pakistan, Poland, Portugal (temporarily), Russia, Rwanda, Senegal, Spain, Sweden, Togo, Tunisia, Uganda, Uruguay, the United States, Yemen, and Zambia.
Strength:	2,385 (instead of the called-for 5,200).
Headquarters:	Abéché.

Basis for deployment:	CM of April 30th, 2008, MC of May 9th, 2008 (dispatch of two staff officers); CM of February 17th, 2009, MC of February 26th, 2009.
Mission:	Assumption of transport duties within the framework of a French logistics battalion for the provisioning of the deployment forces in East Chad.
Appellation:	Austrian Contingent (AUCON/MINURCAT).
Form of dispatch:	FCL-CSD.
Area of operations:	Abéché (field camp), East Chad.
Duration of deployment:	March 15th, 2009 – March 15th, 2010 (three officers in FHQ); March 15th, 2009 – December 23rd, 2009.
Contingent strength:	134.
Composition:	Contingent command with company command and camp operations element; transport element; security element; repair element; medical element.
Commander:	March 15th, 2009 – May 20th, 2009 — Colonel GS Mag. Manfred Hanzl; May 20th, 2009 – September 15th, 2009 — Lieutenant Colonel Bernhard Kundigraber; September 15th, 2009 – December 22nd, 2009 — Lieutenant Colonel Herbert Haller.
Contribution:	Within the framework of both Chad missions 61 vehicles are deployed, with which 650,000 km are covered under the most difficult conditions without personnel damage.
Cost:	34 million Euros.

Development and Training

A deployment under such conditions requires development and training specially adapted to it. This takes place through a specially chosen unit, which fulfills these duties in coordination with the Center for Deployment Preparation (CDP) in Götzendorf, the Deployment Support Command and the special training institutions of the armed forces. In a two-week basic course information specific to the area of operations is conveyed. This includes: the content of the UN mandate, deployment authorizations, cultural "sensitivity" for the area of operations, behavior towards child soldiers, hygiene regulations, language training, mine danger and first aid. In the specialized deployment preparation the use of the communication devices in the area of operations, regulations for transport and securing of loads, the coverage and the special driving methods under desert-like conditions is conveyed.

Top Medical Care

A **"Level 1" field hospital** (first level of general medical care), run by Austrian military medics and doctors, an emergency medical system and an emergency medical helicopter team care not only for the Austrian soldiers, but also for the other nations participating in the UN peacekeeping mission MINURCAT in Chad. Everyone from the Irish staff officer in the UNO headquarters in Abéché, to French logistical soldiers to Finnish nurses is convinced of the high quality of the medical treatment by Austrian medical soldiers. Furthermore, until the end of June 2009, Austria provides the only **MEDEVAC team ("Air Medical Evacuation")** for quick medical aid from the air. This team consists of an emergency doctor and two certified nurses/emergency medics and is equipped with medical tools according to European standards. A civilian "Mi-8" transport helicopter functions as a rescue helicopter. With this the emergency medical care for the logistical convoys, which depending on the target area can last numerous days for the soldiers stationed in the border area to Sudan, are secured around the clock.

Military Dean Dr. Christian Rachlé celebrates an Easter mass with the soldiers (Gerhard Simader). On December 22nd, 2009, at 4:30 PM, a "Hercules" transport airplane with the last ten soldiers of the Chad contingent from the Austrian armed forces lands at Vogler Air Base. With them is Captain Dr. Lorenz Strolz, who has almost continuously served as a legal expert and translator in Chad. Lieutenant Colonel Herbert Haller brings a wooden sign with the inscription "Welcome to Camp Schönbrunn" with him as a reminder of the deployment (Andreas Stadlmayr).

United Nations Disaster Assessment and Coordination Mission in Namibia (UNDAC/Namibia)

Preliminary Events

For decades Namibia, bordering the Zambezi river, has had to battle the most serious floods. At the beginning of the year 2009, after deluge-like rainfall, the regions of Oshana, Oshikot, Changwena and Omusat in the Cuvelai basin in the north and east of the country are under water. The Chobe, Zambezi and Kavango rivers reach their highest water levels since 1963. In total up to 350,000 people are affected by the consequences of the flood, ca. 55,000 people must be resettled. Above all the lack of hygiene, drinking water, accommodations and food are the largest problems in the situation at the moment. Since the last harvest was almost completely the victim of the floodwaters and epidemics begin to spread among the cattle stocks, relief of the situation without external aid is unforeseeable. The Namibian government, which has already taken its own first measures for emergency flood aid, declares a state of emergency in these regions and directs a call for help to the international community.

International Reaction

The **UN Office for the Coordination of Humanitarian Affairs (UNOCHA)** in Geneva carries out an UNDAC alert immediately after the catastrophe is made known and dispatches two UNDAC teams to Namibia, Angola and Botswana. The European Union dispatches a team of the **European Union Monitoring and Information Center (EUMIC)**. In the course of the deployment there is a close and successful cooperation between an UNDAC and an EUMIC team for the first time. Despite the differing mandates a joint "plan of implementation" with a parallel "method" can be found. This expresses itself in smooth cooperation within all three UNDAC/EUMIC joint teams.

Lieutenant Colonel med. Dr. Sylvia-Carolina Sperandio, the previous commander of the field clinic in Hörsching and henceforth consultant for military air medicine, NBC defence medicine and troop hygiene in the Defence Ministry, is called in as an UNDAC expert as a result of her versatile medical training, in particular in the area of disaster relief. In Namibia she also advises the government and the aid organizations, among other, in the area of hygiene and water supplies for thousands of bivouacking refugees and through this helps to introduce concrete aid measures.

> **Basis for deployment:** Alert by UN-OCHA.
> **Mission:** Coordination of the international aid deployment.
> **Duration of deployment:** March 26th, 2009 – April 9th, 2009.
> **Participating nations:** Austria, Estonia, Ethiopia, Great Britain, Norway, South Africa, Sweden.
> **Strength:** 9.
> **Area of operations:** Caprivi.
> **Austrian expert:** Lieutenant Colonel med. Dr. Sylvia-Carolina Sperandio.

Austrian Reaction

On March 25th, 2009, the urgent dispatch of an UNDAC disaster relief expert takes place to Namibia as well as Angola and Botswana for the duration of up to three weeks through the Federal Minister of Defence and Sports authorized in case of urgency according to Sec. 1 para. 1 sub-para. c (search and rescue service) in connection with Sec. 1 para. 2 FCL-CSD.

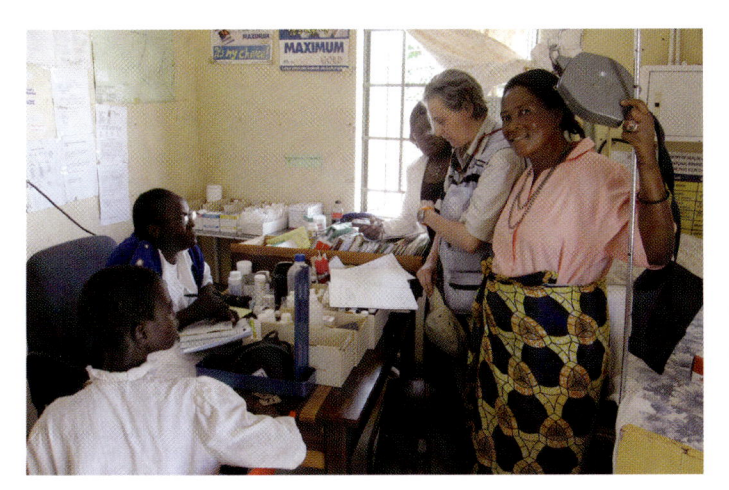

LTC med. Dr. Sperandio making contact in a local medical station (l.) and recording damage (r.).

European Union Monitoring Mission in Georgia (EUMM/GEO)

Preliminary Events

Georgia's march into South Ossetia in August 2008 leads to a massive military deployment of the Russian Federation and to the occupation of South Ossetia, Abkhazia as well as parts of Georgia by Russian troops.

International Reaction

As a result of the Caucasus conflict in summer 2008, the EU decides on September 15th, 2008 to dispatch an observation mission to Georgia. The main duties of the mission are the European contribution to the reestablishment and/or observation of stability and for the normalization of the situation after the crisis, observation and analysis of the situation, in particular the compliance with human rights and international humanitarian law as well as the implementation of the six-point plan agreed upon on August 12th. The area of operations for this mission is Georgia, South Ossetia, and Abkhazia. EUMM/Geo is in close cooperation with the OSCE mission to Georgia and the United Nations Observer Mission in Georgia (UNOMIG).

Basis for deployment: EU Council/Joint Action 2008/736/CFSP of September 15th, 2008.
Mission: Observation of the peace process.
Duration of deployment: October 1st, 2008 – to date.
Participating nations: 22.
Strength: 350 workers in headquarters and staff, 200 observers.
Headquarters: Tbilisi, regional offices are in Mtskheta, in Gori and in Zugdidi.

Austrian Reaction

Political Measures

The federal government decides on the dispatch of up to three policemen and a civilian employed under the leadership of the Federal Ministry for the Interior (FMI) and up to five members of the armed forces.

Military Measures

Basis for deployment: CM of September 17th, 2009; MC of September 24th, 2009.
Mission: Observation of the ceasefire.
Form of dispatch: FCL-CSD.
Area of operations: Tbilisi.
Duration of deployment: January 22nd, 2010 – to date (staff officer); February 10th, 2010 – to date (two military observers).
Contingent strength: 3.

Last reports after going to press:

United Nations Disaster Assessment and Coordination in Pakistan (UNDAC/Pakistan)

Devastating floods occur in Pakistan in August 2010, which put a fifth of the country underwater and make 20 million people homeless. An UNDAC team under the direction of the Austrian Brigadier General Dr. Alois Hirschmugl, an internationally known expert for multinational crisis management, is dispatched to Pakistan on the part of UNO. Furthermore the armed forces contribute immediate aid through the dispatch of 10,000 multipurpose tarps with a total weight for 12.5 tons for the construction of temporary accommodations.

Basis for deployment: Alert by UN/OCHA.
Mission: Preparation and organization of a multinational rescue and recovery deployment.
Duration of deployment: August 24th, 2010 – September 11th, 2010.
Contingent strength: 1.

Austrian Humanitarian Mission Hungary (ATHUM/HU)

On October 4th, 2010, around 12:25 PM, in Kolontár, Hungary, the dam of a chemical waste reservoir used to hold red mud breaks. Subsequently around 1 million cubic meters of the corrosive mud, containing heavy metals, comes out. The mud makes it into the Torna stream, raised by the floodwaters, and floods the surrounding communities. An area of around 40 square kilometers is directly affected by the masses of mud coming out. A state of emergency is called in the region. Ten people die as a consequence of the mud overflow, 150 people are injured, 400 people must be brought to safety. The armed forces dispatches engineering experts to assess the extent of the catastrophe and for support with immediate technical engineering measures.

> **Basis for deployment:** Request from the Hungarian government.
> **Mission:** Assessment of immediate technical engineering measures.
> **Area of operations:** Kolontár.
> **Duration of deployment:** October 14th, 2010 – October 16th, 2010.
> **Contingent strength:** 2 officers and 3 noncommissioned officers from the 3rd Engineer Battalion.

Austrian Humanitarian Mission Albania (ATHUM/ALB)

At the beginning of December 2010, heavy rainfall and snowmelt cause extensive floods in the northwest of Albania. More than 12,000 people must be evacuated. The situation around Skohder is described as "critical", after 2,500 houses and 14,000 hectares of agricultural land are flooded.

At the request of the Albanian government the armed forces participate in the evacuation of people in North Albania. For this two helicopters are temporarily shifted from KFOR to Albania.

> **Basis for deployment:** Request from the Albanian government.
> **Duration of deployment:** December 7th, 2010 – December 11th, 2010.
> **Contingent strength:** 30 soldiers and civilian workers, 1 S-70 "Blackhawk", 1 AB-212.

Crisis Support Team/Egypt (KST/EGY)

From January 28th, military specialists, together with representatives of the Foreign and Interior Ministries, are dispatched to the tourist centers of Hurghada, Sharm El Sheikh and Cairo, in order to advise the Austrian representative authorities in questions of security. The soldiers are part of a crisis support team (KST)[150], which is prepared for such deployments. Subsequently a C-130 "Hercules" transport plane is deployed for evacuations.

> **Basis for deployment:** Alert by the Federal Ministry for European and International Affairs.
> **Mission:** Identification of Austrian and EU citizens and their evacuation.
> **Area of operations:** Hurghada, Sharm El Sheikh, Cairo.
> **Duration of deployment:** January 28th, 2011 – February 8th, 2011.
> **Contingent strength:** 33 (military crisis support team with security element, military psychologist and military doctor), 1 C-130 "Hercules".
> **Contribution:** 112 people (including Australians, Germans, Swiss, French, British and Czechs) are brought to Austria.

Crisis Support Team Libya (KST/LBY)

At the beginning of March 2011, after unrest in Egypt and Syria, there are also demonstrations in Libya against those in power and the dictatorship in the country. During this there are serious armed conflicts in Libya between the regular armed forces and freedom fighters. The latter succeed in taking possession of large parts of the east of the country. In order to protect the liberation movement from attacks by the Libyan Air Force, the UN Security Council establishes a no-fly zone, which is observed by NATO airplanes. Through their deployment, the majority of the Libyan Air Force is destroyed. As a result of this, however, there is solidification of the front between East Libya, which is in the hands of the liberation movement, and West Libya, which is controlled by Gaddafi's troops. Many nations thereupon begin with the evacuation of their citizens in Libya. For Austria's part, a military air transport element with a C-130 "Hercules" transport plane is held ready for this in Malta. This brings the evacuated people to Malta, from where further transport to their homes takes place with civilian aircraft. The first transport of this kind takes place on February 21st. Furthermore, people are evacuated by land to Tunisia under the escort of a military crisis support team.

> **Basis for deployment:** Alert by the Ministry for European and International Affairs.
> **Mission:** Identification of Austrian and EU citizens and their evacuation.
> **Area of operations:** Libya, Malta.
> **Duration of deployment:** February 19th, 2011 – February 28th, 2011.
> **Contingent strength:** 25 (military crisis support team with security element, military psychologist and military doctor), 1 C-130 "Hercules".
> **Contribution:** 62 people are brought to Malta.

---

150 See page 356.

Austrian Humanitarian Mission Japan (ATHUM/JPN)

A serious quake of 9.0 on the Richter scale causes a tsunami off the east coast of Japan on March 11th, 2011. Broad sections of the coastal region are devastated and whole cities destroyed. 850,000 households are cut off from the electrical grid and in around 1.5 million houses there is no more running water. In addition, the nuclear power plant in Fukushima is subsequently so damaged, that the absolute worst case scenario occurs. There is a nuclear meltdown in three of the four reactors. Coolant water contaminated with radioactivity makes its way into the ocean without hindrance.

At the request of Austrian Airlines, a specialist from the military NBC Defence School accompanies a flight to Japan for the first time on March 14th, 2011, in order to carry out radiation tests during the landing approach to Tokyo. The tests on board the aircraft are carried out in order to be able to warn of possible radiation exposure in time. Furthermore an officer is placed on duty in the NBC Defence School for expert support of Austrians and Austrian agencies at home and abroad and/or to prepare and support dispatches of military experts as well as the AFDRU.

> **Mission:** Radiation tests during the landing approach to Tokyo; preparation for the withdrawal of Austrian citizens.
> **Duration of deployment:** March 14th, 2011 – to date.
> **Strength:** 21 officers and noncommissioned officers of the NBC Defence School.

European Union Italian Operational Headquarters (EU IT OHQ)

As a result of the further escalation of the situation in Libya, the European Union plans a humanitarian deployment to support the United Nations Office for the Coordination of Humanitarian Affairs (UN OCHA). On April 1st, on the basis of the UN resolution, the establishment of a military operation for Libya ("EUFOR Libya") is enacted. This is to serve for safe evacuation of refugees as well as support for humanitarian organizations, according the United Nations call. An operational headquarters is established in Rome to prepare for the operations. This is to work out the operational concept, the operational plan and the rules of engagement. As a result of the humanitarian emergency in the region, Austrian participates in the construction of the EUFOR headquarters with two staff officers. A further military deployment is dependent on the plans and a request from the UN-OCHA officer.

> **Basis for deployment:** SC/Res 1970 (2011) and 1973 (2011), EU Council/Joint Action 2011/210/CFSP.
> **Duration of deployment:** March 14th, 2011 – to date (end planned for December 31st, 2011).
> **Contingent strength:** 2 Primary Augentees (PA).

United Nations Office for West Africa (UNOWA)

UNOWA has the mission of coordinating the contributions of the United Nations for peace and security in the subregion of West Africa and/or promoting their efficacy. Austria had already participated in this mission from 2006 – 2009.[151] In May 2011, this deployment is taken up again in rotation.

> **Mission:** Promotion of the cooperation of the United Nations and other partners through the strengthening of an integrative, subregional approach, and support of the coordination measure, the exchange of information, etc...
> **Duration of deployment:** May 5th, 2011 – to date.
> **Contingent strength:** 1 military adviser in Senegal.

European Civil Protection Mission Cyprus (EUCPM/CYP)

On July 11th, 2011, there is an explosion of numerous munitions trailers on Cyprus. Thereupon Cyprus requests international aid within the framework of the European Civil Protection Mechanism (EUCPM). Brigadier General Dr. Alois Hirschmugl is volunteered as an expert on July 15th on the part of the Defence Ministry. He is assigned as the team leader of the European expert team and set on the march to Cyprus on July 16th. From July 19th, the armed forces provide a further expert, Ing. Günther Povoden from the NBC Defence School, for the disaster area.

> **Mission:** Coordination of rescue deployment.
> **Duration of deployment:** July 16th, 2011 – to date.
> **Contingent strength:** 2 experts, including the team leader.

---

151 Seep page 354.